THE FILM FINANCE

C000056422

HOW TO FUND YOUR FILM

How To fund your film

by Adam P Davies and Nicol Wistreich

chapter 2 by James MacGregor

further research by Catharine Allen and Hiu Wan Au-Yeung

with additional interviews by Stephen Applebaum and Tom Fogg

for **free** updates and information, please **register** at
www.netribution.co.uk/book

Interior design by Playne Design - www.playnedesign.co.uk

PUBLISHED BY
Netribution Limited
Suite 19
100 Drayton Park
London
N5 1NF
www.netribution.co.uk

ISBN-10: 0955014328
ISBN-13: 978-0955014321

A catalogue record for this book can be found in the Britsih Library

Printed in Spain by MCC Graphics - www.mccgraphics.co.uk - on FSC Paper.

FSC

What's in this book?

For this new **global** edition, the Handbook has been split into three parts: **Theory and Practice, International Incentives**, and the **Funding Directory**. The **Reference Section** has also expanded with a new 400-entry Glossary.

Part I, covering **Theory and Practice,** takes you through all the aspects of independent film finance, and includes various case studies and interviews throughout.
Chapter 1 gives an overview of the film industry, with essential background information and advice on how to prepare yourself and your project in the best way to attract finance. **Chapter 2** looks predominantly at ways to reduce budgets for *low* and *microbudget* films - while still putting the maximum value onto the screen - through tips, interviews and case studies with independent filmmakers.
Chapter 3 describes in-depth all the various aspects of production financing. It explains the types of financier that tend to provide funding, what type of deal they want in return, how they need to interconnect with each other, and what needs to happen for the film to turn a profit. We cover step-by-step the entire range of film finance currently available, including *Soft Money, Equity, Deferments, Pre-Sales, Gap, Sales Advances, Negative Pick-ups, EIS and Venture Capital, Sponsorship* and *Product Placement*. We also illustrate the roles of the various other companies integral to the financing process, including *Sales Companies, Distributors, Discounting Banks*, and *Completion Guarantors*.
Chapter 4 explores how tools, networks and services on the web collectively offer the independent filmmaker great power for financing, marketing and distributing their films, and some of the ideology which underpins these developments.

Part II provides information on **International Incentives** for **50 countries**, in many cases written together with local specialists. If a government has put in place a scheme to entice you to shoot there, we will tell you about it. We cover all the popular countries in depth, and bring to your attention a number of others with attractive and interesting regimes.

Part III is the **Funding Directory**, and provides a full breakdown of **1,000 public funds** available from over **300 organisations** around the globe. Wherever possible, we include details on their criteria, objectives and (most importantly!) the amounts they are willing to provide.

Contents

Chapter 3: Production Financing 96

Part III: Funding Directory 297

Acknowledgements

Many thanks to: Aisling Curran, Aly Lewin, Anna Yasmin Highet, Bernie Topper, Carl Kestens, Carlo Dusi, Caroline Hancock, Catharine Allen, Charles-Edouard Renault, Charlotta Denward, Chris Chandler, Chris Jones, Chris Locke, Claire MacMillan, Clare Playne, Cristian Conti, Daniele Cop, David Harris, David Tonna, Declan O'Neill, Dr Andreas Penser, Ed Parsons, Eelyn Lee, Einar Hansen Tómasson, Emmet Walsh, Eric Dubois, Francis Morgan Giles, Francois Gouliardon, Heather Mansfield, Herman Croux, Hiu Wan Au-Yeung Jan Dunn, Jan Ravelingien, Jan Ravelingien, Jenny Wistreich, Jeremy Stimpson, Jeremy Thomas, Jim Gilliam, Jodi Smith, Julia Giede, Ken Dhaliwal, Kieran Fairnington, Laurence Boyce, Leslie Lowes, Lindsay GIlmour, Linsey Denholm, Lloyd Chater, Luis A. Riefkohl Miranda, Lulu Black, Mario di Stefano, Mario Galavotti, Mark Playne, Markus Booms, Matt Hanson, Nicholas Reville, Nick Cain, Nils Klevjer Aas, Patrick Roe, Peter Mullan, Peter Thompson, Rachel Harris, Rebecca Greenfield, Roland Wigman, Sara Nordström, Sean Walsh, Sonja Hernicki, Stephen Salter, Sung Park, Susan Numan Baudais, Tamara Gregory, Tamas Cstak, Tina McFarling, Tom Fogg, Tom Selz, Stephen Applebaum, Wendy Bevan Mogg and Younes Jama as well as the various organisations and bodies who provided information the directory.

Note

To make things easier, we refer throughout to anyone who puts money into a film as a **financier**. In fact, this is not always technically accurate, as in certain quarters the term 'finance' relates solely to banking facilities, and not equity investment. But for the purposes of this book and the sake of simplicity, we refer to any monetary contribution to a budget as **production finance**, and to those who provide it as financiers. We also refer to '**Producers**' throughout as *human beings* (**s/he**, **his/her**, etc), mainly to help distinguish them in the text from any other entity (company, partnership, fund, etc), which we will always refer to as an '**it**'. In practice this won't always be correct (the Producer, for financing purposes, will nearly always be a limited company or specialist partnership), but we felt it helps differentiate between the various parties when describing multi-party transactions. Most people reading this Handbook will probably relate mostly to the Producer, and so we are allocating to you the privilege of humanity!

Preface: Going Global

You want to know more about financing films?

The fact that you're reading this means you must be at least partly interested in making films. Or financing them. Or perhaps both.

It could be that you already have a string of Oscar® winning hits behind you, but just need clarification on the new UK *20% tax credit rules*, how the new *German Production Cost Reimbursement Model* works, or on which US states now offer incentives to shoot there (and what you have to do to qualify).

Alternatively, you may be about to embark on your first attempt at producing a short or feature film, and wondering where on earth you can get your money from. You've heard that there are funds available for filmmakers, but have no idea where they are, what you need to do in order to access them, the kind of deal to strike, or how to keep your budget low enough to avoid having to put in half the money yourself.

Or maybe, despite being in the game for a while now, you're still not quite sure how a *discounted pre-sale* actually works, or what the difference is between *gapping* and *bridging*, and are too embarrassed to ask your colleagues. Maybe you are one of those colleagues and, having just been asked, can't actually remember the answer.

Whatever the case may be, we hope that we can help. Having been involved with or advised on the production, financing and/or sales of more than 200 films between us (ranging from £200 shorts to features costing nearly US$100 million), and consulted on film funds from England to New England, and from South America to South Africa, we have written this Handbook for anyone and everyone who wishes to understand the mechanics of the financing process, or who just needs specific information about where the money comes from.

These are exciting times to be following the success of the previous UK Handbooks with a new **Global** edition. In response to our fast-shrinking world, the book has almost doubled in size. Following increasing demand for a single book with a fully international outlook, we have added a completely new section setting out, in clear terms, the various finance incentives available in **50 countries** around the world. The **Theory and Practice** part has been expanded with various new sections and fuller explanations (with straightforward examples), and we have included a new chapter on the emerging trends heralded by the **Internet**, and its impact on financing, marketing and distribution. James MacGregor has expanded his chapter on low and **microbudget** production, covering countless tips and tricks to make a small budget go a long way. Our step-by-step guide to mainstream production financing, accompanied with a vast new **glossary**, illuminates more clearly a world that has long been mysterious and elusive.

> **'While awaiting the Grand Jury prize announcement, Claire wondered if the anxiety she felt at maxing out 5 credit cards to finish her film was as great as the anxiety her competitor felt investing $50 million to make his.'**
> **Hollywood Reporter advert in Cannes Market Guide**

The world is getting smaller

So it finally happened. After over a century of cinema, the power of moving image is in the hands of anyone with so much as a camera-phone and a web connection. Years of talking about it, wishing for it, questioning it, and it finally happened, much more quickly and effortlessly than many of us imagined. A filmmaker or artist can now get a bigger audience through a video sharing website than via TV or cinema. And this audience doesn't seem to care what film school you went to, what your budget is, or if you live in London, LA or Calcutta; simply that you have something worth watching.

The other side of the world is no longer just a place from cinema and the news, but the home of the person we're chatting to, working with, watching, commenting on. The web shrinks the world: for the independent artist it removes the need for a studio distribution network; for the studio it opens up a conversation with its audience which it hasn't often entered into. Globalisation is a reality for anyone online and as we wrote this book, dealing with contributors in six continents, the 'global village' we're now part of was impossible to miss.

But the story is perhaps bigger than that. Bigger than the new international collaborative and creative possibilities of the web. Bigger even than the arrival of a level playing field, which the independent producer — long forced to compete for shelf and screen space with the major studios — has until now been denied. The real blockbuster story is about people around the world beginning to communicate with each other through moving image. It's as if after a century of watching a select few play in the symphony, millions have been handed instruments and an open mic. It's loud, raucous, tacky often, but genuine and fresh. The introduction of the printing press led to the Renaissance across Europe and we are only just beginning to imagine where the web, as a new mass market tool for personal and creative expression, will take us.

And in the midst of this, the independent filmmaker has a brief head start before the studios stop focusing on the web's uncertainty and risks, and join the party. The rules of the game are shifting — as we wrote this, and no doubt further still as you read it — but one thing is clear. Where once a carefully managed, demographic-specific marketing message was enough to capture a potential audience's interest, online — amidst the millions of voices competing for attention — it is authenticity, honesty, and a certain 'humanness' that seems to stand out and resonate.

For cinema this isn't exactly a new idea; from Cinéma Verité, Italian neo-realism of the '40s and British Free Cinema of the '50s, through to Dogme and contemporary American independents today, filmmakers have constantly sought to better represent 'reality'. The new breed of 'User Generators' – who produce around half of video watched online —are not so different, if more international and less organised.

Knowledge of the industry can get you so far. It may tell you how to ink a distribution deal or close multi-party financing. All of which this book should help you understand, and perhaps achieve. But it won't necessarily find you an audience. And if, in the hunt for finance, you lose the qualities that made you unique as a filmmaker, you may abandon your most valuable asset. Which is yourself, your stories and your voice. And there, perhaps, is the web's greatest miracle and also it's big challenge. Online someone, somewhere, wants to hear it.

These are remarkable times and, amidst a backdrop of challenging world events, it's easy to forget that. Much is uncertain about the future, but that the world has begun a long overdue conversation seems without doubt and full of promise.

Why a book on film finance?

Of course, it would be great if, once you have a film financier interested in your project, s/he would simply write you a cheque for $10m (or whatever you need) and you could just go off and make your film. In return, you would give him/her some of your profit, and keep the rest. Easy.

Instead, in the 'real world', we involve *banks, production funds, tax funds, equity investors, sales agents, distributors, completion guarantors, public bodies, governmental culture ministries, tax authorities, lotteries, lawyers, financial engineers, accountants, collection agents*, and so on. But who exactly are all these people? What do they do? And how do they fit together into the financing puzzle?

The problem is that, at anything above 'microbudget' levels, you are unlikely to find a single financier to fund your entire project. Most investors like to share their risk with others, and so will want to see other people co-financing the same project. This means that you're likely to have to deal with more than one financier from the word go. Even this wouldn't be too much of a problem if all financiers were the same. If, instead of an offer of $10m, you had ten identical $1m offers, you could just give each person exactly the same deal, splitting the pie ten ways and giving each $1m financier a tenth of what the single $10m financier might have expected to get.

Unfortunately, that too almost never happens. In the real world of film financing, each financial contributor tends to approach the project from a different angle, looking for a different type of deal, and a different form of reward. In fact, it's often impossible to have more than one 'type' of financier on board at the same time. So the problem facing the Producer (or his/her rep, EP, etc) is how to glue all these pieces together into one happy family, such that everyone feels like they are getting the deal they want, even if it's completely different from the next person's.

And that's where we can help. If you want to source production funding for your picture, in whatever country, this Handbook should be a vital tool. Our aim is to empower you with the knowledge you need to feel comfortable with the many concepts involved and, with all the relevant information at your fingertips, to know how and where to tap into public funding. In essence, we want to provide you with your own comprehensive guide to all the ins and outs of production financing for independent films. Of course, the information is not limited to features, and can (and should) be applied to documentaries, short films and films made specifically for TV.

It's been a mammoth task to compile what we believe is the first book to pull relevant information about film financing for independent production from across the world into one place. It is a bold testament to the hard work of dozens of people in nearly 30 countries across all six continents who have contributed towards it. We sincerely thank them for their input, and hope you find here what you're looking for.

Good luck,

Adam P Davies and Nicol Wistreich, April 2007

PART I
THEORY & PRACTICE

The Bigger Picture

A quick reminder of why you're here...

So you have an idea, story or a script that you want to put on film. And you want someone else to pay for it, so you bought this book.

But before we launch into a full-scale discussion about the workings of the industry, the mechanics of independent film financing and sources of public funding, there is one question worth considering.

What are your reasons for wanting to make your film in the first place? Having a clear understanding of your aims and objectives will help you choose the financing approach you should take in order to reach your goals. This means stepping back from your project for a moment, and reminding yourself what it is you want to achieve from the 'bigger picture'. In the words of Kevin Spacey's Buddy Ackerman in *Swimming with Sharks* (an interesting insight for anyone daring to try to enter the Hollywood machine): *'What is it you really want'*?

You might be looking to build a business that can support you and yours over a number of years. You may simply love filmmaking, and want to enjoy the process itself as much as possible, without being tied down with bureaucracy, market demands or delivery issues. You could be looking for complete control over your work, or the security of having fully financed employment.

If you are driven by love, you might get away with credit cards, guerilla filmmaking techniques and a website to stream and sell from, as did **Susan Buice** and **Arin Crumley** for their debut feature and Slamdance hit, *Four Eyed Monsters* (see **page 91**). If that's the case Chapter 2 will provide you with numerous tips on reducing your budget considerably. The same concepts apply if you have $120,000 in savings, a series of spare weekends to shoot, and are hoping to replicate the success of **Chris Kentis** and **Laura Lau**'s *Open Water* with a 2,700 screen release and $31m gross in the US (see **page 83**).

Having been shunned by traditional sources, you may choose to email 170,000 people in order to net $270,000 for your documentary about how private contractors in Iraq dubiously profiteered from the invasion, as did **Jim Gilliam**, producer of *Iraq for Sale* (see **page 158**), did in ten days. Chapter 4 should give you some ideas on using the Internet to fund, promote and distribute your film online. If your aims are to be one of the first companies to shoot in a particular country, especially if there are real financial incentives available to you if you do, Part II of this book should help point you in the right (geographical) direction. **Jeremy Thomas**, for example, used the bait of new market opportunities in China in the late 1980s to attract banks to almost completely finance his multiple Oscar winner, *The Last Emperor*, to the tune of $25m (see **page 47**), using locations no-one had ever gained access to before. And for those who consider themselves in the mainstream of commercial independent film-making (or are intending to get there), Chapter 3 will teach and/or remind you of all the concepts behind typical financing deals and structures on the commercial side of the industry, from pre-sales to completion bonds, soft money to bank gap, and equity to actor, producer or sales agent deferments.

> 'The highs and lows are going to be a constant thing and you have to ask yourself, what do you want out of this? Is it kudos, is it awards, is it money? I want to achieve an emotion from an audience and that kind of makes it a lot easier than being motivated by money or fame.'
> **Janey de Nordwall, Silver Films**

AUTONOMY

SELF FINANCED

INDEPENDENTLY FINANCED

STUDIO FINANCED

BUDGET

Whatever you motives, unless you can fund your project yourself or do it for free, you're going to need to blend film and finance; commerce and creativity. These pairs have often made ugly bedfellows. On one side lies a creative person or team with a story that they wish to bring to life, and on the other is a multi billion dollar business filled with financiers, executives and so-called professional experts seeking their cut as specialised gamblers on the illusive nature of art and success. At every step of the way, the producer or filmmaker dances a duet between the integrity of the project, and the profit motives of those financing, selling, distributing and exhibiting it. And then of course there is the producer's own financial needs; to see a return and make some form of a sustainable living.

Naturally, knowing what you want to get out of making a film can, to a large extent, determine the size of your budget and the type(s) of finance you are likely to need. In many ways, the issue is a question of creative freedom. The less experienced you are, the less autonomy conventional financiers are likely to give you, while the size of your budget will typically be inversely proportional to the amount of control you have over the finished film.

Ultimately, it is about finding the finance and business model that most suits your particular project, your intended audience, and the way you want to live and work. It is said that there are as many ways to get a film made as there are filmmakers to make them. But by combining the advice of those who have already navigated the industry with practical facts regarding the nature of the business and law as it currently stands, we hope to provide an armoury of tools to protect your vision and help bring your story to light. We are sure the information we provide on 1,000 or so funds and international financing incentives won't be lost on you either.

Whilst bearing in mind your overall motives as you read this book, also remember that there always has been, and always will be, an audience for stories well told. With the advent of the Internet, a filmmaker today is lucky enough (potentially at least) to reach over a billion people, and that itself can be a pretty strong motivational force. In America, which employs half a million people in the film business, wanting to become a filmmaker has never been considered a sensible career path. In the UK, which is currently producing less than 50 locally financed mainstream theatrical features a year, it's even more uncertain. But if you know what it is you want to achieve before setting out, you're already at least one step along the way.

After a look at where independent production is in relation to technology and the industry as a whole, this Chapter looks at the basic mechanics of film as a business, before exploring the path you would typically take from idea to closing finance.

A brave new world?

Since its inception, the film industry has had a love-hate relationship with technology. On the one hand — through the advent of sound, colour, 3D and CGI - technology has kept driving cinema forward, ensuring this year's blockbuster looks newer, fresher and better-made than last year's. Ever since 1888, when Louis Le Prince shot the first moving picture in a garden in Leeds, England, technology

'The thing that has kept me going every day is what happened at the test screening. After the film they asked, 'How many of you in the audience think she was vicious and did some horrible things?' 95% of the audience raised their hands. Then they said, 'How many of you felt tremendous compassion for this character?' 95% of them raised their hands. It just destroyed me. I burst into tears because if anything, what I care about the story for is shades of grey and compassion.' **Patty Jenkins, director, Monster** has brought the means of production – and, more recently, distribution — closer to the public, who today can buy a DV or HiDef camera the size and weight of a toaster for less than the price of a flat screen TV. But with this greater freedom, new technologies have always brought uncertainty, and as such potentially unnerve the established control structures on which major studios and other industry stalwarts have built their businesses. Although today the issues might be the protection of expensive products, whose values are stored in easily reproducible ones and zeros, together with concerns over freedom, access and future control of internet distribution, the whole concept of addressing, embracing and clashing with modern technology is nothing new.

Back in December 1908, the main US film inventors and industry leaders joined forces to create the Thomas Edison-run Motion Picture Patents Company (MPPC), demanding licensing fees from all film producers, distributors, and exhibitors. Within a few months, unlicensed outlaws – who referred to themselves as **independents** – emerged, carrying on business without submitting to the Edison monopoly. By the summer of 1909, the independent movement was in full-swing, with producers and exhibitors using illegal or unlicensed equipment and imported film stock to create their own underground market. These independents, such as William Fox (who later founded 20th Century Fox), Carl Laemmle (one of the founders of Universal Pictures) and Adolph Zukor (whose company became Paramount Pictures), eventually headed West to California, far from the watchful eye of the MPPC, who had taken to confiscating equipment and shutting off content supply to cinemas who showed unlicensed prints.

These rebels at the birth of cinema grew into the six **major studios** that now in turn control the vast majority of films released theatrically in the US and other English-speaking countries. However, the independent 'rebellious' never went away, rebounding with great vigour towards the end of the twentieth century. Some say that the independent renaissance in the US started with Steven Soderbergh's 1989 debut *Sex, Lies and Videotape,* which helped catapult the reputation of those involved, including Miramax who distributed it, and the Sundance Film Festival where it premiered.

Typified by Robert Rodriguez's Hollywood success after shooting his self-financed movie *El Mariachi*, the 1990s were a period where barriers to film production continued to fall. Cheap digital cameras and desktop editing, coupled with a refuse-to-be-defeated guerrilla attitude, allowed filmmakers to bring in feature-length films on microbudgets. These self financed films became a springboard to bigger budgets, with filmmakers such as Chris Nolan, whose £80,000 *Following* led to *Memento* and then *Batman Begins* and Darren Aranosfky who went from the microbudget *Pi* to *Requiem for a Dream* and *The Fountain*. The pioneering spirit of these low budget indies inevitably filtered upwards through the film food-chain, with bigger features, such as Danny Boyle's high-concept zombie movie *28 Days Later* (made for £4m), using digital to shoot at cost. Even the *Harry Potter* films use desktop editing tool Final Cut Pro on set to make rough assemblies of scenes as production unfolds. A number of public film funds also now seek to support the trend for microbudgets. In the UK, for instance, Film London's £100,000 microwave scheme and North West Vision's £250,000 Digital Departures will 100% finance features shot on a minimal budget.

By the end of the 20th century, festivals such as Sundance were receiving a plethora of self-financed and microbudget features, all hoping to be the next *Pi* or *Blair Witch Project*. However, while the means of production had become available to an ever-increasing pool of potential filmmakers, the platforms for

'Internet distribution is the future of the industry. Theatrical will remain attractive to consumers as a real event to share with an audience but niche films and library exploitation will find their new business model in internet distribution. The ease of use and title availability will make internet distribution the winner in the next decade.'
Carmen Menegazzi, former head of Columbia TriStar'

distribution did not expand at a similar rate. The phenomenal success of DVDs also saw an increase in the number of distributors specialising in 'niche' titles, yet the shelf space at Wal-mart or Blockbuster remained limited and targeted at sure-fire hits. Likewise cinema expansion worldwide and the rise of the multiplex was accompanied with a move towards saturation opening weekends where films take a number of screens in a single venue. In short, the empowerment brought about by digital was not initially matched with increased access to audiences.

Forced to in-fight for the limited screen space at cinemas dominated by the majors, while attempting to stand out against an average studio marketing spend of $36m per picture in America alone, contemporary independents today still face massive competition to get their films distributed and seen.

Like film festivals, the Internet is a platform beginning to offer a level playing field for independent producers. By allowing anyone with a broadband connection either to upload or watch near-VHS quality video, the Internet has removed the need for a separate entity (such as a distributor or broadcaster) to act as interface between creator and consumer. Where previously film distribution has been mediated by entities which, in addition to selecting content they deem suitable for commercial exploitation, also manage (and take the vast majority of) revenue, the only barrier between filmmaker and audience online is technology, and access to it. And while much of this technology is controlled by media conglomerates such as Google (YouTube) and NewsCorp (MySpace), web software systems do appear to gravitate towards systems that are transparent, open, affordable, unbiased and impartial (see Chapter 4).

> 'The movie industry fights changes at every turn, but technology is like a freight train. You can slow it down with obstacles like litigation, but eventually, it will hit you. Microsoft loses more money than the movie industry to piracy, but that is a cost of doing business.'
> Todd Wagner, 2020 Entertainment

And so the film producer now has instant access to potentially over a billion viewers, with the cost of — and barriers to — distribution dropping to next to nothing. At the same time, the viewer has access to a huge and diverse range of content from around the world – far broader than any video store or TV channel – and all available on-demand, tagged and user-rated to increase the chances of finding something of interest Ultimately, both the producer and viewer are in control as never before, making DVD and TV appear pre-historic by comparison.

Amidst all the new excitement, there are still a number of core questions to be answered, such as *how* will people watch, *what* will people watch, *who* is going to pay and — the biggie for the business — *how much*? Internet film releases change the nature of presales and global release patterns, and in Chapter 4 we explore the range of new models being used, from Creative Commons to ad-supported, download-to-own, as well as the threat of piracy and the promise of the 'longtail'. As with the introduction of video, famously compared to the Boston Strangler by then MPAA head Jack Valenti, the studios have been cautious about entering the web distribution market whilst so much uncertainty remains. Their impasse, however, gives independents prepared to operate in a rapidly changing environment a head-start for building up relationships with online audiences around the world.

The numbers

Revenues at the **box office** continue to grow, rising 9% worldwide in 2006. After a global cinema slump in the '80s, **cinema admissions** rose during the '90s and early '00s by a phenomenal amount. In the US, box office receipts skyrocketed from $5.3bn in 1994 to $9.5bn in 2006, while the global box office between 2001 and 2006 increased by some 52.3% to $25.8bn. Admissions in America have dipped slightly from a peak in 2002, but this is considerably offset by international performance. With US admissions now rising again (by 5.5% in 2006), these dips do not appear to be part of an ongoing trend. Admissions in **Europe** in 2006 rose 4% to an estimated 924m, with the biggest gains seen in eastern Europe. In the UK, admissions fell to 156.5m in 2006 for the second consecutive year, from a peak of 175m in 2002, yet showed signs of recovery in early 2007 hitting the highest level since 2003. In France admissions rose to 188.5m from 184.4m in the same period.

DVD sales are finally beginning to level off, after the total spend on home entertainment in the US effectively doubled between 1999 and 2006. **Digital TV** has allowed broadcasters to put out more channels in their distribution — be it through cable, satellite (direct-to-home/DTH) or terrestrial (co-axial) — and have therefore increased the number of specialist channels to buying content, However, with greater competition for viewers, channel budgets are shrinking as a result.

US Box Office performance 1997 – 2006

Year	US box office gross (US$m)	Annual change	Admissions (million)	Annual change
2006	9,490.0	5.5%	1,450.0	
2005	8,991.2	-5.7%	1,402.7	-8.7%
2004	9,539.2	0.5	1,536.1	-2.4
2003	9,488.5	-0.3	1,574.0	-4.0
2002	9,519.6	13.2	1,639.3	10.2
2001	8,412.5	9.8	1,487.3	4.7
2000	7,660.7	2.9	1,420.8	-3.0
1999	7,448.0	7.2	1,465.2	-1.0
1998	6,949.0	9.2	1,480.7	6.7
1997	6,365.9	7.7	1,387.7	3.7

Source: MPAA

Worldwide box office 2002 — 2006

US$Bn	Box office (US$Bn)					Admissions (Bn)				
	2002	2003	2004	2005	2006	2002	2003	2004	2005	2006
US	9.52	9.49	9.53	8.99	9.49	1.64	1.57	1.54	1.40	1.45
Europe / Middle East / Africa	4.95	5.58	8.53	7.40	–	1.14	1.11	1.17	1.06	–
Asia-Pacific	3.79	3.79	5.46	5.25	–	3.92	4.16	4.38	4.57	–
Latin America	0.90	0.79	0.91	0.90	–	0.32	0.32	0.37	0.32	–
Canada	0.60	0.69	0.80	0.69	–	0.13	0.13	0.12	0.10	–
TOTAL	19.76	20.34	25.24	23.24	25.82	7.15	7.28	7.57	7.45	–

Source: MPAA, Informa Media & Screen Digest

As film audiences have flocked to the cinema in ever-greater numbers, film producers have also found an increasing number of potential platforms for exploiting their product, through DVD, video on demand (VoD), and the explosion in pay-TV channels. **DVDs** are one of the most successful consumer products in history, with sales rocketing from 350m units in 2001 to 1.2bn in 2005 in the US alone. The combined spend on VHS and DVDs in the US effectively doubled between 1999 and 2006. In the 1950s, ancillary media (mainly TV in those days) was considered a threat; nowadays, they make up the vast majority of a film's total revenue.

Between 2004 and 2006, DVD sales finally started levelling off in the US, with growth falling to less than 1%. Free distribution of DVDs has also increased. For example, in the UK in 2005, 130m discs were given away free with newspapers (etc), against 211m actually sold, according to Screen Digest.

US Home Entertainment Sales & rentals 1999-2006 US

(In US$Bn)	DVD Sales	DVD Rental	Total spending on VHS & DVD
1999	0.7	0.1	12.8
2002	8.7	2.9	20.3
2004	15.5	5.7	24.5
2005	16.3	6.5	24.3
2006	16.6	7.5	24.2

Source DEC: Digital Home Entertainment

Another trend on the rise is the **costs of production, release and marketing**, which has made distributors keener to bring fewer, more bankable, films to market, but with a greater marketing push per film. In the US, the average combined production budget ('negative cost', including an overhead element) and print and advertising (P&A) expenditure for a studio feature exceeded $100m in 2006 for the first time; almost double that of 1994. On the other hand, films from the mini-major divisions cost an average $47.5m in combined production and P&A spends, considerably less than the $61.5m in 2003.

US Motion Picture Costs & Revenues 2002 — 2006 ($m)

Year	Gross	Films Released	Average Gross per film	MPAA Member Averages			MPAA Subsidiary Averages*		
				Production cost	Print cost	Marketing Cost	Production cost	Print cost	Marketing Cost
2006	9,490.0	599	15.84	65.8	34.5		30.3	17.2	
2005	8,991.2	535	16.81	60.0	3.83	32.36	23.5	1.85	13.31
2004	9,539.2	474	20.12	62.4	3.74	30.61	29.0	1.29	10.13
2003	9,488.5	459	20.67	63.8	4.21	34.84	46.9	1.87	12.80
2002	9,519.6	449	21.20	58.8	3.31	27.31	34.0	1.42	9.76

*Source MPAA * MPAA Subsidiary/Affiliates includes studio classic divisions such as Miramax, Sony Classics & Fox Searchlight*

Recognising that a successful film can offer considerable **benefits to the local economy** both during production and, from subsequent film-inspired tourism, the past decade has seen an escalation of production and tax incentives from around the world. One German regional film fund claims that every euro invested in film production by the state results in another three euros being spent locally. The UK Film Council estimates that British films contribute £800m to the country annually through tourism, while 10% of visitors to New Zealand in 2003 quoted *Lord of the Rings* as one of the motivating factors for going. *Lord of the Rings* is also one of the more famous examples of the use of local tax breaks; it is claimed that $200m of the $400m budget for the three films was offered to producer New Line as an up-front deduction by the government. Parts II and III of this book cover in some depth financial incentives and funding opportunities offered in some 50 countries around the world.

The studio and independent sectors

So, if this book is aimed at describing what financing options are available for the independent sector, and how they work together, it makes sense to take a look at what 'independent' actually means, so we know what kind of animal we are dealing with. It may come as no surprise to you to learn that there is no hard and fast definition as to what the **'independent'** sector is, or whether a film falls within it.

The term 'independent film' has long been associated in the minds of the cinema-going public with quirky, arty or unconventional pictures, made on a shoestring by maverick *auteurs* without regard to commerciality. But within the industry, the most widely used interpretation ascribed to 'independent film', whatever its budget (and irrespective of whether it is considered art-house, commercial, neither or both), is simply one that 'is not a **Studio** picture'.

So then what *is* a Studio picture? There are now currently only six remaining so-called Studios (also known as **'the Majors'**), being Time Warner, Disney, Paramount, Universal, Fox, and Sony (which now incorporates most of MGM). These Studios are all located in the US, mostly around the Los Angeles area. Traditionally they have been based on their own, huge, production 'lots', where they have physically produced their own pictures on their own studio sound-stages (hence the term **'Studio'**). Over the years, the Studios became powerful enough to be able, without outside help, to develop, finance, produce, sell, distribute and even exhibit — although not in the US as this contravenes local competition laws — the films they made. These six major film Studios each operate massive international multi-platform distribution networks, offering finance, development, production and, most significantly, marketing and distribution across cinema, video and TV.

While there are tens of thousands of film production companies across the world, it is claimed that the six studios control the production and/or release of the vast majority of all films screened theatrically in the US.

So, an independent film might therefore be considered as one which is *not* developed and produced solely by an individual Studio. Or even if it were, it could still be considered independent if it didn't get sold and distributed around the world by the same company that produced it. In fact, the term 'independent' actually comes from the premise that, as a direct result of a film's production finance (or a substantial part of it) coming from non-Studio sources, the major creative, production and distribution decision-making process (ie. 'control' over the picture) is also **independent of** the Studio system.

It's interesting that in the last decade or so, the Studios themselves have slowly moved away from the 'one-stop-shop' approach on more and more of their

> **'The main business of the major studios is distribution — not production. Essentially they only produce films to ensure that they have the right number of films to feed their distribution activities.'**
> **Gareth Wigan**
> **Vice Chairman, Columbia Tristar**

pictures. In order to spread the risk on their films, some of which have massive budgets (regularly over $100m), they have begun to share an increasing proportion of the financing, production, distribution and exhibition elements both with other Studios, and with selected non-Studio companies within the mainstream sector. In fact, many of the larger independent production and distribution companies (known sometimes as '**mini-majors**', such as Miramax, DreamWorks, New Line, and Working Title) that originally began to partner with the Studios have since been bought out by them. The picture becomes a bit cloudier still with the Studios' 'classics' divisions – such as Sony Pictures Classics, Fox Searchlight – increasingly putting out more 'independent-style' films that were traditionally the mainstay of the truly independent sector.

Nevertheless, even the Studios continue to seek outside financing partners for a large proportion of the pictures that they are developing and producing. This off-balance-sheet financing helps to mitigate their risk and spread their available capital further. They are looking to partner with worthy independent producers who not only provide both commercially attractive and star-driven projects at a discounted budget (given lower overheads and the talent's willingness to work

Studio (Parent company)	Film companies	Other parent company interests include:
Buena Vista Motion Pictures Group (The Walt Disney Company)	Walt Disney Pictures, Walt Disney Feature Animation, DisneyToon Studios, Pixar Animation Studios, Touchstone Pictures, Miramax Films, Hollywood Pictures	*ABC Television & Disneyworld resorts.*
Fox Entertainment Group (News Corporation)	20th Century Fox, 20th Century Fox Animation, Fox Searchlight Pictures, Fox Atomic, Blue Sky Studios, Atomic Fox, DNA Films (50%)	*The Sun & The Times Newspapers, Fox News, BSkyB, Harper Collins, (controlling stake) & Myspace.com.*
NBC Universal (General Electric & Vivendi (20%))	Universal Studios, Focus Features, Rogue Pictures, Working Title Films, WT2	*Other parent group interests include NBC (General Electric), Canal Plus and Universal Music (both Vivendi)*
Paramount Motion Pictures Group (Viacom)	Paramount Pictures, Paramount Vantage/ Paramount Classics, DreamWorks SKG, Go Fish Pictures, United International Pictures (joint venture with Universal Studios), MTV Films, Nickelodeon Movies, Republic Pictures	*Blockbuster video, MTV, iFilm.com & AtomFilms. com.*
Sony Pictures Entertainment (Sony)	Columbia TriStar Motion Picture Group (includes Columbia Pictures, TriStar Pictures, Sony Pictures Classics, Screen Gems, Triumph Films, Destination Films, Sony Pictures Animation) and Metro-Goldwyn-Mayer (MGM) (co-owned by Comcast, including, United Artists and The Samuel Goldwyn Company)	*Sony consumer electronics (Playstation, Walkman, etc), Sony BMG (music), Sony Ericsson, and Sony Broadcast equipment.*
Warner Bros. Entertainment (Time Warner)	Warner Bros. Pictures, Warner Independent Pictures, Castle Rock Entertainment, New Line Cinema, HBO Films, Picturehouse (co-owned by New Line Cinema)	*Warner Music, AOL, CNN, Moviephone, Time Magazine.*

Source: Wikipedia

for substantially reduced fees), but also to provide a significant proportion of the financing. Independent films can be made at a fraction of the budgets that typify major studio productions, yet may still have equivalent production values and major star names. Top-level talent is often willing to appear in independent films for a fraction of their normal fee, and are attracted to independent productions for a number of commercial and artistic reasons. Independent films often give them a better chance of Oscar® nominations; some are their own personal projects that might be commercially viable on a lower budget, but would struggle to break even at the $50 to $100m (plus) typical studio level; and some are projects which the stars believe will ultimately be more profitable for them, because they can negotiate a percentage of the revenues more easily, rather than just an up-front Studio fee. Another reason why Studio budgets are higher is because many of the production services companies that they use (from caterers to costume designers) are actually group companies or on the studio payroll, so less of the money spent on production actually leaves the group.

For the purposes of this book, we use the phrase '**independent**' to relate to any film whose *financing* has come, at least in part, from outside the Studio sector. We imagine that for most of the readers of this Handbook, this will relate to films that are *produced* outside the Studio sector too. It might be interesting to note that in recent years, most nominees and winners in the major categories at the Oscars were either independent pictures or, again, from the 'classics' divisions of studios, using independent financing as part of their production strategies.

Non-profit films

In his book *The Gift*, Lewis Hyde suggests that *'works of art exist in two "economies", a market economy and a gift economy'*; an artwork can be both a commodity with a value, and something experienced — for both creator and viewer, reader or audience — that cannot be priced. For this reason, while most of Part I of this book largely considers the world of commercial film production, ie. films produced to make a profit for their investors and producers, it is worth noting that a huge number of films are made with an alternative driving purpose.

There are a number of reasons for making non-profit-making films. The most common, and no doubt the motivating factor behind most of the 65,000+ odd films uploaded onto YouTube each day, is simply the enjoyment of communicating in a visual format. Then there is production for the purpose of being noticed and recognised, perhaps in order to get finance for another short or feature. Some produce as a learning experience; countless films made each year are considered masterpieces until the dust and egos settle ultimately get shelved, but nevertheless act as a mini film school for those involved. There are campaigning films, produced to highlight a specific issue, organisation or cause; and promotional films or 'corporates' that act as extended advertisements or 'infomericals'. Video art and experimental film are as popular today as they ever were. Then there is community video, a massively growing area whereby specialist groups — eg. students, prisoners, homeless or socially excluded — produce work where the process is as, if not more, important as the outcome.

Ultimately, given how few of the estimated 5,000 feature films produced each year ever see any profit, if your motivation is simply to tell stories to the widest possible audience without concern for financial returns, then it is worth exploring production and distribution models which do not depend on back-end profit.

'**Art that matters to us — which moves the heart, or revives the soul, or delights the senses, or offers courage for living, however we choose to describe the experience — is received as a gift is received... when we are touched by a work of art something comes to us that has nothing to do with the price.**' **Jonathan Lethem, The Ecstasy of Influence**

Producers – what's in a name?

'The key issue
about making
a feature is that
politics plays a
huge part. I had
to get constant
approval from
three executives,
not just the basic
costs and crewing
but on everything.
They were all
supportive but I
had to constantly
communicate to
them that they
were all being
treated equally
well… I've since
realised that that
is a principal
element of
producing.'
**Gavin Emerson,
producer
Ratcatcher**

People are often confused by the number of 'producer-type' credits that roll at the beginning (and end) of a film. Who are all these people, and what do they do? Below is a brief explanation of the different 'categories' of producer. See also the Glossary in the reference Section towards the back of this Handbook.

Producer — The person, either corporate or individual, who oversees and is ultimately responsible for the management of a film from concept to marketplace, and at all stages in between. The Producer typically acquires the rights to make the film, engages the cast and crew, is ultimately responsible for obtaining and repaying finance, and ultimately owns and controls the copyright in the finished project.

Production company – An entity incorporated for the purpose of producing a film (or films). It may be an ongoing business, developing and producing a number (a 'slate') of films, or simply a company formed specifically for the making of a single project (or SPV: Single Purpose Vehicle)

Executive Producer — Often an abused title in the film industry, the 'EP' is the person engaged by the producer to make sure the whole thing gets off the ground; the person who 'made it all happen', who 'executed' the project. This usually means arranging for the film's financing, packaging other elements of the deal, and sometimes overseeing the project to keep it on budget. The on-screen executive producer credit increasingly is given as a contractually negotiated 'perk' to a financier or talent agent, or someone else who (loosely) made the film possible.

Associate Producer — Usually a producer brought in to a make a special creative contribution to a film where special expertise is required. The title acknowledges the creative status of their contribution to the film. The associate producer might be the person who initially owns or acquires the rights to the film, but ultimately takes it to a 'bigger' producer to get it made. The associate producer stays on-board to a greater or lesser extent, sometimes with consultation or approval rights relating to how the project gets made., and often with a share of the profits

Line producer — Similar to a production manager, a producer with expertise in managing film production, particularly where this is complicated (ie with global locations). Technically, the line producer is responsible for making sure that each 'line' of the budget is properly spent.

Production Manager — Manages the hands-on elements of the production of a film, from greenlighting to wrap. Accountable to the film's producer. Sometimes overlaps with the line producer, although not technically a producer at all.

Assistant Producer — Not really a producer either, but an assistant *to the* producer; the producer's 'right-hand (wo)man'. Often a great stepping stone for learning production techniques, especially where the production is too much for the producer to manage alone.

Co-producer — where the responsibilities for producing a film are split between more than one producer, each is referred to as a co-producer, and the film a 'co-production'. This may be done specifically for financial reasons (see Chapter 3 in particular for a further discussion on co-production).

Timing – from concept to screen to bank account

As you will no-doubt know by now, nothing in this industry is absolutely standard or written in stone, and neither can you take the following paragraphs as gospel. However, if you think by making a film in the Spring you will solve all your debts by the Summer, you are of course somewhat mistaken. There follows an explanation of the time it typically takes to get from scrip to screen, and to reap the rewards.

Once you have an idea it needs to be developed fully (see *Development*, below) in order to attract production finance. The **development** process, which includes completing the script, can take anything from a couple of months (unlikely!) to several years. Many films do not get made until more than a decade after they were first conceived. But, if focused throughout, a typical length of time for developing a film from inception to the point where you are looking for finance is probably a year or two.

Then, looking for finance itself will often take up to another year. If you can't **find finance** with a fully developed project by then, you might want to consider making changes to your package, especially the talent and/or budget. Of course, the ease or difficulty of attracting finance is dependent on the quality of the script, level of budget, genre, status of talent, time of year (especially in relation to taxed-based money) and so on. If you have all the elements in place and still can't attract any money, you might want to step back and ask yourself seriously if your entire approach ought to be re-considered from scratch or (worse still) if your project might actually be fundamentally flawed in some way. Of course, there are countless stories of films that get stuck in 'development hell' for years on end before eventually making it big (so don't necessarily give up!), but for every one of these that make it, the reality is that there are many more that don't.

However, once you have your money secured, you can then start spending it, first on **pre-production**; ie. getting everything ready for your shoot. This preparation period can take up to six months depending on complexity, but four to twelve weeks is a more typical period. Then you roll the cameras (known as **principal photography**) for another month or two (or three or four if you are a big studio picture), before heading into the labs to do your **post-production**. This involves everything from editing the film to adding all your special effects, sound, CGI and so on. It is therefore very much dependent on both the speed of the teams and complexity of the picture, but two to twelve months would be typical (it always, *ALWAYS*, takes longer than planned).

Whilst the film is being made you can start **selling** it, but money doesn't come in until after completion and 'delivery' of the finished product. If all territories have been sold by then (see relevant section in Chapter 3 for more information on how films make money through sales), your money could be in the collection account within weeks, and then divided up between financiers, the producer, and anyone else entitled to it, within months. Unfortunately this is rarely the case, and the first round of sales of a finished film will typically continue for a year or two. Once sales are made, as in any business, it can take some time for payment to be received, and then the collection agent requires a bit of time (weeks, not months) to calculate what needs to be paid out to whom.

Then, after sales are made, if the film is very successful in various territories, additional income know as **overages** may also come in to the collection account,

'There was always that nagging question in my head about how long would I wait and what would I do if it didn't come together. But every time that doubt got really strong, we would have a breakthrough and that's what kept me going. Every six months there would be something that just reminded me or encouraged me to believe in it and keep going. So I did.'
Nicole Kassell, director, The Woodsman

and that depends on the release pattern and individual payment terms for the territory(ies) concerned. Subsequently, as 'sales' actually only last for a limited period of time (see Chapter 3), further sales can be made at later dates throughout the copyright life of the film, and a successful picture can continue to generate income (eg. from repeat broadcasts on television) for many years.

All these activities are explained in much more detail throughout this Handbook, particularly in the relevant sections of Chapter 3. The important thing for now is to see that, with (say) 12 months for development, six months to get financed, a further six months to make the film and another year to receive most of the income from it, you are typically in for at least **three years** of hard labour from the time you come up with your film concept to buying your yacht and Lear jet, and that's if you have a particularly smooth run at it.

How do films earn money?

Revenue streams

Film revenues are generated during an ongoing cycle that normally starts with a cinema ('theatrical') release, continues through DVD rentals and sales to pay and free TV broadcast, and ultimately library sales. Although there is no fixed proportion that applies to every film, it is said (at least in relation to studio films) that box-office tends to account for about **30%** of primary worldwide exploitation revenue, with DVD contributing approximately **45%**, and TV **25%**. However, these figures will vary dramatically depending on who you ask and what you read. Finance executives within the industry are often loath to disclose sensitive information about the relative performance (or otherwise!) of their films.

> 'The problem with new filmmakers is — quite naturally — they all think that their film is the best thing since sliced bread. Unfortunately, this gives them a false sense of security. They think that they are going to get more than it cost them to make the film from their first sale alone. This rarely happens. They need to talk to other producers to find out what the likely sales are.'
> **David Nicholas Wilkinson, Distributor, Guerilla Films**

When this income is received will typically depend on when the relevant 'sale' (licence of rights) takes place. This can be any time from the beginning of production to several years after the film is finished. Typically, if the film is being sold successfully on the international market, a number of territorial 'pre-sales' (see Chapter 3) will be made during production, although payment won't be received until the film is '**delivered**' (completed and handed over to the distributors), the remaining countries being sold within another year or so. One might expect about 60% of total sale income generated by the film to be received within that year, with 20% in the following 6 months, and the remaining 20% in the next year or two. Should you be lucky enough to be entitled to **overages** (see Chapter 3), they are likely to be received soon after DVD release. In this case, you might expect about 50% of total overages to come in within 18 months of the film's initial release, 30% in the next 18 months, and 20% in the following two years. Of course, as with everything else, these figures are general approximations rather than scientific formulae; some films will generate income more quickly, others less so, and some for many, many years after their initial release.

Income from a film in any given territory will arise from a number of different sources (see over). The distributor for that territory will collect the income from all these sources, take off its own out of pocket expenses (known as '**prints and advertising**', or '**P&A**', costs), and then **split** the rest with the producer in agreed ratios (depending on the format to which the income relates). Often, but not always, the distributor will pay the producer an '**advance**' (known as an **MG**) against these splits at the time it buys (acquires) the relevant distribution rights. The following is a simplified breakdown of the ways in which films generate income, and how (some of) that money finds its way back to the producer. For a much more detailed explanation of how these deals work, see *Pre-sales and Distribution Deals* in Chapter 3.

Theatrical release
'Net theatrical rentals' are the revenues paid to the distributor by the exhibitor (cinema owner) and range from 45% to 55% of box office gross in the US, to 30% to 40% in the UK, with the rest of the world somewhere in between. A worldwide average of 45% (received by the distributor) would be a fair assumption to make. Of this, at least half will be paid over to the producer (the pre-agreed '**split**'), but in most cases only *after* the distributor retains an amount to cover its costs of prints, advertising and any advance it paid has been recouped.

Video/DVD rental
The distributor typically offers the producer a royalty fee of about 25% (of income it derives from rentals), but has to deduct the costs of producing and marketing the DVDs from its own share. Other ways of splitting income are also popular.

Video/DVD sale
This tends to be the most profitable part of the release cycle, where a film can take 30% to 40% of its total income (or all for a straight-to-DVD title). As with rental, deals are usually on a royalty basis, but with only 12% to 20% paid to the producer, and again the distributor paying its own costs. If instead the distributors costs are taken 'off the top', the percentage of net income (after the costs) attributable to the producer will be much higher.

PPV/Video-on-demand (VoD)
The pay-per-view provider (broadcaster) typically gives 50% to 60% of the end-users' viewing fees to the distributor (after recouping any advance it may have paid). Of this, the distributor will typically pay 50% to 70% over to the producer.

Pay-TV
The channel broadcaster pays a fixed fee to the distributor for an agreed number of screenings, usually linked to box office performance, and anywhere from $10,000 to several million. The distributor keeps a commission, typically between 25% and 35%, and the rest goes to the producer.

Free-TV (eg. BBC1)
As with pay-TV, the fee paid by the broadcaster is linked to box office performance. The distributor retains fees of 25% to 50% before paying the remainder over to the producer.

It should be noted that, as between the distributor and producer, television as a whole is often 'bundled', without separate splits for each of PPV, pay and free television. In these circumstances, the distributor tends to retain a fee from all television sales of roughly 30%, with the producer entitled to the other 70%.

Other sources
In addition to these 'primary' sources of income, a film also generates 'secondary' (or 'ancillary') revenues from other platforms such as '**non-theatrical**' (ie. airline, hotel and similar sales), **soundtracks** (of the film's score and/or related songs), **merchandising** (clothing, fast-food tie-ins, books, crockery, etc). Sponsorship and long term library sales can provide further revenue streams.

Release patterns
Release patterns are the timings at which point a film becomes (legally) available to the general public on respective formats. The last decade has seen significant changes, with more films released '**day-and-date**' worldwide and a shrinking

'People think they can make anything and it will find an audience. This is not the case. You have to be really honest about your film. Go to the video store and hire five successful films like yours and ask yourself how does yours stack up? Too many new filmmakers are so wrapped up in the excitement and glamour they forget about the end purpose of a film.' David Nicholas Wilkinson, Guerrilla Films

interval between first cinema screening and sale on DVD (where the most revenues are usually earned). This '**holdback window**' for the DVD release is still decreasing, and at the end of 2006 the US average was 4 months and 8 days, a total of 10 days less than in 2005. In the fourth quarter of 2006, it broke under the 4 month barrier for the first time, with an average of 3 months and 25 days, although blockbuster movies continued to have longer windows. This 'window' represents the amount of time, from the first day of theatrical release, that the distributor has to 'hold back' the DVD (and video) distribution in any particular territory. DVD *rental* and *sale* used to have separate windows (DVD rental permitted first), but this distinction is now all but gone. TV sales, whose window from DVD release is also decreasing steadily, are still — for the time being at least — very important, with total international feature film earnings from TV sales equal to approximately $12bn in 2006 (according to the BBC).

Theories abound as to what the most profitable release patterns should be with the advent of internet and other new media options. Some commentators suggest day-and-date (on all media and/or in all territories) will erode theatrical takings and kill the cinema industry. Others, such as Todd Wagner of 2020 Entertainment, suggest that such scheduling is inevitable with the reality of current technical advances, but that the cinema experience will withstand this and continue its popularity as a social 'event'. (www.netribution.co.uk/2/content/view/819/182/)

A day-and-date release across all platforms would give the consumer a choice of watching the film in a cinema, buying a DVD to watch at home, or downloading it from the internet (see in particular *The Future of the Independent Financing Model* section in Chapter 3, below). It may only be a matter of time before an independent film premiering online will be of sufficient quality to attract publicity, a distributor and a subsequent theatrical release.

'We have been very specific about what we want to achieve with the release. We could have gone much wider but we would have lost a lot of money. This way we focused everyone into two cinemas, got our reviews and got out with great screen averages.'
Chris Jones, Producer, Urban Ghost Story

For now, the three most common release strategies for independent feature films are:

- **General cinema (theatrical) release**, followed by DVD and TV. In the majority of cases, despite everyone's optimism that the film will score billions at the box office, the theatrical release often effectively turns out to be just a publicity vehicle for the video release. As it is chronologically the first format for 'exploiting' the film, the majority of publicity costs (**P&A**) are associated with it, and most of the income goes to repay these. Even a very limited one or two screen run can attract significant media attention and press reviews, which can potentially be invaluable for the later DVD release and television broadcasts.

- **Festival release**, followed perhaps by some theatrical screenings but mainly DVD and TV sales. A festival run can build up acclaim, as well as bring the film to the attention of buyers and press around the world. This path often generates industry recognition, which helps to progress onto higher budget work with a greater chance of theatrical release.

- **Straight to DVD**. Traditionally seen as the poorer cousin of a theatrical release, and often considered to be reflective of inferior quality. However, the sheer number of films produced make it unfeasible to distribute them all cinematically on profitable terms. For films that have a core fan-base, such as genre-specific (horror, sci-fi, etc), a cult leading actor (Jean-Claude Van Damme being an obvious example) or which cover special interest (eg. Yoga, Travel), this path can, however, prove highly profitable.

How are films financed?

It is extremely rare for a film to be financed from a single source. One exception is where a Studio or other backer gives 100% of the film's budget in return for full ownership of the film (and, unless it's a very favourable negative pick-up deal — see Chapter 3 — usually control over its production). The likelihood of getting such deals is determined by the strength of the project, the track record of the producer and any key 'named' talent attached. This type of financing is not really an option for a first or second-time feature producer of a mainstream feature, unless they surrender up all control. That said, at the microbudget level, financing *will* often come from a single private investor.

The most common form of film finance structuring, therefore, is '**multiparty**' financing, whereby the independent producer attracts money from a host of sources. These types of deals are all covered in full in Chapter 3, but below is a summary of the typical options.

Deferments. Cast and crew effectively part-financing the film out of their own fees.

Financing (co-)producer. A partnering producer who provides or sources money in return for an equity stake in the film (participating in future income) and sometimes taking certain distribution rights. Co-producers on the same film are often based in different countries in order to access multiple local benefits.

Foreign incentives. International co-productions allow native producers to tap additional oversees sources of '**soft money**', such as tax breaks and public subsidies, by partnering with foreign producers.

Friends and family. The first films from Stanley Kubrick, John Waters, Ed Burns and countless others were financed by close family.

Gap financing. Banks occasionally provide a gap loan to match a shortfall between a film's budget and other funds raised from elsewhere, using projected sales income as collateral.

National screen and media agencies. Over €1.5bn of public money was available in 2004 in Europe alone for audiovisual content and related activity. Funding can support development, slates of projects, company and personal development, production, distribution, festivals and cultural activity.

Negative pick-up. A distributor or Studio contracting to pay an amount on delivery of a completed picture in return for all rights (ie. it will own the whole picture), such contract then being used as collateral to borrow money to use in the production.

Pre-sales. In advance of the film being made, a distributor or broadcaster contracts to pay for an agreed set of rights to distribute or broadcast it (when finished), and this contract is used as collateral to borrow money to put towards making the film.

Private equity. Recoupable investment provided in return for a share of the profits.

Product placement and sponsorship. Companies provide cash or in-kind services in return for screen-time or marketing associated with the film.

Regional funds. The location of both the production company office and principal photography allow producers to tap into extensive regional investment.

Soft Money. Money ultimately from the public purse (through national film funds, tax breaks, etc), that typically doesn't have to be repaid, or if it does, then on less-than-commercial terms.

Tax-based Funds. Structured funds utilising film-specific legislation offering private investors tax relief in order to encourage investment in film.

Tax credits and rebates. Funding based on legislative tax breaks typically aimed at producers (rather than investors).

Venture Capital. VC financiers typically invest in high-risk, high-return products, and if convinced on the strength of the team and project, may get involved.

Web funding. Also known as **'crowd sourced financing'**, whereby a number of people invest in a project, usually in return for an incentive such as a credit or even a role as an extra. Successfully used in shorts and at least one feature *(Iraq for Sale)*.

….Inventive alternatives. If all else fails, there's always original funding sources that can be of greater publicity benefit than the money they raise, such as Robert Rodriguez offering himself for medical tests to finance *El Mariachi* or Rocliffe Films collecting sperm donor fees for the short *No Deposit No Return*

Your Picture

In this section, we take you through the process of getting your project off the ground, from assembling a team and forming a company, through to preparing relevant documents and closing your deal.

Prepare yourself and build the right team

Film is an industry with thousands of people with viable projects fighting to get in, and a relatively small and close-knit group of people acting as gatekeeper. It's easy for frustration to boil over at what can feel like an impenetrable old boys club, but more often than not it is just about presenting yourself without coming over as a potential risk. If you're trying to raise a substantial amount of money for your first feature, you need to be in it for the long haul, take your project seriously (if you don't, they won't), and consider the knock-backs as part of the training. Of course, you would rather be making films than filling in forms, networking and making presentations, but proving that you can jump through hoops with a level head is the reassurance the market is looking for. Ultimately they want to feel confident you won't be a risky green light.

Who exactly are you?

There are two drivers to a movie – the creative vision that makes a film great, and the entrepreneurial energy that gets the film made. While some filmmakers do successfully combine both producer and director roles, this is generally the exception rather than the rule. At one extreme, the film might get made and sold, but suffers artistically. At the other end, the project has 'creative masterpiece' written all over it, but it runs out of money and is never finished, or isn't sold at the prices needed to make it a commercial success.

'I was both the producer and the director, a situation I don't ever want to be in again. The conflicts between the artistic imperatives of the director and the financial and practical considerations of the producer are bad enough when they are fought between different people but when that battle is raging constantly in your own head, it's enough to drive you stark raving mad.'
Owen Carey Jones – Baby Blues

When approaching and presenting to financiers, sales companies and (co-)producers, you must be clear as to what your role is going to be, be it writer, director, and/or producer. If they think you may have control-freak or multiple personality tendencies, they will get nervous. They may be interested in (or insist on) 'helping' you put together your team, and will not be comfortable if there are not clear lines of responsibility in place. Of course, you may well be taking more than one role (particularly if you are a writer-director), but make sure you have thought this through, and can present clear, sensible reasoning for your decisions to those that are bound to ask you why (and if you can cope).

And who are they?
The old film adage that 'No-one knows anything' might be a bit harsh, but it is certainly true that 'No-one knows *everything*'. No matter how long you have been working in this industry (profitably or not), there is always something more to learn, particularly as nothing stays the same for too long anyway. Getting a feature film made successfully requires an inordinate amount of knowledge, experience, and — importantly — time, from the financing and legals 'behind the scenes' right through to the mechanics of physical production. Even if there were enough hours in the day, it is simply impossible for one person to manage the entire process, and any financier will know that. As a producer, you should start identifying your team from the earliest opportunity. And this means approaching lawyers, accountants, line producers and production managers as much as it does a director, writers and a production designer. Financiers tend to be more business-minded than creatives, and illustrating an impressive team with notable experience will go a long way towards securing your production money.

Of course having good people around you is not just about getting the finance. Building the right creative and business team is also the prime factor behind success in your actual production, and eventual sales. With a deemed shortage of good producers in proportion to writers/directors, some teams, such as *Guerrilla Filmmaker Handbook* authors Chris Jones and Genevieve Jolliffe, tend to take it in turns to produce each other's movies.

Stepping back, moving forward, and preparing for a long ride
While developing and promoting your project, it is very easy — almost inevitable — to get caught up only in that part of the process where you are at any given moment, be it networking, development, or fundraising. Taking a step back to remind yourself of the bigger picture can help in understanding why you may not be moving forward with your project as quickly as you would hope. The production executive who isn't returning your calls is beholden to his/her management and must field dozens of potential projects at any one time. In turn, the management is dependent on the company's backers, and the company as a whole is investing vast sums of money in product that it must be able to sell on the international market in order to stay afloat. The distributors in turn need to acquire a certain number of 'hits' to ensure their survival. The studios and corporations that own these distributors are accountable to their shareholders. At every step of the way the success of your project is dependent on an awful lot of people believing that backing you won't risk them their job.

That's the bottom line, and while it can feel like you're a Kafkaesque cog at the bottom of a giant machine, film is a $70bn a year industry and, until you are a proven safe bet with a commercial or critical hit under your belt, it's not going to be any other way. You may have the best script in the world, but as far as the gatekeepers are concerned, you may be just as big a risk as anyone else (at least until you've proven otherwise).

'Experience teaches you that there are no external forces capable of preventing you achieving what you've set your mind to. I've come up against some pretty intransigent forces in my time, but the only true obstacles are internal ones like self-doubt and pessimism. Once you've conquered these, the outside world is a relative pushover.'
Omid Nooshin, director, Panic

Ambition and drive tend to come hand-in-hand with wanting success fast, which is often followed by despair when this doesn't happen. Filmmakers and producers with a long term game-plan tend to be better equipped to cope with the constant let-downs than those expecting overnight recognition. How many short films do you realistically need to make both to get noticed, and to equip yourself with the necessary skills to make a feature? For how long are you prepared to push your feature project forward, and how many compromises will you make on the way? Each project that doesn't attract finance or a release can be a useful learning experience if you are honest enough about the mistakes you made along the way.

And remember, by focusing solely on the end product, you may miss the chance to enjoy the process itself. It is an unfortunate irony that film, whose main objective is to give something positive to an audience, can be an incredibly stressful experience for the producers and key players involved in making it.

Do the research

'If you know there are millions of teenagers out there desperate to see your film then go online, do your research and get your statistics. So many independent filmmakers have the passion but not the interpretation that convinces those with the money that there is some commercial, and I don't mean formulaic, but financially sound reason to make it and that you are trying to reach a certain audience.'
Amanda Posey, producer, Fever Pitch

While the script is the basic vital asset in financing and packaging a successful film, any investor is going to want to see that you understand your market and that the numbers for your film add up. Most individual private investors capable of providing money for your film will have made their fortune in industries where a business plan and long-term financial strategy are vital for success. A good **pitch** (see below) and the promise of getting 'that guy from *Bend it Like Beckham*' may grab their attention for a few moments, but will never persuade them to take your project seriously as an investment vehicle.

At the most basic level, a business plan (see below) needs to convince a potential investor that your film, or slate of films, can comfortably make a return on the investment and provide a profit in a certain number of years down the line. Making this argument sound convincing requires you to prove that the creative team have the skills and experience, your management team possess the know-how and contacts, and, most importantly, that the market displays the demand and the ability to pay.

To present a convincing argument, you need to be very honest about your film's strengths and weaknesses in relation to similar films that have successfully come to market. How does your company's creative and production skills match the film and its likely audience? Your project may be a moving personal story of the toils of childhood in a Scottish village in the '70s, and you could certainly point to *Ratcatcher's* success, but had NFTS graduate Lynne Ramsay not already established herself as an art-house auteur with two Cannes nominations and one Special Jury Prize for her short films, raising £1.8m to make a film destined for the festival circuit rather than multiplexes would have been very difficult.

Indeed whether or not you are planning to produce a mainstream commercial feature, it may well be worth factoring in the production of a series of shorts to gain an international festival reputation as part of the business plan. Janey de Nordwall, producer of BAFTA and TCM-winning short *About A Girl,* part-financed her first three shorts by selling an equity stake in her company to individuals found through a business angel network. She pitched making shorts as 'research and development' expenditure, allowing her to form creative relationships, introduce herself to the industry and master the art of producing for a world cinema audience.

Not another 'Blair's Open Funeral'!

If you are looking to produce more straightforward commercial films, you will need to illustrate how similar films have succeeded and why your film is similar to those (yet still unique). Many filmmakers believe that their idea is commercial because 'it contains all the elements – sex, action, comedy' or because it is comparable to a breakout critical hit. How many financiers get told that the film they are considering will be bigger than *Pi*, *Being John Malkovich*, *Open Water* or, worse still, *Blair Witch* or *Four Weddings and a Funeral*?

You will also need to indicate that – at the very least – you have talked with suitable distributors and sales agents about your project and feel confident that it meets the criteria for the sort of films they are looking to acquire. The process allows you to form a relationship with a distributor early, and get an assurance that you are not planning to produce something completely unsuited to the market's appetite, or that the way in which you wish to shoot will only hinder your success. If you plan to shoot in black and white, the success of *Schindler's List* should not form the basis of your argument. Likewise if you plan to shoot on DV, the success of *28 Days Later* is not enough to prove that your film will be released theatrically. A proportion of sales agents and distributors refuse to look at DV-based projects, no doubt partly because of the vast number of them out there, but largely because they know it will be harder to sell. Theatrical exhibitors aren't yet equipped to deal with them, and many industry executives still feel that the quality is lacking when compared with film.

You will also need to find out how much similar films have actually sold for; not box office revenue, but sales to theatrical, TV, and video distributors. This information can be tricky to track down as it is not formally published, but a trawl through industry websites such as screendaily.com, indiewire.com, boxofficemojo. com, hollywoodreporter.com or variety.com, and a working knowledge of internet search engines usually throws up the goods. This also gives you an idea of how much your film could expect to make, which in turn allows you to figure out how much money you can spend making it.

The business plan (see below) should illustrate that you have done all this research and are confident that the budget of your film, your company overheads and the costs of selling it once complete, are considerably less than its realistic potential value at market. This may mean rethinking the film's budget, or deciding to target straight-to-video, or TV sales instead.

Know your potential audience

The 'if I build it they will come' philosophy can be a way of putting off facing the unpleasant realities of the film business until the end of post-production, when the filmmaker hopes that their skill and imagination will be sufficient to attract a magical distributor and sales agent who will sign up their film and whisk them away to a studio to start work on their next project. This never happens. The rare low-budget success stories were still made with a focus on who would want to see that film at the end of the process. Robert Rodriguez knew that there would, at the least, be a video audience for his $7,000 *El Mariachi* especially if he got a few 'money' shots to put into a trailer. *The Blair Witch Project* raised finance with a solid business plan that identified who would go and see the film once produced, backed up with a well-planned debut at Sundance.

Once you know who your audience is (clubbers, couples on dates, genre-hungry film-geeks, Playboy or Forbes-readers), you can look at the films competing for that audience's attention and see what your project has to offer that will make it

'You can't take the anomaly and make that the rule, that just doesn't work. Everyone all of a sudden goes out and makes Blair Witch, there were probably 20 Blair Witch knock-offs that did nothing.' **Steve Mackler, Bedford Entertainment**

stand out. Find out as much as you can about the audience, and make sure that your film is better than anything else they are currently being offered.

Networking

It's a sad reflection of reality but in this business, perhaps more than any other, it is definitely a question of *who you know* at least as much as it is about *what you know*. Striking up decent and legitimate relationships not only helps in the sourcing of production finance, but also when it comes to obtaining general advice on various topics, without the need to pay for it. People in-the-know really can be an indispensable reservoir of information.

That said, networking is too often seen as the process of convincing everyone in a room that you are great, when in fact just making friends with a few people at a party can set-up more useful long-term relationships. It is not always the quantity of contacts, but the quality of the relationships. And once you've got a bursting contact book, think before using it — there's only so much you can ask for before needing to give something in return. Of course, networking is not just a question of buying people drinks in the hope that they'll give you money. It involves being present at relevant industry events, doing the business card swap, knowing who to speak to and — importantly — when. No-one likes to be hounded for information (or worse, money) the minute they give out their number, so you have to build up a level of trust, and get to a position where people are comfortable taking your call. The gatekeepers to the film business — be they financiers, festival chiefs, journalists or successful producers — are in constant demand, so remember that you are only one of many people attempting to get as much as you can out of them. And few successful people in this industry are purely altruistic, so always consider what a contact might get in return from you.

'I think another common mistake people make is to tire the contacts they make or approach people the wrong way — they think they have to pitch to everyone all the time. I think that when making contacts you need to be as natural as possible, not harassing them with phone calls.'
Pikka Brassey, Wanton Muse.

Doing relevant research before approaching people always helps, so keeping an eye on the **trades** is an important exercise. They are often the best source for knowing what major deals are going down, what companies are moving into which sectors, what films types are being picked up by which companies, who is changing executive position through what revolving door, and so on. Signing up to emailed daily reports, such as those provided by Screen International and Variety, will send the information you need straight to your computer before you've finished your breakfast.

Attending **festivals** and **markets**, where industry execs (such as distributors, producers, sales companies, financiers, talent, agents etc) hang out in the bars, restaurants and screenings, is also a priceless exercise if you can afford it. Certain festivals focus on certain type(s) of product or certain types of format (such as buying and selling TV rights to films), so make sure you are not wasting valuable resources on a plush suite at the Cannes Film Market if you are a first-timer looking to finance a 20 minute short film. Likewise you're unlikely to find money for your $50m blockbuster romantic comedy at the Rhode Island Horror Film Festival. The predominant international festivals and markets for mainstream feature films include **Sundance** (Utah, USA, January), **Berlinale** incorporating the European Film Market (Berlin, Germany, February), the Hong Kong **Filmart** (Hong Kong, March), **Cannes** Film Festival and Marche du Film (Cannes, France, May), **Venice** Film Festival incorporating MIFED (Venice, Italy, August / September), **Toronto** International Film Festival (Toronto, Canada, September), **MIPCOM** (Cannes, France, October), the **London** Film Festival (London, UK, October /

November), and finally to end the year the **American Film Market** ('AFM', Los Angeles, USA, November).

Observers often say the best thing they get out of a festival is the **Market Guide**, the official book containing contact details of all the attendees. The one at Cannes runs to over 1,000 pages, and is probably worth the market admission fee alone. Other good reference books include Kemps (www.kftv.com), Kays, the Production Guide, Mandy.com, the Knowledge, the Producers Masterguide, and the Hollywood Reporter's Blu-Book.

Major film districts such as the west side of Los Angeles, or Soho in London, have their own bars, clubs and restaurants where media executives hang out, take meetings, and generally chew the film cud. The popularity of these places is at the whim of fashion, and change on a regular basis (especially in LA). Stalwarts in London such as Groucho's, Soho House (also New York) and Century can often provide interesting conversations with industry insiders.

A number of film 'community' or learning organisations also exist, and provide invaluable advice, lectures, conferences, seminars, and so on. Some are more net-based (such as Netribution, Shooting People, filmmaking.net, buzznet.com) and others concentrate more on providing seminars and teaching (eg. UCLA Extension, Raindance, APT, IFP and numerous film schools).

Development

Before trotting off to all the contacts you've made to look for production finance, you need to be sure that your project is fully developed. This means getting absolutely everything you need ready before you start approaching financiers for production money. The development process is a whole exercise in its own right (and not really the subject of this handbook), with certain private and public funds set up specifically to help finance it. Established production companies have executives who do nothing else but work on development, turning a project from an initial idea or concept into a fully scripted package with all the elements necessary to attract millions of dollars of production finance. Smaller independent producers will often undertake this exercise themselves, but the important point is that any film should be fully developed before asking financiers to seriously consider putting up money for production. **Development finance** is available from most public screen agencies, especially where it looks like a viable project may – with development support – make it into production, or shoot in a region that it might otherwise not consider. Most *production* financiers will want to see that the film script is fully developed before they get involved, and are therefore not in the market for providing development finance.

Perhaps the most important aspect of the development process is getting a fully polished **script**, capable of attracting financiers to invest their hard-earned cash in your film. This means a script that you are actually happy with. Of course, it will probably continue evolving right up until the final day of shooting, but that doesn't mean you should approach production financiers with something that's basically clearly still a working draft. Before showing the script *for Four Weddings and a Funeral* to anyone, Richard Curtis wrote five drafts working closely with his script editor and wife Emma Freud. Then came further rewrites for his producer, for Working Title, for the director, and more for budget cuts, subsequent budget cuts, responses after the first read-through – a total of 17 re-writes in all. And this from a screenwriter who had already demonstrated his skills in writing some of the most successful British TV comedy of the previous 20 years. As Curtis, himself, said,

'Let the work speak for itself; don't try too hard to convince anybody that it's any good (it can easily sound like desperation). I've gone to a lot of festivals now and seen how other filmmakers operate. Some cruise the jury, some even buy them presents. I like to keep out their way until after the adjudication. Best strategy is be yourself and meet as many people as you can.'
Irvine Allen, director Daddy's Girl (winner short Palme D'Or 2001)

'Don't resent the rewrites – the awful painful truth is that the script probably did get a bit better each time.' It does cost money to get a script written and polished (and re-polished), and certain development financiers specialise in paying for script commissioning and re-writes.

Optioning Underlying Rights

Development isn't only about getting the script ready. It also includes **optioning** any necessary **underlying rights**, ie. ensuring the copyright owners of any book(s), article(s), programme(s) or play(s) on which the film is to based have agreed to the adaptation of their work, and will definitely grant the licence(s) you need to produce and exploit the film once you have secured your production finance. Any production financier will want to know that you have, or are unequivocally able to obtain, the rights you need to make the film. Taking out an **Option Agreement** with the original rights owner will prevent him/her from selling the rights to anyone else for an agreed period (say, 6 months or a year). It will also force the owner to sell you the rights (under an **Acquisition Agreement**) when you are ready, for a pre-determined fee and on pre-agreed terms. The agreed form of Acquisition Agreement should be attached to the back of the Option Agreement (and will therefore be negotiated at the time the Option Agreement is entered into), so that if/when you get your production finance, and are ready to **exercise** the option, you just sign the pre-drafted Acquisition Agreement, and don't have to worry about whether — or not — you will agree all the relevant acquisition terms at that later stage. Of course, negotiating all the terms of a draft Acquisition Agreement, when you have no idea yet whether you will ever sign it because you don't know if you'll attract any production finance, can be very expensive. But without it, the option could become ineffective if you can't agree terms when you are ready to exercise it. In case the **option period** runs out while you are still trying to obtain production finance, it is wise to try to agree an automatic renewal for an additional period or periods, on the payment of a pre-agreed fee.

Preparing the budget

Another major element of the development process is the preparation of a **budget**. If you don't know how much it will cost to make your film, you don't know how much to ask for. Production financiers will want to know that your budget is accurate and has been calculated on a realistic basis (including a sensible contingency). You should therefore make sure that you engage a line producer or production accountant who actually knows what they are doing. It might be that you have to prepare more than one sample budget, in different currencies, because you might not at this stage know exactly where you will be shooting the film, and that may in any event depend on where some or all of your production finance comes from (see *Co-productions and International Options* in Chapter 3 for more detail). Costs vary from country to country, so it is important that the person preparing your budget has good local knowledge. The first budget you draw up should be a fully funded model that puts the director, producer, all crew and cast in at the appropriate fees, and all post-production in at industry standard prices. The chances are that you will then want (or need) to reduce this figure. You may ask for all manner of favours, and probably end up deferring some or all of your own fees and those of other key creatives. Chapter 2 sets out all sorts of ways of bringing budgets down, particularly on lower budget films, and the way in which deferments affect your production finance is illustrated in Chapter 3. The amount of money you need to actually shoot and finish the film (ie. ignoring any deferred fees), including creating the delivery materials needed to satisfy a sales agent or distributor, is known as a **cash budget**.

'Don't rush development, and don't abandon the script the moment it looks like your funding has fallen into place. It can always be made better.'
Working Title executive

It is worth noting that few films financed with budgets between $5m and $20m ever become profitable. Films under $5m are more likely to be able to recoup their budget through ancillary sales such as DVD, while films over $20m can afford to payer the higher salaries to well known directors or stars that increase the chance of box office returns.

Attachments

Development also involves securing your **above-the-line attachments**. This basically means persuading your director and lead actors to commit to your project, subject to you finding the production finance required to make it. Naturally, the better the calibre of talent on board, the easier it is to attract finance. You will likely be asked (and required to prove) the extent to which your above-the-line personnel are 'really' attached to your project. Of course a letter direct from Johnny Depp saying he has read your script, loves it, and has already blocked out next Summer from his diary in order to be available for you goes a long way. But this level of commitment at the development stage is very unusual, and you are more likely to get some form of **letter of intent**. This will probably come from the agent rather than the actor him/herself, saying that, subject to agreeing a fee, the actor's prior commitments, and your obtaining full production finance (by a certain date), the actor will make him/herself available for a certain number of weeks during a specified period. The letter might state what that fee will be (this would be a good time to start those negotiations), and may even require a proportion of it to be put in **escrow** to show a commitment on the part of the Producer. Note this is *not* the same thing as a **pay-or-play** deal, where under an executed Talent Agreement, the producer is required to pay an actor his/her *full* fee whether or not s/he actually ends up using the actor at all. Where a letter of intent is not forthcoming, a **letter of interest**, which might not say much more than that the actor has read and likes the script, and is interested in doing the picture subject to further negotiations, is still far better than nothing. The same process is true for director, producer and other above the line line talent.

In the absence of any letter from actors or their agents, a sensible cast 'wish list' should be prepared with the help of a professional **casting director** (who will have a feel for the appropriate talent based on scripted characters, level of fees available, genre, budget, etc). S/he will help identify and secure not only your lead actors, but also most of the other scripted parts. Some casting directors require payment from the outset, so this needs to be borne in mind when preparing a development budget.

Other considerations

Other balls that need to start rolling during the development period are the preparation of documents supplementary to the budget, such as a Production Schedule and Cash-Flow Schedule, and the identification of suitable locations (perhaps by engaging a professional **location scout**), costume designers, other heads of department, and so on. Depending on the type of production financier you are thinking of approaching, a full **Business Plan** (see below) might also be prepared at this stage, usually with the help of an accountant or other professional adviser.

The cost of development can range from a few thousand dollars / pounds ./ euros, to several hundreds of thousands. Development costs are, however, usually **repayable** out of the production budget, in which they will appear as line items. In other words, when the overall production funding is made available, those that financed the development process can be repaid immediately, usually with a hefty return and often with the right to a share in the film's profit (see Chapter 3).

Packaging

One question often asked is 'In what order should I **package** my finance' and, to be honest, there really isn't a right answer. Often people go for soft money first, and try to attract an equity investor at about the same time. This might make up about a third or two-thirds of the budget. It then might be time to approach a sales agent, who may be able to bring the rest in by way of pre-sales and gap (maybe from its own regular bank).

There simply is no 'correct' order, although certain financiers will typically require that other types of finance are in place before they commit (such as a bank wanting to see secured pre-sales). All of these options are explained in more detail in Chapter 3. When it comes to packaging talent, you are often left in a Catch-22 situation, as actors will not normally commit to a film until production finance is in place, and financiers will not commit funds until they know the actors are secured. Obtaining **letters of intent** (see Development, above) from both 'sides', worded as strongly as possible, is often the best way around this. Some producers have been known to promise each side that the other has already committed, in the hope that they can secure both at the same time. This does work occasionally, but not as often as you might think, and you have to consider your own scruples and reputation (and potential legal liability!) before taking this approach.

> 'The producer's job is to end up with a script that will attract talent, the talent attracts the money, that's how it works, there aren't any real shortcuts.'
> Nik Powell, producer, Head of the UK's NFTS

Budget size and sales projections

Size is important, no matter what anyone might tell you, but this doesn't necessarily mean big is beautiful. The important thing to keep in mind, when working out how much your film is going to cost to make, is whether or not it will sell for enough to make its money back (see *Recoupment and Profit*, Chapter 3). Like in any industry, there's no point making something for $10m if it will only sell for $1m. The best way to anticipate how much your film will sell for is, of course, to ask a sales agent. Obtaining these 'projections' can be quite tough, particularly if the sales agent is not asked (or willing) to actually sell the picture when the time comes. Beware of some sales agents who simply take your budget and tell you it will sell for (say) 110% of it. See *Pre-sales and Distribution Deals* in Chapter 3 for more details.

Naturally, different films simply will cost different amounts to make, depending on the quality of production, type of content, length, above-the-line talent, and so on. Digital techniques have become much more advanced, allowing a picture to be made at a fraction of the amount it would have cost if shot on 35mm film, without sacrificing the level of quality that would have been lost only a few years ago. That said, if you are looking at releasing theatrically, despite use of digital on blockbusters such as the *Star Wars* prequels, 35mm film is still expected by many buyers.

There is a rule of thumb stating that, subject to a few considerations, you should be able to make any live action, full-length feature on 35mm film for between $1m and $5m (and films regularly cost less than that). Those additional considerations are crowd scenes (people cost money), period pieces (where specific-era costumes and sets need to be specially designed and/or adapted), post-production requirements (the amount of CGI and other effects can greatly increase the budget) and, of course, above-the-line talent (some A-list actors charge upwards of $25m per film). These aspects can turn a film that could otherwise be made for a paltry few million(!) into a medium budget picture costing $20m, $40m or $60m and requiring a significant level of guaranteed distribution to be in place before production funds will be committed.

Finance plans

As we stated above, the first thing you need to know before approaching any financier is how much your film is actually going to cost. For this, you need to prepare a **budget**, preferably together with an experienced line producer. As opposed to the budget, which lists the things on which the production finance will be *spent* in making the film, the **finance plan** sets out *where that money comes from* in the first place; the various sources of production finance. It is a very important document for any Producer who isn't being financed from a single source, and will usually be the first thing production financiers will ask to look at. They will want to see where you expect to source finance from, who else is putting money in, and therefore what the relative recoupment positions are likely to look like (see relevant section in Chapter 3, and for a sample **Recoupment Schedule**, the Reference Section).

Production finance for a film will often come from different countries, so finance plans should set out the amounts in the currency in which they are being provided, and then translate these into a single currency (typically US dollars) for the sake of clarity.

Below are some example Finance Plans for pictures of varying budgets and financial sources, just to give you a flavour of what people will be expecting to see.

Micro-budget — $100,000 and under

DigiBeta, ghost story, no named cast, inexperienced producer, director and writer all unpaid, intended to sell to DVD/Video		
Development	Self-financed	nil
Production	Private Equity	$20,000
	Small Grant	$10,000
	Deferred Fees	$60,000
TOTAL		**$90,000**

Ultra-low budget — $750,000 and under

Super16mm, Horror, one named TV actor, producer and director with micro-budget experience on productions which have sold to distributors and has sales agent on board — intended for worldwide TV and DVD/video release.		
Development	Private Equity	$20,000
Production	Private Equity	$160,000
	Grant / Lottery	$100,000
	Deferred fees	$50,000
	Sales agent as Co-Producer	$300,000
TOTAL		**$630,000**

...KAGING 25

...ANDBOOK

Low budget — $3m and under

Super16mm, Black Comedy, 2 x TV / feature cast, up-coming director and producer, intended for print blow up for theatrical release		
Development	Regional Funds	$20,000
	Private Equity	$20,000
Production	TV Broadcaster	$300,000
	Soft Money Fund	$220,000
	Bank loan based on distributor minimum guarantees	$100,000
	Private Equity	$190,000
	Tax Relief	$150,000
TOTAL		**$1,000,000**

Low-Mid budget — $10m and under

35mm, Drama, Shot in the UK, 1 x US named cast, 1 x UK named cast, experienced director and crew intended for theatrical release		
Development	UK Lottery Development Funds	$20,000
	Private Equity	$20,000
	Foreign co-producer	$20,000
Production	UK Lottery Premiere Fund	$1,200,000
	France & German presales	$1m
	Bank loan based on distributor minimum guarantees	$1,300,000
	UK TV Pre-sale (cash)	$250,000
	Private Equity	$1,250,000
	UK Tax Relief	$1,290,000
	Foreign co-producer	$1,150,000
TOTAL		**$7,500,000**

Mainstream medium budget film — $50m and under

2 A-list stars, 3 other 'named' actors, UK Co-production with top directors and crew, intended for theatrical release		
Bank / Gap	ABC Bank	$3,412,500
Deferments	Producer / Prod company	$780,000
	Above the line / actor / director	$195,000
	TOTAL DEFERMENTS	**$975,000**
Recoupable Finance	X Equity Fund	$4,875,000
	Y Equity Fund	$1,950,000
	TOTAL EQUITTY	**$6,825,000**
Non-recoupable finance	Lottery grant	$1,969,500
	Discounted Tax Credit	$2,788,500
	Regional fund	$1,267,500
	TOTAL NON-RECOUPABLE	**$6,025,500**
Arranged pre-sales	UK & Republic of Ireland	$1,950,000
	France	$1,750,000
	US	$5,100,000
	TOTAL PRESALES	**$8,800,000**
TOTAL		**$26,038,000**

Writing the business plan

In addition to a Finance Plan, many financiers (especially equity investors) will want to see a full business plan illustrating where your project fits in the market, and how (and why) the financier is likely to get repaid and, hopefully, enjoy sharing in a profit. These business plans should be put together in a similar way to a standard corporate business plan for a normal business. It should set out who the team is, their general experience, any success they've had, what the product is, what its unique selling points are, how much it will cost to make, how well similar products fare, how much it is likely to sell for, when income is likely to be received, and so on. Facts should be backed up with source references and numeric tables where relevant. This is where your research (see above) is vital

There are various models of business plan for film investment, depending on the type of funding being sought and the project itself. Ideally, you should work through your business plan with an accountant (if you can afford it), as s/he will be very familiar with what needs to be included, and how it should be set out. In her book, *Filmmakers & Financing, Business Plans for Independents* (Focal Press, ~~~~) Louise Levison — who wrote the Business Plan for *the Blair Witch Project* h this process step-by-step. She suggests that a typical plan ollowing:

Executive summary. This section should be written last, as its objective is to summarise the rest of the plan in a clear and concise manner. You should also state the amount of investment you are looking for and, if you wish, indicate the nature of your proposal and the amount of profit you are offering (see Chapter 3, below).

Company background. This should outline why the company has been formed, what its objectives are, and how it is placed to achieve those objectives, as well as describing the legal nature of the company and how long it has been running. You also need to provide details of your management team, illustrating the skills, experience and contacts of key individuals. If any member of the team lacks substantial experience, it is vital that your other partners have experienceo find other partners with experience, or at least form an advisory board of your best contacts to illustrate that your inexperience is compensated by the involvement of people who know what they are doing.

The film(s). As well as outlining the project(s) you are seeking finance for, and their budgets, this is your opportunity to convince the investor that you have a hot property. If you own an option on a book, have the confirmed interest of a named actor or director, have crew attached with well-known credits, have the support of your regional film agency, or a foreign distributor, state this here. Testimonials from seasoned producers who have already read the script will help, as will a sensible budget illustrating how the film is being made inexpensively (never use the word 'cheap'!) without sacrificing quality.

The industry. You should provide an overview of how the film industry operates, as many investors will not completely understand it, and provide market data to illustrate its workings. Of course, we might suggest you recommend that they read this Handbook! Likewise, the BFI Handbook provides useful figures for the UK industry, and the MPAA provides in-depth analysis of the US (www.mpaa.org). Describe each of the different exploitation opportunities – theatrical, video/DVD-rental & retail, pay-per-view, pay-TV, free-TV, and so on.

The market. Here you should describe why there is a market for your films. What films similar to yours have been released successfully and why is your film comparable to those? What similar films have failed, and what are you doing to ensure this won't happen to yours? How do you intend to bring your products to market, and why in such a competitive environment do they stand out? How will you find a distributor and/or sales company (unless you have one already – which would be great), and what would your/their distribution strategy be?

Financing and forecasts. You should list your planned sources of finance to fund start-up, development and production and, together with a knowledgeable industry accountant (or lawyer), prepare the meaty part that any investor will look most closely at; your projections, cash-flow forecasts and assumptions. List the budget and returns — across all platforms — of successful films similar to yours. Use these numbers as the basis for sales forecasts for your film(s) which should be broken down by territory/region and platform. Use this, combined with the film's budget to make a quarter-by-quarter cash-flow statement for the first three or five years of operation. The key is to show that the numbers balance and that the investor could make an X% profit over Y years, based on a number of assumptions (which you should identify).

If you can't get a sales agent to provide sales estimates to support your forecasts, then you should at least provide a table of worldwide returns of similar films across platforms (theatrical, video/DVD, TV-sales) and territories. A lot of this data is available online through sites such as www.showbizdata.com, www.variety.

> 'It's one of the most frustrating, irritating and problematic jobs around. And one is constantly dispirited and crushed by the system in trying to get your film forward and struggling for the available funds. But there's always that possibility you will get to make your film. And once you're actually there standing in a field and the cameras are turning over and the actors are just doing what they're doing, there's nothing more exciting in the world and it's all worth it.'
> **Ben Hopkins, Simon Magus/ The Nine Lives of Tomas Katz**

com, www.bfi.org.uk, and in the industry **trade papers**. However, be careful with quoting box office data – a film that grosses $100m does not equate to revenues of $100m for the producer: the exhibitor typically takes off 40% to 60% and a further 10% to 20% goes on consumer tax (VAT or equivalent), while prints and advertising costs, and the distributor's share of gross receipts (30% to 50%) come off before the producer sees a cent. Chapter 3 goes into this in much more detail.

Pitching

The spoken pitch

Try to **find out as much as you can about the person** who you are pitching to ahead of time — the films they've financed, the people they've worked with and their reputation in the industry. Use this knowledge to understand what they are looking for and in turn what it is about your project that will attract them. Here are some pointers to help with your preparation:

- Bear in mind that any producer or financier you're pitching to is likely to be looking at the project as **a business prospect** and is going to want to know how much the film will cost, to whom it can be marketed, and what other films it is similar to. You don't need to answer these questions explicitly, but be sure to provide enough information about characters, location and period for them to be able to work this out.

- **Know your story backwards** and try to pre-empt challenges and questions about all aspects of it, from character motivation to possible plot weaknesses. Try to identify a hook – the thing about your film that will make it interesting to an audience, and to the person you're pitching to.

- Have at least one more developed pitch in case you're asked for **'any other ideas'**.

- If the process still sounds terrifying, one technique used by Terry Rossio and Ted Elliot (*Shrek*, *Pirates of the Caribbean*) involves detailing the story on 18-21 **index cards**, attached to a portable noticeboard (Spielberg reportedly said 'this is how all films should be pitched' after Rossio pitched him *Mask of Zorro* in this manner). Talking through the story like this focuses the executive's attention onto the board, rather than the speaker, while allowing them to visualize the narrative and its key elements.

- As well as presenting your project, the pitch is also a chance to **present yourself well**, showing, as Terry Rossio writes on WordPlayer.com *'Here I am. I'm serious. I'm capable. I'm talented. I know the business, and I'm ready to do this job.'*

- Spoken pitches typically come in two forms: a **1-2 minute teaser** to attract interest, and a **10-20 minute story outline** if the teaser works. This should outline the story and illustrate the fundamental elements — heroes, their goals, the conflict, any pivotal events or turning points, and the conclusion.

- If you're not excited and passionate about the film, it's unlikely the person you are pitching to ever will be. If you're friendly and witty they'll remember you positively even if they pass on the script. Whatever happens, **don't plead**.

'If you're "good in the room", then half the battle is won. For written pitches, it's down to your talents as a writer, the appeal of your concept, and the special spin of your pitch. Whatever its form, pitching is the key element that kick-starts the whole exciting process of getting something made... Conversing, querying, and communicating. We do it all the time. It's only when we become consciously aware of the "pitch" that our mind begins to generate nervous excitement and the fear of fluffing it up. Fear not. Tell the story. And everything else will follow'
Danny Stack, Screenwriter, dannystack. blogspot.com

> 'I got situated around Soho in a 20-quid-a-night stinky bedsit, and captured a yellow pages with film company addresses. I pounded the streets, occasionally walking into soft porn production companies by accident. On my last day, I almost gave up. I then got a meeting with Victor Films. They gave me twenty minutes but most of the time it was hard to get people just to sit down and listen so I pitched it as if I was making Citizen Kane!'
> **David Paul Baker, Director, Pasty Faces**

The written pitch

Find out — before sending anything in — what it is they want to see, and in what format. Written pitches can take many forms, and you are more likely to get a positive response if yours is written in exactly the style they like to read. Here are the main options for a written pitch:

- A **synopsis** summarises the characters, concept and plot, taking anywhere between a paragraph and six pages.

- An **outline** is an extended script synopsis covering the essential aspects of the story, turning points, subplots and the key characters. This could run anywhere between 6-12 pages.

- A **treatment** details the film action by action, describing the film visually in greater detail and actions and can run up to 30 pages though some argue it should be no more than 10.

- A **one-page outline** is a single page document outlining the key elements related to your script, including genre, format, target audience, box office potential, tag line, premise, brief synopsis and a statement of intent.

- A **two page outline** covers the same areas with a fuller synopsis and character backgrounds for the key roles.

Thoughts from a professional script reader

'Shorthand descriptions of characters makes it really hard to put yourself in the script's world. I particularly dislike films about filmmaking, and find that all too often our 'hero' is simply reactive rather than active and can be the hardest person in the script to get to know. Too much dialogue is often a turn-off; as is any script that copies films we already know as if they expect no one to notice. Scripts that aren't formatted properly make me want to throw them out before I've even started, as it suggests an ignorance of the process likely to show in the writing... Filmmaking is all about pictures, and scripts that have economical but punchy dialogue are usually promising. More than anything though it's just a good story told through strong characters — a script that you read all the way through without any teabreaks!'

UK Film Council script reader (and producer) Wendy Bevan Mogg

Completing funding applications

By Rose Cupit on behalf of Film London www.filmlondon.org.uk

When preparing an application for funding, be sure to thoroughly read all information provided by the funding body. It is also important to familiarise yourself with the organisation, its aims or mission statement, and previous projects they have funded so as to have an idea of the work they support. Most organisations will answer questions and be happy to discuss your eligibility for their specific funding program. Some require this by default.

Documentation

Most funding applications will require you to send some documentation of examples of your work. It is vital that you do your work justice by sending in high quality, professional, clearly labelled examples. Never assume that the funder knows your work. It is unlikely that the person or panel reviewing your application will have time to view large amounts of material, so you will need to carefully select clips and short pieces that are a good representation of your work. The LUX Distribution Guide (distribution.lux.org.uk) outlines a good approach to preparing promotional materials for artists' moving image works. This relates to general promotion of work but is just as relevant for funding applications, particularly in relation to CVs and showreels.

Budget

You will usually need to prepare a balanced budget showing all your other income sources and everything that you will need to spend. A simple way to prepare a budget is to write out a 'shopping list' — an itemised account of everything that you will need to purchase, hire, and spend money on. It is a good idea to be as detailed as possible. For example, rather than put an entry like 'film stock = £396' make sure to give more detail, for example '16mm Fuji colour negative stock 500T = £56.13 per roll x 6 rolls'. Include any 'in-kind' support — anything that you are getting for free, including goods and people's time. This needs to be included in your expenditure list, and also as an income — you are simultaneously spending it and having it paid for, making it free!

Some examples of funding application budgets for arts projects can be found at http://www.artscouncil.org.uk/publications/information_for_subject.php?sid=24 (example travel and film projects from an artist applying to the Arts Council England 'Grants for the Arts' scheme).

General tips

- Be aware of funding deadlines — many funds only have one per year so be sure not to miss it.

- Research the funding source you are planning to approach, and contact them directly to make sure that you are eligible.

- Have someone read over your application before you submit it. This is helpful in picking up on typos, but also is useful in making sure that your application makes sense and that there are no gaps.

- Double and triple check your budget.

- If your application is unsuccessful, don't be discouraged as the number of suitable applicants normally far outnumbers the amount of support available. In many cases the funder will give feedback so it is worth asking why your project was unsuccessful to help you better target future applications.

Working with an accountant

Michael Lerman, *Lerman and Co*

Viewing your accountant as a business adviser, not just as a professional trained in traditional accountancy and tax compliance services, could greatly assist a film producer's business. In addition to performing routine accountancy duties, a large part of the professional accountant's duties are those of advising clients on their budgets, profitability improvement, and operational procedures — and performing

'I take the view that if you get the right people around you, not having any money can be a creative thing. You are not throwing money at problems, so you've got to find other ways to solve those problems. If you've got very young and very talented, very passionate people around you, on both sides of the camera, they find interesting creative solutions.'
Karl Golden, Director, The Honeymooners

other tasks not often associated with accountants. Always keep your long-term goals in mind. Running your business more cost-effectively can be achieved only if you have the vision to project your goals into the future. Frequent cash shortages, lack of a solid business plan to guide the business, and steady decreases in profitability are all warning signs that a business could be heading towards a potential financial crisis. It is crucial to evaluate your business's structure, the projects undertaken and performance before it displays these danger signals.

An accountant can help you to boost your profitability by analysing all the elements of your business. Reporting on profitability is a standard procedure, but helping create it by providing intelligent, entrepreneurial advice is what an accountant strives for. Dealing with your accounts doesn't have to be a problem, even though it sometimes feels that way. For film producers, more important than making a huge profit, is controlling your finances and covering your costs. With control of those key elements of the business, the profits will flow.

Often, a film producer's accounting system will need to record transactions related to a number of projects, over a number of years. This is a complication that is a challenge and should be used to the producer's advantage for monitoring cash-flow and profitability.

The key to financial control is knowing what's happening. Therefore you need to monitor your financial situation at all times by regularly reviewing elements such as debtors, creditors, financial commitments, cash balances and borrowings.

All money that comes into or leaves your business should be documented. It is this documentation that will form the basis of your year-end accounts and your financial records. All sales should be receipted or invoiced, as should all costs and purchases. It is important to ensure that you have a working relationship with your accountant. When meeting prospective advisors, make sure you choose someone who you feel comfortable with and who gives you a feeling of confidence in their abilities. Items to consider, when choosing an accountant range from: -

Costs – most accountants today will consider quoting a fixed fee for the work being undertaken. Whilst costs will vary, the purchaser of accounting services must be sure that s/he is receiving 'value for money'.

Experience in the particular industry – althought this is not necessarily essential amongst professional accountants, it is a useful pointer to obtaining relevant and useful advice.

Accessibility – the cost of traveling to an accountant far away may be prohibitive. See if the prospective accountant will travel to you, to see your business as opposed to always expecting you to travel to him/her.

Qualification – A professional accountant will have the ability to advise you on most areas affecting your business. Many accountants who are not qualified under the many recognised institutes, will only have experience in limited areas of business.

Annual accounts
All businesses should produce accounts on a regular basis. For management purposes, accounts will be in a format that is most useful to the owner, and produced at times most relevant to the running of the business (e.g. monthly, quarterly, or at the end of a particular production). Annual accounts are required for tax purposes and for submission to providers of finance and banks with different requirements depending on legal entity. In the case of Limited Companies

and LLPs in the UK for instance, annual accounts in a format governed by statute, must be prepared and submitted to companies house within a certain time limit.

Annual accounts will include a balance sheet, profit and loss account, certain notes relating to the financial items in the accounts.

A **balance sheet** shows the financial position of the business as at the date to which the statement is prepared. It represents the balance of assets and liabilities at that moment and is presented on a historical cost basis. This means that no 'valuations' are carried out on the figures (except in the case of land and buildings or certain other appreciating assets). The general format of the balance sheet is to start with 'long term assets' such as cars, equipment and buildings. Then short term assets, such as bank balances and debtors are matched against short term creditors, for example overdrafts, loans, payables and taxation. Long term creditors (e.g. bank loans), are then deducted and you arrive at a figure for 'net assets'. Whilst this is not a value of the business, it measures, to a large extent, its financial health.

An **asset** is generally described in accounting terms as anything on a company's books considered to have a positive monetary value. Assets include holdings of liquid value (cash, debtors), less liquid items (stock, aging equipment), and other quantities (pre-paid expenses, goodwill) considered an asset by accounting conventions but possibly having no market value at all. Assets are shown on the balance sheet.

An asset that is utilised in the business for, generally, more than one year, is shown on the balance sheet as a 'Fixed Asset'. The costs of such assets are spread over their useful lives. **Depreciation** is the term given to the process of 'writing off' the fixed asset over its lifespan.

For more information see www.lermanandco.com

Negotiating your deal

Once you have managed to garner sufficient interest that someone actually says they want to put money into your film, you will need to sit down around a negotiating table and strike a deal. The negotiation process can be the make-or-break of any contract, and to some is the most intense and nerve-wracking part of financing. Hammering out a deal is never easy, and ending up with the exact deal you wanted is near-on impossible. However, there are a few tools you can arm yourself with which, at best, will help get close to what you want and, at worst, will stop you looking like a completely naïve novice. The following pointers will also be useful to you when dealing with buyers, or with key talent whose commitment you may need to help package the film in the first place.

Who to take with you for company
If you are going to be negotiating face-to-face at a meeting (rather than over the phone or internet), then unless you are supremely confident in your own abilities, it is usually best not to go alone. However, taking a lawyer with you too early in the deal-making process will sometimes appear a bit heavy handed. You might instead go with a colleague who can 'take notes' while you are thinking, or just to provide general moral support. It gives you the opportunity to duck out of the room occasionally and use someone as a sounding board, and to make sure you keep focused on the plan you arrived with. However, it is not usually advisable to turn up with your entire team, because you might be forced into making a decision

there and then. When you need time to think, the line 'I need to check this with my colleagues and get back to you' can work wonders in relieving the pressure.

Dress code

Many people who negotiate contracts or deal with finance for a living, especially lawyers, bankers and accountants, are often by their very nature instinctively less willing to give money to someone wearing jeans, t-shirts and trainers, and carrying their papers in a carrier bag. This doesn't mean you necessarily need to be suited and booted (especially in LA, where that can even be off-putting), but dressing smartly gives off a certain air of professionalism which will usually work in your favour.

Know the market

By understanding the typical 'going rates' for various elements of a deal, you will be prevented from asking for something which, although might seem reasonable to you, is in commercial terms so far from the market norm that you will be laughed out of the room. Some people who are used to negotiating deals will form an opinion of you based solely on your worst mistake, so 'knowing your stuff' will help you command a certain amount of respect. Of course, reading books like this is a great way to get an understanding of typical deals, but things can change frequently in this industry, and keeping abreast of movements by reading the trades and asking your own contacts about recent trends prior to entering into negotiations will stand you in good stead.

Know who you're dealing with

'Opponent' might be a bit of a strong word to describe the person about to dip into his/her pocket and give you all the cash you ever wanted in order to make your film, but the person you are negotiating with will still want to get the best deal s/he can, and probably 'score' as many points as possible along the way. Knowing a bit about him/her personally, and engaging in a general conversation (perhaps about mutual hobbies or interests), before you start thrashing out the details, can help find common ground. Having prior knowledge of his/her standard business terms is also very useful. It may be that s/he tends to deviate from the market norm a little, and it's always good to be prepared for that. And knowing his/her negotiating style (direct, vague, aggressive, 'good-cop-bad-cop', sly, etc) in advance can help you understand what their thinking is, eg. if they throw something at you from 'left field', is it likely to be just for effect, or of real substance. If the other party knows less than you, don't rub it in their face, but you can always start sentences with 'As I'm sure your lawyer (or whoever else is there advising them) will confirm to you,...', which can subtly put them under pressure if they don't actually know what is the norm.

Your bottom line

You must *always* work out, before starting any negotiations, what your bottom line is; ie. the point below which you will *never* agree, no matter what other terms are offered to you. Then, during the negotiation conversations, you should keep this in mind throughout, in case you get asked to agree something that, with hindsight, you know you would never accept. Otherwise it can be easy to get caught up in the excitement of it all and agree terms that you will feel bitter about for years to come, and which might even put you in a loss-making position right from the start. Everyone has their 'line in the sand' which, if asked to cross, would be a 'deal-breaker', causing them to walk away from the negotiating table and, thereby, the deal.

> 'There a few factors that are essential, that excite backers. A filmmaker's passion and vision for a project. My dedication to it was total. I could tell you what colours the heist corridors should be, tell you how the characters walked or talked. Nobody will part with money if you go 'eehhhhh' and you think about it. If they ask a question about the project, you have to KNOW what they will ask, before they know.'
> **David Paul Baker,**

Your general parameters

In addition to your 'bottom line', you should also — before starting the negotiating process — have thought about what you actually really want out of the deal. For each main deal point of a potential contract (eg. the ownership of rights, fees, time periods, credits, recoupment, profit share), decide in advance what you would actually be happy with, and work out how far away that is from both the best you could realistically ask for, and your bottom line. These are effectively your deal parameters (the best possible result, what you would be happy with, and your bottom line). Knowing these in advance will enable you to approach the negotiation methodically, and help you interpret how far away from closing a deal you are at any stage.

Win-win scenarios

Of course, you want to avoid the farce of a *Life of Brian* market-stall scenario, but you will almost always need to 'haggle' at least a little bit when trying to agree numbers on your deal. The trick is to look like you are giving something away (allowing the other side the false satisfaction of thinking s/he has 'scored a point' or won something) whilst still agreeing terms you are happy with yourself. When two parties start off far apart, they in fact rarely meet exactly in the middle, so don't ever assume that will be the case. If you are seen to accept something a long way off from what you originally asked for, you are in danger of getting a reputation for caving in and/or not knowing your market in the first place. It is often therefore prudent to go in, say, 10% or 20% away from what you really want and hold as firm as possible for as long as you can. This way you have still something to give away whist at the same time giving the impression you are true to your word rather than playing games. Someone with a reputation for meaning and sticking to what they say is usually taken more seriously. That said, if you really feel that the person you are dealing with knows less about the business than you do, you could always try starting with your 'dream deal' and working down!

The important point is that everyone wants to think they got something out of the deal, whilst also wanting the other party to think they scored points (even if they didn't). If someone is offering you money, you probably want to do future deals and build up a relationship with them, so it is often better settling on less-favourable terms and taking a less aggressive approach, rather than screwing your 'opponent' into the ground so much that, although they may have signed up to this deal, they will never want to work with you again.

Reacting to offers

If the other party opens negotiations, remember that they will most probably be employing similar tactics to you. You should therefore not necessarily accept the first thing that's offered (even if it's beyond your wildest dreams), as you can probably do better by holding tight.

Special bargaining chip

This is another tactic often employed, particularly by lawyers who are used to negotiating as part of everyday life. The idea is to hold firm on a point that you actually don't feel too strongly about, but that you know is important to the other side. If there is another point that you particularly want them to concede, you can then — towards the end of negotiations — use this as a bargaining chip by offering to 'give' on your position in return for them moving on theirs. You end up getting what you want whilst relinquishing a position you were never really that bothered about in the first place. People always like to feel they are in a win-win situation.

Firm, polite, but fair

The days of banging fists on tables and throwing tantrums in meetings are thankfully over. You don't want to appear a soft touch, but being polite and firm will usually give you respect. Also, be prepared to be asked to justify the position you are taking at any point in the negotiations. If you are seen to be taking a reasonable stance, it may help the other side to concede the points you are asking for. Again, knowing the standard market terms helps considerably in demonstrating that you are taking a fair and rational view.

Take your time, and know what you're getting in to

Always be prepared to put something on hold or 'park the issue'. Make sure you don't agree to parts of the deal or terms that you don't understand, and avoid being pressed into agreeing terms on the spot. It is rare that a deal has to be settled in full during the negotiation meeting itself, so you should be able to ask for time to consider. Anyone who denies you this and insists on an immediate decision should be treated with caution. Asking for time to consider an offer should always be respected, and will help you avoid rushing into things.

Follow up in writing

You must keep notes on as much of what is said as possible. Follow up each meeting in writing confirming what was agreed and what is still outstanding. This removes the likelihood of disputing later, when memories have become a little fuzzy, as to what was actually agreed. Make sure your letter or email does not end up committing you to the deal unless you actually want it to (see Subject to Contract, below). If you later realise that terms agreed are in fact less favourable than you first thought, you shouldn't try to renegotiate the deal unless absolutely necessary. If you can, simply put it down to experience.

When is a deal a deal — contract basics

Don't panic! We're not about to launch into a dry, boring, academic text on the intricacies and complexities of contract law. But it is vital you understand the basics of deal-making, so you don't end up thinking you've done a deal when you haven't, or having to sue someone (or worse still, being sued yourself) for 'breach of contract' when you have. **Contract law** also varies somewhat from country to country (see Law and Jurisdiction, below), so a complete technical analysis would only cover contracts made in the country whose laws are being discussed, and therefore only be relevant for some readers. Instead, below is a practical explanation of some of the main principles (or 'doctrines') of contract law that apply similarly in most industrialised countries, to the extent they relate to deals generally made in the film financing arena. We've based the following loosely on UK law, but the basic concepts are similar, if not identical, in most other jurisdictions. It goes without saying, however, that our explanations are merely simplified illustrations to help the non-lawyer grasp various concepts. They are not exhaustive, nor are they intended as a replacement for formal legal advice. You should always engage a professional lawyer wherever and whenever you are entering into any kind of important deal.

Some basic contract terminology

The **parties** are the various people or other entities (see below) that enter into the contract. Some contracts are between just two people, and others are 'multi-party', with many different entities contracting on the same deal. For simplicity's sake, we will assume for the explanations in this section that there are

> '**Don't keep going back and trying to tinker with a deal once it has been set. It looks unprofessional and can damage chances for more successful dealings in the future.'**
> **Dorothy Viljoen, The Art of the Deal**

only two parties, but the same principles will normally apply if there are more. The contractual provisions are the various terms and conditions, ie. the individual and cumulative rights and obligations of the respective parties. In a written contract, most **provisions** are clearly set out as express terms, but some contracts (especially, for example, consumer-type contracts in Europe) may have additional terms **implied** into the contract by the general law, even though they are not actually written down (eg. that consumer goods are of a decent quality).

The **term** (not to be confused with terms and conditions generally) is the length of time the contract runs for (which, on a distribution deal, is usually the licence period). **Executing** a contract means bringing it into force, for example by signing and dating it, and/or applying a company seal. Failure to observe or uphold the terms of a contract is referred to as a **breach**, which can lead to court proceedings to force the defaulting party to remedy the breach or, more likely, to claim damages (ie. compensation) against them for any loss suffered by the other party as a result of the breach (other remedies may also be available).

Rights are basically legal powers, such as the right to *do* something, or (as in the case of copyright, see below) the right to **prevent** someone else from doing something, and they can be enforced in a court of law. Rights can generally be transferred, ie. bought or sold under a contract, this type of agreement often being referred to an **Assignment**. Most rights can also be **licensed**, which effectively means given (or granted) to someone else for a specified period of time and under certain conditions. Licences (spelt 'licenses' in the US) are sometimes **sole and exclusive**, meaning that no-one else can be granted the same rights at the same time. The rights are effectively the 'benefits' you get from a contract, and the obligations are the opposite, the things you are compelled to do or get done.

Sometimes certain other documents (such as long lists or **Schedules**, or a budget or script) are specifically referred to in a written contract, and in order to avoid any uncertainty as to which version is relevant, they can be attached to the back of the contract as an **appendix** or **annexure**. At the front of a contract, there might be a definitions section, which sets out the precise meaning of expressions that are used (usually with a Capital Initial Letter) throughout the rest of the contract.

Oral and Written Contracts

Probably the first myth to dispel is that all contracts have to be in writing. In most countries, if there is a clear intention to enter into a binding contract, and all the necessary provisions (contractual terms) are clear in the minds of all the parties, the deal will usually be binding and enforceable. Of course, if it is 'oral' (ie. verbal, and not in writing), and one party alleges a breach by another, it can be near-on impossible to prove in court what was or wasn't actually agreed in the first place. This is in fact the main reason for putting everything in writing; certainty and clarity.

Another important reason for having written contracts is that, under the laws of some countries, certain types of contract (eg. assignments and/or licences of copyright — see below) are not effective *unless* in writing.

A written contract doesn't necessarily have to be a formal document signed and sealed by all parties. It could potentially be a string of emails or an accumulation of letters or faxes. For this reason, it is important to keep copies of everything that was discussed and agreed along the way, so no-one at a later date can deny what was said (written). This set of written 'documents' (emails, letters, etc) covering all the negotiations and culminating in the final agreement, is known as a **paper-**

trail, and something that your lawyer will be very pleased you kept when you turn up to see him/her about a contractual dispute.

Types of written documents

A written contract can be formed (or 'construed') from cumulative emails and letters, or alternatively (and preferably) set out in a single document covering all the agreed terms in one go. Contract documents can be in short-form or long-form. **Long-form** agreements are generally multi-page, formal documents with a front 'title' page, and a special 'attestation' part for the signatures. They set out almost every conceivable provision that can go into a contract, including at the end a number of standard-type provisions called **boiler-plate**, which cover various peripheral, less commercial terms (such as how to notify each other of information, how and where to resolve disputes, whether the agreement overrides previous or subsequent agreements, etc). On the other hand, **short-form agreements** tend only to include the main commercial terms. They might be in the form of a **letter agreement**, where you'll usually ask the other party to sign and return a copy of your letter to confirm it is all agreed, or a **Deal Memo** (also known as a term sheet), setting out the main terms almost in a bullet-point fashion. Short-form agreements are generally legally binding in relation to the terms they contain, although they are often replaced in due course by a long form agreement containing all the additional terms. A **Memorandum of Understanding** is similar to a Deal Memo, but may go into more detail, and may sometimes in fact expressly state that it is *not* legally binding, and therefore may not be relied upon in a court of law.

Intention to bind, and the concept of consideration

For a contract to be binding, there usually has to be an intention by the parties to enter into a legally enforceable agreement. This usually goes without saying (especially if the agreement is in writing), the most notable exception being some agreements between family members.

Contracts themselves are basically two-way agreements. One party promises something, and another promises something in return. Generally (and ignoring a special form contract known as 'deed'), each party to a contract must have some form of obligation, even if it's an obligation to refrain from doing something. This concept is known (confusingly) as **consideration** for entering into the contract, and is based on the idea that you can't get something for nothing. Each party's consideration does not need to be equivalent in value to that of the other party, so long as some obligation actually exists. For example, if I simply promise to give you my car, there is no enforceable contract, even if I put it in writing. However, if you promise to give me $1 in return, or promise not to buy a car from someone else, or even simply to wait at home until I deliver it, you have given sufficient consideration for a binding contract and, if you keep to your side of the bargain, you can sue me if I don't turn up with the car.

Offer, acceptance, and 'Subject to Contract'

Technically, a contract is made (concluded), and thereby comes into force, at the point one party agrees to (ie. accepts) a set of terms offered by the other party. Before then, some terms might have been agreed in principle, but it may be that one or both parties don't want them to become enforceable until all the other provisions (ie. the contract as a whole) are also agreed. This is why many people agree to certain terms, but only 'subject to contract'. However, simply scribbling this at the top of pre-contract correspondence might not prevent it from being treated as an enforceable agreement in the eyes of the law if it's not clear on the face of it that there are still other terms yet to be agreed. So, in order to avoid the

...uation where letters discussing a potential contract, which agree various (but not all) terms in advance, are construed as the contract itself, it can be safer to state somewhere clearly 'subject to entering into a long-form agreement' (a letter is not a long-form agreement). Also, clearly marking a document 'draft' will (unless it's signed and dated) usually prevent anyone from claiming it to be an agreed, finalised and enforceable contract, even if it is in the long-form style.

Clarity/Certainty

A contractual provision is not likely to be enforceable if, on the face of it, it's not clear what it actually means. This is why some clauses seem to go on for ever explaining in minute detail the intention of the provision. Usually a decent definitions clause (typically at the beginning of the contract) will help to resolve this problem. But the important thing is to avoid ambiguity in a contract, and that's when formal legal advice can become invaluable.

Warranties and indemnities

A warranty is basically a contractual promise that a particular fact is true, rather than a promise to do (or not to do) something. For example, a promise that a script is original, non-defamatory and non-obscene, or that you have taken out all necessary insurance, or that you are authorised to enter into the contract in the first place. If the statement turns out to be false (eg. the script wasn't actually original, despite a warranty saying it was), the party giving the warranty can be sued by the other.

An indemnity is a no-nonsense obligation to reimburse in the event of a breach of contract (such as a warranty claim). Take for example a situation where a producer is sued because the script s/he commissioned from a writer turns out to be an illegal copy of someone else's work. Assuming that in the producer's contract with the writer there is both a warranty as to the originality of the script, and a full accompanying indemnity, the producer can reclaim from the writer any loss at all that s/he suffered as a result of the writer's breach of warranty, including the costs of fighting any case with the original owner of the script. Even without the indemnity, the Producer can sue for breach of warranty, but the added indemnity makes it clear exactly what can and can't be claimed (eg. legal fees, etc), so that there is no argument as to what loss suffered by the producer is to be compensated.

Law and jurisdiction

This provision is often tucked away amongst the boiler-plate. It is, however, an important consideration for anyone entering into a contract. The 'law' part it sets out what country's law should be used to interpret the contract. As most country's laws are fairly similar (although differences in copyright and moral rights do exist), this isn't necessarily too much of a worry. However, your lawyer will usually only be authorised to give advice on one country's law, and so will always prefer for the contract to confer with the law of the country in which s/he is legally qualified.

The 'jurisdiction' part states where you have to fight any case that results from a claim under the contract. If, as is often the case in the film business, the parties to a contract reside in different parts of the world, it becomes important to try to get your local courts (rather than those of the other party, thousands of miles away) agreed as the forum for resolving disputes.

What you need to know about copyright

Just as for contract law, copyright rules vary from country to country and so the following really is simply a basic explanation of the main principles rather than any kind of detailed legal advice. Most progressive nations have signed up to the *Berne Convention* which effectively gives copyright protection to anyone in any country that is a signature to the Convention, in respect of potential infringement in any other signatory country. Again, the following is based on UK law, but most concepts will apply for other jurisdictions.

Protecting expressions (in the form of 'works'), not ideas

The first thing to be aware of, is that copyright can *not* protect an idea, only the *expression* of it. In other words, if you come up with a concept, you cannot stop someone else from using or 'nicking' it unless you can show that they actually copied (or adapted) something that recorded or represented that idea. This 'something' that they copy must be a legally protected **copyright work**. For our purposes, the 'work' in question is likely to be something *literary* (ie. written, such as a script, book or computer program), *dramatic* (acted), *artistic* (painted, drawn, sculpted), *musical* (played or sung), *recorded* (sound), *filmed, broadcast* and/or a *cable* programme. To attract copyright, the work itself must generally be **original**. A first-draft script will normally be an original literary work, even if it is based on a previous book (unless the book is exactly 'copied'), but see adaptations, below.

Who can sue?

The person able to enforce copyright law is the work's **owner** (or, depending on the terms of the licence, a licensee). The initial owner will be the original **author** of the work, although s/he may subsequently sell (assign, transfer) or license this ownership to another person. For a film, the authors will normally be the producer and director, although as it is the producer who ultimately needs to own the copyright in order to exploit the film, s/he should obtain an assignment of all rights from the director. Note also that any work created in the course of employment will automatically be owned by the employer as author, and not by the employee. This is why most production contracts are described as '**work-for-hire**' agreements, an American term suggesting an employment contract between the producer and the worker s/he is engaging.

A bundle of restrictive rights

Contrary to popular belief, copyright doesn't actually give the owner any real right(s) to *do* anything at all. It is instead a bundle of restrictive or 'negative' rights, ie. the ability to *prevent* someone else from doing various things (or at least to claim compensation if they do). These six **restricted acts** are (i) **copying** (ie. reproducing in any form), (ii) **issuing** copies to the public (distributing), (iii) **performing in public** (including playing recordings to the public, as in a cinema / theater), (iv) **broadcasting**, (v) making an **adaptation** (eg. a script from a novel, film from a script, cartoon from a film, etc), or (vi) doing any of the above to an adaptation. To be able to exploit a film properly, a Producer needs to own all these rights. Note that an original adaptation (such as a script from a novel), unless a direct copy, will itself attract copyright protection despite potentially infringing the copyright of the original work. The point is that no-one can carry out any of these restricted acts without the owner's permission, or by actually becoming the owner by buying the copyright.

Some other legal bits you ought to know

Generally, the length of time that a work is protected for is until **70 years** after the death of the author.

Copyright is not infringed unless a **substantial part** of the original work is used. Even if it is, many countries have a **fair use** defence whereby there is no infringement for (say) using copyright material when doing a review or criticism on it, or (except for photographs) if it is used in the reporting of current events. If one work is included in another (eg. a picture in a film), but its use was merely incidental (and not 'featured'), there is also generally no infringement unless, in the case of music, the inclusion was deliberate.

A film's **title**, itself, can not attract copyright protection (and so can be used for another film), although the graphical description of it when used as a logo will be protected (both through copyright law and as a **trade mark**), and the use of the name — or one strikingly similar — will be illegal under '**passing off**' laws if it confuses the paying public into thinking the latter film is connected with the earlier one.

The need for transfers, assignments, licences and clearances

Copyright dealings can be compared with real estate. You can sell a piece of land, lease it for a period of years, subdivide it, keep hold of the freehold, and so on. Likewise, with copyright, you can sell it — or part of it — outright (known as a transfer or assignment), thereby retaining no rights in it, or license it for a period of years under certain conditions. Either way, you are effectively transferring to someone else the right to prevent a third party from carrying out the relevant restricted act(s) in relation to the work. You don't have to sell or licence the whole shebang in one go. For example, you can give the right to broadcast a film (the work) to one person, the right to distribute (issue copies to the public) it on DVD to another, and the right to adapt it into a book to another.

A producer needs to be the owner of all the copyright in a film so that s/he can grant the necessary rights to distributors in order for them to exploit it. An actor will create a dramatic work whilst performing his/her part, and so this copyright must be assigned to the producer. In fact, where anyone creates copyright specifically for the film (such as actors, writers, the director, composer, set designer, art director, costume designer), the Producer will require an assignment of it to obtain the necessary ownership. This might be in the form of a present assignment of future copyright, in the event that the contract is entered into before the copyright is created (as for actors, commissioned writers, etc).

Where copyright *already* exists, the producer will need permission to use it for the film. For example, the owner of copyright in a novel (usually a publisher) will have to grant the producer the rights to 'adapt' the novel into a film, along with all the rights necessary subsequently to 'exploit' it. This means the copyright in all formats for the entire period of copyright throughout the whole world. The producer will therefore need an assignment of the aspects of the copyright (adapting the novel, and then distributing, broadcasting (etc) that adaptation), which are known as the **underlying rights**. An exclusive licence of these rights, rather than an assignment, could also work if there are no major restrictions and if it is granted in perpetuity (thereby avoiding problems where copies of the film could outlive the licence period), but an assignment is always preferred. Under the assignment (or exclusive licence), the Producer effectively becomes the owner of the copyright, something that any financier will want to see by checking through the **chain of**

title documents (the string of contracts that demonstrate the transfer of the copyright from all the original authors to the ultimate Producer).

Where existing copyright is to be used in a film (other than where the film is actually based on the relevant work), such as a picture appearing on a wall, or a song playing on the radio, the Producer will only need **clearance** (a type of non-exclusive licence) to use the work in his/her film. S/he will not normally require the right to stop anyone else using the same work in another film. Such use will often be 'incidental', and therefore technically not an infringement of copyright, but obtaining clearance (a form of licence from the copyright owner) will avoid any doubt as to whether the work was incidental or, alternatively, 'featured' (in which case a licence is definitely required).

Practical ways to protect your work

In many countries, copyright protection exists automatically under the law, so you do not actually need to place the © symbol on the work for it to be protected. However, it is always good practice to mark a work with the symbol, together with the date of its creation, and the name of the author. This gives notice to potential infringers that it is a copyright work which you intend to protect. Another useful tool is to send yourself or your lawyer a copy of your original work through the recorded post / mail, and then do not open it when it is received (write on the outside of the envelope so you know what's inside!). This package can then be taken, still sealed and with the postal date marked on the envelope, to court and opened in front of a judge (so s/he can see it has not been tampered with), to prove it was in existence at the recorded date, during any proceedings for infringement.

Moral rights, performance rights and rental/lending rights

These rights are connected with copyright, and were brought in across the whole of Europe in the last 20 years or so. The main Moral Rights include the right to claim authorship (to have your name attached to your work), to have no derogatory treatment done to it, and to prevent false attribution (eg. unauthorised body-doubles). A Producer should, in each talent contract, get an express waiver of all of these rights. There are a few other European rights that have been brought in as a result of various recent EU legislation, such as the Performance Right (the right to income whenever a work is performed) and Lending Rights (the right to get paid if the work is rented, such as a video or DVD). When contracting with talent, a Producer should always, of course, take professional legal advice to make sure s/he acquires all the rights s/he needs, and will therefore be able to make and exploit the film without fear of being sued, having to pay damages or worse still, having the film injuncted (prevented from being released).

Creative Commons.

Created by Laurence Lessig in 2001, **Creative Commons** are a set of 'copyleft' licenses available 'off-the-shelf' for most countries worldwide to cover works where the creator actively wants end users to freely distribute, or remix, sample, remake and even sell their work (but still wishes to limit certain uses and be credited as author). Some 170 million content items online are tagged with the licenses, with Creative Commons sound effects now used in large budget Hollywood films. More information in Chapter 4 and at CreativeCommons.org.

Companies and Limited Liability

Let's say you are lucky (or clever) enough to be offered money for your film. Where does this money actually go? Who will it be given to? The chances are, nobody is going to give you millions (or even thousands) of dollars personally and, to be frank, you probably wouldn't want the responsibility or potential legal exposure anyway, should something go drastically wrong. As an individual, if you get sued, you can lose everything you own if you are judged to owe substantial damages.

The most common way to protect yourself from this potential liability is to produce the film through a limited company. That way, if the company gets sued (eg. for infringing copyright or breach of contract) and doesn't have enough money to pay, it simply goes bust. You, as director and/or shareholder of your company will not normally be at risk personally — unless you have been fraudulent or grossly negligent — and you will get to keep your house (and yacht). This is because the company, in law, is a different 'legal person' (or **entity**) to you. It can own things (such as copyright), do things (such as enter agreements, carry on a business, or produce a film), earn money and pay debts. If it does something wrong, it will get sued in its own right and will pay damages out of its own resources. It won't die of 'natural causes', but can be wound up (ie. dissolved), either voluntarily or because of insolvency.

Unlike an individual, a company has 'owners', called **shareholders**, who appoint (and may in fact be the same people as) **directors** to run and manage its business and other affairs. In turn, the company owns the business it runs. If it makes money, the profits get shared amongst the company's shareholders. Like an individual, the company will pay taxes on profits it makes, but not necessarily at the same rates (especially in so-called 'tax-havens', where corporate taxes, if they exist at all, can be very low). However, if a company makes a loss, the liability of the shareholders is limited to the amount they agreed put into the company when they started it up. Generally, the directors have various legal duties towards the company (and its owners), and their administrative requirements — such as filing annual accounts — can be quite high. The company will be 'registered' in a particular jurisdiction (such as a country or state) and must abide by the local corporate laws, although it can usually do business outside that jurisdiction. In most cases, companies must pay some form of income tax in respect of their employees, and those of a certain size typically have to be audited annually by independent accountants.

The cost of setting up a company depends on the jurisdiction and the type of company, but these days costs have come down in many countries, and you should be up and running for a few hundred dollars (or much less if you're willing — and able — to do the work yourself). There are, however, specialist organisations who will help you get off the ground, and their fees have also dropped considerably in recent years. By using one of these firms, you will reduce the chance of messing up the incorporation process.

Importantly, a company can have its own bank accounts, and it is into one of these that the production funds are paid. Usually the production money for any particular film is kept in a 'segregated' account, separate from the company's other money, so that it is used solely for the film, and not any other affairs (or to makeup for any losses) of the company. If the company, as **producer**, is the entity making the film, it will own the copyright, engage cast and crew, enter into all the production contracts, contract with financiers, and appoint the sales agent to

'Form the business skills to put a company together and keep an accurate record of accounts. It forces you to be business-like, makes you put better preparation into your film, make a better account of all the numbers and overall you'll get a better result because of this. The other thing is of course, that you can claim back VAT [consumer tax] if you are a registered company, which not all filmmakers will be aware of!'
Tom Swanston, Producer, The Ultimate Truth

sell the film. It will be accountable for all the contracts it enters into (as arranged by its directors), and as the film makes money, it will be responsible for repaying financiers their contributions and any profit.

Sometimes actors and other above-the-line talent will contract through a **loan-out company**, which is a specialised company they set up and own (again, to avoid personal liability). They technically work for the company, which contracts with the producer, promising to provide the services of the actor.

Company names can have different 'suffixes' (such as LLC, Limited, Inc, Ltd, plc, BV, SarL, Pty, etc, etc), depending on the country of incorporation, and the type of company it is. *Public* companies typically have greater filing and accounting disclosure requirements than private ones, and much of their corporate information is available for public inspection. *Listed* companies have their shares traded on a recognised stock exchange, so its shareholders will continually change.

Partnerships and LLPs

Sometimes, you will come across an entity known as a **'limited liability partnership'** (**LLP**), especially when dealing with a film fund. This is a particular kind of **partnership**, which is a different type of entity to a company. A partnership is basically a group of individuals (or other entities) that want to join up to do business together, and share in the costs and rewards of doing so. The partnership is not incorporated, so has less formalities than a company, and does not confer on its owners (partners) limited liability, as each partner is potentially personally responsible for the acts of any and all of the other partners. The partnership is not normally taxed in its own right, with each partner separately paying taxes in relation to profits from his/her/its partnership 'share'. An LLP is a special type of partnership whereby (if a film fund) the rights and obligations of the investors in the fund are considerably different to those of the fund's manager. It may have certain registration and reporting requirements, and as such can be considered as a kind of company-partnership hybrid.

Your accountant or lawyer should be able to advise you if there are any particular implications in carrying on a business through, or entering contracts with, an LLP or other partnership. They will also help you set up a company when the time comes, and assist with preparing the formal documents and filing at the relevant registry.

And finally... the film festival
Laurence Boyce, Hull International Short Film Festival,

With modes of distribution changing and the method of exhibition increasingly in the hands of the filmmaker, the question as to what exact role the film festival plays within the industry has become a pertinent one. Whilst the glitz and glamour of Cannes or the prestige of Berlin are well noted, they are only two of more than approximately 4000 film festivals from around the world. Are Film Festivals really worth the hassle of submitting to (especially the lesser known ones)? And, if you do, just how exactly can you make them work for you?

Film Festivals are often seen as a shop window for product and, in the case of the majors, the shop window displays are pretty damn large. The Cannes Market – which runs alongside the more visible competitions and galas – screen 1000s of films around the clock in the hope that distributors will attend and decide to pick up the film. And it doesn't matter who you are: anyone can get a screening in the Cannes Market as long as you prepared to stump up the cash. But with so many films vying for attention in a comparatively short amount of time, it's difficult to get yourself noticed amongst the general chaos, a similar situation to many of the other festivals/markets across the world.

Yet beyond the buying and selling, film festivals – at least the good ones — provide an important function. Firstly, as they're outside the normal constraints of distribution, they can take risks with their programme. From screening 'difficult' films to showcasing the work of debut directors, festivals can help encourage audiences to discover things that they may have never sampled before (and if the audiences go for it, the distributors will follow...) whilst also giving life to those films that have slipped through the cracks of distribution.

Secondly, they provide a forum for audiences, filmmakers and industry professionals to discuss films and filmmaking. On one level, there's the opportunity to meet people to work together with in the future and discuss new projects. But there's also the chance to gauge audience reactions to your work and get some real life feedback. It's certainly much better then having a sterile set of test scores on a sheet of paper. There's also the chance to see the work of your peers, an especially important fact when it comes to younger filmmakers. One of the biggest complaints from programmers – of which I include myself – is that people don't watch enough films. We wade through 1000s of submissions and see countless films which we have seen executed much more competently by someone else. How can you improve if you don't know what your being compared to? A film festival is the best opportunity to catch this work and it's one that every self-respecting filmmaker should take.

And, don't forget that if your film gets entered into competition, there's always a chance you could win. Any award at a Film Festival is a great promotional tool and a potential money earner – not only if there's a cash prize attached to the award but if there happens to be a distributor on the jury, there's an extra opportunity to sell your film. Let's not forget that festivals can also provide a host of fringe benefits such as parties and freebies. Which is never a bad thing in my blagging book.

If we agree that – generally – film festivals can be a good thing, just how do you decide which one(s) to enter? The answer is simple: research. Whilst everyone will know the 'biggies' by heart, you can find plenty that will offer the perfect place to screen your film. Go through websites to see what festivals have programmed previously and ask colleagues to recommend events that you should try. Just try and avoid the slapdash approach that many filmmakers employ by submitting to every film festival that you can think of. Have a strategy for what you are doing as it will save you a lot of hassle and heartache.

For some, the notion of being stuck on the 'film festival circuit' can fill them with dread. It conjures up images of niche screenings towards small audiences with – crucially – little or no money. Whilst this does sometimes happen, the role of film festivals — especially those that aren't considered 'A List' — has sadly been somewhat downgraded over the past few years. Yet, films can only be considered for distribution if they're actually seen, and film festivals provide this. Tastes for new types of films can only be cultivated when programmers take risks and educate them, and film festivals provide this. New projects and ideas take off when people are able to meet new collaborators, and film festivals provide this too.

Whether it be the red carpet at Cannes or a red welcome mat at a small cinema, festivals come in all shapes and sizes and – provided that you know what you want – can prove invaluable to selling, distributing and exhibiting your film. And, often, the free drink isn't bad either.

Currently the Director of the Hull International Short Film Festival, Laurence Boyce has been involved with film festivals since 1999, previously programming short films and the UK Film Week for the Leeds International Film Festival. He has been on the jury of numerous international film festivals as both a festival representative and as a film journalist.

Jeremy Thomas
Producer, Recorded Picture Company, Dream Machine

Jeremy Thomas is one of the UK's most seasoned international producers, who has embraced international productions with the fearlessness of a jungle explorer. 1988's *The Last Emperor*, which won Thomas an Oscar, was the first film from the west to be shot in China, and Bernardo Bertolucci's film crew were the first to get access to The Forbidden City. In another collaboration with Bertolucci, *The Little Buddha*, Thomas' team became the first crew to ever shoot in Bhutan, filming Buddhist monasteries which had never before been recorded. A genuine director's producer, Thomas has released a number of films with leading names including Takeshi Kitano (*Brother*), Terry GIlliam (*Tideland*), Richard Linklater (*Fast Food Nation*), David Cronenberg (*Naked Lunch, Crash*), Nic Roeg (*Insignificance*), Julian Temple (*Glastonbury*) and Jonathan Glazier (*Sexy Beast*).

What qualities would you say are most useful for a producer?
Well I suppose to be personable, or a combination or false form and being personable, with your own raft of ideas and dreams. You have to have some ideas and dreams to be a producer and you've got to be able to get them over many hurdles to get your film made. So the desires and dreams follow the idea, and the stronger the idea is, the easier it is to make whether it be a little three minute film or a big epic.

You went straight into epics early on — what was the genesis of The Last Emperor?
Well I had been working for years and years. I entered the film business in the late 60s, in 1967 in fact. I had been working since 17 in the movie business as an employee at the laboratory of Denham, processing film. Then I moved forward as a runner, then an assistant editor and then finally graduated to become editor, then I went on to produce my first film when I was 23-24, which was very young to produce a first film, but I had already been going a long time. And *The Last Emperor* was halfway through my journey, it was something that happened through chance meetings with people, and (Bernardo) Bertolucci giving me the autobiography of Puyi, and then the long journey to make that film. But that was something that had happened after making films for a long time and I had already learned a lot about making films.

How did you go about pulling together the team for it?
Well I was a big fan of Bertolucci, so when he proposed the film to me it was an easy decision, I want to make it. Especially a film about 60 years of Chinese history, the last Emperor, son of heaven, lord of 10,0000 years, absolute ruler of a quarter of the world who died as a gardener, it was an extraordinary story. It has an extraordinary history running behind it. But the size of the film was so gigantic, it was a day at a time. And the people who came to work on the film were all wonderful in the various capacities from Vittorio Storaro who is a great cameraman to fantastic designers, costume designers and production people who had worked in China before, and then of course the Chinese themselves who were very, very involved in the mounting of the film and delivering that incredible thing you saw on the film. Including the Forbidden City, as a location, which was open to us, we were one of the first people to take a camera into this place. I'm a great believer in shooting films for real if you can and will always go

and make a film in the real place rather than build it if I can.

How hard was it to get access?
It was very difficult and took a long time. But they wanted the film. Initially we had to get permission to proceed with it and they wanted this film. And there was this idea that it would be great to have Bertolucci to be making a film in China but particularly in China a film about a man who was born as an Emperor who could die happily as a gardener. This was a story they were very happy that we wanted to come and tell, and spend tens of millions of dollars making a film which endorses an ideology in certain respects.

Did you have to present their version of the story?
We had to have the screenplay read for accuracy, but the changes they asked for were minor and factual, not political at all. We shot the film, the film was sent back every night to Italy from Peking or wherever we were, back to Rome, to Technicolor, and then the film was edited and then they saw the movie. There was maybe one person on the set listening to what was being shot. But there was no surveillance and we were pretty free once we got these permissions.

The main difficulty was communication, and making arrangements: we're gonna be here on this date to shoot and we need that, and you'd arrive and they'd got the wrong day, or didn't know the time, didn't understand that making a movie with 100s of people, there's a time factor. When you have 100s of people, trucks and lights and cameras, and actors, you need the place to be open so you can get through the front door. Those kinds of little annoyances.

Taking on a project of that scale, how did you psyche yourself up for it?
It was a day at a time. I suppose, coming back to what it takes to be a producer, there was a dream, and I shared that dream with Bertolucci, and we made it happen. With a lot of other people of course, but there was a push, some kind of energy and effort in terms of pushing that thing into reality from being an idea on the page, it was a mass of work, and cost a mass of money.

Later you made The Little Buddha in Bhutan, was that the first film shot there?
First cameras in there, yeah. That was an exciting thing to do, and you hope that you can deliver to the cinemagoer something amazing by going to such a place with a camera and filming drama in it. You couldn't have built these things, it's unbuildable, the Forbidden City is unbuildable. We'd seen it in things like 55 Days of Peking, but the sets are just a little bit of wall. It's not the Forbidden City as we knew it. And the same with Bhutan, we wanted to find the most impressive monasteries in the Himalayas, and they exist in Bhutan, so we had to go there to get that. And all those ceremonies, and Buddhist events that we filmed they were real, with our actors in them. So you had this reality going on and it would have been very difficult to get extras to do that. Plus of course equipment now is getting smaller and smaller and you can go to more and more extraordinary places to shoot your movie, if you can persuade your actors to come with you.

Are there skills a producer needs in a situation like that?
Well they're personal skills, it's like being a diplomat, they are skills of intelligence, and again finding the right help. So I found the right help to get into Bhutan, to help with the various problems that we encountered. We were in Katmandu and there was a lot of unrest when we were filming there. We were there for months between Katmandu and Bhutan. It sounds very exotic but the story took us there. It's not a case of gratuitously going to these places, you needed to go to these places to make the movie.

And in The Sheltering Sky in the desert, going right through the desert with a camera crew. You can feel it in the film, in the middle of no-where, you can feel that you are with them in 360 degrees of desert all around. It takes a lot to take crew and actors out there to a place where you can die in a second, you have to look after the crew, you have to plan it like a military campaign. You have to think about everything.

These were high budget films for an independent..
These were the three high budget films I've made. I'm not a specialist, I mean, I live in London and make my films out of the UK, I'm not in a Hollywood system of studio movies that make that size of films, it's a very difficult mountain to climb, and I've done it three times. I'm not sure if I'll ever do a film like that again, maybe I won't.

How did you go about raising the finance for The Last Emperor?
In the same old way, the begging bowl, you know, please (cups hands). And you do it with some idea of what the film is and where you're going to find the money. That film, of course, it was difficult promoting the first western film to be shot in China. Can you

do it, will you be able to do it, can we believe we can do it? But in fact the Chinese authority's open door policy to us enabled me to bring lots of banks into the film because they all wanted to come into China and I managed to persuade them that coming in was an artistic endeavor, approved by the Chinese authorities and good for the bank. And I arranged meetings with the head bankers, and I had some knowledge of who ran the main institutions in China, who had interactions with western companies, and the banks came along and put a lot more money than banks normally put into movies. It was the first and only time that I got banks involved in a movie but there was another reason why they wanted to be involved. And when I came back to the next movie having made them an incredible film, a lot of money and all the Oscars and all that stuff that went with the movie, they said, well, not this time — there was no appetite in the City, but they wanted to be there in that film, China was there as a welcoming commercial arm.

Was it after that you got money from the Japanese?

The French were the first to come in, they came in with some development money, then the Japanese came in with some development money. Because it was a very expensive film to develop. Normally if there's a film set today with no set building and people wear regular clothes you need only a few weeks for preparing it. But if every costume and set has to be designed or made you have a mighty pre-production period to get the film ready for production. So to fund the film and get money for the development, I had to spend $2m of investors money on a film where the financing hadn't yet been completed.

Is most of your day-to-day funding from producers fees?

That's the basic idea, but it's not like that now because of the years of work. But initially I did that. It was hand to mouth at the beginning of course, sleeping on floors as anyone does, but after years of making films after so many years and so many movies it all comes together as one lump, and a lot of my older films are paying for my current life, ie development money is coming from the past. I don't see the film industry today in the way I did at the beginning because then I was producing for fees to make my work pay for my life and development.

Today I don't focus on the fees as much I focus as the movie, and how its structured and set up and what I

can generate out of that film once it's shot and made, so I'm trying to make the film as cheaply as possible. I'm not trying to suck the film, I'm trying to make the film economically and then put it out, so it's more of a longer game plan. It's a company with 30 people covering sales marketing, development delivery, it's a constant going round.

When did Hanway set up?

1997. I have had involvement in many different sales companies over the years. What an indie producer needs in his arsenal of filmmaking tools is a good relationship with a sales company or a sales company of his own.

I imagine it must make a big difference for recoupment?

Well it's not so much that because the money's been prearranged with the people who put the money up, you get your little piece for getting the film out and most of the money would go back to investors initially. You'd normally make a film in a trustee company set up, you don't handle the money, the money is handled by an unimpeachable source with a prearranged waterfall of money, first this, then that. But having a number of things going on rather than one thing at any time, it helps with the cash-flow as our business doesn't have any outside investors in it. It would be difficult making some of these films that we make with investors on our back saying why didn't you make a romantic comedy, why don't you do this, why don't you make a film that's traditionally popular.

How are your current projects being financed?

Every film is different. It always turns into something else, unless you've got financing from a parent, it's like being a kid, unless you can get it all paid for by a parent, you've got to get it financed by someone else. If you work for a major studio, they pay for 100% of the film and they own 100% of the film and give you some piece of the profits and you're doing a job for them and they pay for that and you don't have to worry about where the profits are coming from.

And that is the traditional way of making film, the large industrial companies, the industrialisation of film, the large major companies who control production, that is the normal financing route.

The independent financing route is what's left of the scraps at the end of the table because the majority of the decent stuff is taken up by the big companies who can push their films into the market no matter what the merit of the movie.

We're very dependent on reviews, word of mouth and PR in the independent world because you're making an economical film and you can't afford to spend one or two times the cost of a film to market it, whether it's any good or not, whereas the large international conglomerate make a movie, and the release date for that film and the worldwide plan for that has already been thought out when it goes into production.

If it's $100m film, maybe they'll spend $100m marketing it, it will go out on X-thousand cinemas around the world, it is pre-planned and a very different kind of operation and the money spent on the marketing is so enormous. And whatever the merit of the film, the entertainment value of the film, there'll full page ads and a complete blanketing of the world of media, cable TV and every way you can. They've got the machinery: private jets, junkets, to ensure that that investment is covered, and it's only in exceptionally bad luck that they can not get a film out there and get over the hurdle of recoupment.

When do you start marketing a film?
I'm involved with the marketing in my mind when I begin, but I don't always have the resources to do that so I work on the marketing throughout the film, get together pieces of journalism by people to go with but you can't pay for everyone to come in like a large film, you've got to invite them in and find a clever way to do that, and then you use festivals and other ways of getting your film out. You're thinking about marketing all the time. At the beginning you're thinking about the movie, and then as you develop your skills, that marketing becomes something you do as a producer without thinking about it.

Just looking at the directors you've worked with you're not afraid to work with auteurs
That's personal taste, plus they're filmmakers that I admire and filmmakers I can promote. Many things go for it. You're more likely to get a good movie. First time movie makers I've been working with, you can see where they are and I've had some good work out of that. But by and large I want to work with someone whose work I've seen and I know what they're going to do with something. So I can read a book or think about material with a director whose films I know, and then I can be a producer and I can say, well he's going to do that. It's not a shotgun blast for me, it's more a rifle shot, of what thing's gonna be.

I use this all the time but it's like knowing painters. We all know what a Hockney looks like, or a Picasso, a Dali, roughly, you look and go ooh that's a Dali, that's a Picasso. It's like you say to these painters, you ask them to paint this table, or this bunch of flowers, one will be abstract, one realistic. It's the same with filmmakers, you have a piece of material and you think oh this is definitely one for Ken Loach. Or a first time director and you love the commercials he makes and you know that's going to be good. I want to know the level you're working at, you want to know what the director's doing culturally as a creator and what you want as a producer for your film. And either that happens at the beginning of your career, or you develop that, if you're going to have any longevity.

Are there challenges of working with someone with a big reputation or a way of working — do you have to work around them?
Yeah if someone has developed their own style of work — everyone works in a different own way. Some like to do one or two takes, some like to do 30 takes. Some directors like to to do lots of coverage, some like to do cut to cut, some like no rehearsals with actors, some want to be instant on the set, some like to do to rehearsals till its word perfect. They all want to do it a different way and you just want to come to terms with that. As long as its bearing fruit, you let it happen because you've chosen to work with that film artist for what they do and they get to that place by doing it that way.

Have you got any any advice for making creative relationships work?
It's very difficult, how do you make a marriage work? Give and take. Credibility. Tread softly and carry a big stick I suppose. Have the ability to be in charge of your film but know you're in a creative process which is very technical and exacting, but its still a creative process and you need to deal with creative people in a different way.

Paul Haggis
Writer & director, Crash & Million Dollar Baby

Haggis followed up the screenplay to Clint Eastwood's Million Dollar Baby with Crash, which he wrote, directed and executive produced. The film, which weaves together stories of race relations in LA, went on to win Best Screenplay and Best Picture at the Academy Awards, 2006. Interview by Stephen Applebaum

Unless I'm really uneasy with what I'm writing, I lose interest very quickly. I like to write about things about which I have no answers, questions that trouble me. These things trouble me. You want to dig in and find out what something means to you. And if you do that, I think you have to take risks. I also guess I'm a bit of a contrarian. I left television when everyone was rushing to it. When Jerry Bruckheimer was going 'My God! Television! It's taking over!' I was going, 'You know what? I think I'll go into independent film.' I guess I've never been interested in taking the path that everyone else takes.

I can't say I'm overly political. I'm just as concerned as the next citizen and feel that if you're concerned you have a responsibility to do something about that. So, you know, we're just doing little things here in Los Angeles to make actors, writers and directors a little more aware of what our country is doing in our name. If we can each do our little bit then maybe, eventually, something will happen.

(Funding) it was terrible. No one wanted to do it. First of all I was an unknown director. I had directed for television but that's actually worse. It would have been better if I had been a complete unknown. Also, it's very hard to tell the tone of the movie from

the script, because it could have come off as really preachy, or rather the characters preaching and being didactic, and the film could come off that way, which I didn't want to do. I wanted to lampoon these characters who were saying these great, wonderful things. So we took it out of the studios, no one wanted it, and we took it to quite a few financiers, and they liked the script but didn't want to do it with me as the director. And then, finally, we found Bob Yari and Cathy Schulman, and they said, 'Yeah, we'll put up a little bit of money, to get it cast.' So it took us a year and a half to get the right cast that worked for them so they'd put more of the money up. All the actors worked for nothing. We all waived our fees.

Don Cheadle was great. Don was the first person onboard. I was terrified taking this film to Don. For one, I didn't know him; I didn't know any of these actors. He was the first African-American actor who read the script, and also I have so much respect for him. So when he came to sit in my living room, I had no idea what he was going to say. He might have just come to say, 'Listen, I just want to say what a racist bastard you are, and I want to say it to your face.' He didn't. He sat down and said, 'I want to do the movie.' I said, 'Great. What role?' He said, 'I don't care, any role.' He actually went back and forth between the role of the television director and the police detective for six months. Every week he'd phone and go, 'You know what? I changed my mind.'

He finally made up his mind six months later. We asked him to produce the film with us largely because I knew he'd bring a credibility that I didn't have. People look at him and they know he's associated with quality films. Also, actors want to act with Don Cheadle. He's an actor magnet. He's like Sean Penn.

I don't think it's the job of filmmakers to give anybody answers. I do think, though, that a good film makes you ask questions of yourself as you leave the theatre. The ones that are a total experience in themselves, where you leave the theatre going, 'Yeah, nice film' I think are failures."

Stephen Applebaum

Nik Powell
Virgin, Palace, Scala & NFTS

When it comes to building media businesses, Nik Powell has an unprecedented record in the UK. Childhood friend of Richard Branson, Nik co-founded Virgin Records with him, and then took on the running of the Scala Cinema where he set up producer-distributor Palace Pictures with Stephen Woolley. Palace produced dozens of landmark UK features including *Company of Wolves*, *Mona Lisa* and *The Crying Game*, as well buying for the UK the first films from Lars von Trier, the Coen Brothers and Sam Raimi. When Palace ended, Powell launched Scala Productions with Woolley, and left recently to head up the National Film and Television school.

Is it more important for producers to focus on packaging their film as a sellable product, or in creating a good film?

They're both key. You can be a creative producer if you're in partnership with an entrepreneurial style producer, and you can be a creative producer if you're employed by someone — at Working Title or whatever. But you can't be an independent producer and only creative. You also can't be an independent producer and only entrepreneurial. You know you have to have both sets of skills because they are both required. You need to create a script that will attract.

The producer's job is to create a script that will attract talent; the talent attracts the money. That's how it works; there aren't any real shortcuts. And there are certain kinds of money that are not cast-sensitive, so cast doesn't matter; certain kinds of money that are not director-sensitive, so therefore you can cast a first time director; there are certain kinds of money that are only really interested in tax deductions, so they only real care about you getting the film made — they don't care about quality or anything else.

So you need the different skills, but you need to be able to create things that attract interesting talent. What we're trying to do is make a film that stands up, gets released, and hopefully people go and see, and the critics like. We might not achieve all these things, but that is really our goal; everything else is just a means to get that. So the process in itself is geared to that, it's not geared to whether the distributors like it, whether financiers like it, any of those things. I'm saying the obvious, but we will not change things. Most of my producer colleagues will not change anything if it will lose our main audience, even if it will get us some money. But it can be tricky because you don't want to spend two years making a film that will go down the plug-hole; that no-one ever sees. We've all made those films of course — just look at my CV; quite a few of them — too many!

Sometimes a producer kind of treats it as an end — get the film made and that's all that counts. But it's not actually, its the least important thing. The most important thing is to get a film that the people who you make it for want to go and see.

What was the first sale you made at a market or festival?

Company of Wolves was the first one, and we took that to MIFED, which is a market not a festival, and we sold it to America, to Cannon. And they paid loads of money for it. It was a bit worrying because I did the whole deal with the famous partners at Cannon, Menahem [Golam] and Yoram [Globus], and at the end of the meeting Yoram said to Menahem, 'Don't you think you should see the film?'. Because we were number one at the British box office at the time, he was like 'Oh no it's number one in England, I'm sure it's fine', and Yoram said 'No, before you sign this I think you should go see the film'. And I thought 'fuck me, they're going to hate the film'. I had thought I was going to get away without having to show it to them. So they asked me when the screening was, and I said there's one tomorrow at 9am. I came in at quarter to 9 and I went off to get a coffee. When I came back and it was about ten past nine and I looked in the hall and there was no Menahem in there, where I was showing the film. So afterwards, I went down to the Cannon office and there was Menahem. I just assumed he'd hated it and walked out, and that was the end of it — my first fairly major international deal. I was about to say 'did you hate it?', but fortunately I didn't. He said, 'Ah Nik, we can close the deal now'. I said 'What do you mean? You've only seen like ten minutes of it' — he said 'Nik, my own films I only see ten frames, I seen ten minutes of your films, it's fine'. And the first ten minutes is just a Volvo driving, it's got nothing to do with the rest of the film.

So he signed. It's essentially an art film really, but they released it like a horror film. I remember Steve and I saw it in a house in New York, which was quite a downmarket horror house, and they definitely didn't like the film. But the critics loved it, and it was a big hit here in the UK.

How do you deal with criticism?
I don't care, because most people have lousy taste and judgement. It's like the good script syndrome — every successful film has a great script, but when I've been involved in some of those successful films and taken the script around, 90% of people hated the script. But suddenly its a great script because its a hit, so these things are subjective. There are people in this business whose opinions I take totally seriously, like my ex-partner Steve Woolley, or Jeremey Thomas — you know, heavyweights. But the majority of the industry — they've never made a film, they've never had a hit, it's 'What do they know?'. They may be great script development executives, but they don't have any kind of proven track record.

But if a film is not successful then I always look and analyse that to see where I've gone wrong. Maybe I didn't develop the script enough. Maybe I cast it wrong — or allowed the director to cast it wrong, or maybe it was the wrong story at the wrong time. Whatever. I like to take a good hard long look when things don't work. Maybe it was just the execution of the film and we cocked it up and did a bad job — but I don't need someone else to tell me that. But failure informs you.

And if it's a critical hit and a box office failure then I don't feel so bad because we've got a good film, and we've got it out there and for one or other reason it hasn't worked. People think it's a good film, it just hasn't caught fire.

But a general industry thing — the first screening I ever went to in the industry was a screening of *The Killing Fields*. So I went in and thought, fantastic film, playing *Imagine* at the end was a piece of genius. It's a difficult subject matter; but it really delivers. I couldn't find a single other person who was in that screening room — and it was all people from the industry — who liked the film. They've all got an axe to grind. They all hate Puttnam (I mean they would never say that to him, but they're all jealous of his success). And it was all, 'I don't think that was very good', and 'Playing *Imagine* at the end — what a sell out', and, 'Performance by Sam Waterston, ooh I don't know'. He went on to be nominated for an Oscar of course, and nine months later when all that happened they were all 'Yeah yeah. Thought it was fantastic. That Sam Waterston performance was outstanding.' and you think 'My God, these are people who have to really run to keep their jobs'. But to me, it was just a really fantastic piece of filmmaking and it had to be admired and liked. And it made an important statement about the world. I don't care about how untrendy someone is — Puttnam or whoever — the film speaks for itself. And so often I've been at screenings where 90% of people have walked out. Like my most famous example was *Blood Simple*, the Coen brothers movie. And that was distributors seeing it, not English industry people who would have hated it even more.

I went in with Joel and Ethan Coen, Sam Raimi and Bob Tappert. Sam Raimi had put me onto it and we'd done *Evil Dead* together already. Oh, and Paul Webster – who I had in distribution at the time. We sat down in this crowded screening. Because it was called *Blood Simple*, obviously all these distributors thought it was going to be a fantastic slasher movie, and of course it is a very slow paced movie. So when I woke up from the film at the end, there was only Joel and Ethan, me and Paul, and Sam and Bob Tappert in the cinema. There were about three other people. It had been packed at the beginning, but I hadn't noticed because I'd been so involved in this incredible film. So I knew I could get the film for next to nothing, which I did.

And when I saw Lars von Triers' first film *Element of Crime* — most people have never seen it — I paid $5000 for that, in MIFED again. Very weird film — as one might expect from Lars von Triers' first film. I brought it back and I proudly showed it to all the staff at Palace; showed it to Daniel Battsek who was head of distribution at the time, who now runs Disney [now Miramax]. He and some of the staff came back to my office, and came to see me and said 'Nik, we've just watched this film, it's completely crap, and if you were not our boss, we'd fire you.' That's the advantage of being a boss — employees can't fire you. The banks can fire you, but they can't.

So Steve and I saw *Diva* — we saw *Diva* in LA — we flew from LA to Paris to make the deal because we thought it's gonna be a hit. It's a flash film about absolutely nothing. Beautifully paced, beautifully made, flash superficial film and it doesn't matter that it's in French, and it went onto do huge business. *Evil Dead* Steve saw by himself and just came back and said we had to buy it, and we met this young filmmaker and I decided the only reason Steve wanted to sign this film — I hadn't seen it myself yet — was because this young filmmaker Sam Raimi called Steve 'Sir'. Steve's a working class north London boy and Sam is a mid-western, more middle class. Of course they're trained in those manners — they call you 'Sir'. And so there's this 19-year old Sam calling 22-year old Steve 'Sir', and that was too much for Steve and he had to sign it. No, he loved it, and he thought the movie was fantastic, and he was right.

Very often you're alone and very often you're not. For *My Left Foot* and *Cinema Paradiso* we were up against Harvey Weinstein, who we were also making films for then, so that was kind of tricky. There was lots of double dealing involved, but we won out in the end.

How have you developed your business partnerships?

I've been lucky in my partners. I've had the same number of partnerships as I've had marriages, but the partnerships lasted longer, tho they all ended at the end of the day because I'm not a believer that things need to last forever to be valuable. And you remain friends with your partners even when you stop being their partners. In fact I think one of the secrets of remaining friends with your partners — both in marriage and in business — is stopping them at the right time, and not getting to the point where you want to murder each other. So I've been lucky with Branson and Woolley — and I've always looked for people who are not the same as me, that are very complimentary to me, whom I deeply trust.

Specifically after [the partnership with] Richard ran out, I wanted someone who combined creativity and business and Steve had reprogrammed the Scala cinema (that Branson and I had bought and put some money up to kind of rescue it because it was going bankrupt). And our friend Jo Boyd, who was on the board of it, had recommended this little punk guy to run it. So I met Steve and he impressed Richard and me hugely about what he was going to do to turn it around. And a lot of people do that — they have the mouth, but then they don't actually turn it around. But Steve did, and he turned it around with a mixture of putting on the Clash and the Sex Pistols, who were unknown at the time, and throwing out all the European films and programming it with American absurdist films — early John Waters and suchlike -, good eastern European films, because Steve loves films from everywhere, and he turned it around putting us in profit within 12 months of taking over. It never made big money, but it was creative. Steve knew the value of having midnight shows by the Sex Pistols. It's not easy to organise. So I thought 'That's my man', and when I sold out of Virgin I approached him because he had the qualities I want.

Stephen Woolley and I, and before that me and Branson — I think our very hiring practices were very different to our competitors. We were never very interested in experience, for instance.

First of all, we couldn't afford to pay what our competitors could pay, both at Virgin and at Palace, so we couldn't pay for experienced people. I learnt this off Richard really. We basically employed people who we figured were intelligent; had intelligence and insight and focus and ambition; and we didn't really care if they'd worked for a farm.

And that's what we required. So when [Daniel] Battsek came into my office, he had worked in the mailroom at Hoyts in Australia — and he was dead impressive, I sent him over to Paul [Webster]. Steve had brought Paul in because he'd programmed the Gate cinema and Steve was very impressed — and Steve was saying we did need someone who knew a little bit about distribution.

What would you advise a producer in building a business?

I never believed in this building your company up. I think Tim [Bevan, Working Title] has done it fantastically. But there's only a few. Film producers produce films, that's what we do for a living, and everything is simply to service that purpose. Other than the Working Title model — I think there's not a business model that works. t's only the people who are on salaries who think that there is a business model that works. You can have 500 examples to show that they don't work, and you know producers should concentrate on producing, not on building businesses, and if they happen to have successful films they'll have lots of cashflow and there'll be a business there and if they don't, they don't.

So my advice to a producer is concentrate on producing, because that is your core business, and people should stick with their core businesses. It's not about building a business, unless you're a real entrepreneur, in which case you know, the Working Title or the Palace model (which could have worked). In that case you're an entrepreneur and your core business is distributing, and secondarily producing. And that can work, but that's a different thing. I don't believe a production company in itself is a viable business model. I think producing for yourself is a very viable life, a nice life.

Nicole Kassell
The Woodsman

After watching Steven Fechter's play, *The Woodsman*, first time writer/director Nicole Kassell wrote a screenplay adaptation on spec and sent it to the author, and on eventually finding a producer, insisted he could only have the script if she directed it.

What made you choose pedophilia, one of the last taboos, as the subject of your first film? Aren't first films difficult enough to make without putting further obstacles in your way?
I really felt like the subject matter found me. I didn't search for the most difficult topic to make a film about [laughs]. But I saw Steven Fechter's play, *The Woodsman*, back in March 2000, and was so affected by it that I really felt it was a story that was important to tell. The more research I did, the more I discovered that there was an epidemic problem, and the more committed I came to it. So I knew I was raising the stakes against myself. But the odds of getting a film made period are so slim, and a first feature even harder, I figured why not? You have to be passionate about it and I was. I went for it.'

What was Steven Fechter's reaction when you sent him your screenplay adaptation of his play on spec?
Well the first draft he saw, or when I showed him the first draft, he was impressed that I'd done it period, and liked where it was going. From that point on he was involved in every draft. We would sit down and discuss a draft in detail and I would sit down and write it. So he didn't get surprised in any big way through the writing phase. It was more when I went off to film the movie that he was not involved. But I know when he saw the final film he felt very proud and said the movie was true to the heart of the play.'

What kinds of reactions did you get when you sent the script out in search of finance?
It took a very long time. The big break I got was winning the Slamdance screenplay competition in September 2001. At that point we started sending the script out and we got a lot of reactions of, 'We love the script but it's too dark, too hard to raise the money, too edgy,' so it was a full year before I found Lee Daniels, the producer. He came on in September 2002.

Daniels, of course, produced *Monster's Ball* and seems attracted to dark and edgy material. Did he ask you to change anything?
He was very happy. He didn't ask for any changes. In fact I kept re-writing it and he got irritated! I'm a compulsive re-writer. He supported the re-writing but he was happy with it as it was. Yeah, he loved the script. He said it was the best thing he'd read since *Monster's Ball*. After *Monster's Ball* he thought he'd get offered all these great projects but he was actually getting what he calls 'Leprechaun 3 in the Hood' type projects. So it's really a testament to him that he was interested in more complex material.

And what do you think brought Kevin Bacon onboard?
We sent it out. We went to a couple of people before Kevin got it and it was similar to the producers' reaction: 'It's a great character but . . . ' People did feel it would be putting their career on the line, I guess. Kevin's never been afraid and made choices based on that fear.

Did you have any apprehension, as a first time director, about working with people like Kevin who have been making films for years?
I did but it was also my dream. I got over the intimidation by focusing very much on the material. I had lived with it for three years at that point and that's where my confidence came from.

Were you going to pursue this whatever? Were there occasions where you almost gave up?
There was always that nagging question in my head about how long would I wait and what would I do if it didn't come together. But every time that doubt got really strong, we would have a breakthrough and that's what kept me going. Every six months there would be something that just reminded me or encouraged me to believe in it and keep going. So I did.

Stephen Applebaum

Wendy Bevan Mogg
Producing shorts

After writing the 35mm short *Rare Books and Manuscripts*, Wendy produced a number of successful shorts, including Chris Vincze's *Evol* and Magali Charrier's *Space Between Us*.

How did you get into producing?
I was working as a freelance script editor (after stints in distribution and sales) and came across the short story Rare Books and Manuscripts by Toby Litt. I knew it would make a wonderful short film, and decided that it was a case of now or never to make my first film.

How did you raise the money for your last two shorts?
Space Between Us was fully funded through the Screen South digital scheme. Evol was funded by the director, though by the time this is printed we should have made the budget back in sales. The piece also benefited from a great deal of in kind support.

How easy was the process?
Relatively easy. Public funding tends to mean a good deal of paperwork though!

How should a producer best present themselves to funders?
Honestly. Short films rarely make their money back, and it would be foolish to suggest that a larger budget project will easily break even. Far better just to be upfront about what the project is, where it will be seen, and what the funder will get out of it. If it's a private funder, what is their interest in the project? In terms of a short, they're more likely to be interested in the process itself than in making a profit; if it's a public funder, how do you see the distribution process, and where will this project be taking your team?

What qualities would you say are most helpful as a producer?
Endless patience. The ability to become production manager, location manager, accountant and nanny all at once! It also does help to have an understanding of what the buyers are buying; and the courage to be honest with your director about your thoughts on their decisions. And also the understanding that at the end of the day, short films are a directors'

medium, and that it's only by building up a slate of shorts that a producer will start to get noticed.

Is it worth having a distribution strategy other than festivals from the start?
It's worth knowing your audience and being aware of length and content (useful to have a TV version of films with swearing in, for example!) but generally I would suggest that the film is allowed to 'be' what it is – if you're too aware of the endgame you risk diluting the film's impact. If you concentrate on making a really good film, the festivals will come.

Having said that, it's important to be aware that the more 'commercial' the film, the less likely the film is to get into a festival. This doesn't mean that it's a bad film — but programmers tend to prefer certain themes etc and recently it's certainly been social realism above, for example, comedy.

Jan Dunne and Elaine Wickham,
Gypo

A few months after first meeting short filmmaker Jan Dunn and producer Elaine Wickham met up to discuss possible ideas for a microbudget feature as a calling card. Just two months later they started principle photography on Gypo, with a cast that included Withnail & I's Paul McGann, and Father Tedd/Angela Ashes' Pauline McLynne. After a thirteen day shoot their £50,000 film had wrapped and become the UK's first Dogme certified film. At the film's first industry screening in London it was picked up for UK distribution and international sales. The film premiered at Edinburgh in 2005 to massive acclaim, and went on to pick up the British Independent Film Award gong for outstanding production.

How did you first get the idea for Gypo?
Jan Dunn: I had only recently met Elaine through a Screen South new talent initiative. She'd been selected as a new producer and myself as a new director. She saw my shorts Mary's Date and Joan

and couldn't believe I'd made them for just a few hundred quid and she made this mad suggestion that we hook up together and just go out and make a feature in the same way, simply using it as a calling card to get finance for our first features. The only parameter she gave me was it had to be set and shot in Kent as that's where she lived. I began researching that evening about subject matters that I might use from the region and it became clear I should incorporate the refugees, particularly Romany Czech's. I then pitched about seven ideas, she loved two so I incorporated them and we were shooting eight weeks later.

How long did it take to develop?
I have to stress that our intention was to make it as a calling card, so not very long at all really. I wrote the first draft in two days and then Elaine is a genius script editor, so she made a whole bunch of notes and changes which I followed completely and that's the draft I shot with.

How much was the budget?
Elaine: The actual budget is approximately £250K but we cash flowed on just under £50K and incorporated some specially designed investments that were not really deferments but integrated legally bound investment deferrals from our executive producers at VMI for the camera kit and Molinare for our post production, and even the BBC came in with two days of clear up on sound (there is no track laying or post dubbing under dogme rules). This to us was better than industry support in the traditional way because it meant we started to build relationships with these people and they rarely defer.

Was it cut down much from the original target?
Elaine: Even the original paper budget came in at around £800K but fortunately Jan has a producer's head and it was team work that brought it right down. The leading actors were the only performers we paid, everyone else did it for the break and we cast a lot of parts with Jan's mates as she used to be an actor and from Dover Youth Theatre. Jan was adamant that we cast the younger people from youth theatre rather than stage school. She was absolutely right as they are so real and earthy compared to some stale child performances you sometimes see from teenagers from stage schools.

What changes did you make?
Elaine: We didn't have development time to change anything, we actually set out from the beginning to make a film for the cash we could get our hands on. Jan was great, in that she wrote around the budget

and pretty much from walking around Thanet, here in Kent. She incorporated a whole load of things just in the vicinity, like the Ramsgate Marina for instance, a stone's throw from where the actors were staying. It was all meticulously planned beforehand.

How easy was it raising finance?
Elaine: We didn't raise any, we just went out and shot this film for the cash Jan and I decided we could get our hands on by beg, stealing or borrowing.

How did you go about getting the sponsorship from Pfizer?
Elaine: They have a tiny fund which goes towards helping local people. Jan never had any traditional training and when she (and I) first set out to get jobs as runners, it was near impossible because we were in our thirties. It made us adamant that we would help some selected people (no age discrimination). We also both left school with no qualifications, so we wanted to help bright, intelligent young people who are really talented but didn't necessarily have an academic background. Pfizer gave us £1000 towards us incorporating a trainee scheme. It worked so well that two of the four went on to get places at Ravensbourne to edit and at the New York Academy to train for theatre. It was fantastic and we were so proud when they kept in touch and were so grateful for the help. So successful was the scheme that we incorporated one into our new film that is proving to be equally productive and the boy who went to Ravensbourne came on board as our trainee editor this time and has just secured a job with MotionFX on the new Viper Streaming System, we're like proud mother hens.

Any lessons learnt from the process?
Elaine and Jan: You can't make a film with your own money without making huge, enormous sacrifices (property/relationships etc) and have to be prepared to work seven days a week for longer than a year and not getting paid for it. It's an enormous risk but for us it has begun to pay off with the incredible success of Gypo – which started life as a calling card and ended up not just gaining us entry into the industry but lots of awards and critical acclaim too. Whether it actually makes our money back is yet to be seen but it has achieved much more than we intended. We are still completely realistic and remain humble, grateful and hungry (only for us that has meant literally sometimes!).

Gus van Sant,
Director, Elephant

Elephant was made for TV, and went on to win the Palme D'Or at Cannes in 2003. Covering the Columbine High School shootings, it was a difficult subject to get produced from the very beginning.

How hard was it for you to get Elephant off the ground?
I just addressed it to people that were in the business of making TV movies. I didn't want to make a feature film or something that would be outside of the television realm. The idea was always for television. But I wanted to make a television movie in the sense of a CBS, NBC, ABC television movie, because that was the same forum, or at least the mainstream forum, where the journalistic articles were as well. So they all said no. HBO wasn't the same exact idea, but it was mainstream television.

Hollywood was way too frightened by the whole event. They were coming under scrutiny by the government for violence on television as being a cause for Columbine, specifically. The same week I was pitching the idea was the same week they were actually flying to Washington with the fear there was going to be actions against television violence. So the idea to even consider doing something about Columbine was so far outside their possibilities. And, apparently, HBO's. I mean HBO was a little later. It had been a little while and Colin Callendar [HBO president] had a way to think about it that was not addressing Columbine directly.

Would you say this issue of conformity has become greater since you were at school?
A lot of this is also influenced by my high school years. But when I went to high school it was the Sixties, 1968, '69, '70, and so it was very common to work against the system of conformity -- conformity was suspect, at least in my circle -- and people battled against it. But those same people, the hippie generation, for some reason became ultra conservative when they grew up. I can't figure out how that happened. People that are my age, I oftentimes ask them, 'Were you a hippie?' and a lot of them they were, sort of. But now they drive SUV's and they have very strict, rigid programmes for their children, and they want children to succeed beyond all expectations. They make their children feel that

anybody that doesn't exist like they exist is somehow like cancerous or they're losers, to the point that they'd probably be proud of their children if they picked on their classmates who are 'losers'.

Stephen Applebaum

Patty Jenkins
Writer/director, Monster

Written in seven weeks, financed in just eight, Patty Jenkins' debut feature Monster took a clutch of award nominations for her and star Charlize Theron for her portrayal of serial killer Aileen Wuornos.

As a first-time filmmaker, what attracted you to Aileen Wuornos's story?
I had always read crime stories since I was young, and when Aileen's story broke in 1989, I was in high school and I remember being really struck by the dichotomy of what I was seeing. People were saying, 'Man-hating, cold-blooded serial killer', but she had this defensive, wounded look in her eyes, and it just struck me as so uncharacteristic of a serial killer. She didn't seem like somebody who had bloodlust or enjoyed killing, which I thought was intriguingly heartbreaking. You know, to see this person who looked so victimised, who had killed her johns after being a beat-up prostitute for all these years, I remember just being struck sideways by the combination of things. As the years went by I followed her story, but I never, ever, really thought, 'I want to be a lesbian serial killer director,' which has always felt like what has stood in for whatever was the real story.

How did you get in contact with her?
I think she always wanted her story to be told in a film and I just contacted her and told her I had sympathy with her story, which I saw as a fascinating, classic story in the tradition of good people turning bad. There wasn't something genetic formed in her brain that turned her into a serial killer. It was purely that this series of events led her to this place, and that's a famous, classic tradition. You've got war stories, *Hamlet*, *Badlands*, *Taxi Driver*. So I just wrote her and told her, 'I'm not going to lie to you and make you look like a feminist hero, because I think you killed innocent people. But I also think the series

of events that led you to that place are something that most people can't truly understand.

How difficult was it get the film funded? A lot of the people who fund films are men.
It wasn't difficult at all, probably for all the wrong reasons. I think a movie with the combination of lesbian and serial killer is easier to fund than one would think. And then it just so happened we were making the movie we were making. So I think the ball was already rolling. I decided to do the film a year-and-a-half ago, I wrote the script in seven weeks, and it was set up in two months. So it just went forward.

What lessons do you hope can be learned from Aileen's story and that people will take away from your film?
As I said, I don't like the idea of being an agenda filmmaker. Like I don't think you will see me doing another film like this. I think the thing that has kept me going every day, and that I would love for people to take away from the film, I mean it would be my greatest dream, is what happened at the test screening. After the film they asked, 'How many of you in the audience think she was vicious and did some horrible things?' 95% of the audience raised their hands. Then they said, 'How many of you felt tremendous compassion for this character?' 95% of them raised their hands. It just destroyed me. I burst into tears because if anything, what I care about the story for is shades of grey and compassion.

Stephen Applebaum

Amanda Posey,
Producer, Fever Pitch

Like Paul Webster, Stephen Woolley, Robert Jones and Daniel Battsek, Amanda Posey started out at Palace Pictures. She oversaw films such as the *Crying Game* and *Interview with a Vampire* before becoming Head of Development at Scala. She went on to produce the profitable British feature *Fever Pitch* with Film Four and its US remake, directed by the Farrelly Brothers.

Fever Pitch opened on about 220 screens, which is a big release, but the very big American movies will open on 350 — 400 screens. FilmFour tested it and that's what gave them the conviction to put a certain

amount of money behind it. They spent nearly £1m promoting it and it cost £1.8m to make. You'll never recoup that theatrically but where they made that back was on video because they'd raised the profile so high theatrically. Meanwhile, they were effectively buying themselves a high profile TV broadcast — this was in the days before FilmFour channel. It's just a business; they have to make the pieces of the puzzle fit. That was all without international sales which they did well with too.

The problem comes with the big percentages that get taken off from commission. It has taken something like £3m in actual income but once you take off the commission that FilmFour International took from selling it abroad, and the advertising and promotional budget then it comes down and it's not officially in profit. In terms of the channel they've paid almost nothing for a television broadcast in comparative terms, so for them it's very successful.

Very few people on the creative side have the exposure to the marketing and distribution so they don't know what choices have to be made when putting out a trailer or devising a poster or deciding where to place the ad. I was lucky in that I started in Palace Pictures, which went under for all sorts of reasons, but it was then the biggest independent distributor and producer. You got to see the film from start to finish, so whether it succeeded or failed you learnt lessons throughout. I remember Steve Woolley having huge trouble with *The Crying Game*. No-one wanted to finance that film and he ended up using cash from the Scala cinema and the connected video shop just to live day to day.

You can't rely on anybody else to tell you how to make your movie or to tell you why your movie is going to be any good. If you expect other people to give you money, it's a lot of money and a lot of time and commitment, you have to convey to them that you know what your audience is even if they don't know. And you have to be able to back it up. If you know there are millions of teenagers out there desperate to see your film then go online, do your research and get your statistics. So many independent filmmakers have the passion but not the interpretation that convinces those with the money that there is some commercial, and I don't mean formulaic, but financially sound reason to make it and that you are trying to reach a certain audience. What's often levelled at British filmmakers is that they don't care who their audience is and I think that's something that should be focused on.

CHAPTER 2

Low and MicroBudget Filmmaking

by James MacGregor

There are two major obstacles to successful low budget film production; that is, if you judge success by bodies on seats, no bills outstanding and maybe some profit to put towards the next one: 1) lack of money and 2) lack of distribution.

Fortunately, there are means of managing both situations, but they still require a lot of faith, not to mention the grim determination needed to get through the barriers. The good news is, you can bring home a feature for almost no money – read on for the case studies to prove it – but the bad news is, getting that feature out into the market and into distribution is as tough as making it in the first place, although as the case studies here and Chapter 4 illustrate, this is finally changing. In this chapter, we point to some very practical ways to manage both.

First, don't forget the revolution. That's the digital revolution, increasingly the key to low budget success. It is not the only way though, and photochemical film is not ruled out of lo/no budget filmmaking.

Next, remember it is almost impossible to make a film with no money. You will need to have recourse to some cash, even if just to post your masterpiece off to the Cannes selectors in France.

What you really need to succeed are strategies that ensure you spend as little money as possible as well as, when you do have to spend, strategies to ensure you get best value for it. Finally, having made your film, you need strategies in place to ensure your film can find its audience, but again, at lowest possible cost.

Low budget is not the route for the faint-hearted, because only the most determined filmmakers are likely to succeed on this journey. For those who are single-minded enough to make the trip, there are plenty of lo/no cost aids to navigation on the web and elsewhere, including Netribution.

Good Luck.

The great low budget face-off: Film v Digital

This is almost a pointless argument, because you can shoot low budget on any film medium. Features have been made using industry standard 35mm film for £25K ($50k) or less and some low budget digital films have come in on video at considerably higher budgets than that. The real debate is not about money; it is about if you are up for a challenge, because with the right attitude, you can beat the system.

Putting the film v digital argument another way, the picture that you want to shoot in 35mm film can be shot for a lot less if you shoot digital instead, but if you want to blow up from digital to cinema prints, the cost advantage could disappear. Film is unforgiving of mistakes and doesn't come with instant playback. Video is more forgiving and stock is cheap. It's a case of choosing the medium that suits you and your end purpose best, as much as your budget.

> 'I tried to short-circuit the system. When you make a film here or in any western country it's all about rewrites and script editors, it becomes a collective effort but the more people get involved the more formulaic it becomes. So we just tried to get a small amount of money and make the film without getting other people involved.' Pawel Pawlikowsky. Director, The Last Resort

35MM SAVINGS

Shooting three-perf instead of four-perf film will cut your stock bill by upping a four-minute film cartridge running time to six minutes. More on this in the Chemical Cost Cutters section of this Chapter, below.

SUPER 16 SAVINGS

16mm is less costly than 35mm. In 16mm you will shoot 60% less footage and one foot of super16 stock costs half what 35 mm costs, giving a further saving. You can transfer easily from Super16 (S16) to digital and edit alone at home on a desktop, so further savings are possible there too. S16 has the extra exposure range of film, when compared with video, so in low light conditions, film still has an edge over digital.

Film prime lenses bring depth of field advantages, putting your characters firmly in focus and their background out of focus, forcing audiences to concentrate on your characters. In video everything is often in focus, so the audience's eyes can stray, but these are aesthetic, not cost issues. In the digital domain, DV and HDV camera add-on systems like Movietube are beginning to address this aesthetic.

There are downsides to working with 16mm. A 400ft 16mm camera cassette gives only ten minutes of shooting time, so cameras have to be reloaded far more often. The cameras are bulkier than digital camcorders and more difficult to use. Sound also has to be recorded separately from the camera, so each take must be slated using slate and clapper board to synch sound and vision in post.

THE CASE FOR DIGITAL

Good digital can be hard to differentiate from 16mm film in terms of screen image; the contest is that close. The image capturing chips in digital cameras are generally more photosensitive than film, in turn requiring less light on set. This makes shooting digital generally much quicker and less complicated, needing fewer people. If budget is an important factor, you should consider digital, so here's a summary of what it gives you:

- Cameras are cheaper, smaller and can turn over for longer between tape changes;
- If you shoot guerrilla-style, or for documentary, the cameras are unobtrusive;
- Tape is cheap, so no limit on takes — you can capture the very best performances from your cast;
- Tape makes improvisation affordable;
- Multi-camera shooting is affordable;
- Sound can be recorded on camera;
- Rushes can be viewed immediately;
- Editing can be a one person-and-computer operation.

Looking ahead, an expensive film print is not needed until festival invitations come in, or distribution deals loom. Many festivals already have digital projection facilities and as more and more digital cinemas appear, like the Digital Screen Network in Britain, the need to pay for a film print at some point could be slowly disappearing. At the same time, advancing digital technology means video cameras are able to produce better and better results.

Digital — The New Kids on the Block

Film has served filmmakers well since the earliest days, but the newer digital technologies are making inroads into what was a photo-chemical exclusive domain. And not just in production. There has been a digital takeover in post-production as edit suites displaced splicing machines; in exhibition, where digital projectors run alongside optical ones and increasingly, in distribution, where theatrical distribution appears still to rule, but in actual cash terms, theatrical is usually less valuable than the DVD release that follows. Increasingly, the internet is becoming the showplace for low budget cutting edge work and for viral campaigns and imaginative marketing that are helping filmmakers of all kinds find their audience.

The Relph report confirmed that shooting digital can cut budgets, but film is what cinema audiences are used to, together with its false colours, slightly juddery motion, sharp focus on principal characters and a slightly blurry look of everything else in the frame. With digital the low budget filmmaker now has a new tool that can be used to advantage in two ways; shooting digital can cut production COST, but making the result look like film can also increase production VALUE of the movie.

High Definition

High-end digital (HD) was pioneered in Sweden for many years, but it was George Lucas who made it a commercially viable competitor to film when he finally went digital for the three prequels in the Star Wars franchise. HD post-production costs certainly echo those of film, but HD also produces high quality images for TV drama, where it has often outclassed 35 mm's little film brother, S16mm. TV drama in the States uses 35mm film as standard, but in the UK 16mm was preferred.

In any pixel-versus-chemical-grain contest, high-end digital seriously challenges 35mm film itself. The BBC now plans to shoot quality drama exclusively in HD. In preparation for the change they issued guidelines warning set designers, makeup artists and other key people in production look areas to be aware that the much higher picture resolutions could expose brush stokes from set decoration. The BBC's switch to filming in HD is still underway, but the sort of results they have achieved so far can be measured in the award winning 2005 BBC drama *Bleak House*.

Digital has a little brother too, in DV, which started off as a consumer camcorder format, but in the right hands soon showed it had professional capabilities that punch well above its fighting weight. Ease of use and affordability have made DV the preferred format of many low budget filmmakers, though sometimes to the detriment of their end product. DV cameras used like camcorders do not usually make good films, but used like film cameras, they can and they do. Fixed camera (not moving), used well, makes for another check in that production value box.

Since the the Relph Report appeared in 2002, giving DV a thumbs-up for filmmaking, DV has been further boosted by the appearance of hi-definition digital video – HDV.

HDV bridges the gap between DV and HD, making use of cheaper DV tape transport mechanics that are already in mass production, married to high definition technologies. This offers much higher resolution than standard DV, even when blown up to cinema screen size. Some HDV cameras also offer progressive scan — as in film frames — rather than interlaced scanning of video fields used in TV. This makes it possible to achieve in-frame motion closer to the slightly stuttery motion we are accustomed to seeing in cinemas, compared with the smooth motion we see on television. It also allows for true in-camera slow- or fast-motion.

Still on cinematic feel of images, some HDV cameras can offer interchangeable lenses instead of TV-type zoom lenses. There are specialists who can provide

'The majority of the film is set in one location, a cottage. So much of the film visually was going to be in this one location that we looked for a very long time for the right place. We found a wonderful place in Northern Ireland and that happened to work for us and we found a great crew up there and we were able to access financial resources from the Northern Ireland Film & Television Commission.'
Karl Golden. Director, The Honeymooners

35mm fixed-focus lenses, like the prime lenses used by film cameras, to give that classic film look; pin sharp characters in soft-focus blurry backgrounds. Fixed focus lenses like this keep viewer attention on the characters too, which is why directors love them. Fixed lenses are worth at least another check in that production value box.

Check out the P+S Technik mini-35 website: tinyurl.com/yrx2ex

or Feral Equipment's movietube webpage: www.feralequipment.com/movietube.html

There has been a flurry of new HDV cameras recently, as manufacturers compete for market share, each offering a number of options within their range, so there is a potentially bewildering choice.

One of the best places to look for sound advice is the Urban Fox website run by professional filmmakers Christina and David Fox, who offer buying guides, side-by-side comparison charts and much more besides. They also train camera operators and have used most cameras in action themselves, so what you find here is sound advice. Another good HDV portal is HDV café:

www.urbanfox.tv | www.hdvcafe.com

That concludes this overview of the rise and rise of digital. Film is going to lose the mass-market contest to digital technology eventually, though it can never be discounted altogether. The film aesthetic alone may guarantee that it will continue to be used for artistic reasons. Film archivists say there is no preservation medium for film that can better good old photo-chemical film. The giant conglomerates in film, like Eastman Kodak and Fuji, are re-defining as imaging companies and moving swiftly into the digital realm, while they push the old chemical technologies harder. They continue to supply the still-vibrant market with traditional film stocks as well as many new ones offering newer and ever greater capabilities. Film is far from dead and it is still possible to make a low budget film on film, as we will see shortly. First though, we have to get down and dirty with cutting production costs generally, and, inevitably, cheating. But only in the cause of raising production values and raising the low budget filmmaker's game.

Low budgets – an overview

Cutting Budgets — The Relph Report

Delivered to the UK Film Council in 2002, the Relph Report still has a lot of relevant things to say about cutting budgets in a high-cost filmmaking community like Britain. Relph was talking mainly about budgets above £1m ($2m), but his suggestions are equally applicable to less costly productions. Here's a reminder of Relph's main points:

Development and Pre Production

Write to budget by writing out costs (see below)
Keep development costs as low as possible
Long films cost more money

McGregor's Ten Tips
Be mean
Be twice as mean
Be careful
Plan everything for zero budget
Never pay a full price for anything
Beg, borrow and (almost!) steal
Be resourceful
Think Laterally
Be honest with people (VERY important)
Be prepared to think afresh

3 months prep, minimum
Director and Producer work hand-in-hand
Schedule well, including pickups
Plan with art department to make savings

Production

Use fewer crew
Line Producer and Production manager must be cost cutters
Seasoned cinematographers may cause problems (top gear expectations)
Revenue shares can attract top talent
Crew can be extras
Prizes can lure rentacrowd to a set
Super 16 and DV offer stock and crew savings and speedier production
On 35mm develop and telecine rushes only
Use locations that are good for sound
Engage a recordist who can also mix sound in post
Keep locations and base all within easy reach of each other
A cook and a kitchen can feed most crews cheaper than a caterer
Delivery costs to finish the film need to be kept low.

The full Relph report is available at www.ukfilmcouncil.org.uk/information/
downloads/?subject=27

Carbon neutral filmmaking

Al Gore's climate change documentary, *An Inconvenient Truth* opened up people's
eyes to the devastating potential effects of climate change around the world.

There has finally been an increase in carbon offsetting, whereby carbon used in a
products creation is offset through environmental projects such as tree planting
or energy saving in the developing world. Film such as *An Incovenient Truth, The
Day After Tomorrow* and *Syriana* have all been carbon neutral, with an increase in
the past two years in lower budget independent films also taking this path. Carbon
offsetting may seem like a luxury for a low budget shoot, and can cost around 1%
of the budget.

Ali Selim's *Sweet Land*, for instance, cost $1m to make and a further $5,000 for
London based Carbon Neutral Company to calculate and report on the 8,000
tonnes of carbon used in the process. Offsetting this by investing in a reforestation
project in Germany and windmills and compact fluorescent lighting in Jamaica cost
another US$10,000.

The filmmakers were given incentives to minimise environmental costs during the
production – 'shooting out' each location, by filming all the scenes there before
moving on. Actors used an on-set carpool, while sunlight was used as a light
source wherever possible.

Clerks; The Living End; El Mariachi

In 1992, three young filmmakers proved that exceptional features can be made for less than the cost of a mediocre short. With plenty of creativity, ingenuity, determination and almost no money, these writers-directors made outstanding features that gained festival success, critical acclaim and US national distribution. *Laws of Gravity* ($38,000) and *El Mariachi* ($7,225) were first features that launched the careers of Nick Gomez and Robert Rodriguez spectacularly. *The Living End* ($22,769) was a third feature that boosted Gregg Araki to a new level of prominence and opportunity. Some shorts can cost $100,000 but these features were made for a fraction of that sum. Not only that, these full length features had greater festival play and wider distribution than most successful shorts, while showcasing their directors' talents most effectively.

Kevin Smith's Clerks

Clerks was the feature with the lowest budget in competition at the 1994 Sundance Film Festival. Its 23-year-old director, Kevin Smith, made it for $27,575.

CLERKS BUDGET:

STOCK

37 400ft rolls Kodak Double X Negative	$1600.00
Nagra tapes	$200.00
Camera expendables	$125.00
EQUIPMENT RENTALS	
Insurance	$730.00
Camera	$3400.00
Sound and three lights	$1165.00
PROCESSING	
Negative and work print	$3295.00
Nagra rolls to mag stock transfers	$980.00
EDITING	
Steenbeck/guillotine rental (3 months)	$940.00
Editing expendables	$220.00
Negative cut	$1830.00
MIXING	
Slop print for mix	$900.00
Sound mix and all sound related services	$7280.00
PRINT	
Titles and animation	$800.00
Optical	$990.00
Screening print	$3120.00
Grand Total:	**$27,575**

Araki's The Living End

Araki was experienced in making $5,000 features so his producers, Marcus Hu and Jon Gerrans of Strand Releasing, were confident that The Living End could be made for $20,000, Starting with a family loan, production began. Money was raised in bits and pieces along the way including some from a private investor. Toward the end of post-production Araki received a $20,000 American Film Institute grant which covered more than 85% of the budget.

Lights: Lowell lighting kit (rental)	$390
Lenses: prime (rental)	$1,200
Props: guns (rental)	$150
Food	$1,800
sub-total:	$3,540

Stock

Film stock: 16mm colour Kodak 7296. 12,000 ft = 30 rolls	$2654
Cassette tapes: production sound	$50
DAT tapes: post-production sound	$50
1/2' tape: post-production sound	$100
sub-total:	$2854

Post-Production Expenses

Editing supplies	$50
Dialogue editing, sound effects recording and editing	$5,000
sub-total:	$5,050

Services

Edge code: 24.000 ft x .0 15c -discount + tax	$326
Negative cut. flat deal	$1,000
Film to 3/4' videotape transfer. Incl. stock. for post-prod	$350
DAT to mag transfer used to make optical from	$400
Optical Track	$1,500
sub-total:	$3,576

Titles

Lithography	$150
Processing and printing	$50
sub-total:	$200

LAB

Workprint: (250c x 12,000 ft)	$3,000
1st Answer print: (83c x 3240 ft)	$2,689
Release print: (37c x 3240: (wet gate made from original A	$1,277
Check print: (18 c x 3,240 ft)	$583
sub-total:	$7,549
Grand Total:	**$22,769**

'If you have a good location you probably don't need to build a set, because sets can be expensive. A good location can add a lot of production value to your film. It adds more class. Using someone's front room doesn't necessarily work, but to tell the right story well, you really do need top locations. They just have to look right within the frame. If you don't get good locations, you can devalue your film quite a lot.'
Dean Fisher, Scanner-Rhodes Productions

Robert Rodriguez's El Mariachi

Stock

12 400 ft rolls-Kodak 7292 (indoor)	$1,140
13 400 ft roll-Kodak 7248 (outdoor)	$1,170
1 100 ft test roll (B+W)	$19
sub-total:	$2,329

Processing

25 400 ft roll, (13c per foot)	$1,300
1 100 ft test roll	$23
sub-total:	$1,323

Equipment

2 clip-on modeling lamps	$60
7 bulbs	$67
sub-total:	$127

Miscellaneous

Acting fees	$225
Used guitar case	$16
3 sheets diffuser gels	$15
25 squibs	$50
Blanks (machine gun)	$50
Fake blood, condoms (for squibs), gaffer tape, lens cleaner kit, extra bulb	$122
4 rolls 35mm production still film	$18
10 Maxell 11 audio cassettes	$23
6 197 Ampex 3/4' BLA 60s	$103
sub-total:	$622

Post Production

Video transfer with overall colour correction (28c per foot)*	$2,824
Grand Total:	**$7,225**

Film cheats on camera

Making Video Look Like Film

It is hard to make video look like film because they are two different media and they handle light in completely different ways to record an image, but there is such a thing as a 'film look' dictated by traditional filmmaking methods and equipment. If you emulate them while shooting on tape, they will help you get that desirable 'look' and will not do your production values any harm, either.

In most movies the camera never moves much at all. If it does move, it is rock steady, at the end of a jib, or on a dolly. If the camera moves without being steady, viewers suddenly become aware of the camera. The illusion of the camera being an impartial observer of the scene, is now broken. If you want the illusion to remain throughout your film, resist the temptation to move the camera hand-held, unless there is a very good reason to do so, like in an action sequence. Even so, you would be better to use the camera with some steady equipment. Low cost steady equipment is available for DV and HDV cameras which will keep hand-held motion as smooth as possible. Even a standard camera monopod, with some weight fixed on the bottom works well, eliminating any judder, shake, wobble or jerky movement — which hand-held inevitably produces — in favour of fluid movement, helping maintain the camera-as-an-observer convention. No one is suggesting that the 'rules' may not be broken. Rules always can be broken and always will be broken, but there's a good reason why the 'rules' have become 'rules'. They work. With the odd exception, breaking them doesn't.

Movie cameras have fixed length lenses and are not usually fitted with zoom lenses. Zooming just once generally gives the game away to your audience; you are filming with a video camera. The other quality of movie lenses is that they have shallow depth of field. This means within the distance being covered in front of the lens (the field) only a relatively narrow plane across that field will be in focus (the focal plane) will be in focus. This is where you need to place your characters. Behind them everything else in the frame will be softer, slightly blurred. The audience naturally concentrates their vision where everything is in crisp, clear focus, on your characters in fact, exactly where you want them to concentrate, not on your backgrounds, unless there is a very good reason for it. In this case, the film camera would need a change of lens to one with a much greater depth of field which will do justice to both characters and their background.

Even so, if you are using a DV or HDV camera without additional fixed focus lenses, your TV zoom can still be used to create a softly blurred background with your characters nice and sharp, but your DV camera must be rock steady in fixed position on a tripod to carry it off!

Placing your character far away from the background makes it all the easier to throw the background out of focus. Now set up your camera position so it is a long way from your character, which makes you use the extreme range of your zoom lens to get the character in focus. Zoom in and frame your shot. You will need your aperture wide; there will be a slight drop in resolution, but you will get a shallow depth of field effect, with characters sharp and backgrounds blurred. The wide aperture will have affected exposure – overexposed the shot – so to compensate use a neutral density filter (ND), either one built into the camera or a screw onto lens filter. Running? Now stand-by everyone—and Action!

Film cheats in post

'Cheats' with your digital video start almost immediately in post-production after conforming and colour grading of your movie. You are free to use visual effects, computer generated imagery and digital compositing at this stage, all of which can add to the production value of your film, as will adding foley sound, a soundtrack and proper sound design (see en.wikipedia.org/wiki/Post-production for an explanation of these terms).

Post work like this used to be extremely expensive, but many post houses are sympathetic to the dilemma of low budget filmmakers. If your editor already has a good relationship with a post house, that is a possible low-cost access route, making use of downtime in an expensive edit suite. Alternatively, editing software for a desktop PC is available for a range of budgets from entirely free, like Apple's iMovie, to Final Cut Pro, or Avid in its various guises.

An edit suite is only an expensive array of computer hardware driving some very expensive software, much of it designed to work at speed. Remember, time is money that the client is spending. If the need for speed is removed, so that (for example) rendering times are no longer a factor, DIY post becomes possible.

Walter Murch edited his way through half a million feet of film using FCP to post-produce *Cold Mountain*, the post- US Civil War drama. The Coen Brothers are also FCP desktop post-producers:

www.apple.com/pro/profiles/murch/ and www.apple.com/pro/profiles/coen/

Expensive technology doesn't have to be a bar to progress if you work around it. Could you attempt a low budget fantasy movie involving CGI dragons with just £200 in the pot? No? Those were the circumstances Kenneth D Barker faced at the turn of the millennium when he met a film angel who was prepared to increase the budget a little in exchange for a share of the business. The result was *Kingdom*, which managed, on a shoestring budget, to have dragons flying over Leeds Town Hall, through a 'rendering farm' set up on several PCs by a knowledgeable local operator. *Kingdom* is still selling on DVD and Barker is still making ambitious features for next to nowt, as they say in Yorkshire.

www.netribution.co.uk/features/interviews/2000/kenneth_d_barker/1.html'

Magic Bullet
There are also specialist softwares that are designed to get the look of celluloid film from video, like Magic Bullet. It is not a bargain basement purchase at $799, but it has become the industry standard software for achieving the film look after shooting digital. Everyone is more and more cost conscious and that is one of the reasons they turn to Magic Bullet for the film look.

Full details about Magic Bullet, including before and after treatment pics, user accounts and more can be found here:

www.redgiantsoftware.com/magbulsuit.html

Irish independent director, Patrick Kenny, and editor and VFX supervisor Kevin Hughes, used Magic Bullet to create a softer cinematic look for their debut feature *Winter's End*. Shooting with a Canon XL1, they loved the finished project pictorially, but felt the overall look was just too clean and lacked texture and the reds were too washed out for what they wanted. They chose Magic Bullet to put matters right and give their film the look they needed for the story to be most effective.

www.redgiantsoftware.com/mbsirishuserstory.html

Nattress Film FX Filters
Nattress 'Film Effects' is a 24 frame per second (24p) film effect designed especially for Final Cut Pro. Film Effects does everything you need to make your digital video look like film — whether PAL or NTSC — all for about £60 ($120). These include deinterlacing the video, changing the chroma levels and tweaking several dozen filters and variables.

www.nattress.com

'Manchester wasn't easy to deal with. I think they get large number of requests to film. There's lots of form-filling, lots of bureaucracy and they charge you lots of money. But Leeds/ Bradford Airport is after publicity! They were extremely nice and very friendly, as long as we didn't want to shoot in their busy peak May to October. We shot there at the end of last April when it was about 27 degrees and it looked like June.'
John Williams. Producer, Diary of A Bad Lad

The write solutions to cost cutting

The director's vision does not come foremost from the director's imagination, because it has already been shaped by the script. The first port of call in any budget-cutting exercise is the script as it easier to cut the budget in the script rather than in production.

Dramatic conflict is the essence of good drama. Just two people in conversation can provide that, but **where** and **when** they are having that conversation — and **what** they are saying — can have a huge influence on the film budget. If rent-a-crowd is required in scenes 13, 42 and 66, the writer has well and truly blown the micro-budget.

The lateral thinking alternative may be shooting guerrilla-style, inside or at the edge of a convenient crowd, but you may have to shoot from concealment so your bargain crowd extras don't stare into the lens. Cast will need to be wired, with radio mikes. With careful planning, it can be done, but do make sure the camera doesn't linger for more than a second or two on anyone in frame more prominent than your characters or your cast bill could be in for a rise.

A train derailment at speed down a railway embankment is quite possible using miniatures; Neil Oseman managed it very successfully in his micro budget action adventure *Soul Searcher*, because he felt it was important to the story – but it took an enormous amount of work to get it right. Can you afford to spend that much time on screen effects? It may be easier and cheaper to write it out.

These cost implications of a script show just why low budget producers need to make sure screenwriters have some filmmaking knowledge and keep their eye on the budget as well as on character journeys and the formatting of their script. By the time a script is in draft it may be too late to save the budget, so calling for a treatment before a script is written can save a lot of time as well as a lot of money.

The script needs to come at the end of a development process as the final product of development, whereas a treatment is part of the process. It is often best done as a **step treatment**, each step of the story outlined in short narrative paragraph with no dialogue.

If you were building a lego house, treatment steps would be the bricks. They can be swapped around, changed or altered as often as needed until the first draft script can be written. If big changes are needed in draft scripts, it is often safer and easier to re-write the step treatment and make sure it is working before going full speed ahead with yet another draft of the script.

Of course, some writers prefer to write a script and work back from it, and some of cinema's greatest films have been written this way — there are no absolute rules. However changes are much easier to do at treatment stage than in scripts, which allow for little flexibility and any change can create a great deal of extra work. In contrast, dropping characters, creating new characters, merging characters are all relatively painless in step treatment as part of script development.

Check out some sample treatments at: en.wikipedia.org/wiki/Film_treatment

One of the best explanations of treatment is from downunder:

www.afc.gov.au/downloads/pubs/whatissynopsis.pdf'

Free Treatment Demo is available at www.movieoutline.com/

Writing Treatments at www.writingtreatments.com/index.html

'If you go at it with the right attitude, people are happy to help. I would be honest and say, 'Nobody is paying me to do this production, I haven't got any money, and can I use your place?' - And most people would say 'Yea, OK.' Since then, I've made short films in LA, in places like coffee shops where they regularly charge big movies $5,000 a day and I got them for free. It is all a question of attitude.'
Ian Vernon. Director, Actors

The Canadian site Celtx offers a free scriptwriting and pre-production program which in turn can be shared online, collaborated on, and turned into schedule. The tool can be used for developing a story, writing an industry standard screenplay, or stage play, completing a breakdown, making a storyboard and scheduling the shoot.

www.celtx.com/overview.html

Cutting budgets by design

Thrifty filmmakers love good low-budget production designers and should always start wooing them early, and certainly well before prep time. The designer is another one of those hidden production value factors in a film and it is all to do with encouraging suspension of disbelief by the audience.

Good design work fills your frame with significant details. These details are important. They tell audiences that they are looking onto a real world place, with real action happening. It's not a flimsy studio set. Disbelief is suspended, this place is for real.

'Well we have this wonderful Shooting People you know! I said this is going to be the project, it is going to be in India and if you can afford to pay your way and would not mind working four or five days for free and take a holiday afterwards, here's a script, read it and come along. I am pleased to say that holiday wasn't really the attraction for most people. They read the script and were very interested in it and that's what swayed them.'
Ashvin Kumar. Director, Oscar nominated The Road To Ladakh

Locations dressed by a designer look right. Locations that are not prepped and dressed for their part are like actors without the right costume. They look like they did when you found them and they are certainly not in role. Designers are usually hugely resourceful. Armed with paint and fabric, timber and polystyrene they create screen miracles that support the story being told. Whatever they bring, borrow or build will support the story to be told.

A good designer, appointed early enough, can work with the director, the location scout and the DoP to find the right locations and put production value on screen at lowest cost through careful choice of locations. Good low-budget designers can often source huge amounts of props and set dressing materials, but must cover transport to and from owners, even when the goods are loaned for free.

Early appointment of a production designer certainly pays — and gets another check in the production value box.

PRISON CELL BY DESIGN

Get a brick garage. Paint brick interior white. With 2x2' timber rails and ½' dowel painted matt black, make a frame and bars to shoot through, to cover a window or doorway. Furnish appropriately. Shoot. Cheaper than renting a prison.

SUMMER PLANTS IN WINTER

Make crepe paper flowers. Wire them to evergreen shrubs. All-year-round springtime.

INSTANT HOTEL OR ROAD INN NEON

Rent exterior access to the building you want to use to represent your hotel or road inn exterior. Buy some flashing red Christmas ropelights (about £20 [$40] each.) On a hoistable display board, fix ropelight to spell 'INN, or'HOTEL' (HOTEL might require two ropelights!) or whatever your neon message is to say. Mask the 'joining up' runs of ropelight between the illuminated letters with black tape. Hoist high up on lighthouse accommodation block wall or roof edge. Get sparks to test and power up and see how it flashes. A flashing directional arrow or hand with extended directional index finger can flash separately for an 'American' look.

Cut-price filmmaking kit

Digital has changed a lot of the costs of production. Camera rental made sense when the camera cost two hundred grand to buy, but as long as you are not creating a high-octane, action-packed thriller, you could go low budget and shoot your feature with a mini-DV camera, or HDV camera with a full package costing less than it would cost you to rent a 35mm camera for two months. (Prices below are in British £ - the $ exchange rate would normally be roughly double, but US costs are often lower).

A Panavision 35mm camera costs around £850 per day – and that is just for the camera body. Lenses are an extra £150 per day, each, and you need several. You will also need a cartload of camera accessories from video assists to camera raincovers and the sums just get bigger and bigger. Against this you could buy a complete HDV Sony Z1E Full Monty shooting kit from CVP for £4,680 and that includes tripod, boom and radio mikes, balanced XLR cables, camera bag and a basic 3-Redhead lighting kit can be yours for about £600, or you can buy construction site lights from your nearest hardware stockist from about £15 each.

The important principle is, kitting up this way, you get to keep all the kit because you didn't rent it, you bought it – and you can lose the equivalent amount from your next film's budget. The real clincher is the cost of stock. HDV cameras will happily record on DV tapes at about £2 each, with a tape lasting 60 minutes and no lab costs.

If you are really broke, you can find the same Z1E HDV cameras and shooting kit available for hire through Shooting People for between £80 and £100 a day -shootingpeople.org

UK Film Centre equipment — www.filmcentre.co.uk/equip_main.htm

Now that you are kitted up, you need a few accessories to help you work around those tricky camera moves. You could try a camera dolly at £75pd, or as a low cost alternative try these:

THE STRINGBAG STEADY
If you need moving camera but can't afford a steadicam, a shopper's stringbag may be your answer. You might have to cut a few strings to accommodate the lens, but suspended in a string bag it should stay reasonably steady as you walk it through the shot. If you are budget-rich try these:

www.doggicam.com | www.glidecam.com | www.steadicam.com

THE WHEELCHAIR DOLLY
Probably invented by the legendary Robert Rodriguez for his low budget cult classic *El Mariachi*. It has worked well ever since, though borrowing one from your local hospital might be tricky if they are needed by patients. Red Cross branches sometimes have a medical equipment loan service for discharge patients. If there's not been a glut of wheelchair users discharged a donation to Red Cross funds may get you a low-cost hire. Big-wheel types cope better with dips than small-wheel chairs. Make sure the floor is smooth.

BICYCLE DOLLY
If wheelchairs are scarce, a bicycle can be substituted and is usually easier to find.

SKATEBOARD DOLLY
Very handy for table-top shots.

'The thing that lets most low budget productions down is the sound quality; so if you do not know much about sound yourself, get somebody who is very good with sound. And if anybody uses radio mikes, make sure they switch off their mobile phones! There are lots of shots that get spoiled by bleeps caused by someone's mobile going off, even if it is set just to vibrate.'
**Ian Vernon.
Director, Actors**

RAILCAR DOLLY

As used by Lynn Ramsay in *Gasman,* her award-winning early film, as a tracking vehicle for a trio of characters walking along a railway line in Glasgow. Try and remember to lose wheel rumble and joint clicks, which at that time, Lynn unfortunately forgot.

FX: Getting a bang for your buck

Nothing adds to on-screen value like an explosion or two, or three, but screen effects only work when they are convincingly realistic. Loud bangs and explosions can also look and sound convincing enough to alarm neighbours, so be sure to warn them in advance unless you want to receive a bill from the fire department for an emergency turn-out that did not need to be made. Screen cheats often need practice to work well, but the con is cheaper, and sometimes more achievable, then the real thing. It's all smoke and mirrors, really.

SAFETY NOTE: effects can be dangerous and can maim or kill. Take every precaution to keep safe. Try out an effect remotely before doing it for real. Watch from a safe distance, wear safety goggles and safety clothing. Warn everyone to take cover, and ensure you have read and followed health and safty advice.
www.filmsafety.ca | www.bectu.org.uk/resources/safety/index.html

SMOKE WITHOUT FIRE

Very effective smoke cakes can be made by mixing one part potassium nitrate and two parts of coffee creamer with a little water. After being cooked at 250 degrees for an hour they will not burn, but they do produce lots of smoke for three minutes. More info from www.detonationfilms.com

CATASTROPHIC LIGHT BLAST

A catastrophic light blast is easily created using the manual iris of the camera. Filming begins in the normal way and at the point when the explosion is to happen, the manual iris is opened up rapidly all the way. The scene will flood with light.

INTERIOR CAR FIRE

Set up camera inside the car angled though a window, with space between. Burn combustible material in a large roasting tin or frying pan to get flames. Interpose your flame carrier between camera and window. Shoot through flames.

FOG EFFECT

Dry ice is the secret behind most low budget fog effects. It is produced by warming frozen carbon dioxide and the cloudy vapour that results is heavier than air, so it clings to the ground. You can hire a fog machine or as an alternative, drop pieces of dry ice (from a gloved hand for safety) into a pan of boiled water. The vapour can be directed by using a fan or a hair dryer.

SNOW

Confetti or tiny pieces of polystyrene foam can be used to simulate snow blowing across a scene using a fan as a propeller. It is a very good idea to have a a dust sheet or canvas out of shot on the floor to catch the snow afterwards, or for recycling the material for additional takes.

Do not attempt anything in this section unless you have appropriate experience, supervision and, where necessary, qualifications.

ICE CRYSTALS

Glitter used for Christmas decoration added to whatever you are coating a surface with will add a frosty glint to it. With some light, it will glimmer nicely to make an interesting frost effect.

WATER THE STREETS

Watering the streets before a night shot brings lots of reflections and highlights from streetlights that otherwise would not be there. Watering them through the day can create pools of standing water which can be used to shoot reflections as well as the real thing.

MAKE 'EM SWEAT

Petroleum jelly on bare skin misted with water produces convincing sweat under lights. Don't leave your actor cooking for too long.

MIRRORS

Some of the most convincing effects are made by using mirrors. If you want to show a scene as a reflection on water, fill a paddling pool with an inch of water and place a large mirror in the bottom. Use a second mirror to bounce a reflection of the desired scene onto the water mirror, angle the camera on the water mirror and move the water gently to create movement.

The same two-mirror technique can be used for difficult-to-achieve shots, like a high-angle overhead into a room. One mirror is fixed at a high angle to reflect the scene onto a second mirror, which the action is photographed from. The second mirror helps keep perspective, as well as making sure the image is the right way round, not a reverse image.

SUBMERGED POV

Take a large washing up bowl and cut out the bottom and glue a sheet of perspex over the empty panel. Seal with bathroom sealant. Test with water in for leaks. Sit it in a frame, fill with water, angle camera on the action below the bowl, through the water. Disturb water if required. Shoot.

MOUNTAIN CLIMBING

Cliff faces and mountain sides do not have to be vertical to be effective for climbing purposes if the camera is tilted at an angle and the actors are physically convincing. Eliminate normal background references, like trees which really are true vertical, from the frame, for obvious reasons.

STARSCAPE

No sci-fi epic can be convincing without a starscape for your model space ships to pass in front of. Shoot against a very dense, lightproof black cloth, like velvet, which can hang from a batten in a darkened room. Holes made in the cloth appear as stars when the cloth is lit from behind with a high intensity lamp like a quartz-halogen worklamp.

'You also cannot afford to lose ANY time, so anything that will cause a delay - and over-inflated egos always cause delays - must be kept off the shoot, or kept in control. If you think that someone will be a prima donna on set, don't get them involved. Get someone else.' **Sean Martin. Director, The Notebooks of Cornelius Crow**

Sounds effects

There are plenty of sources for professionally recorded sound effects, but they can still be disarmingly simple to create as well as utterly convincing.

Gunshots sound very like cane smacked down on a vinyl chair seat or leather-covered pillow. Coconut shells famously make horses hooves trot along realistically, but here are a few you may not have heard of.

TELEPHONE VOICE
Record the voice at the other end of the call, talking into a glass.

BREAKING BONES
A handful of spaghetti strands twisted to breaking point

FIST FIGHTS
Best conducted by a wooden spoon smacked down on a large wet sponge.

RAIN
Stretch a sheet of brown paper, tinfoil, cellophane, crepe paper or some other variety, six inches over the microphone. Sprinkle salt on it. Repeat with different materials for different roof surfaces

ROLLING SURF
Ball bearings rolling around in a cardboard hat box

Chemical cost cutters

Some low budget filmmakers can't get away from their love-affair with celluloid. They have an abiding and irresistible affection for silver halide grains. The resolution of 35mm film is about ten times that of image capture chips in DV cameras, equivalent to 5,000 lines of video compared with 500 lines coming from a DV camera, but quite a lot of that advantage is lost during film printing. The film you see screened in a cinema may well be a copy of a copy of a copy of a print which was itself a copy from the original negative. A lot of film's greater resolution is lost by the time it gets to the screen.

Super 16mm is the choice for saving budget. Owing to the smaller gauge you will use 60% less film in S16 than in 35mm shooting, and 35mm not only costs more per foot but it will also cost you more to handle and process. Don't write it off though, because you can still shoot 35mm at low cost. It is just harder to manage, that's all. You can buy at discount, buy short ends and shoot in three perf, which creates more frames per foot than traditional four perf does, so a four minute cartridge lasts for six minutes. This and a few more three perf advantages can bring normal costs down by 25%.

3-Perf Info 1: www.aaton.com/products/film/35/3perf.php

3-Perf Info 2: en.wikipedia.org/wiki/35mm_film

The first thing low budget filmmakers going the photo-chemical route need, is a large fridge. The stock is going to come in dribs and drabs as leftovers, end-rolls, re-cans, whatever. Collection period may be lengthy so starting well in advance of shooting is important and it must be kept refrigerated to maintain useable condition. The second thing low budget shooters need is lots of friends in the film business to help them source these oddments from bigger budget shoots that are wrapping.

UK Film Stock: www.stanleysonline.co.uk/category-232.htm | www. mediadistributors.com

Super 8mm
There is one alternative to both of these film platforms and that is the forgotten format; super 8. That's the small-gauge format that you probably thought passed away when Kodak announced the death of Kodachrome. It didn't die, because there are modern stocks around with far greater capabilities. You simply need to know where to look. There is a substantial super 8 community worldwide, with

'One of the early mistakes I made was in trying to develop a style. I think that is something people out of film school and new filmmakers often try to do, but really, that's not something you can develop purposefully. It is something that just happens because you learn to trust the voice that is talking to you from inside you know. That's one of the things I learned on Road to Ladkh. Style is not something you can create. It either happens or it doesn't happen.'
Ashvin Kumar. Director, The Road to Ladakh

plenty of specialist laboratories and enthusiast websites to help you find what you need to capture images with those warm film tones. There are professional cameras too with specialised companies mounting crystal speed control and a built-in digital film counter to the popular Beaulieu 4008 camera.

The French-based firm Beaulieu, the only company to make professional-grade cameras in the S8 format, was the last manufacturer in the world with a model in production in 2002. They still make replacement parts for their older models, the 4008, 5008 and 7008 series. They feature manual ASA selection, which allows Pro-8 users to use their built-in TTL light meter and aperture controls. Beaulieu's most recent model is the 7008 ProII. The camera takes full advantage of current electronics and microprocessor technologies and its exposure control can be set from 12 to 500 ASA.

The California-based Pro8 company has been in the forefront of many Pro8 developments, where they manufacture Pro8mm cartridges by slitting all of

Kodak's 35mm colour negative motion picture film stocks into 8mm width. They then reperforate the film with Super8 sprocket holes and load it into brand new

Kodak Super8 cartridges. This enables 8mm cinematographers to shoot Kodak's

full range of modern film emulsions, from fine-grain 50ASA Daylight film for use in bright exteriors, to the latest Vision 800ASA Tungsten film used for shooting in extremely low-ight interiors. Sound is recorded separately on DAT or minidisk and synched by using a slate with clapper in time-honoured fashion.

One Pro8 reel of film shoots for ten minutes and will be colour corrected and telecined to mini-DV or other digital format. Processing charges include negative cleaning. Film plus processing packages cost from $278 for a 4-roll package including a five-hour scene to scene colour-correction transfer. A feature with a 3:1 shooting ratio using 24 rolls would cost $1,118 (roughly £600) to colour correct and transfer to mini-DV for editing.

www.pro8mm.com | www.beaulieu.fr (company site – in French) | www.beaulieu.de (spares – in German) | www.movietransfer.co.uk (London-based S8 telecine service)

If you are at all sceptical that 8mm film still has a place in moviemaking you might want to take a look at the following interview with Ben Crowe, who used Super8 for the first time to produce his Cannes Palme D'Or winner, *The Man Who Met Himself*:

'I had never worked with Super 8 before and I went out and picked up a cheap camera. I chose it because I wanted to make a film where the sound and the pictures didn't have to be in sync all the time and I wanted a filmic look. I wanted it to be grainy, I wanted it to hark back to film noir-ish urban thrillers. Super 8 is the cheapest format probably to be able to do that, particularly if you want to re-create something and then tweak it later on, because digital's got its own qualities and characteristics which can be used to do their own thing. So if I wanted to shoot it in a film medium, Super 8 was the choice. And then the idea of non-synchronous music and dialogue, that was also informed by the choice of using Super

'If I'd been with normal British (feature film) professionals it would have been a nightmare. They would have wanted a perfect script and just executed the plan whereas I had a tiny documentary group who all lived in one house and they were all very, very supportive. They all believed in me and the film and it was a great pleasure to work with them. I think it is reflected in the film because there is a chamber-like, organic feel to it.' **Pawel Pawlikowsky. Director, The Last Resort**

8. That also meant that when shooting, I could really focus on the images — sound was to be dubbed later.'

www.shootingpeople.org/shooterfilms/interview.php?int_id=41

Alessandro Machi's website is also worth a visit. He's extremely knowledgeable about small gauge film making, with pointers and links to many resources. www.super-8mm.net

Shooting People member Nathan Coombs came up with a brilliantly simple international documentary project on DVD using Super-8 film. *SUPER-8 CITIES* explored the world in Super- 8, connecting 10 cities, 7 countries and 4 continents. A dozen filmmakers had their work included with a film from each contributor giving their own personal take on their own city and telling it as they saw it by their own off-screen commentary.

Here's Nathan Coombs talking to me about the new Super-8 film stocks now available that were used in the DVD :

'Contrary to the angst surrounding Kodak's shutdown of the Swiss K40 lab, there does seem to be something of a buzz surrounding super-8 at the moment. It has got a bit more difficult for the amateur to pick-up without those convenient mailers that came with K40, but at the same time, the market for pro-stocks has flourished. Not only are more people beginning to shoot the Vision2 neg stocks, which transfer better to digital, but there are several companies re-manufacturing 35mm films and slide films into the super-8 format.

The two most impressive of these are Spectra Film's re-manufacture of Velvia 50D, which for slide photographers is a legendary stock, and Pro-8mm's release of Vision2-50D (7201) in super-8 carts. They are both very slow speed – perfect for super-8 to reduce the grain to a minimum. The Velvia has wonderful saturation, resulting in vibrant colours that just jump out at you, and the 7201 combines a very tight grain with the huge latitude that shooters of Kodak neg stocks have come to love. In fact you can see the Velvia in action in Gavin Lim's film on the Super-8 Cities DVD and I'm hoping one of the participants will shoot the Pro-8 (7201) for the sequel project.'

www.shootingpeople.org/shooterfilms/interview.php?int_id=82

'Sound is so important to a movie. Many new film makers ignore it completely. We were very conscious to make sure that we had an extremely full soundtrack full of atmos. We wanted the tower block in the movie to be its own character so we gave it a constant breathing atmos. You can hardly hear it but it's there adding to the underlying tension. The pipes in the building would have their own throbbing atmos and we would search and search and search for strange animal sounds to add to the mix.'
Genevieve Jolliffe.
Director, Urban Ghost Story

Shedding light on low budget

SAFETY NOTE: Make sure that whoever the person in charge of lighting is (the 'gaffer'), knows what the safety precautions they must take are before touching, plugging in or switching on electrical equipment, indoors or outdoors. Make sure no-one except designated people handle electrical equipment on the shoot. Always have carbon dioxide fire extinguishers near electrical equipment NEVER water-based extinguishers.

The mainstream filmmaker will be using a truck full of lighting equipment and another truck with an on-board generator, so there's a guaranteed power supply wherever it may be needed. This also costs a truck load of money you don't have.

The big budget film comes complete with a whole squad of electricians headed by the gaffer. In a low budget shoot you may be the gaffer.

Lights can come incredibly cheap, if you know where to look for them. In early Hollywood, when they first wanted to shoot in poor light outside they looked around to see what they could use to get more light. Construction firms in California were using quartz-halogen lights as worklights on a stand which were very bright and reasonably portable, but could light up a whole building site. Hollywood adopted them and they've been using them for filmmaking ever since, with a few add-ons like gel filters, barn doors, focus lenses and so on, but those are frills.

QUARTZ-HALOGEN WORKLIGHTS

If you are cutting budgets you need to go back to basics. At the start of 2007 in a builder's toolshop, I found two 500-watt quartz-halogen lamps, complete with a light-stand selling for just £15.99 ($32). Provide your own gels, clipped to the lamp with wooden clothes pegs. They can be streamed though a window to spread a little sunshine on interior locations, or they can be diffused through an opaque shower curtain for a softer effect. The shower curtain diffuser makes for a great backlight too, but keep the shower curtain away from the hot lamps.

SAFETY NOTE: Gel resists melting and shower curtain doesn't, just as wooden clothes pegs are hard to set alight, but plastic ones melt.

Next stop is your local home lighting retail store, which can carry a very useful range of film lighting at minimum cost....

SEALED BEAM HALOGENS

These little beauties are very versatile around a film set. You can highlight props or other special features using the narrow beam varieties; wider beams can spread just too wide. Clamp the halogen lamp socket onto a lamp stand and switch on.

BAG-O-LITE

A soft tube of light that can cantilever up to 6m (20') with support from one end. It provides a soft source useful for lots of aesthetic purposes, gets around rigging problems, saving time and money. Bag-o-lite was used by Ashvin Kumar, Academy nominated low-budgeteer, in his 35mm shoot, *Forest*, involving a man-eating leopard on the loose in India. Slung high above the ground, bag-o-lites picked out crucial important details from the absolute darkness of forest night – just enough to register on film and scare audiences!

Bag-o-lite manufacturer: www.licht-technik.com/eng/index.html

'Once a film is launched you have just 12 months before a whole raft of new films come along and your film becomes a back catalogue item in your Sales Agents portfolio. If you have announced completion to everyone and you do not have a sales agent after 12 months, then you are in trouble.'
David Nicholas Wilkinson. Distributor, Guerilla Films

Do not attempt anything in this section unless you have appropriate experience, supervision and, where necessary, qualifications.

Bag-o-lite in action: www.cirrolite.com/new_product_bagolite_1.html

CHINESE LANTERN DIFFUSERS

Big Chinese lanterns make excellent diffusers for close up work, by using a Chinese lantern on a boom pole close to the actors' faces, just out of shot. They are made of paper and wire and come in different shapes and sizes up to 3 foot diameter. Use a light flex and bulb holder at the centre of the lantern (hot paper can burn!) with a 200 watt bulb in it and you will create beautiful soft close up lighting for faces. If you have the largest globe sizes, two 200 watt bulbs diffuse enough light to fill a corner of a set or a small room. **Again, take care not to get things too hot.**

Alternatively, you can fabricate your own Chinese Lantern using an acrylic globe.

members.aol.com/filmgroup/china.htm

PHOTOFLOODS

Any photographic shop should be able to sell you photofloods. They are more powerful than normal light bulbs so they run hotter, but these can replace ordinary bulbs in 'practicals' on the set; reading lamps, table lamps, desk lamps.

Domestic lampshades that are saucer or scoop shaped can also be used with photoflood bulbs to create extra lighting.

LIGHT STANDS

Professional light stands are rarely cheap. They are designed to carry weight, but alternatives, like sealed beam halogens, are much lighter, so there are lots of substitutes around, like old test tube holders from chemistry labs or music stands, so start looking around (and be careful).

REFLECTORS

Useful for pushing light onto close up subject even in natural light, but they don't come cheap, especially if they are the circular kind that can be flipped over to a quarter size for storage. Kitchen foil makes a perfectly serviceable substitute, pasted on to a piece cut from a large cardboard carton, or on a piece of polystyrene. Foil reflectors work better if the foil is slightly crinkled rather than smooth. If you want the improved two-in-one model, you can have a shiny side up reflector on one side and a duller, diffuse one on the other side, by pasting the foil's shiny side down.

BLUE/GREEN SCREEN

You should not overlook the low budget possibilities that blue or green screen work can lend to your camerawork, well-matched to some stock footage of say, the pyramids, Sydney Harbour Bridge, or some other exotic location that you don't have and are not likely to be able to afford.

You need is a staple gun for anchoring compositing material (blue- or green-screen fabric available from specialist companies) stretched taught to a wooden frame fixed to your garage wall. Twenty feet long and eight feet high gives you great potential for the cost of timber and material. A tryout with a three-foot square screen, to make sure your chosen fabric colour will work with your camera, lights and software, is probably a good idea, but this will save you a lot of money on pro models. Remember, care needs to be taken over lighting the screen to avoid reflection onto actors and their clothes, so it is sensible to get in some practice before it is needed for real. As always, the internet can provide advice on lighting green screens.

Do not attempt anything in this section unless you have appropriate experience, supervision and, where necessary, qualifications.

Down and dirty greenscreens: www.bluesky-web. com/broadcastvideoexamples-greenscreen.html'

How to make a bluescreen: www.jushhome.com/ Bluescreen/Bluescreen.html

Jon Williams
Doing the Cannes Can

Jon Williams produced a darkly-humoured thriller, *Diary of a Bad Lad*, about a filmmaker trying to document the inside story on a shady local businessman. He took it to Cannes but the market failed to impress him. Instead he signed his film to Wysiwyg Films with it set to come out on the Digital Screen Network. Here's some of what happened:

Behind the 'Palais des Festivals'' is an enormous market hall, which also contains several small theatres for 'market screenings'. These can be hired, but most of them are already booked by the producers and distributors of films in the main festival, for the purposes of doing business.

Many of the companies represented in the market hall are small fry, such as American niche market horror producers, but some pretty big fish, such as LionsGate are there too. British companies are conspicuous by their near total absence. In fact it takes a little detective to find out where they are, located in one or other of the five star hotels along the Croisette which specialise in leasing suites and apartments.

UK sales companies are notoriously risk-averse, so if the film hasn't a Richard Curtis script and doesn't star Hugh Grant you have an uphill struggle on your hands. I set off, door-stepping my way down the Croisette and manage to arrange a few meetings for the following week. I'm feeling pretty buoyed up. I'm there with one of the few features that was a British Council supported festival entry, which I know has the potential to become a cult film with potentially many years of shelf-life. So I go in and make my pitch, but no one seems to be listening. 'Leave a screener with us and we'll get back to you,' they all say, trying to get me out of the door as quickly as possible. Most of them don't.

But do you really want to deal with these people anyway? American distribution guru, Peter Broderick

points out that, for indie filmmakers, deals with major companies mean you lose all control over your film for as much as fifteen years, that your film is soon likely to end up being 'left on the shelf' as they pursue the more instant returns (and kudos) offered by the large budget films in their portfolio, that they probably won't do a good job of selling your film in the important DVD and TV markets, and that you'll end up receiving little or no money.

www.netribution.co.uk/2/content/ view/778/277/

Neil Oseman
Soul Searcher

Low budget doesn't have to mean low ambitions. It means some lateral thinking is called for to achieve what is needed at lowest possible cost. Feature director Neil Oseman needed some very good screen effects for his debut fantasy adventure *Soul Searcher* (on DVD from WYSIWYG) but could not afford CGI on a budget. Instead, he used his film skills and Final Cut Pro to achieve what he wanted, like an express train plunging off a railway embankment…

NEIL OSEMAN: I had never filmed any miniatures before so it was a new experience and perhaps it was the one area of effects in the film I had some trepidation about. I originally wanted to shoot all the miniatures on film so we could film them on high speed and then slow them down a lot and get a better sense of weight and scale. When I added up the numbers I realised that wasn't going to be possible with our budget. It did become a worry and I think the miniature shooting became the least pleasant of the whole three-year experience.

Trying to shoot the model train was the most unpleasant part for me. The plan had been originally to film it outdoors in a field, so we spent two nights in a freezing, muddy, cold, Gloucestershire field trying to shoot this train which would not stay on the rails. It just kept derailing time after time. It was the most depressing experience. We spent a day or so, myself and a couple of crew members, digging this 25 metre embankment for it to run along. At the end of these two nights we just had to put all the earth back where we found it without having shot a single frame.

That must have been a very, very low point for you at the time. The end result though, looks very good on screen. One of the best low-budget model shots I've seen. How did you get around the problem?

My father, his brother and his father got together and took the train off me. They are all engineers, whereas the guy who made the train originally, he was in modelmaking. He knew how to make stuff that looked good, but the engineering side and making sure the thing physically worked, he wasn't particularly strong at. So, my relatives were able to remake all the wheels and axles and provide me with some new track and the train finally was able to go along it. In the end, we filmed it indoors by hiring a youth centre hall with a much shorter track using various editing and camera techniques to make it seem like it was travelling a greater distance.

Is miniature and model shooting something you feel people could try for on min-DV?
Yes, I would. My key message on special effects would be don't think, 'This is a special effect. I have got to do it with computer generated imagery.' Yes, CGI can pretty much be done for free if you can get someone who knows their stuff to do it, but if you can film a 'real' thing, whether that's a model that's been made, or some other element, you can create something that is a lot more convincing.

For example, there are effects in Soul Searcher that a lot of people will probably look at and think they are CGI, but in fact they are milk being poured into a fish tank, or my bathroom tap with a few filters on it, or sugar being blasted out of a bowl with a hair dryer. So, if you get creative and learn how to layer up images in Final Cut Pro or After Effects, you can create some stunning effects without having to go anywhere near CGI.

I am actually working on the Soul Searcher DVD extras at the moment and there is a 'How To' element to some of those, where I reveal how these special effects were created with very little money. For anyone interested in low budget filmaking there will definitely be some helpful hints and tips when the DVD version finally gets released.

See The Oseman Diaries : www.netribution.co.uk/2/content/view/243/277/' http://www.netribution.co.uk/2/content/view/243/277/

Alex Ferrari & Sean Falcon
Broken

A Florida-based editor, Alex Ferrari, knew he could make mini-DV look like film and set out to prove it. The result was *Broken*, shot on mini-DV at 24fps, graded and treated in post to get not only the film look he was after, but to add the SFX every action picture needs. The film is a testimonial for what a skilled team, shooting in a hospital basement with no money to back them, can achieve with some standard software and a little imagination. With 5.1 sound and more than two hours of *Broken* extras, the Broken DVD makes for an exceptional value package for a 20-minute showcase action short – and that's just a taster for the full feature he wants to shoot. Director Alex Ferrari with VFX supervisor Sean Falcon and VFX artist Dan Cregan talk us through post to the finished film.

ALEX FERRARI: First off, we hired an amazing young DP named Angel Barretta. We have worked together in the past and I knew he would be able to keep up with my shooting style, which is very fast. We average 110-130 setups a day in the basement. We discussed the look I wanted and told him to shoot it straight. No filters, no gels, no in-camera tricks.

I wanted a clean image that I could manipulate in post. The lighting was key, especially in Mini DV. The camera's spectrum of light is limited so I told him to pump a ton of light in and I'll pull it back in post. The final total was 14 hours on two cameras (2 DVX100As), but I love to let the camera roll so I could capture some magic from the actors when they were not looking. You get some really cool stuff that way.

I edited the first cut in 2 weeks, then started sending out VFX plates to the guys so they could start working. After the FINAL CUT was agreed by Jorge and myself I began colour timing the short to get the look I was going for. As for the colour correction, the filter packages I used were Magic Bullet, G Film, Stib's Simple Levels and a FCP's colour corrector. I found that Simple Levels helped me crush the black in a way that the entire image wasn't affected. I also used garbage matte to cut out sections of the frame and colour correct them individually.

The key is good lighting and having a design in mind before going into post. I did a lot of experimenting and layering techniques in FCP to get the look. I wanted to get three very distinct looks for the short; Bonnie's apartment, the basement and the hospital. I used all my departments, wardrobe, production design, lighting and post to achieve the final looks. I made Bonnie's apartment more blueish for the lighting storm vibe. The basement I wanted dark, crushed blacks, high contrast and overall a very unsettling feeling. The hospital I want a puke green, to give it a very unhealthy vibe.

Sometimes I look back and forget how I got there. I just play around ALOT with the tools. Many independent films do not take the time to design their stories, I did not want to fall into that trap. It also took about 35 hours of rendering all the filters to get the final look for BROKEN.

Now this is where you want us to meet your VFX man, Sean is it? I guess you were responsible for adding in all those muzzle flash effects and explosions?
SEAN FALCON: Yeah, that's me, Sean Falcon, VFX Supervisor.

We knew VFX was going to be an issue before we even started shooting. It had to be done right or it would all be for nothing. So I spent some time playing with different looks for the muzzle flashes. I tried many different approaches, from hand drawn to 3d to procedural. I found that a happy mix between hand painted and procedural yielded the best results.

I started with a very basic flame shape, which was actually a rotoshape in Shake and began layering in different warps. These warps were significant because they really had to sell the look of the flame. I found that using a few different types layered together really gave some nice edge distortion. These were kind of 'global warp nodes'. The reason why the word 'global' was so important to me was that I needed to have a way to make this as 'automated' as possible. One real time saver was that warp setup.

Because Shake is node based, it gives you a great amount of control over the image, so I can easily have the warp effect only certain parts of my script while covering the entire frame. This permitted me to create an effect that never produced the same looking flame twice. In the beginning, I figured that I would just create a library of flame images that I could randomly switch through. This became incredibly time consuming, and there was no guarantee that you would not see the same flame more than once in a shot 'cause there was a lot of shooting!!

Certainly was… I ducked behind the sofa at one point!
Right! Plus, if Alex wanted the flame to come on 3 frames earlier, I would have to go back and change a lot of settings on a lot of nodes. That's why I took the approach that I did. The other way that I saved time was by using expressions. Shake has a scripting language, like Maya's mel scripting, which allows for total flexibility when needed from the app.

Once I had arrived at a muzzle flash that everyone was happy with, I decided to make a template script based on the type of gun that was being fired. For instance, we had Christian's gun producing a multi-flame flash, whereas Tony's gun was a single shot burst. I set it up so that the flame and all atmospheric FX were controlled by one side of the script, and the colour treatment for interactive lighting was controlled by the other side. This made for quick and easy swap-outs of the footage serving as the main plate. The use of expressions came into play heavily on these shots. I basically had a flame 'fader' which controlled when the flame was visible. Linked off of this fader, were expressions that controlled how much interactive lighting was reflected off of the face of the person and surrounding environment, as well as controlling the glows, smoke, dust and camera shake.

This was all done by moving only 1 slider instead of 35. Since the warps were constantly changing on a frame-by-frame basis and the flames only lasted 1 frame, I was certain to have a different effect any time it was visible. I had tons of these shots to complete in a very short amount of time, so these types of set-ups are instrumental in completing complicated or tedious tasks in a much shorter amount of time.

So much for the muzzle flashes, but what about the big bang!
The explosion was kind of a surprise for me. I knew we were going to have that kind of effect, but I didn't get to see the plate until post. We went and got a stock footage CD that had all sorts of fire and explosions, the CD also had some muzzle flashes,

but they were very basic and restrictive as to their integration into many different scenes.

So I did this shot over the weekend starting early Saturday morning, and finishing Sunday night. I wanted the effect to have 'Impact' to it, so I knew the blast would have to be fast and fierce. So I started laying in the explosions, while having to do a LOT of re-timing. That took a little while because these elements were high res. and over 35 seconds long for some of them. I needed these things to fit in a 35-frame window. We didn't have any good smoke elements, so I had to colour correct one of the explosions to look like smoke.

The main thing to keep in mind when doing VFX composites is that it's all in the details. Little things like faint lens flares, subtle camera shake and atmosphere help to sell any shot. Thankfully the explosion was not supposed to break the light housing apart, so that saved me a lot of paint work.

And what about the treatment for Bonnie's bonny blue eyes?
Bonnie's eyes originally were keyed. I ended up using a Shake's colour wheel, warped and colour-corrected to get the eye in the final comp. Then they were tracked into the plate. I wish we could have had more of those shots, but it took too much story for it to make sense. Hopefully we'll see that in the feature....

Chris Kentis & Laura Lau
Open Water

Writer/Director Chris Curtis and producer Laura Lau took a based-on-true-events killer premise – a couple scuba diving in tropical waters is mistakenly abandoned – and turned it into a gripping thriller. Actors Blanchard Ryan and Daniel Travis spent 120 hours in the water and since prosthetic sharks were not an option at the $120,000 dollar level, the shark roles were played by the real thing.

How did the idea for this film come to you?
CK: 'The initial idea was that because of the new DV technology that existed and was affordable, we were very excited about the idea that we could afford to make and finance films ourselves, and have total creative control. I guess we were very

inspired by the Dogme 95 films and the success they were having. Now, at the same time, Laura and I we're married, we've been together many years, and we're recreational divers, we'd been divers for 10 or 11 years and we get all the diving newsletters and everything, and it was in the late 1990s [1998] that we heard about the very specific story that this film was based on, where a couple on vacation went out on a dive boat, and were accidentally left in the water. When I first read about that incident I had a very strong, upsetting, emotional response. Then, I guess around 2000/2001, we decided to make a digital film, and we thought this would be a story that worked very well in that format.'

LL: 'You know digital imparts a very distinct look, a very distinct aesthetic, it gives a very strong sense of realism, so, first of all, we felt that making a digital feature and telling this story on that format would push the format into an area it hadn't been before. We live in New York and a lot of digital features are shot here, and we were thinking, 'What could we do that would be different?' So, once we decided that this story would be well suited to this medium, Chris wrote a script. Shooting in this format, we knew we were going to work with unknown actors, and we knew we were going to have to work with live sharks.'

CK: 'And the reason behind the unknown actors is because we thought the way to make this story work was to make it as real as possible. That's why we used digital video. Working with recognisable stars would have shattered that illusion of reality, and, you know, at the same, we wanted to work out in the ocean, shooting in a documentary fashion. Pretty much everything you see that comes out of Hollywood today, the effects are all computer-generated, and everything in this film is real. We're working with real sharks, and there's a real difference; you're seeing something real on the screen interacting with the actors, and we thought the video format would drive that home even more.'

What expectations did you have when you were making it?

CK: 'One of the challenges that appealed to us was that we were going to wear all the hats here and work without a crew and be doing everything ourselves. For 90% of the shoot it was just Laura and I and the two actors; occasionally her sister would be there as well. The exception was just the two out of six weeks we spent with the sharks, in which case we used professional shark experts that are used to working with sharks in film productions. We worked with them for two days. The bulk of the shoot was just us.'

LL: 'It took us quite a few years to make this movie and since we came out with it, we finished it and we went to a couple of festivals, the response has been incredible. It has been fantastic and surprising to us.'

CK: 'The reactions and comparisons have been surprising to us because we didn't want to do things in a way that we had seen done before. We tried to approach how we were going to structure this story a little bit differently and we didn't really have anything to lose. In a lot of ways we kind of saw this as a little bit more of an experiment.'

LL: 'It's been so gratifying to hear the reactions from film festivalgoers, from divers, from the dive industry, from some of the general public. A lot still remains to be seen.'

There's no way you could have made a film like this at a studio.

CK: 'Yeah, I think if we went to the studio and said, 'Look, there has to be unknown actors, we have to shoot on digital video, we're shooting just in one location, with no back story, with no sub-plot, with nothing dramatic about them being revealed,' forget it. This is what was so ironic to us. I don't think anyone would have gone for this movie in a million years and now that it's done, it's like, 'Why didn't you come to us?' So we're thrilled that so many people are excited about it. We feel really honoured and lucky that that's the case and we don't take that for granted. Also, Laura and I have been working together for about 15 years, so this is not an overnight success story. This has been the result of a lot of long, hard work in educating ourselves. We didn't just come out of film school. It's been a process and it will continue to be a process. So as far as making this film in the studio system, I don't think it would have been possible. And certainly a lot of things we're interested in, we're definitely interested in working independently. But at the same time, we're going to rule anything out right now. We're ruling a lot of things out right now, but when an opportunity comes in we're open to looking at it. You know, if nothing comes in, we're just going to stick to the plan we have. If the movie bombs and nothing comes in, so be it. We're going to continue on our merry way to do what's important to us and work in a way that we had on this.'

Interview by Stephen Applebaum

Writing treatments to cut costs

Adrian Mead
Night People

Adrian Mead, writer and director of *Night People*, developed his very successful £300,000 debut feature in conjunction with Scottish Screen and Scottish Media Group's New Found Films development programme.

Adrian Mead: We were green lit on a second draft script in November and had to have the film ready for a potential screening at the Edinburgh film fest in August. We had to be ready to shoot right at the end of February through March and of course the whole industry shuts down for Christmas and New Year. It was a busy time for us; I think we had Christmas day off. We started full prep about 4 weeks before shooting, everyone had to hit the ground running and we were casting main characters right up to a week before shooting. It was just hard to get hold of anyone until the second week of January. I made the most of the time before that by storyboarding and working with the Editor and DoP who were some of the first crew on board.'

Edinburgh is really an extra character in this film, so did you write for particular Edinburgh locations, or did you write first and then cast your locations later?
With a small budget I knew that the one thing we had to do was to get the most out of our one free resource and that was the city. I knew it really well from walking home in the early hours after working all night on the door and wrote to suit the available locations and also their close proximity to each other. It meant that when we lost a couple of locations due to power cuts etc. we could quickly shift to another spot I knew. I think all in we had 42 locations. However, often we could literally up sticks and walk to the next one.

The New Found Films inititiative appears to have quite a pressured schedule for writers – how pressured was it and how did you cope with that?
It's incredibly tight, but to be fair that was made clear before you applied and at every stage thereafter; 'If you can't do it in this time and on this budget don't apply!'

You were also writing to budget – what sort of feature budget are we talking about?
The budget for the scheme is £300,000 per film and you have to pay everyone at least union rates. Union rates are not very high and these films would not get made without a lot of people being willing to work for a lower rate than they normally do. The crew were fantastic, despite shooting at night in March in Scotland. It was VERY cold.

Alison Peebles
Afterlife

Director Alison Peebles developed her debut feature *Afterlife* with screenwriter Andrea Gibb through the very first New Found Films development process. It was far from an easy ride and the budget had to be increased by 50% from £200,000 to £300,000 – but when the going gets tough…

Alison Peebles You had to apply as a creative team of writer/director/producer with these three key people in place and you would apply with a treatment idea. Ten teams were short-listed. Over the course of the next six months the team ideas were developed. There was an initial meeting and a discussion about treatments with Phil Parker, who's something of a script guru, on what the next stage of treatment should be in moving towards a first draft. We looked at things like who's going to look at it, how are you going to sell it, what's the genre — that sort of thing. Then all the teams went away to create their first draft — in a very, very, very short time. We came up with a first draft, which we looked at and took notes on, then put that into the scheme. Over the course of the next six months we went through three drafts and through this process, in this very short time. Each time we got through to short-listing, we had three, four weeks to do another draft of the script, which would then go to a panel, which would shortlist to next stage.

So did you find this a very intensive process then?
From beginning to end it was very, very intensive, but the development process is extremely intensive

for the writer. An immense burden of work fell on the writer. At each stage we had just a few short weeks to go from treatment to draft, from first draft to second draft, from second draft to third draft. The way the process worked meant we had just three or four weeks to move to next stage, then the draft would sit with the panel for three or four weeks while they would decide. It had to be sent out to people on the panel to be read and then they had to come together, so the panel needed as much time just to read it, as we had to write it. But of course while we were doing that, we needed time for discussions about how to proceed. It was a very, very intensive process.

Was it a good way to develop the story, through treatment and step outline, rather than script alone?
Treatment's a very difficult thing. You can do a fantastic treatment, but the eventual script might bear no relation to it. Writing a good treatment and writing a good script can be very different things, but of course Andrea is a very skilled writer. Her treatment was excellent anyway, but she knew more or less straight away how she wanted the screenplay to go. She had been thinking about it for a long time, so in this case, the treatment and the script were very loyal to each other.

What budget did you expect to have for this feature and how did that affect its development?
The budget was minimal. Scottish Screen and Scottish Television were offering £200,000, which is unbelievable for a feature you are hoping to go into cinema. People can make films on a lot less, I know, but we wanted our film to have a cinema release, to have a quality look about it. We actually ended up with about £300,000 – that's what it was finally made for.

Kenneth D Barker
Kingdom

Kenneth D Barker's debut went against the notion that the first feature should be modest and not too ambitious, but with backing from an angel investor, *Kingdom* set out to get good returns from the family market. The film is set in the world's last dragon sanctuary and is a modern urban fairy tale with full-blown CGI dragons.

I'd left film school and was gagging to make a feature. I figured that once I'd made it, at least I could sell copies at the local car-boot if there was no conventional interest. Most members of the public buy feature films, how many of them will buy a short? All the usual funding agencies said 'nice idea — but bugger off'. Then in a strange twist of fortune, I kept meeting all these talented people who were also looking for a break in films or television. They were model makers, make-up artists and computer graphics geeks. That's when I realised *Kingdom* was achievable on a modest budget.

A month before we were scheduled to start filming, I had £200 and a Hi8 camera to my name, which was not quite enough. It was only after a very convoluted set of circumstances that I heard about a Business Angel network and they were prepared to listen to me. I had a comprehensive business plan I had prepared. All the Angels I spoke to were initially more interested in me as a person, then me as a manager. They wanted to know if I could be trusted with their money — which is a fair way of assessing a risk. Perhaps more importantly, I was genuinely excited about making *Kingdom* and I'm sure my excitement spilt over during my presentation.

I set up a company and the angel sits on it as a non-executive director. Day to day operations are handled by myself, but we both co-own *Kingdom* and all its rights.

My advice to any other film maker looking at the Angel route is — be prepared to give up a lot of the project to get it financed, but ideally you need to retain artistic control. Then be grateful that somebody's interested in backing your wild notion.

Innovative Marketing & Distribution

Lance Weller,
Head Trauma

Lance Weller is a critically acclaimed, award-winning writer and director with a successful and innovative approach to marketing his films. His independent feature *The Last Broadcast* was made for $900 back in 1998, the first all-digital theatrical release of a motion picture and is currently being distributed in more than 20 countries and aired on HBO. To date *The Last Broadcast* has sold 100,000 VHS/DVD units bringing in $4m world-wide.

Weller's new film *Head Trauma* (2006) faces the same hurdles as any other new feature, the sheer number of competing features trying to get into the market; no fewer than 20,000 features are made every year, few of which will see any return on investment. But in the case of an independent film, there's an even bigger hurdle to overcome.

Lance Weller explains: 'The problem is the old business model of supply and demand. Indie moviemakers are creating too great a supply of movies, with little demand from the big studios, who still view the distribution of an indie as a high-risk endeavour.'

In the case of *Head Trauma*, Weller decided to self distribute off the back of the film's acceptance for the Los Angeles Film Festival and use the festival to springboard a platform release.

'Instead of going to look for distribution, I wanted to use the festival for press, networking, the opportunity to see *Head Trauma* with an audience and, most importantly, a way to announce my distribution plan.'

His plan was to roll out the film theatrically in 15 cities, starting in August with a two-month roll-out leading up to a DVD release date of 26th of September. Then in October, he planned to release an alternative sound track to the movie. Head Trauma's acceptance into the L.A. Festival gave Weller the leverage he needed to use on theatres to get them to take up the film.

'I knew from past experience that I could book theatres. I also knew that I could do 'splits' instead of 'four walling,' meaning that I could split costs with the theatre instead of renting the space outright.'

Weller still had to pitch his film to theatre owners, showing a clear vision of his audience and how to reach out to them. Most of all, he knew he had to make a convincing business case to theatre bosses.

'I'm sure most theatre owners love smaller films, but at the end of the day it's business; I wanted to prove to theatre owners that I was thinking of this as a business partnership.'

And that is exactly what he proposed. Theatre managements got a 'favoured nation' deal — a straight 50/50 split, backed up by a low-cost campaign run by Weller with street teams, word of mouth and the internet.

Theatres gave Weller local press lists well six weeks in advance and he let it be known he would attend some screenings to do Q&As, financing his trip by accepting speaking engagements at local schools and film societies, where he was also drumming up custom for his film. At every screening he sold 27' and 40' posters of the film, averaging $200 a night on merchandise.

All of this promotional activity also benefited the sale of the DVD which hit the street quickly as soon as the theatre tour had ended. Weller had spent four years managing his own distribution label for *The Last Broadcast* (1998).

He decided to use a different approach for *Head Trauma* on DVD. This time he went to the Heretic label making it clear he was pitching a special deal to avoid his film being locked up in a 15-year distribution prison from which it could be hard to extract even routine progress and revenue reports.

Weller was bringing Heretic a DVD distribution on the back of a national theatrical release, giving the label the benefit of huge promotion at no cost to them. This advantage was calculable, so he demanded a 60-40 split in his favour and that Heretic would bring to the table a $25,000 dollar package to roll out the DVD. Finally he demanded retention of his digital rights, so that VoD and digital downloads would be his alone and he would also have the right to sell the DVD from his website. He planned on getting $4 to $6 on every DVD Heretic sold.

After theatre and DVD distribution for *Head Trauma*, the third aspect of his marketing plan was the release of an alternate soundtrack. He had liked the Pink Floyd idea of turning down the sound of the TV when it was screening The Wizard of Oz, in favour of the stereo playing Pink Floyd's 'Darkside of the Moon.' This had created an entirely different viewing experience.

His clincher was to be 'Cursed: The *Head Trauma* Music Project,' with tracks from hot talents like Steve Garvey of The Buzzcocks and Marshall Allen of SunRa and The Novenas. Park the Van Records released the album on the 6th of October

This automatically created press hooks and got the papers writing about the album and of course, the film that partnered it. So, to cement the attraction, Weller arranged some screenings of Head Trauma with bonus live performances from some artists on the alternative soundtrack.

Weller's distribution strategy is certainly proactive and has kept him in the business of making films to which he still owns all the rights. Of course, if a distributor was to pitch him a good deal, he will consider it, but it will need to be good one.

Meanwhile he's writing his book on DIY film distribution, due out in 2007.

www.headtraumamovie.com

Gene Cajayou
The Debut (US)

An award-winning family film in English language, The Debut revolves around a talented high school senior, Ben, who has rejected his Filipino heritage. The long-simmering feud between Ben and his immigrant father Roland threatens to boil over and ruin the 18th birthday party of Ben's sister Rose . To Ben's surprise, his sister's celebration challenges his sense of misplaced identity, and the way he regards his father and grandfather (played by Filipino film legend Eddie Garcia). In one night, Ben faces the true nature of his relationships with his family, his friends, and himself.

Despite the changes in distribution that the internet has made possible, the traditional rent-a-theatre-drum-up-a-crowd school of distribution still works. Gene Cajayou's The Debut (debutfilm.com) took $1.7m over two years from a handful of screens each weekend.:

Weekend Gross

Gross	Date	Screens
$5,062	(10 November 2002)	(2 Screens)
$7,028	(3 November 2002)	(2 Screens)
$14,253	(27 October 2002)	(4 Screens)
$641	(22 September 2002)	(1 Screen)
$12,788	(1 September 2002)	(4 Screens)
$12,499	(18 August 2002)	(3 Screens)
$1,929	(21 July 2002)	(1 Screen)
$8,067	(7 July 2002)	(3 Screens)
$11,194	(30 June 2002)	(3 Screens)
$16,937	(23 June 2002)	(3 Screens)
$32,711	(9 June 2002)	(4 Screens)

Gene Cajayou took his film on the road for two years to build up those sort of figures. He was working a potentially large audience that is largely overlooked by distributors in the US, the Asian-American market. He's now signed a home distribution deal with Columbia Tristar, so he won't be lugging cartons of DVDs around main street stores any more and his distributors are no doubt wishing they had spotted the potential of The Debut earlier, but they also realise that with these sort of grosses behind the film, it is never too late to get a piece of the action, even if it is just the tail end.

The Debut on IMDB — www.imdb.com/title/tt0163745

Zack Coffman and Scott Di Lalla
Choppertown: the Sinners

THE PLOT: Custom chopper builder and punk rocker Kutty Noteboom builds his working man's chopper from the ground up with the help of good friend Rico and the rest of his biker brothers in this intimate award-winning documentary about renowned hot rod and motorcycle club the Sinners.

Niche marketing was an obvious way to go for Zack Coffman and Scott Di Lalla after they spent a year with the members of Choppertown Motorcycle Club, filming their custom bike builds, decked out with the very latest chrome and stainless steel add-ons. The film's subjects were all home mechanics in their 20s and 30s who gathered together to pool expertise and tools and build bikes in one garage. Caffman and Di Lalla were garage building a documentary film, so between the subjects and the filmmakers, Choppertown was an ideal marriage.

After a year of getting in the way for close shots and generally holding up bike-building at regular intervals as filmmaking inevitably would, Caffman and Di Lalla felt that at all costs they had to hold on to the goodwill of the Choppertown bikers. Once their film was edited, they arranged a screening for the boys to see their builds immortalised on screen, but they also invited along a selection of the motorcycle and car press, realising that might be good for publicity for their film.

As an idea, it worked splendidly. They were just beginning to plan their next moves with the film when the phone started ringing. The callers all wanted to know when they could see this film about building bikes. Where was it being screened next and when? The motoring press had put the word out directly to the very demographic that would have most interest in the film. A random 'good idea' had turned into a first class marketing ploy.

One of the most frequently asked questions was 'Where Can I Buy a DVD?'

Point taken, Zack Coffman and Scott Di Lalla quickly built a website and started supplying what the callers were asking for. They shifted several thousand copies over just a few months and it is still a strong seller,

having taken on something of a legendary cult status among bikers.

www.choppertown.net/

Scott Pehl
Curiosity is Catching On in the Marketplace

A man walks through a dingy underground car park and something bright and shiny catches his eye, high in some pipework over the exit door. Curious, he reaches up and retrieves a DVD lodged there, looks at it for a moment, then slips it in his pocket. He goes out and crosses to his apartment block. We see him entering his apartment where he slips the DVD into his player and sits down to watch it. The disc shows a man walking through a dingy underground car park and something bright and shiny catches his eye....

It is an intriguing start to a short film that keeps you watching and at its conclusion, chills you to the marrow. Director Scott Pehl describes the borrowed marketing tactic that not only gave them the idea for a remarkable short film, Curious, but got them noticed and well on the way to their first feature deal....

When did the marketing idea for planting the film on discs in public places to get a buzz going come up, exactly?
The idea to put the DVDs out on the street came up almost immediately. As soon as Tim and I had worked out the idea for the short we could see the marketing possibility in planting the DVDs.

People were asked to re-plant the disc for someone else – so could you measure the overall reaction to what people had seen in some way?
We put the request to email us feedback on the cover of the DVD. In the beginning we got a response from one of every ten DVDs we put on the street.

Where did you plant the first discs, how many and what places did you target as planting spots for them?

In the beginning, we planted near the locations we shot the film. All around the East Village. Then we started putting them wherever we went in the city. Dozens of them made it to other cities on trips with us, and with some of the people who originally picked them up. The majority of responses we received were from men and women in their 20's, mostly visitors to NY.

What sort of places did other people plant the discs in, after they had watched them?

To be honest we had little success with getting people to replant the DVD. Most of the people that found them wanted to keep the film for themselves to show their friends.

Some of the people that found the DVD requested copies to distribute back home. That is how it ended up in London, Mexico City and Upstate NY. They replanted them in college cafeterias, subway seats, bookstores and street poles.

Did you ever find any discs yourselves? – where did you spot them?

I have occasionally noticed that a few days after they are picked up they end up back on the same street corner. As far as new places are concerned, I have not run into them, perhaps I am not as inquisitive as other people!

I did have the opportunity in Barcelona, Spain, to watch one of them being picked up. I sat in a café across the street and watched several people look at it, think about it and pass it by. Then a young man did exactly what Cheyenne does in the short. He noticed the DVD, looked around a couple of times, thought about it and quickly grabbed it and hid it in his pocket. He looked around again and quickly went on his way.

Has anyone come to you and offered help with your production plans?

We did sign on with a great distributor, Big Film Shorts. They have single handedly gotten the short distributed on DVD in the US, broadcast on Cinemax in South America and recently got us on Comcast OnDemand across the US. The short has also gotten us a great deal of interest in a feature. We are currently talking with a couple of finance options and distributors about the feature.

What sort of budget did all this take, for filming Curiosity, for the marketing plan?

Asking budget is like asking a lady her age. More than 5k, less than 10k.

Most of the budget was used in shooting and post production. The entire crew worked for free. We spent quite a bit of it on camera, steadi cam, lights, crew meals and transport. We ended up taking it to a Sound Designer to clean up the audio.

As far as the cost of marketing, that continues to come out of pocket as available. I buy a 20 pack of dvds and spend an afternoon burning them. Then we just bring a handful with us wherever we happen to be going.

One of the things I learned while working with publicists is the art of the press release. The internet has made it much easier to distribute news about your film.

I created a publicist, Seth Coptel (an anagram of Scott Peehl), and have him send out releases whenever we have a screening or development with the film. Just make sure what you are sending out is really news. People will get annoyed if you fill up their email inbox with useless information or shameless plugs.

The other hint, and this one takes a lot of time and patience, is to email everyone individually so that your email does not end up in their spam file. You need to be specific about who you are emailing and if they would be interested in what you are sending.

Keep your press release simple. Date, time, place and a small description about what makes this news worthy. Then send them to short film blogs, local film reviewers, etc.

Is living and working in NYC in the East Village an advantage or disadvantage to you as a filmmaker?

Definitely an advantage. NYC is the kind of city where you have no idea where the day will take you. An interaction at a coffee shop can lead to a whole new career. The East Village is filled with creative and amazing people that inspire all sorts of things.

Here are a couple of examples of the questions we sent out to people that have found the dvd and how they responded to us.

FOUND SURVEY

JASON London, England UK

1. What made you pick up the DVD in the first place?

I'm that kind of person.

2. What did you think was on the DVD?
I had no idea, then I imagined it would be a hip hop mix

3. Did you watch it right away or wait awhile... what made you want to watch it?
I stuck it on as soon as I got home, unfortunately there was no one else around and I got a little freaked out, I found myself doing the same as the guy in the short, going to the window even checking the closets. It was then I realised how sad it was that there was only this way of distributing the film and how lucky I was to have found it and experienced it 'as intended'.

4. Did finding it on the street just like the character in the film enhance your experience?
Oh yes ! I was twitchy!

5. Did you put the DVD out for someone else to find it? If so, where?
I hid it between cushions on a train seat (in the UK)

6. If you kept the DVD did you show it to friends? How many?
I gave away one of the copies to a director in the UK, the rest you gave me went on trains.

More information about Curiosity at: www.netribution.co.uk/2/content/view/1030/182/

Susan Buice & Arin Crumley

Four Eyed Monsters Grow Their Own Audience: Romancing – and Distributing — the Web

Susan Buice and Arin Crumley, made a movie about the development of their real-life relationship, podcast it on the web (www.foureyedmonsters.com) to win a massive following and used their audience to decide which local theatres to screen the movie in. They did it on credit cards, racking up an $80K debt.

But there's also a fairy-tale ending. They earned $100K after audiences backed them to win an IndieWire Undiscovered Gems Showcase. That has a cosied-up warm feeling, doesn't it? A nice warm way to get into profit....

How many people are following Four Eyed Monsters and the progress of your emotional relationship on the web just now – do have any idea?
First we should say that the video podcast is a non-fiction depiction of our relationship. As for our audience, we've received over a million views to our videos, but it's impossible to know the number of people that are actually following us.

Is that mostly a US audience or has it spread wider than that through the web?
It's a world wide audience though it's probably mostly a US audience but we've been contacted by people in other countries such as Denmark, the U.K., Australia, Sweden and Germany. To see a map of our world wide web traffic you can scroll down on foureyedmonsters.com and at the bottom right hand corner you'll see a button that says 'geo-visitors'.

How did you meet up and decide to start the project and when did you realise your Four Eyed Monsters was going to have a life of its own, through the web?
As presented in episode 1 of our video Podcast and as portrayed in our film, we met through an online dating website. Our relationship began as sort of an experiment in dating and in communication. We

decided to meet up almost immediately but created the rule that we would not speak to each other but could communicate with one another in any other format. We created hand written notes, drawings, and played music for one another. At certain point we began creating videos for each other. After 4 months of this lifestyle we finally began speaking. We were really inspired by the experiences we had during our non-speaking courtship. We wanted to turn our communication experiment outward and expand our audience from just one another to more people so we created the film to tell the story. The video podcast is a continuation of the same story and the video podcast just so happens to be in a format that can easily spread and be subscribed to.

The focus is on your relationship and how it grows and changes over time, but does it really reflect your real relationship? Is it art imitating life, or has it somehow become a case of art almost dictating life for the two of you?
Everyone who has watched the entire video podcast series to date is aware that it is a depiction of our real lives. Even though we are using a medium and style that is normally associated with fiction, the story we're telling is true. To be fair it's a highly expressive project so when the audience is looking at something that is very obviously constructed, it is an expression of our real experiences. The film works the same way but the film has an even more narrative feel because there is very little real life footage. What we are interested in is working on projects about real relationships; Making stuff up wouldn't provide valuable insights to ourselves or anyone else.

No bust-ups over which way to go or which way to play things??
During the process of making stuff we, of course, disagree all the time but we always agree on the final outcome that becomes public.

There are a lot of people involved creatively – how many exactly?
Who we work with is always changing but we usually work very closely with one other person and for the duration of that time that person is an equal collaborator. The individuals we work with at any given time depends on what the project needs in that moment.

Are they all volunteers or have you had to pay for some things you needed?
We've had volunteers who have worked on basic things but for the most part everyone we have worked with has been a collaborator, some of them close friends and some we've met through working on the project. Other than certain stipends most people have worked in exchange for credit on the project.

Totting up the bills, what were the costs in time and money setting all this up for the web?
We don't really distinguish between the video podcast and the film in terms of financial costs or time costs. The Web hosting of our videos has been donated by Cache Fly and the cost of our website is very little. What has been expensive is time. We've been working on the entire project for the past 3 years full-time and we've racked up a huge credit card debt on living expenses. Our debt to date is somewhere around $80,000.

When you decided you would go for a feature length movie as well as podcasts, how did that work exactly — did you edit pre-existing material together, shoot new stuff; how did you give FEMonsters followers a new and fresh experience?
The film was created first and most of the film is shot fresh, though much of it was based on old footage we had from early in our relationship. The video podcast is a continuation of the same story and it is all new content. Most of the video podcast is documentary footage, but every now and then will shoot something , animate or illustrate something and even use found footage to convey certain aspects of the story we're telling. The video podcast is usually how people find out about the film since we've never had a distributor to release and market the film.

We hear about zero budgets, but we all have to spend on tape, bus fares, pencils and yellow pads... what did you lay out to get from web podcasts to a feature you could screen in theaters?
We owned almost all the equipment we needed for the film: camera, lights, Macs and Final Cut Pro for editing. We did rent a track at one point and for 2 days we rented a space to shoot a restaurant scene. Besides that we bought a lot of mini DV tape. The hard costs of the film totalled to less than $10,000 but like I said before, we worked full time on the project so we put our rent and the cost of food on credit cards, which is how we racked up so much debt.

How did you convince theatre owners that they should let your film into their program and did

you have to pay hire charges or do a 'house split' – how did that work?

On our website we allow people to request our film which means they give us their email and zip code and by doing this they are requesting that we screen our film in their area and that if we do we are free to contact them. Using this information we were able to see where there were people who wanted to see our film. We felt like if 150 people had requested the film in a given area it would be lucrative enough endeavour for us to propose and convince a theatre to arrange a screening. When we called the theatre we explained the request system and explained that we would contact all the requestors and let them know about the screenings and encourage a wider audience to go through our videos on our podcast. In the cities we were going for, we would sometimes hit resistance with a theatre. In that case we would call other theatres until we found the one that wanted to take a chance with us. With most theatres we arranged a 50/50 split of ticket sales. In a couple of cases we were able to negotiate a low four walling fee and all the ticket sales from those venues went straight to us.

You have just had (Dec 2006) a NYC opening week at Cinema Village – how did that go and what sort of box office did you manage to generate?

We opened on split screen with 2 other films. We weren't playing at every slot on every day. Our box office was fairly weak. We did, however, end up the # 5 opening film in New York City that week and got reviewed in the New York Times, Village Voice as well as a slew of other press. We also lead a grassroots campaign using our New York supporters and distributed 4000 stickers, 500 posters, 5000 postcards, and 200 free DVDs which was a cool way to get to know people who have been watching our podcast for a long time. We also held interactive discussions every night after our 7 PM screenings on various topics ranging from net neutrality, to life logging, to internet dating.

Where do you take Four Eyed Monsters from here? I mean has it now got a life all of its own and could go on as pure fiction, or will it have to continue as episodic, waiting for developments in your own relationship?

Well we still have some story left untold which is what we're currently editing into the next few episodes. As for continuing to follow our relationship in an auto-biographical way, we're not going to necessarily continue doing that. We're still interested in discovering things about real relationships, how we go about making those discoveries is something we're currently navigating.

Does it ever feel strange that people you meet seem to know all about you in almost intimate detail, yet they are total strangers. Do you ever feel you have over-exposed yourselves? Are you completely cool about it?

We rarely get recognized in the street so we don't interact with our audience in real life that often, but when we do it's usually pretty cool because some of the introduction bullshit is out of the way. In meeting new people, you have to spend so much time making your first impression and nothing really gets communicated during that first interaction beyond surface things, such as 'well this person seems on the ball' or 'what an idiot,' but when we meet people who have seen the podcast we can quickly get to a point where we're communicating with more depth. Because they know a lot about us, that's less that we have to convey in a less articulate way by talking and they in turn are more apt to be less guarded and reveal things about themselves.

What advice can you give to anyone thinking of attempting the vodcasts to features route – is it a good way to find an audience and is it sustainable long term.

If you're releasing good compelling video on the web for free you will build an audience. If that is your only goal you are set. If your goal is to get that audience to do something else, that becomes challenging. We've been able to get our audience to petition for screenings of our film, come out to theatres and pay

Date	Total Att.	No of Thtrs.	Av.Ticket Pr.	Gross Receipts	Gross per Theatre	Gross to Date
7/9/06	318	6	$8.51	$2,707.75	$451.29	$2,707.75
14/9/06	353	6	$8.28	$2,992.00	$487.00	$5,629.75
21/9/06	499	6	$7.37	$3,679.50	$613.25	$9,309.25
28/9/06	521	6	$8.09	$4,214.50	$702.42	$13,523.75

money to see the film and to help us promote it. At the centre of all this interaction is a community that we are building. The centre of that community is our video podcast. How financially sustainable this will be for us is the next chapter of this experiment. Our prediction is that having a dedicated community around a project has tremendous value that can be creatively leveraged into getting out of debt and lining up a budget for the next project.

Do you feel it is viable to recoup costs and get into a good profit position that way, so maybe you can finance one project off the back of another. Is the market place mature and stable enough for that to be reliable?

There's a bunch of financial information about how our Thursdays in September went here: foureyedmonsters.com/september_stats/ (see below)

You can see in the Total Attendance column and Gross Per Theatre column that each Thursday does better then the previous Thursday. This proves our theory that when you give a film time for word of mouth to spread, you'll see that occur, provided people like the film.

It also proves that this technique of showing the film once a week can be considered pre-release screenings, and theatrical bookings can be made with proof that the film has the ability to spark word-of-mouth. Combine this with what we see on our comments page, with everyone becoming more interactive in the project by posting their thoughts about the film and it starts to really make sense; to get a film out first to some core people that are going to really promote it. Then, from that base start to expand. So that's where we are now, expanding.

Also, we took part in a screening series called the Indiewire Undiscovered Gems showcase which had an audience voted award totalling $100,000 in worth. We were able to get our video podcast audience to go to the screenings and give us a high score to increase our chances of winning. We found out in December that we won the award.

For details on that: www.foureyedmonsters.com/indiewire-2

The couple hae also created a publicly editable databse o 600 US cinemas at foureyedmonsters.com/public-database-of-movie-theaters/

Paul Andrew Williams
London to Brighton

Paul Andrew Williams's debut feature London to Brighton was shot for £80,000, which was enough to attract a number of distributors and the completion funding from the UK Film Council. Described by The Guardian as the best British Film of the year, the film picked up awards at Edinburgh Film Festival, Dinard and the BIFAs.

London to Brighton's full of pace and energy, what sort of look were you going after for your film?
It was always important to try and capture the reality of what was going on and how we would see it if we were there, or we were nearby, or if we were spectating. We wouldn't see it as crisp and clean, as you might get with a really nice 35 mill appearance. It would be rough and out of focus at times and quick, catched glimpses of things. That's what I wanted for the energy of the scene, for whatever scene we were shooting.

And you chose to shoot on film?
I would always shoot on film. We chose to shoot it on 16mm.

That was mainly hand-held then, was it?
It was all hand-held; apart from one scene. I'm not going to give the story away, but it's the scene in the rich house.

Various budgets have been reported, but what was the budget you raised for the film?
We actually shot it and cut it and put the music on for £80,000 and then the Film Council eventually came on to finish the legals and get the film to print. So we made it for eighty grand and then got it to a position where we could show it in cinema with help from the Film Council, pretty much completion money.

We were in a situation where we could have done it on deferred fees for suppliers, but the Film Council brings a lot of support along with it. In order to get it to the screen it cost £260,000 but we made it for £80,000. That was our money. Once we had shown it to distributors and so on, we were showing them what we had shot for eighty grand.

How did you go about raising it?

The exec producer Tony Bolton had put some money into the short films I had made here and there and had been a big supporter for me. I saw him one day and said 'Look if you can give me sixty grand — as it was at that time — then I can make the film. The people who are investing get half the company.' And he said 'OK.' And that was it.

He's a bit of a film angel for you then.
He is a film angel, indeed.

Was that just a cash budget — were there deferrals on top of that?
Yes, we deferred everyone's fees, my fees, everybody's fees they all got deferred.

How does your system of deferrals work? They get deferrals back when? After the cost of making the film has been met?
They get paid on a level with the investors.

Is that cast and crew only or suppliers as well?
The suppliers pretty much gave us stuff for nothing.

You filmed in October and again with pickups in February, but by March you started getting a lot of interest in the film and still more in April – how did all that come about?
Just because we started showing people the odd scene, then, once the Film Council had seen the roughcut we had to start showing it to distributors and about four or five distribution companies wanted to take on the film. That was when the 'The Buzz' started. It hasn't really stopped.

You needed dark, brooding, underworldy locations and grubby tenement flats, but also, luxury apartments and London and Brighton. Where and how did you find all your locations?
We had a location manager who did a great job for us. A lot of the locations are houses of people working on the film, or investors houses. The producer and the location manager did a great job closing deals wherever we were shooting when we had no times. There were times when we would literally turn up on the day without ever seeing where we were filming and have to make do.

Sometimes you can get the best results that way...
Of course, yes. It makes you think on your feet.

London to Brighton Budget

Development and financing	£1,500.
Armourer / Stunts / Prosthetics / Physical FX	£3,000
Set Dressing and Costumes	£2,000
Make Up Consumables	£300
Equipment hire	£10,000
Location fees and facilities	£10,000
Stock	£10,000
Lab Costs	£2,000
Edit Suite Purchase	£4,000
Travel and Transport	£15,000
Hotel and Living	£12,000
Insurance	£2,500
Overheads	£3,000
Contingency	£5,000
TOTAL	**£80,000**

CHAPTER 3
Production Financing

The most prominent, and probably only truly accurate, rule of independent film financing is simply '**There Are No Rules**'. You can do almost any deal you like, so long as it is commercially acceptable to all concerned. There really is no standard way to finance a feature film; it's a question of pulling together whatever you can find.

At any given time, a film could potentially be financed in a number of different ways, depending entirely on what can be negotiated at that particular moment and agreed between the specific parties involved. But, with regular changes in the law (both nationally and internationally), and with a surprising number of financing companies – and sometimes whole sectors – continually entering and leaving the market, the exact same film with an identical cast and budget could be financed under a completely different structure, if made only a year or two later. That said, there would be no point in writing this Chapter (or even this Handbook) if the industry was truly in a state of pure, uncoordinated anarchy. There are, in fact, many 'rules of thumb' that can be used as guidance (if not gospel), and certain types of financier will always deal in a certain way. The purpose of this Chapter is to discuss the range of options currently available in the mainstream independent market, and to see how they might be pieced together in a jigsaw-like fashion to obtain sufficient funds to get your script into the can.

The main reason that film financing can be so complicated, when compared to other financing industries, is simply because in this business there are so many types of financier. Each has a different kind of interest in the film, because each is putting in its money for different reasons. Some financiers are more concerned with how or where the film is made (or at what cost), others with how much it can be sold for on the international market, or how well it may do at the box office in any particular territory or territories, or simply how passionate they are in wanting to see the film in question on the big screen.

A **lending bank**, for example, will only really be interested in its fee, and in receiving a fixed return (interest) on its loan, which it will always expect to be repaid – and usually before anyone else. So long as it is repaid in full, and quickly, it doesn't necessarily care how successful the film then goes on to be.

An **equity investor**, on the other hand, will sit and wait for other financiers to be paid back their contributions first, and will then (after being repaid its own investment) want to share in the profits of the film. It will therefore be very keen for the film to earn a lot of money worldwide for a long period of time, and thereby make a large profit.

A **rights-based financier**, such as a distributor or broadcaster, will put up funds in return for the right to keep any money it makes from distributing (or '**exploiting**') the film in its own territory. It will therefore not be so interested in how well the film does commercially anywhere else in the world (apart from perhaps in the United States), but it will want to be sure that the film is made in such a way as to have the greatest chance of being successful on its home turf.

Alternatively, **governments** that give grants or rebates, or offer tax incentives, will usually be keen for the film, or at least a large part of it, to be made within their jurisdiction so as to bring a benefit to their local economy.

Above are just a few, somewhat over-simplified, examples. Of course for the Producer, each dollar received goes directly into the production of his/her film, no matter where it comes from. S/he must, however, understand that those putting up this money may be looking to get very different, and often conflicting, benefits in return for their cash. It can be a difficult balancing act for the person that the Producer engages to pull all the money together (this person is generally referred to as an '**executive producer**', although this term is regularly misused), to make sure that each of the financiers is happy with its individual deal.

'Building' an Analogy

We have just touched on a few of the different categories of financier within the independent sector. However, before launching into an in-depth analysis of each individual type of finance, it may be useful to compare the various players with those in an alternative and perhaps more familiar industry, in order to understand better the varying roles in the independent financing process. Anyone who's ever bought a new apartment or condominium may be familiar with the role of the Realty (or Estate) Agent, Construction Company, Architect, Land Owner, local government Planning Department, etc. There are in fact many parallels that can be drawn with the construction industry to help demystify the film financing conundrum. As there are a large number of different 'players' being introduced, we have chosen in this Section to use Capitalised Terms to help distinguish between them.

The Players

Imagine you were intending to construct a large, fifteen floor, apartment block containing condos or flats, and costing a total of $10m. Someone owns some land on which s/he would like the block to be built. You, as the Construction Company, buy the land in order to erect the building on it, based upon instructions given by an Architect. At some point, you engage an Estate Agent (known as a Realty Agent in the USA) to sell off the various apartments (usually by way of long lease) in order to bring in revenue. We could say that the original Land-Owner is analogous to the Owner of a film's underlying rights; ie. the script or other property that is going to be used as the basis for creating the film. You, as the Construction Company, are the equivalent to the film's Producer; the person who actually puts the project together, engages the team, arranges the finance, and ultimately intends to own and earn money from the finished product. The Architect can be seen as the film's Director, under whose guidance the creative vision is materialised. The Estate Agent, who may get involved surprisingly early in the process, can be compared to the film's Sales Agent, whose job it is to sell the film to international Distributors, territory by territory, and so on. The analogy may not hold up 100% when analysed in minute detail, but it is a useful tool in helping to understand the basic 'Who's Who' in the film financing arena. Let's explore a little further...

Soft Money

So, once you (the Construction Company) have all your plans and designs finalised, and have obtained the necessary planning consents (which may be conditional upon certain things taking place) and identified the main department heads within your construction team, you will be in a position to go out looking

> It can be a difficult balancing act to make sure that each of the financiers is happy with its individual deal.

for the finance required to pay for the construction of the Building. The first place you may go in order to obtain some of the finance needed could be your local government. You may be eligible for a grant or other incentive specifically available to those who create residential housing in your local area. We could, for the purposes of this example, assume that you are able to get a $1.5m contribution towards your $10m project in this way. This is the equivalent of what we call '**soft money**' in the film industry because, although the money probably comes with restrictions as to how, where and on whom it may be spent, it is unlikely that you will be obliged to repay it in full.

Pre-selling

You may also, at this stage, try to pre-let some of the apartments (or entire floors of apartments) in order to obtain further money to put towards the cost of construction. To do this, you will enlist the services of an Estate Agent (Realtor). The prospective Lessees (or owners) of these apartments would have to commit certain funds having only seen plans of the proposed Building, and would therefore probably obtain their leases at a lower price than if they had waited to see the finished apartments before committing to buy them. We could, for this example, assume you sell three of the fifteen floors (by way of 25 year leases) at $1m each, thereby providing another $3m towards the construction costs. This is the equivalent of '**pre-selling**' a film to foreign distributors, whose '**territories**' could be considered the equivalent to the different floors (the penthouse probably being North America, and the other floors being equivalent to the UK, France, Germany, Japan, Scandinavia, Latin America, etc.).

Although they are committed to buy, the purchasers are unlikely to part with their money until the apartments are actually finished and available, so you will probably have to go to a bank to borrow the money in the meantime, using the sales contracts as collateral. In film, this is known as '**discounting**' the pre-sales.

Deferments

It may be that you and the Architect both believe in the future commercial success of the project so much that you are willing to defer some of your own fees. Although, between the two of you, you may have (say) $1m of fees technically included as part of the budget for the construction, you may choose to defer half of these ($0.5m), and agree for them to be paid out of future income (obtained from selling off the remaining floors of apartments) rather than from funds raised from elsewhere to finance the Building. This will therefore reduce the amount that you have to find from elsewhere by $0.5m. Effectively, you and the Architect are yourselves financing the construction to the tune of $0.5m. The analogy here would be the deferment by the Producer and/or Director or, for that matter, cast and crew, of part of their fees; a common (if often reluctant) sacrifice made particularly by above-the-line personnel when 'passionate' about their film project.

Equity

An Equity Investor may also believe in the long-term profitability of the apartment block. Despite realising that s/he is unlikely to see any money out of the three pre-sold floors for some time (the amounts paid for those 25-year leases went straight into the construction of the building), s/he is comfortable that the remaining 12 floors can be sold off at prices high enough to cover the remaining cost of construction, and make a profit on top. In return for providing equity cash, the investor will require a share of any profit you ultimately make. Likewise in film; an equity investor will share in any profit made from selling off the unsold territories (ie. those not pre-sold). If, in our example, the equity investor puts up another $3m, you are still left with a shortfall of $2m (the total budget was $10m, remember), having sold off three floors for $3m, received $1.5m soft money, and deferred $0.5m in fees.

The Bank
Reluctantly, this is when you probably have to trot off to the Bank for a loan. You still have 12 floors of apartments to sell (including the penthouse), and you only need a further $2m to complete the financing for your block. The Estate Agent (whose sale price projections the Bank trusts) confirms to the Bank that it thinks it can sell the remaining floors for a figure far in excess of this amount, even without selling the penthouse (This is where our analogy is stretched a little as we need to imagine that penthouses – equivalent to the territory of North America – are notoriously and inherently difficult to sell, notwithstanding that if they are actually sold, they are likely to bring in the most money). So, ignoring any possible income from selling the penthouse, if the Bank can be convinced that the potential receipts from selling the remaining floors outweigh - by a huge margin - the amount it is being asked to lend, it will consider lending you the remaining $2m. This will probably be on condition that a) the Bank gets its money repaid with interest (and an additional fee!), b) it is the first in the pecking order to be paid from any receipts generated by selling off the remaining floors (so your deferments may have to wait), c) it takes a security (in the form of charge or mortgage) over the building until such time as it is repaid in full, and d) it has the right to do the discounting for the pre-sales (see above). In the film industry, this type of plugging the hole in the finance is known as '**bank gap**' financing, and depends on the Bank's faith in the Sales Agent to sell the territories on behalf of the Producer at sufficiently high prices.

> **The independent film Producer is likely to need to approach a significant number and range of financiers in order to obtain the $10m needed to produce his/her film.**
> ....

And so you have it. The Construction Company by hook or by crook (no pun intended) has managed to obtain the whole $10m needed to construct its building. And in a similar vein, the independent film Producer is likely to need to approach a significant number and range of financiers in order to obtain the $10m needed to produce his/her film.

The next outstanding issue to be addressed is how, and in what order, each of the financiers gets paid back its contribution. That is, of course, down to the various financiers (and their respective lawyers) to agree, usually before one penny of construction (or, in our case, production) finance is actually spent. Now that we have illustrated (and simplified) the main differences in the various types of financier, we can examine their respective typical deals, attributes and concerns in some more detail. We will revert back to our construction site analogy as and when appropriate, but for the time being, we can leave it and concentrate our minds back on the film industry.

Receipts, Recoupment and Profit

Recoupment
The term '**recoupment**' is simply a film industry expression meaning repayment. As the film gets sold around the world, the buyers (being foreign distributors) pay their respective purchase amounts into a '**Collection Account**' (sometimes fondly referred to as the '**pot**'), which is usually run by a specialist '**Collection Agent**'. The collection agent (often a bank) is charged with (i) collecting the proceeds of sale, (ii) paying the sales agent its commission for the sales it has made (and its expenses), (iii) repaying the financiers their contributions to the financing of the film, and then (iv) distributing the profits to those entitled to participate in them.

The first thing to understand is that it's *not* box-office receipts, but the *sale* proceeds that go into the collection account 'pot' to be shared out between the producers and the various financiers. These are the amounts (known as '**Advances**' or '**MG**'s) that the various *distributors* pay for the right to exploit the film in their territory. How well the film then does at the international box-offices is a matter for each distributor, and not of immediate concern to the financiers. We explain in more detail why this is the case, and how these sales are structured, later in this Chapter under '**Pre-Sales and Distribution Deals**'. The point for now is that, in essence, repayment to financiers depends on the size of the MGs rather than box-office success, and thus on the ability of the sales agent to achieve good purchase prices for the film around the world. Returning briefly to our Building analogy, we're effectively saying the Construction Company is more interested in the amounts it can get up-front for the 25-year leases of each floor, and isn't too bothered about how much money these lessees subsequently make by sub-letting the apartments on that floor to tenants during the 25-year period.

As sales income is received, the collection agent is obliged to repay the financiers strictly in accordance with a '**Recoupment Schedule**'. This is a vital document as it sets out, as between the various financiers, the order of their recoupment, and must therefore be agreed by all of the financiers and profit participants at the time of financing the film. As receipts come in from each territorial sale, there is a specific order of entitlement spelling out exactly to whom each dollar received will go. Sometimes all the receipts will go to one financier until it is fully repaid, and then to the next (the order depending on who had the best bargaining power at the time the financing contracts are agreed). Alternatively, certain financiers might share out between them each dollar received, known as a *pari passu* distribution of income. Where a small(ish) percentage of each dollar received is earmarked for a specific recipient in this way, it is sometimes referred to as the granting of a **corridor**, due to the way it is often represented diagrammatically (see opposite). As mentioned above, the bank is usually the first to be paid off (even if, because of a big-name actor's deferment, it is only able to negotiate an entitlement to take, say, 80 cents of each dollar received on a *pari passu* basis), and all the other financiers have to fight amongst each other for their right to be next in line. Typical repayment terms are covered later in this chapter under the relevant section, and a sample Recoupment Schedule is set out in the *Reference Section* at the end of this Handbook.

The right-hand diagram shows a sample finance plan for '*Project X*'. We've used numbers similar to those in the Building analogy, although to make them look easier for illustrative purposes (remember, nothing is set in stone), we've increased the deferments and reduced the soft money by $0.5m respectively. You can see, therefore, that the $10m budget is made up of $1m soft money (perhaps a grant or a tax break), $3m pre-sales (comprising, say, UK, France and Germany), $3m equity, $1m deferments and $2m bank gap. The diagram on the facing page illustrates the Recoupment Waterfall, ie. the order and amounts the investors get repaid. You can perhaps imagine the money falling into this 'pot' from a height, and filling it up from the

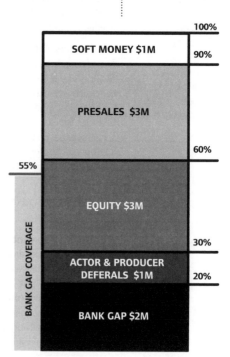

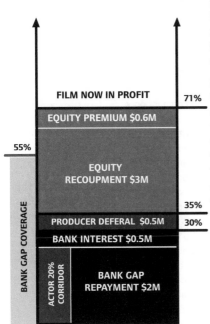

FILM NOW IN PROFIT — 71%

EQUITY PREMIUM $0.6M

55%

EQUITY
RECOUPMENT $3M

35%

PRODUCER DEFERAL $0.5M — 30%

BANK INTEREST $0.5M

BANK GAP COVERAGE

ACTOR 20% CORRIDOR

BANK GAP
REPAYMENT $2M

bottom upwards. As we go through this Chapter, we'll refer back to *Project X* and these diagrams periodically, so by the end, you should have a clear understanding of how each type of deal works, and therefore why the numbers in the diagrams are what they are.

Break-Even and Profit

Ultimately, if the film is sold at high enough prices, sufficient money will flow into the Collection Account to repay all the recouping financiers their respective contributions (together with interest, premiums, and/or whatever else they managed to negotiate at the time). At this point, the film is said to '**break even**'. This does not mean that the aggregate amount of sales exactly equals the budget. In fact, the relationship between the size of the budget and the level of sales required to break even (or 'hit profit') will depend, amongst other things, on a) the amount of soft money involved, b) the number of presales made, c) the level of sales agent's agreed commission and expenses, and d) the amount of financiers' interest and premiums (if any), which will also have to be paid out of sales income. For *Project X*, you can see from the diagram that the break-even point is at 71% of the budget. The financiers that require repayment are the bank ($2m plus interest), the deferments ($1m), and the equity ($3m plus a premium). With interest (say, £0.5m) and premiums (say, $0.6m) taken into consideration, we end up needing $7.1m. If, say, the sales agent was on 15% commission, it would therefore need to do approximately $8.35m worth of sales to reach break-even, because it would be taking $1.25m (15% of $8.35m) itself in sales commission (ignoring its expenses for the moment), leaving $7.1m for the pot.

Once break-even is reached, there is nobody left to be repaid, and the film is therefore '**in profit**'. Any further receipts from sales after this point are usually referred to as '**Net Profits**', or colloquially '**back-end**', and are distributed amongst the profit participants, again in accordance with the terms set out in the Recoupment Schedule. Certain types of financier are more likely to be entitled to a profit participation than others (the most obvious being equity investors). The other main beneficiaries of Net Profits are usually the producers themselves, and any cast or department heads who had enough power to negotiate such an entitlement when they were contracted to contribute their services to the film. All these aspects are explained in much more detail as we go through this Chapter.

Film as an Economic Anomaly

One thing that won't be missed by any reader with an Economics background, is that the film goes into profit *before* sales ($8.35m) exceed the cost of production ($10m). In this regard, the film industry is almost unique. In what other business can you turn a profit when you know the products you make will cost more to manufacture than you can sell them for? Naturally, no-one should go into film production in the hope of making back only 71% of their budget, but the reality is that the more non-recoupable finance you can find, the quicker you can start sharing in the profits. Of course, in truth, the real aggregate sales income for *Project X* was actually at least $11.35m, because we should add back the value of the $3m pre-sold territories too (plus any commission that might have been taken off those sales). However, psychologically, it's the $8.35m gross (or $7.1m net) sales figure that the Producer will be looking to hit.

Gross Receipts, AGR, Net Receipts and Net Profit

Before turning to look at the specific types of film finance in depth, we should clarify a few other terms that are regularly used when referring to the distribution of income.

We know that **Net Profit** is the income received into the collection account once all recoupable finance has been repaid, and all fees and commissions deducted. The term referring to all amounts hitting the pot, which are to be distributed pursuant to the Recoupment Schedule (whether the film has reached profit or not), is **Net Receipts**. We say 'net' because these payments have already had various fees and commissions deducted. On each sale, the distributor will be obliged to pay over a specified amount, but before this hits the collection account, the sales agent will take off its commission, and then deduct its out-of-pocket expenses (see Section on Sales Agents, below, for more detail). The collection agent that runs the account will also take its fee, and there may also be banking fees involved, costs of currency conversion, deductions for taxes, Union expenses (such as residuals), and so on. The remainder will be available for recoupment or, if after break-even, as a distribution to profit participants. The full amounts payable, before any of these deductions, are referred to as **Gross Receipts**, and this term should be carefully defined contractually to make sure it encompasses *all* receipts from *all* exploitation on *all* media from *all* territories. Somewhere between Gross Receipts and Net Receipts there might also be a contractually defined 'AGR', or **Adjusted Gross Receipts**. Quite what is or is not deducted from Gross Receipts to arrive at AGR depends on what is contractually agreed and what the purpose is for the definition (usually someone's entitlement to share in a percentage of revenues calculated before some of the standard deductions are made). The remaining deductions are then made from AGR to reach Net Receipts (or Net Profits if beyond break-even).

> **Net Profit is the income received into the collection account once all recoupable finance has been repaid**

Soft Money and Financial Incentives

Soft on Recoupment

The phrase '**Soft Money**' is often banded about to refer to all sorts of different types of finance. True, it does come in all shapes and sizes, and there are many ways to combine the range of options available. But the common theme is that this type of financier generally take a less aggressive position in relation to recoupment, usually because the financial benefit is ultimately funded by a non-commercial entity (such as a charitable fund) or, more likely, from the public purse (as in the case of national film funds, tax breaks, rebates, etc). This weak, or 'soft', approach to recoupment stems from the fact that a non-profit entity, or public body financed by a central government, has less need (or desire) to be repaid its contribution as quickly as, say, an individual Producer who has deferred his/her own hard-earned fee. Similarly, a private investor who utilises a statutory regulation through which s/he obtains a personal benefit outside the realms of financing the film itself, will tend to take a much 'softer' approach when negotiating his/her recoupment position than another financier who cannot benefit from such a scheme, such as a lending bank. For example, if an investor can somehow get a £4m reduction in his/her personal tax bill, simply by investing £2.5m of his/her own money in a film (which, believe it or not, was actually possible in the UK until fairly recently), s/he will not be as concerned about how quickly the £2.5m gets repaid.

Sometimes soft money can come simply in the form of a gift. If you're very lucky, your filthy-rich great-uncle Albert might just give you a present of $0.5m to play with in your movie, because he heard it was your new hobby, or a 'phase' you are going through. He won't want the money back, and will be happy if he gets two free tickets to the premiere (assuming he's not away on his yacht that week). Unfortunately, this doesn't happen all that often, and the most likely source of soft money will in fact be through an official **financial incentive** scheme established in the region or country where you are making your film. We cover below how the main types of finance incentive work in principle, and in Part II of the Handbook, we go into much more detail on a country-by-country basis as to exactly what is currently available and where, how you qualify, and who administers the relevant regime.

Wherever the money ultimately comes from, it is clear that the more soft money you have in a budget, the better it is for the Producer and other financiers. This is because the smaller the amount you need to pay back to financiers, the bigger the amount left in the 'pot' for everyone else to share. And once all the recouping financiers have been repaid, the Producer can start sharing in the Net Profits. Indeed, soft money is becoming an increasingly essential source of film finance as other forms, such as pre-sales and large 'gap' loans, become harder to obtain. This is why Producers are so keen to understand what is available in various countries around the world.

Note that soft money *does* sometimes need to be recouped by the entity providing it (albeit on weaker terms and/or at a later date than other finance). However, Producers usually distinguish between 'soft' finance and 'recoupable' finance when discussing how a budget is to be sourced, and we will for the most part keep to that distinction in this Handbook.

Financial Incentives

Financial incentives, whether recoupable or not, are by definition offered on less than commercial terms (otherwise there would be no 'incentive'!), and are therefore generally considered 'soft' finance. Most have come about because national and regional governments (sometimes directly and sometimes through screen agencies, film commissions, and the like) want to entice the international film dollar to be spent within their jurisdiction in order to benefit their local economy. As a result, they have created a whole array of schemes, projects, public funds, dedicated tax regimes, and so on, with some countries offering more than one possible option. Before you turn to Part II of this Handbook (**International Incentives**), which goes into great depth on the finance incentives currently available in **over 50 countries**, it is important to understand the various concepts and terminology of the types of options available.

Finance Incentives tend to be divided into three types, although there are of course numerous sub-groups and hybrids. The main categories are **direct support**, **rebates** and **tax breaks**, and below is a brief outline of the principles behind them and their common themes. One thing remains fairly constant no matter which incentive you go for, and that is the need for a local accountant to sign off on the amounts you have spent locally in order to assure the relevant authorities that the deemed investment into their economy really did occur.

Direct Support

Grants, **awards** and other forms of direct support are provided up front and may not have to be repaid at all. The non-recoupable grant is perhaps the most loved type of finance incentive, and is the form of soft money we have used in our

> Producers usually distinguish between 'soft' finance and 'recoupable' finance when discussing how a budget is to be sourced, and we will for the most part keep to that distinction

Project X example. Direct support usually originates from a Government or public body with a remit to promote local film production, such as Scandinavia's various Film Institutes, or the national and regional film funds established in Hungary, the Netherlands, and the UK. Prior to the start of production, a Producer submits an application for funding and, if successful, receives a sum of money which can be used as part of the budget for the production. Sometimes the funding is 'automatic', and calculated with reference to the performance of the Producer's previous films, but usually it is 'selective', with a committee or panel deciding on the merits of the individual application.

These grants do, however, have arguably the tightest qualification criteria, and in some cases require funds to be paid back from income derived from the film (such as for most UK Film Council money). There are countless organisations all over the world offering an assortment of grants and awards of varying amounts, and subject to a huge range of conditions. Part III of this Handbook (**Funding Directory**) provides details on a country-by-country basis of **more than 1,000 funds** that were providing finance at the time of going to press, and how that money can be accessed. The extent to which direct support such as grants can be termed a 'financial incentive' really depends on their size. We feel that those funds that are big enough potentially to entice a Producer to move his/her production to a specific country, simply because there is such a large amount of public money available there, can legitimately be considered financial incentives. Such funds are, therefore, described in Part II of this Handbook as well as having separate entries in the Funding Directory (Part III).

Rebates
Unlike production grants and awards, **rebates** are not received until *after* the production budget is spent. They are usually calculated with reference to money paid out locally, and can take the form of a straight repayment of a percentage of that amount, or a refund of local taxes paid by the Producer. For example, in Iceland, for every dollar spent in the country, the producer will receive (subject to various conditions) 14¢ back from the Government. This is a straight, no-nonsense **cash rebate**. On the other hand, **tax rebates** are a little more complicated. For example, an income tax rebate provides a Producer, who pays local income taxes on wages paid to local crew engaged during the production, with a repayment from the local tax authority of some or all of that income tax. Alternative types of tax rebate would be where the Producer is refunded some of the consumer tax (eg. VAT or Consumption Tax) or entertainment taxes that s/he incurred during production.

Where the governmental or tax authority concerned is totally reliable (aren't they all?), and to the extent that there is no question as to how much will be repaid and when, it can be possible to borrow money against the rebate up-front, before production commences, from a specialist lender, so that it can be used for the production. Of course, these lenders charge a fee and interest (which is usually paid out of the money borrowed, thereby reducing the amount available for the film), and they then pick up the rebate from the tax department or other government body when it is paid in due course. Banks are tentatively starting to move into this business, but can often be reluctant to lend due to the risk that the relevant Government (or body) won't ultimately pay up the anticipated amount, often because the Producer had overestimated how much will be repaid. However, there are various non-banking private funds offering this **'discounting'** service, with the number of rebates available around the world that can now be discounted increasing all the time.

Tax Breaks

Tax breaks tend to be a it more complicated and relate to legislative schemes whereby a taxpayer's liability to the relevant Revenue Department is somehow diminished. They also come in all sorts of shapes and sizes and, in fact, a tax rebate (see above) is technically a type of tax break. Just like grants, tax-based incentives are designed by governments to boost the local economy by attracting investment into a particular sector, in this case the film industry. As for rebates, they are generally calculated with reference to the amount of money spent locally.

The terminology used in relation to tax breaks can be conflicting when compared from country to country, and translations into English are almost never consistent. However, the **Glossary** in the *Reference Section* towards the back of this Handbook provides reliable definitions of most of the terms used, in accordance with the meanings most often given to them. Here, we'll explain some of the main principles in simple terms, although you should of course seek professional advice before making any decision affecting your (or others') tax liability.

Tax Breaks for Investors

Some tax breaks are offered to investors in film, and others to Producers. A **tax allowance** tends to be aimed at the former, and is an amount of income which would otherwise be taxable but which, because of the tax break, you are 'allowed' to receive without paying tax on it. Let's take an example of *Mr Money*, who lives in a fictitious country, *Filmland*, where he made a profit of a hundred million Filmlandish dollars (F$100m) this year from his various businesses. With Filmland income taxes at 30%, Mr Money would potentially have a **tax liability** of F$30m. However, if Filmland offered a tax allowance for film investment, and Mr Money were to invest F$60m of his profits in qualifying films made within Filmland borders, his **taxable income** would reduce from F$100m to F$40m, and his tax liability from F$30m to F$12m (ie. 30% of F$40m), resulting in a saving of F$18m in tax payments whilst still holding a film investment worth F$60m. The following table might illustrate this a little more clearly:

Total Income	F$100m	(profits from businesses)
Tax Allowance	(F$60m)	(film investment)
Taxable Income	F$ 40m	(total income less allowance)
Tax Liability	**F$ 12m**	(applying 30% tax rate to taxable income)

As you can see, Mr Money is 'allowed' to write off his film investment against his other taxable income. As money is (hopefully) made in future years from exploitation of the film he invested in, Mr Money should receive income from it, including the repayment of his investment, and this income will probably be taxable in the normal way (although he may be able to set it off against other losses he may have in those future years). The F$60m allowance is sometimes also referred to as a **tax deduction**, although this term can also be used for the F$18m reduction in *tax liability*, which can lead to some confusion. Depending on the rules in the relevant country, the allowance can be granted in respect of the tax-payer investing in the **production** of a film, or the **acquisition** of a film or film rights (or, as was the case in the UK under the old 'section 48', for both production *and* acquisition).

Note that, for the producer, this type of film finance *is* often repayable (so not technically 100% 'soft'), but generally on weaker terms than much of the other finance, for example by being further down the Recoupment Schedule. Investors take a softer approach because only a portion of the investment (F$42m in Mr Money's case) is seen to be 'at risk'. The rest (F$18m) would be paid to the tax man in any event if it weren't invested in the film. The F$60m film investment is therefore seen as a hybrid between soft money and equity (see relevant Section, below). The benefit to the Producer is that a) this funding exists and is available in the first place, and b) it's on less-than-standard commercial terms.

Producers and film financiers in countries offering this investment incentive can sometimes benefit from specially constructed production **tax funds** (where more than one investor pools their money into a single entity), which utilise the tax allowances when investing in a qualifying film. The 'section 48' regime used until recently in the UK was a tax allowance system, and spawned many different types of financial product, from almost pure equity investment to the notorious niche 'UK Sale & Leaseback' mini-industry. These schemes typically provided a contribution of between 10% and 35% of a film's budget and, without them, some claim that most recent British films would have never seen the light of day. Similarly, in the USA, funds are currently being put together for the relatively new 'section 181' regime, and in South Africa under their 'section 24F' legislation. In these cases, the extent to which the investors can actually lose their own money if the film doesn't perform depends on how the relevant fund is structured (sometimes much of the money is borrowed from elsewhere and is so not the investor's to lose in the first place!), and this in turn will depend on the 'anti-avoidance' legislation in the relevant territory. For example, during the recently curtailed 'section 48' era in the UK, the Government continually brought in more and more supplementary legislation to try to prevent the widespread abuse of the tax-break by increasingly sophisticated investment schemes which were utilising the allowance. Ultimately it gave up, and scrapped the whole thing in return for a tax credit system, introduced in 2006 (see Part II of this Handbook).

> The benefit to the Producer is that a) this funding exists and is available in the first place, and b) it's on less-than-standard commercial terms.

Sale and Leaseback schemes, which generally use a tax allowance system as the basis for their funds, are not now as common as they once were. In the UK, these schemes would often provide upwards of 15% of a film's budget on a *non-repayable* basis. An explanation on a generic level (but based upon the now defunct UK model) as to how these schemes work is set out in the *Reference Section* towards the end of this Handbook. The important thing to remember is that, whereas sale & leaseback schemes were able to provide a certain amount of 'free' (ie. truly soft) money, most funds based around tax allowances require the investments to be repaid, and are therefore akin to normal **equity** funds (see blow), albeit usually with softer terms.

Tax Breaks for Producers

Tax credits (also sometimes known as **tax offsets**) are available in a number of countries (including now the UK). Again, Part II of this Handbook covers where they are available, and how they work in individual cases. The basic idea is, as before, to encourage expenditure in a particular country by foreign and/or local producers. This time, however, the tax bill reduction is aimed squarely at the Producer, rather than investor. Tax credits work in a very similar way to tax rebates (see above), the technical difference being that the money is not refunded directly to the Producer, but deducted from his/her tax bill, or that of a company in the same group. Take, for example, a production company, *Maker, LLC*, part of the small Filmlandish corporate conglomerate *Media, Inc*. Let's also assume that Filmland has replaced its tax allowance regime (above) with a new 20% tax credit scheme. If Maker, LLC produces a F$10m film in Filmland, and 80% of this spend (ie. F$8m) qualifies for the credit, Maker, LLC will receive a tax credit of

F$1.6m (being 20% of F$8m). Assuming Maker, LLC doesn't have a very big tax bill (because it hasn't yet made much profit from its film activities), so there's not much tax liability to set the credit against, but that the credit is legally transferable to the parent company, Media, Inc's simplified tax accounts might look something like this:

Total Receipts	F$20m	(revenue from business activities)
Costs	(F$12m)	(legitimate deductible costs and expenses of Media, Inc's business)
Taxable Profit	F$ 8m	(total income less total expenses)
Tax Payable	F$ 2.4m	(applying 30% tax rate to taxable profit)
LESS **Tax Credit**	(F$1.6m)	(transferred from its subsidiary, Maker, LLC)
Tax Liability	**F$ 0.8m**	

You can see that the credit is a deduction from the tax bill itself rather than from the taxable profit. Note that in some countries, tax credits are **transferable**, not just to other group companies, but to anyone with a tax liability that they want to reduce. In other words, once you receive confirmation of your entitlement to the credit (usually in the form of a certificate), you can literally sell it on to any company who will buy it for cash (so they can use it to reduce their tax bill). This is where the line between a credit and rebate can become quite blurred. As for rebates, it is possible in some countries to discount the tax credit through a bank or other lender, and use the money up front for production.

> **As for rebates, it is possible in some countries to discount the tax credit through a bank or other lender, and use the money up front for production.**

We said that the soft money in *Project X* was a grant. However, it could equally have been a discounted tax credit. In other words if the Producer knew that credit was available and would equate to (say) 15% of the entire budget, and would be available in 18 months time (when production ends and accounts are filed), s/he might be able to use the credit as collateral to borrow the 10% of the budget up-front from a specialist lender, and put that into the film. The lender would then receive the credit in due course, the excess over the amount lent representing its fees, interest and a reflection of the risk (that the relevant authority might not pay up in the end).

Co-productions and International Options

One way to minimise the amount of recoupable finance is to source as much soft money as possible from more than just one country. To access these benefits internationally, a film may (but doesn't necessarily have to) be set up as an **official co-production** between the relevant countries. To qualify as an official co-production, the film will need to satisfy the requirements set out in the relevant **Co-production Treaty** between the countries concerned or, if produced substantially within Europe, the *European Convention on Cinematic Co-production* (see below). Even if the film isn't set up as an official co-production, there are often good financial reasons to produce some pictures in particular territories. Sometimes producers choose to shoot in certain countries not because of a specific soft money incentive, but simply because it is less expensive to shoot there. This was the main reason behind the drive to move scores of productions to eastern Europe in the late '90s, although these countries tend not to be nearly as cheap now as they were then.

As mentioned above, the workings and sources of the main soft money opportunities currently available around the world are set out in more detail in Part II of this Handbook (**International Incentives**). For now, we'll look at the generic benefits and elements of official co-productions.

Benefits for National Films

In many countries, in order to access the main financial incentives, the first test is to see if the film qualifies as a **National Film** for that country. Examples where this rule applies include the UK, Australia, Germany and New Zealand. In order to qualify as a national film for a particular country, the production typically has to be shot locally and to engage predominantly local (or in the case of European countries, EU) nationals or citizens as talent and crew. The thresholds are usually quite high, so if your film qualifies as a national film for one country (say, because you meet a requirement that at least 70% of your budget must be spent there, for example), it is unlikely that it could also qualify as a national film in another country. You can't have more than half your crew from one country, *and* more than half from another! On this basis, you can only access one country's financial incentive. That is, unless you qualify as an official co-production (see below).

Of course, it could be (and has been) said that the provision of national subsidies is just a method for governments to promote their own economies and citizens unfairly and at the expense of other countries, skewing cross-border competition and (in Europe at least) conflicting with general EU principles. But the European Commission has expressly permitted the financial incentive regimes to continue for many years (as exceptions to the general rule), although it does continually review the situation. For example, the 2006 legislation for the recent tax credit introduction in the UK had to be amended *after* it was passed by the UK Parliament in order for the EU to permit it as legally acceptable under its State Aid regulations. Likewise, the new German tax regime had to wait some time to get its EU clearance. The crux is that, in order to pass the State Aid requirements, a country must allow at least *some* (typically 20%) of a national film's expenditure to be incurred outside the relevant country without it losing eligibility for the relevant national incentive. It is politically incorrect to insist that no production funds may be spent on someone or something from another country. But even if 20% of a budget were allowed to be spent in a second country, it wouldn't normally be enough to trigger that second country's incentive in addition to the first's.

Official Co-productions as National Films

And that is exactly where **official co-productions** come in. The idea behind official co-productions is that they allow a film that is made in two countries to access benefits in both those countries, even if it wouldn't otherwise qualify as a national film in bth. This is because official co-productions have a similar status as national films when it comes to entitlement to finance incentives. In other words, whereas a national British Film would be eligible for British benefits, and a national Canadian Film would be eligible for Canadian benefits, a film made as an official UK-Canadian Co-production would qualify for both.

For the Producer, the beauty of the co-production approach is that s/he can access whatever soft money options are available in *all* the applicable co-production country(ies), whether or not it qualifies as a national film in each or any of them. Even for countries which do not have a 'national film' test, qualifying as an official co-production automatically allows access to the financial incentives of each co-production country. Some of these benefits are quite substantial, and it is not unheard of for a carefully structured picture to have 35% or more of its budget covered by soft money in this way.

> **The idea behind official co-productions is that they allow a film that is made in two countries to access benefits in both those countries, even if it wouldn't otherwise qualify as a national film in both.**

So what exactly is a Co-production?

The Producer of any film clearly needs to carry out several tasks in order to get his/her picture made. These include raising the finance, securing talent, engaging the crew, preparing budgets, sourcing locations, overseeing principal photography, arranging and supervising post-production, and so on. There are times when it makes sense to pool resources with another producer, splitting these responsibilities in accordance with their respective means and expertise. Where more than one producer makes a film as a collaborative effort in this way, it is known as a '**co-production**', and the producers involved are referred to as '**co-producers**'. The co-producers (who may or may not be from the same country) will typically enter into a **co-production agreement** that sets out their respective rights and obligations, together with their financial interests in the film.

In industry circles, however, the term 'co-production' is generally used specifically to refer to a film made under the umbrella of a particular governmental co-production treaty ('**Treaty**'), or the *European Convention on Cinematic Co-production* (the '**European Convention**'). It is this type of co-production, better referred to as an '**official co-production**', that is of most interest, as this is the vehicle through which Producers can obtain benefits from more than one country. Those official co-productions made under the European Convention are imaginatively known as '**Convention Co-productions**' (see below for details), and those made under the bilateral Treaties as '**Treaty Co-productions**'.

Qualifying as a Treaty Co-production

> There are times when it makes sense to pool resources with another producer, splitting these responsibilities in accordance with their respective means and expertise.

The exact rules setting out how a film qualifies as an official co-production vary depending on the country or countries concerned, and are set out in agreements, or '**Treaties**', entered into by the governments of those countries. Some countries, such as France and Canada, have entered into co-production Treaties with almost every country that has a semblance of a film industry; more than 50 in all. Others, such as the USA, have shied away from entering into international co-production Treaties, presumably because they want to keep as many film production dollars in their own country as possible. A **co-production table** setting out the most-used bilateral Treaties, on a country-by-country basis, is set out in the Reference Section towards the end of this Handbook. The Council of Europe's 'IRIS Merlin' legal information website has English language translations of many of those between European countries. Go to http://merlin.obs.coe.int/_and search for 'co-production treaty'.

Competent Authorities

Each Treaty country has a 'competent authority' appointed by its government, which has the role of granting official co-production status to films that comply with the relevant regulations. In the UK, the relevant competent authority is the Department of Culture, Media and Sport (www.culture.gov.uk), although the UK Film Council (www.ukfilmcouncil.org.uk) is taking over the administrative function of assessing projects from 1 April 2007. Other competent authorities in some of the more active co-production countries include the Australian Film Commission (www.afc.gov.au), Telefilm Canada (www.telefilm.gc.ca), France's Centre National de la Cinematographie (www.cnc.fr), the New Zealand Film Commission (www.nzfilm.co.nz), the Norwegian Film Fund (www.filmfond.no), and South Africa's Department of Arts and Culture (www.dac.gov.za). The identity of the competent authority will be stated in the relevant Treaty.

Whereas the benefits available in each country range quite considerably, the qualification criteria under the various Treaties - although not identical - do tend to follow certain themes. The following is a summary of the typical requirements which a film must satisfy in order to be granted official co-production status. They are based loosely on the various UK co-production Treaties, but the concepts and requirements are generally found in most Treaties of other countries too. Of course, there are exceptions to the rules in nearly every case and, before applying for official co-production status anywhere, a producer should check carefully the terms of the relevant Treaty under which s/he wishes the film to qualify.

Common Management and Control

The co-producers must be independent from each other, and may not be linked by common management (except to the extent that it is inherent in the making of the film itself).

General Contractual Terms

The Treaties require certain provisions to be included in the co-production agreement between the co-producers. These terms normally include an explanation of the **financial commitment** (including dates) and **recoupment** position(s) of the respective co-producing companies, and must set out the **contingency** arrangement (ie. what happens to the film and any money invested in it) in the event that the picture is not ultimately - or even provisionally - granted official co-production status. Generally, the **income** of each co-producer received from the exploitation of the film should be roughly proportional to that co-producer's financial contribution, and this should be set out in the agreement. **Ownership** of the negative (or, in some cases, the copyright) must also be clearly specified, together with an acknowledgement that each co-producer has the right to **access** and copy the finished product. Producers should always take proper advice when drafting the co-production contract, particularly in ensuring that these provisions are correctly worded.

> The purpose behind the Treaties is to share the benefits and burdens equally with the partner countries, on aggregate and over time

Minimum Financial Contribution

Until recently, most countries insisted that 'their' co-producer provided or bring in at least **20%** (or sometimes 30%) of the financial contribution to the film. However, because the soft money benefits in some Treaty countries were much more beneficial than those in others (for example, the old UK and the current South African tax allowances are/were both calculated against the entire budget no matter where the money is spent), many co-productions have been structured so as to spend as little money as possible to qualify in one country, and as much as possible in the other, thereby maximising the overall attainable benefit. This has annoyed a number of governments because the purpose behind the Treaties is to share the benefits and burdens equally with the partner countries, on aggregate and over time. Instead, there became a huge disparity in the amounts spent between the respective parties to some Treaties. For example, until fairly recently the vast majority of UK-Canadian co-productions were 'majority-Canadian', with 80% of the budget being spent in Canada and the minimum 20% being spent in the UK. These inequalities have resulted in some recent rises in the minimum spend ratios required under certain Treaties (in some cases up to 40%, as was the case for the UK-Canadian Treaty). These rises tend to be *ad hoc*, as a reaction against the way the market is skewing at any given time, and therefore sometimes only temporary. Check with the relevant competent authority before deciding where to shoot or budgeting for a specific amount of subsidy.

Creative Contribution

The general rule is that the 'creative' contribution must be approximately proportional to the 'financial' contribution. Occasionally (as with the UK-France Treaty), a substantial 'finance only' contribution is permitted, where one co-producer may provide only finance (ie. no creative elements), without disqualifying the picture from official co-production status. But this tends to be the exception rather than the rule.

Location

The film must be made (including post-production) in the countries of the co-producers' origin. Generally, the majority of production must take place in the country from where the majority of the finance is provided. Location shooting in another country is (if required by the script) usually permitted, subject to the competent authorities' approval. Personnel involved in making the film who are nationals or residents of one co-producing country are usually granted easy access to the other co-producing country(ies), without the need to obtain work permits.

Qualifying Nationals

This is often the trickiest area, particularly when the project and/or lead cast originate from the United States (which has no Treaties with anyone). The basic rule is that all individuals taking part in the making of the film must be nationals or residents of one of the co-producer's countries (including a third co-producer's country, if any). If the co-production involves a European Union country, this will include a national or resident of any Member State. However, 'exceptional circumstances' (eg. if dictated by the script) will in some cases permit the competent authorities to approve certain talent (often only the leading roles) from another state, depending on which Treaty is being utilised. This is incredibly important where an American director or lead artist is attached to the project. Also, where the authorities have approved location filming in another country, 'necessary' local crew and/or crowd artists can usually be hired.

Credits

Co-production films should all have an on-screen credit indicating that they are co-productions and stating the countries involved. Typically, the majority co-producer's country should be stated first, although this is not always the case in all territories.

Musical Score

Generally, the music must be composed (and sometimes 'directed' and/or performed) by nationals or residents of one of the co-producer's countries (including that of a third co-producer). The rules sometimes vary slightly for music that is not specifically commissioned for the picture.

Third Country Participation

A three-way co-production, with a producer from a third country, will usually be able to access the benefits of all three countries, but *only* if the third country has also entered into a co-production Treaty with one of the other two. For example, as Canada has a co-production Treaty with Algeria, a UK-Canada-Algeria co-production will be permitted under the UK-Canada Treaty, even though the UK has no Treaty with Algeria. Of course, the film will only actually qualify if all the other criteria in the Treaties are also satisfied.

The European Convention

As with the **bilateral Treaties** discussed above, the aim of the European Convention is to allow qualifying co-produced films the benefits that are available to national films in each Convention country. All countries in the EU (and many more in the European geographical area) have now signed up to the Convention, so it applies to nearly every co-production made anywhere on the European continent. As is the case for Treaty co-productions, each co-producer can utilise whatever benefits are available in his/her own country. Again, the creative and financial contributions to the film must be relatively proportional, and must

> **A three-way co-production, with a producer from a third country, will usually be able to access the benefits of all three countries, but *only* if the third country has also entered into a co-production Treaty**

generally exceed 20% (potentially 10% for multilateral co-productions) of the total budget. A financial-only contribution of between 10% and 25% is also permitted under certain conditions. Co-producers from one or more **non-Convention country** *may* be brought into a co-production agreement under the Convention, provided that (i) it/they bring(s) no more than 30% of the total finance to the table, (ii) at least three other 'Convention country' co-producers are party to the co-production agreement, and (iii) the points system (below) is still satisfied.

Note that the Convention is not currently in force in **Bosnia, Norway, Ukraine** or **Lichtenstein** (plus some other smaller jurisdictions). The Council of Europe website has the Convention in full, and also a list of the signatories (including dates when the Convention came into force in each country). The English language URL is: conventions.coe.int/Treaty/Commun/QueVoulezVous. asp?NT=147&CM=8&DF=4/9/05&CL=ENG, or if that's a bit of a mouthful, try conventions.coe.int, and then click Treaties (on the left) and search for CETS Treaty No. 147.

The points system

Unlike the Treaties, where individuals' nationality *and/or* residence tend to be relevant for qualification purposes, the Convention is only concerned with nationality. There is a '**points system**' ascribing values to various contributors (artists, creative department heads etc) if they are nationals of a Convention country, and to qualify as a Convention co-production, the film must have at least **15 of the 19 points**. As the director, writer and first lead artist are each 'worth' **three** points, clearly only one of these may be from a non-convention country. The second lead artist is worth **two** points, and all the other contributors (third lead artist, composer, cameraman, sound recordist, editor, art director, studio or shooting location, and post-production location) are all worth **one** point each. If the film has a strong 'European identity', but only has 13 or 14 points, it may still be possible to make it under the Convention, as the 15/19 points rule can potentially be waived slightly by the relevant competent authority(ies).

Convention or Treaty?

Bilateral co-productions

The general rule seems to be that where a Treaty between two Convention countries exists, any **bilateral co-production** (ie. one produced between two co-producers) should be made under that Treaty rather than under the Convention, and typically the Treaty rules will apply. This certainly is the case, for example, for the UK. Besides, many Treaties between Convention countries are currently being terminated so that the Convention can take over as the sole regulating legislative document, although there are still at least 40 bilateral Treaties in force between various European countries. Where there is no relevant bilateral Treaty in force between two Convention countries, the film should, of course, be produced under the Convention (which then effectively serves as a bilateral co-production Treaty). In such circumstances, the minimum contribution from the minority co-producer must be at least 20%.

Multilateral co-productions

For a **multilateral co-production** (one with co-producers from three or more countries), if there is a combination of Treaties that would cover the film (eg. for a UK-France-Germany co-production), they may be used so long as they do not contravene the specific provisions of the Convention. Effectively, the film will be made, and the documentation needs to specify that it will be made, 'under the terms of the Treaty'. Note that many Treaties require a minimum 20% or 30%

financial commitment from the relevant countries, but the Convention allows for as little as 10% (reflecting the Eurimage position). As there is a direct conflict on this point, the Convention rule will override the Treaties, allowing a 10% minimum contribution. In other words, the 20% requirement in the UK-France Treaty would be overridden by the Convention in a UK-France-Germany 'three-way' Treaty co-production, and a 10% minimum would apply. Where there is no Treaty covering the co-production, the Convention will of course apply, assuming the relevant countries are signatories. As mentioned above, many bilateral Treaties between Convention countries are being terminated to allow the Convention to take over.

Equity

The term 'equity', for the purposes of film financing, basically means 'ownership'. An **Equity Investor** (or simply 'investor') will effectively be buying a piece of the film and will wish to share in the profits of it. It invests in a similar way to a share-holder in a new company, taking a risk that the venture will ultimately become profitable in the hope of participating in profits for as long as it owns a piece of the pie. As mentioned previously, a film goes into profit once all the recouping financiers have been paid back their contributions plus, where relevant, any interest or premium to which they are entitled. The more soft money and pre-sales involved, the quicker the film goes into profit, and the sooner the equity investor gets to share in those profits. This will, of course, be after the investor has been repaid its own contribution (plus, as is usually the case, a premium) as part of the recoupment process. However, because the investor is entitled to share in the profits of the film, whereas other financiers generally are not, it will often be one of the last in line to be repaid as per the Recoupment Schedule. That said, any soft money providers that also require repayment will normally sit behind the equity investor. Once everyone has been repaid (and assuming the film is profitable), the investor will share in proceeds for years to come as the film gets sold and resold during its life-cycle, particularly for television broadcast purposes. Likewise, if the film is so popular from the start that it begins to make overages (see below), it may immediately go into profit and the investor will start to take its share in the rewards straight away.

An investor, being effectively a 'part-owner' of the film, will often own a share in the copyright itself, and the film may therefore form part of its '**library**'. Going back to the Building analogy at the beginning of this Chapter, this is the equivalent to an investor jointly owning the building with the Developer, thereby continuing to share in the income from lease renewals once the other original financiers have been paid off.

Premium, not Interest
Whereas a bank will charge interest accruing on a day-to-day basis (meaning the longer you take to repay, the more you have to repay), equity investors generally require a fixed '**premium**' to be paid on their investment. This is usually quoted as a percentage of the investment so, for example, if a 20% premium on was agreed on a $3m equity investment (as is the case for our *Project X*), the investor would be paid back $3.6m as its recoupment entitlement, and this amount would not increase over time. If, on the other hand, a bank were to charge 20% interest on a $3m loan, it would be repaid $3.3m if repayment took place after 6 months, $3.6m if after one year, $4.2m if after two years, and so on, as interest would continue to accrue daily until repayment (in reality, a bank loan would normally be repaid gradually, so interest would only be chargeable on any outstanding amount).

The level of premium chargeable by an equity investor will depend in particular on a) the share in net profits it demands, b) how far down the Recoupment Schedule the investor sits, c) what any other financiers will allow (especially those, if any, sitting behind the investor on the Recoupment Schedule), and d) how desperate the Producer is for the investor's money. There is sometimes a trade-off between the investor's percentage entitlement to net profits (when everyone has been repaid) and the amount of premium payable to the investor during the recoupment process. Also, the further down the Recoupment Schedule the investor finds itself, the more it can legitimately charge. In the current market, premiums tend to range from 0% to a whopping 50% (or even higher), but somewhere around the 17.5% to 25% mark is fairly standard for equity funds that recoup in second place (after the bank) and require a typical net profit share. Thus the next question is 'What *is* the investor's net profit share?'. Or how much of the profit should go to the investor, and how much should be left for the Producers'?

The Six-Tenths Rule of Profit Share

The rule of thumb is often referred to as the '**Six-Tenths Rule**', and this is how it works. Let's take a simple example of a $5m film where a single Investor will provide all the finance required to fund the entire picture. Although an unlikely scenario, a single, 100% financier is not totally unheard of, particularly on lower budget films. In this example, the only people eligible to share in the profits of the film are the Producer (and possibly his/her cast and crew) who made the film, and the investor who paid for it; otherwise known respectively as the '**creative** people', and the '**money** people'. There are no other financiers, so the spoils are split between the investor and the production team. The Six-Tenths Rule, rightly or wrongly, states that 'money' is worth six-tenths (60%), and 'creative' is worth four-tenths (40%). Producers will argue that it should be closer to a 50/50 split (and that's the direction the market has moved in recent times), but some investors will ask for 75%, or even more. However, for argument's sake, let us assume 60/40 is appropriate in this example. This means that the film breaks even once the net revenues from sales (after deduction of the collection agent's fee, and the sales agent's commission and expenses) exceed $6m, assuming that the investor – who paid for the whole $5m budget, remember - is charging a 20% premium ($1m). At this point, the investor will have been paid back its investment and premium, and any net income from further sales will be pure profit. For each dollar received after this point (film sales are nearly always calculated and quoted in dollars rather than pounds or Euros), the investor would be entitled to 60¢, and the Producer to 40¢. To the extent that any other of the creative team (director, lead cast, heads of artistic departments) have negotiated an entitlement to Net Profits, this must come out of the Producer's share, because they are 'creative', and not 'money'. The Producer will agree the profit entitlements (if any) for its creative team at the time s/he engages them on the picture. A typical structure illustrating which creative team members might get what entitlement is set out in the sample Recoupment Schedule in the *Reference Section* of this Handbook.

Now, if the investor only financed *half* of the film's budget, the Six-Tenths Rule would still apply, but only to *half* of the profits. In other words, the investor would get six-tenths of half of the Net Profit, ie. a 30% profit participation, and the rest would be left for the creative people and/or other financiers. If it financed only a quarter of the film, it might expect to be given a 15% share of Net Profits, and so on. For *Project X*, the equity investor put up 30% of the budget, so it would legitimately be entitled to 18% of the net profits (although we give it 20%). The enhanced recoupment graph opposite illustrates this.

Low- and no-budget films are often funded solely by equity, crew deferments and post-deals (plus perhaps a grant), so the proportion of equity tends to be high.

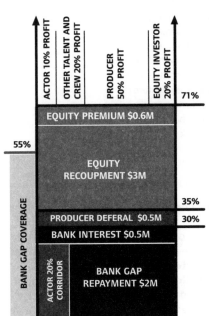

The Six-Tenths Rule is not absolutely rigid, and where equity investors put up a smaller percentage of the budget (especially if they are the last financier to commit), the proportion may go up so that an investor providing only 10% of the budget may get as high as an 8% (or even 10%) participation in the Net Profits rather than the 6% that the Six-Tenths Rule might suggest. Naturally, the actual percentage agreed will depend on the respective bargaining powers, and on whoever else is trying to negotiate a profit share. As mentioned above, if the investor demands an excessive premium, its profit share will probably have to decrease, and vice versa. Ultimately, the Producer will want to be left with at least a 40% share in the film s/he creates, even if s/he has to share some of this with his/her creative team.

Note that many of the so-called '**Equity Funds**' are in fact a hybrid of soft money (utilising the various tax breaks referred to above) and pure equity. This is why many of them take a 'softer' approach to Net Profit requirements than other Equity Investors who do not avail themselves of tax breaks. Producers should try to avoid using any tax-based Equity Fund that insists on applying the 60% Rule in full.

How Much, and Where From?

The proportion of your finance that is made up from equity will depend, amongst other things, on the size of your budget. Low- and no-budget films are often funded solely by equity, crew deferments and post-deals (plus perhaps a grant), so the proportion of equity tends to be high. Larger budget mainstream pictures with a guaranteed theatrical release will be able to finance more through pre-sales, soft money and bank gap, and so the need for so much equity will be lower. Remember, the less equity you have, the less profit you have to give away. But of course your finance does have to come from somewhere, and if the other elements don't provide enough cash to make your film, you will need to attract an investor somehow.

Equity is by definition risk money. It isn't first on the Recoupment Schedule and it may never be paid back at all. Therefore only those who can afford to lose it are likely to invest it. Of course the rewards can be great, but it's a gamble like any other. As we've said before, different people invest for different reasons. The claim that some invest in the business just for the 'glamour' angle is indeed true in some cases, but should never be taken for granted.

At the lower end of the scale, friends and family can be a useful source of finance, particularly if they are very wealthy and/or your budget is very small. But remember that they could lose everything they invest, and bear this in mind before risking any personal relationships you may not want to lose. Private corporate investors, such as business angels, are another potential source, but they tend to be more interested in investing in companies themselves, rather than the films they produce. If you are looking for corporate investment, this is where the Business Plans discussed in Chapter 1 really come into their own, and you can find investor groups easily these days by searching online. Your local Venture Capital Association (or equivalent) might be able to point you in the right direction. Then there are a large number of high net-worth individuals (ie. extremely rich people) who might want to dabble in the film business. Most that do actually come from other fields (it has been said that anyone who comes from the film industry would know never to invest in it!). They will of course be attracted by the potential financial rewards of a runaway hit, but also by the lure of the biz, the thought of rubbing shoulders with the stars in Cannes, and simply the right to boast to their friends that they have financed a real movie. Some are specifically interested in films of a particular genre, or that have a 'message'. If you don't mix in their circles, these gazillioinaires can be hard to track down, but some have actually set up companies specifically with the aim of financing (and/or producing) feature films. Examples include Sidney Kimmel Entertainment, 2929 Productions and the Yari Group, all based out of the USA. Quality networking (see Chapter 1) never goes amiss, and a simple flick through the Cannes Guide (look for 'INV' for investors) is always a good starting point.

Pre-Sales and Distribution Deals

Seller & Buyer, Agent & Distributor, Foreign & Domestic - Confusing Terminology?

Before looking in-depth at how distribution - by way of pre-sales - can aid in the financing of a picture, it is important to understand exactly what we are talking about when considering the role of **sales agents**, **distributors**, **international** distribution, **foreign** distribution, **worldwide** distribution, **domestic** distribution, and so on. These various terms are often used, confused and abused in different ways by industry executives. For the purposes of this Handbook, we will keep our definitions simple (see also the **Glossary**), although you may want to check whenever discussing sales and distribution that the people you are negotiating with have the same understanding as you do.

A **Sales Agent** is the entity appointed by the producer to sell the film on its behalf worldwide (ignoring any pre-sales already carried out by the Producer him/herself). The specific role - rather than geographical scope - of the sales agent is discussed in more detail later in this Section. However, at this stage, you should note that sometimes, especially for US productions, the sales agent is only engaged to sell to '**Foreign**' territories, which rather confusingly actually means those countries outside of North America (no matter where the Producer or sales agent is based geographically). In these cases, the '**Domestic**' (which by way of some weird twist of fate actually *always* means the USA and - usually - Canadian) rights are typically granted directly by the Producer (rather than through a sale by the sales agent) to a **Domestic Distributor** to exploit. Through whomever it receives its domestic rights, be it the Producer directly or from a worldwide sales agent, the domestic distributor will then make the necessary arrangements, or grant relevant sub-licences, for the picture to be shown on the big screen, TV and video (etc) in North America. The term '**International**' tends to be the most confusing as it is sometimes used to mean just 'foreign', but the normal (and correct) meaning is 'worldwide'. In other words, the appointment of an 'international' sales agent would normally be for the sale of domestic rights as well as for the rest of the world (foreign).

An **international distributor** is, for most intents and purposes, the same thing as an international sales agent, although technically it will usually be given a higher degree of control over distribution rights and its ability to make and enforce territorial sale agreements on an autonomous basis, with less influence from the Producer. This is because the term 'Distributor' usually means someone owning or in control of the relevant rights itself, rather than an agent who is simply appointed to sell them on behalf of someone else (the Producer). Naturally, the distinction

Remember that they could lose everything they invest, and bear this in mind before risking any personal relationships you may not want to lose.

can often be pretty vague. We will therefore (unless otherwise specified) use the term **sales agent** generically to mean the seller of the film and therefore to include international distributors, and the term **distributor** to mean territorial buyers who purchase (whether from a sales agent, international distributor or even the Producer directly) the rights to exploit the film in their local jurisdiction, which definition therefore includes the domestic distributors of North America. We explain these terms again in a little more detail in the Sales Advances and International Distribution Section later in this Chapter; see also the **Glossary**.

Distribution Agreements

The next step in understanding pre-sale based film finance is to become familiar with the basics of standard sales agreements, otherwise known as '**distribution deals**'.

We know that to generate income to repay financiers, the sales agent is engaged (on behalf of the Producer) to sell the film to distributors around the world. This is the equivalent job of the Estate Agent (Realtor) in our Building analogy earlier in this Chapter. A large number of film sales occur at special industry 'markets' (such as the *American Film Market* in Los Angeles, the *Marche du Film* in Cannes, or the parallel market at the *Berlinale* festival in Berlin), and behind the scenes at the major festivals (such as, Sundance, Venice and Toronto). At these events, the sales agent gives potential buyers private screenings of the films for sale (or their promotional trailers), or provides details of up-and-coming productions for which it has been appointed to sell internationally. Each sale made will be for a particular **territory**, usually a country or a geographically close group of countries (such as the Middle East, Central America, Scandinavia, Eastern Europe, etc).

The '**sale**' is really actually a licence of copyright; an agreement allowing the distributor to distribute the film exclusively in its territory for a specified period of time (usually between seven and fifteen years). The distributor will normally be granted the rights necessary to exploit the film on all available formats, including **Theatrical** (cinemas), **Non-Theatrical** (airlines, ships, hotels, prisons, etc), **Television** (free, terrestrial, cable, digital, satellite, pay TV, Pay Per View, Video on Demand, etc) and **Home Video** (including DVD and any future formats). It may also acquire Internet rights, Merchandising rights (clothing, crockery, books, fast-food tie-ins, etc), Soundtrack rights and various other '**Ancillary**' rights. The distributor might not itself be a specialist in each one of these fields, but it will know the relevant companies in its local territory, and will be permitted to sub-license to them the relevant rights as necessary. For example, the distributor may book the film into the local cinemas (assuming it has a theatrical arm), sell it for broadcast to the national and local TV stations, and (unless it has the facilities in-house) engage a local video sub-distributor to manufacture and distribute videos and DVDs to appropriate outlets in its territory. The terms of any such sub-licence will normally be subject to the approval of the Producer (sometimes through the sales agent) before it's entered into. Sometimes a sale will not include all formats for a particular territory (for example, when selling to a broadcaster, see Other Considerations, below), so more than one sale will need to be done. Generally, a Producer will be very keen for there to be a theatrical release, and so may negotiate specific clauses in the sale contract about how much money the distributor must throw at preparing and marketing for the film's theatrical release (known as Prints and Advertising expenses, or **P&A**), and the minimum number of screens it will guarantee it will be shown on.

> The '**sale**' is really actually a licence of copyright; an agreement allowing the distributor to distribute the film exclusively in its territory for a specified period of time (usually between seven and fifteen years)

The Minimum Guarantee and Overages

As mentioned earlier, the amount that the distributor agrees to pay for the licence is generally known as a '**Minimum Guarantee**' (or '**MG**'). However, this MG is actually an advance against future revenues payable to the Producer pursuant to the distributor's sale contract (or '**Distribution Agreement**'). This is because every dollar received by the distributor from exploitation of the film in its territory should, in principle, be shared in an agreed proportion between the distributor and the Producer. The MG is just an **advance** paid to the Producer against his/her future share. The important question for the producer and financiers is of course 'How much will the MG be?'. To answer this question, we need to understand how the distribution deals actually work.

The distributor, in deciding what level of MG it is prepared to pay, will need to consider how much it thinks it is likely to earn - *after* recouping its agreed P&A spend - from exploiting the film in its territory. This will primarily be income derived from cinema exhibitors (assuming the film goes theatrical), television broadcasters, video / DVD distribution and, if relevant, associated merchandising.

When the distributor and Producer agree the MG amount, they will also agree how the income received from each of these aspects of the film's exploitation should be split notionally between them. These '**splits**', although roughly in accordance with industry norms, will actually vary from format to format and in different territories, making distribution contracts more complex than you might initially expect. For example, any income received by the distributor from theatrical exploitation (after the cinemas have taken their cut and after the distributor has been reimbursed its costs of advertising, copying, dubbing and shipping the film) might get split 50/50 between the Producer and the distributor - it will in fact be a more complicated allocation than this for the 'major territories', such as the USA, Germany, UK, France and Japan. For video and DVD, the Producer might only get a 12% or 15% royalty on all sales and rentals, leaving the distributor with the lion's share (although the distributor will also be responsible for the costs of duplication, etc). Yet for TV, the split might be 70/30 the other way, this time with the Producer taking the majority of income from a sale to a broadcaster. See *Revenue Streams* in Chapter 1 for a full set of examples.

So, in calculating the level of MG it can afford, the distributor should work out how much in total, during the life of its licence, it thinks it is likely to have to hand over to the Producer. This will be based on the amounts it thinks it will receive from exploitation, and the proportion that it would have to hand over to the Producer pursuant to the agreed splits. Then, rather than agreeing to make drip-feed payments continually throughout the term of the licence (as income is received), the distributor agrees with the Producer an amount to be advanced up-front. This is effectively a guaranteed minimum amount that the Producer will be paid (hence the term '**Minimum Guarantee**') as its share of the distributor's various revenues earned from the film's exploitation in the relevant territory.

The MG is non-returnable, even if the distributor miscalculates and doesn't end up achieving the level of receipts it had anticipated. However, if revenues from exploitation turn out to be so high that the amount attributable to the Producer pursuant to the splits actually *exceeds* the advance (MG) paid at the time of the sale, the distributor will have to start paying additional amounts (known as '**overages**') to the Producer in accordance with the agreed splits. The amount of overages paid to the Producer will therefore depend on the source of the income received by the distributor, so that the right allocation is based on the correct split. These overages are paid into the Collection Account (as were the MGs) for

> Rather than agreeing to make drip-feed payments continually throughout the term of the licence (as income is received), the distributor agrees with the Producer an amount to be advanced up-front.

distribution in accordance with the Recoupment Schedule. It is a sad fact of life, however, that certain distributors in certain territories do not keep proper accounts and/or never admit to earning so much that overages are due. This is why the advanced MG is so important. Psychologically, in many cases, the Producer will assume s/he will never receive another penny after the MG, no matter what the splits are or how much money the distributor makes in the particular territory.

Computing Sales Estimates and MGs using the Budget

Worse still, many distributors do not even go through the above calculation, and instead use a more arbitrary method to decide on how much they should be paying as an MG. In part, this is also due to the techniques used by some sales agents in calculating their Sales Estimates. The idea behind Sales Estimates is, of course, that they are realistic. They should reflect how much the sales agent (who prepares them) honestly thinks it can obtain for the sales it hopes to make to each country. They are usually set out on a territory by territory basis in three columns, indicating respectively what the sales agent thinks is the maximum it can get (the **high** estimates, or **ask** prices), what it would like to obtain (the **mid** prices), and the minimum it thinks it should be able to get in a less-than-buoyant market (the **low** estimates, or **take** prices). Of course, financiers are a prudent bunch, and will only seriously consider the 'lows' (minimums) when doing their internal calculations.

Traditionally, the North American territory would be expected to bring in at least 50% of sales revenue, although these days it is closer to 30% or 40% (assuming a Domestic sale can be made at all). Likewise, certain other territories have also tended to generate a fairly steady, and therefore identifiable, percentage of the total worldwide sales revenue. Of course, these proportions do actually fluctuate on a film-by-film basis, and will in each case be determined by how well the film in question is expected to do in the territory concerned. This in turn will depend on the film's genre, cast, subject matter, and so on.

However, sometimes what happens is that these 'predictable' percentages of worldwide income are used by the sales agent in generating their Sales Estimates. They are then re-calculated with direct reference to the film's budget. In other words, a sales agent may 'estimate' for example that, in its (optimistic) view, 10% of the film's budget can normally be recovered from a sale to France, 8% from the UK and 12% from Germany, and it will prepare its estimates on this basis. Using this method for our example *Project X*, with its $10m budget, the France sales estimate would be $1m, Germany $1.2m, and so on.

These projections are of course used by financiers in determining how much they will invest, what deal they should negotiate, how much profit they think they will make, and so on. Accordingly, they will hope that the numbers are not arbitrarily calculated, but instead realistic estimates based on the specific film's potential in the relevant territory.

The practice of calculating sales projections as percentages of a budget is clearly fundamentally flawed. By way of example, if the 'going rate' for a sale to France was in fact 10%, it would imply that *Project X* should automatically generate twice as much income from a sale to France as would any $5m film. The MG paid for the *Project X* would be $1m, but for the $5m film would only be $500k. For this to make sense to the distributor, it would itself have to generate exactly twice as much income from its territory for *Project X* than for the $5m film. Of course in practice this rarely ever happens. The number of people who actually watch a film at the cinema, on TV or on DVD, is not directly determined by how much

The practice of calculating sales projections as percentages of a budget is clearly fundamentally flawed.

was spent on producing it. The general public rarely even know how much a film's budget is, never mind using that as a basis for whether or not they want to watch it. The amount the distributor makes locally is in fact of course a product of the quality and subject matter of the finished film, the local celebrity of its cast, and the distributor's own ability to market it well.

Nevertheless, certain sales agents do in fact use these percentages to prepare Sales Estimates (although they would probably never admit to it), and certain distributors are coerced into using the same methods in determining how much they are willing to spend for the right to exploit the film. The percentage figures do, however, change over time. During the 2001 'crash' in the German market, for example, German sales dropped from being 'worth' an unprecedented 15% of a budget to under 10%. Below is a rough guide as to what these percentages are, although opinion varies from sales agent to sales agent depending on their own approach and experiences.

Domestic	(33%)	(up to 45%, particularly for North American films, but closer to 20% on lower budget pictures)
Europe	(39%)	Germany 10%, UK 8%, France 7%, Italy 4%, Spain 4%, Scand'via 3%, Other 3%
Far East	(16%)	Japan 10%, S Korea 3%, Taiwan 1%, Other 2%
Lat. America	(4%)	Brazil 1%, Mexico 1%, Argentina 1%, Other 1%
Other	(9%)	Australia / NZ 3%, Eastern Europe 3%, Middle East 1%, South Africa 1%, Other Africa 1%

Ironically, these numbers, which reflect the 'lows' that a sales agent would quote, add up to just over 100% (101% to be precise). Some say this is to give a Producer comfort that, in the worst case, the film will still sell for more than it was made for, so s/he is reassured that it will go into profit. Otherwise the film would never break even, even if a sale were made to every country in the world. However, in reality, the total only needs to exceed that part of the budget that needs to be *recouped* (plus any interest, premiums, etc) in order to go into profit. For *Project X*, this was 71% of the budget (see previous diagrams). However, where a film is 100% financed from recoupable sources, all requiring interest and/or premiums to be paid, this figure will need to be considerably higher than 100%. For example, a low budget film financed entirely from equity, with a 20% premium, will need Sales Estimates far in excess of 120% for it to make sense as a commercial venture. Anyway, the overriding point is that, although these 'standard' territorial percentages may be a useful tool in checking whether a sales agent may have got a good price for a film (which in any event will depend on whether or not it's a pre-sale - see below), they should *never* be used or accepted as the only determining factor in calculating either Sales Estimates or, alternatively, the amount actually to be paid as an MG on an actual distribution contract.

The Pre-Sale
If, at the time of a sale, the film is already completed and the distributor has seen the finished product (for example, during a market such as Cannes, AFM or Berlin, or at a specially arranged screening during the year), it will pay the MG in full as soon as it has checked the technical quality of the elements delivered to it. These elements will be listed in a pre-agreed document called a **Delivery Schedule** (see the *Reference Section* towards the back of this Handbook for an example). The

> The amount the distributor makes locally is in fact of course a product of the quality and subject matter of the finished film, the local celebrity of its cast, and the distributor's own ability to market it well.

MG goes straight into the Collection Account, and the collection agent pays it out according to the Recoupment Schedule (see the Recoupment and Profit, earlier in this Chapter).

However, the Producer may want to start selling the film much earlier, even before it is finished, in order to start paying back the film's financiers as soon as possible (especially if s/he has to pay them interest). When a film is sold prior to its completion, it is known as '**pre-selling**' the film. This is sometimes done by the Producer using his/her own contacts, and sometimes by the sales agent (if appointed at this stage), who may start selling the film straight away. This way, the financiers can start to recoup their financial contributions even before the film is completed, and certainly before it hits the cinema screens.

The advantage to the distributor of agreeing to buy the film early is that it may get a good price because it is taking a substantial risk - ie. that the film will ultimately be as good as is hoped. The rights to the 'finished' film (assuming it turns out well) would usually cost more because the distributor would be able to actually see what it is getting before committing to buy. However, before agreeing to pre-buy the rights to exploit the film, the distributor will want to see and approve a number of '**Key Elements**', including the script, lead cast, budget, shooting schedule and delivery date. Depending on how far down the line the production is at the time of the sale, the Producer may also have some 'rushes' (often called 'dailies' in the US), or selected unfinished scenes, to show the distributor, if s/he thinks these are of sufficient quality to help persuade the distributor to make the purchase (and at the desired price).

Payment of the MG on a Pre-sale

On a pre-sale (unlike a 'straight' distribution deal made after the film is completed – see below), the distributor will not normally be required to pay the entire MG at the time the deal is made. It will typically hand over only a small proportion as a deposit, usually about 20%, although this will depend on the territory and bargaining position of the distributor concerned. The remaining balance is only payable when the film is delivered to the distributor, once it has actually been completed. '**Delivery**' is a whole exercise in itself, and does not just entail giving the distributor a reel of film in a can. In fact, the negative will usually stay in a laboratory somewhere, and the distributor will be given access to it in order to strike the prints that it needs. The Producer will, however, have to deliver (or provide access to) 'masters' for TV broadcast and video duplication, publicity materials, a trailer (if required), information to assist with foreign language dubbing, copies of relevant contracts, an explanation of restrictions that the distributor must comply with, and a large amount of other back-up documentation (including '**Chain of Title**' – legal proof that the Producer had the rights to make the film in the first place). On receipt of these 'delivery materials', the distributor will check that they all conform with what it was expecting (and contractually entitled) to receive, including of course the Key Elements mentioned above, and only then pay the balance of the MG over to the collection account. The distributor will probably by this time have planned its '**Release Schedule**' for the film, and so will also require the film to be delivered bang on time, otherwise it might refuse to pay for it.

Pre-Sales as a form of Finance for the Film

As mentioned in the Introduction to this Chapter, and illustrated to some extent in the Building analogy, a common way to raise finance for a film is to sell off the exploitation rights to the film in certain territories before it actually goes into production. These of course are also 'pre-sales', but specifically ones made

Although these 'standard' territorial percentages may be a useful tool in checking whether a sales agent may have got a good price for a film they should never be used or accepted as the only determining factor in calculating either Sales Estimates or, alternatively, the amount actually to be paid as an MG on an actual distribution contract.

before the film is even started, rather than during production. For the Producer, pre-selling is a way of getting a large proportion of the production funds together without having to give away equity, and therefore profits, in the film. It is also a good way to measure whether or not the concept for the film is attractive to at least some part of the international marketplace before actually spending (other people's) money on producing it. For this reason, a gap financier (see later) may not get involved with a project until it sees that a minimum number (usually at least 2 or 3) of key territories have already been sold by way of pre-sale.

There is one major snag, though. When making a pre-sale for the purposes of financing, the Producer will want to receive the whole MG (rather than the 20% deposit) before making the film, in order to put the entire sale price towards the cost of producing the film. It won't want to wait until it has made and delivered the film to the distributor in order to collect the 80% or so of the MG that it required in order to make the film in the first place.

Once again, this is where the Producer has to turn to the **bank**. As mentioned above, the distributor promises, in its contract, to pay the balance of the MG upon satisfactory delivery of the film. In the meantime, the Producer will ask the bank if it will lend the money to enable the film to be made. This is known as '**discounting**' the distribution contract (sale). The bank lends the Producer an amount of money up front, and collects directly from the distributor when the film is delivered to it by the Producer. Note that this money does *not* go into the recoupment pot (Collection Account) because it is itself production finance to be used for the production of the film, rather than to pay back other financiers. As the sale contract is effectively the bank's collateral, it is unlikely to lend more than the price agreed for the MG. However, the Producer will not be able to use the whole amount for the production itself, as it will have to build in a fairly hefty fee for the bank, and interest during the course of the loan. For example, if the full MG was $1m, the Producer may have to allocate (say) $20k as a one-off fee for the bank (equal to about 2% of the loan). S/he will also need to reserve $100k or so to cover the interest (at 2% or 3% above base rate) that the loan will accumulate from the time the pre-sale was agreed (and the loan entered into - generally being at the start of production) to the time that the bank picks up the payment from the distributor on delivery. In this example, the Producer would therefore only be able to put $880k of the $1m sale price onto the screen itself.

As for the bank, it will only lend against the distributor's promise to pay the MG if it has a good relationship with the distributor, and believes that it is likely still to be solvent (and therefore able to pay) at the time of delivery of the film. It may also require the distributor's own bank to issue a letter of credit on behalf of the distributor, guaranteeing that the payment can (and will) be made, as long as the Producer meets the delivery requirements. It may also agree only to discount a proportion of the pre-sale, particularly if it is uncomfortable that the distributor will be able to pay the entire MG balance on delivery. Of course, the bank must be sure that the film will actually be finished on time and on budget (so as to prevent the distributor from trying to avoid payment), and will therefore usually insist that the Producer takes out a '**Completion Bond**' to ensure s/he (the Producer) complies with his/her obligations to deliver. Completion bonds are discussed in more detail later in this Chapter.

Too many Pre-sales?
Although a Producer will always be optimistic that s/he will one day receive overages from the various territories, financiers will take a more prudent approach. They tend to assume that, after receipt of the full MG, the Producer is unlikely

> If too many pre-sales are made for the purposes of financing the film, there may not be enough remaining territories around the world to be sold in order for the film's other financiers to be repaid or, if entitled, see any profits.

to see any further income from any territory that has been pre-sold. This clearly affects the future profitability of the film. Any **Equity Investor** (see earlier in this Chapter) will be relying on substantial sale proceeds being paid in to the pot, in order for it to recoup its investment and share in subsequent profits. If too many pre-sales are made for the purposes of financing the film, there may not be enough remaining territories around the world to be sold in order for the film's other financiers to be repaid or, if entitled, see any profits. This is because the income from these pre-sales effectively goes straight onto the screen, rather than into the pot for distribution amongst the financiers pursuant to the Recoupment Schedule.

It is therefore not healthy to do too many pre-sales for financing purposes, and the Producer must maintain a balance between obtaining the finance s/he needs to make the film, and leaving enough territories available for future sales so that his/her other financiers will be satisfactorily paid off. It follows that the film's other financiers will normally have a right of approval over any deals pre-selling rights in this way.

Split Rights Deals

One method of financing pictures through pre-sales is the '**split rights**' approach, where one financier puts up about half the production funds money in return typically for **foreign** rights, and another for **domestic**. Actually, these days the split tends to be closer to 60/40, with the domestic side representing the lesser amount. Often the financiers will either be sales agents or distributors themselves, or have close connections to them. They might not use their own money, but rather take the responsibility for arranging their agreed proportion of the budget, using their rights (be they foreign or domestic) as collateral. In these circumstances, there are nearly always two different companies appointed to sell the film, one an international sales agent for foreign rights, and the other a domestic distributor or agent for North America. By their very nature, split rights deals are often the result of some form of co-production arrangement.

Straight, Flat and Outright Sales

Unfortunately, the term '**Straight Sale**' has a couple of different meanings depending on who you ask, which can make life a little confusing. One interpretation is a distribution deal that is not a pre-sale; in other words one that is made after the film is completed. It is 'straight' in the sense of 'less hassle' because the MG is paid in one go, no deposit needs to be taken, and the deal does not need to be banked ('discounted') in order to be used for production financing. The other - different and potentially conflicting - meaning attributed to the term 'straight sale' is a sale that does not have an MG at all. In these cases, the distributor simply pays the Producer (via the collection account, of course) in accordance with the agreed splits from day one (although usually the distributor is permitted to recoup its own costs and expenses from income before it has to start paying the Producer as per the splits). These are becoming more and more common, particularly in the Domestic market, and also for sales to any territory that occur post-completion of the film.

> The combined optimism of the parties, both hoping that the film does better than expected, usually incentivises them enough to enter into an MG-style agreement and negotiate the splits for the potential of overages.

Alternatively if, as happens occasionally, the parties agree that the distributor will never be required to pay the Producer any more than the original purchase amount, it is known as an '**Outright Sale**' or a '**Flat Sale**' (rather than an MG). In such cases, there is no need to negotiate the splits for each format because the sales price is not a minimum guarantee advanced against them, but a simple one off payment. These deals are fairly rare as the combined optimism of the parties, both hoping that the film does better than expected, usually incentivises them enough to enter into an MG-style agreement and negotiate the splits for the potential of overages. However, sometimes only certain aspects of a distribution deal are considered '**flat**', where the Producer is not allowed to share in revenues from certain formats. For example, if the distributor is permitted to keep all income from TV sales (ie. there is no 'split' for TV), the sale is referred to as being 'flat for TV'.

Some Other Considerations

Hold-back Windows
Sometimes a pre-sale may be made directly to a broadcaster, for television rights only, particularly if the broadcaster (eg. Channel Four and the BBC in the UK, or HBO and IFC in the USA) has been in some way involved in developing the project from inception. One point to note is that a pre-sale to a TV network will have an effect on any future sale made to the theatrical (and/or video) distributor in the same territory. A TV pre-sale made without an appropriate '**hold-back**' window will affect the timing of a potential release in the cinemas (and therefore reduce the attraction of the film to a theatrical buyer). The subsequent buyer of theatrical rights will not, of course, be able to acquire the opportunity to sub-license the film for TV in its territory, so its offer price to the Producer will be lower than it would have been if it could have acquired all rights in all formats. That said, any sale is better than no sale at all, and a sale to one buyer might increase the status of the film, thereby helping to secure a sale to another buyer. A recent example of these issues is the award-winning docudrama *Death of a President,* which the UK's Channel 4 (who developed and part-produced it) insisted on broadcasting on British terrestrial TV before it went theatrical in the USA (or anywhere else, for that matter).

New Producers and Project Commerciality
Pre-sales as a form of financing work well for established producers with a good reputation and a good project, but increasingly buyers are becoming less keen to enter into this kind of deal (or to pay the traditional prices), due to the very real risk of not being able to achieve the estimated box office figures. Naturally, this has had a negative impact on established production companies' ability to raise finance. Today, a reputable producer with a good script, cast and production team might expect to raise maybe 10% to 50% of the film's budget this way, compared with upwards of 70% a few years ago. As the internet - which is less easily segmented geographically - becomes more and more prominent as a distribution channel, financing structures involving traditional pre-sales will also evolve. For a fuller discussion on these topics, see the Section on The 'Net' Effect on Financing Models, below.

The sad but true state of affairs currently, however, is that a mainstream film without a distribution deal (pre-sale) in place for at least one major territory is likely to be a less attractive proposition for other potential financiers, especially public funding bodies and banks. This is because, as noted above, the existence of pre-sales is often considered a 'signal' that at least some distributors in the market (ie. those who really should know, first-hand, the commerciality of a film in a particular territory) believe the project to be a good enough commercial prospect to take a financial risk. Additionally, a less experienced Producer will benefit more from the market experience and guidance of a distributor who is already on-board while the film is being made. It would be unfortunate if the film, once completed, was turned down by other distributors for reasons that could easily have been addressed during production, had the Producer only known.

A mainstream film without a distribution deal (pre-sale) in place for at least one major territory is likely to be a less attractive proposition for other potential financiers, especially public funding bodies and banks

Letters of Intent

Whereas selling a finished film is common practice for both established and non-established filmmakers, pre-selling can be much more difficult for Producers with less of a reputation. However, sometimes a distributor can be persuaded to sign a '**letter of intent**' rather than an enforceable distribution contract. This letter acknowledges an intention to buy the film for an agreed price once it has been completed and delivered. As with a normal pre-sale, the letter will indicate certain conditions that the Producer and the finished film must meet in order for the distributor to proceed with the acquisition. Although possessing a letter of intent would be better than approaching a potential investor without any distribution deal at all, it is by no means proof of an actual sale, and in itself would probably not be enough to persuade financiers looking for a reasonably secure investment. At the very least, a letter of intent would establish a relationship with a distributor, and might be a useful way to demonstrate that the film is potentially of commercial interest.

Gap Financing

Not to be confused with '**GAAP**' funds (discussed later in this Chapter), **gap financing** is a form of loan, traditionally issued by a bank — although there are a number of specialist funds entering the market — which provides the finance for the shortfall (the '**gap**') between other finance raised, and the total budgeted amount needed to make the film. Unless stated otherwise, reference below to a gapping 'bank' includes these specialist gap funds too.

Sales Estimates, Coverage and the Domestic Sale

Generally, a gapping bank will lend against the projected '**sales estimates**' relating to unsold territories, as provided by a reputable sales agent. As explained above, sales estimates are figures representing the amount that the sales agent reasonably thinks the film will sell for in the market place, once completed. In preparing them, the sales agent will take into account a number of factors, particularly the Key Elements (budget, cast, director, Producer, genre, etc) and how they might be received by the general worldwide public. They are prepared on a territory-by-territory (and sometimes even format-by-format) basis, showing the likely 'best case' and 'worst case' prices attainable. For more information on the computation of sales estimates, see the relevant Section under Pre-Sales and Distribution Deals, above.

> **The bank will also want to see a clear 'margin' between the sales estimates and the amount it is being asked to lend, in order to provide it with sufficient comfort that enough income will in fact be generated for the loan to be repaid**

The bank will only lend if it is satisfied with the reputation of the sales agent providing the estimates, and then only if the sales agent is actually 'attached' to (ie. committed to sell) the project. The bank will also usually want to see that at least one or two pre-sales have already been made to 'major' territories (being Germany, the UK, France, Italy, Spain, Scandinavia, Japan, Australia or - ideally - the USA). This illustrates to the bank that members of the worldwide distribution industry believe that the film has commercial potential, and also confirms that the sales estimate figures given are in fact realistic. The bank will also want to see a clear 'margin' between the sales estimates and the amount it is being asked to lend, in order to provide it with sufficient comfort that enough income will in fact be generated for the loan to be repaid. The margin required (or, as it is known, '**coverage**' – not to be confused with 'overages'!) will often be 200% or 300% of value of the loan being requested (although 150% has been known to be accepted from time to time, particularly by some of the gapping funds).

In other words, if the Producer of a $10m picture has already secured $8m of production finance, s/he will have a gap of $2m (ie. 20%) to plug. This reflects the position in our example *Project X*, where $8m had been sourced as a mixture of pre-sales, equity, soft money and deferments. A gap-financing bank will require that the 'worst case' sales estimates for all unsold territories (but often ignoring North America) are at least $4m to $6m, being 200% to 300% of the gap required. This will provide the bank with reassurance that, even if the sales agent misses its targets by some way, there should still be enough income for the bank's loan to be re-paid (plus interest) out of those sales actually made. Coverage of 200% (or 300%) should ensure full repayment of the loan, even if the film sales ultimately only make half (or a third) of the revenue anticipated by the sales agent. In fact it means that the sales agent only needs to show projections that the film will be sold for 40% (or 60%) of its budget for the bank to be satisfied and commit to a gapping loan. For *Project X*, we have suggested that the gapping bank required 275% coverage for the $2m loan, meaning that the 'low' sales projections would have had to exceed $5.5m for the bank to provide gap finance. This is illustrated diagrammatically by the shaded area on the side of the *Project X* diagrams above.

As mentioned in our Building analogy earlier in this Chapter, sales to North America (which, as we stated above, is referred to as the '**Domestic**' market, even by non-Americans), although usually the most lucrative, are also often the hardest to conclude. The North American market is incessantly flooded with films from every angle and, although American filmgoers are among the most prolific in the world, there are only so many pictures a person can see. Once a Producer has secured a North American theatrical release (ie. through a Domestic sale), many foreign distributors feel that the film will automatically receive a higher profile globally (particularly as it is likely to be released in the USA, with full fanfare, before the distributor's own territory), and they will therefore often agree to pay a higher price for it. But the fact that Domestic sales are so hard to secure, particularly prior to the film's completion, results in the banks usually ignoring potential income from a Domestic sale (or at least limiting it to a TV / video-only sale) when looking at sales estimates and calculating the required coverage.

Repayment

Banks will always insist on being the first to be paid back out of income received from exploitation of the film. This suits the Producer to some extent, because the bank usually charges higher interest than any other financier, so the sooner they are paid off, the better. Sometimes they will allow for other financiers (usually just government bodies and 'deferments') to take a small '**corridor**' and recoup *pari passu* (see Recoupment and Profit section above), but this will typically be given only after strong negotiations. Even the sales agent may have to defer some of its commission until the gap loan is repaid (see below). In our example *Project X*, the bank has permitted a 20% corridor for the lead actor to recoup the deferred element of his/her fee. In reality, to be entitled to such a large corridor, the actor concerned would normally have to be a fairly big name. Producers are typically not so lucky, and in *Project X* they have to wait until after the bank has been repaid before recouping their deferments (see previous diagrams for illustration). One major advantage of gap finance is that a bank will never hold an equity share in the film so, once it has been repaid, it will receive no share in the future revenues.

> **Banks will always insist on being the first to be paid back out of income received from exploitation of the film.**

Security

The bank will also usually take **security** (such as a charge and/or mortgage) over the film, or even the entire asset base of the production company, until it has been fully paid off. This is another reason why the Producer will want the bank to recoup as soon as possible. The costs of effecting the security (particularly the legal fees) can be substantial, and certainly contribute to the high price of this type of finance. In addition to the security documents themselves, the banks will often require sales agents to enter into a Notice of Assignment with each distributor, effectively obliging the distributor to pay the bank directly upon delivery of the film (until it has recouped its loan), rather than paying into the Collection Account. This gives the bank an added level of security.

New Gap Funding Opportunities

As mentioned above, with the demise of a number of tax-based funding opportunities, there are now an increasing number of private, almost equity-type funds entering into the gap market. Their terms are generally a little softer than those of a traditional lending bank, but harder than those of a pure equity fund. Advantages over the banks are that they tend to provide more money (up to 40% of the budget, whereas most gapping banks these days still tend to be limited to about 20%) and charge lower fees and interest (or premium). The downside is that they usually require a back-end participation (banks never ask for this), although because they recoup in first position, they don't generally apply the six-tenths rule in full. In other words, for each percentage point of the budget that they put up, they take less than the 0.6% profit-share that a straight equity fund recouping in 2nd place would typically require. Note that some of these funds are in fact tied into certain tax-breaks around the world, and will require that a proportion of the production budget (often at least equal to the amount of the gap finance) is spent locally in order to qualify for the relevant benefit.

Completion Bond

The gapping bank will often insist on being the bank that discounts any existing pre-sales too.

Just like a bank that discounts pre-sales (see above), a gapping bank will also normally require a **Completion Bond** to be put in place to ensure that the film is delivered by the Producer on *time*, so that buyers will be obliged to pay the balance of their MGs as soon as possible, and on *Budget*, so that no further money needs to be borrowed from elsewhere ('**rescue finance**' needed to finish a project that has overspent will often knock the bank out of first position on a Recoupment Schedule). In fact, the gapping bank will often insist on being the bank that discounts any existing pre-sales too. That way it gets more fees and interest, and the whole operation is more streamlined, with only one bank (and therefore one set of lawyers!) doing all the necessary lending. The basic workings of Completion Bonds are explored later in this Chapter.

Costs of Gapping

The costs relating to gap loans will typically include a 'gap fee', a separate arrangement fee, and/or a loan fee, together with a particularly high interest rate (due to the risk factor) payable on the loan. It is therefore an expensive form of financing. The total fees may amount to 8% or 9% of the value of the gap, interest will probably be 2% or 3% above base rate, and the Producer will also have to cover the bank's legal fees (which can be over $100,000 (£50,000) for a complicated transaction).

The Rise and Fall of Insurance-Backed Gap

Traditionally, gap finance was fairly easy to come by, and banks were always prepared to put up about 20% of a film's budget in this way. Later, particularly in the late 1990s, a number of insurance companies wishing to expand their exposure to high-risk markets offered to 'insure' the gap loans on individual films. The bank would insure against the risk that the anticipated sales levels were never reached, so that it could call upon the insurance company to pay back the loan if the Producer couldn't. This additional security (ie. the risk of the film not meeting its sales expectations now being moved to some extent from the bank to the insurance company) allowed the banks to increase the size of the gap loans dramatically, sometimes up to 50% - but more usually 30% to 40% - of the budget. Naturally, many films did not meet even their 'worst case' targets (low estimates), and numerous insurance policies were 'called in' by the banks to cough up the difference when gap loans were left unpaid. Mass litigation ensued (some of which is still on-going) as the insurance companies claimed that they were misled as to the risks of the projects, either by the banks or the Producers (or both). As a result, insurance-backed gap financing has all but disappeared (although not necessarily for TV projects), and banks are now reluctant even to put up the 20% which was common before the insurance companies' heightened involvement. In addition, many of the traditional gapping banks have left the scene altogether, and others have merged and/or severely tightened up their requirements.

Summary

A typical gap loan in the current climate will provide a Producer with between 10% and 18% of the budget of the film, assuming all the bank's other criteria are met. However, one or two banks are quoting 20% or 25% in certain circumstances, probably in order to remain competitive as private funds continue to enter the market. Gap finance is often the only way for a Producer to meet the full budget costs of his/her film, despite not really being his/her preferred form of finance due to the high costs attached. Banks that are currently still active in this field include the Royal Bank of Scotland, Bank of Ireland, Comerica and Anglo Irish Bank.

The new private gap funds that are emerging seem to be charging lower fees and interest than the traditional lending banks, and sometimes have less stringent coverage requirements (perhaps as low as 150%). They will also usually offer a larger percentage of the budget (up to 30% or 40%) — but in return they will require a piece of the back-end (ie. a Net Profit participation) — which a traditional bank will never require, creating in reality a type of hybrid between a pure gap loan and an equity financier. It follows that Producers should try to avoid private gap funds that charge bank-comparable interest (and fees) *and* apply the six-tenths rule in full to their Net Profit entitlement.

Completion Bonds

A **Completion Bond** (also known as a 'Completion Guarantee' or more usually, using the American spelling, '**Completion Guaranty**') is not actually a form of financing at all. But as the presence of a Bond is integral to so many financing transactions, it is important to understand the basics of how they work, and they therefore a deserve a few explanatory paragraphs of their own.

Protecting the Financiers

In essence, a Bond is a kind of insurance taken out by a Producer in order to guarantee that the film will be completed without running over budget or (equally importantly) schedule. Financiers, especially the banks, will normally require a Producer to take out a Completion Bond (and to be party to those agreements) in order to help secure their investment; the film becomes worthless if it is ends up unfinished because funds run out, or if delays result in losing cast or a particularly

> **Gap finance is often the only way for a Producer to meet the full budget costs of his/her film, despite not really being his/her preferred form of finance due to the high costs attached.**

desired exploitation opportunity. Even a good film finished late will be a financial disaster if the distributors refuse to pay for it due to late delivery, which they are often contractually entitled to do.

Should it be impossible to finish the film on time and on budget, the **Bond Company** (a term which is interchangeable with '**Completion Guarantor**') will, under the Completion Guarantee, be required to repay all financiers who are party to the Completion Guarantee their *entire investment* to date. This means that if the Producer runs out of money, the bond company has to find the sums from elsewhere (any money already contributed will of course have already been used) in order to pay back the financiers in full – or, alternatively, pay to finish the film itself. It will usually take out its own insurance policy with Lloyds of London (or similar institution) to protect itself against this Armageddon scenario. Naturally, no bond company will ever want to do this unless absolutely necessary, and so it will not get involved with any project that it feels, following careful consideration of the script, budget, shooting schedule, people involved, locations, special effects, technical requirements (etc), is likely to be a no-hoper. If it chooses to bond a project, it will in any event require rights of '**take-over**', allowing it to step in to replace the production team (or part of it), including the Producer and/or Director, in order to manage the production directly, if it feels that targets are being missed and there is a chance it will have to cough up some extra cash. In reality, it is almost unheard of for a bond company to repay financiers in full. It will nearly always step in and (as a last resort) take over, preferring to find **finishing funds** from its own pocket, rather than to give the financiers all their money back. Producers know that the bond company has this power, and so will usually do as it says whenever budgets or schedules start to slip. The uncompromising documentary feature *Lost in La Mancha*, which recorded the events around the doomed attempts at producing Terry Gilliam's 2002 film *The Man Who Killed Don Quixote*, famously demonstrated the devastating consequences of what can happen when a shoot goes wrong, and how and why a bond company might get involved.

How the Bond works

There are two principal agreements entered into in relation to a Completion Bond. The first is the **Completion Guarantee** itself, between the bond company and the financiers whose position it is protecting. This states that the Guarantor will make sure (or 'guarantee') that the film is finished (or 'completed') and delivered on time, or else the Guarantor will repay all the contracting financiers. In practice, as stated above, if it becomes inevitable that the project is going to run out of funds, the Guarantor itself will usually prefer to muster up the extra cash needed to get the film finished on time, rather than have to repay all the financiers the entire amounts spent to date (which would usually, by this stage, mean repaying most of the budget – probably a much higher amount than the additional 'finishing funds' required).

The second agreement is the **Completion Agreement** with the Producer, which gives the bond company its requisite rights of take-over and to receive certain documentation (in the form or reports) throughout the production. It is in the interests of both the bond company and the Producer that they work hand-in-hand with each other throughout the production. A representative from the Guarantor will periodically visit the set, and the Producer will be required to send in daily and weekly reports, setting out over-costs and over-runs to date (and how they expect to make up this time or money), and so on. These give the bond company a clear picture on how the production is going at any given point in time.

Financiers, especially the banks, will normally require a Producer to take out a Completion Bond (and to be party to those agreements) in order to help secure their investment; the film becomes worthless if it is ends up unfinished because funds run out
....

Its personnel are usually experienced producers who have a full understanding of the quirks of film production, and have an array of ideas for when things start going wrong. Where problems look imminent, the bond company will offer advice and, in extreme circumstances, will remove and/or replace the director, Producer, or other key elements in order to get the film finished on time and delivered to the sales agent and distributors. In such circumstances, the bond company will not necessarily be overly interested in the artistic quality of the finished film; its concern will be getting the job done, and the film delivered in accordance with the various technical delivery requirements set out in the Completion Agreement (which approximately mirror those in the Distribution Agreements and Sales Agency Agreement – albeit not necessarily in their entirety).

This is because the Completion Bond is there to protect the rights of the various financiers - the '**beneficiaries**' to the Bond - and *not* those of the Producer. As you can imagine, the bond company can be a bit of a burden (albeit arguably a necessary one) for the Producer, who in an ideal world would want to keep total control of the film s/he is producing, and not spend the substantial fees (and time) on a Completion Guarantee that s/he often thinks will never be necessary. This is one reason why on very low budget pictures, or those where there is no bank (or other financier requiring equivalent protection), the Producer will simply avoid taking out a Bond altogether.

It should also be noted that neither the sales agent, to whom the Producer delivers the film, nor the distributors (to whom the sales agent then delivers on), are typically beneficiaries to the Bond, unless they themselves have put up any money for the production. For example, a distributor whose 20% pre-sale deposit is being used directly for the financing, will only be a beneficiary to the extent that if the film collapses, it will be repaid that amount. The discounting bank, on the other hand, will ensure it is fully protected.

The Producer will initially have to provide the bond company with a script, schedule and budget, as approved by the financiers and (where relevant) those distributors that have already agreed to buy the film. The bond company will examine these documents, and any others it requests, in order to satisfy itself that the film can realistically be completed within the proposed budget, and that the Key Elements, insurance and locations are all properly dealt with.

Strike Price and Contingency
The financiers will have to guarantee that they will all actually pay up their agreed contributions, to ensure that the entire budget required to make the film is made available before production starts. Otherwise the Guarantor will not be willing to guarantee that there is enough money to complete it, and therefore won't issue the bond. The amount needed to complete the film, from the Bond's perspective, is known as the '**strike price**', and is usually roughly equal to the film's **cash budget**, being the total budget less certain **deferrals** (see below). However, the Guarantor will sometimes refuse to bond certain delivery items if it feels they are unnecessary, and may also refuse to bond certain costs relating specifically to the financing of the film itself (such as financing fees and legal expenses) as it believes these are not costs of making the film and should therefore be borne by the financiers, even if the film ultimately collapses. The bond company will also require that a '**contingency**' equal to about 10% of the budget is specified as a line item and set aside to cover any unforeseen budget overruns. Likewise, the fee for the Completion Guarantee will be agreed as a line item, and is often calculated as a percentage of the budget (usually in the region of about 2% to 6%, depending mostly on the confidence the bond company has in the project). If the Guaranty

is not 'called upon' (ie. the bond company is not required to pay up any money), it will often give a rebate equal to approximately half of the original Bond fee, especially if the original bond fee was at the higher end of the scale.

Bond Companies' track records

As an aside, it is also important for the Producer and his/her financiers to establish whether or not the completion guarantor would actually be able to pay up if called upon. The bond company will have taken out an insurance policy to cover itself in the event of being required to pay large sums back to the investors, and the Producer and financiers have every right to enquire about this, as well as the bond company's track record. Two of the more established Guarantors in the field are Film Finances and International Film Guarantors.

Deferments

Many people don't think of deferments as a source of financing and, technically, perhaps they're not. But they do reduce the amount of 'up-front' finance required from elsewhere, and so therefore make a positive contribution to the budget. We touched on deferments briefly in our Building analogy at the beginning of this Chapter and there are only a few points to add.

They do reduce the amount of 'up-front' finance required from elsewhere, and so therefore make a positive contribution to the budget

As mentioned, the simple concept is that certain cast and/or crew (usually starting with the Producer!) agree to their fee being paid part up-front, and part out of future sales revenue. The entire fee is included in the budget (for it is contractually payable as a cost of making the film), but the Producer does not need to find production finance to cover the whole lot. Let's say our $10m example *Project X* has an A-list actor charging a $1m fee (OK, these days probably a B-list actor at that price). If the actor is willing to defer $0.5m of this, the Producer only needs to find $9.5m from elsewhere to get his film on the screen. It is almost as though the actor him/herself is financing the film to the tune of $0.5m. The net amount required ($9.5m in this example) is known as the '**cash budget**', as it reflects the amount of cash actually needed to physically make the film. Actors may be willing to defer some of their fee if they really believe in the project, especially if they are taking a break from the studio system to do a 'worthy' independent picture. But they will, in return, probably require a piece of the back end.

A high-level actor or director who defers part of his/her fee will usually be the first person to receive income from sales of the film, even before the gapping bank. This is because the first sales are effectively just completing the financing of the film (the deferred $0.5m was still included in the budget), rather than actual income. And without the actor being on board and happy with his/her deal, the film probably wouldn't get made, so the bank may succumb to his/her demands. It won't necessarily allow the actor to recoup out of 100% from first dollar, as in our example *Project X*, where the actor is given a 20% corridor (see earlier diagrams) from which to recoup the deferred part of his/her fee. On the other hand you can see that the Producers' deferral in *Project X* (also $0.5m) is recouped *after* the bank.

The producer often has to wait until after any bank gap has been fully recouped before receiving the deferred element of his/her fee, as banks will often take a harder line against producers than actors when negotiating the Recoupment Waterfall. Gapping funds can take a softer line when it comes to corridors for recoupment of deferments.

There is clearly a fine line between, on the one hand, a $10m film with $1m fees deferred (such as *Project X*), and on the other hand a $9m film where the actor simply has first position on the Recoupment Schedule until Net Receipts equal $1m. The financiers will generally want to claim the higher budget if they are looking to benefit from, for example, tax breaks based on budget size. Accordingly, there is legislation in a number of countries restricting the inclusion of deferments in budgets of qualifying films for tax purposes. For example, producer fees are often limited to around 10%, so that they can't claim (say) $5m fees, $4m of which are deferred, on a $6m project (ie. with a $2m cash budget).

In practice, it is not the actors who need to be most aware of the possible need to defer their fees. The first fees to go this way are usually those of the Producer, usually because the financiers demand it. To them, it is a sign that the Producer believes in the project enough to put his/her money where his/her mouth is. If s/he produces a turkey, no sales will be made and the Producer will not get paid his/her full fee. Where the Producer has sourced almost enough money to make the film, the financiers may require the budget to be squeezed a little to make it fit (rather than bring another financier on board), and the Producer's fee is usually the first to go. That said, many actors complain that, even on larger budget pictures that appear to make lots of money, they never get to see the deferred element of their fees, despite supposedly recouping it in first position.

Sometimes, particularly on very low budget films, it is the Producer him/herself who requires deferments from the rest of the cast and crew. This way s/he reduces the cash budget as much as possible, so that the amount of finance ultimately required from elsewhere is at an absolute minimum. And it is not just cast and crew who may be asked to defer in these cases. It is not unheard of for printers, laboratories, prop providers, film stock suppliers, screenwriters, (etc) to be asked to take their fees out of sales receipts (usually being repaid *pari passu* with each other) in order to get the film made for tuppence ha'penny. See Post-Production Deals, below.

There is one other major consideration regarding deferments, and that relates to the strike price for a Completion Guarantee (see previous section). The strike price will be reduced on a bonded film by the value of any deferments because the completion guarantor will not need to pay back any 'financier' who has not actually put up any money and, using our *Project X* example again, will acknowledge that only $9m is needed to ensure that the film gets made and delivered on time.

Post-Production Deals

Post-production Deals can be a vital element of any financing plan, especially at lower budgets where cash is not always forthcoming. They are a sort of hybrid between equity and deferments, whereby a laboratory or other post-production studio offers to work at a significant discount (sometimes at cost, sometimes even for free), in return for deferred fees and, usually, a Net Profit participation. Naturally, this significantly reduces the cash budget, and therefore the need to find finance from elsewhere. Sometimes the lab or studio will take specific territories as collateral, particularly the one where it's based. For example, a post-production outfit in Germany might offer to do work on a film at cost (or less), but in return require the German territorial rights (because it has contacts there to do a sale, or even the facilities itself to distribute the film), together with a piece of the back-end (profit), and maybe even get a corridor from 1st dollar from which it can

> Sometimes, particularly on very low budget films, it is the Producer him/herself who requires deferments from the rest of the cast and crew. This way s/he reduces the cash budget as much as possible, so that the amount of finance ultimately required from elsewhere is at an absolute minimum.

recoup some fees as a deferment rather than waiting until the film hits profit. The value of the work that the studio is performing It will determine what deal it gets.

GAAP Funds

Not to be confused with gap financing (see above), GAAP funds are based on the concepts of **generally accepted accounting principles**, hence their name. The idea is to structure a film fund in such a way as to allow the investors in it to get some form of tax benefit by applying the normal rules of taxation, rather than by accessing a film-specific legislative incentive. GAAP funds for films are a relatively new creature, having only really come into their own in the last 5 or 10 years. However, they do tend to come and go regularly, as many governments typically don't like them, so introduce legislation to shut them down (as happened in the UK as recently as March 2007, effectively killing the anticipated raising of over £500m - equivalent to $1bn - film finance). This is because, although the funds are financially engineered as **tax-avoidance** schemes (as opposed to **tax-evasion**, see Glossary for an explanation of the distinction), the tax authorities feel they are losing revenue they never intended to lose. The basic rationale behind these funds is the structuring of transactions through special partnerships in such a way that a film investment will appear, technically, as a *loss* in a the partnership's accounts. This loss can then be set off against the partners' other profits in order to reduce their overall tax bills. GAAP funds tend to offer finance as an equity-type provider, recouping after a gapping bank, and taking a Net Profit participation. Some funds actually replace the gapping bank (and therefore recoup in first position), and have been known to provide up to 30% or 40% of a budget.

A laboratory or other post-production studio offers to work at a significant discount (sometimes at cost, sometimes even for free), in return for deferred fees and, usually, a Net Profit participation.

Sales Agents' Commission

As has been illustrated in previous Sections in this Chapter, the role of the sales agent is fundamental to the likelihood of a film going into profit, as it is the sales agent whose job it is to sell the film and thereby bring in the income from which the financiers will be repaid. Before we look at the sales agent as a potential financier (in the next section), we should remind ourselves of the basics behind the sales agent's role in the whole process, and take a look at its typical deal and commission structure.

The Cost of Selling

The sales agent performs a function similar to any other agent in a distribution-based industry (see, for example, the comparison with an Estate Agent in the Building analogy earlier in this Chapter). A good sales agent will strive to form business relationships with as many distributors around the world as possible. If it has many potential buyers in each territory for a 'must have' picture, it can pitch them against each other to get the best price attainable. Unfortunately, most films are not so easy to sell, and the sales agent has to work hard promoting them at festivals and markets around the world. This costs money. A plush suite at Cannes can cost anything up to $100,000 for the week, and when coupled with the costs of putting on screenings (at $2,000 to $5,000 each), throwing the obligatory party (up to $100,000), and paying for A-list stars to fly over in their private jets to attend market premieres (anywhere up to $200,000), expenses quickly add up. These costs (known as '**Sales Expenses**'), although laid out initially by the sales agent, are recoupable immediately out of the proceeds of any sales made (although after the deduction of the sales agent's '**commission**'). This means that they are recoupable before the film's financiers (the first recouping financier, of course, usually being the gapping bank).

Deferred and non-deferred Commission

The level of commission payable to the sales agent depends on a number of factors. Often (but not always), commission on a US ('**Domestic**') sale will be a few percentage points less than on a sale to other territories. And there is usually no commission payable on pre-sales that the sales agent didn't itself arrange (eg. where the Producer organised some pre-sales to help in the financing of the film before appointing the sales agent). Typical commission rates will usually, however, be in the region of around 10% to 25%. If the sales agent has been instrumental in helping to source other finance for the film, has been involved in the packaging from the beginning, and/or has contributed creatively to the development and production of the film, it is likely to charge a higher commission (plus, usually, an executive producer's fee). Conversely, where the sales agent has been appointed later in the day to do nothing else but simply sell the picture, a typical deal might be to award it 15% on international sales, and maybe 10% on any Domestic sale.

Any bank providing gap finance will often try to insist that, whatever commission the sales agent is ultimately entitled to, it should not be permitted to actually get its hands on all its commission until the bank has been paid off in full. The bank will always want to paid back first (although after the sales agent's pre-agreed out-of-pocket expenses), and by taking as much of each dollar of income as possible. The sales agent may therefore be required to '**defer**' a proportion of its commission, and **claw** it **back** once the bank has recouped.

Let's take an example and run through the numbers. Say a bank providing the gap finance for the $10m *Project X* requires that the sales agent - who would otherwise be contractually entitled to 15% commission on all sales - takes only two thirds of its commission (ie. 10%) until such time as the bank has fully recouped. Ignoring any collection agent's fee (usually less than 1%), this will allow the bank to be paid back 90¢, instead of 85¢, out of each dollar received from the gross sales (ie. from '**Gross Receipts**'). The bank had put up 20% of the budget as gap finance, so the loan amount is $2m (ie. 20% of $10m), and this is the amount it will need to recoup, together with interest (let's say, of $0.5m), giving a total recoupable amount of $2.5m. Let us also suppose that the pre-agreed sales agent's expenses amount to $500k. The receipts from the first $555k of sales will therefore go straight to the sales agent and not the bank. This is because the sales agent first takes off its *non-deferred* commission (10% of $555k, being $55k), and the remaining $500k is taken as recoupment of its sales expenses. The bank then recoups its gap loan through the next $2.777m of sales. During this time, the sales agent takes off its 10% non-deferred commission ($277k), leaving exactly $2.5m for the bank. By this stage, the total sales made to date are $3.333m (the initial $555k plus $2.777m), the bank is 'out of the picture' having now fully recouped, and the sales agent's commission can therefore go up to 15%. However, it still has 5% *deferred* commission owed to it from the *previous* sales (equal to $167k, being 5% of the $3.333m), which it is entitled to recoup (or '**claw back**') next. So the next $196k in sales (Gross Receipts) goes straight to the sales agent again ($29k in commission - now increased to the full 15% - plus the $167k that had been deferred from the previous sales). Sales have now reached $3.529m (£3.333m plus $196k) and, from then on, the sales agent takes its standard 15%, and the rest gets distributed in accordance with the remainder of the Recoupment Waterfall.

Both the amount of commission that a sales agent takes, and the proportion that it is willing to defer, are dependent on a number of things, but mostly in relation

Unfortunately, most films are not so easy to sell, and the sales agent has to work hard promoting them at festivals and markets around the world

to how much involvement the sales agent has had in the project. One thing that is fairly standard is that it will only defer commission until the gapping bank is 'off', and not beyond that point. If a sales agent is required to defer too much, especially on a poor performing film that might not recoup more than the bank's finance, there is clearly little incentive for the sales agent to push for further sales whilst getting minimal commission. This is why a sales agent will rarely defer its entire commission, and will nearly always be allowed by the bank to take at least 5% on a non-deferred basis to keep it incentivised.

Commission on pre-sales

Another point to note is that where the sales agent is in fact entitled to commission on pre-sales (because it arranged them), it may not be able to take it from the sale proceeds if they are being used in full for the financing of the film. In this case, the sales agent will get its commission paid out of the next sales it does. In other words, it will recoup this commission in first position from future sales, even before the bank. It may, of course, be persuaded to defer part of this commission too, but most sales agents will try to resist that. All of this will, of course, be set out clearly in the Recoupment Schedule.

Sales Advances and 'International Distribution'

Sometimes, the sales agent itself will actually contribute finance to the film. This is typically known as a '**sales advance**' (although beware because this term is sometimes also used to mean an MG), and works in a similar way to gap finance. In fact it is very rare for there to be a sales advance and gap financing on the same film, as they will both want to be in first position on the Recoupment Schedule, and are both effectively advances against future sales. If there is no gap financier, the sales agent may agree - if it has the financial clout - to advance money against its first few sales, wherever they may be. By contributing finance to the production, the sales agent can normally negotiate for itself get a much better commission rate of up to 25% or even 30% on all future sales, depending on how much of the budget it puts forward.

> **By contributing finance to the production, the sales agent can normally negotiate for itself get a much better commission rate**

Most sales agents do not themselves have enough cash of their own to be investing in film production. Those that are willing to put up a sales advance usually do it through an arranged facility with their own bank. That bank will provide the sales agent with some form of credit line, but will usually ask similar questions to those asked by a gapping bank. There are also some specialist funds looking to step into the market of backing sales agents' advances.

One advantage to the sales agent (other than the obvious higher commission rate) is that it does not have to defer any commission behind a gapping bank. Another advantage is that, when advancing production finance, the sales agent is more likely to be granted the rights as an '**International Distributor**' rather than be appointed as a pure '**Agent**' (see Section on Presales and Distribution Deals, above). This means that, rather than just being appointed to sell the film on behalf of the Producer, the sales agent would take an actual licence of the distribution rights themselves, and then sublicense these around the world. Returning to our earlier Building analogy, this is similar to taking a lease on all floors and then subletting them, rather than acting as an estate agent and just arranging leases directly between the landlord and the tenants. Naturally, if the sales agent takes the rights itself, it will have more control over them and will not be obliged to seek as many approvals from the original rights owners when doing its deals. In fact, technically, a sales agent who takes the role of an international distributor is not really an 'agent' for anyone at all.

To recap, the amount an international distributor contributes to a budget is also similar to what would otherwise be provided by a gap financier; ie. usually under 20%. It will take its full commission (at a higher rate than if it hadn't put up the advance) from the first sales it makes, and will recoup its sales advance from the net amount left. Once it has recouped, it continues to take full commission on future sales, and the net (remainder) is distributed according to the agreed Recoupment Schedule. In some cases the advance may be against a limited number of territories (ie. the sales agent can only recoup the advance from sales to certain countries), although this obviously puts the agent in a conflict position as to where it focusses its sales efforts, and so should be avoided.

Negative Pick-ups

As '**Negative Pick-ups**' are becoming less common, and are not really a direct form of financing, there is no need to go into much detail about them for the purposes of this Handbook. However, a brief explanation may be useful.

A Negative Pick-up is an acquisition of all the rights to all territories, often by a Studio. If the Studio (or other prospective purchaser) likes the concept of a film but does not want to commit itself to financing or paying for it until after it has seen the finished article (or at least some attractive work-in-progress), it may agree to buy the whole film at a later date. After paying over the purchase price, it would effectively own the entire film (having 'picked up the negative' from the Producer), and can then exploit it throughout the world, by itself, and without having to pay anything back into the pot. The price it pays to the Producer for the film will hopefully exceed the cost of producing it, so that the Producer can pay back all the financiers with the proceeds of the sale, and (hopefully) keep any left-overs for him/herself and any other profit participants. The buyer will then go on to sell and/or distribute the film itself (if a Studio), or alternatively appoint a third party sales agent. Unless they managed to negotiate a continuing interest in the film after the acquisition, neither the Producer nor the original financiers will see any further income from it.

If a Producer has enters into a negative pick-up agreement with a reliable studio (or other purchaser), it may be able to discount the contract at a bank in order to access the funds for production purposes. The buyer will then pay the bank the sale price upon delivery of the finished, completed film. Of course, if s/he needs the money for production, the Producer should always check that the buyer's contract is 'bankable' before entering into the negative pick-up deal in the first place. Banks do not trust as many buyers as they used to, and will not discount any old deal, so the Producer could be left with an agreement to receive payment for a film on delivery, but without the cash to make it in the first place.

Bridging Finance

One type of finance that is often confused with gap finance is bridging finance. Whereas gap finance 'closes the gap' in the **budget** between the amount of money needed and the amount raised (usually up to about 20%), bridging finance closes the gap in **time** between the film's finance being needed, and actually being ready. This gap in time occurs if *all* the finance is agreed in principle for 100% of the budget of the film, but due to legal technicalities, the financiers

> Unless they managed to negotiate a continuing interest in the film after the acquisition, neither the Producer nor the original financiers will see any further income from it.

will not let go of their funds until all 'i's have been dotted and 't's crossed in the numerous contracts that need to be completed in order to effect the overall financing transaction. The concern here, for the Producer, is that s/he will not be able to begin on time and that cast, crew, locations, and weather opportunities, amongst other things, will be lost. This is where **Bridging Finance** comes into play. In assessing the risk, the bridging financier takes a view on how far down the line the relevant agreements have progressed, and how soon after the commencement of '**principal photography**' (when the bulk of the money is needed) they will be finalised and tied up. If it feels that there is little chance of the entire financing falling apart, it may lend the Producer the money s/he needs in order to start production before it's too late. Independent productions can be incredibly time-sensitive, especially when big-name stars offer to work at a very low fee, but only for a brief 'window' of time, so any delays in starting could kill the whole picture. As soon as the financing agreements are closed, the entire *production* finance will be made available for the film, and the bridging financier can be paid back whatever it has advanced to date (plus a hefty fee and huge interest!).

A Producer should try to avoid using bridging finance by making sure all financing agreements are tied up before the film actually goes into production. This is because bridging finance - if available at all - is very expensive (and usually not budgeted for), and the film will not be benefit from any Completion Bond until the main financing contracts have been agreed. Rates of interest charged can exceed standard bank rates several times over, with substantial penalty clauses if the loan is repaid late, although with a recent influx of new bridging financiers coming onto the scene, the competition may drive down these fees.

Bridging finance closes the gap in time between the film's finance being needed, and actually being ready

Venture Capital and Enterprise Investment

Venture capitalists make high-risk investments in growth businesses with a high potential return. They may be willing to put money into projects that other financiers, such as banks, would turn down due to the risk level. The venture capitalist typically becomes a shareholder in the production company (rather than taking an equity stake in the individual film(s)), and will often take on an executive role in forming long-term business strategy. **Business Angels** are venture capitalists that invest specifically in small and medium-sized enterprises (SME's), which can benefit from their knowledge and experience as well as their finance. They tend to be looking for businesses with at least a medium-term strategy, with a view to 'getting out' or 'exiting' within 3 to 5 years, either by way of a share sale (for much more than their original investment) or a floatation on a listed stock market (such as Nasdaq or AIM).

Many countries encourage private investment in new and small companies, and have set up specific tax incentives for doing so. In the UK, for example, the **Enterprise Investment Scheme** ('**EIS**') provides tax breaks to those who invest into qualifying companies. A qualifying individual who subscribes for new shares in a relevant company (which, in the UK, will be an unquoted public company), can deduct from their income tax liability an amount equal to 20% of the amount s/he has invested. There is a minimum and maximum subscription amount, and any individual is limited to investing in up to 30% of the company. The investors get a number of different tax breaks in relation to the amounts they invest, and to any profits or losses they make on a subsequent sale of the shares. The shares have to be held for a minimum period (currently 3 years), and the company has to spend most of the invested money within a limited timeframe. If the company goes in the wrong direction and the shares become totally worthless, there are further mitigating provisions to soften the blow to the investors, thereby reducing the risk of the investment.

Many other countries have similar regimes providing investors with significant tax benefits if they invest in start-up and relatively new companies. We do not go into detail in Part II of this Handbook on these schemes because the incentives are *not* film-specific. However, the general rule is that if the business or trade of the company receiving the investment is the production of films (which should be the case for a production company), it can accept the investment and then use it to pay for an entire film production (especially for lower budget films), thereby reducing the need to obtain and piece together other forms of finance for the picture.

The UK's **Enterprise Investment Scheme** has indeed been used by a number of film producers to finance their films. Although the idea behind the regime is to build sustainable businesses, a large number of companies set up under the scheme have only ever, and will only ever, produce one single film, most of which (it has to be said) are unprofitable. If you want to use the scheme for your production company, you should instruct professional accountants or similar advisers, who in addition to helping with putting together the legal structure and share subscription documents, often have a reservoir of potential investors to approach.

> **The investors get a number of different tax breaks in relation to the amounts they invest, and to any profits or losses they make on a subsequent sale of the shares.**

Some people buy listings of individuals who have already invested in similar types of film or business from specialised companies. These listings are quite expensive to buy and to mail, so it is very important to hit the targeted investors precisely, and to make sure the 'invitation' letter is properly and professionally drafted.

In the UK, the EIS is regulated by the Financial Services Authority (FSA), and a Public Limited Company (plc) must be created in order to launch one. A written proposal for the project (known as a 'prospectus') must be approved by lawyers, and potential investors must be contacted through official means, with all correspondence drafted in a specific way.

The cost of a launch is therefore quite high (between £30,000 to £60,000 depending on the complexity of the project and the scale of the mailing), and it is necessary to retain accountants or other specialists in order to make sure the enterprise is run within the requirements of the legislation. One drawback of EIS-type schemes is that the company will be dealing with hundreds of small investors, which can involve heavy spending on mailing, staff and the running of a well-oiled organisation. Also, the amount of capital raised via an EIS is never very high (compared to other available schemes), with £1m the maximum capital you can currently raise.

Of course, other money such as soft money, film equity and bank loans can be added to the share capital raised in order to reach the amount needed to produce a film (remember, much of the corporate money invested will need to go into the company's infrastructure). EIS is therefore an interesting scheme if you are doing a low- or no-budget feature (below £1m) or if you have other money already in place.

For further information, see the official website at www.hmrc.gov.uk/eis/eis-index.htm, or the EIS Association's site at www.eisa.org.uk.

Sponsorship and Product Placement

Sponsorship

Sponsorship generally involves a business paying a company in cash or in kind to promote the sponsor's products or services. In the film industry, for example, a drinks company may supply free beverages to the crew throughout the production period in return for a screen credit and/or some other form of exposure, perhaps on the film's marketing and promotional literature. In some cases a producer may also be able to secure a cash payment from a company in return for a screen credit. For example, Adrian J MacDowall's £3,000 BAFTA winning short *Who's My Favourite Girl* is said to have a sponsor credit list at the end of the film longer than that for the cast and crew. That said, for larger budgeted pictures in particular, the amount of time spent trying to identify and secure a sponsor may not be justified by the amount of money received in the deal.

There is room to be creative when conceiving a sponsorship deal, which can come from the most unlikely of sources. In fact, a Producer may have a better chance of securing a sponsorship deal with a company not directly related to the film industry; the perceived glamour might be a more effective pull to a company that is not trying to make its living within it. The sponsor will want to feel like it is going to get a real return for its donation, and this can make it difficult for an inexperienced Producer to attract sponsorship, unless s/he is a great marketeer. Some companies have specific sponsorship budgets as part of their advertising and/or marketing allowances. *First Light*, the initiative that brings production companies and young filmmakers together, has produced short guidelines on approaching sponsorship (see the excerpt at the end of this section below).

Some have predicted that, with possible revenues from TV and DVD sales diminishing (see *The Future of the Mainstream Financing Model*, below), we may return to large-scale sponsorship deals , similar to the original TV "soap opera" arrangements with washing detergent companies, to make up the gap. The suggestion is that a big-name company would put substantial money directly into a film in return for a front-end 'Presentation Credit', and it's logo on all packaging and advertising. Something like '*Kellogg's presents…*' or '*Cadbury's presents…*' at the beginning of the film and on the DVD case. The money would come out of the company's advertising budget, but unlike most advertising, would actually be recoupable from film income, and form part of the Recoupment Schedule. There would also be the opportunity to cross-promote by having tie-ins on the packaging of the sponsor's own products. Naturally, there would have to be some compatibility between the film and the sponsoring company.

Product Placement

Product placement has become a common source of finance for big-budget US productions, and is increasingly being used by independent Producers. It works in a similar way to sponsorship in that a company contributes to the production in cash or in kind. However, product placement specifically refers to the product, its brand name and/or logo, actually appearing on screen in the body of the film itself, rather than simply a credit for the company in the end-titles or marketing materials. As with sponsorship, it is more likely that an experienced producer working on a strong project will secure a product placement deal, because the advertiser will want to ensure as far as possible that the product will be seen by the general public. One notable deal in recent years is photographer Rankin's debut feature *The Lives of the Saints*, which was paid £1m by an Italian fashion company, in return for all the characters wearing the label's clothes.

Critics of this form of film finance question the involvement of advertisers in production and how much creative control they can exert over it, being anxious that filmmakers do not abandon artistic integrity to get the deal. How often do you see a drink or mobile phone in a modern film where the brand is so 'in-yer-face' that you momentarily lose focus on the film itself?

A very real problem for a director and editor is keeping the required product placement shots in the final cut if they coincide with scenes that they would otherwise choose to cut out. The brand owner will usually specify in its contract a minimum number of seconds or minutes, and sometimes even maximum intervals, for when the product must be clearly visible on screen.

Another important factor, when considering product placement, is how it might affect a television distribution deal. Most broadcasters have rules about advertising, and there is sometimes a very fine line between product placement and full-on advertising. In the UK, for example, the Independent Television Commission (now succeeded by OfCom) produced comprehensive guidelines (*The ITC Code of Programme Sponsorship*, first issued in Autumn 2000 but since updated) on product placement and advertising within television programmes and broadcast films. Although most of the guidelines concern television production, the regulations are applicable to films acquired for television broadcast, although the stipulations are a little more flexible. The full regulations can be accessed and downloaded from the OfCom web site (www.ofcom.org.uk).

'Businesses tend to sponsor arts activities to develop their corporate image in three ways: their relationship with their own employees, their relationship with other companies, and their relationship with their local community. Sponsorship is generally part of a wider marketing strategy and most companies won't sponsor you simply because you are deserving. You should approach potential sponsors with a sense of what you may be able to offer them, of how your film project will help their profile in the community. Sponsorship can be a time-consuming process, often for relatively small amounts of money, which are 'one-offs', so it may be best to focus your energy on getting to understand public funding, rather than pinning all your hopes on private sources. If you do find a sponsor who has never sponsored the arts before, it may be possible to get matching funds from Arts & Business'.

The Future of the Mainstream Financing Model

The Tangling of the Web
No discussion about the future of the financing 'model' is complete - or should even start - without serious thought being given to the impending changes from the growing impact of the internet. Not just from the perspective of the end-user's experience, but also the implications for distribution methods, real-time transfer of money, sources of production finance, piracy and so-on. It is true that no-one can unequivocally proclaim through a crystal ball exactly how the business will be run in ten years time. But what is clear is that the various 'possibilities' thrown up by the internet that everyone was hypothesising about five years ago have now

> A very real problem for a director and editor is keeping the required product placement shots in the final cut if they coincide with scenes that they would otherwise choose to cut out.

been replaced by 'probabilities'. At the numerous over-priced seminars regularly addressed by top-brass industry executives discussing forthcoming issues, the phrase 'This is how things could change' has definitely switched to 'This is what we are currently planning and testing'.

Chapter 4 (below) provides a full discussion of the impact of the web on filmmaking, financing, marketing and distribution. For now, though, we will look specifically at how the finance models discussed earlier in this Chapter might be affected by developments over the next few years. Of course, nothing in this section should be read as gospel as no-one knows for sure precisely how things will turn out. But there are some serious issues being raised right now that need to be addressed imminently if independent films are to continue being funded at the budget levels we are currently witnessing.

The key question to be addressed is: If, today, an independent film is typically funded predominantly from **soft money**, **equity**, **pre-sales** and **gap**, how is that likely to change? The answer simply depends on the extent to which these elements are sensitive to current developments in technology and, in particular, internet use.

First, soft money tends to be linked to the *location* in which the production finance is spent, so its availability is not directly affected by technological advancement. Equity is invested with a view to *profit*, ie. the excess of income over the repayable costs of production. In principle, an investor will not mind how this income is received (via new technologies or otherwise), so long as there is a surplus in which to share. If s/he believes that, commercially, the project is likely to turn a profit, s/he will invest, period. Gap finance is based on the risk that sales income will reach certain minimum levels so, if the structure of film sales doesn't change, neither will gap financing (all other things being equal). Which leaves us with the sales themselves.

> **For those films that will continue to require pre-sales as part of their production financing there are some pretty harsh realities hiding just around the corner**

As illustrated earlier, sales are territorial acquisitions of distribution rights, and (in the form of pre-sales) can typically provide between 10% and 60% of a budget. And this, in our view, is where the current financing model faces a serious potential clash with the future. If a film can be financed without the need for territorial pre-sales, either through alternative traditional means or via new technologies (see, for example, Chapter 4 below), then there isn't necessarily a problem, as the finance plan will not be affected by any changes to the way pre-sales work. However, for those films that will continue to require pre-sales as part of their production financing (remember, a bank, fund or other financier might want to see pre-sales in place to demonstrate the project's commerciality), there are some pretty harsh realities hiding just around the corner relating to the established territorial pre-sale structure.

The key word here is 'territorial'. A distributor puts up a certain amount of money based on how much it thinks it can make in its own territory. However, the internet, by its very nature, is not categorised on a territory-by-territory basis. So if the future *is* all about the web, it is likely to have a huge impact on a) the structure of distribution deals, b) thereby, the value of sales advances (MGs), and c) in turn, the contribution of pre-sales to the budget. The web is potentially a major spanner in the works.

MGs today are calculated with reference to anticipated earnings (see above), primarily from theatrical, TV, and DVD (video) exploitation. Distributors can forecast how much they think they will make during their licence period from TV broadcasts, video rentals and sell-through, cinema exhibition and the like, and decide how much they are willing to advance against it. But if these formats (or some of them) are to undergo wholesale change, then so will the income derived from them. Which leads us to the next question: What formats will be available for the distributor to sell in its territory, how much will it get for them, and how (and when) will it get paid. But before speculating about how much income the distributor will get from where, we should consider how the end-user will in fact be viewing the product where s/he will get it from, and how much (and when) s/he is likely to pay for it.

Split Screens - only two valuable formats?

Taking the film industry as a whole, the current school of thought gaining ground the quickest is based on a 2-format model. The idea is that in future, the general public will think of film-watching in one of only two ways, being on a **large** screen, or on a **little** screen. Conceptually, they will distinguish between, on the one hand, watching a film in public with dozens (or hundreds) of other people laughing, crying, and screaming alongside them and, on the other hand, watching it in private, either alone or in the presence of a few family members or friends. The former could be called the '**big screen experience**' with an 'event' feel to it, and the latter the '**small screen experience**'.

> in future, the general public will think of film-watching in one of only two ways, being on a large screen, or on a little screen

Commentators argue that the big screen, or cinematic, experience is here to stay, despite (or even because of) technological advances, and the statistics, at least so far, seem to back this up. On the whole, cinema attendances seem to be fairly stable, notwithstanding a few countries bucking the trend by experiencing significant short- or medium-term drops or rises. But there appears to be no wholesale desertion of the movie theaters, and no earth-shattering worldwide increase either. And this pattern looks to remain fairly steady, at least under current forecasts.

The cinema's robustness as an entertainment option might, in Economics terms, be part-explained by the fact that a trip to the cinema can display certain '**Geffen good**' characteristics. This means that, for some people, should their income drop, they are actually *more* likely to go to the movies instead of, perhaps an expensive meal out or a visit to the live theatre. Conversely, spending on a 'normal' (rather than Geffen) good would tend to *fall* as income decreases, but the cinema (like the humble potato) bucks this trend, certainly for those who are fairly well-off to start. On the other hand, for those in lower income brackets, a *rise* (rather than fall) in earnings will increase the chances of a trip to the movies, as the cinema becomes a more affordable option, when they might otherwise stay in to watch a video or participate in other low-cost entertainment activities. The cinema thereby behaves more like a 'normal' good for them. These two phenomena, when combined, make cinema-going a fairly tough animal with higher than normal chances of survival in most economic circumstances.

In *non*-Economics terms, people simply enjoy going out to the movies, and supposedly always will. It's a different experience to watching live theatre, and there are not many new technological inventions which are likely to compete with the atmosphere and tradition of the 'big screen experience'.

On the other hand, the viewing of films on other formats seems to have a very different future. At present, the choices are watching on television (whether paid for or free, scheduled or on-demand), on DVD / video (rented or owned), on the internet (downloading or live streaming), on mobile phones and, increasingly, on handheld gaming consoles (HGCs). It seems widely accepted that all these formats will, over the next few years, 'converge' - probably eventually into just one, single format. Conceptually, a viewer will not distinguish between watching a movie through any of the above means. The suggestion is that s/he will download a movie on-demand via the internet, and then decide whether to watch it on a fixed screen or on the move, either immediately (streaming) or at a later date (downloading). This assumes that films will not spontaneously combust after a period of time (replicating the current 'rental market'), although with current technology, that option shouldn't be totally ruled out. So after purchasing a film one morning, say, the viewer should - at the press of a button - be able to switch from viewing it over breakfast on a home entertainment system (the large screen in the dining/living room) to some form of mobile device (a hybrid of today's mobile phone, PDA, MP3 player and HGC) whilst travelling to work. Then, on reaching the office, a flick of another switch and the film 'jumps' to the computer screen so s/he can watch the ending during lunch-break. In the viewer's mind, all of these are the same 'small-screen experience', and a single price should be paid for the right to watch - perhaps for only a limited period of time - on any or all of these devices. The purchase itself would take place either wirelessly (perhaps through a mobile network) or via an internet download, but the viewer will not distinguish between these options when it comes to paying the purchase price and then viewing the movie. All this technology is already with us ('Blue-tooth' being one example of a wireless switching from one device to another); it's just a question of rolling out the products to the consumer market at sensible speeds and prices, and that should take just a few years to achieve. To summarise, a 2-format theory would suggest that, conceptually, people will consider the right to watch a movie anywhere in private - as opposed to on the big screen - as a single product, and will therefore pay a single price.

The important thing to note here is that at no stage does the viewer watch a 'TV channel' (paid or free), or hire or buy a hard copy of the film, such as a video or DVD. This means that, if the entire public does end up watching movies in this way, there will be no market for TV or DVD sales as we know it, and distributors buying film distribution rights in the way they do today will not be able to make local sub-sales of those rights. It follows that format-to-format '**holdback windows**' would become instantly confined to history. In fact, if you take the 2-format approach to its logical conclusion, as the big-screen and small-screen experiences themselves are considered different products, they do not actually compete with each other, and so 'day-and-date' (ie. simultaneous) releasing across both formats would become the norm.

The only 'territorial' rights a distributor would buy would therefore be *theatrical* and so, if **internet rights** (ie. the right to transmit content online, through the web) are not acquired by these distributors because they cannot be split territorially, the value of territorial MGs will drastically decrease. Where film rights are sold on a pre-sale basis, as an element of the production financing, this would clearly leave a huge hole in the budget as MGs plummet.

The Need to Sell Internet Rights
It follows that, in order for rights pre-sales to maintain their current levels of contribution towards production finance (and assuming theatrical receipts don't miraculously increase so much that they cover the deficit from loss of TV and DVD revenues), either more theatrical-only presales need to be made - to make up for the loss in the TV and DVD element - or some element of internet rights might also have to be pre-sold. Pre-selling more of the world theatrically is not necessarily a huge problem if recoupment for other financiers - and a decent profit - can be expected from income resulting from subsequent sales of internet rights.

Of course, returning to large-scale 'soap'-type sponsorship is another option (see section on *Sponsorship,* above), but for now we will concentrate on the internet issue.

Note that the licensing of internet rights is a fundamental legal requirement for the purchase of films to be made online. The problem is that internet rights, by their very nature, are *not* territorial, and so cannot be sold to territory-based distributors in the traditional way. Ironically for many existing films, internet rights have in fact been sold to distributors, but on condition that they may only be exploited when sufficient, reliable and industry-acceptable geographical safeguards are in place, so as to ensure each distributor cannot sell to an end-user outside its granted territory. Despite inordinate amounts of money being thrown at creating this type of technology, in truth the internet is no closer now to having hack-free geographical safeguards as it was when these contractual clauses first started appearing in the late '90s. And if territorial exclusivity is not a realistic option (some still argue it is only a matter of time before the technology will arrive - we'll see if they are right), a traditional territorial distributor is unlikely to be the purchaser of internet rights in the future.

> **Does it mean that internet rights can only be sold in one go on a worldwide basis?**

This throws up a few more questions. Does it mean that internet rights can only be sold in one go on a worldwide basis? If so, who would buy them? Could a *pre*-sale of internet rights be possible, to help finance the film? In order to address these issues, it's necessary to consider how a buyer itself would make money. If it buys these internet rights, it needs to know that it can recoup the purchase price, and turn a profit. It must therefore understand how - in practice - it can exploit these rights once it purchases them. To consider this, we need to start by looking at the other end of the supply chain, and working our way up to the Producer see how the business model might work.

Websites as the End-User's Point-of-Sale

First and foremost, we have to presume that the future model relies on consumers legally purchasing films online, as the alternative would look like a pretty grim prospect indeed. In this regard, a quick comparison with the music industry over the last few years should present a stark warning. For now, though, we won't address *how* the industry - through encryption software or otherwise - will prevent a similar collapse in revenues from illegal acquisition of content (again, see Chapter 4, below). But to provide any financial model for the future, the assumption has to be that there *will* be a consumer market for acquiring films at a price. Besides, a Producer, having spent substantial sums in getting his/her film made, cannot receive income to repay the financiers and make a profit unless the public ultimately forks out cash to watch the film. It's all well and good saying 'But I can get my film to millions of viewers through Google Video', but if they're not paying to watch it, and they are effectively replacing your TV and DVD revenues, how are you going to fund your $10m film in the first place, or repay any financiers who were mad enough to give you the cash?

So we assume that the end-user, the consumer, will be prepared to pay a certain amount to buy the film for his/her small-screen experience. Unless mobile phone networks' bandwidth increases dramatically, and the associated costs to users reduced even more significantly, the initial download of a movie is likely to be via the internet rather than straight to mobile. In other words, films will be bought online. This also means, of course, that they must be priced in such a way so that the prospective viewer isn't enticed to obtain an illegal copy for free instead. Current research suggests that the average net user in Europe and North America would choose to pay approximately $2 online for a music album rather than download it illegally, but at any higher price, s/he is more likely to download it for free from an illegal site. Accordingly, the price of mainstream albums has continued to fall towards these levels, and it appears that an equilibrium is not far off. According to some reports, by the end of 2005, for the first time, more albums (not yet singles) were being downloaded from the net legally for a price than illegally for free , although track-by-track buying may make album sales obselete very soon.

Let's suggest, for argument's sake, that the 'natural' market price to watch or own a feature film turns out in due course to be $3 (some say it will be even lower than this, but it doesn't look likely to remain above $5 for many more years). This means that $3 would be the maximum amount a consumer would typically be prepared to pay to buy the film, and so it follows that this can be taken as the price that films will sell for at the point-of-sale. It might not sound too much, but with substantially less distribution costs involved than for TV broadcast and DVD manufacture, a larger proportion of the end-user's payment should end up in the Producer's collection account. Plus the fact that, at the right price, more people might buy (although not necessarily watch) the small-screen experience than do today.

So who gets the $3? As far as the end user is concerned, s/he will pay the website from whom s/he is buying the movie. This will be the site(s) s/he feels most comfortable visiting and purchasing from, which in turn will depend on a number of factors, including the site's branding, the ability to search for films that might appeal (by genre, stars, director, length, language, even price), download speed and, importantly, the general ease of use. This doesn't necessarily mean the site with the biggest size of library will succeed. Research shows that a prospective viewer will tend to use a site where s/he can quickly and easily find a film to match his/her mood, price, or other personal requirements.

> **As far as the end user is concerned, s/he will pay the website from whom s/he is buying the movie. This will be the site(s) s/he feels most comfortable visiting and purchasing from**

These popular consumer 'film sale' websites, which we will call '**filmsites**', may be run by established brands in movie retail (such as Blockbuster, HMV and Virgin), 'refocused' TV film-channel brands (such as IFC, HBO, Showtime, and FilmFour), mainstream TV channels (ABC, Fox, BBC, MTV, Sky, Channel 4), dedicated arms of studios (Warner, Sony, Fox, Disney, etc), general retailers (K-Mart, Wal-Mart, Tesco), current online content sellers (Real.com, Amazon, emusic.com), internet community sites (Orkut, MySpace, bebo), film-specific websites (IMDb, RottenTomatoes, aintitcoolnews.com), video sites (Revver, Blip.tv, iFilm, Youtube), standalone players (iTunes, Joost, Miro), internet service providers (NTL, AOL, BT), web portals (Google, Yahoo, MSN), or new emerging site brands that simply manage to get the marketing right. They may also, for those viewers who prefer to be 'told' what to watch, 'stream' content to paying subscribers in a similar way to current-day television channels.

What is abundantly clear, however, is that no Producer will want to grant any one of these filmsites a totally exclusive right to sell his/her movie, as s/he will almost certainly lose end-user sales from the numerous other competing sites. In fact, s/he will probably want his/her movie available to buy from as many sites as possible in order to maximise sales. So why would any filmsite pay up-front (ie. pre-buy) for the right to sell a movie to the public? If it is clear that the seller (Producer) wants the product on as many websites as possible, would market forces really create competition amongst filmsites or encourage them to scramble to pay money up-front in return for the 'privilege' to sell the movie? Further, with technology allowing each $3 paid by the end-user automatically to be transferred electronically to those entitled to it, the risk element of pre-buying is taken out of the equation. The ultimate income payable to the Producer can be calculated directly with the reference to the number of actual purchases, and paid over in real time (at the exact point the end-user buys the film).

Who would pay an MG?

However, Producers might argue that, with the loss of TV and DVD revenues in pre-sales, they *need* an up-front payment for internet rights to put towards production costs. Their argument would simply be 'If you want it, you have to pay for it'. One option might be to offer certain filmsites exclusivity after all, but only for a limited time period (from initial release). In other words, Site XYZ could pay the producer an MG of $XXX in return for the exclusive right to sell the film online for a limited period, maybe a week or two, or perhaps a day or even just an hour. Only then would the film be released to all the other filmsites (by which time the pirates will probably have got hold of it anyway!). Site XYZ would have to estimate how much it thinks it will make during the exclusivity period in order to calculate how much it is willing to pay for the MG (as distributors similarly do today). This would probably depend on the negotiation of an agreed 'split' of the consumer's $3, with this split being dressed up as either a **royalty** payable to the Producer (with the filmsite keeping the rest), or a **commission** being retained by the filmsite (with the remainder being paid over to the Producer). Only market forces will determine whether this kind of pre-sale would generate a high enough MG to fill the production financing vacuum. The length of the exclusivity period would probably be a determining factor (but marketing policies and the risk of piracy might dictate a natural limit to this), as will any premium the filmsite might be able to charge the end-user during the exclusivity period. There is also the question of whether a particular filmsite's contract will be sufficiently bankable (ie. reliable enough for a bank to discount it) in order to get the film made in the first place.

Although territorial exclusivity is unlikely to be a realistic option , it might be possible to enhance revenues by pre-selling to different filmsites on a language-by-language basis. In other words, if Site XYZ (an English-language filmsite) pays for the exclusive right to market the film in English for the first week of release, Site ABC could be given the equivalent right concurrently to market it exclusively in French. This would allow more than one filmsite to sell the film during the exclusivity period, but each to a different customer base, in a similar way to the territorial distribution model in use today. The reference to language would more likely to refer to that used on the filmsite rather than the language of the film itself, as any one filmsite may have the film available for purchase in more than one dubbed language, but its market would be defined by the language (be it English, French, German, Japanese, etc) of its interface with the public.

Middlemen and a New Breed of Buyer

Under this 2-format scenario, the traditional sales agent would still sell to territorial theatrical buyers for the big screen experience but, in relation to selling the small-screen experience, it would have to familiarise itself with a whole new breed of buyer. These buyers would represent the various filmsites, and sales agents will need to create new relationships and networks, possibly with output deals, first-look deals, alliances and so on. It may be that a new type of '**middleman**' materialises specialising in having all the relevant filmsite contacts and relationships, and is appointed specifically to make internet rights sales to the filmsites. These middlemen could be seen as pseudo-distributors, taking a fee or commission for their services. They might be appointed by the lead sales agent (as a kind of sub-agent), or even by the Producer directly, effectively meaning there are two sales agents, for big and small screen rights respectively. It may even be

> It might be possible to enhance revenues by pre-selling to different filmsites on a language-by-language basis

that these distributors themselves put up the MG in return for the right to make sales to filmsites. They would then keep any income received from such sales until the MG is recouped. In particular, if it turns out that giving exclusivity periods to certain filmsites just doesn't work, it might be that these 'middlemen' distributors simply agree splits with *all* the filmsites, and calculate the MG based on projected income from those splits. In other words, if the end-user's $3 is to be divided (say) $1 to the filmsite and $2 paid over to the distributor, the distributor might pay the Producer an MG based on how many $2s it thinks it will ultimately receive as end-user purchases of the completed film take place. Remember, money moves on the web in 'real-time' these days, so payment terms, accounting procedures and auditing become much easier. Some have even suggested that, with technology, these middlemen might even turn out to be not much more than a piece of software, into which you submit your film, and it automatically distributes it to all the relevant film sites and collects money on your behalf. Others have suggested that, ultimately, end-users will simply refuse to pay for online content at all, and income will instead come solely from a share of advertiser revenue on the filmsites.

The Future is Nigh

All this still leaves open a number of questions, not least who is responsible (and who pays) for marketing and advertising the film on the web, who these new middlemen would be (specialist arms of existing sales agents, studios and/or distributors?), and what happens to the internet rights to existing films already 'sold' on a territory basis (would they all be bought back for a dollar - because they're currently worthless - and then resold?).

All of the above is really mere speculation, but most of these technologies are actually already in place

Of course, all of the above is really mere speculation, but most of these technologies are actually already in place, money already moves on the web in real time, movies are already available to end-users online for a fee, and internet rights are already being valued and their ownership negotiated hardball in sales contracts. If you also consider that, today, mobile phones are capable of 'playing' entire feature films, TV advertising revenue is dropping like a lead balloon, and DVD sales have already peaked in many countries, perhaps the future is not so far away after all. Any distributor buying rights these days for 7 to 15 years *must* think seriously about these internet issues, as they will clearly have a huge impact on the distributor's ability to receive income from traditional sources (TV, DVD, etc) well before the expiry of the distribution contracts. Likewise, any Producer reading this should already be considering the impact of internet rights on the ability to finance for his/her next film.

Mira Nair, Vanity Fair
Working with a studio

After winning the Golden Lion at Berlin for Monsoon Wedding, Mira Nair returned to the studio system for the first time since The Perez Family to produce a big budget adaptation of William Makepeace Thackeray's Vanity Fair with Reese Witherspoon.

How did you become involved in this project?
It was an extraordinary coincidence, really, because I have loved this novel since I was 16 years old. But I had no hankering to make it into a film, and I usually originate my own films, I don't look for work. The studio had Monsoon Wedding in distribution and it was a big hit for them, and they simply offered me their best, or biggest, next thing. They didn't know that I loved this novel, and I pretty much said yes instantly.

You had quite a bad experience with a studio when you made The Perez Family?
It was a terrible experience.

Did it make you wary of working within the studio system?
It depends entirely on who you work with, you know? Vanity Fair is also a studio film and it's been a completely respectful and wonderful experience, because they came to me for my sensibility. I gave them my sensibility and they were dazzled -- that is the word they used – by it. You know, they let me be. Not so with Mr Samuel Goldwyn, who saw the piece [The Perez Family] and, you know, Four Weddings and a Funeral was out that year, and basically when they tested Perez in America, the results were so high and fantastic that he began to think that maybe it will be even better if it's just a total comedy. So the problem was that my film was this rhythm of memory and exile, which was tragic-comic, like the Cubans are, and theirs was, 'It's reading funny, let's go for the broad comedy.' That's where the fight began. It's very sad because even if you think you're winning, if you tamper with the essential rhythm of a picture, you're lost. So I lost.

What did you learn from that?
Just to trust myself even more and to rely on myself even more. I am an independent filmmaker and an independent producer as well, I produce my own films, so I have never looked to be on any A-list. To me the reason I do what I do is to do what I do, you know what I mean? [Laughs] That's the privilege, rather than wanting to be on an A-list.

Were you involved in producing Vanity Fair?
Yes. The main producer on it was Lydia Dean Pilcher, with whom I have done everything since Mississippi Masala. We work very closely. Like in this movie, Vanity Fair, I can't even believe it myself, but we shot this in 55 days. It's a huge movie, you know, and the only way we can do that is to organise the production, that is extraordinarily organised, which is how I do my own movies. You know, cutting my cloth to size, but making you believe I have all the cloth in the world. That's the trick and that's what I do with my producing partner. I have to plan it very, very carefully otherwise it doesn't look as it looks.

Stephen Applebaum

Jacqueline Swanson, *Checkout Girl*
Product placement

Rupert Grave's Checkout Girl, staring Pauline Quirk, is a comedy short set in a supermarket. Producer Jacqueline Swanson spent a year raising almost £25,000 in product placement fees, as well as stocking an entire supermarket with produce.

We were first scheduled to shoot in December of 1998 on an RAF base leased to the US Airforce. The whole place was in the process of being decommissioned but the base commissary (the supermarket) was still open and they were very happy for us to use it as our set over their three-day weekends. About five weeks before we were scheduled to shoot I got a call saying that the LA press office were unable to let us continue. Films shot on US bases need to promote the US armed forces and it's recruitment. In all fairness everyone at the base felt terrible that we had gone so far down the line without being aware of the protocol but in the military I guess rules are rules and we were, unfortunately in breach of them. No amount of script doctoring was going to make us fit their criteria.

After having to call everyone to cancel the shoot I hid under my duvet for a week before resurfacing to reconsider our position. I reckoned the budget was going to go up by another £25,000 if we were going to even consider building a supermarket. To my surprise when I consulted the key cast and crew they all wanted to continue with the project and were happy to re-discuss their fees further down the line should it be necessary. It would be inappropriate for me to discuss the actual final fees but let's just say that as filmmakers Rupert and I are totally indebted to everyone who worked on the film from our runners and local extras right up to the HoDs and main cast. In a perverse way the production was so big and had so much support I did not really have the option of giving up, although we often felt that we really had bitten off too much.

Because of Pauline's schedule her next available slot was going to be December 1999 which gave me just under a year to raise the rest of the budget. We had already received production funding from Southern Arts (Rupert was from Southampton) who also then came through with post production funding. I had a very good friend at Saatchi & Saatchi who had put the script forward to a couple of account directors with some positive but ultimately non-committal feedback. Product placement was a fairly uncharted territory at that point. However, when Sunny Delight was about to launch in the UK they had generous budgets and more scope for taking risks. It was pretty much left to me to structure the deal and suggest a fee. Although it was a significant amount for the production it really was not a big commitment for the agency so the whole process was fairly straightforward. I had suggested a four-tier payment structure; a sum on first day of photography, another on completion of shoot, a third on sale to a UK broadcaster and the final installment on sale to a US broadcaster or Trans Atlantic in-flight entertainment programme. We also received product placement monies from HP Beans. That was also fairly straightforward. I explained to them how much the set was costing to build and asked them for a portion of the costs up front. They were happy with my proposal in the knowledge that their product was going to 'colour' the film rather than the distinctive colour of their main competitors.

Tom Fogg

Roy Disney,
Director Emeritus, Walt Disney Corp, the Studio

The secret of Disney's success? — Great story telling I think. Great stories, great characters, great music — it's a lot of things, music is an amazing part of people's memories of film. When you play 'when you wish upon a star' it conjures up a whole movie for you and The Lion King is like that as well. We have such a tremendous tradition of what was done in the past, (uncle) Walt kinda looks over our shoulder and says 'this is what you have to live up to — be this good, be this good.'

I like comedy. I like to go into a theatre and sit back and relax, not to have too many heavy social messages crammed down my throat and if so I'd like to be entertained by that too. I'd like to understand that if people have problems that they have funny sides and sad sides, I want a picture with memorable characters in. I find a lot of disaster movies, shoot-em-ups and exploding planet movies don't really work that way for me, I'd rather be entertained by something small and charming than by someone blowing up the world — unless it's funny!

I found my way into the business by way of nature movies — turned out to be the greatest film school you could have gone to. We'd go out with a 16mm camera and an endless supply of film and literally shoot pictures of animals for months and months throughout the seasons. Many of the movies involved the birth and growing up of different animals, we'd take that back to the studio and they'd have to try to make a story out of it. The craft of story telling was implicit in everything we did.

www.netribution.co.uk/2/content/view/130/35/

Janey de Nordwall *Silver Films*

Business angels

Janey de Nordwall founded Silver Film in 1996, and in 2000 decided to focus the company solely on film production. She approached the North West Business Angel Network – Techinvest – and sold a percentage of her company to raise capital to part-finance two shorts – About a Girl and Jump - and a relocation to London. About A Girl was a runaway success for her and director Brian Percival, nabbing the BAFTA for Best short in 2002 and winning first prize in Turner Classic Movies short film award.

Few people really understand business angels. Back in 2000 I did my first presentation to 70 angels in the same room. They were not investing in the films, they were investing in the company – I pitched doing a slate of three short films as a research and development process to build awareness of Silver Films in the industry and build relationships with creative talent, ahead of producing features.

I also saw making shorts as the route to learning about producing films. I already knew how to produce, production manage and build a budget and so forth from my time doing promos, but realised very quickly how different film is to commercials. I wanted to see if I could pick up on a script that I believed in and take it forward. When I sent the About A Girl script to people in the industry, they all said the same thing 'you don't want to make that, it'll do you no good, you want to make a comedy'. I had to sit back and think am I right, are they wrong, and after a while I decided 'this is what I believe in and want to move forward with'. What I had wanted to learn as a producer was how to trust my instinct, and the success of About A Girl proved to me, and the industry, that I could.

My angels are advisors as well as investors, they offer help with the business, planning, legal issues and so forth - we have monthly board meetings – they're there for the long haul, and may not get a return on investment in the next five or six years. At the end of my presentation to the business angel network I said, 'this is long term, high risk, but potentially high return' and three guys came along and said lets go for it. One in Manchester, one in London and one in Chicago. They all reinvested for more money, and I'm currently looking to a fourth investor with a bigger lump for development on the feature slate.

If you can get a slate of films together it allows the investors choice on what they want to put their money into. They may dislike foreign films for example so its nice to have a range of films on your slate, there's also slate funding out there through the Film Council and other organisations that appreciate the slate over the individual film. It adds to the longevity of production companies and of the industry. It lets people hedge their bets! Out of five films maybe one will be OK. I had three shorts slated and made just two of them: *About a Girl*, which cost £35,000 and *Jump*, which cost £55,000. My first year at Silver Films, which included moving from Manchester to London, was funded by £100,000 of investment – a mixture of money from selling equity in the company to the angels, matched by the same amount from North West Vision, my own money, sponsorship and product placement cash.

The sponsorship and product placement came from my contacts in the gaming industry. Sponsorship was from 3DO, who were making a new PR marketing campaign about how gaming crosses over so many mediums, ie. that gamers are interested in sport, fashion and film. The campaign was that they are supporters of new talent in the industry, they sponsored someone in music, fashion and film and gave us £10,000 in return for a logo at the end of Jump and use of us as marketing on the website and so forth. And they gave £2,000 for the premiere at Planet Hollywood. For product placement, we sold ad space to games that were coming out around the time of the film's premiere so we had Final Fantasy 9 on a t-shirt in a bus for £1,000.

About A Girl was winning awards at the same time as Yousaf Ali Khan's *Skin Deep*, which got 3rd in TCM, was a BAFTA nominee and Kodak award winner. Yousaf and myself looked at working on a feature project together, and decided to test the relationship by making a short film– *Talking With Angels*, made in Salford with much of the 80 cast and crew sourced from locals. It cost about £50,000 just to shoot and the funding on it is very different to the other two shorts: we got money from the LFVDA, from North West Vision, and some cash from Fox SearchLab which finances shorts. SearchLab is the little sister of Fox Searchlight, with whom we have a first look deal. I began discussions with them after *About A Girl* was the only British short to be accepted into Sundance. I then met up with them in LA whist I was on the Inside Pictures course. They were great and said do it in your own timescale, we want to work with you, they didn't want to read the script, they just trusted my instinct. We got funding also from B3 Projects who give money for ethnic minority work and are going to get involved in the distribution and marketing. We've also, unusually, got regional government cash, because we are making a big difference to the Salford community by using locals. There's money from Salford Council, Salford University, the Regeneration and Employment Agencies and the Cornerstone Community centre. Mike Knowles who runs the Northern Film Network, is my co-producer on this and helped set that up as he's based in Manchester still.

I'm getting my feature slate together. While it's very important to have a slate I only want to work on films that I believe in. I just go for things that turn me on – my films tend to be very social issue films, very personal, that have a message, that have social awareness – but not depressing regional drabness.

You get used to having that feeling of hitting walls. You're kind of living on the edge all the time, and there are these big highs and then these incredible lows when you don't want to have anything to do with this industry. I do get really down, in fact recently I was about to write the email saying I was about to quit the industry and go sit on a beach and plaid my hair – when you hit that sort of point you need to take some time out and think about what you're doing and what you want to achieve. The highs and lows are going to be a constant thing and you have to ask yourself, what do you want out of this? Is it kudos, is it awards, is it money? I want to achieve an emotion from an audience and that kind of makes it a lot easier than being motivated by money or fame.

NW / Tom Fogg

David Thompson
BBC Films

From Oscar winning *Iris* to the $100m grossing *Billy Elliot*, David Thompson has steered BBC Films through a string of critical and commercial successes. With a £10m annual budget for mainly co-productions, including Woody Allen's *Scoop* and *Match Point*, and the first film from Leonardo DiCaprio and kate Winslett since *Titanic*, BBC Films has become one of the UK's most active and inspiring producers.

What sort of skills are you looking for in the new producers you work with?
We're looking for a combination of skills which is hard to find because producers don't get many chances to make films. Sadly, producers get a chance to make one film and then not another one for a long time.

You need a combination of creative ability, ability to work with scripts, and an understanding of casting. You also need to be able to put deals together and run productions, so it's a very complex list of skills that are required which is not easy to achieve, except on the job. And that's the paradox and the challenge for the British film industry really.

Unless you've been working, say, in television, where you're acquiring many of the same skills, or up to a point, in commercials, it is very hard to learn on the job.

But you do need a big range of skills. You need tact, diplomacy, creativity, some vision, and a kind of mad, manic drive really. A manic belief in turning the impossible into the possible.

And generally the first time feature producers you've worked with, have they all come from a particular background?
No they come from all kinds of backgrounds; documentary, commercials, theatre, all kinds of worlds. I wouldn't say there was a particular way in, but I would say TV and commercials are really good as a way in. But also coming up through the production line - a lot of big first ADs or big script editors become producers. There's all different ways. Through the script editing route; through the production route; up from runner. No one way is better than the other. You also need to have also an understanding

of how the creative process works. Both the nuts and bolts and the creative process are really important.

At what stage should an indie producer approach BBC Films? How developed are you looking for projects to be?

You can come with an initial idea. We often get treatments, scripts; a mixture of things. There's no right or wrong. You can come early or late. Come early with a treatment if it's a really hot idea. If it's just 'lets do an adaptation of a classic book' and you've got no take on it then it's kind of pointless. But if you've got the rights, or nearly got the rights on a really interesting book, then that's worth coming to us. Or a really unusual idea - albeit in a short treatment form - then its still worth coming to us.

What kind of films is BBC Films looking to develop?

Well we do all kinds of film. If you look at our past range, from comedies to drama, strong drama like Iris, to uplifting films like Billy Elliot, to more gritty social films reflecting the many aspects of our culture like Bullet Boy, through to musical comedy, like Mrs Henderson, there's all kinds of films we are doing.

We're particularly looking for comedy, and particularly lighter, more uplifting films. They're the harder ones to find. Films that can play on BBC1. Ones that can really cross over and be hits. We have more drama, and so does the industry in general.

We're not looking to do horror. We would do spoof horror maybe, if it was the right kind of thing. Comedy, entertainment uplift, and some strong dramas but we're quite well stocked with strong dramas.

So the emphasis is on films that can cheer people up and make them feel better about themselves and the world. Which are harder to find. Which is not to say we're not only going to do those films. Of course not. The bulk of the films we do will be more on the edge, that's the truth of it.

But we've got a big range in the films that are up and coming. From Michael Winterbottoms new film Cock and Ball Story, to Danny Boyle's new film Millions, which is more of an uplifting family film. And we're still doing period films from time to time, but not so many.

I should rephrase that slightly, we are particularly looking for comedy.

How much is your commissioning strategy defined by programming for BBC channels?

We're trying to find more that will play on BBC1. In the past the bulk has been on BBC2, but we're trying to shift it a bit more so more of it will fit on BBC1. The bulk of it will probably still go on BBC2.

It is remarkable how much you achieve with the £10m budget

I must admit there is a kind of slight of hand and magic, a bit like the feeding of the five thousand with not many fishes and loaves. The truth is we do make our money go a long way because we gear up more money. In other words we co-produce so much. Everything we do, almost, is co-produced. A little seed money can go a long way. It's a big strain to get a film going on those terms. And it's harder and harder to do it. Us trying to put in a tiny bit of money into films where we still want to retain very strong editorial involvement. Which is always what we want to do. Even if we get more money we'll still have to make the money go a very long way, it's not suddenly going to be bread and jam tomorrow. It's still going to be a strain, because some of the money we get will only go to replace the tax funding that has dropped away. So it's not going to suddenly be all easy, but I hope it will be a little bit easier because right now it's very tough. Certainly we've got a very strong co-production team. And co-production, co-financing and partnership is at the heart of what we do. Almost every project we do is partnered. But that of course has its problems, because sometimes partners don't see eye to eye and the film suffers in that mix, because people take different views and the film ends up in a hole down the middle.

Much more straight forward if you're fully funding your own thing.

Do you fully fund anything?

Hardly ever. We sometimes regret we haven't. We very much regretted not fully funding My Summer of Love. But we couldn't do it, and very rarely can we do it. Can't remember the last film we fully funded, actually. It was a long time ago.

Last Resort was done on a £400,000 budget.

We did fully fund that. Often we are in the invidious position of where we have so little cash we end up selling off rights not necessarily in the way we want to just to get the film financed. So we weaken our own position in films, but because we only have £10m for the whole operation we have to do that. It doesn't involve us adopting the soundest commercial principles.

Billy Elliot was a classic example of that, if we had lots of money we could have fully financed the film and we'd be very rich by now. But there we are.

Do you come in at a certain stage as a co-producer. Are you usually first in?
We're often first in, we're usually first in, but we sometimes come in right at the end, We look for opportunities when things are fully developed, we're not adverse to that, particularly where people are looking for smaller sums. The bulk of things we do we developed ourselves, but we're not exclusive about that or precious about that. We'll take a good script from wherever it comes, even if we haven't developed it; more than happy to.

How many projects have you got in development at any one time?
We've got about 30 projects in active development, maybe a little more.

And how many will go into production?
Well in Hollywood it's one in a hundred. We'd like one in four to get off the ground at one stage or another. One in four, one in three, somewhere in between the two. That's quite a difficult thing to pull off. Because in the film industry it's not good enough just to have a good script, like it is in television where it will get made properly. You need a good script that will attract finance at that particular time, that will attract actors at that particular time. So what you need is many more good scripts that are ready to go.

It's not always the best script that tickles someone's fancy at a particular time. You need to have a lot of scripts ready. We'd be happy to get to a ratio of three to one, compared with Hollywood which is hundreds to one I think we do pretty well.

And do you see BBC Films moving into microbudget as some screen agencies are exploring?
We want to be in all the sectors. We want to do lower budget films and bigger budget films. I do think that many British films are far too expensive for what they are; unnecessarily expensive. And made in old fashioned ways. And we've been trying very much to pioneer new ways to make films. And the films that we've done with Dominic Savage, Francesca Josepf and Pawel Pawlikowski have been good examples of that. Working with different technology in different ways. But British indie films are far more expensive than American indie films, and that's not really sustainable in the long term.

And what do you think will be the key thing that changes that?
There won't be the money around any more. There won't be these tax breaks, it won't be so easy to do it. So we'll have to find ways to make films more cheaply.

Multi crewing, multi-tasking, all this stuff. Using different equipment; the equipment is getting cheaper all the time so the process should get easier. Michael Winterbottom has pioneered this, with In this World which was done with very small crews and new technology. There needs to be more of that going on.

With a new Director General, the culture seems more positive towards BBC Films
For years film at the BBC was quite an equivocal process. People weren't sure if they did or they didn't want it. Because it wasn't top of the agenda. But now the BBC has got right behind it and stated its commitment to backing British Films, and that's really good news. It makes it a much more positive environment to work in. We're very much part of the proposition for the charter renewal and that's obviously a good position to be in. We can offer something valuable to the British film industry and indeed the BBC.

Let me just say one more thing, which I think is really important. There will have to be more speculative script writing. I think that's the way to get started, I'm afraid. It happens much more in America. People can't hang around waiting to get a commission. Having said that, there is money for commissioning with all the money from the Film Council for development. But people will have to be more prepared to write spec scripts and do more work on spec, because that's how the industry works in the rest of the world.

Dirty Pretty Things was kind of a spec script. We didn't commission it in the first place; we got the script and then commissioned further drafts of it. We got that from Steve Knight who created Who Wants to be a Millionaire, but he hadn't been a writer before that, or not much. We got one before called the Theory of Flight that literally came through the post, for Ken Brannagh and Helena Bonham Carter.

To summarise, you just have to be slightly insane, totally driven, never give up and be prepared to suspend all disbelief to make a film, and push through and make your vision happen.

CHAPTER 4
The Internet

The Seventh Major

Traditional film studios are massive networks of people, resources, knowledge, creative products and screens. They have expertise in producing and packaging films and extensive relationships around the world and knowledge of local markets and audiences. Most importantly they have access to the significant sums required to produce and market a film at a high budget, and the output deals to ensure such films get seen. As discussed in Chapter 1, the big six studios: Sony, Universal, Disney, Fox, Warner Bros and Paramount together control the overwhelming majority of films screened, sold and broadcast. While recent years have seen a growth in the popularity of independent films, most of these have still been produced and released by the specialty divisions of the major studios.

In the same period, we have seen the gradual emergence, very loosely, of a seventh major studio-like power. It is neither owned by a single organisation or individual. It does not even have a manager. Rather it is a collection of tools, networks, information and communities which collectively could be said to be beginning to offer similar functions to a traditional vertically integrated studio. From script development, through funding, to crewing, management, procurement, communications, marketing and distribution, the Internet offers cheap, and effective tools. And of most interest to the independent producer, this 'studio' is neutral, largely meritocratic and completely global.

A writer in Wales can connect with a production team in Oslo, to produce a film shown at international festivals found via the web, and streamed from a service in California through a social network based in London to a viewer in Venezuela. While accessible capital and infrastructure is still currently a long way behind a traditional studio, these new connections between ideas, creative people and audiences, which aren't dependent on being based in LA or having access to a great local cinema, makes the spectrum of stories told far broader than ever before, something as exciting for audiences as for the independent filmmaker.

In this chapter we begin to explore the finance, marketing and distribution 'divisions' of this new 'studio' and how they can both help you fund your film and connect with an audience, who sometimes - as two interviews illustrate - are the people providing the finance. We also look at some of the new ideas — including Cluetrain, the Longtail, the Wisdom of Crowds, Open Source and Creative Commons — which are driving 'Web 2.0', the term currently used to describe the internet's evolution from publishing platform to open operating system.

> **'Just as the spread of literacy in the late middle ages disenfranchised old power structures and led to the flowering of the renaissance, it's been the ability of individuals to share knowledge outside the normal channels that has led to our current explosion of innovation.'**
> **Tim O'Reilly, O'Reilly Media**

Finance 2.0

'Somewhere… somehow… someone's going to pay!'

While producers have for some time been using the Internet to advertise their film to potential investors, the notion of '**crowd-sourced**' financing (sometimes known as 'crowd-funding') is a relatively new concept. By spreading the cost of producing a film between scores of individual investors who may put in no more than the cost of a DVD, significant sums of money have been raised. In

June 2006, producer Jim Gilliam emailed the buyers of the previous films he had made with Robert Greenwald asking for help with their next documentary, *Iraq for Sale*. Nine days and four emails later over 3,000 people had collectively raised $267,000, enough to release a further $100,000 in funding and cover the costs of production.

Crowd-sourced financing doesn't have to offer money back to the micro-investor in the event of the film making money; the offer could be a copy of the DVD, a role as an extra, or as in the case of *Iraq for Sale*, simply their name on the credits. The type of incentive will ultimately depend on the project's kudos (cast and key talent involved, web buzz, etc.) and the reasons people are likely to support it will vary with different types of project.

Iraq for Sale worked because the filmmakers are well known and a large group of people wanted the documentary's issue about the use of private contractors in Iraq to reach a larger audience. For supporters of PouringDown.TV's Daniel Liss - who raised $2,000 from his viewers for *7 Maps*, a series of viewer-inspired films off the back of a popular web vlog – the chance to be involved with something original and groundbreaking was probably the motivating factor.

Where a project has a guaranteed audience but no easy way of raising cash, one option would be to pre-sell DVDs ahead of production to finance it, (though this would obviously jeopardize any possible DVD distribution deal). As well as offering a chance to raise cash, crowd-sourced films also increase exposure, engaging the potential audience at the earliest stage. In the case of *A Swarm of Angels* (see below) investors also have a say in posters, trailers, script development, casting and so forth. Some examples of web-based financing follow:

Fundable.org
Fundable is an early pioneer of crowd-sourced financing. An individual creates a project bid for a set amount of money and invites a group of people to pledge support by providing credit card or paypal information on Fundable. If enough money is raised, everyone is billed and the money is paid to the project creator, less a 7% commission to the service. If the full amount isn't raised within a set time limit, then all pledges are deleted.

The system could be used to fund

- Group purchases, such a video projector for a screening group or camera for a film workshop;
- Bulk purchases for a number of organisations, eg. 100 DigitBeta tapes;
- The production budget for a film or video project;
- Distribution costs to secure sufficient sales before going into production, e.g DVD pressing costs of $1,000 could be raised by pre-selling 100 copies for $10.

Typical bids for funding are between $500 and $3,000 with individual pledges usually around $20 to $50. Projects successful in raising money on Fundable include the short film *Signage* (www.idlerichpro.com) from Doug Hertz and Claudia Myers. The film raised over $2,000 to cover completion costs including final sound mix, colour correction and graphics laid in for titles and credits. Donors offering more than $250 were listed in the credits.

The documentary *Polly's Global Walk* (www.pollysglobalwalk.com) sought minimum donations of $30, offering funders a copy of the finished DVD and their name on the credits. The project raised $1,440, almost double the $750 originally asked for.

Have Money Will Vlog

HaveMoneyWillVlog.com is a website where a group of volunteer 'advocates' act as an informal commissioning structure for video-blog (vlog) and online video proposals. The advocates promote projects they believe in to potential donors, be it friends, family, the site's visitors and related mailing lists etc. Projects are usually funded within several weeks at a level of between $1,000 and $2,000. Those looking for funding must first 'find an advocate' who will promote and vouch for the project, details of which are then posted to a Wiki (tools that allows visitors to add and edit content) and discussed before being promoted formally by the site and other advocates. Some of the projects funded include:

LostinLight.org – a website dedicated to preserving 8mm films, raised over $1,500 through 'Have Money Will Vlog' to buy equipment to digitise footage. The site will digitise and host (under a Creative Commons license) the 8mm films of anyone who sends in their film.

7 Maps. Vlogger Daniel Liss of PouringDown.tv raised $2,000 to support a seven day trip through Canada writing, shooting, editing and posting one film a day in response to instructions from subscribers to his vlog.

SustainableRoute.com pulled together $2,000 for a documented road trip across America filming individuals and communities attempting to live in an environmentally sustainable way.

ColumbiaMigrationProject.net is an ethnographic/videoblog project following Colombians in the US and in Colombia about their experience and hopes about immigration, which raised $2,100.

Kinooga

Kinooga (kinnoga.com), created by founder of the Hollywood Stock Exchange Max Keiser, allows micro-investors to pre-buy downloads of a film, typically for a nominal $10-$15. These presales also act as an investment, allowing the funder to enjoy a profit share in the event of the film making a profit. No funds are released to the filmmaker until all the money has been raised, although most films listed on the site at publication were yet to raise 10% of their total asking price.

Sellaband

An interesting model from the music world is **Sellaband.com**, where artists encourage 1000 fans to fund the burning of an album to the tune of $50 each, upon which the fans get both a limited edition CD and investor status. Once mastered, the songs are offered as a download for free, and for sale at gigs and online, with money earned shared between artists, funders and the service (which owns a share of all future publishing revenues). At publication, four bands had been financed in this manner, having used the service to raise a full production budget. A similar service could realistically be created for film production (and by the time you read this probably will have been!).

The One Second Film

Crowd-funding can also be done directly via a single website with links to PayPal or another online payment system. Nirvan Mullicks' *1 Second Film* (the1secondfilm.com), raised over $150,000 from over 7,000 backers, most of whom paid just $1 for a producer credit. The 70mm film, made up of one second of animation followed by 90 minutes of producer credits and documentary, garnered enough interest to bring in backing and 'investment' from the likes of Stephen Colbert, Spike Jonze, Kiefer Sutherland and Samuel L Jackson. Any profits from the film are set to go to the Global Fund for Women. In early 2007 the IMDB stopped listing the films' full 7,000 producer credit list – which split up executive, associate and standard producer depending on the level of investment, fearing that it set a bad precedent.

New thinking
Open Source & Free Software.

'Open source gives us a better tool for innovation, not because of any magic in its development methodology (although there is great power in distributed peer review), but because it is part and parcel of an environment in which multiple players can take us in unexpected directions... I'd like to argue that open source is the "natural language" of a networked community, that the growth of the Internet and the growth of open source are interconnected by more than happenstance. As individuals found ways to communicate through highly leveraged network channels, they were able to share information at a new pace and a new level.'
Tim O'Reilly

If the large software companies such as Microsoft, Apple and Adobe are the tech equivalents of the major film studios, then the open source movement would be the independents. However, unlike the indies who have been forced to compete for ever shrinking shelf space and cinema screens, open source software - by virtue of normally free and often better developed products – has grown in popularity.

Since Linus Torvalds unveiled his own version of Unix (Linux) in 1991, the open source software movement has become one of the most active and energetic areas of software development and human collaboration. In short, coders create and distribute modifiable, and 'open' software packages. These range from the Apache web server, used by the majority of webhosts worldwide, the Firefox web browser, which is second in usage (and fast growing) to Microsoft's Internet Explorer, OpenOffice, which offers an alternative to MS Office, through to 3D animation (Blender), content management (Joomla) and blogs (Wordpress).

The most surprising aspect of the Open Source movement has been the speed with which autonomous development communities have formed, and the high standard of work such a disparate collection of people from around the world work can often produce. Like much microbudget film production, the contributors will never profit financially directly; though they may in the long term through associated businesses such as training, consulting and a more marketable skillset (some such as Linux distributor Redhat are valued at over $3bn). Once complete, however, these tools are generally - without the duplication or distribution costs of conventional products - completely free.

In the last five years the movement has influenced the non-software creative sector, notably Creative Commons (see below) and Wikipedia, the content of which is distributed under a General Public License (GPL), making it free to copy, modify and distribute.

Elephant's Dream, an 11 minute animation which premiered on the Internet in May 2006, describes itself as an 'open movie' and acted as a test case for a more complex production. It was animated on the open source 3D package Blender, was distributed, with the soundtrack, under a Creative Commons license - and almost all the tools used in its creation were open source. Furthermore it provided an early outing for an EU backed project spanning 6 countries - the open source UniVerse - which allowed 3D animators in different countries to connect their computers and 3D software in order to collaborate more closely. The film is an allegorical story of a hopeful boy and embittered man traveling through the internal workings of nightmarish machine that responds to their every move. In less than a fortnight of online release it was downloaded more than a million times. See www.netribution.co.uk/2/content/view/611/267/ and www.elephantsdream.org

With less fanfare but on similar lines, video social networks such as YouTube have seen a growth in unmediated collaborations. For example, a number of musicians have filmed themselves which others have downloaded and added their accompaniment to creating an impromptu virtual jam, or someone has started a story which others continue. In one notable example user MadV invited fellow YouTubers to write a message for the world on their hand on the theme of 'one world', receiving over 2,200 submissions, which were selected and cut into short film *The Message* (www.youtube.com/profile?user=MadV).

'One of the more difficult things to comprehend is that the gift economies—like those that sustain open-source software—coexist so naturally with the market...'
Jonathan Lethem
The Ecstasy of Influence

and we've done *Outfoxed* and *Walmart* and now *Iraq for Sale*.

A lot of people I'm sure would like to make the leap from a desk job into making films that they believe in, how did you find that transition?

It worked out really well for me, because I hooked up with Robert Greenwald, who is a really respected director; he'd made many many films. But he didn't know much about technology and I did, so I was able to provide a whole lot of insight and skills for the project that helped us get it done much much faster than we would have before. Even little things like being able to download video from the White House website so we could start cutting them straight away – we wouldn't have to wait for screeners to come in. It was amazing how helpful things like that were, like being able to do research online. It was a great opportunity for me to learn the filmmaking stuff from a great filmmaker, and he got a lot out of it, because I was this tech guy.

Were you involved in fundraising for his earlier films?

Fundraising was always a case of us having no idea where the money is coming from. Robert would take out loans, he would try to scramble, we got some money from MoveOn.org, we got a little money from this group or that group. But basically we couldn't raise any money, that is what it boiled down to. Nobody really wanted to touch it. And he took out a lot of loans and we ended up doing alright from DVD sales so that we could keep going.

Can you talk me through what happened with the funding for Iraq for Sale?

I was involved in the funding for that one. That was one of my big dreams. We basically put a lot of effort after *Outfoxed* into collecting all of the emails and contact information for all the folks who had bought *Uncovered* and *Outfoxed*, all the folks who had bought those DVDs. So the very first thing you think right off is OK, we can get them to organise screenings. But then we were like, what if we can go to these folks to raise money. What if we can solve our big fundraising problem and make any film we like if we can convince them that it is a good idea. So that was the idea from the get go, but we thought it would be a long while before we could get to that.

And, to do *Iraq for Sale*, we basically got desperate. We were like, 'it's a great story, we've got some great great research, we really want to do it, we're at the end time wise, we've got to make a call whether to

Jim Gilliam,
producer, Brave New Films

In just 10 days and from four emails, Jim Gilliam raised over $267,000 to fund the documentary *Iraq for Sale* from more than 3,000 people. With a background in the Internet, Jim has used the Internet to pioneer new financing and distribution models while producing political documentaries with Robert Greenwald.

How did you come into producing?

My whole professional background is on the internet. Until about three and a half years ago I was doing dotcom stuff, I was the CTO (Chief Technology Officer) of business.com, I'd done some things with eCompanies, which is an incubator like Idealab. Then I decided that I didn't want to do that with my life and so I ditched it a little after September 11, and eventually decided I wanted to do more political things, which by happenstance led me to doing documentary films, because of what Bush was doing with Iraq. And there was a story which no-one was paying any attention to, which was that the intelligence [for going to Iraq] was all completely bogus. You had all these CIA people saying it was totally bogus, and no-one was paying any attention to them. And we had to get that story out there, so that became *Uncovered*, which we started in July 03 shortly after the war was 'over'. And we got it out in about October of that same year. And since then I've worked on all these films. That one totally took off

do the project or not, lets just go for it'. And so we did, we went for it. We went back and forth in the meeting internally about how much to ask for and I was like, well how much do we need?

And basically we figured out we needed $300,000. Well we had a commitment for $100,000 and none of us thought we could raise more than $100,000 online. I was the most optimistic, I thought we could do $100k, everybody else thought it was more like $50k. But we pulled it off, we asked for the whole thing and we raised $220,000, basically through our email list. Which was incredible. They really believed in the project and what we'd done.

How many names were in the email list?
At the time it was 170,000.

It worked partly because you had built up a relationship with these people over a number of films?
Oh yeah there was a lot of work that had gone into putting that together, and a lot of these were folks we'd come into contact with because of *Walmart*. This was not like putting a blog post up and all of a sudden everybody comes and knocks our door down. We'd carefully cultivated an audience and put a lot of effort into the technology to pull them all together so that we could email them all at the same time.

And did you offer them anything?
We did, we offered them a credit. We told them we could offer them their name at the end of the film which we thought was the coolest thing we could do. We thought about offering a copy of the film, but decided that it was obvious. But we thought the credit thing would be cool, and of course it would be cheap. It didn't really cost us anything and people did a lot of things with it too, they put in the names of soldiers, loved ones, even their website names, names of their peace groups, stuff like that.

Presumably it also meant that by the time the film was finished there was a huge audience who were really into the film and wanted to see it succeed?
Oh yeah. I mean, that was the reason we really wanted to engage the audience with *Walmart*, we wanted them to be invested, just emotionally in the project overall. The sooner they were engaged, the more they would care about it being a success.

That was definitely a goal. It's a great opportunity for filmmakers these days to be able to build an audience themselves and interact with them directly, because then you can make whatever kind of movie you want

to make because they'll be with you. If you've got faith in them they'll be with you, to support you.

Brave New Theaters seems another similar idea, mobilising people to do something that previously a big film organisation needed to do?
So the idea is to take our distribution model - people call them house parties, we just call them screenings - and make it available to all filmmakers. And seeding it with all of the folks who have screened our own films, the 1000s of folks that we've already been engaged with. It's basically just a place where we match up filmmakers with screening hosts. And so both sides want to reach more people for their cause or whatever reason - for fundraising or just to have fun. And by hooking them up with the right films, and the right activists or the right screening hosts both sides can win, and we provide tools for everybody to reach a bigger and bigger audience.

So you can invite people to the screening, you can put buttons on your website, send out an email, various RSVP tools.
And we'll keep building out that functionality over time to create a fully-fledged people-powered movie distributor. And really engage the audience to reach more people. The hope is that it becomes this virtuous circle, where the films are both being marketed and distributed by the people that are really engaged and care about your films, so that no matter what size, or no matter how small the niche might be there is someone out there who cares about it and will want to screen it and show it to people. Stuff like that.

How many screenings or films have been listed on the services?
So we've had (checks computer) 8400 screenings, I think we're up to about 60 films.

Documentary seems to have become increasingly popular with audiences recently?
I think there's been an increase in people finding out what's going on and it's only been because the mainstream media hasn't been covering this stuff that filmmakers have gotten so frustrated and said look, we're just going to do this ourselves. You don't want to distribute this? We'll just go and do this ourselves. People want to know what's going on. I think the documentary thing is about telling these true stories that the mainstream just won't touch. And if they had then they wouldn't have been getting this threat - it wouldn't have become so powerful.

Marketing 2.0

'This time it's personal'

'Content isn't king. If I sent you to a desert island and gave you the choice of taking your friends or your movies, you'd choose your friends - if you chose the movies, we'd call you a sociopath. Conversation is king. Content is just something to talk about.'
Cory Doctorow, BoingBoing

The **Cluetrain Manifesto** (www.cluetrain.org) was published in April 1999 and suggested that the future of the internet (and hence most business) stood in conversations. The web had exploded, it argued, as a communications medium within which traditional corporate top-down marketing just wouldn't stand up. To get anywhere online amidst the billion or so voices competing for attention, companies would need to enter into a two-way dialogue.

While it could be argued that few major corporations have yet to successfully pull this off, web users have embraced the concept in the same time it takes a class of students to break silence once a teacher has left the room. The explosion of blogs, podcasts, social networks like MySpace and Bebo and community-driven services like Digg and Del.Icio.Us – not to mention flickr, eBay and YouTube - have shown Cluetrain to be right on the mark.

The most interesting conclusion of Cluetrain for independent filmmakers is that success on the web seems to demand originality and integrity. Where producers may have often been encouraged to pander to the mainstream market, reaching the broadest possible appeal with their work to the point of homogenization, on the web the vast competition for attention makes uniqueness and honesty a strong 'selling point' (especially when coupled with creative talent!). The idea has echoes of the Free Cinema Movement, a creative force in filmmaking in the 1950s.

Approaching the web

Online marketing can be as cheap as the work you put in and can be incredibly effective. Films such as *Snakes on a Plane* and *The Blair Witch Project* generated such strong online buzz that the web campaign became a news story in itself. Yet the Internet is a massively competitive marketplace for ideas and stories with, by the end of 2006, some 1.5million blog entries and 65,000 new videos on YouTube published daily.

Getting noticed online may be free, but it is rarely easy, and the most effective web promotion methods, such as blogs and social networks, take time and a long-term commitment. If you spend all your time building and updating a website, you'll never get a chance to finish the masterpiece or business plan.

But of course a good website isn't just about drumming up interest from strangers, it also provides a place where those potentially involved with a project – financiers, buyers, cast, crew, journalists and, of course, audiences – can learn more. Not having even a basic single page presence can suggest a company is at best aloof, or at worse not serious or trustworthy. While at the development and financing

'Tell us some good stories and capture our interest. Don't talk to us like you've forgotten how to speak. Don't make us feel small, remind us to be larger. Get a little of that human touch.'
Chris Locke, The Cluetrain Manifesto.

'As filmmakers we believe that no film can be too personal. The image speaks. Sound amplifies and comments. Size is irrelevant. Perfection is not an aim. An attitude means a style. A style means an attitude. Implicit in our attitude is a belief in freedom, in the importance of people and in the significance of the every day.'
Lorenza Mazetti, Lindsay Anderson, Karel Reisz, Tony Richardson The Free Cinema Movement

New thinking
The wisdom of crowds

'Sometimes... these nonmarket collaborations can be better at motivating effort and can allow creative people to work on information projects more efficiently than would traditional market mechanisms and corporations. The result is a flourishing nonmarket sector of information, knowledge, and cultural production, based in the networked environment, and applied to anything that the many individuals connected to it can imagine. Its outputs, in turn, are not treated as exclusive property. They are instead subject to an increasingly robust ethic of open sharing, open for all others to build on, extend, and make their own.'
The Wealth of Networks, Yochai Benkler

To support the launch of the film *AI*, Warner Bros hired Microsoft developers to create a massive online game with hidden puzzles across a number of websites. Within days of it being launched, a community had formed to help each other out with the increasingly fiendish puzzles. The game's creators later joked that they were so blown away with the speed at which puzzles were solved that had they sought a cure for cancer it would have been found. The 'wisdom of crowds' argues that by collectivising knowledge and experience online the total output is greater than the sum of its parts. An obvious example is Wikipedia, where a number of people work together to create a single encyclopedia entry. On Digg.com users vote on articles to appear on the front page of the site, while user voting and commenting is integral to most community sites, from YouTube to Flickr.

According to James Surowiecki, author of *The Wisdom of Crowds*, which discussed the idea and coined the phrase, four key criteria separate wise crowds (such as those who build open source software that works better than commercial alternatives) from irrational ones (such as those who fuel stock market bubbles):

- Diversity of opinion - each person should have personal views even if it's just an eccentric interpretation of the known facts.
- Independence - people's opinions aren't determined by the opinions of those around them.
- Decentralization - people are able to specialise and draw on local knowledge.
- Aggregation - some mechanism exists for turning private judgments into a collective decision.

The full implications of such network effects for the film industry are yet to be seen, but are beginning to be explored. onedotzero founder Matt Hanson is exploring the area through *A Swarm of Angels* (see below) a collaboration to build an open source film. In 2006, The Beastie Boys created a concert movie *Awesome, I fuckin' Shot That*, (www.beastieboysmovie.com) by distributing 50 Hi8 cameras to fans in the crowd. In terms of distribution, an example from the music world shows how the wisdom of crowds can match people with content they might otherwise never discover. Last.fm builds user specific radio stations based on the tracks and artists members say they like (if you say you like Radiohead, it may play Explosions in the Sky). Like Amazon's recommended products feature, it helps the user find things which they would otherwise find hard to locate but probably appreciate.

stage there may not be time – or even need – to develop a full blown web strategy, some form of presence is increasingly expected.

Domain name

If you aren't able to build a website just yet, it is still worth registering a domain name for your production company and/or project (the shorter the better) before anyone else does. This can forward to a blog or social network page until you have a full site, while also allowing you to have an identifiable email address. While it makes sense to have the domain name for your country (ie .fr, .co.uk), if you intend to operate and distribute internationally, a top level domain (TLD) - .biz, .com, .org, .net, ,info and .tv (not strictly a TLD) can make a better impression. Dotorgs are normally reserved for non-profit organisations.

Search engines

The art of getting good search engine rankings would fill a book in itself, but could roughly be summed up as designing your site's pages to be search engine friendly, and encouraging as many people as possible to link to you. The first step to being found by the main search engines is registering with them – Google, Yahoo, AskJeeves, MSN, Live, Alexa & DMOZ, all of which have a form for alerting them to new sites.

Search-friendly sites are built with consideration to the way a 'spider' (automatic robots which 'crawl' the web, looking for content) may index them. A site designed entirely in Flash (an animation tool) may look nice but cannot be indexed by the search spiders. Keywords, which you would want people searching for, ie. 'disaster comedy' or 'Helen's Film Company', should appear prominently on pages, links and titles. Some tips at searchenginewatch.com/showPage. html?page=2168021

Google ranks pages based on how many other sites link to them (and how reputable these sites are). If you have a links page, you can offer reciprocal links to people you know, while there are plenty of web directories where you can submit your site and company details, all increasing links to your site. Similarly, linking to the site in every email, piece of publicity, forum posts, web articles and comment items, will increase the number of sites linking to you.

There's plenty of room to be creative. For example if you want to get high search rankings for a phrase like 'food movie' you could write an in-depth, researched article about 'The 10 Greatest Food Movies' with plenty of links to other sites. Then submit a link to the article to forums, communities and websites relating to food, asking people to read the article and give you comments. It can take time, but as more people link to the article, your page should become strongly associated with the keywords. Although there is a fine line between this and spamming - make sure the information is of interest and use.

Further info: www.SearchEngineWatch.com | SEO Wiki entry - en.wikipedia. org/wiki/Search_engine_optimization | List of search engines Wiki - en.wikipedia. org/wiki/List_of_search_engines

Video hosting

Again, this is a subject that could fill a small book in itself. The key question to decide is where to host your video:

- On a **centralized service** (eg. Google, DailyMotion, Revver, etc.) – this is usually straightforward to set up, and connects you to a network of people who may otherwise never stumble across your work. Some of the video sharing sites are becoming more producer-friendly. Blip.tv, for instance does not brand its video viewer, which is good for embedding in your site without promoting them, and allows you to apply usage licences, such as Creative Commons. On the other hand you will be putting your content in the hands of a separate organisation, and will be subject to their user agreement, server stability, encoding, business health and so forth. For example after Viacom sent takedown notices to 120,000 YouTube users believed to have been posting copyrighted content, a number of people whose content had similar names to Viacom properties found their work taken offline.

- **Hosting video yourself** (eg. Broadcast Machine, Brightcover, custom) ensures you are in full control at all times, but requires some technical knowledge to ensure it will work on the majority of websites. You first need to encode your film(s) in a workable format, such as QuickTime, RealPlayer, Windows Media Player or more commonly Flash Video. Flash can then be embedded within pages and has become increasingly popular, because of the ubiquity of the Flash player (almost every web user has a copy, regardless of browser or operating system).

One of the simplest ways to create a channel of videos is through Broadcast Machine – an open source system which allows the end user to publish a channel of videos on their website which people can subscribe to via iTunes or RSS (see below), and even distribute their files as BitTorrents (which shares the bandwidth costs). Download from www.getmiro.com/broadcast

Where to host your video: pros & cons

	On a centralised service (eg Blip, Google Video, etc)	On your own site (either directly hosted, or through Broadcast Machine, etc.)
Pros	Large potential audience, and accompany social network; File hosting and management costs covered; Easily embeddable in your own site and others.	Greater control over your content and usage; Build up a community around your website, rather than someone else's; Retain full independence.
Cons	Sharing ad revenues with service provider; Subject to site's policies, stability and content licensing; Little control over comments or who embeds your video.	Higher technical know-how required; Potential bandwidth costs; Need to actively promote your site / video to encourage visitors.

The blog
A simple blog (short for web log) is a user-generated website, presented in a journal style with the most recent entries at the top. A blog shows that a website is active, while providing an insight into how the production is coming along, allowing people to 'build a relationship' with your film or company over a long period of time. Blogs can be hosted on a larger blogging service, such as the Pixar insider blog Luxo (pixaranimation.blogspot.com), or within a blogging programme like WordPress on a standalone site such as Colin Kennedy's blog for *Hallam Foe* (www.getyourpeople.com), who as assistant to director David MacKenzie had a unique position to see the workings of the production from start to finish.

Once set up and after your first post, submitting an **RSS** (really simple syndication) feed of the latest entries to the main tracking services such as feedster.com and technoratti.com will increase the chances of people finding you. RSS also allows, for example, a development executive to subscribe to your blog's feed to keep abreast of news on your project without having to keep going back and forth to check the site.

Further info – blog software comparison chart www.ojr.org/ojr/images/blog_software_comparison.cfm | legal guide for bloggers - www.eff.org/bloggers/lg/

The website

At a minimum, a **company site** should include full contact details and background to the company, projects and key individuals involved. A newsletter signup, mission statement, press release and clippings archive are almost standard, while a blog is increasingly the norm for net savvy companies (eg. googleblog. blogspot.com). Relevant videos, artwork, stills, links and articles of interest will increase the site's stickiness (amount of time people stay on the site). In addition, social network sites, such as Blip.tv, YouTube, IMDb and Netribution profile pages should both increase traffic to the site while appealing to those who stay within social networks.

Standalone **websites for films** typically include synopsis, production notes, clips, trailers, image galleries, a forum or chatroom, screening information (depending on the stage), free downloads, latest news or blogs, a newsletter and frequently puzzles and games. Most importantly, the site, if intended for a potential audience as opposed to investors or buyers, is expected to extend the universe of the film into the web. Elaborate full screen flash animations and embedded video, with atmospheric sound can recreate the world of a nightmare (hostelfilm.com) or existential riddle (donniedarko.com).

Some general tips:

- Put content on your website in an **easily re-usable format**. If a blogger cannot easily copy and paste parts of your site's text, or hotlink stills from the film into their own site, you are making it much harder for them to promote your film for you. Likewise, provide trailers and film footage that can be embedded in other sites, eg. via YouTube or Vimeo or VideoEgg.

- Provide Creative Commons (see below) or similar open copyright notices on materials you want to be used in the marketing (eg press releases, stills, trailers, footage etc) to **encourage people to freely use** in their own sites and blogs. Being protective of marketing materials can be self-defeating.

- Have a no-spam **email newsletter**. Even if you don't plan to send one out for several months, collecting email addresses on your site helps you to build a lasting relationship with interested visitors and is of increasing value over time.

- **Test your site** and its content on low quality kit. The trailer may sound great on your studio-grade monitors, but on a home PC with built in speakers it could sound terrible. Likewise, not everyone has fast web access or big monitors. If your site looks good on a low-fi set up, it will definitely look good on a higher spec system.

'Kids are more powerful than ever before.. They are able to get content and make it their own. That's a scary thing for people who own properties but it's also good for us because kids are more invested in the process and feel more connected to it.' Leigh-Ann Brodsky, President of Nickelodeon and Viacom Consumer Products

Generating word of mouth

The holy grail for a film is the situation where fans produce trailers, artwork, posters and reviews, running their own fansites covering every new story and announcement relating to the film in great detail. This is most common for large projects with cult appeal such as *Harry Potter*, *Star Wars* and *Lord of the Rings* as well as unexpected titles such as *Snakes on a Plane*, as opposed to an independent project with no named talent or cast. Such communities can be powerful as NewLine discovered after plans to drop Peter Jackson from *The Hobbit* backfired as users of the OneRing.net community planned a general boycott of the studio and an attempt to discourage key talent from working on the project.

Word of mouth, 'viral' web phenomena can generate a huge peak of hits and interest in a very short space of time, although they are almost impossible to predict, and once unleashed are very difficult to control. Common themes include mashups (*Brokeback to the Future*, *Scary Mary*), clever display of initiative (*Million Pixel Homepage*, *One Red Paperclip*), cult or retro factor (*Starlords*, *The Meatrix*); special or impressive skills ('*Robot Dance Kid*'); cool and futuristic technology (Steve Jobs keynotes); triumph over corruption, bureaucracy and greed (*Al Gore's Penguin Army*); the stupidity of other people, and of course celebrity.

Mashups, a phenomena with roots in the live visuals / VJ world, mix together a number of often contrasting pieces of video (or music) to create a single form, which in the case of, for example, *Little Miss Sunshine (horror)* or *Requiem for a Toy Story* can arguably widen the audience to people who may otherwise be unaware of the film (see more at TheTrailerMash.com). Some general tips

- **Form meaningful relationships** with the right communities and social networks. Finding and maintaining these can be time consuming, but if well targeted, immensely powerful. As with all marketing this comes down to understanding who the audience for your film is (it will rarely be just one group) and finding communities where such people exist. A meaningful relationship, like in life, is a two way exchange so let them tell you what they need.

- **Appeal to people's desire to help**. If you find a website or group that would appear to be interested in your project, rather than forcing them to fit with a marketing plan of your own, take time to understand how their community works, and if needs be ask for help. A posting in a chess community saying 'I'm working on a film about a chess grand master and would love to know how best to find people here who would like to see it' will probably get far more response than 'buy chess film here with a discount'.

- **Give something away**. Give things away for free: content, prizes, tickets, credits, exposure for their films/blogs and so forth. Many sites are hungry for content, so breaking up your press pack into articles or behind the scenes video which can be republished for free is cheap press coverage.

- **Be honest.** Frauds soon get found out. Sony suffered a massive credibility backlash online when it was found out to be hiring PR company Zipatoni to create a fake fan site (alliwantforxmasisapsp.com). It's easy to pretend on the web to be something that you are not, but some of the most successful sites are those that are honest about their aims and the people behind them.

- **Stay human.** The internet is driven by human beings, not corporations, so make sure you act like one.

Matt Hanson,
A Swarm of Angels

Like *Elephants Dream, A Swarm of Angels* is an attempt to bridge the world of cinema with the bottom-up networked world of open source and the Internet, creating a fully financed feature film to be released under a Creative Commons non-commercial licence. Yet if the finished film can be distributed freely upon release - why would anyone bother paying to see the end result? Instead, people pay to be part of the process of creation. £25 ($50) gets you membership of the Swarm, and you can start voting on scripts, posters and production, while discussing decisions and direction directly with project conceiver Matt Hanson, who founded the pioneering **onedotzero** festival, and has written extensively about the future of cinema.

What are your main goals with Swarm of Angels?
I'd like to push feature film form forward because of its iconic status. There's a great quote I use in *The End of Celluloid* from William Gibson: 'Digital video strikes me as a new platform wrapped in the language and mythology of an old platform. Lamb dressed as mutton, somewhat in the way we think of our cellular systems as adjuncts of copper-wire telephony. The way we still 'dial' on touchpads. We call movies 'film,' but the celluloid's drying up.'

Essentially *A Swarm of Angels* is an idea I've been circling around for a while to direct a film that starts to eject the assumptions of the old platform. For example, many directors focus on wanting their work to be distributed on the big screen. To me that's an old mindset, based on an outdated hierarchy of the screen. Yes I'd like it to be projected on a great swathe of cinema screen, but also on a video ipod, and a computer monitor.

How is the Swarm structured: how are decisions made and is the process democratic?
This is totally new, so we are evolving it as we go along. I wouldn't call the process democratic, but it is collaborative. I have overall control, much more than I would in a traditional project by a first time feature director. But in the same instance members get unprecedented access to the creative process of feature filmmaking, and the chance to influence and shape the film. That can be through direct contribution of skills and materials. Or it can be through voting — we have series of polls on creative and production decisions. For example a member vote recently chose the version of the film project poster we are to use.

How do you apply the 'hive mind' to a medium which has often been auteur driven?
Hive mind implies a kind of conformity, a uniformity of vision, so I don't like the term compared to the idea of the 'wisdom of crowds', which is more about a diverse collection of independently-thinking individuals. I could argue you get a 'hive mind' in Hollywood cinema, or 'Euro co-productions', or US indies... there is a certain view held by organisations and individuals who can fund and distribute those productions as to what is commercially acceptable and artistically viable for them to produce.

The idea of my 'swarming angels' model is actually that we are not beholden to this spectrum of artistic taste and commercial payback. The eventual size of the Swarm — 50,000 — is a global niche audience that means I'm able to make something far more distinctive because I essentially only have to make them and myself happy. If someone else likes it that is a bonus, but I am free from commercial bonds. The members act as an echo chamber and feedback loop, so the film evolves into something that is more inclined to our cultural tastes. Forum postings on books, soundtracks, and movies we like suggest we are already self-selecting particular 'cult' tastes.

Do you think the idea of auteurship in cinema is outdated?
On the contrary, I think it can regain ground with digital tech as the enabling force. The Internet allows you to create a large enough group of people who share niche tastes, to create media specifically suited to them and you. Paradoxically by including similar-minded people in his/her creative process the filmmaker can have more control and authorship over their vision. I'm essentially trying to invent a new relationship between filmmaker and audience. But it needs a landmark project of this size to work, and for people to support it, to show that there's a viable alternative filmmaking model to the current ones.

Do you think this ongoing dialogue with the swarm will help you better understand the ultimate audience for the film?
Ultimately they are the audience. At the same time they are the tip of that particular iceberg of people who share similar cultural tastes. This type of participative cinema means the Swarm develops into an ongoing focus group, and generator of ideas.

Why should someone pay £25 - what do they get?
Access to exclusive media including video, audio, podcasts, and limited edition merchandise including a member-only DVD. An Angel also gets editorial access to the process through member-only forums, and being able to post and communicate with the filmmakers, and vote on key creative and marketing decisions.

Most of all, this is a chance to be part of a revolutionary filmmaking experiment.

It's Creative Commons licensed - what was the thinking behind that?
I've been involved in producing VJ and remix cinema projects. I like the idea of sampling other work, and doing it legitimately. So this is a digital community project, as I want to give something back to the community by opening it up for free sharing and non-commercial use, as well as commercial sampling.

There's a huge opportunity in more open content that Hollywood and the music industry haven't realised or been able to move toward because their business models are predicated on something else.

As consumers we are all becoming used to creating our own media, and viewing it how we want. As such, personally, I don't want to cripple my media with bad DRM (Digital Rights Management, see below) and punish viewers/users of my material. A Swarm of Angels has Cory Doctorow as an advisor who is a far more eloquent expert on the issues of copyright, open content, and opponent of DRM than myself. You should check out his arguments against it.

Do you worry about piracy?
I understand artists and creators should be paid for their content. Copyright was invented to protect those rights, but it has shifted dramatically to become a protection for commercial exploitation by companies. Often this actually harms the rights of artists now. So the idea of piracy has changed, and there is not a sensible debate on this because of the vast lobbying power of current commercial interests.

I'm not advocating piracy, but I am saying that artists can create viable business models which allow much more freedom and open access to their content, so more people can enjoy it. After all I think most filmmakers are more interested in communicating with their audience, rather than milking them dry of their cash.

What are the advantages of an open source model for filmmaking?
Making truly digital-age cinema opens up the possibility of more artistic diversity, experimentation and risk-taking. More of what people want without it being lowest common denominator.

Tapping into the strength and vitality of a community centred around this creative process.

Utilizing the expertise and local knowledge of members to come up with more exciting creative possibilities.

Do you think the film industry could be facing a 'linuxisation?'
Possibly, it takes a large enough group of committed individuals working in harmony to render the first working 'operating system' to show that an alternate entertainment eco-system can exist. *A Swarm of Angels* can do that with enough people subscribing.

www.aswarmofangels.com

Distribution 2.0

'... and remember, the next stream you see could be your own!'

For those motivated and driven by telling stories to the widest possible audience, the internet offers over a billion potential viewers through some 300 million broadband households.

Parallel to this, for commercial producers and distributors, there lies uncertainty. Traditional distributors face competition from two fronts: 'pirates' seeking to circumvent tech controls on the use of content; and the vast scores of so-called 'user-generated' content producers who now compete, if not yet for Oscar awards, for 'eyeballs', making up some half of video viewed online. According to a report by Screen Digest, 47% of video watched in the US on the internet in 2006 was 'user-generated', a level forecast to rise to 55% by 2010 — with some suggesting the figure to already be 60%.

As with the early days of cinema, the most popular of these films have been novelty: dance displays, animals performing tricks, titillation, disaster and buffoonery. But as the quality of the top bloggers now rival newspapers for

New thinking
The Long Tail

'Our culture and economy is increasingly shifting away from a focus on a relatively small number of 'hits' (mainstream products and markets) at the head of the demand curve and toward a huge number of niches in the tail. As the costs of production and distribution fall, especially online, there is now less need to lump products and consumers into one-size-fits-all containers.'
Chris Anderson, longtail.com

Wired Magazine editor Chris Anderson's landmark book *The Long Tail* looked at how the scale of the web and the ease of mass digital distribution creates a significant market for smaller and niche titles - be it books, music, film or special interests. Where shops have traditionally only been able to sell as much stuff as they can fit on their shelves, the web allows retailers to offer near unlimited catalogues. Indications seem to suggest that the effect of this is that far more books, films and media are sold in the 'long tail'; the part of the sales chart that tails off after it peaks on the bestsellers.

For instance, Amazon each day sells more things that didn't sell at all the day before than things that did.

On web music services such as iTunes with a library of millions, it transpires that almost every track has been purchased at least once. To the independent filmmaker, traditionally left to fight for shelf and cinema space against better resourced and more crowd-friendly blockbusters, the long tail offers hope.

While an obscure film may attract a paying audience of 100 in one city, scaled up through the web to people with similar tastes around the world, there is potentially a substantial audience. Instead of creating something generically mainstream, where there is huge competition for attention, focus on 'limited appeal' ideas and stories, traditionally seen as uncommercial, could potential be just as successful. Film libraries that have traditionally cherry-picked the most commercially viable titles for DVD release, potentially can earn as much for the collective value of their unreleased titles as their current hits.

'TV is not vulgar and prurient and dumb because the people who compose the audience are vulgar and dumb. Television is the way it is simply because people tend to be extremely similar in their vulgar and prurient and dumb interests and wildly different in their refined and aesthetic and noble interests.'
David Foster Williams, A Supposedly Fun Thing I'll Never Do Again

investigative reporting and comment, so too 'user generated' video is likely to evolve. As with other industries the film distribution industry will need to change to embrace rather than battle these new creative voices. The nature of that change, however is far from certain, and for a sector famous for its control-freak nature, it's a future driven by consumers and web-surfers, not the other way around.

Change for the music industry came fast, with IBM suggesting the industry as a whole lost $90 - $160bn in its transition to digital. Some, such as Wired Magazine editor Chris Anderson, now argue that the music industry cannot realistically build a business model around selling tracks, it needs to be around live performance, special editions and merchandise. Others suggest the key factor is trusting users (see below). The approach taken by eBay was dismissed when it first appeared as a decentralised community driven marketplace, yet it now makes more money than its traditionally modeled cousin, Amazon.

'In the traditional world, content produced by professionals and distributed through proprietary platforms still dominates. But in the new world, content is often user-created and accessed through open platforms. These polarised tendencies mark the clear and present conflict between incumbents and the new entrants.'
Steven Abraham, global industry leader,
IBM media and entertainment

Piracy

'We understand now that piracy is a business model... It exists to serve a need in the market for consumers who want TV content on demand. Pirates compete the same way we do - through quality, price and availability. We don't like the model but we realise it's competitive enough to make it a major competitor going forward.'
Clare Sweeney, Co-Chair, Disney

2006 saw two forms of pirates triumph. One, played by Johnny Depp in *Pirates of the Caribean 2*, became the third film to pass $1bn at the global box office. The other, the BitTorrent tracking site The Pirate Bay withstood attacks from the Motion Picture Association of America and Swedish authorities. With every new legal attempt to shut the site – which links to hosts of copyright infringing Bittorrent files, but does not host the files themselves - the site fought back with greater resolve, still standing in early 2007. The site argues, and the industry tends to agree, that if shut down it would soon be replaced by another.

At the heart of the piracy debate facing the film studios is that, while online distribution offers vast benefits to consumers and distributors, in terms of breadth of content available and reduced costs, the ease of making perfect digital copies has forced the inclusion of Digital Rights Management protection systems. However, DRM systems on legitimately purchased digital content currently allow the consumer to do less with the file than with a physical item, simultaneously frustrating consumers and arguably limiting uptake.

For example, a purchased DVD can be lent to a friend to watch in their own time (or even just taken over to their house to watch with them), or a track from a CD recorded to a mixtape or birthday compilation. Downloaded films or music, however, often don't share these same rights, or if they do require both parties to install special software, which has been show to cause security issues for the end user. At the very least, the strategy slows uptake, at worst it pushes the user to piracy where, for example, unable to play their legally purchased DVD on their computer – or to play the iTunes purchased track on their non-Apple MP3 player, they download a version 'illegally'.

In addition, many DRM systems require users to sign an off-putting (tho rarely read) digital End User License Agreement (EULA), which in the case of Amazon's UnBox download service – appears to ask the user to surrender their rights to privacy, integrity of personal data, and control over their computer. In the infamous case of Sony BMG's rootkit, which made computers vulnerable to spyware and hacking, the EULA on the 8 million later recalled CDs bound its purchasers to destroy their music if they left the country or had a house-fire, and to promise not to listen to their tunes while at work. As seen in the disputes between European countries and Apple over the FairPlay DRM licensing used on iTunes, and Apple boss & Disney's largest shareholder Steve Jobs' announcement that he would like to strip all DRM out of iTunes sales, this is an ongoing issue, and arguably something holding back the development of legal services, and worse, fuelling the uptake of illegal ones. The second most popular music service after iTunes has already done that – offering all its tracks for download without any form of copy protection. Indeed just before this book went to print one of the big four record labels, EMI, announced a partnership with Apple to sell DRM-free versions of their entire catalogue, ahead of similar deals with other labels.

At its most extreme DRM limitations have driven consumers to break the system, notably coder 'Muslix64' who was the first to break the HD-DVD encryption standard because a HD-DVD he had bought would not play on his computer monitor as it did not have the compliant connector demanded by the movie industry. 'Not being able to play a movie that I have paid for, because some executive in Hollywood decided I cannot, made me mad' said the hacker.

The rapid rate of technological change on the Internet has put the film industry in the rare and uncomfortable position of catch-up. The introduction of DVDs was carefully, slowly and – with the exception of the region coding which forced those who bought DVDs while on holiday to get their player illegally 'de-chipped' to watch them - successfully managed. On the other hand, online video has been fueled by consumer demand limited only by the ever expanding reach of technical capability. However, the majors' reluctance to put substantial amounts of content online in user-friendly formats provides a window of opportunity for independents to meet a huge and rapidly increasing hunger for video on the web where – for once – the bulk of the competition is produced on no budget.

'We take the view that we have to trust consumers-- the fact that some will disappoint us and continue to steal the music is inevitable... we have always argued that the best way to combat illegal traffic is to make legal content available at decent value and convenient.'
Eric Nicoli, Chair of EMI on plans to release the EMI catalogue without DRM

Options for making money online

For filmmakers the web is still largely unproven for making money. The most common area is currently advertising-supported content, with the majority of video streamed online being offered for free and surrounded by ads. Download-to-rent or to-own aims to offer an experience somewhere between video-on-demand and DVD, sometimes allowing the end user to burn a disc. Many download services involve a special player which the end user needs to install. Subscription services have yet to make a substantial impact, but potentially allow users' fees to be distributed proportionally to producers in relation to what has been watched.

Other options include the 'busker's hat' approach used by some blogs – ie 'if you liked this film please make a donation so we can make more' for filmmakers with a strong rapport with their viewers. Micropayments within an environment where every view deducts a few pennies from a user's account have long been discussed.

For an updated list of paid-for video services, see the list from Cinematech's Scott Kirsner, author of *The Future of Web Video*, which this is based on: www.scottkirsner.com/webvid/gettingpaid.htm.

New thinking
Creative Commons

'If the Internet teaches us anything, it is that great value comes from leaving core resources in a commons, where they're free for people to build upon as they see fit.'
Lawrence Lessig, founder, Creative Commons

While copyright aims to provide a creative with the protection to limit distribution to those who've legally acquired it, both those at entry level and seeking the widest possible audience may not want to do anything which limits the potential audience for the work. Furthermore, as novelist Jonathan Lethem illustrates very clearly in his essay *The Ecstacy of Influence* (www.harpers.org/TheEcstasyOfInfluence. html), the reuse of creative goods is a fundamental part of culture – from Shakespeare's stories, the bulk of Disney's classic films, through to Hip-Hop sampling and blog and mashup culture. At the same time, however, some form of licence may be useful to prevent, say, someone else changing it and claiming it's their work, or selling copies of something intended to be free.

Creative Commons (www.creativecommons. org) licences aim to provide a 'wired' 21st century copyright framework for the multitude of uses which fall outside the standard restrictions of IP law. It claims to be consumer friendly in that it encourages redistribution, and for those who cannot afford an IP lawyer but want some kind of copyright protection, creators can apply a custom built licence to their work, specifying aspects such as commercial use and the creation of derivative works. Some producers use Creative Commons licenses to get widespread distribution and awareness, increasing the chance of sufficient recognition to get a sale. 170 million creative items were available under a CC license by the end of 2006. Some notable uses include:

Magnatunes (www.magnatune.com). An entire record label built around Creative Commons, which seeks to embrace peer-to-peer as a viral distribution method. Users can download and share music at a low quality for free and, using an honour system, pay for a higher quality version of the album (physical or digital) for a price the end user decides. Despite setting a minimum fee of $5, the average payment is $8. The label is also film friendly: filmmakers can download tracks to use in their films for sales and festival screening purposes for free and in the event of a sale or commercial release, a full licence can be purchased.

Archive.org. As well as hosting the only historic snapshot of the web, Brewster Kahle's service also offers tens of thousands of hours of CC licensed video for use including old adverts, propaganda films, news reels and stock footage.

Flickr. At publication some 32m photos were available on Flickr.com with some form of Creative Commons licence.

Creative Archive (creativearchive.bbc.co.uk) Before his departure BBC Director General Greg Dyke promised to make all of the BBC content library freely available online. While this is a long way from materialising, the Creative Archive project - in partnership with Channel 4, ITN and the Open University - offered limited amounts of archive material under a psuedo-Creative Commons licence allowing filmmakers to use the content for most non-commercial uses in the UK.

Cory Doctorow (www.craphound.com) The science fiction writer and self-declared 'copy fighter' has released CC versions of all of his books available to download for free alongside the printed published versions. His publisher claims that in spite of free versions being available, commercial sales were double forecasts. The licences have enabled people to legally translate his works into their own language, create audio books and even graphic art based on them, which otherwise would have been unlikely to have happened for a niche sci-fi novelist. In commercially licensing content that has previously appeared under a Creative Commons non-commercial license, Doctorow's agent adds a clause as follows:

'The exclusive rights granted to Licensee hereunder are subject to a pre-existing Creative Commons licence which grants members of the public the irrevocable and nonexclusive right to create their own adaptations of the Licensed Property. Such Creative Commons-licensed works may not be sold or distributed for profit. Licensee acknowledges that under the terms of this Creative Commons licence, members of the public may create comic book [or whatever format] version of the Licensed Property for non-commercial distribution. Licensor agrees not to license the rights which are granted to Licenee hereunder to any competitor of Licensee or to any commercial enterprise intending to create adaptations of the Works for commercial distribution.'

Download to rent or own

Downloads are playable forever, or a short period of time, often – as in the case of Amazon's UnBox and Apple's iTunes – a special player, normally DRM restricted (see piracy above). Questions remain over what happens if a user upgrades, damages or changes their machine, or if they want to watch the downloaded content through other video players. The current situation is analogous to buying a Columbia TriStar DVD that would only play on a Sony TV.

Apple's iTunes store claimed 40 million TV episodes and 1.3m feature films downloaded by January 2007, while other providers have yet to provide details but are believed to be much less. iTunes has also limited access to major studios and distributors, with some exceptions such as shorts screened at Sundance 2007. Pricing is typically around $1.99 for short form content and $9.99 to $14.99 for a feature. Rentals on UnBox cost $3.99. Some of the major services include:

CustomFlix - www.customflix.com
Part of Amazon, CustomFlix allows producers to get their film listed in Amazon's UnBox download to own/rent programme. Download-to-own videos must be at least 20 minutes long; rental videos must be at least 70 minutes. Producers can set the price with 50% of revenues going to Amazon.

Cruxy - www.cruxy.com
One of the most affordable options for producers, Cruxy takes 3 percent of the retail price, plus ten cents, and passes on PayPal fees (5 cents plus 5%) which should bring costs to a little over 10% depending on price.

Panjea - www.panjea.com
Offers a generous 80% of revenues on paid downloads, and 50-85% for ad supported films, with a $25 limit for payments to start.

Brightcove - studio.brightcove.com
Producers can offer content of any length either for free, with adverts inserted (30% goes to BrightCove) or priced above 99 cent (with 50% going to BrightCove). The site suits library owners as it does not acts as a destination, instead enabling producers to embed and promote films in their own site. By February 2007, the service claimed 3,000 commercial producers using the service.

GreenCine Video-on-Demand - www.greencine.com
The site selects films to promote on its video-on-demand service, reportedly offering a 50-50 revenue split. 12,000 on-demand titles are offered for rent with far less for the download-to-own service.

EZTakes - www.eztakes.com
Offering non-exclusive distribution for downloads allowing DVD burning, EZ takes 30-35% for delivering full-length features and documentaries, including the Troma Entertainment library.

DivX Stage6 - stage6.divx.com
For Windows users only, and costing a 10% transaction fee plus a bandwidth charge – around $3.30 for a gigabyte. Videos must be in DivX format which is a full screen video compression format.

Google Video - video.google.com
For anyone with more than 1,000 hours of video content the company allows people to offer paid downloads.

Advertising revenue share

YouTube announced in early 2007 that it planned to share revenues with users, although no details were available at publication. Many sites offer 50% - sometimes up to 85% - of advertising revenues, with Blip.tv also offering to negotiate sponsorship deals for popular content. Sponsor funded films have also had some popularity, such as through BMW's *Hire Film* series of web virals (bmwfilms.com), with a huge increase in sponsor backed competitions on the popular video sharing websites. These include the Shooting People RudeBox Shorts competition with a £15,000 prize to make a film based on a track from Robbie Williams' last album, and the UK MySpace MyMovies Mashup, which offered a £1m feature film budget and distribution deal to the winning filmmaker.

Blip – www.blip.tv

Splits advertising revenue 50-50 with the producer quarterly for streamed video. The site also claims to negotiate sponsorship deals for its most popular content, and allows the producer to chose the advertising to appear alongside its content. Embedded video in other sites do not have any Blip.tv branding, which is attractive to producers not wanting to advertise another company in the video on their site.

Revver - www.revver.com

50% of advertising revenues from a commercial played at the end of any short film are returned to the filmmaker. A viral video of exploding bottles of soft drink on the site by Fritz Grobe and Stephen Voltz earned the makers well over $25,000. Revver values clicks at between 75 cents to $1 per view (ads are at the end of the video, so the entire video has to be watched), with potential earnings for a 1,000 views of $22.50 - $40, with a click through of between 3 and 4 percent. Affiliate sites, which embed the video, get 20% of ad revenues.

Metacafe - www.metacafe.com

Every 1,000 views earns the filmmaker $5 with payment starting after views hits 20,000 (if the rating averages over 3/5). A video that is seen two million times would earn $10,000. At publication the top earner on the Isreali site, Reel Stunts, had made over $26,000 for home videos of martial arts displays, with others earning five figures including massage tutorials, how-tos and general novelties.

Babelgum.com

Headquartered in Ireland the site offered at launch $5 per 1000 views, with payment from 40,000 views, and a focus on 'professional content'.

Lulu - www.lulu.tv

Pools advertising revenues each month and distributes to all content creators proportional to the popularity of their video, after a 20% deduction.

Rights purchase

A number of websites operate closer to conventional broadcasters, commissioning and acquiring content, including Atom Entertainment (www.atomfilms.com), Addicting Clips (www.addictingclips.com), Expert Village (www.expertvillage.com), Break.com and early pioneer **Current TV** (www.current.tv). Unique among other online offerings, films uploaded to the Al Gore–backed website can be selected to appear on an accompanying Current TV cable channel, whereupon a special fee is negotiated with the creator. Current also sometimes commissions content from site producers, and pays up to $1,000 for user-generated adverts.

'Obscurity is a far greater threat to artists and authors than piracy'
Tim O'Reilly, O'Reilly Media

Sliding pricing

While not film-based, music site **AmieStreet.com** has an original and promising model. Music is offered initially for free, with its price increasing depending on the popularity of a song. Users who recommend a song or artist in turn receive a small share of money earned from music sales, both encouraging the user to listen to new work, rewarding 'early adopters' with free tracks, while an ever escalating price encourages further sales reflecting the 'value' of popular work.

'Realworld' distribution

As well as distributing films, the web has an increasing relationship with cinema's home, the big screen. Asides from marketing, where the web makes up less than 5% of distributor's budgets, sites such as Brave New Theaters provide a realworld version of online video whereby filmmakers can connect to audiences without a distributor, while digital looks set to shake things up even further.

Digital cinema – the Digital Screen Network

Long touted as the distribution solution for independents, digtial cinema removes almost all print costs and allows an exhibitor to take risks with content by changing programmes rapidly in response to popularity. Uptake of digital projectors by cinemas has been slowed in part by debate between exhibitors and distributors as to who most benefits from the technology and therefore should cover the installation costs. In addition digital projectors are estimated to have a 10-15 year shelf life, against 40+ years for film projectors, and the cost of upgrading in some markets makes a full digital transition unlikely for some time.

> 'The big screen is cinema's natural habitat. There are convenient "zoos" like television, video and the Internet, but you can never emulate the experience of seeing a film on the big screen.'
> **Omid Nooshin, director, Panic**

The UK has used this impasse to try and become a global pioneer through the 240-screen Film Council backed Digital Screen Network. The £12m scheme, operated by venture capital firm Arts Alliance, funds the installation of digital projectors in return for exhibitors committing to showing a certain proportion of 'specialised films' which can include work from local and community organisations. The UKFC Distribution and Exhibition department will consider any film for inclusion on its specialised film list, whether from producers or distributors, although it is up to the exhibitor to then book the film. Specialised films are defined as 'films that do not sit easily within a mainstream and highly commercial genre' (a full definition at www.ukfilmcouncil.org.uk/cinemagoing/distributionandexhibition/dsn/specialisedfilms/definition/)

For rights holders, digital exhibition offers a flexibility that traditional film-dependent distribution can't. Producers or cinemas could invite people to commit to buying tickets for niche, undistributed or little-known films, and when enough people in the area commit to make a screening cost effective it can be organised at minimal risk (subject to scheduling). This could fit with the trend whereby films build an audience through an online presence ahead of a cinema release, such as *Four Eyed Monsters* (see case study chapter 2), where people vote for the film to screen in their neighborhood, and then they are screened in areas with enough votes. More info: www.ukdsn.org | en.wikipedia.org/wiki/Digital_cinema

Brave New Theaters (bravenewtheaters.com)

Bypassing conventional theatrical distribution altogether, Brave New Theaters links filmmakers directly with related interest groups, providing the tools to organise and advertise screenings. The site, which largely covers documentary and political films, provides a means for filmmakers to advertise their films to potential hosts, sell them a screening copy (usually a DVD), publicise screenings and reserve tickets. At publication over 9000 screenings had been run through the network (see interview with Jim Gilliam, who created the network, above).

PART II

INTERNATIONAL INCENTIVES

'People change, hairstyles change, interest rates fluctuate, actors become presidents' –
Top Secret, 1984

Things Change!

There. Have we made the point? Governmental incentives do not last forever. Tax breaks come and go, sometimes with very little notice (such as the sudden abolition of GAAP funds as a source of UK tax-based soft money in March 2007). Most of the research undertaken for this Part of the Handbook took place between October 2006 and February 2007 and, even during that period, a number of announcements were made, new schemes introduced and old ones abolished. The chances are, something referred to in this Handbook will change between the time you buy the book and the time you get it home. So check with the relevant tax authority, government department, film commission, screen agency or whatever, before making any major decisions about where to film. Note that even government and public body websites are far too regularly out-of-date, so don't automatically rely on them as gospel. If necessary, engage a local accountant and/or lawyer to give you formal, up-to-the-minute advice on the current state of play. Producers should check their eligibility at any given time, and make sure that, where necessary, their films are completed in time in order to access the relevant benefit before it disappears (assuming its phasing out is actually announced in advance!). However you do it, there is no substitute for taking proper advice before embarking on a production.

That said, as far as we are aware, this is the only major publication setting out all the major international financial incentives in detail, and it is a pretty accurate snap-shot of nearly 50 countries from around the world, as at 1 March 2007. Most of the information has been prepared in conjunction with, or verified against information provided or published by, relevant public bodies and/or specialist local law firms, with accuracy and applicability confirmed in 2007 before going to print. We don't pretend that the list is exhaustive, but it should serve as a fairly comprehensive guide to the most popular incentives at the time of going to press.

In this Part II, we cover all the main benefits that are considered large enough potentially to entice a Producer into choosing to shoot in one particular country over another. These include tax-incentives, such as rebates, allowances, deductions and credits, and public money, such as subsidies, grants, and other direct support. For the majority of these countries (those which have proved more popular in recent years), for each incentive on offer we set out a brief description of WHAT benefit is available (what type, how much), WHO is eligible to apply for it (producer, investor, local, foreigner, etc), HOW one actually qualifies (numerous eligibility criteria typically apply, often relating to size of budget, amounts to be spent locally, nationality of cast/crew/producer/investor, ownership of copyright, level of investment, etc), and WHERE the application for the benefit should be made (together in some cases with details of the procedure and documentary requirements). For the remainder of the countries, generally those less prevalent, we set out more briefly at the end of this Part II — under The Best of the Rest — the benefits available and aimed at attracting production. In all cases, relevant contact details and web resource information is provided. Unless specified otherwise, reference to any currency is to the local currency of the country referred to (ie. reference to '$' in the Canada section means Canadian dollars, and so on).

Note that we do not cover taxation issues that are not specific to or directed at the film industry, such as withholding tax and double taxation treaties. For guidance on these issues, you need an accountant with expert knowledge in these fields. Specialist collection agents like Fintage House (www.fintagehouse.com) and Freeway (www.freeway-entertainment.com) also have a lot of useful information and can provide excellent advice.

The Sections on Soft Money and Financial Incentives, and Co-productions and International Options, in Chapter 3 of this Handbook will help you to understand the meanings of the various terms and concepts referred to in this Part, and we strongly advise you to read that section carefully prior to launching into the next 100 or so pages. So, assuming you have done that, and before hitting you with a detailed country-by-country analysis, below is a brief sample of what's available and where.

Awards, Grants & Subsidies

So-called 'automatic' support is available in Australia, Austria, France, Germany, the Netherlands and Italy, amongst others. Significant selective support is also available in Australia, Austria, Colombia, Croatia, Denmark, Estonia, France, Germany, Greece, Hong Kong, Hungary, Iceland, India, Isle of Man, Israel, Italy, Macedonia, the Netherlands, New Zealand, Norway, Poland, Singapore, Slovenia, South Africa, South Korea, Sweden, and the UK (see Part III for UK funding).

Cash & Tax Rebates, Credits, Refunds & Offsets

These are available usually in respect of locally qualifying production spend. The figures given in this paragraph are the maximum net amounts potentially available, and can be totally misleading if taken in isolation without reading the detail in the relevant country section. They should definitely not be taken as sound-bites or used alone for comparison purposes. Schemes currently exist in Australia (12.5%), Canada (15% or 16% plus regional credits), Czech Republic (12.5% announced but not yet in place), Fiji (15%), France (16%), Germany (16%), Hungary (20%), Iceland (14%), Malta (20%), New Zealand (12.5%), Puerto Rico (40%), Serbia (21.5% announced but not yet in place), South Africa (15% or 25%), the UK (20%) and some states in the USA (eg. 30% in Connecticut).

Regional Funding

Substantial regional (as opposed to national) funding and/or tax breaks are available in Australia, Belgium, Brazil, Canada, Germany, the Netherlands, Sweden, the UK (see Part III) and the USA. Almost 1,000 regional funds are set out in Part III of the Handbook.

Tax Allowance / Deduction for Investors

Tax allowances (deductions) for investments in qualifying films exist in Australia, Belgium, Brazil, Colombia, France, Hungary (16% credit), Ireland, Jamaica, Luxembourg, Malta, Mexico, New Zealand, Romania, South Africa, and the USA.

Other Benefits

Other benefits for the film producer include those in China (lower taxes for foreign businesses), France (loan support guarantees), Indonesia (tax-free for foreign artists), Italy (soft-term loan guarantees) and Jamaica (income tax relief), amongst others.

UNVERZAGT · VON HAVE
RECHTSANWÄLTE

ENTERTAINMENT LAW & MEDIA FINANCE

HAMBURG

ΟTHENBAUMCHAUSSEE 43
148 HAMBURG
ΕL +49.40.41 40 00-0
MAIL hamburg@unverzagtvonhave.com

• BERLIN

MONBIJOUPLATZ 2
10178 BERLIN
TEL +49.30.28 87 63 33
E-MAIL berlin@unverzagtvonhave.com

• COLOGNE

FROHNHOFWEG 16
50858 KÖLN
TEL +49.221.346 82 16
E-MAIL koeln@unverzagtvonhave.com

www.unverzagtvonhave.com

AUSTRALIA (NATIONAL)

Prepared with the assistance of Clare Mirabello at TressCox Lawyers (www.tresscox.com.au)

I. INTRODUCTION

There are considerable commercial incentives and opportunities for filmmakers producing film and TV programmes in Australia. The Australian Government presently offers various taxation incentives such as **taxation rebates**, **credits**, **refunds** and **deductions**.

In certain circumstances, foreign producers are able to share the benefits offered by the Australian Government with the local producers, and take advantage of these benefits by producing films and TV programmes in Australia as official co-productions through the Official International Co-production Program.

The principal forms of assistance provided by the Australian Government to the film and TV industries are:

- Indirect assistance to producers through **tax concessions** granted to private film investors under Division **10B** and Division **10BA** of the Income Tax Assessment Act 1936 (the 1936 Tax Act).
- **Direct funding** to producers via the Film Finance Corporation Australia Limited (FFC).
- A **refundable tax** offset available to producers of large-budget film productions under the *Tax Laws Amendment (Film Incentives) Act 2002* (the Refundable Film Tax Offset).
- **Investment** by Film Licensed Investment Companies (**FLICs**).
- **Co-productions** via the Official International Co-Production Programme administered by the Australian Film Commission (AFC).
- Incentives provided by **State** bodies and State based government agencies.

II. THE 10B AND 10BA TAX ALLOWANCES

(a) WHAT is available?

DIVISION 10B

Division 10B entitles an investor to an **accelerated deduction** for the **capital cost** of **producing** or **acquiring copyright** in an **Australian film** (see below). It allows for a **100% deduction** to initial investors over **two financial years**, whereby up to 50% may be claimed in the financial year in which the film is made, and 50% in the subsequent year.

DIVISION 10BA

More popular than Division 10B is Division 10BA, which seeks to encourage private investment in culturally relevant, high quality **qualifying Australian film** (see below) and TV productions. Investors in 10BA certified films can claim an **immediate deduction** for the **full amount** of their investment in the year the investment is made, if the relevant requirements (see below) are met. Both 10B and 10BA can potentially be used for sale & leaseback, although no 'mini-industry' has popped up as it did in the UK during the late 1990s and early 2000s.

Producers cannot claim under both Division 10B and Division 10BA, and will generally make a choice between Division 10B and Division 10BA depending on the film's budget and the financing structure being used.

(b) WHO can apply?

DIVISION 10B

The Division 10B deduction is available to investors who are either residents or non-residents of Australia.

DIVISION 10BA

The Division 10BA deduction is available only to **investors** who are **residents** of Australia for taxation purposes, and who have spent capital in producing a film or as a contribution to its production.

(c) HOW do you qualify?

DIVISION 10B

The film must be an 'Australian film' (see below). Formats that are eligible for the Division 10B deduction are feature films, documentary, mini-series, short drama, multimedia, promotional, variety, educational, training and large format.

DIVISION 10BA

In order to qualify for 10BA, the following requirements must be met:
- The film must be Australian (see below);
- At the time the money was spent, the investor must expect to become one of the **first owners** of **copyright** in the film;
- The investor must intend to use the copyright for the **purpose of producing income** from the exhibition or broadcasting of the film or from granting rights to exhibit or broadcast the film;

- The investor's expenditure must be 'at risk', ie. s/he must suffer a loss if no income is derived from the exploitation of the film (this does *not* apply to pre-sales or distribution guarantees, as long as the pre-sales or distribution guarantees are not available to the investor to make the actual investment) - in other words, the investor cannot use distribution guarantees or pre-sales as investment funds.
- Where the investor contributes to the cost of producing (rather than acquiring) the film, a **declaration** must be given to the Commissioner of Taxation stating (amongst other things) that a production contract exists for the film.

The Division 10BA taxation deduction will be disallowed if in fact the investor does not become the first owner of copyright, or if the copyright is not used for the purpose of producing assessable income **within 24 months** after the end of the financial year in which the investment was made.

Those formats that are eligible for the 10BA certificate are feature films, telemovies, documentary, TV, mini-series, or children's TV mini series.

As the deduction is only available on money spent on **production**, finance and brokering fees will *not* be included as deductible.

Certification as an 'Australian film' or a 'qualifying Australian film'

An absolute and threshold requirement for obtaining this Australian Government assistance is that the film must be certified as either an '**Australian film**' (for the purposes of Division 10B) or, more restrictively, a '**qualifying Australian film**' (for the purpose of Division 10BA). Decisions on whether a film is an Australian film or a qualifying Australian ilm are made by the Minister for the Department of Communications, Information, Technology and the Arts (**DCITA**), or the Minister's delegate. See the DCITA website (below) for more details.

Australian Film

A film will be an '**Australian film**' if it is either:
- made wholly or **substantially in Australia** and has '**significant Australian content**'; or
- an **official co-production** made under a treaty or similar arrangement between the Australian Government and another government (see below).

Qualifying Australian Film

A **qualifying Australian Film** is an Australian Film (see above) which is a feature film (including an animated feature length movie), a telemovie (including half hour adult and 15 minute children's animated telemovies), a mini-series or a documentary which has been produced for exhibition to the public in cinemas or on TV (an eligible film).

Television commercials, chat shows, quiz shows, panel shows, variety shows, series or serials, training films or films of public events, which may be 'Australian Films' are not eligible, and together with productions which are not sufficiently Australian, do not qualify.

Australian Content

Ministerial guidelines concerning the criteria used to assess whether a particular film is an Australian film state that '*the determination of significant Australian content is a matter of judgment by the Minister based on consideration of all the elements of a particular project*' and if there are non-Australian elements, the producer should provide justification of these elements and there should be other strong Australian elements. According to the guidelines, the factors that will be considered include:
- the **subject matter** of the film;
- the shooting **location** of the film;
- the **nationalities** and places of **residence** of the producer, writer, director, lead actors and other cast and crew;
- the effective **ownership** of the **production company** (which would normally be expected to be exclusively Australian);
- **sources of finance** for the film;
- the **owners of copyright** in the film;
- details of **production expenditure**; and
- any other matters the Minister considers relevant.

Many of these factors are relevant to determining who ultimately has creative and commercial **control** over the film. The Minister may still refuse certification as an Australian film or a qualifying Australian film, even though the film has significant Australian content, if the film also has significant non-Australian content.

Certificate from DCITA

A prerequisite for obtaining either the Division 10B or 10BA deduction is that at the time the investment was expended, a **provisional certificate** must have already been issued by the DCITA, confirming that the film is an Australian film or (as the case may be) a qualifying Australian film. Provisional certification may be obtained by the producer early in the production process and can be used by producers to attract and secure investment for the project. In order to obtain provisional certification, applicants need to apply to DCITA together with a budget, script or synopsis, and a list of intended cast and crew.

In the case of a Division 10BA Deduction, the producer of the film must following completion obtain a **final certificate** from the DCITA confirming that the film was in fact made as a qualifying Australian film. Application for final certification must be made within six months of completion of the film and should set out the final budget of the project, script, and DVD or video copy of the film.

ATO Product Ruling

Although this is not a legal requirement, it is a useful tool often obtained by a producer in order to give potential investors a degree of comfort. An **ATO product ruling** is a determination by the Australian Taxation Office (ATO) on the certainty of the taxation benefits that investors will be able to claim (for example Division 10B or Division 10BA deductions) if they participate in the investment fund for the film. Product rulings are binding on the ATO so long as the investment scheme is implemented in the way it is described in the product ruling application. As a matter of practice producers generally seek an ATO product ruling after obtaining preliminary certification from the DCITA (see below). Obtaining a product ruling can be an expensive and time consuming process and will often not be applied for unless the fundraising is for a substantial amount.

More information about the product ruling system can be found in the ATO document PR 1999/95 'Income Tax and Fringe Benefits Tax Product Ruling System'. The ATO website at www.ato.gov.au also provides information on product ruling applications in respect to film schemes, including the application form.

(d) WHERE do you apply?

The finance itself is usually accessed through specialist brokers. Applicants seeking 10B and 10BA certification must apply to the **DCITA**:

Film Incentives and International Section
Department of Communications, Information, Technology and the Arts
GPO Box 2154, Canberra ACT 2601
www.dcita.gov.au/arts_culture/film

III. THE REFUNDABLE FILM TAX OFFSET

(a) WHAT is available?

The **Refundable Film Tax Offset** is available for domestic or foreign film production companies in respect of **qualifying Australian production expenditure (QAPE)** that the company incurs on a film, so long as that expenditure exceeds A$15m. It provides an incentive for large foreign film and high-budget TV series productions to be produced in Australia.

The tax offset reduces the applicant's tax liability by an amount equal to **12.5%** of its qualifying Australian production expenditure. Due to the minimum QAPE requirement (see below), this will equate to between **8.75% and 12.5% of the total budget**.

If the offset exceeds the company's tax liability, the excess is **refundable** as a payment to the production company.

Note that those productions that access any other incentive scheme, such as Division 10B or Division 10BA, will not be eligible for the Refundable Film Tax Offset (although simply obtaining a 10BA provisional certificate will not disqualify the film).

(b) WHO can apply?

The benefit is available to the main production company (or, if QAPE exceeds A$50m, then the production company responsible for the Australian element of production) of any feature film, mini-series, or telemovie (and has recently been extended to TV series), irrespective of the source of funds or control or degree of Australian content. Foreign companies may apply if they have an Australian Business Number.

(c) HOW do you qualify?

The eligibility requirements are that:
- the film is **certified** by the Minister of the DCITA as being completed on or after 4 September 2001;
- it has a **minimum QAPE of A$15m**, and
- **70%** or (if lower) **A$50m** of the total production expenditure (see below) must qualify as **QAPE**.

Total Production Expenditure
This is the cost of production incurred effectively from pre-production to delivery, but *excluding* the following:
- Financing and development costs;
- Copyright acquisition;

- Overhead;
- Distribution, advertising, publicity (etc) costs;
- Deferments;
- Depreciating asset acquisitions.

QAPE

However, some of the above (eg. copyright acquisition, overhead, development and certain publicity costs), if spent in Australia, *are* included in QAPE, mainly to encourage these activities to take place in Australia. Of course, this increases the chances of hitting the 70% minimum mentioned above.

Generally (subject to a few specific exclusions), to be included for QAPE, expenditure must be on goods and/or services **provided in** or, at the time they (including land) are used in the production, **located in,** Australia.

(d) WHERE do you apply?

Applications should be made to the relevant Australian Taxation Office at the time the company lodges its income tax return.

IV. FFC FUNDING

(a) WHAT is available?

The Australian Film Finance Corporation (FFC) is a company wholly owned by the Australian Government which provides substantial financial support to feature films, telemovies, mini-series or documentaries that have been issued a **provisional certificate** under Division 10BA of the *1936 Tax Act* (see above for eligibility criteria). It does not provide funds by means of grants or subsidies, but principally by means of **equity investment**.

In the last few years the FFC's policies have become more flexible, leading it on a case-by-case basis to provide support by way of **production loans** (which are generally non-recourse loans whereby the FFC recoups in first position from the theatrical exploitation of the film, and then from exploiting all other rights in the film until the loan is repaid), **print and advertising (P&A) loans** to facilitate the theatrical release of feature films (both in and outside Australia), and **distribution guarantees** for the purpose of producers securing private investors (whereby the FFC agrees to advance money to the Producer to be repaid to the FFC upon distribution of the completed film, the financial benefits of which can be used as an incentive to obtain private investment).

The Australian Government is the principal source of the FFC's funds. For each of the three financial years up to 2006/2007 the FFC received A$50m in base funding from the Government as well as an additional A$10m per year specifically for feature films and A$10.5m per year specifically for TV drama. The FFC's total funds for the year are also derived from revenues earned from investments in previous years that are still active in the marketplace. The investment terms are generally determined on a case-by-case basis depending upon the private sector participation.

The FFC is unable to fully fund productions, and FFC funded productions must have some form of private sector participation (such as Division 10BA investments and/or pre-sales to broadcasters).

(b) WHO can apply?

Any producer may apply direct to the FFC for funding if the project concerned meets the FFC's requirements (see below).

(c) HOW do you qualify?

The applicant must have already received a **provisional certificate** under Division 10BA (see above) and some form of private-sector finance. Different guidelines apply to different types of production, such as feature films, adult TV drama, children's TV drama, documentaries and co-productions. Generally, when determining whether to provide funding the FFC will consider the potential market support for the production, and the production's creative, market and audience potential. The FFC also has administrative requirements that must be met by applicants who apply for funding. The full FFC funding policies are set out in published guidelines which are available on their website (see below).

(d) WHERE do you apply?

Film Finance Corporation Australia Ltd (FFC)
Level 12, 130 Elizabeth Street
SYDNEY NSW 2000
www.ffc.gov.au

V. FILM LICENSED INVESTMENT COMPANIES (FLIC) SCHEME

(a) WHAT is available?

FLICs were introduced in 1999 as a way of attracting private **investment finance** for the production of certified Australian films and TV programmes by offering concessions to the FLICs' own investors (they get a 100% tax deduction for the cost of their shares). A licensed FLIC may raise up to A$10m (for 2005/06 and 2006/07), and will be required to invest all of the capital raised by 30 June 2008 in a range of productions, thereby resulting in up to A$20m being invested in the Australian film industry in this way. The terms offered by FLICs are not necessarily any better then other commercial terms; they are merely another source of funds for filmmakers in an environment where funds are generally very limited. The FLIC scheme was introduced as part of the federal Government's 2004 election package in order to inject additional funding into the film industry.

(b) WHO can apply?

Any producer of a qualifying Australian film can attract FLIC investment from a licensed FLIC.

(c) HOW do you qualify?

The film must meet the eligibility and content requirements of a **qualifying Australian film** (see Division 10BA, above).

Note that those qualifying Australian films that receive assistance from a FLIC will not be able to access other concessions, such as the Refundable Film Tax Offset.

(d) WHERE do you apply?

The FLIC scheme is administered by DCITA, but the relevant FLIC licensee determines how to invest the funds in qualifying Australian films. At the commencement of the pilot FLIC scheme two companies, Macquarie Film Corporation and Content Capital were given two years to raise A$40m in concessional capital. The only existing FLIC single licensee is Mullis Capital Film Licensed Investment Company Ltd, whose website is: www.mulliscapital.com

VI. OFFICIAL CO-PRODUCTIONS

Co-productions in general and their benefits are discussed in more detail in Chapter 3 in this *Handbook*, but the following may be useful in relation to their specific administration in Australia.

Foreign filmmakers may co-produce films with Australian producers in certain circumstances. The Official International Co-Production Programme is administered by the **Australian Film Commission** (AFC). In order for co-productions to qualify as official co-productions, they must be made in accordance with the terms of a treaty or a 'less than treaty arrangement'.

The Australian Government has entered into formal co-production treaties with the governments of the United Kingdom and Northern Ireland (**UK**), **Canada**, Republic of **Ireland**, **Italy**, **Israel** and **Germany** (each with a minimum 30% Australia creative contribution, see below). Memoranda of Understanding or arrangements described as 'less than treaty status' (MoUs) have been made with the governments of **France**, **New Zealand** and **Vietnam** (with a 40% minimum Australia contirbution). An agreement with China is planned for the future.

To obtain approval of a film as an official co-production, the Australian producer must first apply to the **AFC** using the form of application provided by the AFC. Relevant documentation will need to be provided to the AFC including the budget, the script, the script chain-of-title, presentation credits, producer's undertakings, copies of the executed co-production agreement between the co-producers and executed financing agreements. The foreign co-producer must make a separate application to its equivalent foreign authority. The AFC will assess the application based on set criteria such as:

- The underlying work must either be out of copyright, or written by a national or resident of Australia or the co-producing country;
- There must be a co-producer from each of the relevant countries and the producers, between them, must contribute 100% of the cost of the proposed co-production film;
- The Australian producer's **creative contribution** to the production must meet a set percentage (which varies depending on the individual co-production treaty, but is typically 30% for treaties and 40% for 'less-than-treaty' arrangements).

There is a **points test** used to determine the level of creative contribution, whereby one point is given to the director of photography, composer, editor, production designer and each of the four lead cast, and two points given to the director and writer (totalling 12).

Consultation will also take place between the AFC and the foreign competent authority. AFC approval will not be given until both the AFC and the foreign body have approved the production as eligible.

Once the project is approved as an official co-production by the AFC, the Australian producer must apply to the **DCITA** for a **provisional certificate** as a qualifying Australian film.

VII. THE AFC AND STATE BODIES

The Australian Film Commission (AFC) has additional funds available, mostly for development. However it does sometimes provide production financing for low-budget films which would otherwise find difficulty in obtaining finance from more traditional sources (see Part III).

A number of State government agencies also provide **development funding** as well as incentives or inducements to attract film production to their relevant State, and in doing so actively encourage international production. They also offer free assistance with location, liaison and advice on local product and post-production facilities. These bodies include:

Australian Film Commission: www.afc.gov.au
NSW Film & Television Office: www.fto.nsw.gov.au
Film Victoria: www.film.vic.gov.au
South Australian Film Corp: www.safilm.com.au
Screen West: www.screenwest.com.au
Screen Tasmania: www.screen.tas.gov.au
Pacific Film & TV Commission: www.pftc.com.au

Some regions within States provide further incentives to produce films in their region. For example in New South Wales (NSW), the following organisations provide support to the film industry:

Film Broken Hill (www.filmbrokenhill.com) assists filmmakers with various resources such as location, crew, facilities, transport, financial incentives, and travel. Film Central NSW (www.filmcentralnsw.com) offers assistance to filmmakers in relation to locations. Film Illawarra (www.filmillawarra.org.au) works with 5 regional councils in NSW to promote the Illawarra region to filmmakers, and provides information on local resources and locations. Film Mid North Coast Armidale (www.filmmnca.org/about.asp) represents the screen industry of the Mid North Coast region of NSW. Northern Rivers Screenworks (www.screenworks.com.au) provides crew, location and other information in relation to the Northern Rivers region of NSW.

More useful information is available at www.ausfilm.com.uk

AUSTRALIA (REGIONAL — QUEENSLAND)

Prepared with the assistance of Pacific Film and Television Commission (www.pftc.com.au)

I. INTRODUCTION

A number of Australian regions (states and territories) provide significant financial incentives for film production. Set out below, as an example, is the regime currently in place in Queensland, where there are a number of film-related studios and facilities, including the world-class Warner Roadshow Movie World Studios on the Gold Coast. Recent films made in Queensland include *Scooby Doo*, *Peter Pan* and *House of Wax*.

The Queensland Government's **Pacific Film and Television Commission** (**PFTC**) facilitates and celebrates quality film and TV production in Queensland. PFTC's key roles are to attract international production to Queensland, develop and support the local film industry and celebrate an active screen culture across the State. To help achieve these objectives, the Queensland Government through PFTC offers **four film incentives** and a range of development and investment schemes to encourage producers and production companies to film in Queensland and to generate production and employment opportunities for Queenslanders. The production incentives include a **State Payroll Tax Rebate**, **12.5% State Labour Incentive**, **Head of Department Incentive** and a pilot **Post-Production Incentive**.

II. TAX REBATE AND INCENTIVES

(a) — (c) WHAT is available, WHO can apply, and HOW do you qualify?

GENERAL REQUIREMENTS

To be eligible for all the production incentives, the **production office** must be based **in Queensland** and the Production Company or Production Services Company applying for the incentive must have an **Australian Business Number** (ABN) and be registered for the Goods and Services Tax (**GST**).

Feature films, telemovies and TV series (including reality, drama, animation and mini-series) are the types of projects eligible to apply for these incentives.

THE STATE PAYROLL TAX REBATE

The aim is to increase production of film and TV projects in Queensland by providing **full rebates** of Queensland **Payroll Tax** to all eligible productions.

There are two options for this rebate, being (i) a project with a **minimum A$3.5m** spend during production in Queensland, or (ii) the bundling of two or more productions with a minimum **individual** Queensland spend of **A$1m** and a minimum **combined** Queensland spend of **A$5m** within a **four-year** period by one production company or production services company.

The rebate will be eligible to be processed at the conclusion of principal photography, or upon the cessation of the liability of a production company to pay Queensland payroll tax in respect of the relevant production, whichever occurs the later.

THE 12.5% STATE LABOUR INCENTIVE

This aims to increase employment of Queensland **cast** and **crew** by providing a cash incentive for all *bona fide* Queensland cast and crew employed on the production. This incentive is calculated at **12.5% of the basic salary/wage costs** (other than rebatable payroll tax) of *bona fide* Queensland cast and crew employed on the production. The incentive is subject to a remuneration package ceiling of **A$2,500 per week per employee**.

There are two categories of eligibility for the 12.5% State Labour Incentive.

Drama productions (including animation productions) *not* receiving PFTC equity investments are eligible to apply for the following maximum incentive, based on qualifying production expenditure in Queensland (please note all $ are Australian dollars):

- Expenditure between $2.5m to $4.99m: maximum incentive of $100,000
- Expenditure between $5m to $9.99m: maximum incentive of $200,000
- Expenditure between $10m to $14.99m: maximum incentive of $400,000
- Expenditure between $15m to $19.99m: maximum incentive of $550,000
- Expenditure between $20m to $24.99m: maximum incentive of $700,000
- Expenditure between $25m to $29.99m: maximum incentive of $850,000
- For expenditure of $30m and above, the applicant should approach PFTC directly.

Non-drama productions (including reality) and productions in receipt of PFTC equity investment are eligible to apply for the following maximum incentive, based on qualifying production expenditure in Queensland:

- Expenditure between $2.5m to $4.99m: maximum incentive of $75 000
- Expenditure between $5m to $9.99m: maximum incentive of $100 000
- Expenditure between $10m to $14.99m: maximum incentive of $200 000
- Expenditure $15m and above: maximum incentive of $300 000.

THE HEAD OF DEPARTMENT INCENTIVE

This aims to increase employment of Queensland **crew** by providing up to **A$50,000 cash incentive** for *bona fide* Queensland Heads of Department employed on the production. The maximum incentive available is **A$25,000** per Head of Department for a **maximum of two** eligible Heads of Department employed on a Production. Eligible Heads of Department are those who are currently enrolled on the Queensland **Electoral Roll**, and have been for a minimum of **six months** or if not on the Queensland Electoral Roll, those that can substantiate proof of residency in Queensland for at least six months prior to the production commencing. To qualify for this incentive, a production must satisfy the following minimum spend requirements:

For the maximum incentive of **A$50,000** for two Heads of Department, a minimum Queensland spend of **A$5m** on production; or for a partial incentive of **A$25,000** for one Head of Department – a minimum Queensland spend of **A$3.5m** on production.

In addition to the above, each Head of Department must be employed by the production for a minimum ten-week period, and s/he must hire a minimum of four Queensland-based crew.

It is recommended that applicants contact PFTC prior to applying for the incentive to clarify which department areas are eligible.

THE POST-PRODUCTION INCENTIVE

This aims to increase **post-production** of film and TV projects in Queensland by providing cash incentives to production companies contracting Queensland post-production facilities. It is a pilot scheme. Incentives will be available to maximum limits per production based on qualifying expenditure in Queensland as follows:

- Qualifying expenditure between A$1m to $1.99m incentive of **A$100,000**
- Qualifying expenditure between A$2m to $2.99m incentive of **A$200,000**
- Qualifying expenditure A$3m & above maximum incentive of **A$300,000**

For the purposes of this incentive, post-production is defined as those activities that enhance or finish a film or TV product, in preparation for its distribution. While the process by definition typically takes place away from the production, it is not limited to those activities undertaken at the completion of principal photography. Rather, it is acknowledged that digital technology has caused substantial structural change to the post-production process and as such some elements may be undertaken during the production shoot.

The definition of 'post-production' is detailed in the production incentive guidelines.

(d) WHERE do you apply?

Applications must be submitted at the start of **pre-production**. PFTC approval for the incentives must be **in place prior to the start of production**. Bundled approvals should be sought prior to the start of the first production. Applications are open all year for incentives. Decisions are subject to approval of PFTC's Industry Development Committee (IDC) and are based on both the applicant having met the eligibility criteria in the guidelines and the availability of funds.

For a copy of PFTC's Production Incentives Application Form or the full incentive guidelines visit www.pftc.com.au/incentives or contact PFTC on the following details:

Pacific Film and Television Commission
PO Box 15094, Brisbane City East
Queensland 4002, Australia
T: (+617) 3224 411
www.pftc.com.au/

Note that other states in Australia also have incentives including, for example, **South Australia** (www.safilm.com.au) and **Victoria** (www.film.vic.gov.au) (see part III).

AUSTRIA

I. INTRODUCTION

In Austria, independent films make up a considerable proportion of the national film industry. The **Austrian Film Institute** (*Österreichisches Filminstitut*, or '**AFI**') is the federal funding body. It awards funds in the form of **soft loans** for film production, and also grants for script and project development. Money is available for Austrian and international filmmakers with Austrian participation. Other sources of support include **regional funds** (such as the *Vienna Filmfund*) and awards from the **Austrian Broadcasting Corporation** (ORF) under the *FilmFernsehabkommen* (Film/TV Agreement). Austria is a member of Eurimages and the EU MEDIA programme (see Part III), and has a co-production agreement with Canada.

II. FEDERAL PUBLIC FUND

(a) WHAT is available?

Funding from the AFI supports film production chosen on the basis of quality of project (**selective funding**) or performance (**reference film funding or automatic funding**). It is available in the form of **soft loans**, **conditionally repayable** or **non-repayable contributions**. Production funding that is repayable to the AFI can be reimbursed by converting it into automatic funding.

In the 2006 film industry report published by the AFI, the annual amount of public financial support totalled €33.475m (which included funding for TV productions).

(b) WHO can apply?

The applicant (usually the producer) must be an **Austrian national** with a **residence** in Austria. If the applicant is a non-individual legal entity (eg. the production company), it must have a **registered seat** in Austria or have an Austrian **branch** if it is an EU company.

(c) HOW do you qualify?

The applicant must show that funding is **essential** for realisation of the project, and the film must be an **Austrian film** or official **co-production**.

To qualify as an Austrian film, the **creative and managerial decision-makers** must be **Austrian nationals** along with the **majority** of the **crew**.

A final version of the film must be made in **German**, and the film shot **in Austria** (except any scenes necessarily requiring foreign locations). A foreign film, where its Austrian contribution is limited to financial participation and with no less than 10% production cost, may be considered as an Austrian film under certain conditions.

To qualify as an international co-production, the must fulfil the requirements of the relevant intergovernmental treaty (if it exists), otherwise the Austrian participation in the financial, creative and technical aspects of the film must be no less than 30%. The AFI may choose only to award funding to the Austrian financial share.

To be eligible for **automatic** funding, the producer must have produced a 'reference film' that has achieved 'artistic success' (participation or award-winner in an Austrian recognised international film festival) or 'economic success' (admissions in Austrian cinemas).

'Commissioned' films cannot apply.

(d) WHERE do you apply?

Applications should be sent to the AFI, and applicants must submit auditable financing and production schedules with their applications.

Österreichisches Filminstitut
Spittelberggasse 3
1070 Wien
T: +43 1 526 97 30
F: +43 1 526 97 30 440
www.filminstitut.at/
office@fiminstitut.at

BELGIUM

Prepared with the assistance of Marx Van Ranst
Vermeersch & Partners (www.mvvp.be)

I. INTRODUCTION

In Belgium, private investors can benefit from a
tax shelter system. Being a federal country, the
Flemish and **French** communities have their own
public funding schemes. The **Walloon** Region has
also set up a regional programme for **funding** the
local audiovisual industry. The different communities
provide various types of support for producers based
on different criteria and classification systems. These
can be spend-related, and may be repayable in
certain circumstances.

II. GENERAL TAX ALLOWANCE FOR PRIVATE INVESTORS

(a) WHAT is available?

Under the **Belgian Cinema Tax Shelter**, a
corporation tax allowance is available to **private
investors** (including foreign companies that pay
non-resident corporate income tax) for investing
in a qualifying Belgian audiovisual production (see
below). The investing company can deduct **150%**
of the investment from its pre-tax profits. The
maximum tax-deductible amount is capped at €750k
per company in each taxable period, which
corresponds to an investment of €500k.

The actual tax-deductible amount must not exceed
50% of the investing company's pre-tax profits.

More than one company can obtain the
tax allowance by investing in the same film. It
may therefore be worthwhile trying to attract
several investing companies, despite the rather
'unsubstantial' individual amounts available from
individual investors.

These tax shelter investments can provide
producers with **up to 50%** of the film's **budget**.

(b) WHO can apply?

The investing company must be either a Belgian
company who pays the Belgian corporate income
tax, or a foreign company who pays the Belgian non-
resident corporate income tax.

The investing company itself *cannot* be a
production company, a TV company, or a bank.
At the same time, the production company (which

benefits from the investing company) cannot be a TV
company.

(c) HOW do you qualify?

The investments must be made in the production
of feature films, 'long' fiction TV films (since 2006),
documentaries or certain animated films.

The investing company can provide the tax
shelter investments in two forms: as a **loan** to the
production, or as **equity** (thereby being entitled to
a share of profits). Up to **50%** of the production
budget can be funded this way, a maximum of 40%
of which may be by loan, and the remaining 60% (or
more) of the investment in equity.

The production company must also agree to spend
an equivalent amount of 150% of the tax shelter
equity investment in production or exploitation
costs *in Belgium*. These conditions must be listed
as a guarantee in the general financing framework
agreement (see below). As an example, for a
production budget of €10m, only €5m can be raised
as tax shelter investments, of which no more than
€2m is in loan. Also, the producer has to spend €4.5m
(150% of €3m) in production or exploitation costs in
Belgium.

A general financing framework agreement between
the parties should set out how the tax shelter monies
get recouped.

(d) WHERE do you apply?

The **financing framework agreement** must be
filed by the investing company, together with a
tax declaration. Within four years, the production
company needs to obtain and deliver to the investing
company two certificates, one from the Ministry of
Finance, and the other from the Ministry of Culture
concerning completion and that all conditions have
been met.

III. PUBLIC FUNDING (FLEMISH COMMUNITY)

(a) WHAT is available?

The **Flemish Audiovisual Fund (VAF)** provides
public funding for films in the form of **cash grants**
(see Part III). The funding principles of VAF are laid
down in the management agreement (renewed every
three years) between the Flemish Community and the
VAF, and in the regulations of the VAF.

At the time of writing, the 2006/08 management
agreement, which had been expected at the end of
2006, was still to be finalised. For 2006, the total

funding was set at €12m, and is expected to rise in the coming years.

There are four categories of funding ('support'), being **scenario**, **development**, **production** and **promotional**. The maximum amount of support depends on the type and length of the audiovisual production, the kind of support sought, and other criteria such as the promotion of Flemish culture. Depending on the type of film to be produced, the current maximum amounts of funding are €7.5k to €12.5k for scenario, €75k to €250k for development, **€87.5k to €1250k** for production, and €25k for promotion.

The total amount cannot exceed 50% of the production budget.

In principle, the support is non-repayable, except for the production support, which is recoverable when the film goes into profit.

(b) WHO can apply?

The applicant has to be independent, meaning that s/he can only be limitedly involved in or owned by a broadcasting organisation or a governmental institution. VAF can participate in the financing of Flemish productions as well as in the financing of the Flemish share of co-productions.

(c) HOW do you qualify?

Four categories of audiovisual productions can qualify, being animation, documentaries, fictional films, and experimental media art. They *exclude* sitcoms, soaps or formats, commercial productions, educational projects, pornography and/or (s)exploitation films, or productions ordered by a governmental institution or by companies and individuals with their seat in Belgium.

The support must be **spent** in the **Flemish Community** (the Flemish Region or the Region of Brussels Capital City), unless this condition is waived by agreement with VAF.

The VAF will base their granting decision on the advice given from one of the following five assessment committees: animation, documentary, experimental media art, short-length fiction and long-length fiction.

The applicant chooses and files the application with the appropriate committee. Support will only be granted when the applicant provides satisfactory proof of financial standing and ability to fulfil its financial obligations.

Each type of support requires a different application form.

(d) WHERE do you apply?

VAF
Handelskaai 18/3
1000 BRUSSELS
T: +02 226 0630
F: +02 219 1936
www.vaf.be
info@vaf.be

Depending on the type of support required, e-mails should be sent to specific persons within the VAF. Visit the website for details.

IV. PUBLIC FUNDING (FRENCH COMMUNITY)

(a) WHAT is available?

Cash grants are available from the **Centre du Cinéma et de l'Audiovisuel** (**CCA**) of the French Community. Similar to funding from the Flemish community, the maximum amount depends on the category of support and the type of production. Grants are given after selection of projects by the Film Selection Commission, which distinguishes between '**majority**' (if the director, at least one principal cast and one lead technician are Belgians) and '**minority**' productions.

Grant limits are set differently if previous support has been granted.

The support is spend-related, and all of it must be spent in Belgium or on the benefit of persons or companies whose tax domicile is in Belgium.

For long-length features, production support can be awarded up to €150k for minority productions, €375k for first majority productions, €500k for other majority productions, and €625k for third and subsequent fiction cinematographic majority productions with a budget of over **€2.5m**. Finishing funds (for completion of the production once shooting is complete) are limited to €75k, and Scenario support is capped at €12.5k.

The support is recoverable from profits, capped at **200%** of the amount awarded. The CCA is entitled to **50% of the Belgian producer's share of profits** until 100% of the awarded amount has been recovered. After that, the share of the CCA is **reduced to 25%**.

Production support can also be granted for short-length features, documentary, fictional films for TV, and animation films.

(b) WHO can apply?

For long-length features, producers (and co-producers on official co-productions) are entitled to apply for funding. To be eligible, the project must be presented by a production company based **in Belgium** and **run by EU citizens**, and the company cannot be connected, directly or indirectly, to broadcasters or public authorities.

For other films, additional rules may apply (eg. for fictional films for TV, the director or the cinematographer, plus one principal cast and two lead technicians, must be EU citizens; for documentaries, the cinematographer must be an EU citizen; for TV production, the director or cinematographer, and two lead technicians must be EU citizens).

(c) HOW do you qualify?

As mentioned above, for length features, a distinction is made between majority productions and minority productions. A **majority production** is one where the director, at least one principal cast and one lead technician are Belgian. Otherwise it is considered a **minority production**. Support cannot be granted to two subsequent minority productions from the same producer (the 'alternation rule'). For minority productions, the producer must have already secured **at least 30%** of the budget.

Production support can also be granted to short (up to 60 minutes) fiction, documentary and animation films of cinematographic type, if the producer is a Belgian company, owns the majority of the production's share and if the director is a citizen of an EU member state.

For fictional TV production (films and animation), a distinction is also made between majority and minority productions (it being a majority if the producer is a Belgian company and owns the majority of the production's share). Support can be awarded if the director, one principal cast and two lead technicians are citizens of an EU member state, and if the producer has secured at least 15% of the budget from a broadcaster.

Documentaries, animations and shorts made for TV, as well as TV series can also be awarded support, under various conditions.

(d) WHERE do you apply?

The projects are first presented to the **Film Selection Commission**, who will decide if they are eligible. Eligible projects must then be presented to an **Approval Group** within 12 months. The Approval Group will grant provisional approval if it considers the project viable after examining the provisional documents. These documents contain details such as the listing of involved technicians and actors, the budget and the financing plan, intention letters of partners, drafts of contracts, etc. If the project is considered viable, it must be re-submitted to the Approval Group, with the finalised documents within 12 months, for a final approval. Applications must be filed with specific forms, and the exact number of copies required depends on the type of support (between 7 and 12 copies).The applications should be sent to the following address:

Madame Marie-Louise Van Durme
Secrétariat de la Commission de Sélection des Films
Communauté française de Belgique
44 Bvd Léopold II, Local 4B051
1080 BRUXELLES
www.cfwb.be/av

V. PUBLIC FUNDING (WALLOON REGION)

(a) WHAT is available?

The Wallonian incentive is awarded by the agency **Wallimage**. Usually this is split as a **40% loan** and the rest as a 'co-production investment share' (here the 'co-producer' being Wallimage).

This system is spend-related. At least **€250k** must be spent **in Wallonia** on expenses for products or services in relation to the audiovisual sector (an exception applies for documentaries where local expenditure must be equivalent to 15% of the production's total budget). The amount of the total incentive may not exceed the amount spent in Wallonia and is capped at €500k (it generally equates to about €300k). If the amount spent in Wallonia exceeds the incentive granted, the share of the loan in the total incentive can decrease, with a minimum loan share of 10% (which can be obtained if the eligible expenses amount to 250% of the total incentive granted by Wallimage).

The loan is granted at a yearly rate of **2.5%** interest and must be reimbursed in four half-yearly payments, beginning 18 months after signature of the relevant agreement. No interest is due for the first year. The investment's share gives Wallimage first ranking on the film's revenues until the investment is recouped and, after recoupment, to a further right in a share of the revenue, equal to the Wallimage's share of investment in the film. There must also be co-ownership of the material and immaterial rights, including copyright, in proportion to the amount of Wallimage's share of the budget.

(b) WHO can apply?

To be eligible, the project must be presented by a **production company based in Wallonia** and **run by EU citizens** (Production Companies can be set up in the same way and under the same general conditions as other companies, and there are no specific taxes on production companies). The company cannot be connected, directly or indirectly, to broadcasters. Co-productions with foreign producers are permitted.

(c) HOW do you qualify?

Most types of cinematographic or TV production is eligible, although commercials, shows, news and sports productions are not. The producer must have **already raised 30%** of its budget, and must also present evidence of the planned expenditures in Wallonia.

Wallimage selects the granting of incentives based on the following criteria:
• The structural effect on the audiovisual sector in Wallonia;
• The viability of the project and the possibilities for return on Wallimage's investment;
• The credibility of the project's promoter and his team; and
• The budget funds still available that year.

(d) WHERE do you apply?

Four copies of applications must be filed, and sent to the attention of the director of Wallimage.

WALLIMAGE sa
Rue du Onze Novembre, 6
7000 Mons
T: +32 65 40 40 33
F: +32 65 40 40 39
www.wallimage.be
info@wallimage.be

BRAZIL
Prepared with the assistance of Code 7 (www.code7.com)

I. INTRODUCTION

Brazil has several specific film-related Tax Waiver Laws for promoting the film industry, and has co-production treaties with Argentina, Canada, France, Germany, Italy, Portugal, and Spain. The tax incentives are aimed specifically at direct investment, usually through funds set up to utilise the relevant incentive program. Recent Brazilian international successes include the highly acclaimed and multi-awarded films *Central do Brasil* (*Central Station*), *O Quatrilho*, *Four Days in September* and *City of God*. The exchange rate is (very) approximately US$1:R$2.

II. TAX DEDUCTIONS

AUDIOVISUAL LAW

(a) WHAT is available?

The **AUDIOVISUAL LAW** incentive is aimed specifically at film investment (as opposed to cultural investment generally — see below). An **income tax allowance** is available for **private investors** under the Audiovisual Law, which allows a deduction for up to 3% of the investor's Income Tax liability. These private investors (or 'backers') need to obtain an **investment certificate** from the production company in order to access the tax allowance. The investor becomes a partner in the film, receiving **quotas** (shares), and earns a percentage of the film producer's net income. In Brazil, companies pay two taxes simultaneously. The first is known as Income Tax (to which the allowance and 3% cap apply), at a rate of 15%. The other is called Additional Income Tax, at 10%, although companies cannot benefit from a deduction to this tax. The amounts invested by corporate taxpayers under the Audiovisual Law can effectively be deducted twice, once generally as operating expenses, then again as a deduction from income tax, thereby giving a kind of '**double benefit**'.

(b) WHO can apply?

The production company applies and issues an **investment certificate**, which is then given to the investor ('the backer') to obtain the tax allowance. Any company that pays income taxes and any individual persons who file their tax declarations under the 'complete model' can deduct up to 3% of their due income tax.

(c) HOW do you qualify?

The audiovisual project must be approved by the **ANCINE** (National Cinema Agency).

(d) WHERE do you apply?

First, confirmation of approval must be obtained from **ANCINE**, and then the taxpayer's accountant will make the necessary application for the deduction on submitting the tax returns.

CULTURAL ACTION PROGRAM (PAC)

This is a **MECENATO** (Patronage of the Arts) programme based in São Paolo. However, the majority of Brazilian States offer a similar benefit, but all of them require that there be a local company among the co-producers and/or that the project be developed inside the State.

A Producer can obtain up to R$600,000 for the funding of a cinematographic project, which must be listed in the Project Manager Registry of the State Secretariat of Culture of São Paulo. The benefit comprises a partial or total deduction from the amount of taxes owed under the Taxes on Operations Related to the Circulation of Goods and on the Provision of Services for Interstate and Intercity Transport and Communication (ICMS).

III. SPONSORSHIP

SPONSORSHIP OF FILMS UNDER MECANATO PRINCIPLES (ROUANET LAW)

There is also a tax deduction available for the 'sponsorship' of shorter films. It is based on the so-called **ROUANET LAW**, which aims to support all art forms through physical and inspirational heritage under the principle of '**MECENATO**' (Patronage of the Arts). Sponsorship generates a lesser tax benefit than the Audiovisual Law (above), but sponsors benefit from the publicity associated with it.

The sponsor may participate in a number of different ways, including the donation of finance, providing services, or a temporary transfer of real estate or other property.

An Individual who sponsors **short** (under 16 minutes) and **medium** (16 to 69 minutes) length films has the right to a maximum 4% deduction from income taxes. For corporate entities, the ceiling for

the discount is 6% of payable income taxes. **Long** (70 or more minutes) length films cannot benefit.

SPONSORSHIP IN SÃO PAULO (ETC) UNDER MENDONCA PRINCIPLES

In São Paulo City, a filmmaker may obtain donations, sponsorship and investment to fund his/her project in conjunction with a **tax waiver** of the ISS (Service Tax) and IPTU (Property Tax). The sponsor/backer may use up to 20% of his tax (ISS and/or IPTU) and invest it in a project approved by the Secretariat of Culture of the City of São Paulo. A similar benefit is available in other cities.

There are limits to the amounts that can be used according to the length of the project, being R$500,000 for a long-length film, R$150,000 if medium-length; and R$80,000 for a short.

Once the relevant certificate is obtained, the sponsor will have up to 24 months to use the amount to pay IPTU and/or ISS taxes, at a 30% discount of face value. In other words, an investor with a tax bill of R$100,000 can invest up to R$20,000 (20%) in a qualifying film, giving an immediate deduction of R$20,000 (the value of the certificate) in taxes payable, but $14,000 of this will ultimately have to be paid to the tax authorities within 2 years.

Applications should be made to the São Paulo Secretariat of Culture, Mendonça Law Benefits (IPTU and/or ISS) within the published deadlines.

IV. PROCEDURES

(a) PREPARATION of Documents

The applicant for the above schemes generally needs to submit the following documents: summary/synopsis, objective, justification, execution plan/descriptive brief (project steps), project/product destination, distribution plan, production plan, technical analysis of the project, qualifications of the proposing company, qualifications of the person responsible for the proposing company, qualifications of those responsible for the project, professional Registration (DRT) of those responsible for the management/coordination of the project. Local advice should be sought in preparing the necessary papers.

The applicant will also have to obtain the relevant 'certificates of compliance with tax and labour laws' in the name of the appropriate party.

(b) FILING with the Relevant Public Organisation

Applications for **Audiovisual Law** waivers of Income Taxes should be made to the **ANCINE**. Delivery of applications can be made up to 15 November in order to be considered in the same year. There is generally a 45 day turnaround.

The **Rouanet Law** benefits (waiver of Income Taxes) and support from the **National Culture Fund** should be applied for at the Ministry of Culture. Submissions may be made at any time of the year, although projects sent after 30 October will be analysed only after February of the following year.

Applications for the **Mendonça Law Benefits** (IPTU and/or ISS) should be filed at the São Paulo Secretariat of Culture. Submission should be made after publication of the annual 'Public Notice', and within the relevant deadline. Most applications are made between February and May, for presentation in the following three months. In 2006, for example, the Public Notice was published in February allowing submission at any time up until 24 March 2006.

For other state and city schemes, each region will have its own specifications, and deadlines are variable.

(c) PUBLICATION in the Official Diary

The project will only benefit from the relevant tax waiver after publication in the Official Diary. Any expenses incurred before this occurs *cannot* be included in the expense accounts.

(d) REGISTRATION of the project

The audiovisual project must be registered in the **Securities and Exchange Commission** (**CVM**) and in its inspectorate, the CETIP, through a **DTVM Securities Broker**, who will need paying at 3% of the value registered in the CVM.

The company proposing the project will need to pass a corporate resolution, effecting the relevant transformation into investment quotas. It must draw up a preliminary prospectus containing the rights and obligations of both the investor and the proponent of the project.

(e) FUNDRAISING issues

The agents carrying out the fundraising will have the right to commission for their service, at a rate ranging from 5% to 10%, depending on the type of project and various other factors.

The amounts raised under the **Audiovisual Law** will be deposited at the Securities Broker, which will then transfer them to the fundraising account of the proponent company, at the Banco do Brasil. Amounts benefiting from the **other laws** will be deposited in specific fundraising accounts, opened in the name of the proponent and consigned exclusively to the approved project. No other amounts may be deposited in these accounts.

(f) DRAWING Down Funds for the Projects

The project may use the funds raised strictly in accordance with the percentages deposited in the fundraising accounts. The authorising organisation will release the funds according to the type of project. The relevant organisation will be ANCINE for audiovisual law funds, the Ministry of Culture for the others at the federal level, and São Paulo Secretariat of Culture for ISS and IPTU taxes.

Audiovisual projects will only be allowed to withdraw funds from their fundraising accounts when they have **50%** of the total cost of the project. For the other cultural projects benefiting from the **Rouanet** and **Mendonça Laws**, it is possible to utilise the financial resources once the amount reaches 20% of the total cost of the project.

(g) POST-COMPLETION Documentation

Proof of completion of the production will need to be provided, and should comprise various legal documents, together with appropriate 'filming of' footage, newspaper reports, posters, leaflets, brochures, and a copy of the finished product when available (on film, DVD, etc). The relevant authority will also want to be reported to in relation to the categories of public reached by exploitation, the characterisation of this public, results obtained and accounting documentation, with copies of all registered documents and contracts.

V. INTERNATIONAL CO-PRODUCTION

Projects made in association with companies from other countries through international co-production agreements with Brazil, must present, in addition to the documentation specified above, the following complementary documentation in duly notarised form:

- documentation relative to the conformity to the international co-production convention or agreement, referring specifically to the project, duly consularized and translated;

- the proponent's co-production contract with the foreign company, duly consularized and translated, containing the following information:
- specification of amounts and origin of the financial contributions;
- specification of the equity rights distributed among the co-producers;
- corporate charter of the foreign company, duly consularized and translated.

Projects made under co-production or in association with foreign companies from countries with which Brazil does *not* maintain co-production agreements must, in addition to supplying the documentation specified above, satisfy the following requirements (and include them in the co-production contract):

- utilisation of at least **two-thirds Brazilian artists** and technicians or of foreigners residing in Brazil for more than three years, for the production of the work;
- **ownership** of at least **40% of the equity** rights of the work in the name of the proponent.

VI. LEGAL DEFINITIONS FOR THE ANCINE AND VARIOUS OTHER REGULATIONS

Proponent: Brazilian production company whose corporate purpose includes the activity of audiovisual production, that, upon delivering the project of the audiovisual piece to the ANCINE, becomes responsible for all the procedures and commitments necessary for carrying it out, being answerable to the ANCINE for administrative, civil and legal matters, as well as to the various other public organs and entities in terms of the current legislation.

Television programmes of an educational and cultural nature: Brazilian audiovisual piece of independent production, produced for initial distribution in the (…broadcast and electronic transmission…) markets, whose subject matter is Brazilian culture, education or environment, and whose content is made up of at least 95% of images produced in Brazil.

Synopsis: Summarised description or synthesis of the project, its history and its characters, when applicable. **Film plot**: Text including dramaturgical development, without dialogues, with or without division of sequences. **Script**: Text prepared on the basis of the plot of the audiovisual piece containing a description of characters, the dramaturgical development, the dialogues and its division into sequences.

International festival: competitive or non-competitive exhibits of Brazilian audiovisual works carried out abroad or of foreign audiovisual works carried out in Brazil.

VII. CONTACT DETAILS

Ancine
Audiovisual Laws
www.ancine.gov.br

Ministry Of Culture
Lei Rouanet 8313/91
www.cultura.gov.br

Government Of The State Of São Paulo
PAC – PROGRAMA DE AÇÃO CULTURAL
www.cultura.sp.gov.br

São Paulo City Hall
Lei Mendonça – Lei Municipal de Cultura
www.prefeitura.sp.gov.br

CANADA

Prepared with the assistance of Heenan Blaikie LLP
(www.heenanblaikie.com)

FEDERAL TAX CREDITS

The Canadian federal government assists domestic and foreign producers by offering a number of tax incentives and funding programs that are available to both 'serviced' productions and 'Canadian-content' productions. The Canadian Audio-Visual Certification Office (**CAVCO**), a branch of the Department of Canadian Heritage and the Canada Revenue Agency (CRA), jointly administer the **Canadian Film or Video Production Tax Credit Program** (CPTC) and the **Film or Video Production Services Tax Credit Program** (PSTC). Only one of these tax credits may be claimed for a particular production.

CANADIAN FILM OR VIDEO PRODUCTION TAX CREDIT PROGRAM (CPTC)

(a) WHAT is available?

The CPTC was established to aid in the development of the Canadian film and TV production industry and to promote Canadian TV programming. The key features of this credit is:

A refundable tax credit equal to *25% of eligible labour expenditures*, capped at 60% of total production costs, giving an effective rate of 15% of production costs (25% of 60%).

(b) WHO can apply?

The CPTC provides tax incentives to qualified Canadian **production corporations** that **produce** *and* **own the copyright** in 'Canadian Film or Video Productions'. Canadian Film or Video Productions are those productions that satisfy the criteria established by the Income Tax Act Regulations, as interpreted and administered by CAVCO. The applicant production company must also be **owned and controlled**, either directly or indirectly, by **Canadian citizens** or permanent residents in accordance with definitions found in a combination of the Citizenship Act, the Immigration Act and the Investment Canada Act.

The credit is a **refundable** tax credit (that is, it is fully payable to the production company even if it owes no taxes).

(c) HOW do you qualify?

Eligible labor expenditures exclude amounts paid for the services of non-Canadian residents, unless the person was a Canadian citizen at the time the payment was made. Eligible costs may be incurred as early as two years before principal photography begins, so that in-house development labor costs of an initial draft of a script, as well as the cost of further revisions become eligible.

The holding of an interest in the film or video production by a person other than the actual production corporation used to disqualify the production from eligibility for a federal tax credit, but that is no longer the case unless the production or one of the investors is associated with a tax shelter.

The credit is calculated in conjunction with provincial credits such that the eligible production costs are reduced by any applicable provincial tax credit amount.

FILM OR VIDEO PRODUCTION SERVICES TAX CREDIT PROGRAM (PSTC)

(a) WHAT is available?

The key features of the PSTC are:

A refundable tax credit equal to *16% of labor expenditures* paid to Canadian residents.

There is no cap on the amount that can be claimed under this credit. The credit is also a refundable tax credit, and is calculated in conjunction with similar provincial tax credits.

(b) — (c) WHO can apply and HOW do you qualify?

A production that does not meet the Canadian content criteria for the CPTC may instead be eligible for the PSTC. To access the PSTC, the applicant company performing production services must be either a Canadian-owned or foreign-owned corporation with a permanent establishment in Canada. 'Permanent Establishment' for this purpose generally means having a **production office in Canada**, even if it is only on a temporary basis while shooting in Canada.

Another eligibility requirement is that the applicant production company must either **own the copyright** in the film during the production period, or be engaged directly by the copyright holder to provide production services.

The production must also meet the minimum expenditure requirements, which are C$1m for feature films, C$200,000 for a one-hour TV episode and C$100,000 for a 30-minute TV episode.

Excluded Productions

The following types of programs are *not* eligible for either the CPTC or the PSTC: news programs, talk and game shows, sporting and award events, reality TV, productions that solicit funds, pornography, advertising, and industrial or corporate productions. CAVCO has posted guidelines on their website that help clarify which types of programs are classified as excluded productions.

For further details, refer to:

www.pch.gc.ca/progs/ac-ca/progs/bcpac-cavco/definition_e.cfm

PROVINCIAL INCENTIVES: ALBERTA

ALBERTA FILM DEVELOPMENT PROGRAM (AFDP)

(a) WHAT is available?

The Alberta Government, through the Alberta Film Development Program (AFDP), provides incentives to filmmakers shooting their productions in Alberta by way of **direct grants**. Depending on the level of Albertan **ownership** in the production and the amount of Alberta residents in **key creative positions** (writer, director, art director, editor, DOP, composer and 2 performers in lead or supporting roles), the AFDP will make available between **14%** and **23%** of **all eligible Alberta expenses**.

(b) — (c) WHO can apply and HOW do you qualify?

For the purposes of the AFDP, productions are classified into the following three categories to determine the level of incentive that can be accessed:

(1) Majority (51% or more) Albertan ownership of production and a majority financial and creative control. Albertans employed in at least 2 out of 8 key creative positions. Eligible to receive grant for **up to 21%** of eligible Alberta expenses. The project will have enhanced eligibility if there are 3 or more Albertans in key creative positions, and can receive a further 1% for each additional Albertan employed in a key creative position, up to a **maximum of 23%**.

(2) Equal or Minority (10% to 50%) Albertan ownership of production and at least 1 Albertan employed in a key creative position. Eligible to receive a grant for **up to 19%** of eligible Alberta expenses. The project will have enhanced eligibility if there are 2 or more Albertans in key creative positions, and can receive a further 1% for each additional Albertan employed in a key creative position, up to a **maximum of 21%**.

(3) Nominal (0% to 10%) or no Albertan ownership of production. Eligible to receive a grant for **up to 14%** of eligible Alberta expenses. The project will have enhanced eligibility if there are 2 or more Albertans in key creative positions, and can receive a further 1% for each 2 additional Albertans employed in a key creative position, up to a **maximum of 16%.**

To be considered eligible for funding, all projects must be supported by a **broadcast license or distribution agreement** (in the case of theatrical releases) at fair market value. A broadcast license includes any of the following: (i) A commitment by a licensed broadcaster (this includes all private, public, and educational broadcasters and all specialty, pay and pay-per-view broadcasters) to participate financially in the production; (ii) A commitment to broadcast the program within two years of its completion; or (iii) Participation by the broadcaster in the form of a cash contribution. Theatrical distributors must be able to demonstrate sufficient financial stability and expertise to arrange for distributions in all markets for which they have acquired rights.

Recipients of AFDP funding must be **incorporated in Alberta**, and the amount spent in Alberta for the project must be greater than **C$25,000** (before GST).

The maximum funding available to any project is **C$1.5 million**. Except with the prior approval of Alberta Economic Development (AED), which may be granted at the discretion of AED solely for time-sensitive events, principal photography must not have commenced prior to AFDP submission. Applicants must provide written evidence of **65% confirmed financing** at the time of submission.

Genres of production *not* eligible for funding are: news, current events or public affairs programming, or a program that includes weather or market reports; talk shows; production in respect of a game or contest (other than a production directed primarily at minors); sports event or activity; production that solicits funds, Reality TV (this includes production that consists of scenes recorded on amateur home video cameras or private or public authority surveillance equipment, and programming currently known as court TV and similar formats); Pornography; Advertising; Production produced primarily for industrial, corporate, or institutional purposes; Production other than documentary, all or substantially all of which consists of stock footage.

(d) WHERE to find more information?

For more information on the programs offered by the Government of Alberta, visit:

www.alberta-canada.com/aed/afdp.cfm and www.abertafilm.ca.

BRITISH COLUMBIA

THE FILM INCENTIVE BRITISH COLUMBIA (FIBC)

(a) WHAT is available?

The FDBC Film Development Society of British Columbia (British Columbia Film) administers the Film Incentive British Columbia (FIBC), which is a package of refundable corporate income tax credits which are divided into three specific categories: (i) **Basic Incentive**, (ii) **Regional Incentive**, and (iii) **Training Incentive**.

(b) — (c) WHO can apply and HOW do you qualify?

Basic Tax Incentive: This tax credit is equal to **30% of eligible British Columbia labor costs** up to a **maximum of 48%** of total eligible production costs. To be eligible for this incentive the production company must be British Columbia **controlled**, and the producer must control the ownership of the **copyright**. In addition, the producer must be both a Canadian resident and a **resident** of British Columbia.

Regional Incentive: This tax credit is equal to **12.5%** of **eligible British Columbia labor costs**, pro-rated by the number of days of principal photography outside the designated Vancouver area, divided by the total number of days of principal photography in British Columbia. It assists production companies who shoot their productions *outside* of the Vancouver designated area. To be eligible, **principal photography** of the production must occur in British Columbia outside the designated Vancouver area for a minimum of **five days**, and more than 50% of the total number of days in which principal photography is done in British Columbia. This incentive must be accessed in conjunction with the FIBC Basic Incentive.

Training Incentive: This tax credit is the lesser of **30% of trainee salaries** or **3% of eligible British Columbia labor costs**. To be eligible for the training incentive tax credit a trainee must be registered in an **approved training program**. This incentive must be accessed in conjunction with the FIBC Basic Incentive.

The above three tax incentives allow a production company to claim a combined benefit in the amount of eligible British Columbia labor **capped at 48%** of total production costs. In addition to the individual eligibility requirements above, a production must also satisfy *all* of the following:

- *75%* of **principal photography** must occur in British Columbia;
- The production must attain **6** of the possible 10 **CAVCO points**;
- A minimum of **75% of total production costs** must be spent on goods or services provided in British Columbia by British Columbia residents or companies. In addition, a minimum of 75% of post-production costs must be paid in respect of post-production work carried out in British Columbia and be paid to British Columbia residents or companies;
- The production must be distributed by a **Canadian distributor or broadcaster**;
- The production must be shown in Canada within **two years** from completion of the production.

Some genres are *excluded*, such as pornography, talk shows, news, live sporting events, game shows, reality TV and advertising.

It should be noted that special rules apply to treaty co-productions and inter-provincial co-productions.

PRODUCTION SERVICES TAX CREDIT (PSTC)

(a) WHAT is available?

The PSTC is a package of refundable corporate income tax credits which are divided into two specific categories (it should be noted that a particular production may access only one of the FIBC *or* the PSTC, but not both): (i) **Basic Incentive**, and (ii) **Regional Incentive**.

(b) — (c) WHO can apply and HOW do you qualify?

Basic Incentive: This tax credit is equal to **18%** of accredited qualified British Columbia **labor costs** incurred in making the production.

Regional Incentive: This tax credit is equal to **6%** of accredited qualified British Columbia **labor costs** incurred in making the production, pro-rated by the number of days of principal photography outside the designated Vancouver area, divided by the total number of days of principal photography in British Columbia. To be eligible, **principal photography** of the production must occur in British Columbia *outside* the designated Vancouver area for a minimum of **five days**; and more than **50%** of the total number of days in which principal photography is done in British Columbia. This incentive must be accessed in conjunction with the PSTC Basic Incentive.

Other Programs

Other programs available in British Columbia include the British Columbia Arts Council Project Assistance for Media Artists Program British Columbia Film Programs, Equity Capital Programs, TELUS BC New Media and Broadcast Fund.

(d) WHERE to find more information?

For more information on programs offered by British Columbia Film, visit www.bcfilm.bc.ca. Other useful local sites may include:

> www.filmcolumbiashuswap.com
> www.filmnanaimo.com
> www.northernbcfilm.com
> www.okanaganfilm.com

MANITOBA

MANITOBA FILM AND VIDEO PRODUCTION TAX CREDIT

(a) WHAT is available?

The Manitoba Film and Video Production Tax Credit is administered by the Manitoba Film and Sound Recording Development Corporation (MFSDC). The basic **tax credit** is equal to **45% of eligible Manitoba labor expenditures**.

Productions may also be eligible for two additional bonus credits:

(i) **Frequent Filming Bonus** equal to **5%** of eligible Manitoba **labor expenditures**. In order to qualify for this bonus, the company must produce 3 films in Manitoba within 2 years (the third film will be eligible for the bonus);

(ii) **Rural and Northern Bonus** equal to **5%** of eligible Manitoba **labor expenditures**. To qualify for this bonus, at least 50% of a production's Manitoba production days must involve shooting at locations 35km (22 miles) *outside* of Winnipeg. If both of the foregoing bonuses are combined, the Manitoba Film and Video Production Tax Credit can be as high as **55%** of eligible Manitoba labor expenditures.

(b) — (c) WHO can apply and HOW do you qualify?

In order to be eligible for this tax credit applicants must:

- have a **permanent establishment** (as defined in the Income Tax Act) in Manitoba;
- be **incorporated** in Canada (either federally or provincially); and
- be a **taxable** Canadian corporation primarily carrying on a business that is a film or video production.

In addition:

- There are *no* Canada or Manitoba **content requirements**;
- **Copyright** ownership is *not* required;
- There are *no* **caps** on the amount available; and
- There is no requirement to work with Manitoba producers, co-productions qualify for this tax credit.

Eligible projects include fully financed TV movies, documentaries, features, dramatic series, animation, children's programming, music programming, informational series, variety, multimedia, digital and CD-ROM productions.

Other Programs

Additional MFSDC Programs include the Market Driven Television Development Financing Program, Market Driven Feature Film Development Financing Program, Market Driven Television Production Program, Market Driven Feature Film Production Program, Low Budget Feature Film Development Financing Program, and the Emerging Talent Matching Funds Program.

THE FILM/VIDEO SCRIPT DEVELOPMENT GRANT

(a) WHAT is available?

This grant is administered by the Manitoba Arts Council and offers up to **C$6,000** per project to aid in the creation of scripts. The grant may also be used as a living allowance.

(b) — (c) WHO can apply and HOW do you qualify?

The applicant must be a professional filmmaker, writer or artist who:

- is a Canadian citizen or landed immigrant;
- has maintained principal residence in Manitoba for at least one year prior to making application; and

- is recognized as a professional in his/her artistic discipline.

Eligible genres include drama, documentary animation, and experimental film and video.

Ineligible projects include TV pilots and instructional, promotional and industrial films.

THE FILM VIDEO PROJECT GRANT

(a) WHAT is available?

Also administered by the Manitoba Arts Council, this grant offers up to **C$6,000** for costs related to project development.

(b) — (c) WHO can apply and HOW do you qualify?

The eligibility requirements are the same as those listed above for the Film/Video Script Development Grant.

THE FILM/VIDEO PRODUCTION GRANT

(a) WHAT is available?

This grant is also administered by the Manitoba Arts Council and offers up to C$20,000 for a range of production-related costs.

(b) — (c) WHO can apply and HOW do you qualify?

The eligibility requirements are the same as those listed above for the Film/Video Script Development Grant.

(d) WHERE to find more information?

For more information on these and other programs, visit the MFSDC website at www.mbfilmsound.mb.ca, and the Manitoba Arts Council website at www. artscouncil.mb.ca.

NEW BRUNSWICK

NEW BRUNSWICK LABOR INCENTIVE FILM TAX CREDIT

(a) WHAT is available?

The New Brunswick Labor Incentive Film Tax Credit is equal to **40% of eligible labor expenditures** paid to New Brunswick **residents, capped at 50%** of the total production cost.

(b) — (c) WHO can apply and HOW do you qualify?

To be eligible for these credits, the production company must:
- be **incorporated** in Canada, but **cannot** hold a **broadcasting license**;
- be primarily in the **business of film-making**;
- have a **permanent establishment** in New Brunswick; and
- pay a minimum of **25% of labor costs** in New Brunswick, to New Brunswick residents.

Eligible projects include feature films, TV series and movies, children's programs, documentaries, animated productions, educational productions, dramatic, experimental, non-theatrical and variety programming.

Inter-provincial and international co-productions are eligible for this tax credit provided that they satisfy the New Brunswick content requirements.

NEW BRUNSWICK FILM EQUITY INVESTMENTS

(a) WHAT is available?

New Brunswick Film ('NB Film') will make **equity investments** in projects where the potential for recoupment and profits is, in the opinion of NB Film, sufficiently high. Where there is an expected significant benefit to the New Brunswick film industry, and where the New Brunswick content requirements have been met, NB Film may invest up to **10% of the total production budget**, to a **maximum of C$250,000**. NB Film equity investments are subject to the following caps:

Dramatic Series, Children's programming C$250,000, Theatrical Feature Films C$250,000, Television mini-series and MOWs C$250,000 Documentary, Features or series C$200,000, Documentaries (60 minutes or less) C$200,000, Short Films (educational, experimental or non-theatrical) C$50,000.

(b) — (c) WHO can apply and HOW do you qualify?

- The applicant must be a New Brunswick business, and must have as its primary purpose the domestic or collaborative production of film or video products (note that there are specific requirements relating to private and publicity traded corporations);
- Distributors and broadcasters are *not* eligible to apply;

- A majority of voting shares must be owned by New Brunswick residents;
- A minimum of 51% of the voting members of the Board of Directors must be New Brunswick residents;
- The 'mind and management' of the corporation must be controlled by a New Brunswick resident.

Eligible projects include feature films, TV series and movies, children's programs, documentaries, animated productions, educational productions, dramatic, experimental and non-theatrical programming. Inter-provincial and international co-productions are eligible for equity investments provided that they satisfy the New Brunswick content requirements.

(d) WHERE to find more information?

NB Film also offers a Development Loan Program. For more information on programs offered by the Government of New Brunswick, visit www.nbfilm. com.

NEWFOUNDLAND AND LABRADOR

NEWFOUNDLAND AND LABRADOR FILM AND VIDEO INDUSTRY TAX CREDIT

(a) WHAT is available?

The Newfoundland and Labrador Film and Video Industry Tax Credit is limited to the lesser of **40% of total eligible labor expenditures** in Newfoundland and Labrador or **25% of the total eligible production costs**. There is a corporate cap of C$3m for a 12-month period. There are no provincial or CAVCO Canadian **content requirements** for this tax credit.

(b) — (c) WHO can apply and HOW do you qualify?

To be eligible for this tax credit, a production company must:
- be incorporated under the laws of Newfoundland and Labrador, another Province of Canada or Canada;
- have a permanent establishment in Newfoundland or Labrador;
- be primarily in the business of film, TV or video production;
- have a minimum of **25% of salaries and wages** paid within Newfoundland and Labrador to provincial residents.

Broadcasters and cable companies are *not* eligible to apply for this tax credit.

Eligible genres include feature films, TV series and movies and video programs in the following areas: drama, variety, animation, children's programming, music programming, informational series or documentary.

The following genres are excluded from the program: news, talk shows, sporting events, galas, pornography, advertising, projects contrary to public policy or projects the government determines are not eligible.

NEWFOUNDLAND AND LABRADOR FILM DEVELOPMENT CORPORATION

(a) WHAT is available?

The Newfoundland and Labrador Film Development Corporation administers an **equity investment program** to assist in scriptwriting, production, post-production, distribution and marketing. This assistance is **capped at 20% of overall costs** of a given project.

The Newfoundland and Labrador Film Development Corporation has set the following maximum equity contributions:

Dramatic series: C$250,000; Theatrical feature film or TV: C$250,000; Documentary (stand alone or series): C$150,000.

(b) — (c) WHO can apply and HOW do you qualify?

To be eligible for this equity investment program, film and video production companies must be incorporated in the province, and be at least **51% owned** by residents of Newfoundland and Labrador.

The project *must* meet Canadian **content requirements** as set out by CAVCO.

Eligible projects include feature films, TV movies, mini-series, TV specials and non-theatrical films, provided that a market can be demonstrated.

Inter-provincial and foreign co-productions may benefit from this program so long as the Newfoundland producer holds a minimum of **33% interest** in the project.

(d) WHERE to find more information?

For more information on incentives provided by the Government of Newfoundland and Labrador, visit www.nlfdc.ca.

NOVA SCOTIA

NOVA SCOTIA FILM INDUSTRY TAX CREDIT

(a) WHAT is available?

The Nova Scotia Film Industry Tax Credit is administered by the Nova Scotia Film Development Corporation (NSFDC). It is a **refundable corporate income tax credit**, available to both productions and co-productions.

There is *no* **corporate** cap, *no* Canadian **content** requirement, and *no* **copyright** ownership requirement.

Effective from 1 January 2005, this credit is equal to **35% of eligible labor expenses** (paid to Nova Scotia **residents**) to a **maximum of 17.5% of the total eligible production budget**.

The **regional bonus** would increase these rates **up to 40%** of eligible labor expenses to a maximum of **up to 20%** of the total eligible production budget.

An additional 5% of eligible labor expenses is available for productions which qualify for the **frequent filming** bonus.

(b) — (c) WHO can apply and HOW do you qualify?

Eligible production companies must:
• be **incorporated** under the laws of Nova Scotia or another province of **Canada**, or federally incorporated;
• have a **permanent establishment** in Nova Scotia (which could include a production office); and
• be registered by NSFDC as producing an eligible film.

In addition, at least **25% of Canadian salaries and wages** must be paid to Nova Scotia **residents**.

Eligible categories include TV, videotape, feature film, non-theatrical production or interactive websites associated with TV or feature film projects, with the subject of drama, variety, performing arts, animated or information series, documentary or music programming, including music videos.

Other Programs

NSFDC also administers an equity investment program, a development loan program, new media equity investment, a travel assistance program, partnerships in training, sponsorships, a feature film distribution assistance program, and the CBC/NSFDC bridge award.

(d) WHERE to find more information?

For more information on programs provided by the NSFDC, visit www.film.ns.ca.

ONTARIO

ONTARIO MEDIA DEVELOPMENT CORPORATION FILM FUND (OMDC)

(a) WHAT is available?

The Ontario Media Development Corporation (formerly the Ontario Film Development Corporation) jointly administers the following tax credit programs with the Ontario Minister of Finance. The OMDC Film Fund has been developed to increase the level of indigenous film production in Ontario. It will provide support to Ontario producers for feature film projects in the final stages of development and **production financing**. The OMDC Film Fund consists of two components:

> **(1) Development** — Provides funding in the form of an **interest-free loan** of up to **C$25,000** for the final development stage.

> **(2) Production** — Provides funding in the form of a **repayable advance** of up to **C$300,000** on a last-in basis **to complete the financing** of a feature film.

(b) — (c) WHO can apply and HOW do you qualify?

The eligibility requirements are fairly extensive but outlined in full in the OMDC Film Fund Production Guidelines and the OMDC Film Fund Development Guidelines at www.omdc.on.ca.

ONTARIO FILM AND TELEVISION TAX CREDIT (OFTTC)

(a) WHAT is available?

Effective from 1 January 2005, the OFTTC is equal to **30% of eligible labor costs**, with *no* **cap**.

First-time producers are eligible for an enhanced rate of **40%** on the first C$240,000 of labor costs.

(b) — (c) WHO can apply and HOW do you qualify?

To be eligible to receive this credit:
• at least **75% of total final productions costs** must be **Ontario expenditures** (in the case of inter-provincial and international treaty

co-productions, 75% of total expenditures is in respect of the Ontario portion of the production);

- production company must have a **permanent establishment** in Ontario;
- the production company must be **Canadian controlled** and must be a qualified corporation for the purpose of the federal credit;
- the production company's **primary business** must be the production of Canadian films and videos;
- **all production costs** must be **Ontario expenditures** and a minimum of **95% of post-production costs** must be incurred in Ontario other than in the case of co-productions;
- the producer must be an Ontario **resident** for at least two years prior to the commencement of principal photography;
- the film must be **shown in Ontario** within two years of completion by an Ontario-based film distributor or Canadian broadcaster **during prime time** (that is, between 7pm and 11pm);
- the production must attain at least **6 of the possible 10 CAVCO points**;
- a minimum of **85%** of the total number of days of **principal photography** or key animation must be done in Ontario, unless it is a documentary or treaty co-production; and
- the Ontario Minister of Culture must **certify** the production as an **Ontario production**.

Ineligible productions include: TV programs not shown in prime time other than children's programming and non-Canadian controlled service productions; talk shows; reality TV; and sport shows.

Inter-provincial and international treaty co-productions are eligible for this tax credit. In such cases, the calculation is based on Ontario's portion of the production budget.

Regional Bonus: Productions shot in Ontario entirely *outside* of the Greater **Toronto** Area (GTA) or productions that have at least five location days in Ontario (in the case of a TV series, the number of location days must be at least equal to the number of episodes in the series) and at least 85% of the location days in Ontario are outside of the GTA are eligible to receive a **10% bonus** on all Ontario labor expenditures.

ONTARIO PRODUCTION SERVICES TAX CREDIT (OPSTC)

(a) WHAT is available?

Effective from 1 January 2005, the Ontario Production Services Tax Credit is equal to **18%**

of **Ontario labor expenditures**. This credit is available to both **Canadian** *and* **foreign** production companies producing in Ontario.

No **content** requirements need to be satisfied to be eligible for this tax credit provided that the production company has a **permanent establishment** in Ontario (which includes a production office set up in Ontario during filming), and either **owns the copyright** in the production or contracts directly with the copyright owner.

(b) — (c) WHO can apply and HOW do you qualify?

To be eligible to receive this credit:
- The corporation must be primarily engaged in the **business** of film or video production;
- The production must meet **minimum budget levels** of C$100,000 per 30-minute episode or less of a TV series, C$200,000 per episode greater than 30 minutes and C$1 million for all other productions.

The OFTTC and the OPSTC cannot both be claimed for the same episodes of a TV series.

Ineligible genres include news shows, talk shows, game or contest productions, sports events, gala or award presentations, pornography, reality TV and advertising or industrial productions.

Other Programs

Other Ontario funding programs include The CJOH-TV/CTV Television Incorporation Development Fund, MCTV/CTV Television Incorporation Development Fund, DGC Entertainment Ventures Corporation, The Ontario Arts Council, Toronto Arts Council Grants to Media Artists Program, and TV Ontario.

(d) WHERE to find more information?

For more information on programs provided by the Ontario Media Development Corporation, visit www.omdc.on.ca, and for Hamilton in particular, www.hamilton.ca/film.

PRINCE EDWARD ISLAND (PEI)

INNOVATION AND DEVELOPMENT TAX CREDIT

(a) WHAT is available?

Technology PEI's film funding programs are not refundable tax credits. Rather, the Film, Television and New Media division **provides funding** to eligible PEI production companies through a number of programs including a **labor rebate program** and **development loans**.

Effective from 1 January 2006, this incentive — which despite its title is effectively a **labor rebate** — will be available to assist film and TV productions which utilize PEI labor. All **non-owner labor** is eligible for a rebate of 35% of 150% (for an **effective rate of 52.5%**). Similar to tax credits, this incentive will be paid upon completion of the production and submission of the required project and labor cost reports. This program covers more than film and TV, however, and at the time of writing, Technology PEI was in the process of preparing specific guidelines on the program's applicability to film and TV.

(b) — (c) WHO can apply and HOW do you qualify?

This rebate is available if the following criteria are met:

- PEI **owned and operated corporations** which have a **permanent establishment** in PEI;
- A minimum of **25% of salaries and wages** paid to employees of the corporation must be paid to **PEI employees**;
- **Co-productions** qualify for this tax credit;
- There are *no* Canada or PEI **content** requirements;
- The PEI production company (the applicant for the incentive) must own and control at least **25% of the copyright** in the production;
- There are **caps** on the amount of **producer fees** paid to producers with an ownership interest in the production or the production company: only C$40,000/per project in such fees will be eligible for calculation of the incentive.

DEVELOPMENT LOAN

(a) WHAT is available?

Technology PEI provides **loans** to production companies for **up to one third** of the proposed **development budget** to a **maximum of C$25,000**. This non-interest bearing loan is to be repaid in full on the first day of principal photography, or on the optioning, sale or transfer of the property to a third party, or on a specified date in the loan agreement between Technology PEI and the producer.

Eligible expenses include the optioning and purchase of literary property, script development, writers' fees and story editing, development related travel, market research, financing, packaging, marketing, related consulting and professional expenses, producer fees and corporate overhead

(up to 15% of the total development budget) and the preparation of a detailed production budget or production schedule.

There must also be financial commitment from a **broadcaster** for the development process.

(b) — (c) WHO can apply and HOW do you qualify?

To be eligible for development loans from Technology PEI, applicants must be corporations incorporated in Canada that have a **permanent establishment** in Prince Edward Island and whose **primary business** is film and TV production. Eligible corporations require financial participation from **Broadcasters and/or Distributors**.

Note that the eligibility criteria are different for **co-productions**.

Other Programs

Technology PEI also offers the following programs: Short Film Program; Professional Development Program; Capital Assistance Program; Professional Services Assistance Program; Atlantic Canada Film Partners Program and Marketing Assistance Program.

(d) WHERE to find more information?

For more information on incentives provided by Technology PEI, visit www.techpei.com, and for the Government of Prince Edward Island, visit www.gov.pe.ca.

QUEBEC

REFUNDABLE TAX CREDIT FOR QUEBEC FILM AND TELEVISION PRODUCTIONS

(a) WHAT is available?

The **Refundable Tax Credit** for Quebec Film and Television Productions, which is administered by the Société de développement des entreprises culturelles (SODEC), is generally equal to **29.16% of eligible labor expenditures**, to a **maximum of 50% of production costs**. The general maximum **effective rate is 14.58%** of a production budget. The **tax credit** is capped at **C$2,187,500** for each production or series.

An **additional credit** of **10.21%** is available for labor expenditures which are directly attributable to the creation of digital **animation or visual effects**, so that the effective rate may reach **19.69% of a production budget**.

A **higher effective rate** of **19.69%** applies for giant screen films and for certain French-language feature films and single documentaries which meet higher content criteria.

The effective rate for regional productions (in the Province of Quebec but *outside* the **Montreal** region) produced by regional producers is increased to **24.28%**.

(b) — (c) WHO can apply and HOW do you qualify?

To be eligible for this tax credit:

- a production company must first obtain an **advance ruling** or a certificate from SODEC;
- a production company must be a corporation having its **principal establishment** in Quebec, which carries on a Quebec film or TV production **business** and which is not directly or indirectly controlled by a person or persons not **resident** in Quebec for at least 24 months prior to the year in which the tax credit is claimed;
- **private broadcasters and corporations** that are not at arm's length with broadcasters are *not* eligible;
- the production must meet **6 of the possible 10 Quebec content points** (the Quebec-content point scale is similar to that of CAVCO but is based on residence of key personnel in Quebec rather than on Canadian citizenship);
- for productions of **75 minutes or more** (per episode in the case of a series), **75% of post-production costs** must be incurred and paid with respect to services rendered in Quebec;
- for productions of **75 minutes or more** (per episode in the case of a series), a minimum of **75% of production costs**, excluding payments to key personnel for purposes of the point scale and those related to financing, must be paid to individuals resident in Quebec at the end of the previous year or to corporations having an establishment in Quebec during the year;
- for productions of **less than 75 minutes** (per episode in the case of a series) and for **all co-productions regardless of duration**, the **content** points requirement relating to key personnel does not apply but the production must meet the requirement that **75% of all production costs**, except those relating to financing, must be paid to individual **resident** in Quebec at the end of the previous year or to corporations having an establishment in Quebec during the year;
- a production must have a commitment from a **Canadian broadcaster or distributor**

undertaking that the production will be broadcast or exhibited in theatres in Quebec. However, for a giant-screen production, the production company needs an undertaking that the production will be screened in Canada in a public performance venue.

Eligible projects (live action or animation) include features, movies of the week (MOW's), documentaries and documentary series, children's programs, and certain variety and magazine programs.

As noted above, co-productions are also eligible for this tax credit if a minimum of 75% of production costs relating to the Canadian portion of the co-production are paid to Quebec residents or incurred for services rendered in Quebec. In such cases, the tax credit is calculated based on **Quebec's portion** of the budget.

REFUNDABLE TAX CREDIT FOR QUEBEC FILM PRODUCTION SERVICES

(a) WHAT is available?

This **refundable tax credit**, administered by SODEC, is equal to **20% of qualified labor expenditures**.

An **additional credit** of 20% is available for labor expenditures which are directly attributable to the creation of digital **animation or visual effects**, so that the **combined rate** for these expenditures **amounts to 40%**.

(b) — (c) WHO can apply and HOW do you qualify?

To be eligible for the Refundable Tax Credit for Film Production Services, the following must be satisfied:

- a production company must first obtain an **advance ruling** or a certificate from SODEC;
- the corporation must have an **establishment** in Quebec;
- the corporation's **primary business** must be the operation of a film or TV production business or production service business;
- the production company must either **own the copyright** in the production or have directly contracted with the copyright owner to render production services for the production;
- the production must meet a **cost minimum** which varies depending on the type of production and duration.

Official Treaty Co-productions are eligible for the Quebec Refundable Tax Credit for Film Production Services.

Eligible projects (live action or animation) include features, MOW's, documentaries and documentary series, children's programs, and certain variety and magazine programs.

(d) WHERE to find more information?

For more information on programs administered by the Société de développement des entreprises culturelles, visit its website at www.sodec.gouv.qc.ca.

SASKATCHEWAN

SASKATCHEWAN FILM EMPLOYMENT TAX CREDIT

(a) WHAT is available?

Administered by the Saskatchewan Film and Video Development Corporation (SaskFILM), the Saskatchewan Film Employment Tax Credit is equal to **45% of eligible labor expenditures**, to a **maximum of 50% of the total production costs**.

'Eligible labor' refers to Saskatchewan and deemed non-Saskatchewan labor. There is a **bonus** equal to **5% of the total production budget** for productions shot 25 miles (40 km) *outside* of **Regina** or **Saskatoon**, which increases the maximum credit to 22.5% of the total production budget. This bonus is calculated on any expenditures incurred in Saskatchewan.

There is also a **key creative position bonus** equal to **5%** of eligible labor expenditures. This bonus is designed for projects with **budgets of C$3m** or more, and the production must attain a minimum **6 out of 10 points** based on the hiring of Saskatchewan crew into key positions.

There are *no* corporate or project **caps**, and *no* copyright requirement for this tax credit.

A unique *advantage* of the program is the producer's ability to **deem non-resident labor** as eligible when no qualified Saskatchewan resident is available. Above-the-line salaries and wages are included in the calculation of the tax credit. Government assistance is deducted from the eligible amount with the exception of Telefilm Canada, the Canadian Broadcasting Corporation (CBC), the National Film Board (NFB), the Canadian Television Fund (CTF) and the federal tax credit.

(b) — (c) WHO can apply and HOW do you qualify?

To be eligible for this tax credit, the following must be satisfied:

- The production company must have a **permanent establishment** in Saskatchewan;
- The production company must pay at least **25% of all labor costs** to Saskatchewan residents;
- The production company cannot be **controlled** by a corporation based outside of Saskatchewan;
- The production company must be **incorporated in Canada** or in a province of Canada.

Ineligible genres include news, current affairs, talk shows (except for children's shows), sports events, gala presentations and award shows, reality TV, advertising and commercials, stock footage (other than documentaries), productions that solicit funds and pornography.

Eligible productions need *not* meet Canadian or Saskatchewan **content** requirements.

Eligible genres include: drama, variety, animation, children's programming, music programming, education resource programs, information series or documentaries. Canadian broadcasters and specialized channels are not eligible applicants.

Other Programs

SaskFILM also provides financial support through the following programs: Development Loans Program, Scriptwriter's Program, Equity Investment, Filmmakers Program, Documentary Fund, Marketing Travel Assistance Program and Festival/Competition ravel Assistance Program.

(d) WHERE to find more information?

www.saskfilm.com.

YUKON

Since **no taxes are paid in the Yukon**, no tax credit is available to production companies that produce in this territory. Instead, Yukon Film has developed other incentive programs to attract production companies to the area.

YUKON FILM INCENTIVE PROGRAM LABOR REBATE

(a) WHAT is available?

This **labor rebate**, created to increase the number of high quality employees in the production industry, is equal to **35% of eligible Yukon labor**, to a **maximum of 50% of total expenditures** incurred in the Yukon.

(b) — (c) WHO can apply and HOW do you qualify?

To be eligible for this labor rebate, productions must be either dramatic TV programming or feature films or movies of the week (MOW's) and must be shot on **16mm** film capture or better. In addition, Yukon residents hired for the production must work at least **25% of the total person days** in the portion of the production shot in the Yukon. A production company does *not* have to be registered in the Yukon to be eligible for this rebate.

YUKON FILM INCENTIVE PROGRAM TRAVEL REBATE

(a) WHAT is available?

This travel rebate is available to dramatic TV productions and feature films and MOW's. Yukon Film will pay up to **50% of travel costs** from Calgary, Edmonton or Vancouver to Whitehorse. This rebate is calculated as the *lesser* of **C$2,000** multiplied by the number of days of production in the Yukon to a **maximum of C$15,000**, or **15% of the total cost** incurred in the Yukon.

(b) — (c) WHO can apply and HOW do you qualify?

For the Travel Rebate, the minimum Yukon **crew level** must be **15%** or more of the total person days for the Yukon portion of the production. Additionally, the rebate is **reduced** by **C$1,000** for each new member or service who is out-of-territory when there is a capable Yukon resident available for the job.

FILM DEVELOPMENT FUND

(a) WHAT is available?

This fund can provide in the form of a **grant** up to **50% of the Yukon expenditures** to a **maximum of C$35,000**, or **33% of the total project expenses**, whichever is *less*. This includes the following four phases: concept to fully developed script; treatment to first draft of script; first-draft to final-draft screenplay; polish/rewrites and preproduction expenses.

An additional C$10,000 may be awarded for costs associated with training and mentoring a Yukon screenwriter. The total contribution may not exceed 75% of the total project costs.

(b) — (c) WHO can apply and HOW do you qualify?

Applicants must be Yukon **residents** or Yukon registered **corporations** (majority owned by Yukon residents) whose **primary business** is film production. Applicants must **own 51%** of the project, and must have a **broadcast development** agreement with a licensed broadcaster or a **distribution arrangement**.

Broadcasters and distributors are *not* eligible.

FILM PRODUCTION FUND

(a) WHAT is available?

This **fund** offers a maximum project contribution of **C$500,000**. For productions controlled by a Yukon resident or corporation, the contribution will be based on **30% of Yukon expenditures**, or **30% of total production costs**, whichever is *less* in the form of a **grant**.

For **co-productions**, the contribution will be based on 30% of Yukon expenditures, or 20% of total production costs, whichever is *less*.

(b) — (c) WHO can apply and HOW do you qualify?

The applicant must be a Yukon-registered **corporation** (at least 51% owned by Yukon residents) whose **primary business** is film production, and must **own controlling interest** in the project.

In the case of **co-productions**, the co-production company must be **registered** in the Yukon.

Broadcasters and distributors are *not* eligible.

In general, interpersonal communication systems, transactional services and corporate promotion titles are not eligible.

(d) WHERE to find more information?

For more information on incentives provided by the Yukon government, visit www.reelyukon.com.

Canada: Summary of Provincial and Federal Government Tax Credits

QLE = Qualifying or eligible labor expenditures as per the relevant legislation
CAP = Capped at a fixed % of production costs

AREA	TAX CREDIT (or * for GRANT/REBATE)	BASIC TAX (as % of QLE)	CAP?	CAP CONDITIONS (if applicable)
FEDERAL	Film or Video Production Tax Credit	25%	Yes	At 60% of production budget (approx. 15% budget)
	Film or Video Production Services Tax Credit	16%	No	N/A
ALBERTA	* Alberta Film Development Program - GRANT	N/A	N/A	N/A
BRITISH COLUMBIA (BC)	Film Incentive BC	30%	Yes	At 48% of total eligible production costs (approx. 17% of budget)
	Production Services Tax Credit	18%	No	N/A
MANITOBA	Film & Video Production Tax Credit	45%	No	N/A
NEW BRUNSWICK	Labor Incentive Film Tax Credit	40%	Yes	At 50% of total production costs
NEWFOUNDLAND & LABRADOR	Film & Video Industry Tax Credit	40%	Yes	lesser of 40% of QLE or 25% of the total eligible production budget
NOVA SCOTIA	Film Industry Tax Credit	35%	Yes	At 17.5% of total production costs
		40%	Yes	At 20% of total production costs
ONTARIO	Film and Television Tax Credit	30%	No	N/A
	Production Services Tax Credit	18%	No	N/A
	Computer Animation and Special Effects Tax Credit	20%	No	N/A
	Interactive Digital Media Tax Credit	30% or 20%	No	N/A
PRINCE EDWARD ISLAND (PEI)	* Labor Rebate Program see Technology PEI	N/A	N/A	N/A
QUEBEC	Refundable Tax Credit for Film and Television Productions	29.16%	Yes	At 50% of production costs (approx. 14.58% of budget)
	Film Production Services Tax Credit	20%	No	N/A
	Dubbing Tax Credit	29.16%	Yes	At 40.5% of eligible dubbing costs
	Multimedia Production Tax Credit	37.50%	No	N/A
		30%	No	N/A
		26.24%	No	N/A
SASKATCHEWAN	Film Employment Tax Credit	45%	Yes	At 50% of total production costs
YUKON	* Film Incentive Program - REBATE	N/A	N/A	N/A

CHINA

I. INTRODUCTION

The film industry in China is fairly active, and is regulated by the **State Administration of Radio, Film and Television (SARFT)**. Traditionally, only state-owned companies were allowed to produce, distribute and exhibits films in the republic. There are currently **no specific tax incentives** concerning the film industry, although there has been talk and speculation of their imminent introduction. Major English-language productions of recent years include the period drama *The Painted Veil*, directed for Warner Independent Pictures by John Curran and starring Ed Norton and Naomi Watts, which was shot in studios and locations in and around Shanghai, Beijing and Guangxi province in the south of China. However, Warner has since announced the scaling back of its Chinese activities. *Mission: Impossible 3*, starring Tom Cruise, also shot scenes in mainland China. Low costs, a growing number of facilities and a relaxation of the laws are encouraging international shoots on an unprecedented level.

Recent changes to Chinese laws, overseen by SARFT, have permitted majority foreign-owned joint ventures to produce film and TV content, increased the annual quota on imported films, and raised the foreign content limits on domestic TV channels.

However, in December 2006, SARFT temporarily halted permissions for foreign companies to invest in local programme-makers. Note that although it was announced as a temporary measure, at the time of going to press, we had not heard anything to suggest if or when the ban will be lifted. The descriptions below assume that, by the time you read this, the temporary ban will hopefully be lifted.

II. CO-PRODUCTIONS AND INTERNATIONAL PRODUCERS

Since joining the World Trade Organisation in 2001, China has continually revised and relaxed its tax laws to favour foreign investments. Currently foreign companies pay up to **14% less** on corporate profits than the 24% paid by local companies. However, a new tax law, scheduled to come into effect in 2008, is proposing a 'unified' tax of 25% on corporate profits across the board. In 2004, SARFT issued new rules regarding film production, distribution and exhibition. Under these regulations, foreign investors can undertake co-productions in the form of **joint production, collaborative production** and **designated production**. In all cases, producers must obtain a **Sino-Foreign Cooperative Film Production Licence** and various other approval documents. The rules can potentially allow foreign companies to co-invest with state-owned studios (ie. enter into equity joint ventures), whereas previously the only cooperation allowed was only on a project-by-project basis. However, the relaxation in the rules means that foreign productions now no longer have to co-produce with a state-owned studio. They can partner with any company registered in China, and which has capital of at least RMB1m (US$130m). In 2005, three out of four of the top-selling films were co-productions. Co-productions are classed in two main categories. **Joint productions** (or **full co-productions**) are when a Chinese and a foreign producer share in the rights and risks in the production of a film. They can be more difficult to arrange, but the films are classed as domestic productions and can thereby bypass China's import quotas when it comes to exploitation in China. Merchant Ivory's *The White Countess* reportedly qualified in this way. An **assisted production**, on the other hand, is where a foreign producer makes a film in mainland China, and the Chinese Government provides **compensated assistance**.

The benefits of co-productions generally include a corporate tax as low as 10% instead of 25%, **no restriction** on the percentage of co-production sharing or on location use, and there is supposedly a 20-day approval process for a project. That said, at least **one-third** of the cast should be **nationals** from China, Hong Kong, Taiwan or Macau, when working with foreign producers.

Recently, most foreign producers have chosen to opt for the full co-production option, which involves co-investment from Chinese partners, rather than assisted co-production, in which state-owned studios provide services for a fee. Either way, the master negative is expected to be kept in mainland China and all prints struck from it there. In 2006, eleven co-production deals were signed between China and European producers.

III. FUNDS FOR SMALL TO MID-BUDGET FILMS

SARFT has recently (January 2007) confirmed its intention to set up a fund to support young Chinese directors in the making of small to mid-budget films. During the first year of the fund, 16 filmmakers will each receive RMB0.5m (approx $64,300) to help finance a low-budget project, in addition to assistance in obtaining script approval and distribution of the finished film.

Beneficiaries of the fund will include a number of renowned filmmakers who have won acclaim on the international film festival circuit, but who have found it difficult to secure finance and distribution within Chinese borders. The idea is to support filmmakers who are under 45 years old and who have gained a certain degree of recognition either nationwide or overseas, and to encourage production of a more diverse range of genres. According to reports, the scheme is seen by industry players as a reaction to the 'polarised box office performance' of Chinese films. They claim that big-budget international co-productions, such as Zhang Yimou's *Curse Of The Golden Flower*, have achieved substantial box office returns, while award-winning art-house pictures find it difficult to remain on the theatrical circuit for more than a couple of weeks. The 16 filmmakers can apply to the fund in respect of any one of their current projects, so long as it has a shooting permit. Each director is only allowed to apply once with one project during 2007.

IV. THE NEW MARKET AT THE SHANGHAI INTERNATIONAL FILM FESTIVAL

The Shanghai International Film Festival (SIFF), the country's main festival with an international focus, has announced that it will be launching a film market at its 2007 event. The 'Film Mart' is specifically aimed at encouraging the formation of co-productions between China and producers from other countries in a market environment. The festival will also create various audience awards for both Chinese and international pictures.

V. OUTLINE OF RECENT LEGISLATION

The Interim Provisions on the Entry Qualifications for Film Production, Distribution and Projection became effective on 1 December 2003. The provisions permit minority foreign owned equity or cooperative film production joint ventures between foreign companies and existing state-owned film production units. Foreign investment enterprises (FIEs) may also engage in upgrading film production and projection infrastructure, technology and equipment, and, upon approval from the provincial or municipal authorities, the foreign investors in an FIE whose activities are limited to upgrading may have a controlling interest. The provisions do not, however, permit foreign investment in enterprises engaged in the trading and distribution of films.

The Provisions on the Administration of Sino-foreign Cooperative Film Production, also became effective on 1 December 2003. The provisions, which replaced similar rules issued in 1994, permit domestic film producers with a Film Production License to co-produce films, digital films and TV programmes in China with foreign film producers. Co-production takes one of three forms: (1) **joint production**, where the Chinese and foreign party jointly invest (in capital, labour or kind), produce and share the risks and benefits; (2) **assisted production**, where the foreign party contributes capital and the Chinese party provides the site, equipment, facilities and labour; and (3) **commissioned production**, where the foreign party commissions the Chinese party to produce the film on its behalf. The provisions also set out requirements regarding the use of the Chinese language and Chinese personnel, including creative personnel, and require certain production and post-production activities to be carried out in China.

Source: www.perkinscoie.com/content/ren/ updates/china/june2004.htm

More info at:

www.sarft.gov.cn

COLOMBIA

Prepared with the assistance of Dynamo Film Production & Financing (www.dynamocapital.net)

I. INTRODUCTION

Colombia has one of the highest growth rates in theatrical attendance in Latin America, with the quality of local productions now comparable to other international product. This is mainly due to the increasing skill of the film community and the new film tax incentives known as the 'Ley de Cine' (the Film Law) introduced by the Ministry of Culture through the 'Direccion de Cinematografia Colombiana' (Colombian Film Office).

In addition to affordable and experienced crews (transferring over from the massive TV and advertising production community), Colombia has a multitude of impressive and versatile locations, including urban Latin American metropolis (Bogota), colonial gems (eg. Cartagena), the Amazon rainforest, woods, deserts and endless oriental plains.

The tax breaks are also encouraging the appearance of innovative private equity film investment funds that can also contribute finance to productions. Partnering with a local production service company is advisable in order to ensure the best results. Recent features made in Colombia include *Rosario Tijeras*, *Satanas* and the $40m US production *Love in Times of Cholera*.

II. TAX ALLOWANCE

THE DIRECCION DE CINEMATOGRAFIA COLOMBIANA

(a) WHAT is available?

Investors who invest capital into a film project can **offset 125% of their investment** from their income tax bill on the year of the investment. The tax break is made available to the investor in the form of a **transferable certificate**. Importantly, if the investor does not have a high enough income tax bill in the relevant year (and thereby can't make use of the certificate), it can sell the certificate to a third party (corporate or individual) in Colombia who *can* make use of the certificate. The original film investor typically sells the certificate for cash at a discount, and the buyer then applies it to their own tax bill. This means that foreign investment capital (which can also benefit in this way) is also being channelled into the Colombian film industry. The allowance can be used for feature films, shorts and documentaries.

(b) WHO is eligible to apply?

Any **Colombian investor** who declares income tax in Colombia is eligible. However, the fact that the tax break certificates can be sold to third parties means **foreign investors** can also access it to through specialised funds.

(c) HOW do you qualify?

In order to receive the certificate, the film has to qualify as a **Colombian production** or co-production under the regulations of the 'Direccion de Cinematografia Colombiana', who will require from the producing entity proof of expenditure. The film must be produced via a Single Purpose Vehicle (SPV) using a fairly straightforward '**trust**' mechanism.

The Colombian qualification requirements are:

For 100% Colombian Production:
- **100% Colombian investment**
- **Artistic Department:** Director plus two leads OR two leads or secondary actors and one of the following — Director of Photography, Art Director, screenwriter, music composer, animator or editor to be Colombian; and
- **Technical Department:** two of the following — sound man, cameraman, camera assistant, light, script, mixer, makeup, dress designer, set designer, casting.

For Co-Production
- **20% of budget** invested by **Colombian investors**
- Director or two of the following — Director of Photography, Art Director, screenwriter, music composer, animator or editor, lead actor or secondary actor.

There is no need to shoot in Colombia in order to qualify as a co-production

(d) WHERE do you apply?

The film cannot qualify (as an official Colombian production or co-production) until it is in an advanced stage of development, which includes having a budget, identified heads of department, lead cast and scouting among others. For more information on application and qualification, see www.proimagenescolombia.com or write to:

Fondo Mixto de Promoción Cinematográfica — PROIMAGENES en Movimiento
Calle 35 No 4, 89 (Barrio La Merced)
Bogotá DC, Colombia
T: (+57 1) 2870103
F: (+57 1) 2884828
info@proimagenescolombia.com

III. OTHER BENEFITS

Under the '**Ley General Cultura**' (**General Cultural Law**), there are other benefits for international distributors with a Colombian subsidiary as well as benefits for reinvestment in cinema by Colombian companies. For more information see:

www.proimagenescolombia.com and
www.mincultura.gov.co.

IV. OTHER USEFUL WEBSITES

www.dynamocapital.net
www.proimagenescolombia.com
www.mincultura.gov.co
www.enrodaje.cinecolombiano.com

FRANCE

Prepared with the assistance of Olivier Cousi & Charles-Edouard Renault (www.gide.com)

I. INTRODUCTION

France has an extensive range of financial support for the Film industry, with one of the highest number of public grants available for members of the European Union.

First, a fairly new **tax credit** regime, the 'credit d'impôt', can provide up to **16%** of production expenses.

At the national and regional levels, various public organizations provide filmmakers with a range of funding schemes. The **National Cinematography Centre** ('Centre National de la Cinématographie', or '**CNC**'), whose funds come from industry sources rather than from Government, provides an extensive range of financial support systems, offering up to about 33% of a budget. There is in fact no official maximum, since funds are provided on a case-by-case basis, and some of them can be cumulated with others in some scenarios.

The French Departments of Cultural Affairs (through museums and cultural centres) and Foreign Affairs also have regulations allowing producers to obtain governmental grants. Further, most French regional councils have recently increased involvement in movie production support, and French collective management organizations (such as the Society of Dramatic Authors and Composers) can also provide financial support.

The Film industry is also financed by **private investors**, through specially created investment corporations called **SOFICAs**, and **guarantees** to film lending banks from the **Institute for the Financing of Cinema and Cultural Industries** ('Institut pour le Financement du Cinéma et des Industries Culturelles' or '**IFCIC**').

France has also adopted an extensive number of international and European financial grants systems, mainly through the conclusion of **co-production** treaties. Like Canada, France seems to have co-production treaties with almost every country that has a semblance of a film industry.

Because of the vast number of grants available, and the complexity of some of their mechanisms, we only cover the most significant schemes below. Note there are numerous other incentives, including selective financial support for productions in foreign (non-French) languages, for the development of new projects, for the writing of screenplays, and for the use of new technologies in image and sound.

II. TAX INCENTIVES

THE TAX CREDIT (CREDIT D'IMPOT)

(a) WHAT is available?

Introduced for film at the beginning of 2006, the **credit d'impôt** is a relatively recent arrival, and works as a tax credit on certain qualifying expenditure. It only applies to **French language** films (see below), and provides a **20% credit** on **eligible expenses** which themselves are capped at **80% of the budget** (or 80% of the French spend on an international co-production). It is credited against the corporate tax due for the year in which the expenses are incurred, any excess being **refundable** to the company.

The credit itself is **limited to €1m** (£680k, US$1.2m) per film. It is also capped at €1,150 to €1,200 per produced and delivered minute, depending on the nature of the film (fiction, documentary or animation).

The strict qualification criteria (see below) can make it difficult to combine with soft money from other countries.

(b) WHO can apply?

The credit can be obtained by a film's 'executive' income tax paying **production company** ('*producteur délégué*'), who must obtain the necessary licence from the **CNC**. For these purposes, **executive** means the company taking responsibility (with a co-producer if an official co-production) for the film's financing, its technical and creative input, and completing the final production. Although it doesn't have to be French, the company must be submitted for French corporation tax ('*impôt sur les sociétés*'). Further, to be eligible for the Financial Production Support system, the company must satisfy the **nationality criteria** set out below.

A maximum of two companies can apply and, for a co-production, each co-producer will be allocated the '*crédit d'impôt*' proportionally to the amount it has invested.

(c) HOW do you qualify?

The film must be eligible for the **Financial Production Support** system ('*Soutien Financier de l'Industrie Cinématographique et Audiovisuelle*') (see III, below) and additionally meet certain other requirements, including that:

- the film should be totally or partially **in French** a French regional language;
- the film should be **produced** predominantly **in France** (including the scriptwriting and, in particular, pre- and post-production where the location is not dictated by the script);
- the film must **contribute** to the development and the diversity of the French and European film industry (ie. the artistic and technical staff should be mainly French, French residents, or citizens of the European Union).

The costs to which the credit applies must be paid to people established in France and carrying out their services there. It includes payments to authors, script, cast, crew, production staff. The general rule is therefore that the producers should hire French/ EU crew. The full list expenses to which the tax credit applies are listed in full in the *20 March 2006 Executive Order* (see IV below for web address), and includes the compensation and social benefits of the authors, cast and crew, as well as shooting and post-production costs.

Any subsidies already received for the payment of such expenses will be deducted from the relevant costs.

Pornography and violence-inciting films are *excluded*, as are advertisements, commercials, news and current affairs programmes, sports programmes, variety and game shows, and films containing mostly previously-made footage.

(d) WHERE do you apply?

The application is a two-stage process. The first is to obtain **temporary approval** of the CNC who, along with a commission of experts, checks that all eligibility criteria are met in accordance with a pre-established scale.

The request must be sent by certified mail with acknowledgment of receipt to the CNC Director **before** shooting starts, and must contain basic information (title of the film, name of authors and directors, as well as shooting dates), along with a file including the available authors' contracts, a financing plan and available preliminary sales estimates.

The right to the tax break is available from the date the request is made, so that the **funds** might become **available immediately**, should the producer be able to get them discounted by a bank.

The temporary approval certifies that the film is eligible to the credit d'impôt, so that the production company may benefit for the fiscal year to come from the deduction, instead of waiting until the end of principal photography. The tax deduction will then be apportioned at the date of the payment of the remaining corporation tax due by the production company.

The producer then has to obtain a **final approval** of the CNC in the 8 months following the issuing of the distribution certificate. Should the final approval **not** be granted, or if the film is never achieved, the production company will have to reimburse the tax credit that was perceived.

The current contacts at the CNC are:

Jean-Pierre Guerrieri (jean-pierre.guerrieri@cnc.fr)
Caroline Cor (caroline.cor@cnc.fr)
Philippe Lang (philippe.lang@cnc.fr)
Chargés de mission, Direction du cinéma
Service du soutien à la production et à la distribution, 12, rue de Lübeck, 75116 Paris
Tel: 01 44 34 36 12
Fax: 01 44 34 37 24

THE SOFICA SYSTEM

(a) WHAT is available?

Certain specially created entities known as *Societes pour le Financement de l'Industrie Cinématographique et Audiovisuelle* ('**SOFICAs**') are tax efficient vehicles for their investors. They part-finance qualifying films (technically, 'audiovisual works'), usually by taking shares in the relevant production company (thereby always **participating in the profits** from the film). They have a limited amount of money (90% of which they must invest within 12 to 18 months of raising it), and they usually hit their maximums. Having started in 1985, the scheme has recently been extended and there are now more than 15 SOFICA companies looking for films to invest in (see (d) below). SOFICA investment may comprise either:
• contractual monetary contributions of **up to 50%** of the final cost of production, with a participation in profits (ie. an **equity** stake in the film); or
• subscription for shares in the capital of companies which exclusively produce cinematographic works (ie. a **shareholding** in the production company).

In aggregate, SOFICAs have between about €30m and €40m per annum to spend, and tend to invest an average of **7% to 13%** (capped at 50%) of the budget, more often in larger productions. They cannot invest more than 20% of their share capital per cinematographic work.

The money is raised in the form of a trust, and any tax relief gained is repayable to the tax authorities if the individual investors sell their shares in the SOFICA within five years of the acquisition.

SOFICAs take a commercial approach to the selection of film projects for investment, and they take a negotiated recoupment position.

(b) WHO can apply?

The tax deduction is available to individuals and companies who invest In SOFICAs and are resident in France. Producers then apply to the SOFICAs for production finance.

Individual investors may deduct 40% of their contributions to the capital of SOFICAs from their taxable income (subject to an upper limit of 25% of taxable income as well as being capped at €18,000). Production companies may also invest in SOFICAs, and the benefit to them is an immediate write-off of 50% of the amount invested (so long as the money is made available for at least a 5-year period). These elements of the scheme were modified recently (December 2006), so be sure to take up-to-date advice.

(c) HOW do you qualify?

SOFICAs can only invest in qualifying French or European films. The films should be in the French language, although a SOFICA can invest up to 20% of its share capital in co-productions made in the language of one of the co-producers from a Member State of the European Union. The film must also satisfy the eligibility criteria for the Financial Production Support system of the movie industry ('*Soutien Financier de l'Industrie Cinématographique et Audiovisuelle*', see below).

The investors in a SOFICA must also be French, and the shareholding must be approved by the French Treasury Department.

Each SOFICA develops its **own** qualification and application **criteria**, on a commercial basis, although the films must be approved by the CNC.

(d) WHERE do you apply?

The producer does not need to make any specific application in relation to investment by SOFICAs. The tax break is offered to SOFICA shareholders, and so the burden of qualification and application process falls ultimately on them rather than the film company.
www.senat.fr/rap/r98-011/r98-01115.html
Since they offer pre-financing, SOFICAs should obtain necessary approvals from the French Treasury Department prior to the start of production.

The French Authority of Market Regulation ('*Autorité des Marchés Financiers*', or 'AMF') provides on its website the list of the latest approved SOFICAs at the following address:

www.amf-france.org/affiche_page.asp?Id_Tab=0& lang=fr&urldoc=sofica_sofipeche.htm

LOAN SUPPORT GUARANTEES

(a) WHAT is available?

The **Institute for the Financing of the Cinema and Cultural Industries** ('*Institut pour le financement du Cinéma et des Industries Culturelles*' or '**IFCIC**') assists in the discounting of pre-sales and shares in the credit risk with banks who lend to European (but not necessarily French) productions for production purposes. The IFCIC was established in 1983 by the two French Departments of Cultural Affairs and Treasury, to contribute to the development of cultural industries by facilitating access to bank financing by film companies.

The IFCIC offers its **guarantee** to specific credit institutions, such as Natexis Coficiné or Cofiloisir, that are aggregated in bank syndicates, and that finance cinematographic and audiovisual projects, the guarantee being directly addressed to the credit institutions themselves. If the production company defaults on repayment, the bank's loss will be shared with the IFCIC. It generally represents **50%** of the value of the amount lent, and can be increased to 70% for certain types of subsidy.

The IFCIC guarantee fund comprises a portion of the CNC subsidies, and the IFCIC also offers general financial expertise.

(b) WHO can apply?

The credit institution approves a production company and files an application to the IFCIC. However, the IFCIC might ask to meet the borrower directly.

(c) HOW do you qualify?

The qualification requirements are set by the Department of Cultural Affairs, the Treasury Department, the CNC and the IFCIC. The request for a guarantee will be subject to the opinion of a committee of experts, as well as the IFCIC's approval committee.

The decisions are made by the general manager of the IFCIC or his/her representative.

There are no specific criteria. The IFCIC will look at the general financial state and background of the production company, specifically by analysing its last two balance sheets and income statements, in order to make a decision of approval or rejection. The IFCIC will also take into account the legal, financial, artistic and technical features of the project contemplated by the production company. It will also try to assess the risk-taking of the operation and evaluate the value of the securities attached to the loan approved by the credit institution to the production company.

(d) WHERE do you apply?

The application forms should be sent to the **IFCIC**:
   Laurent Vallet
   General Manager
   Institut pour le Financement du Cinéma et des Industries Culturelles
   46 avenue Victor Hugo
   75116 Paris
   www.ifcic.fr

III. PUBLIC MONEY

Initially created in 1948, the financial support system for movie production is well-matured and has strictly defined requirements for the eligibility of production companies and films applying for support. Several types of financial support are available, depending on the **length** of the film (full length or short) and the nature of the support (**automatic** or **selective**). The following are the two main examples:

LE SOUTIEN AUTOMATIQUE À LA PRODUCTION DE LONG MÉTRAGE

(a) WHAT is available?

This is an **automatic** financial support for **finished** feature films. French (or international co-production) **full-length** movies — ie. more than 60 minutes — can obtain automatic support from the CNC, based on the level of commercial exploitation obtained for the film (theatrical distribution, TV broadcasts, etc).

The exact amount of support is calculated on a pre-established scale. For example, a scale of 100 points is used both (i) to determine whether the film may obtain the investments agreement mentioned in c) below; and (ii) to calculate the amount of the financial support if granted. This scale includes seven sub-categories of technical and artistic criteria (nationality of the production company, of the crew, the authors, comedians, etc.). The number of points obtained is then used to determine the amount of the support.

This calculation takes into account three categories of elements:

- first, the benefit perceived from the **tax** on the ticket's price, on the sale or renting of the film and on the purchasing of the diffusion's rights by TV services;
- second, a legal calculation issued from executive orders specific to each mode of support (theatre, video distribution or broadcast support); and
- third, consideration of the number of points previously obtained.

The money is then credited to a bank account held by the CNC in the name of the beneficiaries (production company), who will be able to use it later to invest in **future** movie productions.

(b) WHO is eligible?

The **production company** of the film is eligible if it satisfies the following nationality criteria:

- The chairman and directors of the production company must either have French nationality or be European citizens (ie. European Union or a country party to the European Convention on Transfrontier Television or other official treaty ratified with the European Community); and
- The production companies may not be controlled by one or more individuals or companies of countries that are not European (as defined above).

The executive production company (there is a maximum of two executive production companies) is entitled to specific rights on the financial support, according to which the support may be allocated in a minimum proportion of 25% on the executive production company's account (12.5% each if two executive producers).

(c) HOW do you qualify?

The movie needs to have obtained **two** types of approval from the CNC:

- before shooting starts, it needs approval of the finance structure (depending of type(s) of funding). Only the executive production company is entitled to request this approval, which aims to check that the film meets the criteria set forth in (a), above, and may therefore, benefit from the support.
- then, final approval for the production has to be requested within the 4 months of the issuance of the distribution certificate. This final approval will often accompany the granting of the sums.

These approvals are granted by the Director of the CNC after examination of a special commission.

(d) WHERE do you apply?

Applications must be filed with the **CNC**. The current relevant contacts are:

Jean-Luc Douat
Chef de service, Direction du cinéma
Service du soutien à la production et à la distribution
12 rue de Lübeck,
75116 Paris
T: +33 44 34 37 91
F: +33 44 34 37 24
jean-luc.douat@cnc.fr

Marie-Hélène Colinet
Adjoint(e) au chef de service, Direction du cinéma
Service du soutien à la production et à la distribution
12 rue de Lübeck, 75116 Paris
T: +33 44 34 36 05
F: +33 44 34 37 24
marie-helene.colinet@cnc.fr

SOUTIEN SÉLECTIF À LA PRODUCTION

(a) WHAT is available?

This is **selective** production financial support, and consists of **advances against receipts** either **before** or **after** the first day of principal photography ('**PDP**'). Both types are effectively **interest-free loans**. The total budget allocated to these types of advance is generally around €20m per year.

(b) WHO can apply?

Screen-writers and **directors** of the film can apply only for the advance against receipts *before* PDP, and only if they have French or European state member nationality or residency.

Production companies which satisfy the nationality criteria required for automatic support (see above) can apply for both types of selective advance.

(c) HOW do you qualify?

The film must be a full-length featured movie with its original version primarily in the **French language** (unless animation, adapted from opera, or one of a couple of other exceptions), and must also meet the following requirements:

- At least one of its **production companies** must be established **in France**;

- The film must be **produced** with studios or laboratories established in a **Member State** of the European Union;
- The film shall contain a minimum proportion of French or European nationality cast and crew (being at least 25 points on the abovementioned scale).

If the advance is requested **before** PDP, one of the two following reimbursement options should be elected in the agreement between the production company and the CNC:

- reimbursement of the support on **receipt of income** from the commercial exploitation of the film (at least 10% of the total receipts must be allocated to the reimbursement); or
- reimbursement of the support on **receipt of other financial support** generated by the film (at least 25% of the receipts must be allocated to the reimbursement, but capped at 80% of the advance to be reimbursed).

The requests for these advances are reviewed by a special commission of the CNC dedicated to the selective financial support, divided in 3 sub-commissions:

- the first sub-commission reviews requests and determines the level of advance on receipts before PDP of a first full-length feature film;
- the second reviews requests and determines the level of the other advances on receipts before PDP; and
- the third is dedicated to requests for advances after PDP.

Each sub-commission is competent in its own field to determine whether the requests meet the eligibility criteria abovementioned, and then is in charge of the pre-selection and selection of the projects that will be granted the advances.

(d) WHERE do you apply?

Applications must be filed with the **CNC**, the current contacts being:

Catherine Siriez (catherine.siriez@cnc.fr), chargée d'études, and
Nadia Brossard (nadia.brossard@cnc.fr), gestionnaire
Direction du cinéma
Service des aides sélectives à la production et à la distribution, 11 rue Galilée, 75116 Paris
T: +33 1 44 34 38 03
F: +33 1 44 34 38 40

IV. USEFUL CONTACTS AND INFORMATION

The CNC: www.cnc.fr

The French Department of Cultural Affairs: www.culture.gouv.fr

The French Department of Foreign Affairs: www.diplomatie.gouv.fr/fr/actions-france_830/diversite-culturelle_1046/diversite-culturelle-actions_14111/cinema_14115/index.html

Society of Dramatic Authors and Composers: www.beaumarchais.asso.fr

20 March 2006 Executive Order available at: www.legifrance.gouv.fr/WAspad/Ajour?nor=MCCK0600228D&num=2006-325&ind=1&laPage=1&demande=ajour

Natexis Coficiné: www.nxbp.fr/

Cie pour le financement des loisirs
48 avenue Poincaré 75016 Paris
Tel: 01 53 65 73 30

Conseil Supérieur de l'Audiovisuel (CSA): www.csa.fr

Fondation GAN: www.fondation-gan.com

IFCIC: www.ifcic.fr

Médiamétrie: www.mediametrie.fr

Listing of types of aid (regional, shorts, foundations): www.analysescript.com

Film France: www.filmfrance.net

Ile de France Film Commission: www.iledefrance-film.com or www.idf-film.com

GERMANY

Prepared with the assistance of Dr. Andreas Pense,
law firm Unverzagt–von Have
(www.unverzagtvonhave.com)

I. INTRODUCTION

German film incentives have been the centre of
much interest, change and speculation over recent
years as the future of the various famed tax funds
under the new political reality has become a little
uncertain. In the past, German money had been the
biggest non-US contributor of production finance
to the worldwide independent film sector, despite
complaints locally that much of the funding given at
the expense of the German tax authorities went into
films that did not benefit the German economy or
promote its culture.

In October 2006, the German Government
agreed on the main principles of a new *production
cost reimbursement* model as a future financing
tool for film production in Germany. A first
draft of the proposed regulations ('*Eckpunkte
Produktionskostenerstattungsmodell*') was published
on 18 October 2006, and the final guidelines
('*Richtlinie des BKM, Anreiz zur Stärkung der
Filmproduktion in Deutschland*') were published and
approved by the European Commission for state aid
purposes on 21 December 2006, and came into force
on 1 January 2007.

II. FINANCIAL INCENTIVES

THE NEW GERMAN PRODUCTION COST
REIMBURSEMENT MODEL

(a) WHAT is available?

The official title of the German Production
Cost Reimbursement Model is the Deutscher
FilmFoerderFonds or German Federal Film Fund
(DFFF), and it consists of an automatic non-recourse,
non-repayable and non-recoupable **reimbursement
of production costs** based on expenditures for
film production in Germany (**German Spend**). The
Government has €60m pa to spend on this scheme in
each of 2007, 2008 and 2009.

Productions will be eligible for the reimbursement
of **20% of qualifying production costs** incurred in
Germany (in other words 20 cents for every Euro of
German Spend), up to a **maximum of 80%** of the
total budget.

The **cap** per film is **€4m**, but it can be increased up
to **€10m** if the German Spend amounts to **at least
35%** of the film's total production costs, *or* if **two-
thirds** of the points of the cultural test (see below)
are attained.

(b) WHO can apply?

The applicant must be a company or a subsidiary or
branch of an EU-company or a non-EU-company
having its seat in Germany. It must be the film's
producer or co-producer who is (jointly) responsible
for and **actively involved** in the production of
the film throughout. It (or in the case of a Single
Purpose Vehicle (SPV), a group company) generally
must also have **already produced** (or been a co-
producer on) a theatrical feature film in Germany or
any other member state of the EU or EEA within the
five years preceding the application. In the case of
an international co-production, the applicant's own
contribution must amount to at least 20% of the
film's production budget. However, the applicant's
contribution can be reduced to at least €5m if the
film's total production costs exceed €25m.

(c) HOW do you qualify?

To be entitled to receive the Production Cost
Reimbursement, the relevant **film** must meet
the following conditions (see below for fuller
explanation):

- a **theatrical feature** (usually minimum 30 prints),
  with an unconditional distribution contract *in
  place*;
- a total **production cost** of at least **€1m** (or a
  theatrical documentary with total production costs
  of at least €200K, or a theatrical animation film
  with total production costs of at least €3m);
- the applicant must also provide financing of
  at least **15% of the production budget** (for
  international co-productions, 15% of the German
  contribution) which can be provided in the form
  of producer's equity, deferments, distribution
  advances or loans;
- a minimum **German Spend** of **€15m** or (if lower)
  25% of production costs (reduced to 20% for
  films with budgets over €20m);
- it must satisfy the German equivalent of a **Cultural
  Test**; and
- principal photography must **commence after 1
  January 2007** but no later than **30 June 2009**.

Cinema release in Germany must be secured by a
binding and unconditional distribution agreement.
A list of approved distributors will be provided

by the German Federal Film Subsidy Board, the 'Filmförderungsanstalt' (**FFA**). A release of a German subtitled version of the Film will suffice.

German Spend is defined as film-related goods and services manufactured, used and rendered in Germany by companies, their employees, freelancers or independent contractors. Wages and fees for services rendered by individuals qualify as German Spend if they are subject to German taxation. This means that foreign cast and crew can also qualify. Fees for services rendered or goods manufactured by companies qualify as German spend if:

- the company has its seat or a subsidiary situated in Germany and is registered in the local registry;
- the company or its German subsidiary has at least one employee in Germany;
- the services or goods are accounted for in the books of the company or its subsidiary; and
- the services or goods are rendered or manufactured fully in Germany and the necessary technical equipment is actually used in Germany (mobile technical film equipment needs to be acquired, leased or rented from Germany).

The following will *not* qualify as 'German Spend':

- costs for development (including location scout), acquisition of **underlying rights** (incl. music);
- **legal**, **financing**, and insurance costs;
- **travel** and transport of actors;
- **overhead**;
- actor's compensation above **15%** of the film's total production costs; or
- contingency.

Note that if (and only if) the script requires non-German location shooting, **up to 30% of non-German spend** on features can be **included** as 'German Spend', assuming it meets all the other relevant conditions.

The film will also have to satisfy the German **Cultural Test** for Theatrical Feature Film, where it needs to achieve **48 out of a possible 94 points** (these numbers differ for documentaries and animation). The relevant categories are Category A, for cultural content, talent and crew, and Category B for physical production (ie. photography, VFX, SFX, music, sound, laboratory etc). The test covers content, contribution and country of origin of cast and crew, and location of production. As for other European countries, the cultural test is substituted by the European Convention points test in the case of *European Convention* co-productions. Details of the Cultural Test can be found on the FFA website (www.ffa.de).

(d) WHERE do you apply?

The application has to be filed with the **FFA** (address below). Approval will automatically be given once the requirements have been met. Generally, the film's financing needs to be closed no later than 3 months after approval has been given and principal photography needs to commence no later than 4 months after approval has been given; otherwise the approval will become void. However, a producer can reapply for a project twice.

Shooting should *not* start before approval of the rebate is given. And, before applying, the applicant must have, as a formal requirement, **75% of the film's financing** already in place.

Normally, disbursement of the financial aid will take place **upon completion** of production, audit of the final cost statement and evidence that all requirements have been met. However, in return for an administrative fee, the reimbursement can be paid out in three **instalments** of 33% each, payable respectively upon commencement of principal photography, completion of the rough cut, and following the auditing of the final cost statement. In the case of instalments being paid **before completion**, and the total reimbursement amounts to at least €2m a **completion bond** or bank guarantee in the amount of the rebate need to be in place.

Formal text (on pdf) of the regulations in English can be found online on the website of the FFA:

Große Präsidentenstraße 9
10178 Berlin
T: + 49 (0)30-27577-0
F: + 49 (0)30-27577-111
www.ffa.de

REGIONAL STATE GUARANTEES BACKING FILM PRODUCTION INVESTMENT

(a) WHAT is available?

In addition to regional subsidies (see below), some federal states ('*Bundesländer*') offer **state guarantees** for film production investments. These state guarantees are aimed at attracting the production of international films into specific states of Germany. In some states, the schemes have been tested thoroughly, whereas in others they are still at the discussion stage, *vis*:

Brandenburg — established and tested

Lower Saxonia (Niedersachsen) — it is established and tested

North Rhine Westfalia — established (but not thoroughly tested)

Hamburg — established (but not thoroughly tested)

Berlin — in discussion.

The way this works, in essence, is that the relevant state will **guarantee up to 80% of a third party loan financing a German co-producer's equity contribution**, subject to the contribution being **capped at 30%** of the total budget. The contribution can represent more than 30% of the budget, but only 80% of 30% is guaranteed by the state. The amount invested in this way must, of course, be matched by **local spend** in the relevant state.

The guarantee works as follows: if after 4 years from the start of exploitation of the film, the lender has not been repaid its entire loan by the German co-producer through revenues generated by the film, it may draw on the state guarantee in order to recover 80% of the outstanding loan amount. Generally, the recoupment position of the German co-producer will need to be after any gap financing and *pro rata pari passu* with other equity investors.

It should be possible to mix the state guarantee-backed financing with the DFFF incentive (above) as long as the total amount of the public incentives and aid per film stays within 50% of the film's budget (the threshold under EU law). However, note that the European Commission is currently debating regulations to restrict state guarantee backed financing, the outcome of which is expected to be published by mid-2007.

(b) WHO can apply for the State Guarantees?

The applicant must be a company or subsidiary of an EU company having its 'seat' in the region.

(c) HOW do you qualify?

Qualification as a 'German Film' is *not* required, but the following requirements must be fulfilled at the time of the application:

- the local spend generated by the realisation of the film project in the region must be at least 100% of the co-producer's contribution;
- distribution deals in at least 2 key territories, or a sales agency agreement for worldwide rights, must be in place;
- revenue projections by reputable sales agent must lead the State's auditors to give a positive

prognosis that the equity investment is likely to be recouped; and

- evidence of closing of financing needs to be produced.

(d) WHERE do you apply?

The application has to be filed with the competent **regional ministry of finance represented by its auditors**.

III. PUBLIC MONEY

FEDERAL FILM SUBSIDY

(a) WHAT is available?

The **Federal Film Subsidy** is granted by the FFA in accordance with the German Film Subsidy Law ('*Filmförderungsgesetz*', '**FFG**'). There are two types of production funding, **project funding** and **reference film funding**.

Project Funding

The Project Funding subsidy is a selective funding for films which look set to improve the quality and profitability of German Cinema. The maximum subsidy awarded by the FFA, in the form of a non-recourse production loan, is **€1m** per film. The Federal Film Subsidy Project Funding's annual budget is approximately €76m.

In recouping the loan, the FFA corridor starts once the German producer/co-producer (the Borrower) has received net revenues (ie. net of distribution fees, sales commissions and distribution expenses) of 20% of the production costs (in case of international co-productions, the German share of production costs) as audited by the FFA. The FFA's corridor is capped at 50% of Producer's net revenues.

Reference Film Funding

Reference Film Funding (*Referenzfilm*) subsidies are granted to producers of previously successful German Films for their next 'German Film'. They benefit from an **automatic** (non-recoupable) **grant**, which depends on the German **box office results** and/or the prizes and awards won in film festivals.

The maximum grant is €2m per film. Producers have no obligation at all to reimburse these grants.

(c) WHO can apply?

The applicant, ie. the producer or co-producer of the film, must be a company or a subsidiary of an EU-Company or an EEA-Company having its **seat** in Germany.

(d) HOW do you qualify?

To be entitled to receive Project Funding, the following conditions must be fulfilled:

- Qualification as '**German Film**'. Note that a German national qualifying film can use elements (cast, crew, etc) with nationals of any member state of the European Union – as opposed to being restricted to German nationalities;
- At least one version of the film shall be in the **German language**;
- Closing of financing must be substantiated;
- Distribution deals for German speaking territories must be in place;
- Regarding German domestic (co-)productions (ie. with no international co-production):
  - The studio shoot and technical services shall be undertaken by service companies located in Germany or in other EU-member countries;
  - The Director must have German or EU nationality (although an exception is possible if, with the exclusion of script writer and two main cast, all other cast and crew, are German or EU national);
  - The film shall have its premiere in the German language in Germany or be a German contribution at a recognised Festival.
- Regarding international co-productions, there are two alternatives:
1. If an International Co-Production Treaty applies:
   - The German co-producer's financial contribution must be **at least at 20%** of total production costs; and
   - German and/or European creative and technical elements must balance with the co-producer's financial contribution.
2. If no International Co-Production Treaty applies:
   - The German co-producer's financial contribution must be **at least at 30%** of total production costs;
   - If the German co-Producer is the majority co-producer then the film shall be world-premiered in the German language in Germany or be a German contribution to an international Film Festival; and
   - German and/or European creative and technical elements must balance with the German co-producer's financial contribution.

To be entitled to receive Reference Film Funding, the above conditions must be met, and the applicant must additionally have produced a German film which has attained **150,000 'reference' points**

in Germany within one year of initial release. The 'reference' points are calculated in relation to the success at the German box office and important international festivals and awards.

(d) WHERE do you apply?

The application should be filed with the **FFA** (see address above).

Qualification as a **German Film** has to be obtained by written application from the **German Federal Office of Economics and Export Control** ('Bundesamt für Ausfuhrkontrolle und Außenwirtschaft' or **BAFA**), whose address is:

Frankfurter Straße 29 – 35
65760 Eschborn

Preliminary approval is given 2 months before the beginning of principal photography, and final approval follows the completion of the film.

REGIONAL FILM SUBSIDIES

(a) WHAT is available?

In addition to the Federal Film Subsidy, there are **regional film subsidies** which are granted in the form of **non-recourse production loans**. Regional film subsidy boards have been established in Northrhein-Westphalia, Bavaria, Berlin/Brandenburg, Baden-Württemberg, Hamburg, Lower Saxonia, Thuringia, Saxony, Saxony-Anhalt, Hessen and Schleswig-Holstein. The aggregate amount of subsidy granted by the above-mentioned States in 2005 were:

North Rhine Westphalia (approx €36m)
Bavaria (approx €30m)
Berlin/Brandenburg (approx €21m)
Baden Württemberg (approx €10m)
Hamburg (approx €7m)
Lower Saxonia (approx €10m)
Thuringia, Saxony, Saxony-Anhalt (approx €12.5m)
Hessen (approx €2.1m)

The **recoupment** corridor starts after the German producer/co-producer (the Borrower) and other financiers have recouped their respective equity contributions. The corridor is capped at 50% of Producer's net revenues (ie. net of distribution fees, sales commissions and distribution expenses).

(b) WHO can apply?

The applicant must be a company or subsidiary of an EU-Company based in the region.

(c) HOW do you qualify?

Regional film subsidy boards do not require a qualifying German national film but they do require a certain local spend; as a rule of **100% to 150%** of the loan amount has to be generated as local spend by production of the film in the relevant region. A **distribution deal** for German speaking territories must be signed, and evidence of closing of financing must be substantiated.

(d) WHERE do you apply?

The application has to be filed with the corresponding competent regional subsidy board:

Baden-Württemberg:
MFG Medien-und Filmgesellschaft Baden-Württemberg mbH, Breitscheidstraße 4, D-70174 Stuttgart. T: +49 (0)711/90 715 400. Fax: 0711 / 90 715-450. www.film.mfg.de

Bavaria:
FilmFernsehFonds Bayern GmbH, Sonnenstraße, 21, D-80331 München. T: +49 (0)89 544 602 50. Fax: 089 / 544 602 60. www.fff-bayern.de

Berlin / Brandenburg:
Medienboard Berlin-Brandenburg GmbH, Postfach 90 04 02, D-14440 Potsdam-Babelsberg. Tel: 0331 / 743 87 0. Fax: 0331 / 743 87 99. www.medienboard.de

Hamburg:
Filmförderung Hamburg GmbH, Friedensallee 14-16, D-22765 Hamburg. T: +49 (0)40 398 37 0. F: +49 (0)40 398 37 10. www.ffhh.de

Hessen:
Hessische Filmförderung, Am Steinernen Stock 1, D-60320 Frankfurt a.M. T: +49 (0)69 155 45 16. F: +49(0)69 155 45 14. www.hessische-filmfoerderung.de

Lower Saxony:
Nord Media, Die Mediengesellschaft Niedersachsen/Bremen mbH, EXPO-Plaza 1, D-30539 Hannover. T: +49 (0)511 123 456 0. F: +49 (0)511 123 456 29. www.nord-media.de

North-Rhine Westphalia:
Filmstiftung NRW GmbH, Kaistraße 14, D-40221 Düsseldorf. T: +49 (0)211 930 500. F: +49 (0)211 930 505. www.filmstiftung.de

Schleswig-Holstein:
MSH Gesellschaft zur Förderung audiovisueller Werke in Schleswig-Holstein mbH, Schildstraße 12, D-23552 Lübeck. T: +49 (0)451 719 77. F: +49 (0)451 719 78. www.m-s-h.org

Thuringia, Saxony, Saxony-Anhalt:

MDM Mitteldeutsche Medienförderung GmbH, Hainstraße 19, D-04109 Leipzig. T: +49 (0)341 269 87 0. F: +49 (0)341 269 87 65. www.mdm-online.de

IV. CO-PRODUCTIONS AND OTHER USEFUL WEBSITES

Germany is a signatory of the *European Convention on Cinematographic Co-Production*, and has entered into international co-production treaties with the following countries: Australia, Austria, Belgium, Brazil, France, Great Britain (although superseded by the *Convention*), Israel, Italy, Luxembourg, Canada, New Zealand, Portugal, Sweden, Spain, South Africa, Switzerland. In addition, at the time of writing, treaties are in negotiation with Argentina, Hungary, Ireland, India, South Korea, Poland and Russia.

A few other film commissions and related websites that might be of use include:
www.bbfc.de
www.ibhh.de
www.shfc.de
www.film-commission-bayern.de

HUNGARY

Prepared with the assistance of Abacus-Consult Kft (www.abacusconsult.hu)

I. INTRODUCTION

The Hungarian government has recently introduced **tax incentives** that enable film producers to obtain up to **20%** of their production budget through a local 'corporate sponsorship' scheme. The 'sponsors' themselves can benefit from a number of tax incentives, including a tax credit *and* an additional tax deduction. Possibly as a result of the introduction of this scheme, the money spent on film productions has more than tripled in 2005.

Direct **public funding** is also available to films that satisfy a points system (see below), and an additional 'development tax' allowance is available for investment in local film infrastructure.

Hungary is a signatory of the *European Convention on Cinematographic Co-Production* ('*European Convention*'), and has also entered into a co-production treaty with Canada. High-profile productions made in Hungary include *Munich*, *Severance*, *Ten Commandments*, *8mm 2* and *Eragon*, and the country offers a sophisticated film production workforce. Hungary is a member of the European Union (EU) and the Euro is currently worth about 250 Hungarian Florints (HUF).

II. TAX-BASED INCENTIVE

(a) WHAT is available?

This scheme is a little more complicated than other jurisdictions, so it is recommended to take specialist advice from the start. The following is a simplified explanation of how the regime works (Note that an additional tax benefit in the form of a 10-year right-off also exists for investments over HUF100m, but is not covered below).

The Producer's Benefit

In essence, the *Producer* receives an **uncapped**, **non-repayable**, **cash 'rebate'** from the 'sponsor' (see below), equal to a maximum of **20%** of the **Hungarian eligible production costs**. The rebate (also known as the '**support**') is discountable by local banks.

The Sponsor's Benefit

In return, the *sponsor* obtains a '**Sponsorship Certificate**' entitling it to both a **tax credit** equal to the amount it invests, *and* an **additional income tax allowance** (**deduction**). The tax credit reduces the sponsor's corporate tax liability, effectively serving as a form of compensation for the support by allowing the sponsor to recoup the amount it invested from the tax-man. The income tax deduction is generally also equal to the amount invested, so the overall tax relief regime in fact provides the sponsor with up to a **16% return** (equivalent to the Hungarian corporate income tax rate) on its investment. This allowance can be used in the year of investment or any of the subsequent three years.

(b) WHO can apply?

Any company (including for example a non-Hungarian co-producer, provided it has a Hungarian branch) that is **registered** with the **Hungarian National Film Office** ('**HNFO**') is entitled to the tax benefits. Any EU company with a Hungarian branch may register with the HNFO.

(c) HOW do you qualify?

The tax benefit is capped at 20% of **Hungarian spend**, being money spent on **Hungarian taxpayers** (corporate or individual), regardless of where they physically perform their services. Hungarian spend can *include* finance, insurance and bond fees, and is subject to the following restrictions (for all films, not just co-productions):

- Copyright costs may not exceed 4% of the budget;
- PR costs may not exceed 2% of the budget;
- Capital costs may not be included (but depreciation is);
- Travel costs are limited to journeys within, or to/from Hungary;
- Only costs of accommodation in Hungary may be included;
- Up to 80% of production overhead may in some circumstances be included (if invoiced by an appropriate SPV — take local professional advice!);
- Services delivered by foreign sub-contractors are excluded; and
- *per diems* should not be paid (again, take local advice)

It follows that none of the money needs to be spent in Hungary, so long as it goes to Hungarian taxpayers.

Any interest or fees charged by a bank **discounting** the rebate can be included in Hungarian spend.

Both the **production company** and the **film** must be **registered** with the HNFO (see above), who will not sanction the benefit for films with pornography or violence.

Copyright does *not* need to be given in return for the sponsorship.

The sponsors may *not* hold any interest in the production company and, as the support must be non-repayable, they may *not* receive any distribution revenues or other compensation for their involvement in the film.

(d) WHERE do you apply?

The application, accompanied by the standard array of documents (script, budget, finance plan, packaging, etc) should be made to the **HNFO** before the start of principal photography (or, in the case of co-productions, at least 45 days prior to the start of principal photography). The HNFO then issues a statement specifying the amount of Hungarian spend that will potentially qualify. On completion (or quarterly before completion if these costs exceed HUF150m), the HNFO will audit and verify relevant invoices and issue the certificate usually within a month, and the cash should then be forthcoming from the sponsors within days.

Hungarian National Film Office
H-1075 Budapest Wesselényi utca 16
T: +36 1 327 70 70
F: +36 1 327 02 20
www.nemzetifilmiroda.hu
info@filmoffice.hu

III. DIRECT STATE FUND

(a) WHAT is available?

A maximum of HUF100m (approx €400,000) per film is available from the **Hungarian Motion Picture Public Foundation** ('**HMPPF**'), depending on the amount of Hungarian participation, and based on a points system (see below).

(b) WHO can apply?

Producers must involve a Hungarian film production company as a co-producer registered by HNFO (see above).

(c) HOW do you qualify?

The level of Hungarian involvement is categorised through a points system, and the more points attained, the more funding is available (subject to the HUF100m cap).

It is a '**Hungarian film**' if it has more than 75 out of a possible 100 points, a '**co-production**' if 30-74 points, or '**other qualifying film**' if 15-34 points. Points are given to the director (12), writer (8), composer (4), production company (10), co-producer (5), lead actors (10), supporting cast (5), location (3), post-production (between 1 and 4 points for different activities) and crew (between 1 and 3 points for each department). For full details, see HNFO website.

The **HMPPF** provides the funding and audits how the money is actually spent. According to the points system, a film qualified as an official *European Convention* co-production with a total budget of over €4m can get the maximum fund of €400k, other films scoring between 30 and 74 points can obtain the €240k award, and other 'co-productions' scoring at least 15 points can obtain a €120k award.

Again, the **film** must be registered and classified by the HNFO.

(d) WHERE do you apply?

The HNFO registers and classifies the films (see above). Applications for the fund should be sent to the **HMPPF**. The application must be filed between the period of registration and classification.

Hungarian Motion Picture Public Foundation
H-1068 Budapest, Városligeti fasor 38
T: +36 1 357 7696
F: +36 1 352 8789
www.mmka.hu
mmk2@axelero.hu

ICELAND

Prepared with the assistance of the Film In Iceland
(www.filminiceland.com)

I. INTRODUCTION

In recent years Iceland has become a popular location
for films seeking rugged and dramatic landscapes.
International productions such as *Flags of our
Fathers*, *Batman Begins* and *Die Another Day* have all
filmed in Iceland and benefited from local incentives.
The originally famed 12% rebate was due to expire
on 31 December 2006, but was replaced from 1
January 2007 (until 2011) with an enhanced **14%
of all production costs**, based on substantially the
same rules.

Note that Iceland is a member of the European
Economic Area (EEA), giving it the same status as
EU members for most matters that pertain to film-
making.

Note that where an applicant for reimbursement
has already received a grant from the Icelandic Film
Fund for the production of the **same** motion picture
or TV programme, the grant is **deducted** from the
amount that is considered domestic production cost.

The combined total of any grant from the Icelandic
Film Fund and the reimbursement may not exceed
50% of the total production costs of the same
motion picture or TV programme.

II. THE 14% REBATE

(a) WHAT is available?

A fairly straightforward **14% reimbursement** from
the State Treasury is available to any production (film
or TV with international distribution) which incurs
production costs in Iceland between 2007 and 2011.
When more than 80% of the total production cost of
a motion picture or TV programme incurs in Iceland,
the reimbursement shall be calculated from the total
production cost incurring within the EEA.

Production costs covers all costs incurred in Iceland
that are tax-deductible for income tax purposes.
Payments pertaining to employees and contractors
can only be included as production costs if they are
verifiably taxable in Iceland.

(b) WHO can apply?

Any company established in Iceland for the
purpose of production is eligible to apply for the
reimbursement. Registering a company in Iceland is a
fast procedure that can be done in one day, and can
be established as the Icelandic branch of a company
registered in another EEA member state. Icelandic
companies are charged only 18% corporation tax.

(c) HOW do you qualify?

In assessing whether a proportion of the production
costs of a motion picture or TV programme shall be
reimbursed, the following conditions shall be fulfilled:
- the production should promote Icelandic culture
  and the history and nature of Iceland;
- the production should enhance the experience,
  knowledge, and artistic ambition of the parties
  involved;
- a company must be established in Iceland
  specifically for the production (an Icelandic branch
  or agency of a company registered in the EEA will
  suffice);
- information on the principal parties involved in the
  film or TV programme must be made available;
- information on the Icelandic parties and their share
  in the production of the film or TV programme
  must be made available;
- an itemised estimate of the production costs
  and sources of funding must be made available,
  together with various confirmations, statements
  and declarations by the funding parties and/or
  applicant;
- information about the content of the proposed
  production must be made available, such as the
  script and location information;
- a statement of intent for general distribution to
  cinemas or broadcasters must be given; and
- the subject matter of the film or TV programming
  must not violate the provisions of law relating
  to film inspection and the ban on violent films,
  nor the provisions of the General Penal Code
  concerning pornography.

(d) WHERE do you apply?

An application, submitted to Iceland's Ministry
of Industry and Commerce **before production**
commences, must include:
- a comprehensive cost breakdown for the
  production;
- information about the production including
  content and filming locations and how the
  production intends to portray Iceland, its culture,
  people, and landscape;

- a production schedule (the production must be completed within three years of receipt of the 14% rebate); and
- evidence that the film or TV programme is intended for distribution by a broadcasting company and/or in cinemas.

Further information about the application procedure is available for download on the website of the **Film in Iceland Agency** (an independent agency of the Ministry of Industry and Commerce) who offer free assistance and information about filming in Iceland at www.filminiceland.com.

A conditional letter of intent is issued by the Ministry of Industry and Commerce within two weeks. Refunds are issued on **completion of the production**, usually within two weeks of the Ministry's receipt of required documentation and payment of State and municipal taxes.

III. PUBLIC MONEY

The **Icelandic Film Fund** is set up under the Icelandic Film Centre (**IFC**), which works to promote, distribute and support the production of Icelandic films, as well as to promote stronger ties between the Icelandic and international film-making communities. The Icelandic Film Fund provides financial support to films which are produced by **Icelandic nationals**, or **co-productions** between Icelandic and foreign companies. To qualify for this Fund, a production must have connections with Icelandic culture, although allowances can be made if special cultural grounds exist for the Fund to decide otherwise.

The grants cover a whole gamut of film-making activities, including script-writing, general development, production and (in certain circumstances) post-production. Production grants are subject to the remainder of the budget being fully financed, and the applicant (a company with film-making as its principal activity) having extensive film-making knowledge. The IFC works together with specially appointed 'film consultants' who assist in the decision-making process.

For the full rules on the film funding scheme, see: www.icelandicfilmcentre.is/law-and-regulation/

IV. OTHER USEFUL CONTACTS AND INFORMATION

Film In Iceland
Borgartun 35
P.O. Box 1000
IS-105-Reykjavik
Iceland
T: +35 4 561 5200
F: +35 4 511 4040
www.filminiceland.com
www.icelandicfilmcentre.is

INDIA

FILM PRODUCTION IN INDIA – AN OVERVIEW

By James MacGregor

Films have been produced in India since the dawn of the 20th century and are the country's single most popular form of entertainment. Funding of the industry works in a very different way to the English-language film financing model, and almost invariably comes through private finance.

In terms of the number of films produced and released each year, India's is the world's biggest film industry. In 2004, certified production was 934 films, of which 245 were films in the Hindi language. Three billion people a year are admitted to cinemas in India, almost double the US market and three times that of the rest of Asia.

The term 'Bollywood' has become synonymous with Indian cinema, especially in western countries, derived from a fusion of the names of two places long associated with filmmaking – Bombay (now officially known as Mumbai) and Hollywood.

The Indian film industry as a whole is fragmented in language clusters. Mumbai in the west is India's biggest filmmaking centre, and is most closely identified with films produced in the Hindi, Marathi and Kannada languages. Other major film production centres are Kolkata (Calcutta) in the north east, which typically makes films in Bengali, Chennai (Madras) in south eastern India, which produces mostly in Tamil, Cochin (in Kerala) in the southwest from where most Malayalam films derive, and the south-central city of Hyderabad which focuses mostly on the Telegu language and reportedly has the second biggest output after Mumbai. As you can see, production clusters tend to be associated with India's many languages, which makes the Indian film industry one of the most fragmented of national film industries.

Film studios in India are vertically integrated from finance through production and post-production to distribution, with some extending to ownership of cinema chains, as with the original Hollywood studio system.

Finance in Film

Film production has only recently (2000) been officially recognised as an industry in its own right by the government of India, so never received any official backing. This made it difficult for Indian producers to raise capital from normal commercial sources, like banks, driving many producers towards private funds for essential investment to float screen projects.

Some of this capital came from alternative sources in cash, leading to claims in some quarters that 'hot' money in need of being laundered was being pumped into film in order to legitimise it. Although a lot of film capital has of course always been quite legitimate, the underworld connection has — rightly or wrongly — tended to stick to Bollywood in the same way the US entertainment industry became linked with the underworld in prohibition days.

However, with the recent official recognition, banks in India have become more willing to offer loans to producers and overseas investment has also started to emerge, with US and other producers coming in with an eye to co-production and also looking at what many observers believe is the historic under-performance of Bollywood compared with Hollywood productions in terms of return.

The Bollywood product itself has continued as India's number one source of entertainment and has extended its popular reach outside the mother country to expatriate Indian communities throughout the world, with Bollywood films often out-performing local produced films in areas with sizeable populations of Indian origin and culture. In addition to the rest of South Asia, Indian films find sizeable audiences in the UK, USA, Canada, Australia, Singapore, Malaysia, the Middle East and parts of East Africa. Many new distribution companies have set up to exploit Bollywood movies internationally.

At the same time, new markets have appeared within major Indian cities, among the rising middle income economic groups, who have gained from India's economic boom. These are well-educated graduate Indians who seem to have an appetite for more than standard Bollywood song and dance dramas offered on screen. These cinema-goers have chosen to patronise a new wave of films that feed off Indian culture and family life, but often in off-beat settings (such as ex-pats living in American cities), and delivered as pure drama in English, which is widely understood by this type of audience.

Official Investment in Film

In 2006, India's Minister for Information and Broadcasting, Priyaranjan Dasmunshi, announced during the inaugural ceremony of the 37th International Film Festival of India (IFFI) that he will campaign to increase the **National Film Development Corporation (NFDC)'s** financial base.

In July of that year, Dasmunshi told the parliamentary consultative committee of the Information & Broadcasting Ministry that NFDC would, by 2007, once again be in a position to finance two to three films a year. He said, 'I want to create a scenario in which young and promising filmmakers looking for funds will not have to go to any other sources of finance.'

Dasmunshi's decision to aid the resurgence of NFDC follows an earlier ministry decision to set up five different committees to advise the government on addressing issues that confront the film production business, including taxation, piracy and creative processes.

'These committees will submit their reports by January next year and their recommendations will be implemented at the earliest,' the minister revealed.

Said Dasmunshi, 'With all responsibility I admit that the government has done precious little for the film industry, but the film industry has done a great deal for the country'.

It's payback time, the minister assured representatives of India's film industry.

Indian and UK governments have been actively working towards a film co-production treaty since December 2005 when UK Culture Secretary Tessa Jowell met Indian Film Minister, Shri Jaipal Reddy, in Delhi, to discuss developing such a treaty for mutual advantage. These treaties aim to share risk, get tax benefits and encourage new business for the film industries at either end of co-production partnerships. As this book was being set for printing, word reached us from India that the treaty would be signed in May 2007. 'It makes sense for our industries to join forces so that we can raise our game even further. A co-production treaty would create the means to do this' said Clare Wise of the UK Film Council.

MAJOR PRODUCERS

National Film Development Corporation (NFDC)
www.nfdcindia.com

The National Film Development Corporation, under the Ministry of Information & Broadcasting, is the Indian government's presence in the film industry, run broadly along commercial lines. It serves as a production company that also hires out equipment and production services and arranges permissions as well as offering access to investors and some funds of its own that are earmarked for co-production. NFDC

began life as the Film Finance Corporation way back in 1960 and assumed its present name in 1975.

NFDC is a major producer of motion pictures, having produced, co-produced and/or financed more than 300 films over the last 25 years. Major successes include the Academy Award winning film *Ghandi*, directed by Sir Richard Attenborough, the Academy Award nominated film *Salaam Bombay* directed by Mira Nair, and films like Ketan Mehta's *Mirch Masala*; Kundan Shah's *Jaane Bhi Do Yaaron* and Satyajit Ray's *Agantuk*. One of the last films it financed, ahead of its planned reinstatement in 2007 was the Kashmiri-language *Bub* in 2001.

Yash Raj Films Pvt. Ltd.
www.yashrajfilms.com

Founded by Yash Chopra, one of India's most successful directors of commercial films, in 1971, Yash Raj films has grown to be one of the wealthiest and most powerful studios in Mumbai. The Yash Raj company handles distribution overseas as well as in India.

Mukta Arts Ltd.
www.muktaarts.com

Since its establishment in 1978, Mukta Arts has become one of the fastest-growing companies in the Indian entertainment industry. Film production, studio and post-production work, music production, including albums, graphics and special effects, promotional and advertising films, film sales and distribution. The company set up Whistling Woods International as an institute dealing with film, TV, and media arts generally.

Rajshri Productions (P) Ltd.
www.rajshri.com

Established on August 15, 1947, the Rajshri group is one of India's largest, oldest, and most successful studios. Rajshri has produced 49 Hindi feature films and among them are some of Indian cinema's biggest hits. Rajshri owns and controls India's biggest film distribution network, controlling over 13,000 screens throughout India.

Shekhar Kapur Films
www.shekharkapur.com

Shekhar Kapur is an internationally acclaimed director. Notable films include *Elizabeth*, *Bandit Queen*. His productions are strong on theme and cinematic presentation.

Dharma Productions Pvt. Ltd.

www.dharma-production.com

Established by Yash Johar in 1976, Dharma Productions is a leading feature production company noted for very popular family entertainment films.

FILM FINANCE

National Film Development Corporation (NFDC)

The NFDC has a scheme for investment in co-productions. Scripts must be in English, registered with the Writers' Association (www.uwaindia.com) together with a Letter of Commitment for an assured minimum fiscal investment of 30% of the total cost of the film project. The proposals are then evaluated by an NFDC committee drawn from the entertainment sector.

A maximum of five scripts annually will be selected by the committee. These scripts can be backed by NFDC with an investment of an additional 30% of the budget or Rs 1 Crore (ie. Rs10m, approx $225,000), whichever is less. Scripts need to be submitted by 30 September each year.

The NFDC investment will be subject to the filmmaker being able to raise the balance of the finance within one year from the date of the NFDC's selection of the script. Once all the finance for the project is in place, NFDC's stake cannot be substituted under any circumstances without NFDC's specific written consent, even if the filmmaker is able to attract 100% financing, or in the event of an escalation in budgets, reducing NFDC's investment of Rs.1 Crore to a smaller equity stake in the film.

After the selection process, the producers of the successful scripts will be given a platform at the IFFI event in Goa, where they can meet with potential Indian and foreign investors to raise the balance of investment required. NFDC support to the producer will include providing a screening room with DVD projector for the filmmaker to make a presentation of his project and screen any previous works, as well as facilitating meetings between the filmmakers and the potential investors.

Once 100% finance for the project is finalised, co-production agreements will be drawn up between the stakeholders on mutually agreed terms and conditions. Any interpretation and/or questions arising from NFDC involvement with the production will be decided by the Chairman of NFDC whose decision shall be final and binding on the parties.

Scripts (in English) along with the required application duly completed together with all required enclosures should be submitted before 30 September each year, to the following address:

The Managing Director,
National Film Development Corporation Limited,
Discovery of India Building, Nehru Centre,
6th Floor, Dr. Annie Besant Road,
Worli, Mumbai-400 018.
coproductions@nfdcindia.com

EXPORT-IMPORT BANK OF INDIA

The Export-Import Bank of India (EXIM) has so far sanctioned loans in excess of Rs 33.15 Crores (approx $7.5m) for film production. The first three films financed by EXIM Bank were commercially successful across India and overseas markets.

The bank offers cashflow financing for film production; cashflow financing for film distribution/exhibition in overseas markets; term loans for fixed assets finance; and term financing for export market development.

Films financed by EXIM Bank include: *Fanaa, Bunty Aur Babli, Salaam Namaste, Veer Zaara, The Rising, Dhoom, Hum Tum.*

INCOMING FILM PRODUCTION WITHIN INDIA

NFDC

THE NFDC functions as a one-stop screen commission for incoming filmmakers. As a corporation under the Ministry of Information & Broadcasting, NFDC can ensure speedy clearances and permissions for shooting from both central and state governments and other regulatory authorities.

Headquartered in Mumbai (Bombay), NFDC is backed by an all-India network of offices in production centres all over India; Mumbai, New Delhi, Kolkata (Calcutta), Chennai (Madras) and sub-offices in Secunderabad, Bangalore, Thiruvananthapuram (Trivandrum) and Guwahati.

NFDC claims access to the best professionals in the Indian film industry and promises the expertise to source all services needed, from equipment hire and casting to transport, travel, visas, insurance, taxation, hotel and catering arrangements at the lowest cost, anywhere in India.

Contact — lineproduction@nfdcindia.com

Pitching in Bollywood
Ashvin Kumar

Arun Kumar's directorial debut feature *Truck of Dreams* won the World Cinema Award at the 2006 Washington DC Independent Film Festival.

It was an inspired idea – creating a feature around the ultimate fantasy of a girl from village India dreaming of Bollywood stardom and to fulfil it, running away with *Truck of Dreams*, the mobile cinema that rumbles around the dirt roads that pass for off-the-beaten-track in rural India. It was a dream also for London-based director Arun Kumar, a first feature with global themes, financed and shot in India, combining his western expertise with his mother culture. In fact, it was the dream that sometimes appeared to be turning into the ultimate nightmare, as everything began to go wrong. But this is India, where everything is possible – eventually.

Arun Kumar takes us on the road with his *Truck of Dreams*…

It all started when my friend introduced me to an Executive Producer, Claire Lewis, who showed me a picture of a travelling cinema. She said she wanted to make a documentary about India's travelling cinemas and would I get involved.

I wrote a short treatment of how I saw the film and Claire attempted to raise money from UK broadcasters. No one was interested until she had a meeting with Shailendra Singh, the head of an Indian production house, who was in London looking for a producer for another project. The idea appealed to him and he said he would consider it.

GO EAST YOUNG MAN

I said to Claire that if she could pay for my flight and give me some expenses money I would go to Mumbai and find a travelling cinema. Whilst there I would also trawl around Indian producers and try get finance for the film. Claire agreed and a couple of weeks later I was in Mumbai.

Back in England, Claire had run the film idea past an old friend of hers, Steve Hawes who was a drama producer and writer. He said it was an interesting idea but what it really needed was a dramatic narrative and that it should be a movie not a simple documentary. Claire called me in Mumbai and related his comments and I said I'd have a think and come up with a storyline, which would integrate with the travelling cinema story.

INSIDE BOLLYWOOD

I spent the next few days calling Bollywood producers/distributors and arranging meetings. I got used to Bollywood time quickly which basically means that people are hours late for meetings or don't show up at all. Partly this is due to the horrendous traffic and general chaos of the city. Once I got to meet people though everyone was very friendly and helpful and my request of making contact with a travelling cinema was met with a cheerful 'No problem'. However no one actually seemed to be able to connect me with a travelling cinema operator.

THE STORY UNFOLDS

At the same time I mulled around various storylines in my head and decided on a scenario where the film narrative would be the story of a village girl in love with movies since childhood. Her exposure to movies had come from the annual visit to the village of a travelling cinema and in our film the arrival of the travelling cinema would be the film's climax and where two threads of narrative would come together. Her scenes would be everyday village life told from her point of view, where we would hear her own thoughts and dreams of the cinema. These would be intercut with the travelling cinema's tour of the region. I decided to structure the film so her thoughts would be heard over point of view shots so that we would actually experience her mundane day-to-day life whilst listening to her dreams. The travelling cinema's story would be told more conventionally through conversations between the cinema's owner and his grandson in which he passed on his experience and knowledge. Our girl would be at the stage where she was about to be married off and she would change her life by running away with the cinema. The whole story would be told in retrospect at the moment when she was about to achieve her dream and walk onto set to play her first role in a movie.

Happy with the structure and story I now had to find the cinema, the actress, a village and characters and also a writer who was versed enough in village life to write realistic scenes for the girl's character. I would need someone who could write poetically in English and then I'd get the scenes translated into Marathi which is the state language of Maharashtra where I planned to film. My actress would need to also speak fluent Marathi and be happy to spend a couple of weeks in the village becoming a villager which is not something most Bollywood actors are prepared to do. In Bollywood films most actors work on several projects at the same time and basically play themselves.

THE HUNT FOR A CINEMA

I then got the breakthrough I had been waiting for. A Bollywood distributor, Aditya Shroff, called me and gave me the number of a rural distributor who supplied films to the Alankar touring cinema operated by the Deshpande family. He said that this guy would connect us. I spoke to the rural distributor and got the usual 'no problem' from him but I'd have to go and meet him out in Sangli —a 12-hour drive from Mumbai. He would then connect me with the travelling cinema operator.

Before I left London I'd made contact with a young producer Raadha. She was originally from London and had relocated to Mumbai after getting frustrated with the lack of opportunities for Asians in film/TV in the UK. She was now working for Percept Picture Company, whose MD Shailendra Singh, Claire had met in London.

I met Raadha at an ocean side café in Bandra and both of us marvelled at the difference between where we were right then and meetings in stuffy offices with moody people in the UK. She loved the idea and said to be patient as it would take some time but she was confident that eventually Percept would fund the movie. I told Raadha that I had a lead on a cinema but was looking for an actress to play the village girl and also a writer to work with. She connected me to a writer Anisa Mukerjea Ganguli and her boyfriend suggested an up and coming actress Peeya Rai Choudhri who had recently completed Gurinder Chadha's film 'Bride and Prejudice'.

THE SEARCH FOR A STAR

I met Peeya in the coffeeshop of the Marine Plaza Hotel in downtown Mumbai. I set up a video camera and did a little screen test. I got her to talk about herself and why she thought she would be good for the part, which I had described to her. She was perfect. She could speak fluent Marathi, had spent lots of time as a child in her maid's village and most importantly said she would give the film her full and total concentration. She was more than happy to live in the village and connect with the people. I was totally convinced. I had an intuitive feeling that she was the one and said to her that I was happy for her to play the role. I said that I would convince Claire and whoever else that needed to be convinced.

I called Claire and outlined my story idea to her and said that I had found the actress to play the lead. She was happy with the story but cautious about Peeya saying she wanted to meet her. She also said that she had met Shailendra Singh from Percept again in London and told him I was in Mumbai. He would be back the next day and wanted me to call him and go in and pitch the film to him. Which was great, apart from the fact that I had no script to show him. I convinced myself that this was no obstacle and spent the rest of the night expanding my story idea.

PITCHING TO PERCEPT

So the next day I arrived at the Percept offices and was shown into the boardroom to meet Shailendra. He was tall and had the looks of a classic Bollywood hero. He smiled and said, 'tell me about your film'. I launched into my pitch with passion and verve and **after five minutes of me he banged his hand down on the table and shouted, 'I love this and we're going to make this movie'**. It was a surreal moment and I was stunned as he picked up a phone and called for assistants to start taking notes on what I needed. He introduced me to a woman called Priti and said she would be running the project along with Raadha. I called Claire and told her it seemed to be all happening and she was also a little taken aback. After years of bland meetings at UK broadcasters where no one can take a decision without months of internal meetings I guess we were both unused to such forthright decision making. All very old school and a refreshing change.

The first thing I said they needed to do was arrange transport for me to go to Sangli to meet the travelling cinema, which they assured, wouldn't be a problem. I told them I wanted to cast Peeya and that I was planning to shoot her village POV scenes on film and the rest digitally to give a clear visual distinction between the narratives. Also from a budget point of view it would save an enormous amount, as the scenes with the travelling cinema would use a lot of stock. I planned to improvise these and shoot them almost documentary style with a small, unobtrusive crew. Well that was the plan anyway...

Full story at · www.netribution.co.uk/2/content/view/408/277/

The Forest
Ashvin Kumar

Ashvin Kumar is an Academy-nominated director who was born in India, learned his film-making in London and now makes films in India with mixed crew of Indians and westerners. His films include *The Road to Ladakh*, Academy-nominated *The Little Terrorist*. His debut feature, tense thriller *The Forest*, is the first Western feature to be shot and post produced entirely in India.

The Little Terrorist is set in Rajahstan — can you set the scene there for us?

The story reflects the political situation in Kashmir, in Rajahstan, in Gujerat, all three states that share the border with Pakistan. Metaphorically though, it also represents conflicts across borders between Israel and Palestine, where a border has been drawn between two peoples.

These are two peoples where they used to be together until a border was drawn between them, which I suppose generally is also the case with Palestine and the Arab situation there.

Basically the film is questioning geographic boundaries, you know, where have these boundaries come from? What do they actually mean to people who have to live with them rather than what they mean to the people that made them?

You have been quoted in the Indian press as saying India is like a laboratory for you — what do you mean by that?

What I meant was backlot. There are so many stories to be told out of India. Bollywood so totally dominates the cinematically cultural Indian landscape that very few alternative voices can come out

through any fissures that may be in the system. As India moves rapidly to capitalistic meritocracy from a heaving feudal socialistic background we find very little time to want anything but escapist, mindless, entertainment. I think the positive fall out of that is, there are a lot of people with a lot of money to spend. he negative fall out of that is, the number of people who can make stories that are important and good and need to be heard, are few. Cinema in India was much more vibrant in the 60's and 70's when we had the avant guard so-called alternative Indian cinema and there were a lot of young filmmakers coming up with films. Since then there has been almost complete silence. I find that there are many, many stories to be told that are not being told. And I also find India is such a varied and culturally interesting country, especially the last 200 years with its contact with the English language, which has opened it very uniquely — unlike China and other countries in South East Asia — to the rest of the world. We can watch *Ali McBeal* or *Friends* on TV and understand the humour that happens — that's kind of rare for a country that can't put together two square meals and drinking water. These kinds of dichotomies exist in India, which I find fascinating. There are so many interesting stories to be told and a laboratory is a place where you bring lots of interesting things that you want to explore. You bring them together, put them under the microscope and look at them. That's my film laboratory.

What is your advice for anyone contemplating shooting in India?

Expect everything to go wrong. People expect standard things to go wrong, but in India you must apply that to every single thing. If someone says he will be there at 2.00 o'clock, expect him at 3.30. Discount everything you hear by about one-and-a-half times. If someone says something will be ready, discount that by one-and-a-half times, because it will not be ready, not at the time you think it is going to be ready. Dubiously, it might be ready somewhat later.

Is India a good place to make films?

You have to make a switch to the kind of mindset that operates in India. A lot of things are still done on request, there's never a command structure, it is always a request structure. So you request someone to do something for you and if he's in the right mood, he'll do it for you. If you demand, or command, or order, it will be misinterpreted as bad manners, heavy handedness, et cetera. It is the East, you know, it is very much part of the whole culture there.

How did Forest come about?

Forest came about in a funny way; three or four unconnected and unrelated things came together. One was the need to do something significant after *Little Terrorist* as a debut feature film. I was tiring of *Road to Ladakh* by then. I had written the script six months prior and it had done the rounds of Hollywood and been passed by several lead actresses. I had started getting a little disillusioned by the whole story and it just didn't feel right any more for some reason. So, I decided to start writing another film but at that time I had no idea what I wanted to do.

I had some ideas and I like to jockey my ideas and I had a document on which I had jotted down interesting possibilities and one of them was a story of this young, urban couple who go out into the jungles and meet dark characters from their past and it all ends very badly. That's as far as that story goes. I decided to pick that up and it felt — now that I was two years from the *Road to Ladakh* — that it would be strategic for me to do a genre film for my first feature film.

I'm also very aware of the safety of having a sales agent on board before you start making a picture. The only way I could see myself doing that in the absence of any lead actor who would then bring in distribution and so on, was to do a genre picture, because I couldn't see myself being in the position where I would have been able to attract the interest of any major American star.

So what is the story of The Forest?

The film concerns a couple on the point of divorce and separation who decide to escape city life in the Forest alone. However they are unexpectedly met by someone from both their pasts whose presence threatens to throw their marriage into turmoil. Just as the drama of their relationship unfolds and heightens, a more sinister development takes place — a hungry man-eating leopard on the loose forces a re-examination of priorities and the fragile guise of relationships torn asunder. The leopard, a victim of poachers' traps driven wild by hunger, unremittingly attacks them — obsessed with his kill — until all four are trapped inside the Resthouse that was to be their holiday home — unable to escape. Will they manage to? Even if they do — what state will their relationship be in by the end?

This film is a much bigger budget and on a much bigger scale than your previous two films shot in India — did that throw up any particular challenges for you?

I pretty much produced both my other films in guerilla style you know, where I have had a very clear understanding, a grip and handle, on how my money was being spent and where my money was being spent. This time I felt very out of control at that level you know? — because of the scale. I had to appoint people to take care of that side of things. And rightly so.

It is not my preferred vocation to be producer. I am a producer by force. But it does give you a tremendous sense of being in control of how and when you do things, so that is the one factor I found it a little uncomfortable to deal with.

What were your priorities for the film given the relatively limited budget you had available?

This movie was made on a low budget, which doesn't go far when you have two French leopards that have to be flown to Thailand. Incidentally those leopards belong to the guy who did the animals in Gladiator!!

The thing we did on the production side that saved us money was to shoot on 3-perf film, which saved us 25% on film cost. Doing all my post-production here in India, we went the digital intermediate route, so you can grade the film digitally and do all kinds of things with the footage through edit windows and all that kind of thing. My 25% saving on film stock pretty much paid for that digital intermediate route.

We spent money in all the right places, we had a great guy doing our make up and prosthetics, so the blood and false limbs look great, we used good visual effects, a western crew and gear, our music was recorded at Abbey Road, we had an excellent French production designer, sets, a Swiss cinematographer and a British sound designer — I like to think we did well on that score and we're proud of that. And it was the first western film to be shot and post produced entirely within India. We are very proud of that, too.

IRELAND

Prepared with the assistance of Declan O'Neill, Ernst & Young, Ireland (www.ey.com/global/content. nsf/Ireland/home)

I. INTRODUCTION

The introduction of **Section 481** ('**s481**') of the Taxes Consolidation Act (formerly Section 35 of the Finance Act 1987) has made Ireland one of the more competitive and attractive destinations for film production. This has led to an increase in the level of film production locally, with Ireland being the chosen location for a number of recent blockbuster films such as *Saving Private Ryan*, *Braveheart*, *Intermission* and Laws *of Attraction*. The result has been the development of an experienced Irish film sector with the qualifying period for s481 further extended in the Finance Act 2004 to 31 December 2008.

II. SECTION 481

(a) WHAT is available?

General
s481 provides a tax deduction for **investors** who invest in a qualifying company which has been authorised to raise s481 funds for the purposes of making a qualifying film. The regime was substantially improved in 2006, allowing producers to obtain up to 19% (see below for sample calculations) of their global budget funding through s481.

A producer can raise the *lower* of the **eligible Irish spend** on Irish goods and services, or **80%** of the total global **budget** for the film, in either case with a **cap of €35m** (approx US$45m).

For example, if the global budget for a film is $100m and the eligible Irish spend is $5m, the maximum that can be raised would be $5m. Where the eligible Irish spend is $50m, the maximum that can be raised is €35m (approx €45m). Where the budget is less than €35m, and 80% or more of the spend will be in Ireland, the maximum that can be raised is 80% of the budget. As a general rule, because of the fees involved, the budget must be in excess of €1m for a s481 deal to be worthwhile.

The s481 funds must be made available to the production company at the latest before 25% of the total production budget has been incurred.

The Investors' Benefit
The film investment is obtained by the producers retaining a specialist intermediary firm (such

as Ernst & Young) to raise the s481 funds from various investors. The maximum any individual can invest in any one year is **€31,750**, so to make the numbers meaningful, the intermediaries source subscriptions for shares in a special purpose company from a number of individuals, so they all invest simultaneously in the same film. The investors tend to borrow a large proportion of the €31,750 from a bank (this transaction is often organised through the intermediary), typically as much as 75% (approx €23,250). This would mean the investor puts up only €8,500 him/herself, but the whole amount will be regarded as a qualifying investment.

The tax break works to give the investor an **80% deduction** of his/her investment from taxable income. With tax rates currently at 41%, this correlates to a reduction in taxes payable of €10,414, being 80% of €31,750, multiplied by the 41% tax rate. If only €8,500 of the finance is the investor's own money (the rest being borrowed), s/he is approx €1,914 up on the deal (€10,414 less €8,500), which might be considered a pretty good low-risk return on investment (22.5%). This is the benefit to the investor, and s/he is unlikely to see any further income from the film.

The Delivery Payment
On closing of the s481 fundraising, the production company receives up to 80% of the Irish production budget. In exchange, however, the production company must procure the balance of the production budget (in this case 20%), *plus* a '**delivery payment**', which must be paid over **upfront** (see below), to be used to repay the s481 investors (or, more specifically, the bank that lent to them) a large proportion of their investment in 12 months' time.

This delivery payment is usually held in escrow pending 'delivery' of the film once production has finished and the film completed. Alternatively, if the producer can procure one, a **bank guarantee** will be accepted in lieu of an upfront delivery payment. This would allow the producers to take the benefit of the deal at the start of production, provided the bank can be satisfied that the producer already has the cash resources available to finance the delivery payment upfront. Usually there are no further payments made by the producers to the investors.

As a general rule, the higher the amount that can be raised under s481, the greater the benefit to the producer. Suppose a producer has a film with a €35m global budget. If 80% or more of the budget is spent in Ireland and qualifies for s481, this would allow the producer to raise up to €28m in s481. If 75% of this (ie. €21m) was borrowed by the investors, the delivery payment will have to cover this amount plus interest (say, €22m in total). From this upfront cash benefit, the producer generally has to meet his own legal costs in putting the deal together. If these fees were a further €100,000, the remainder left over, being the **net gain** to the producer, would be in the region of €5.9m, or **17%** of the total production budget.

It follows that if the producer has a film with a €35m global budget, of which only €5m is to be spent in Ireland and qualifies for s481, the producer would only be able to raise €5m in s481, and could expect a net benefit before legal costs of around €1.25m.

(b) WHO can apply?

The producer must establish a new **special purpose vehicle** (an 'SPV') for the production. This 'commissioned' (see below) SPV must be **incorporated** and **resident** in the Republic of Ireland for it to be a 'qualifying company' for s481 purposes, and its **sole purpose** must be the production and distribution of the film in question. An **Irish-based producer** should be involved in the production, and that producer must be responsible for compliance reporting and must be a director of the SPV. Financial arrangements involving persons/entities located in territories outside the EU or with which Ireland does not have a double taxation treaty, or even a flow of funds through such territories, will come under particularly close scrutiny.

The SPV is the entity which secures the s481 certificate from the Irish Revenue Commissioners ('the Revenue') (see below). The s481 investors subscribe for new shares in the SPV for the amount of funding allowed under the certificate (ie. up to 80% of the budget). The **commissioning producer** (ie. the 'real' Producer) procures the balance of the production budget and the fixed price delivery payment (see above) which is paid to the SPV on the delivery and acceptance of the film to/by the commissioning producer.

(c) — (d) HOW do you qualify and WHERE do you apply?

The scheme is available for feature films, TV drama, animation and creative documentary. The relief itself is **spend-related**, and investors do *not* need to own any **copyright** in the film.

Usually, an established Irish film producer is commissioned to deliver the Irish elements of the overall production. A production, finance and distribution agreement is entered into, setting out the key terms of the deal, including any rights in the project that the Irish production company may be entitled to.

The relevant Minister (see below for details) will consider the contribution that the film will make to either or both the **development** of the film **industry** in Ireland and the promotion and expression of **Irish culture**. The Revenue will examine the financial aspects of the proposal with regard to the legal, commercial and corporate arrangements for the production of the film. They will look to see that the appropriate level of non-s481 funding is provided and that the budget and financial structures are appropriate for the proposed film. In particular, the Revenue will want to understand the flow of funds between the various parties involved in the production and distribution of the film, as well as the role of each of those parties in the structure. It will look at each film on a case-by-case basis. Typically, the type of expenditure which is acceptable to the Revenue as expenditure on the production of a qualifying film is **all expenditure necessary** to produce the film from the **development** phase up **to** and including **post-production**, together with the cost of providing an archive print.

The Regulations also specifically detail expenditure which is *not* acceptable, including such items as costs relating to the distribution or promotion of the film, professional costs associated with raising finance for the film, and costs of organising the pre-sales monies.

One other key requirement which the Revenue will be monitoring is the fact that the investment must be at the **risk** of the investor. Essentially, the Revenue wants to ensure that the investment is being made for *bona fide* commercial purposes and is not part of an elaborate tax avoidance scheme. Therefore, contractual provision cannot be made to protect investors from the normal commercial risks of such investments.

After obtaining the authorisation from the Minister and after a detailed review of the SPV's proposal, the Revenue will determine what they deem to be **eligible Irish spend**, and will issue the s481 certificate, which governs how much can be raised from the investors. The s481 certificate issued will also be subject to certain conditions as both the Minister and the Revenue may consider necessary.

Eligible Irish spend means expenditure in the State on employment of eligible individuals, as well as expenditure in the State on goods, services and facilities. An eligible individual means an individual who is a citizen or resident of, or an individual domiciled in Ireland or of another Member State of the European Community. Where, however, a person provides goods, services or facilities, the person must operate from a fixed place of business in the State.

The Revenue may *refuse* to issue a certificate if they are not satisfied with any aspect of the SPV's application and, in particular, where any of the following situations apply:

- where the principal photography, the first animation drawings or the first model movement (as the case may be) has **commenced before an application** is made by the SPV to the Revenue;
- where they have reason to believe that any item of proposed expenditure in the budget is **inflated**;
- where they are not satisfied that there is a commercial rationale for the corporate structure proposed for the production, financial, distribution or sale of the film; or
- where they believe that the proposed structure would hinder them in verifying compliance with any of the provisions governing the relief.

There will normally be a requirement that a **completion bond** should be in place before the s481 investors will be prepared to release their funds into the production company. As mentioned above, the delivery payment must also be handed over before the s481 funds are released. Alternatively, a bank guarantee can be used.

s481 deals can often run into difficulties where the producers do not give themselves sufficient time to get the s481 certificate from the Revenue. If more than **25%** of the global budget has been spent before the s481 deal is closed, the investors no longer qualify for their tax break and the deal must be **aborted**. The Revenue has indicated that this requirement will only be waived in exceptional cases.

When applying to the Revenue for a s481 certificate, the SPV must make a detailed application, outlining the proposed spend in the Republic of Ireland and the detailed production budget. On subsequent review of the SPV's proposal, the Revenue are required to seek authorisation from the Minister for Arts, Sport and Tourism (the Minister) as to whether they may, following a full examination of the SPV's proposal, issue a certificate to the effect that the film may be treated as a qualifying film for the purposes of relief under s481.

Each application effectively goes through a two-stage review process, and both the Minister and the Revenue have specific requirements which must be met.

An application for a Certificate must be made in writing, in the form prescribed by the Revenue (form available at www.revenue.ie). The application form incorporates both the requirements of the Minister and the Revenue. All application forms should be made to the Revenue at the following address:

Office of the Revenue Commissioners
Direct Taxes
Business Incentives
Stamping Building
Dublin Castle
Dublin

III. OTHER USEFUL CONTACTS

Film Institute of Ireland: www.fii.ie
Irish Business and Employers Confederation:
 www.ibec.ie
Irish Film Board: www.filmboard.ie
Irish Film Board Incentive information:
 www.filmboard.ie/incentives.php
Irish Revenue Office:
 www.revenue.ie/services/film.htm,
 www.revenue.ie/service/sect35.htm
Minister for Arts, Culture and the Gaeltacht:
 www.ealga.ie

ISLE OF MAN

I. INTRODUCTION

The Isle of Man, situated half way between Ireland and England, has become in recent years one of the busiest areas for film production in the British Isles with over 8 productions per year. Recent productions include *Miss Potter* and *Stormbreaker*.

II. TAX INCENTIVES

There are no fiscal incentives in the form of tax breaks currently available in the Isle of Man. However, the **Media Development Fund** has been created by Isle of Man Film (wholly owned by the Isle of Man Government) to provide direct equity investment to qualifying films.

III. PUBLIC MONEY

(a) WHAT is available?

The Isle of Man Media Development Fund offers **25%** of the production budget in the form of **direct equity investment**, without upper or lower limits, to qualifying films.

(b) WHO can apply?

Producers (of any nationality) who are otherwise fully-funded and have a proven track record in film-making.

(c) HOW do you qualify?

To be considered for the fund, at least **50%** of principal photography must be filmed **on the Isle of Man**, and at least **20%** of the below-the-line budget must be spent with **local service providers**.

Additionally, your project must otherwise have **full funding**, and you must have a **completion bond** in place. Isle of Man Film look to recoup their investment from the **North American** territory and therefore priority should be given to films receptive to that market.

Emphasis is always placed on the **commercial** aspect of the project, with the sales and distributions aspect of the application being a vital element in the decision making process. The Production must also be in the **English Language**.

All investment decisions are **discretionary**.

(d) WHERE do you apply?

Applications should be submitted to **Isle of Man Film** (details below) as early as possible.

In order to evaluate a project for investment, Isle of Man Film needs to receive the following information:
- A final draft of the screenplay;
- A long synopsis or treatment;
- Biography or filmography of all key elements including principal cast, producer(s), writer, director and heads of departments;
- Full budget incorporating Isle of Man expenditure analysis and where appropriate, expenditure analysis demonstrating British film qualifications; and
- Finance structure including principal conditions attached to all investment.

It is a **rolling scheme**, so applications may be made at any time with no deadlines.

Isle of Man Film
1st Floor, Hamilton House
Peel Road, Douglas
Isle of Man
IM1 2EP
T: +44 (0) 1624 687173
www.isleofmanfilm.com
iomfilm@gov.im

ITALY

Prepared with the assistance of Gallavotti Honorati & Partners (www.ghplex.it)

I. INTRODUCTION

There are no specific tax incentives for *investors* in Italy. The Italian government does, however, offer **loans** and **contributions** to *producers* as benefits to encourage the production of films in Italy.

II. PUBLIC MONEY

Italian film funding legislation has undergone substantial changes in the recent years. The former law on cinematography (known as *'Legge Cinema'*, originally issued in 1965), was replaced by *Legislative Decree No. 28* (the **'Decree'**) in January 2004. Subsequently, there have been a number of ministerial regulations (*Decreti Ministeriali*) which have introduced new rules for financial support to production companies, distribution and export companies, technical industries and exhibitors.

Each of these business categories can access different public funds and subsidies, which themselves can be categorised roughly into two types: **public financing** (such as interest-free or 'soft' terms loans, and secured loans) and **subsidies** (such as non-refundable contributions, based on box office revenues).

The new film funding legislation introduced the so-called **'reference system'** by which each project is rated by screenplay and cast, and by taking into consideration the producer's track record with specific reference to its prior capacity to repay previous public funds granted to it (or him or her) in the past.

Access to public funds is also granted to 'debutant' directors, since a portion of public financing is also reserved to new directors for their 'first' and 'second' feature film.

The Decree grants funds to several categories of film industry business, such as:
- production companies;
- distribution and film export companies;
- exhibitors; and
- technical industries.

The funding of feature films themselves is generally reserved for **production companies**, while the other categories can benefit from funds and contributions relating to their own specific area of business activity. So for present purposes, we will only focus on the type of funds reserved for production

companies, together with the conditions imposed and process involved.

(a) WHAT is available?

Public funding in Italy is mostly based on **'soft'** terms loans, which may or may not be secured by a specific governmental **'Ministry's Fund'** (*Fondo per la produzione, la distribuzione l'esercizio e le industrie tecniche*).

'SOFT' TERMS BANK LOAN SECURED BY THE MINISTRY FUND FOR CULTURAL INTEREST FILMS

This element of public funding is based on the so-called **'Industrial Cost'** (*Costo Industriale*) of the film. The Industrial Cost of a film is made up of both the **Production Costs** (which *includes* the costs of creating the master print; general expenses; financial costs related to loans and the producer's fee) *and* the **Distribution Costs** (which includes the distribution costs both for Italy and for export).

General expenses and producer's fees are limited to 7.5% of the final budget, while costs related to production staff members may not exceed 25% of the overall Production Costs.

Such financing is in the form of a **three-year, low interest rate loan** (see below), secured by the Ministry Fund. The loans are granted to full-length Italian feature films having a **'Cultural Interest'** (ie. a film which has significant cultural, artistic or spectacular qualities, and meets most of the **Italian Nationality** requirements, being all those elements listed below (under 'Italian National Film') in a), b), c), d), e), f), n), o), p), and q), and at least four of the five listed in g), h), i), l) and m). Note that exceptions can sometimes be granted with reference to the elements in f), n) and o).

As far as Cultural Interest films are concerned, the **interest rate** is equal to only **30% of the normal reference rate** set and periodically updated by the Ministry of Productive Activities.

The loans cover **up to 50%** of the film's budget, limited at **€5m** for **'first class'** production companies and of **€3.75m** for others (see *(c) HOW do you qualify*, below for definition of classes). Therefore the loans are capped respectively at €2.5m or €1.875m, so a first class producer with a budget over €5m will be eligible to access a maximum loan of €2.5m, and a second class producer with a budget over €3.75m will be eligible to access a maximum loan of €1.875m.

First and second feature films of **'debutant'** directors are also eligible for such funding, up to **90%** of the Industrial Cost of the film, within limit of

€1.5m. So a producer appointing a debutant director and a budget of €1.5m will be eligible to access the maximum loan of €1.35m.

Short length Cultural Interest feature films (ie. a film which has significant cultural, artistic or spectacular qualities, and meets most of the **Italian Nationality** requirements, being all those elements listed below in a), b), c), d), e), f), g), h), i)) are also granted a three year, low interest rate loan, secured by the Ministry Fund, which covers up to 100% of the Industrial Cost of the film within the limit on the loan of €40K. Note that exceptions can be sometimes granted under artistic or cultural grounds.

Public financing is **secured** on the film's revenues and copyright. Should the producer fail to repay the loan within three years, the Ministry will acquire a share of the ownership of the film equal to the outstanding unpaid loan balance. Should the same producer fail — for two consecutive films — to repay at least 30% of the loan (or 15% for short length feature films), s/he will become ineligible for financing for a three year period.

Loans are recouped, as follows: initially, all revenues arising from the film's exploitation, less pre-sales and a 'prints and advertising' cost allowance (not exceeding the 20% of the film budget), are allocated **in first position** to repay the **first 20%** (or 10% in case of a short film) of the funds secured by Ministry Fund. Then, any further revenues can go to recoup any the other distribution costs incurred in Italy and abroad, and to cover recoupment of the remainder of the Industrial Costs. Any further balance will be allocated to the State and to the production company on an 80:20 basis until the loan is entirely repaid.

'SOFT' TERMS BANK LOANS UNSECURED BY THE MINISTRY FUND FOR FILMS WITH NO ITALIAN CULTURAL INTEREST

The Decree also prescribes benefits for Italian or EU producers of full-length feature films with *no* Italian Cultural Interest.

These benefits consist of **three-year, low interest rate loans** which are *un*secured by the Ministry Fund, and cover **up to 70%** of the Industrial Cost of the film. In this case, as the loans are not secured by the Ministry Fund, but on the production company's assets and film's revenues, so a greater share is granted to the producer.

The interest rate is equal to the **40%** (ie. more than the 30% for films with Cultural interest, see above) **of the normal reference rate** set and

periodically updated by the Ministry of Productive Activities.

There is a budget limit of €5m, so should the budget exceed such maximum amount, the loan will be capped at €3.5m.

A three-year, low interest rate loan is also available to production companies duly listed in the Public Register who are **developing** film projects from original screenplays which have some social or cultural importance.

SUBSIDIES TO PRODUCTION COMPANIES

The Decree also allows for further post-exploitation, non-refundable subsidies for production companies, based on the gross box office success of the film. Subsidies are granted to companies that have produced full-length Italian feature films (including animation) which, in the first 18 months of *Italian* theatrical exploitation, earn at least €50K gross at the Italian box office. Should this condition be met, the subsidies are calculated — from the very first Euro — as a percentage of each of the following gross box office revenue brackets:

BOX OFFICE REVENUE	CONTRIBUTION
From €1 to €2.6m	25%
From €2.6m to €5.2m	20%
From €5.2m to €10,329,137	10%
From €10,329,137 to €20.7m	7%

In addition, an amount of 1.5% of gross box office revenue is also granted to the director and authors of the script/screenplay.

These subsidies **must be allocated to repay** the secured and unsecured third party loans received to produce the film in the first place, and then to cover any loan for the Industrial Cost of the film or, if no loans were made, to recoup the entire Industrial Cost of the film. The production company is then required to invest any balance left over in a new Italian feature film, within five years, or else the subsidies will be revoked.

'QUALITY AWARD'

Production Companies, again only if duly listed in the Public Register held by the Ministry of Culture, can with reference to an Italian Nationality Film effectively released in Italian theatres, be eligible also for a **Quality Award** (ie. *Premio di Qualità*).

At the time of writing, the award amounted to **€250K** and, once received, must be shared between the production company (71%), the director (10%), the script author (3%), the screenplay author (7%), the director of photography (3%), the set designer (2%), the editor (2%) and the composer (2%). Quality Awards are granted for acknowledged cultural films selected by a special jury formed by qualified experts appointed by the Minister.

(b) WHO can apply?

Production companies are allowed to apply for public funds on condition that they have their **registered offices** and **tax domiciles** in Italy. The same rights are granted, under reciprocity regulations, to **EU** companies with a **subsidiary** office in Italy. In order to access public funds, both Italian and EU Production Companies must be listed in a Public Register set up by the Ministry of Culture (the *Ministero per i Beni e le Attività Culturali*).

(c) HOW do you qualify?

For public funding purposes, production companies are divided into two different **classes** (first and second) with different prerogatives as far as the maximum amount of the loan is concerned (see *(a)* above).

The categories are determined by the '**quality**' of films already produced by the company concerned (eg. participation in any film festival and/or winning festivals' prizes), their financial stability (based on the number of years of activity, the number of produced films, and with specific reference to the repayment of prior funds previously granted), and its ability to demonstrate its commercial skills in the business (such as the average and total revenues arising from its films and sales outside Italy).

Italian National Film

In addition, before allowing access to public funds or subsidies, the film project itself must qualify as an **Italian National Film** (Nazionalità Italiana), either by meeting the test below or by qualifying as an official Italian co-production (with no more than 20% non-EU contribution).

Italian Nationality is granted by the Ministry of Culture, and is based on a type of **Cultural Test** relating to the Italian (or EU) citizenship of the crew and cast. The relevant elements relating to the nationality test are:

a)   The director;

b)   The script author(s);

c)   The screenplay author(s);

d)   The leading actors;

e)   The supporting actors;

f)   Live sound in Italian;

g)   The director of photography;

h)   The editor;

i)   The composer;

l)   The set designer ('director of scenography');

m)   The costume designer;

n)   The crew;

o)   The use of Italian studios and locations;

p)   The use of Italian technical industries;

q)   At least the 30% of the costs related to crew, shooting, studios and technical industries (see n), o), p) above), including social security costs, must be spent in Italy.

(Note that there is no j or k in the Italian alphabet!) In relation to the above elements, Italian Nationality is granted to films having each of:
- **all** the elements listed in a), b), c), f), n) and q);
- at least **three** elements out of those listed in d), e), g) and h);
- at least **two** elements out of those listed in i), l), m); and
- at least **one** element out of those listed in o) and p).

Exception can be sometimes be granted with reference to conditions f) and n).

The film itself must also be registered in the Public Register for Cinematography (*Pubblico Registro Cinematografico*), held by the Italian Society of Authors and Publisher (*SIAE*). The eligibility of a film for public funds is then evaluated by a special Committee (*Commissione per la Cinematografia —* referred to below as the '**Commission**'), formed by experts appointed by the Minister. The Commission evaluates the film by reference to its artistic quality, technical quality, the consistency between the artistic and production elements and the original proposed film project, the quality of the work of the director and of the screenplay writer.

Importantly, financing is only granted if a **theatrical distribution** deal **for the Italian territory** is in place, and the production company finds the balance of the overall **production costs** within one year from the Commission's decision to grant the funds.

Advances can be permitted based on a satisfactory producer's guarantee. The guarantee is based on the producer's patrimony.

(d) WHERE do you apply?

To access to public funding, the production company must file all the necessary application forms with the **Ministry of Culture** at the following address:

Ministero per i Beni e le Attività Culturali
Dipartimento per lo spettacolo e lo sport
Direzione Generale Cinema
Via della Ferratella in Laterano 51 — 00184 Roma

Forms can be downloaded (in Italian only) from the following web address:
www.cinema.beniculturali.it/cinema.html

III. OTHER USEFUL CONTACTS

Autoritàa per le Garanzie delle Communicazioni (AGCOM): www.agcom.it

Associazione Nazionale Industrie Cinematografiche Affini: www.anica.it

Associazione Nazionale Esercenti Cinema: www.cinetel.org

Film Commission: www.filminginitaly.com/

Dr Francesco Ventura
Il Dirigente Ministero per i Beni e le Attivita'
Culturali Ufficio II – Ripartizione 1 Attività
Cinematografiche Via della Ferraratella in Laterano
n. 51, 00184 Roma Italy
Tel: 00 39 06 773 2424
Fax: 00 69 06 773 2468

LUXEMBOURG

Prepared with the assistance of DI STEFANO & SEDLO Avocats à la Cour (www.mds-legal.com)

I. INTRODUCTION

Since December 1988, with what was initially intended as a temporary fiscal regime, Luxembourg has had in place a specific fiscal incentive for filmmakers to choose the Grand Duchy of Luxembourg ('Luxembourg') as the place to produce and finance their pictures. The legal regime (the 'Regime') is specifically targeted at promoting risk capital investments. Though sporadically amended over the years, it remains in place today and has fostered the creation of a small but active audiovisual industry in the country, and continues to attract international producers and financiers. Since its inception less than 20 years ago, more than €200m has been invested and 400 audiovisual productions completed. Today, there are about thirty active production companies in Luxembourg producing feature films, animation and documentaries. There are several film studios, and more than 300 technicians and other professionals permanently working in the audiovisual sector. In 2005, there were tax investment certificates issued for some €8.8m under the Luxembourg Film Industry Fund. At present, the Regime is due to expire in 2008, although there is a draft bill underway aiming to extend its application to the year 2015.

II. THE TAX ALLOWANCE

(a) WHAT is available?

An audiovisual production financed and produced pursuant to the *Law of 13 December 1988* ('the Law') will entitle the producer, subject to approval by the Luxembourg authorities, to receive **transferable audiovisual investment certificates** that are deductible from taxable income. These certificates can be transferred once (and only once), so that if the initial beneficiary does not have sufficient taxable income to deduct from, it will be able to obtain a return from effectively 'selling' the certificate to give a tax advantage to the transferee.

The amount of the audiovisual investment certificates are fixed in accordance with certain eligibility criteria (set out in the **Law and the Grand-Ducal Regulation of 16 March 1999**). The reduction can not exceed **30%** of the taxable income of the beneficiary or transferee, as the case may be. It has to be recorded in the accounts for the tax year specified by the audiovisual investment certificate.

The corporate tax and municipal tax amount to an aggregate of just under 30%; so this is the potential advantage for the buyer of the certificate. However, the extent to which this is split between investor and producer is open to negotiation.

(b) WHO can apply?

Fully **resident** and fully taxable capital **companies** (as opposed to partnerships) whose **main corporate object** is audiovisual production, and which actually do produce audiovisual works under the conditions determined by the Law, may apply for approval. The applicant company has to prove that it has fulfilled all the obligations under relevant legislation governing working conditions, taxation and social security. It must have stable and **long-term** administrative structures, as well as an accounting organisation and internal control procedures which are suitable for the proper execution of their activities and duties. The shareholders or associates, as well as the members of the management bodies, must prove their **moral integrity** (usually by signing an affidavit and submitting a certificate of good character). The executive director must also show the required level of professional competence and moral integrity.

(c) HOW do you qualify?

In order to be eligible, the film (an 'audiovisual production') must fulfil the following criteria:
- **contribute** to the development of the **audiovisual production sector** in Luxembourg, taking into account a reasonable balance between the advantages given and the economic, cultural and social consequences in the long term of the production of these works;
- be conceived to be **produced principally** In Luxembourg;
- be produced or co-produced by the production company, notably through the effective and long-term holding of a significant portion of the **rights**; and
- offer **reasonable prospects of return** on investment.

Excluded from the Regime are films which are pornographic, incite violence or racial hatred, condone crimes against humanity or, in general, infringe public order and good morals. Also excluded are audiovisual works intended or used for advertising purposes, news programmes, reality shows, as well as sports broadcasts.

The production costs incurred must be **'appropriate'** for the needs of the production of the film in the Luxembourg. Thus, the amount of the issued certificates are calculated on a case-by-case basis and may cover only a certain proportion of the stated production costs and expenses incurred.

Personnel costs are eligible only if they are borne and paid in the Grand Duchy of Luxembourg or contribute to the training of people working in the audiovisual industry residing in Luxembourg, and if the applicant company proves that it has fulfilled in this regard all the obligations of the applicable legislation governing working conditions, taxation and social security.

Costs borne by 'affiliated' companies may be eligible to the extent that the company uses goods or services of the affiliate in the production.

In general, certain other restrictions will also apply, and the eligibility of the various types of expenses (above-the-line, below-the-line, contingent expenses and general expenses) is dealt with more in detail by the Grand-Ducal Regulation of 16 March 1999, available in English on pdf format from the Luxembourg Film Fund website:

www.filmfund.lu/imperia/md/content/pdf/4.pdf

Taxpayers holding an audiovisual investment certificate at the end of the tax year can on application obtain a **reduction of their taxable income** (the corporate tax and municipal tax amount to an aggregate of 29.63%, so this is the advantage for the buyer of the certificate; the split can then be negotiated.

(d) WHERE do you apply?

The **National Fund in Support of Audiovisual Production** (the '**Film Fund**') is the public body in charge of the administration, supervision and control of the Regime.

The production company must file an application in writing to the Film Fund at least six weeks prior to the start of that audiovisual production. Once the film has been completed, the company then submits a file containing a copy of the audiovisual production, together with documents evidencing the production costs ultimately incurred and spent in the Luxembourg. The Film Fund may require further documents and information if it deems necessary.

The application should specify the maximum amount for which it is being made. The Film Fund examines the application and advises on the amount of eligible production costs. It will issue a detailed written notice to the attention of the **Competent Ministers** (see below), who take the final decision on the amount for which certificates are to be issued.

The application is examined by the board of directors of the Film Fund and then forwarded to the so-called Competent Ministers, consider the Film Fund's advice and make the final decision. The Competent Ministers must render their decision by the end of the second month following receipt of the application, assuming the application, the information and the supporting documentation are complete.

Approval is valid for two years. The application must be renewed if there are changes in the company's objects, capital, corporate name, legal form, shareholding, executive management, ability to continue, etc, and the Competent Ministers can withdraw approval if the conditions for approval are no longer fulfilled, or if no use is made of the approval for an uninterrupted period of twelve months, or if the company is in a state of serious default with respect to its legal, regulatory or contractual obligations. The Film Fund can enquire on such matters and may request from the company documents and information enabling it to verify whether the conditions of approval are still fulfilled.

The Competent Ministers' decision (assuming positive) becomes the subject of an agreement to be concluded between the Film Fund and the beneficiary (or, in the case of a co-production, beneficiaries).

On completion, the production company must deliver to the Film Fund a copy of the completed work, as well as a copy of any available promotional material, in a format to be defined by the Film Fund.

The applicants must immediately inform the Film Fund on any **transfer** of the certificates. Audiovisual investment certificates are nominal and may be transferred **only once**, the transferee having to be a capital company. They may not be sub-divided.

The relevant approvals are issued by the Ministers competent for finance, the audiovisual sector and culture (the 'Competent Ministers'). The decisions are taken jointly by the Competent Ministers.

Production companies wishing to file applications for audiovisual productions under the Regime in order to obtain audiovisual investment certificates will have to be approved by the Competent Ministers. The application for such approval is to be filed in writing with the Film Fund. The board of directors of the Film Fund will examine the application and forward it to the Competent Ministers together with a recommendation as to the eligibility of the company.

III. USEFUL CONTACTS

Film Fund Luxembourg
Fonds national de soutien à la production audiovisuelle
5, rue Large
L-1917 Luxembourg
T: (+352) 478 20 65
F: (+352) 22 09 63
www.filmfund.lu
info@filmfund.etat.lu

Service des médias et de l'audiovisuel:
www.etat.lu/SMA

MALTA

Prepared with the assistance of MAMO TCV
Advocates (www.mamotcv.com)

I. INTRODUCTION

Malta has for some time attracted bigger budget studio-type films such as *Gladiator*, *Troy* and *Munich*, but more recently has made efforts to create its own internal industry, rather than settling for a mere filming location of choice.

Incentives for the production of feature films, TV films, commercials and documentaries in Malta were first made available under the *Business Promotion Act*, aimed at encouraging the private sector to invest in certain sectors of Maltese industry, including film. Then in 2005, the *Malta Film Commission Act* (referred to below as '*the Act*') was adopted specifically to provide for a legal framework for the promotion, development and support of the audiovisual industry, including the film servicing industry. The Act also formalised the role of the *Malta Film Commission* and the *Film Commissioner*, who is responsible for the implementation of Malta's audiovisual policy.

The incentives presently available under the Act are a **cash rebate** in relation to film productions carried out in Malta, and a **tax credit** for investments in local audiovisual infrastructure. Malta is also a member of the *European Convention on Cinematographic Co-production*, and has a co-production treaty with Canada (see below for details). These international agreements make it possible for co-productions falling within their scope to use the benefits granted to 'national' films of the various countries covered.

II. TAX INCENTIVES

CASH REBATE under the MALTA FILM COMMISSION ACT

(a) WHAT is available?

This benefit, set out in the *Financial Incentives for the Audiovisual Industry Regulations, 2006*, is a cash rebate of up to **20% of eligible expenditure**, given as a **cash grant** to qualifying companies on completion of a qualifying production in Malta.

The current incentive applies to audiovisual productions started after 1 June 2005 and in respect

of which an application for provisional approval is made before 31 December 2008.

(b) WHO can apply?

The cash rebate is available to **qualifying companies** in relation to **qualifying productions**. A 'qualifying company' is any natural or legal person which carries on, or intends to carry on in Malta, a trade or business which consists in the production of films, and which is certified as such by the Film Commissioner. The qualifying company is the entity responsible for all activities involved in making a qualifying production and having access to full financial information for the total production worldwide.

(c) HOW do you qualify?

A 'qualifying production' is an audiovisual production satisfying the criteria and conditions laid down in the Schedule to the Act and certified as such by the Film Commissioner. The audiovisual work must be:

- A feature film, TV drama, animation or 'timeless' creative documentary;
- **produced** wholly or partially **in Malta** on a commercial basis with a view to profit;
- produced wholly or principally **for exhibition to the public** in cinemas or through TV broadcasting;
- **make a valid contribution** to the expression of creativity and culture in Malta through the development of production capability skills in the media of film and TV; and
- based on a format **approved by the Film Commissioner** in accordance with the Guidelines established by the Film Commissioner.

The cash rebate is calculated on the basis of **eligible expenditure**, calculated with reference to the overall budget of the production concerned. The items of eligible expenditure are described in the *Guidelines* for the certification of audiovisual productions, which are attached to the *Financial Incentives for the Audiovisual Industry Regulations, 2006* ('the Guidelines'). They include, for example, expenses related to local labour, accommodation, *per diems*, catering and craft services, telecommunications, ground transport services, air travel, shipping, location fees, professional services and rental of facilities and equipment. The Guidelines can be read in full at:

mfc.com.mt/filebank/imagebank/pdf/financial_incentives_guidelines.pdf

Additional specific conditions and requirements that need to be complied with will be set out in the certificate of provisional approval given to the company.

Note that the work will not qualify if it comprises or is substantially based on:

- any public or special performances staged for filming or otherwise;
- any sporting event;
- games or competitions;
- current affairs or talk shows;
- demonstration programmes for tasks, hobbies or projects;
- review, magazine-style, or lifestyle programmes;
- unscripted or "reality"- type programmes;
- advertising programmes or advertisements; or
- pornographic or sexually explicit content.

(d) WHERE do you apply?

The application for provisional approval must be submitted to the Film Commissioner by the qualifying company or its local branch or agent. Then the application for final approval must be submitted within six months of completion. The application procedure is described in detail in the Guidelines.

Office of the Film Commissioner
Malta Film Commission
Enterprise Centre
San Gwann, SGN 09
Malta
T: +356 21 497970
F: +356 21 499568
www.mfc.com.mt
info@mfc.com.mt

THE TAX CREDIT under the MALTA FILM COMMISSION ACT

(a) WHAT is available?

The Tax *Credit (Audiovisual Infrastructure) Regulations, 2006* provide for a **tax credit** in respect of **allowable expenditure** incurred by a qualifying company in carrying out an approved project. The tax credit is allowable for the year of assessment immediately following that in which the expenditure is incurred or in which the employment condition is first satisfied, whichever is the later, and is equal to:

- **25%** of expenditure for the acquisition, construction, development or improvement of any industrial building or structure, including a warehouse, and including related labour costs which are capitalised as part of the cost of any

such acquisition, construction, development or improvement; and

- **40%** of any other allowable expenditure.

However, the tax credit may not exceed (in aggregate) 50% of the total cost of the project in the case of a small or medium sized enterprise, or 40% in the case of any other qualifying company.

The tax credit is effectively a deduction from the tax chargeable on gains or profits derived from the relevant film. Any amount of tax credit due for a year of assessment that is not absorbed in that year may be carried forward (up to the year of assessment 2013) and deducted from tax chargeable in subsequent years on income from the same film. The Regulations apply to qualifying expenditure incurred on or after 1 January 2005.

(b) WHO can apply?

Applicants must either be companies established or with a place of business **in Malta**, whose **business** consists solely or mainly of activities that form part of the **film servicing industry**, that are **certified** as a qualifying company and are in possession of a valid certificate issued by the Film Commissioner.

(c) HOW do you qualify?

The tax credit is available to '**qualifying companies**' which incur **allowable expenditure** in producing an approved project, and which satisfy various employment and other conditions laid down in the Regulations. A 'qualifying company' is one established or having a place of business in Malta, whose business consists solely or mainly of activities that form part of the film servicing industry, and who has a valid qualification certificate for the allowable expenditure.

The **employment** condition is satisfied where, during the project period or within three years from the termination thereof, the qualifying company in question employs at least four additional employees for an indefinite period (at least 3 years).

The project must **contribute** towards the development, improvement or expansion of the **audiovisual infrastructure** in Malta.

The qualifying expenditure incurred in such project *includes*:

- the acquisition, construction, development or improvement of any industrial building or structure (including a warehouse any related labour costs which are capitalised as part of the cost of any such acquisition, construction, development or improvement);

- the acquisition of plant and machinery (but usually excluding motor vehicles);
- works of art and antiques;
- any assets whose use is wholly or mainly of a decorative nature;
- any assets whose cost is related to their intrinsic value rather than to their specific usefulness for a qualifying investment; and
- the acquisition of intellectual property rights from third parties under open market conditions the cost of which is amortisable.

One further condition for this tax credit is that **no other benefits** are claimed by a person on the same activity or project under any other legislation granting fiscal incentive schemes.

Projects will not be approved if their realisation requires a period of more than five years and if the application for their approval is not made before 31 December 2008.

(d) WHERE do you apply?

Applications for the certification of qualifying companies and the approval of qualifying projects are to be made to the **Film Commissioner**. Within sixty days of completion of the approved project, the company has to deliver to the Film Commissioner a certificate drawn up by a person who is recognised by the Commissioner as competent for this purpose.

> **Office of the Film Commissioner**
> Malta Film Commission
> Enterprise Centre, San Gwann, SGN 09, Malta
> T: +356 21 497970
> F: +356 21 499568
> www.mfc.com.mt
> info@mfc.com.mt

TAX REBATE under the BUSINESS PROMOTION ACT

(a) WHAT is available?

Until December 2008, income tax rates for qualifying companies are reduced to 5%, 10% or 15% (from the standard rate of 35%) with respect to the profits derived by companies from the various qualifying businesses carried out in Malta.

(b) WHO can apply?

Local and foreign companies whose business involves the production of audiovisual productions consisting of feature films, TV films, advertising programmes or advertisements, and documentaries, may benefit from the reduced tax rates.

(c) HOW do you qualify?

The benefits set out in the *Business Promotion Act* cover trade or business in Malta which consists solely of the production of feature films, TV films, advertising programmes or commercials, and documentaries. Any company that falls within this field qualifies for the reduction in tax rate (rebate).

Where a company satisfies the above condition throughout a relevant accounting period (see *(d) WHERE do you apply,* below), the profits derived by that company from its trade or business carried out in Malta shall:

(a)　with effect from the relevant year of assessment and for the six subsequent years of assessment, be subject to income tax at the rate of **5%**;

(b)　for the next **six** years of assessment, be subject to income tax at the rate of **10%**; and

(c)　for the next **five** years of assessment, be subject to income tax at the rate of **15%**.

For newly established companies, the year of assessment from which these provisions become applicable is any of the first three years of assessment of the company. Note that the scheme is currently due to run until **2009**.

The **maximum** profits taxed at the reduced rates of tax in any relevant year of assessment, are the amount produced by multiplying the **number of employees** by:

(a)　**Lm25,000** (at 2002 prices, annually increased according to the inflation index) where the profits are taxed at the rate of **5%**;

(b)　**Lm28,000** (at 2002 prices, annually increased according to the inflation index) where the profits are taxed at **10%** or **15%**.

(d) WHERE do you apply?

The authority administering the incentives under the *Business Promotion Act* is the **Malta Enterprise Corporation**. Applications for the incentives should be submitted by the company to Malta Enterprise, which will certify the company's eligibility.

The conditions to be satisfied essentially pertain to the company's business activities (see above), and the company must apply for a determination by Malta Enterprise Corporation that it is eligible to qualify for the benefit. On being satisfied that the company meets the above condition (that its trade or business, in Malta, consists solely of one or more of the above qualifying activities), the Malta Enterprise Corporation will provide it with a certificate signifying the accounting period for which the conditions are satisfied. The company's entitlement to the benefit is conditional upon the production of this certificate (together with various declarations by the company's directors and auditors) on submission of its income tax return for each year of assessment in respect of which it claims the reduced tax rate benefit.

Malta Enterprise Corporation
Enterprise Centre, Industrial Estate
San Gwann SGN 09, Malta
T: +356 2542 0000
F: +356 2542 3401
www.maltaenterprise.com
info@maltaenterprise.com

INVESTMENT TAX CREDIT under the BUSINESS PROMOTION ACT

(a) WHAT is available?

Tax credits in relation to investment are also available in Malta. Income tax can be reduced or eliminated by tax credits of up to **50% of eligible expenditure** (based on investment or job creation). As of 1 January 2007, the maximum levels for investment tax credit are **50%** in the case of a company which qualifies as a small-sized enterprise, **40%** in the case of a company which qualifies as a medium-sized enterprise, and **30%** in the case of any other company.

Unutilised investment tax credits may be carried forward to the following year of assessment, and increased by 7%. These incentives currently remain available until the 31 December 2008.

(b) WHO can apply?

Local and foreign companies whose business involves the production of audiovisual productions consisting of feature films, TV films, advertising programmes or advertisements, and documentaries, may benefit from the tax credits.

(c) HOW do you qualify?

The benefits contemplated by or under the *Business Promotion Act* concern trade or business in Malta which consists solely of the production of feature films, TV films, advertising programmes or commercials, and documentaries. The company must satisfy the eligibility criteria applicable for tax rebates under the *Business Promotion Act* (see above). In addition, the investment project must be approved

in writing by Malta Enterprise Corporation before its setting up.

(d) WHERE do you apply?

The authority administering the incentives under the *Business Promotion Act* is Malta Enterprise Corporation. Applications for the incentives should be submitted by the company to Malta Enterprise Corporation, which will certify the company's eligibility (address above).

III. INTERNATIONAL CO-PRODUCTIONS

Malta has been an active signatory of the *European Convention on Cinematographic Co-production*, since 2001. See the Section on European co-production in Chapter 3.

A Memorandum of Understanding between the Government of Canada and the Government of Malta on audiovisual relations has also been in place since September 1997. Co-productions made under this Treaty must have a minimum financial participation from each country of at least 20% of the total budget (for both bilateral and multilateral co-productions). It is the Film Commissioner's task to approve international co-productions and to issue any relevant certificate granting 'nationality' to such co-productions.

THE NETHERLANDS

Prepared with the assistance of Versteeg Wigman Sprey Advocaten (www.vwsadvocaten.nl)

I. INTRODUCTION

The Netherlands' film industry is renowned for features, documentary and animation. Two Dutch feature films have won Oscars for best foreign films, and two Dutch animation shorts have also won Oscars in their category.

Though a very professional industry, it is also relatively small, possibly due to the limitation of the Dutch language, the fact that the home market is small, and financial limitations.

The year 2007 will see the end of the infamous structure of tax incentives for productions through limited liability partnerships, and the start of a new fund tentatively called the '**suppletion fund**'. The government has **increased** its financing of the film industry with a structural €20m. There are a number of large-scale funding options, the most prominent of which are set out below (see also Part III).

II. THE DUTCH FILMFUND

(a) WHAT is available?

As of 2007, there are **no longer tax** driven or tax based incentive schemes available for the Dutch film industry. Instead, the government has ordered a reorganisation of the **Dutch Filmfund** and has added €20m to its annual film budget. As the restructuring is due to take place during the first six months of 2007 and final documents had, at the time of writing, not yet been published, both the structure and the criteria set out below are tentative and potentially subject to the final outcome of the reorganisation.

Essentially, there will be one overall organisation, the Dutch Filmfund, financed by the Ministry of Education, Culture and Science, which will be responsible for two separate and different funding schemes. One scheme will be the continuation of the current fund and the other scheme will be the 'suppletion fund'.

ORDINARY FUNDING

Financing is available to producers in the form of a **loan** for a specific film project, which is repayable from revenues of that project. It is **non-recourse**, so that if there are no revenues, there is no repayment.

No **interest** is charged, no profit points are taken and the Fund's **recoupment** position is **negotiable**.

Funding is available for screenplay development, project development, production and, under certain circumstances, money may also be available for post-production. Support is allocated to features, shorts, documentaries, animation and *avant garde* film (under the title of 'research and development'), as well as distribution and promotion.

Feature films are divided in artistic films and commercial ('broad audience') films.

As of 2007 there will **no** longer be a **maximum** to the possible loan.

This scheme will have a budget of **€15m** for feature film alone and it is expected that on average 15 to 20 films per year will be supported (therefore providing an assumed €1m or so average per film).

'SUPPLETION FUND'

This is the new fund. It is meant as an '**automatic**' fund, so that if you already have **65%** of the budget in place, the fund will finance the remainder.

(b) WHO can apply?

Ordinary funding
Applications may only be made by producers with a minimum of two years in the Netherlands. Directors may not be producers of their own film.

Suppletion Fund
At the time of writing it was still unclear as to exactly who may apply. The government was seeking to introduce a distinct Dutch criterium to the fund. However, in the absence of any approval or guidance from the EU in Brussels, it appears that applications may be made by any European producers with a minimum of five year standing.

(c) HOW do you qualify?

Ordinary Funding
All projects will be judged on a number of criteria, including artistic merit and content.

Suppletion Fund
25% of the budget needs to be funded by **private parties** (which includes (public) broadcasting companies), at least one of which must be a **theatrical distributor** funding a minimum of **10%** of the budget.

There will be more criteria set out in due course. It is understood that **theatrical distribution in the Netherlands** will be one of them, and it is expected that the **quality of the funding** in place will be important to qualify.

(d) WHERE do you apply?

Nederlands Fonds voor de Film
Jan Luikenstraat 2
1071 CM Amsterdam
T: (31) 20 570 7676
F: (31) 20 570 7689
www.filmfund.nl
info@filmfund.nl

II. ROTTERDAM FUND FOR THE AUDIOVISUAL INDUSTRY

(a) WHAT is available?

Apart from the National Filmfund (above), the **Rotterdam Filmfund** is an active regional fund, supporting the production of films in the area of the **city of Rotterdam**. Its structure is based on the German regional film funds.

Funding comes in the form of an **interest-free loan**, with **repayment** due from revenue. The available loan is currently capped at **€200,000** for Rotterdam-based producers and **€100,000** for international co-productions. These caps may be increased if a production plans to shoot entirely in the city of Rotterdam.

(b) WHO can apply?

Since the beginning of 2003, the Fund has limited applications to producers who are **based in Rotterdam**.

(c) HOW do you qualify?

Projects are solely assessed on their **economic benefit for the region** of Rotterdam and their commercial potential. **150%** of money allocated by the Fund has to be **spent in the region** of Rotterdam or on companies or individuals resident there.

(d) WHERE do you apply?

Rotterdam Fonds voor de Film en Audiovisuele Media
Rochussenstraat 3c
3015 EA Rotterdam
T: (31) 10 436 0747
F: (31) 10 436 0553
www.rff.rotterdam.nl
info@rff.rotterdam.nl

III. OTHER SOURCES OF FINANCE

CO-PRODUCTIONS WITH PUBLIC BROADCASTERS

A film project that is co-produced with a Dutch public broadcaster is eligible for additional funding from two funds, known respectively as the CoBo Fund and the Stifo Fund.

CoBO Fund

Applications for a loan need to be made by the **broadcaster** concerned, even though the loan agreement itself is made with and the loan is paid to the producer. The Fund's own money comes from a levy on cable companies distributing Dutch public TV in Belgium and Germany. Each broadcasting company supplying programmes has an allocation within the Fund and, provided sufficient money is available within that allocation, grants are awarded more or less automatically.

The available loan is based on two criteria, being the level of the **budget** and the **Dutch content**. For example, CoBO might lend up to **20%** of a €1m budget film, but if the director is not Dutch, then the loan will be a maximum of 88% of that 20%. Filming in a foreign language will decrease the loan by another 30% and so on.

In the event the budget is also partially funded by the Dutch Filmfund, other criteria apply.

Repayment is from all revenues, and the Fund requires a **share in any profits**, pro rata with its investment.

Stifo Fund

The Stifo Fund has been set up to stimulate Dutch culture, and one of its conditions for funding is that the project be in the **Dutch language**. Grants are applied for by — and made to — the **broadcaster**. The Fund's money comes from the Dutch Ministry of Education, Culture and Science and needs to cover support for cultural radio and TV programmes (including feature films).

Repayment is from box office and other revenue and the Fund requires a **share in any profits**, pro rata with its investment.

Note that for both the CoBO Fund and Stifo Fund, applications may only be made by a **Dutch public broadcasting organisation**.

THUISKOPIE FUND

The Thuiskopie Fund (literally the 'home copy foundation') is the collecting agency for levies on blank video and audio-cassettes and DVDs in the Netherlands. 15% of its net revenue is allocated to social and cultural projects relating to musical and audiovisual culture. Film projects fall under this banner and are regularly supported.

The applicant need not necessarily be Dutch; there is no minimum or maximum support, no obligation to repay and no profit points taken. Since any money from the Stichting is, as a result, **100% subsidy**, the emphasis is on the **Dutch social and cultural nature** of the project.

Stichting de Thuiskopie
Siriusdreef 22-28
2132 WT Hoofddorp
Postbus 3060
2130 KB Hoofddorp
T: (31) 23 799 7811
F: (31) 23 799 7700
www.cedar.nl/thuiskopie
thuiskopie@cedar.nl

SOME OTHER USEFUL CONTACTS

Commissariaat voor de Media: www.cvdm.nl
Dutch Film Fund: www.filmfund.nl
Film Investors Netherlands bv: www.find.nl
Holland Film: www.hollandfilm.nl
Rotterdam Film Fund: www.rff.Rotterdam.nl

NEW ZEALAND
Prepared with the assistance of the law firm Bell Gully (www.bellgully.com)

I. INTRODUCTION

New Zealand's huge diversity of landscape and range of attractive fiscal incentives have attracted a number of small- and large-budget pictures in recent years, including of course *The Lord of the Rings* trilogy, *The Last Samurai* and *Whale Rider*.

II. 12.5% CASH REBATE

(a) WHAT is available?

This incentive is officially known as the **Large Budget Screen Production Grant** ('LBSPG'), and works along similar lines to the Australian refundable film tax offset. Eligible applicants can receive a **cash rebate** (so technically not really a 'grant' — which would normally be up-front) equivalent to **12.5%** of '**Qualifying New Zealand Production Expenditure**' (QNZPE).

Since its inception in 2003, only about half a dozen productions have benefited from the LBSPG (albeit including *The Lion, the Witch and the Wardrobe*, *Boogeyman* and *King Kong*).

A film that receives the LBSPG will *not* be eligible for any other New Zealand (NZ) grants, or for the accelerated tax deduction for expenditure referred to below. It will, however (despite the official LBSPG guidance confusingly stating to the contrary), be eligible for the deduction for acquisition (see below). Whilst producers might seem to prefer the LBSPG grant to the deduction if they had a choice, most productions in NZ do not in fact qualify for the grant in the first place.

(b) WHO can apply?

The applicant must be the entity **responsible** for all activities involved in making the production in New Zealand, and who must also have access to full financial information for the production worldwide. It must be a New Zealand **resident** company **or** a foreign company operating with a fixed **establishment** in New Zealand for the purposes of lodging an income tax return.

(c) HOW do you qualify?

The project must incur **QNZPE** (see below) of **at least NZ$15m** and, unless it exceeds NZ$50m (in which case no minimum threshold applies), the QNZPE must represent **at least 70% of 'Total Production Expenditure'** (**TPE**).

It is not possible to bundle separate films in order to reach the QNZPE thresholds (although the NZ Government has undertaken to review this policy). It is, however, possible to bundle episodes of a TV drama series if they have completed principal photography within the same 12-month period and there is an average spend of at least NZ$500k per commercial hour.

QNZPE

Broadly speaking, **QNZPE** covers expenditure on goods, services and facilities in **New Zealand**, and **TPE** is the **worldwide** cost of making the production. QNZPE is effectively defined as production expenditure by the applicant on the screen production, where that expenditure is incurred for, or is attributable to:

- goods and services **provided** in New Zealand;
- the use of land located in New Zealand; or
- the use of goods **located** in New Zealand at the time of use.

The New Zealand Film Commission (the government agency that administers the scheme — see below), determines what expenditure constitutes QNZPE, and has issued guidelines and examples, with the following costs specifically *included*:

- **development** and **pre-production** work in New Zealand, including location surveys, scriptwriting and casting;
- the **acquisition** of **New Zealand copyright**;
- general business **overheads** in New Zealand (up to the lesser of 2% of TPE or NZ$500,000);
- **publicity and promotional** expenditure incurred before completion of the production;
- **travel to New Zealand** for work on the production;
- **advances** paid for deferments, profit participations or residuals, where these advances are non-recoverable;
- international **freight costs** paid to a New Zealand provider;
- **production insurance** purchased from a New Zealand provider (except errors and omissions insurance);

- **audit costs** incurred in New Zealand; and
- certain **agents' costs**.

For **non-cast** personnel (ie. those other than actors), there is a requirement that the person works in New Zealand for at least 14 days in total. The following costs are specifically *excluded* from the calculation of QNZPE:

- **financing** costs;
- the cost of goods delivered to New Zealand (which would otherwise qualify) where those goods embody the cost of services predominantly performed outside New Zealand;
- **perks** to cast or crew; entertainment costs; and
- **gratuities**.

The grant is available for feature films, TV movies and TV drama series. Neither documentaries nor reality TV shows qualify.

(d) WHERE do you apply?

Interested applicants should apply to the **New Zealand Film Commission** for an initial (and non-binding) assessment of eligibility.

The full application should be submitted to the Film Commission within three months of completing the production, or when the QNZPE has exceeded NZ$50 million. If QNZPE exceeds NZ$50 million, another final application must be submitted on completion. Applications should include an audited expenditure statement, the supporting documentation specified on the application form, sample footage, and a statutory declaration certifying the truth of the information provided. The application will be audited by the Inland Revenue Department and approved (or not) by the Film Commission. The Film Commission aims to make payments within three months of receipt of applications.

Applications should be sent to:

Large Budget Screen Production Grant
NZ Film Commission
PO Box 11 546
Wellington
New Zealand
www.nzfilm.co.nz/regulatory_approvals/large_budget_grant_scheme.aspx

III. TAX DEDUCTION

(a) WHAT is available?

Big-budget productions that do not receive the Large Budget Screen Production Grant (for example, documentaries) may instead be eligible for an **accelerated tax deduction** for film rights **acquisition** and **production expenditure**, under the *Income Tax Act 2004*. In fact, even if a film does receive a Large Budget Screen Production Grant, it may still be eligible for accelerated tax deductions in relation to the cost of **acquiring** the film rights, but *not* for production expenditure. The normal income tax rate is 33% of worldwide taxable income, net of allowable deductions, for companies tax resident in New Zealand, or if non-resident where income is sourced from New Zealand.

The rules are a little tricky and expert advice is highly recommended from the outset. However, below is a fairly simplified explanation.

Relative Timings for the Deduction

Significantly different timing rules can apply for the deduction, depending on whether a) the deduction is in relation to acquisition or production expenditure, b) the film qualifies as a national New Zealand Film, and c) the film is or is not a feature film. We will take a brief look at a) and b) and assume in each case that the film in question is a feature.

For the **acquisition** deduction, the deduction is apportioned over a 24-month period — possibly therefore involving three accounting years — starting from the completion of the film (or immediately if the rights are disposed of sooner).

For the **expenditure** deduction, the deduction depends on whether the film is a **New Zealand film** (see below for qualification criteria). If it is, then the deduction for pre-completion expenditure (note for these purposes 'completion' simply means fully edited rather than actually finished, delivered and ready for release) occurs in the year the film is completed (any post-completion production expenditure being deducted in the relevant subsequent year). If the film is *not* a qualifying New Zealand film, half of the deduction is allocated to the year of completion (or, if greater, an amount equal to the income received that year) and the other half (or remainder) the following year — unless the rights are disposed of in the first year, in which case the entire deduction can be allocated immediately.

Deductions for film production expenditure (FPE) may have to be deferred if a film is financed by limited recourse loans until the borrower is actually at risk. Other anti-avoidance measures exist where, for example, a second deduction is claimed for what is, in substance, the same expenditure (a type of '**double dipping**').

(b) WHO can apply?

Broadly, any New Zealand income or corporation taxpayer is allowed a deduction for the relevant expenditure incurred. While the guidelines do not formally define a 'New Zealander' for these purposes, the *New Zealand Film Commission Act* refers to both **nationality** and **residency**.

(c) HOW do you qualify?

A taxpayer is generally allowed the deduction for all **film production expenditure** ('**FPE**') which, not being directly linked to New Zealand spend, can be more inclusive than QNZPE. FPE is defined for tax purposes as:

- the **expenditure** or loss incurred **in producing a film**;
- an amount of depreciation loss on property used in producing a film; and
- depreciation loss arising from the disposal of depreciable property used in producing a film.

FPE does *not* include the cost of acquiring a film right after a film is completed, or the cost of **marketing** a film.

For a film to qualify as a 'New Zealand film', it must be certified as such by the **Film Commission** (see criteria below). These special timing rules for treating FPE on New Zealand films are only available to taxpayers in receipt of a final certificate from the Film Commission.

For tax purposes, 'film rights' include various rights and interests in films, including primarily copyright in the underlying property.

New Zealand Film

To qualify for a single-year tax production expenditure deduction (but not necessary for acquisition deduction), or for a payment from the Film Fund (see IV below), the film must be certified as a '**New Zealand film**'. To qualify, the film must have '**significant New Zealand content**' and, in determining if this requirement is satisfied, the Film Commission will look at the following criteria:

- the **subject** of the film;
- **location(s)** of production;
- **nationalities** and places of **residence** of those involved in making the film;
- those who **own** shares or capital in any company or partnership concerned with making the film (ie. typically the **producer**);
- those who **own copyright** in the film;
- **sources of funding**;

- ownership and location of **equipment** and technical facilities; and
- any other matters that, in the opinion of the Film Commission, are relevant.

(d) WHERE do you apply?

During production, you should apply to the Film Commission for provisional certification as a New Zealand film, and apply for final certification once the film is completed. If the film is produced in accordance with the provisional application, it is likely that final certification will be granted. Payment from the Film Fund (see below), or the deduction of tax, can then be made.

More information is available on the NZ Film Commission site at www.nzfilm.co.nz.

IV. FILM FUND

(a) WHAT is available?

The Film Fund was established by the New Zealand government in 2000 to help develop a sustainable film industry. To date, it has supported films such as *Whale Rider*, *Perfect Strangers*, *Perfect Creature* and *The World's Fastest Indian*. The Film Fund can invest up to NZ$2.5m per production. Investments can be made in several ways but the majority is likely to be invested as equity. The production should have a total budget of at least NZ$4.5m and around 40% of the total budget should be in the form of offshore market attachments (with a commitment from at least one reputable theatrical sales agent).

(b) WHO can apply?

Funding is only available to New Zealand filmmakers, which means a New Zealand producer and a (separate) New Zealand director. These filmmakers should both have made at least one previous feature film.

(c) HOW do you qualify?

The Film Fund will only invest in the production of feature films that qualify as **New Zealand films** (see above). It will be disqualified if the investors in the production receive a tax advantage in New Zealand for the production (other than on the net amount of their own direct investment). The film must be budgeted at over **NZ$5m** (although the **New Zealand Film Commission** also has a fund for **smaller pictures**).

There must also be reasonable evidence that the film will enjoy market success and that the investment will be recouped.

(d) WHERE do you apply?

Applicants are encouraged to consult with the **Film Commission** *before* lodging an application, which should include the latest draft of the script, details of the production company, its directors and a certificate of incorporation, details of principal cast and key creative personnel, a detailed budget and cash flow schedule, and a detailed production timeline.

Full details on application materials can be found on the Film Fund's website at www.filmfund.co.nz. Applications should be couriered to:

The Film Fund
119 Jervois Quay
Wellington 6000
New Zealand

The Film Fund's board aims to meet within six weeks of receiving an application and will advise the applicant within seven days of the board's decision.

V. CO-PRODUCTIONS AND OTHER USEFUL CONTACTS

A film will be deemed to have 'significant New Zealand content' if it is made following the terms of an official co-production treaty. New Zealand currently has treaties with Australia, Canada, France, Germany, Italy, Singapore and the United Kingdom. Generally they require a minimum 20% financial contribution and/or 30% creative contribution from New Zealand. Unlike many other countries, there is no formal points system relating to key positions. In addition, the following criteria will be used to decide whether to grant certification to a co-production: there should be a producer in each country; there should be a minimum 30% New Zealand participation (both creative and financial); creative and financial percentages should equate – so if 40% of the budget is to be spent in New Zealand, then at least 40% of key positions should be filled by New Zealanders; either the writer or director should be a New Zealander and a New Zealand actor should be cast in one of the major roles; and if there is public funding from New Zealand, it should only be spent on New Zealand costs and the investment should not be subordinated to foreign equity investors.

The Film Commission will consult with its equivalent organisation in the country of co-production.

Other useful websites include:

www.filmsouth.com (Film South New Zealand) and www.filmwellington.com (for city of Wellington).

NORWAY

Prepared with the assistance of the Norwegian Film Fund (www.filmfondet.no)

I. INTRODUCTION

Public support for film production in Norway goes back to 1950. Modified on several occasions, support is now referred to as pertaining to 'audiovisual' production and – in addition to film – covers TV drama and documentaries and development of interactive ('video') games. The **Norwegian Film Fund** is the Government's executive body for film policy and handles the Government's schemes for support.

Government funding schemes for audiovisual productions have their legal base in *Regulations on Support for Audiovisual Production*. These were last amended on 28 January 2005 and have been extended until 7 August 2008.

The Government has announced that it will present a White Paper on Film Policy to Parliament in March 2007. This paper may propose measures that could affect what types of support that will be available as well as the conditions for obtaining such support. It is also expected to deal with the organisation of governmental executive bodies. However, no major changes to the system described above are expected before 2008.

II. PUBLIC FUNDING

(a) WHAT is available?

Government funding is available for:

- **Production** support for full-length features, including for project development and marketing (Regulations chapter 2);
- Support for the Norwegian (minority) participation in an **international co-production** (Regulations chapter 3);
- Production support according to **commercial criteria** (Regulations chapter 4);
- Production support for short films and TV **documentaries**, including support for project development (Regulations chapter 5);
- Production support for **TV series** (drama and documentary), including support for project development (Regulations chapter 6);
- Support for project development for **interactive** productions (Regulations chapter 7); and

- **Box Office Bonuses** (Regulations chapter 8).

In addition, a support scheme for company development focuses on **slate development** funding (legal basis Regulations of 18 September 2002; available only in Norwegian at www.filmfondet. no/icm.aspx?PageId=595).

Funding is made available on an annual basis by decision of Parliament, within the framework of the budget for Culture in the National Budget. The 2007 appropriation for audiovisual production purposes administered by the Norwegian Film Fund is NOK292m (approx €35m).

The amounts available for support under each support scheme is determined by the Film Fund's Board of Governors at the beginning of each budget year. The Board has a mandate to adjust the repartition of funds between schemes during the course of the year. They therefore do not publish official amounts of allocation for each support scheme. A general guide to funds available under each scheme may be deduced from the allotment of funds published in the Film Fund's annual reports. Thus, in 2005 (the latest report available at time of writing) funds were repartitioned as follows: Feature production and development (chapters 2, 3, 4) 56%, feature film promotion (chapters 2, 3, 4) 5%, short films 4%, TV documentaries 4%, TV series (drama and documentaries) 7%, interactive productions 2%, box office bonuses 21%, and company development 1%.

No single project may receive more than **NOK30m** (€3.6m) in combined support, and this figure is CPI-indexed from 2002.

Support for any project is **repayable** at a rate of 35%, *pari passu* from net receipts starting at the point when they exceed **130%** of combined third party equity (and any producer's) investment.

The authoritative text of the Regulations – in Norwegian only – is available at:

www.lovdata.no/cgi-wift/ldles?doc=/sf/sf/sf-20050128-0071.html

An unofficial English translation can be found at: www.filmfondet.no/iCM.aspx?PageId=118 (click link on the right-hand column to access in Word format)

(b) WHO can apply?

Support may be applied for by **independent**, **professional** production companies **registered** in Norway. Subsidiaries of foreign companies are eligible for support if formally registered in Norway and **represented** by a Norwegian citizen or a person holding permanent residency status in Norway.

Foreign companies established in the **EEA** (EU countries plus Iceland and Liechtenstein) may apply on the same conditions as independent Norwegian production companies.

(c) HOW do you qualify?

Only films and other audiovisual programmes that comply with the criteria for a '**Norwegian production**' (set out in Article 1.3, 6th paragraph, of the Regulations) are eligible for support.

The basic criterion for a Norwegian production is quite simply 'a film recorded in the Norwegian or Sami **language**, produced by an **independent Norwegian production company**'. Exemption for productions in other languages may be granted, provided a) the Norwegian company is the delegate/main producer, b) that it is the biggest (co-)producer (minimum 33,33% of budget) and c) that the film 'includes a significant artistic or technical contribution that serves to promote audiovisual art and culture in Norway', such contributions being calculated on the basis of a points scale.

Support under chapter 2, chapter 3, chapter 5 (short films only) and chapter 6 (drama only) is selective. Applications are evaluated by the Film Fund's **commissioning executives** (sometimes erroneously referred to as 'consultants') on the basis of **artistic, production-related, economic, technical** and **market-related** criteria. The Commissioning executives can grant support at any time, and operate under the **Guidelines of 5 December 2006**, which can be found on online at:

www.filmfondet.no/iCM.aspx?PageId=4

Support under chapter 5 (TV single documentaries), chapter 6 (TV documentary series) and chapter 7 are also selective (commissioning executive review), but deadlines apply (see (d) below). Support under chapter 4 (commercial criteria) is **automatic**, and application deadlines apply (see (d) below). Awards under chapter 4 are, however, restricted by the amount allocated to this type of support each year. If there are more applications than funds allow, the Board will make a selection on the basis of evaluations made by a panel of anonymous readers. Box office bonuses (chapter 8) are **automatic**. Any Norwegian film released commercially in Norway is eligible for this type of support, which is calculated in proportion to the level and amount of equity investment. Application for eligibility must be made before the start of principal photography.

(d) WHERE do you apply?

Applications are made to the **Norwegian Film Fund** (www.filmfondet.no). The working language of the Fund is Norwegian, and all documents are issued in Norwegian only.

There are no deadlines for the schemes under chapters 2, 3, 5 and 6; projects may be proposed to any one of the Film Fund's commissioning executives at any time. Application deadlines for support under chapter 5 (TV single documentaries), chapter 6 (TV documentary series) and chapter 7 are posted on the home pages of the Norwegian Film Fund. When applying to support schemes with specific deadlines, the **electronic** application forms must be used.

The names and contact details of the commissioning executives and their respective areas of responsibility can be found at www.filmfondet.no/iCM.aspx?PageId=129.

All applications for support must be submitted electronically. Electronic application forms may be accessed via the link at www.filmfondet.no/iCM.aspx?PageId=616. Other relevant documents (budget breakdown sheets, key concept definitions, etc) are available via the Fund's homepages.

III. OTHER USEFUL CONTACTS AND FUNDING POSSIBILITIES

Norwegian Film Commission: www.norwegianfilm.com/

Norwegian Film Institute: www.nfi.no (these guys are really helpful!)

Nordic Film & TV Fund: www.nftf.net

Norwegian Ass'n of Film & TV Producers: www.produsentforeningen.no/

Government funding is also available for **short films** and **documentaries** through the 'Fund for sound and image' (www.fondforlydogbilde.no/flb2/index.php?section=3), the Film Centre of Northern Norway (www.nnfs.no/) and the Film Centre of Western Norway (www.vestnorskfilm.no).

Several **regional funds** are currently under establishment. These funds normally combine local and regional public and private funding. Their status in relation to government funding schemes has not been finally determined. Links to regional funds and relevant public and audiovisual sector organisations may be found at:

www.filmfondet.no/iCM.aspx?PageId=117.

PUERTO RICO

Prepared with the assistance of the Puerto Rico Film Commission (www.puertoricofilm.com)

I. INTRODUCTION

The Puerto Rico incentives for the production of series, mini-series, films and 'telenovelas' (latin soap operas) are claimed to be the highest anywhere in the world (at a wapping **40%**), and unique in the Latin production market. The incentives, combined with first class infrastructure, commercial and banking laws akin to those in the USA (with whom there are no trade barriers), the US dollar as its currency, internal labour subsidies, local talent, and general fiscal autonomy (with no federal taxes) make Puerto Rico a very attractive destination for many productions.

II. FINANCIAL INCENTIVES

THE 40% REBATE

(a) WHAT is available?

The main fiscal incentive for shooting in Puerto Rico (PR) is the huge **40% rebate on expenditure**, in the form of a **transferable tax credit**. There is a stated US$15m yearly cap on the aggregate amount made available by the authorities, but there is potential to increase this on a project by project basis.

There is a clearly defined market for the credit (because it is transferable), which goes to the investor. Further, up to $1.2m in the form of **investment guarantees** is available to certain local people and/or productions for cash-flowing a proportion of the rebate (seek local advice for eligibility and accessibility).

The rebate will usually **net**, after transaction costs, about 36% of the PR spend. The transaction costs are (a) the appropriate Film Entity Licence fee, at 1% of the total budget (but negotiable), (b) the discount on the transfer of the tax credit (about 5% to 9% of the credit itself — equivalent to about 2% to 4% of the budget), (c) monetisation and incentive request process services (being documents to be filled out, submission of application packages, follow up with local government agencies, etc), and (d) the cost of any guarantees the production company needs to put up in order to obtain the rebate advance.

(b) WHO is eligible?

The incentive is given to an investor who **invests** in a 'Film Entity' (being the production company)

dedicated to producing a film project, in exchange for stock or unit participations. There is no nationality requirement, and the rebate is available to both individual investors and corporate ones.

(c) HOW do you qualify?

At least **50% of principal photography** has to be shot in Puerto Rico (based on the number of days or script pages) and the payments must be made to either a Puerto Rican Company or a Puerto Rican (PR) resident.

The rebate is based on '**Puerto Rico spend**', meaning money spent on development, pre-production, production and post production, such as equipment, crew, actors, travel (if through a local travel agency), hotels, and stage rental. It includes both above- and below-the-line costs. Puerto Rico spend means all expenses paid to any PR resident (working in PR or abroad) and any payments made to locally established companies, be they for services, purchases, stores, hotels, or anything where PR are paid.

(d) WHERE do you apply?

Applications should be made to the Puerto Rico Treasury Department. The application must be accompanied by a Puerto Rico budget. The rebate is paid around 90 days after all paperwork has been submitted following completion of principal photography.

For addresses of the Treasury Department and others, see the Film Commission's website at:

www.puertoricofilm.com

Since this is a fairly new program, there are few local specialists that can assist in the application process, such as Antonio Sifre at Production Advisory Services (787) 413 5262, Carlos Rios-Gautier at Rios Gautier Law (787) 753-7750, or Rosana Moreno-Rodríguez at McConnell Valdés (787) 250 5651.

III. GOVERNMENT HOTEL TAX WAIVER AND FREE LOCATION

(a) WHAT is available?

A waiver of the local hotels tax, which for 'casino' hotels' is 11%, and for non-casino hotels is 9%. Puerto Rico also offers Government Fee-Free Locations, meaning public facilities will not charge productions for per-day usage.

(b) WHO is eligible to apply?

Any production company shooting in Puerto Rico.

(c) HOW do you qualify?

The producer (or co-producer) should obtain an appropriate letter from the Commission prior to anyone turning up at hotels (etc), in order to obtain the automatic waiver of entertainment taxes.

(d) WHERE do you apply?

First port of call should be the **Puerto Rico Film Commission**

www.puertoricofilm.com

Another useful contact is the Puerto Rico Convention Bureau. The person to contact there is

Marilia Juarbe, Regional Sales Manager, at (787) 725-2110 or: mjuarbe@prcb.org.

ROMANIA

I. INTRODUCTION

Romania joined the EU on 1 January 2007, and amendments are therefore being made to bring the Romanian audiovisual law in line with EU policies. The effect on local prices — which have recently been more competitive than those of nearby rivals Hungary and the Czech Republic — is yet to be seen, but in all probability likely to go up. Currently, specific tax incentives (again, probably also subject to changes) are available for producers and investors in film production and distribution who re-invest their profits in the industry. A further **income tax reduction** of up to **20%** is available in certain circumstances (see below), and investors may get additional deductions on their corporate income tax for larger investments.

The **Romanian National Cinema Centre** (*Centrul National al Cinematografiei*, or '**CNC**') was created in 1998 and offers **reimbursable loans** to productions film involving Romanian participation.

Romania is a member of the *European Convention*, Eurimages, and the South Eastern Europe Cinema Network (SEE Cinema Network). **Co-production grants** are available on satisfying the relevant conditions.

It is important to note is that there is a relatively high level of red tape in Romania. Any individual or company (resident or not) who carries out cinema-related activities or services in Romania, **must register** with, and obtain approval from, the **Romanian Cinema Registry** at least ten days before work commences. Recent major productions have included Miramax's $80m *Cold Mountain*, which apparently saved itself $20m in production costs as a result.

II. TAX INCENTIVES

(a) WHAT is available?

For **investors and producers** directly involved in film productions, a tax **exemption** is available for **customs duties** payment related to **imports** of cinematographic equipment and installations.

Specifically designed for the film industry, an **income tax deduction** also exists in two forms. First, **production profits** that are **reinvested** in the local film industry are totally **exempt** from income tax.

A further **20% reduction** on income tax payable is applied if new jobs are created and if there is an overall increase of at least 10% in the number of registered employers compared with the previous calendar year. These deductions were valid until the end of 2006 and, at the time of writing, details of possible extensions had yet to be announced.

Additionally, **corporate tax incentives** provide a **20% deduction** on the value of the new investments (if over US$1m) which have a significant impact on the economy (which can potentially include the film industry), effectively giving a 120% deduction of the cost of the investment. Specialist advice should be sought as the application of this incentive to the film industry is not straightforward.

Additional tax incentives may in some cases be granted by local authorities or various public authorities.

(b) WHO can apply?

Any **registered production company** (or individual investor) involved in film productions can apply.

(c) HOW do you quality?

The producer or production company must obtain authorisation from the CNC. It must also be registered with the Romanian Cinema Registry and the Trade Registry. The Cinema Registry is administered by the CNC. For further requirements, see (a) WHAT is available, above.

(d) WHERE do you apply?

Register with the relevant bodies (**Cinema Registry, CNC** and **Trade Registry**).

> **Centrul National al Cinematografiei**
> Str. Dem. I. Dobrescu nr. 4-6
> Sector 1
> Bucuresti 010026
> T: +40 21 310 43 01
> F: +40 21 310 43 00
> www.cncinema.abt.ro/index.aspx
> www.centrul-cinematografiei.ro/
> cnc@cncinema.ro

III. REIMBURSABLE LOANS

(a) WHAT is available?

Reimbursable loans (with or without interest) are available to **producers** for features, shorts and animation. The CNC provides the loans and agrees the amount to be granted through a 3-member commission.

There is a **budget limit of 65%** for features of which 50% is available up-front, and the remaining 15% during production. The 65% can be increased to 80% for shorts and first-time directors and, again, 50% is available up-front and the remainder (30% of the budget) during production.

The funding is offered in several forms: repayable advance on receipts (maximum of 50% of the granted amount), loan (with or without interest), co-financing, co-production, distribution agreement, acquisition of work by the fund.

Repayments are made over a maximum of seven years for the interest-free loan, or three years for those bearing interest (which is linked to the National Bank of Romania's rate). Interest-free loans are available for international co-productions involving Romanian companies.

(b) WHO can apply?

Producer or production company registered and authorised by the Cinema Registry. This includes foreign producers involved in Romanian co-productions.

Broadcasters, distributors, and promotion agencies can also apply for the fund regarding film distribution, exhibition and exploitation.

(c) HOW do you quality?

The producer (or co-producer) must:
- pay, **register** with and obtain approval from the **Cinema Registry** for all crew at least ten days before work commences;
- **provide** a minimum of **6%** of the total production **budget** him/herself, of which **half** should be made in cash or via a bank letter of guarantee, and the other half in services (but see below regarding co-productions);
- obtain written approvals from the author of the screenplay; and
- carry out at least **two-thirds** of the production work **in Romania**.

The production budget is subject to the following preset **maximum quotas**: 12.5% producer's fee, 10% contingency, 5% director's fee, 4% executive producer's fee, and 4% screenplay. Costs included in the production budget must not exceed market prices.

At least **two 'authors'** (screenplay writer, director, composer), at least **50%** of **leading roles**, at least **50% of technicians** and specialists must be Romanian citizens.

Interest-free loans are available for **international co-productions**, under the following conditions:

- the project must involve a **Romanian** legal entity which has co-ownership rights over the negative, reproduction rights over the film, and exploitation rights;
- the applicant must **register** with the CNC;
- the producers themselves must provide **at least 10%** (for multilateral co-productions) **or 20%** (for bilateral co-productions) of financial participation; and
- the CNC must be credited in the main titles and promotional materials.

In all cases, films which are intrusive or prejudicial to the private lives of individuals, pornographic, instigate violence, and which engage in political or religious propaganda are *excluded* from public funding.

(d) WHERE do you apply?

The applications should be sent to the **CNC**.

The standard application form should be accompanied by documentations, legally translated into Romanian if applicable, detailing activities to be carried out in Romania and the list of artistic and technical elements.

Centrul National al Cinematografiei
Str. Dem. I. Dobrescu nr. 4-6
Sector 1
Bucuresti 010026
T: +40 21 310 43 01
F: +40 21 310 43 00
cnc@cncinema.ro

SOUTH AFRICA

Prepared with the assistance of Bowman Gilfillan Inc.(www.bowman.co.za)

I. INTRODUCTION

Filmmakers, both local and international, are increasingly holding South Africa's production film industry in high regard. The Republic of South Africa has, over the past 10 years or so, nurtured and encouraged its fledgling film industry into producing local and international films that reflect a truly South African flavour. This nurturing has allowed the South African film industry to develop into an industry which is growing in depth, stature and, ultimately, accolades. One example of the achievement of the South African film industry is the recent Best Foreign Language Film Academy Award won by Peter Fudakowski and Gavin Hood's *Tsotsi* in 2006. In addition to that, a number of local films have achieved international recognition as film festivals such as the Berlin Film Festival (*U-Karmen eKhayelitsha* being one of those). Other noteworthy productions, such as *Hotel Rwanda* and *Yesterday* (itself an Academy Award® nominee in 2005) and the recent award winning documentary *A Lion's Trail* by Francois Verster serve to indicate the level of talent, quality and excellence in South Africa's film industry.

On the co-production side, South Africa has become a skilful and beneficial partner to involve in international productions, owing in part to the financial instruments that have been put in place by each of the Department of Trade & Industry ('DTI') and the South African Revenue Services ('SARS') to encourage both foreign and local productions. These headline incentives are a **rebate** on South African spend of **15% or 25%**, a **deduction** from South African **income tax** of amounts invested in qualifying films (known as **s24F**), and **direct funding** from the **National Film and Video Foundation**.

II. THE DTI REBATE

(a) WHAT is available?

The Department of Trade & Industry ('DTI')'s **film rebate scheme** entitles eligible applicants to a rebate of a certain portion of qualifying South African production expenditure, namely **15%** for **foreign** productions and **25%** for **South African** productions.

The rebate has a minimum **R25m** activation threshold (local spend — see below) and is capped at **R10m** per project. A 12-month time frame is applied on **bundling** films for purposes of attaining the R25m threshold, and no more than 3 feature films, documentaries or TV movies can be bundled. If the films are sourced from an offshore producer, that producer should be the same source for all 3 bundled films. Sourced is defined as the common beneficial holder of the copyright in and to those works.

This incentive is not specifically a tax incentive, but rather a cash rebate payable by the **Department of Trade and Industry** (DTI), and is itself exempt from income tax.

An eligible applicant will receive a rebate equal to **15%** for foreign productions, and 25% for South African productions and **official co-productions**.

(b) WHO can apply?

The applicant must be an entity **incorporated in South Africa** for the purpose of the production of the film(s). In addition, that entity needs to have at least one South African **resident director** (of the company, not necessarily the film) who should have an **active** participation in the production of the film. The applicant must be the entity in fact **responsible for all production activities** involved in making the film in South Africa.

The rebate is available to applicants who meet the expenditure criteria set out above within a 12-month period.

(c) HOW do you qualify?

To become eligible for the application of the rebate, a production would need to meet the following criteria:
• The **majority** of the production's principal photography should be filmed in South Africa, provided that **no less than four weeks** of the principal photography should be filmed in South Africa;
• Productions must have commenced principal photography on or after **1 April 2004** in order to apply;
• Productions covered include feature films, TV dramas, mini-series, animations and documentaries, but specifically *exclude* reality TV, advertising programmes, news and current affairs programmes, public events such as sport events, and training programmes. A feature film can include animation, must be no less than **60 minutes**, or in the case of a large format (IMAX) film, no less than 45 minutes, and be shot and processed to **commercial release**

standards, for cinema exhibition, TV broadcast or direct-to-video;
• The **minimum South African production expenditure** incurred must be **R25m**, with the rebate **capped** at **R10m** per production. As mentioned above, this can be achieved by **bundling** up to three projects;
• All beneficial rights must be owned or **co-owned** by a **South African entity**;
• The persons involved in the production process need, unless special circumstances exist, to be **South African citizens or residents**;
• Live action shooting and animation films must, subject to certain allowances, in principle be **conducted in South Africa**, although shooting may be conducted outside of South Africa if the NFVF approves the production as an official 'co-production', or where South Africans remain involved.

Qualifying South African production expenditure is defined as the production expenditure spent by the applicant on copyright and goods and on all facilities and services **provided by a South African entity** to individuals, but *excluding* certain non-qualifying items, such as financing expenditure, general business overheads over a certain benchmark level, producer fees (to the extent that they exceed the lesser of 10% of the total production expenditure or R1m) or other associated party fees that exceed a certain maximum amount, deferments, profit participation, residuals, advances, buildings and land, and costs of services embodied in goods.

Any expenditure must be calculated on an 'arm's length' basis, in other words at an independent market value.

The film allowance granted in terms of **s24F** (see below) remains *unaffected* by the rebate, and will be available for the same productions. However, it is important to note that the film allowance is only allowed to the extent that payment has actually been made without using credit or loans, or alternatively to the extent that the film owner is at risk of suffering an economic loss if the film fails to generate income. Since guaranteed rebates will reduce any economic loss that might be suffered, the s24F film allowance will generally initially be reduced, and the balance claimable only once the loan finance (lent against the rebate) has been settled.

(d) WHERE do you apply?

Applicants are required to apply for a **provisional certificate** from the **DTI**. That certificate provides the applicant with certainty that their production satisfies the eligibility criteria set out above. This, in turn, allows the DTI to budget the rebates and also serves the purpose of discouraging applications for projects that are not likely to reach fruition. An applicant may hold **up to three** provisional certificates for projects that have not yet commenced principal photography.

A provisional certificate will lapse if the applicant does not confirm that it has **commenced principal photography within six months** of it being issued.

Applicants are required to submit a **final rebate application** to the DTI **within three months** of completion of the film production (being the date on which the cut master negative and conforming soundtrack are married to an answer print). Payment is made after a DTI panel (consisting of representatives from the NFVF, SARS and the National Treasury) has assessed the application.

Application forms can be downloaded from the DTI website at www.dti.gov.za.

Three complete copies of the completed application must be sent to:

The Investment Services Manager
Film and Television Production Rebate
Department of Trade and Industry
Private Bag X86,
Pretoria, 0001
South Africa

III. TAX DEDUCTION

(a) WHAT is available?

In summary, **s24F** entitles a **film owner** (see below) to secure an immediate deduction from its South African income of its **production costs** in the tax year in which the completion date of the production falls. In that year too, the film owner may claim its **post-production** cost. Subsequently the film owner claims post-production costs as it incurs them.

The application of s24F is relatively complicated, and parties should always obtain comprehensive local legal advice before seeking to deduct production costs in terms of s24F.

With the aim of encouraging the production of South African films, the film allowance is targeted at expenses incurred and paid/payable **in South Africa**. The view of the **SARS** (South African Revenue Service) is that South African tax expenditure in the form of the film allowance should be focused on South African film productions in order to grow and support the local film industry.

Accordingly, the **production and post-production costs** (which we'll call '**Film Costs**') which may be allowed to a film owner is limited to expenditure incurred and paid or payable in South Africa to persons who are **subject to tax there** on the receipt of those costs.

In order to allow for co-productions and the use of **foreign talent and expertise**, the **total** amount of all Film Costs incurred may be deductible if **at least 75%** of the total amount of those Film Costs is incurred and paid or payable in South Africa to persons who are subject to tax there. Alternatively, the total qualifying Film Costs can be deducted where the film is an **official co-production**.

Where **neither** the 75% nor the co-production requirements are met, the film owner will be entitled to an immediate s24F allowance for those Film Costs incurred as are payable in South Africa in respect of services rendered or goods supplied in South Africa. Any remaining Film Costs will be deductible over a 10-year period.

The effect of the accelerated allowance in terms of s24F is that a film owner gets the benefit of a tax deduction before the related income from the exploitation of the film is taxed. In order to limit the deduction of expenditure to closer reflect the economic cost to film owners the concept of an **at risk** rule was introduced (see below).

Tax rates in South Africa are currently 29% for corporations (34% for some exceptions, such as foreign companies) and 40% for individuals.

(b) WHO can apply?

Any entity which is required to submit South African income tax returns can apply, assuming it is an **owner** or **part-owner** of the film. For these purposes, a film owner is a party that owns any portion of a film, but in practice a person will not be regarded as a film owner where s/he is a mere lessee, financier or has a limited right to income for a period of time, without the risks and rewards incidental to actual ownership. In other words, if an investor in a film is looking to avail itself of this tax deduction, it must become an at-risk (co-)owner of the film itself.

Of course, it must also comply with the eligibility criteria set out below.

(c) HOW do you qualify?

As mentioned above, for the **entire budget** (subject to exceptions — see below) to be deductible, at least **75%** of the Film Costs incurred by a film owner must be **paid or payable in South Africa** and in respect of services rendered or goods supplied in South Africa.

In order to fall within this limitation, **foreign** actors should be paid, and taxed, in South Africa. Although legislation has been drafted regarding withholding tax on amounts payable to sportsmen and entertainers, it is not yet been finalised nor promulgated.

As previously stated, if a film is approved in terms of one of the **co-production** agreements concluded by the South African government, the **total** Film Costs incurred by a film owner in respect of the film will automatically qualify for the s24F allowance. Therefore, if (say) only 40% of the budget is spent in South Africa on an official co-production, s24F will still be calculated on the entire budget (as was the case in the UK until recently). South Africa has entered into co-production agreements with **Italy**, **Canada** and **Germany** and the **UK**.

The 'at risk' rule

Where the Film Costs incurred by a film owner were partly or wholly financed by a loan or credit and such loan or credit is partly or wholly **outstanding** at the end of the year of assessment during which the s24F allowance is claimed by the film owner, the s24F allowance must be **reduced** by the amount for which the film owner is deemed not be 'at risk' as provided for in s24F.

A film owner is deemed to be at risk to the extent that the payment of the Film Costs incurred by the film owner, or the repayment of any loan or credit used by the film owner for the payment or financing of such costs, would result in an economic loss to the film owner if no income was received by or accrued to the film owner in future from the exploitation of the film.

Put simply, if the film owner took a loan out to pay for the Film Costs, but income from the film is not sufficient to repay the loan, the film owner will **not** be **at risk** if s/he is not still required to pay back the rest of the loan. In particular, if the **full** amount of the loan or credit is not **repayable within** a period of 10 years from the completion date, the film owner is deemed not be at risk for that portion of the Film Costs financed by the loan for s24F purposes. This is because it had become clear that in a limited number of cases, film owners were extending the period within which a loan or credit which was used to finance Film Costs of a film was repayable for as long as possible. This had the effect of creating an unacceptably long period between the tax year in which the expenditure was deducted and the date of settlement of the loan or credit. Internationally, limits are imposed in different forms on the tax deferral by investors in films. So, in South Africa, a film owner is now treated not to be at risk for purposes of the film allowance to the extent a loan or credit used to finance production or post-production cost is not repayable within a period of 10 years from the completion date of the film.

The 'at risk' rule may also apply to **soft money** to the extent that its terms result in the film owner not being at risk for that finance.

Finally, an expenditure amount incurred in respect of Film Costs will not be allowed as a s24F allowance unless there is a **binding, unconditional obligation to pay** that amount within **18 months** after the completion date of the film (in other words, if it's claimed as a Film Cost for s24F purposes, it *must* be payable as a budget item).

The s24F allowance is available in respect of Film Costs (ie. **production** and **post-production** costs) which would, but for this rule, have constituted capital expenses. **Production costs** are defined in s24F as the total expenditure incurred by a film owner in respect of the **acquisition or production of a film** *including*:

- any remuneration, salary, legal, accounting or other fee, commission or other amount paid or payable to any person for the purpose of or in connection with the production of the film (ie. **wages** and **fees**);
- the costs of acquiring the story rights, script, screenplay, copyright or other rights in relation to the film (ie. **underlying rights** acquisitions);
- insurance premiums in respect of **insurance** against injury to or death or persons, or loss of or damage to property employed or used, as the case may be, in the production of the film;
- premiums or commission payable in order to secure a guarantee that the cost of the film will not exceed a specified amount (ie. **completion bond premium**);
- **interest, finance charges** and raising fees incurred for the purpose of or in connection with the production of a film;
- the cost of acquiring or creating *music*, sound and other effects which will form part of the film;
- in certain circumstances wear and tear allowances in respect of any machinery, implements, utensils or articles used in the production of a film; and
- expenditure incurred in respect of the purchase, hire or construction of sets and the hire of any

machinery, implements, utensils or articles used in the production of the film.

Production costs specifically *exclude*:

- expenditure incurred in the erection, construction or acquisition of any **buildings** or other structures or works of a permanent nature;
- expenditure incurred in the **marketing**, **promotion** or soliciting of orders for a film; and
- **print costs** in relation to a film incurred after the completion date.

Previously, the cost of acquisition of a film was included under the definition of 'production cost' and qualified for the accelerated write-off under the previous version of s24F. It has become clear that this allowance was used by some persons who are involved in transactions with connected persons to artificially increase the value claimed for tax purposes. In order to limit the potential for abuse of the film allowance, the acquisition cost of a film acquired directly or indirectly from a connected person is now expressly limited to the cost of acquisition or the actual production cost incurred in producing the film, whichever is lower.

(d) WHERE do you apply?

SARS can be contacted via their website at www.sars.gov.za, or at their address as follows:

299 Bornkhorst Street
Nieuw Muckleneuk, Pretoria, 0181
or
Private Bag X923, Pretoria,
0001, South Africa

IV. NATIONAL FILM AND VIDEO FOUNDATION

(a) WHAT is available?

The **NFVF** is a statutory body formed to encourage and develop the local film industry. The NFVF provides to eligible applicants funding assistance in the field of education and training, and development funding.

(b) WHO can apply?

Independent South African-owned production companies with **reasonable experience**, or **writers** who hold exclusive rights or options for at least a period of 24 months. The NFVF will support new and emerging filmmakers only in the production of documentaries and short films and where those parties have production companies attached.

(c) HOW do you qualify?

The NFVF will, in its discretion, consider applications based on the **likelihood** of the project reaching its target audience, the likelihood of the project obtaining production finance and local and international distribution intent. Preference is shown to products with local creative control and local distribution intent.

In the case of a co-production, **recoupment** will only apply to the South African distribution component.

The following principles must be in place in order to qualify for production funding:

- Credible **track record** in production;
- **Distribution intent** or **financial commitment** from other partners, particularly theatrical or video distributors and broadcasters;
- Guaranteed **rural** or **township** exposure on screen;
- Language **diversity;**
- Proven commitment to **empowerment** and **training** in pre- and post-production as well as during production;
- Technical **production standards** that are of broadcast quality, consistent with international film distribution trends;
- **South African** perspectives and leading roles for South African actors; and
- In the case of **co-productions**, South African involvement in production must be at least **50 per cent** or meet the requirements of the relevant co-production treaty.

(d) WHERE do you apply?

For further information or to obtain an application form for funding visit the NFVF website at www.nfvf.co.za or contact them by phone on +27 (0)11 483 0880.

SOUTH KOREA

Prepared with the assistance of AJU International Law Group (www.ajulaw.com)

I. INTRODUCTION

The Korean film industry has grown dramatically since the 1990s. In particular, the *Promotion of the Motion Pictures Industry Act of 1995* ('the Act') has been a major trigger of growth for independent filmmaking, providing filmmakers with access to public funding. These grants are also available for international co-productions with a South Korean entity as one of the parties, but such grants are generally available for a maximum of two international co-productions each year. In October 2006, South Korea signed its first legally-binding international co-production treaty with France.

The basic purpose of the **Korea Film Council** (**KOFIC**)'s financial support is to enhance the Korean film industry by encouraging Korean producers to make films which might otherwise be under-financed without the financial support from the Council.

Today, the major source of film production capital still comes from private investors, with other financial institutions such as banks still reluctant to lend. Individual investment is typically made through a collective investment association.

II. PUBLIC MONEY FOR INTERNATIONAL CO-PRODUCTIONS

(a) WHAT is available?

In order to attract more foreign investment into the Korean motion picture industry, every year two international co-productions can receive financial support of up to **50% of the production budget in cash**, subject to a KW200m (US$200,000) cap. For these purposes, the budget must not include any office rent or operational costs, script copyright or development fees, print production costs, or publicity and marketing costs. After the financial support is approved, 70% of the amount granted will be immediately available to the producer at the start of production, and the rest will be remitted during the second half of production.

In October 2006, South Korea entered its first international co-production treaty with France, allowing an official Korean-French co-production to

benefit from domestic or 'national' film status in both countries.

(b) WHO can apply?

The **Korean co-producer** who is properly registered as a professional film producer in accordance with the Act should be the one to apply for the grant.

(c) HOW do you qualify?

The co-production must involve two or more entities from two different countries with at least one being from South Korea. The registered Korean co-producer should additionally file for the approval for 'co-production' status from the KOFIC, who will consider the application in accordance with KOFIC's regulations. KOFIC has lengthy regulation relating to qualification for both international co-production and Art Film status. The basic requirements for the grants are that the film must be made for **theatrical exhibition**, and the co-production should be evidenced by a **contract** (or planned contract) between at least one overseas production company and a local entity. KOFIC financial support will not be granted if the participants for the international co-production are owned by the same person. Further, net production cost of the co-production should be less than KW3,000m (approx. US$3m) and a foreign producer's investment proportion shall accord with the Act (specifically, Article 4 of the enforcement regulation). For example, to qualify as an official co-production with France, investments from each country need to be no less than **20%** and no more than **80%** from either side.

(d) WHERE do you apply?

The application must be submitted to the **KOFIC** at the pre-production (planning and before principal photography) stage.

KOFIC
206-46, Cheongnyangni-dong, Dongdaemun-gu, Seoul, Korea (130-010)
F: +82 2 9587 500
www.kofic.or.kr

III. PUBLIC MONEY FOR INDEPENDENT FILMS

(a) WHAT is available?

The KOFIC also provides **non-repayable** financial support for local independent filmmakers who have *not* registered as a professional film producer in accordance with the Act. The support can cover all costs, including the purchase of film and/or DV tapes, rent for equipment, recording, lighting, costs of transportation, labour, and location accommodation. There is a **cap**, determined by the film's running time. A film running less than one hour is entitled up to KRW20m (approx. US$20,000), and up to **KRW40m** (approx. US$40,000) if over an hour. Each project can receive up to **50%** of the **net production cost**. Financial support is available at the pre-production stage (planning and before principal photography), as well as at post-production stage (during or after principal photography). The intellectual property of the completed film is left with the applicant or producer(s).

(b) WHO can apply?

Any Korean national producing an independent film is eligible for KOFIC's financial support. However, if an applicant falls within the definition of a 'movie enterpriser' in accordance with the Act, it *cannot* qualify for the grant. Under the Act, a 'movie enterpriser' means a person generally engaging in film production for business purposes, which would imply that the support is only available for new entrants to the business.

Although KOFIC's instruction materials do not explicitly state that the financial support for independent film production will be granted only to South Korean nationals, a foreign national would be unlikely to enjoy support from KOFIC considering its fundamental purpose is to encourage Korean independent film production.

(c) HOW do you qualify?

The fund is available for any individual producing an independent film of any genre, with the exception of animation and certain HD films. The application for the fund can be filed any time during the period of planning and production of the film (ie. pre- and post-production). A 'completed' film, however, can not qualify.

(d) WHERE do you apply?

The application should be filed with the **KOFIC**. The submitted documents should include a plan for the film production, proposed financial statement, resume and self-introduction of the applicant, scenario and synopsis of the film, and storyboard or continuity of the film. The applications are accepted and evaluated by a committee once every six months. (see above for KOFIC address).

SWEDEN

I. INTRODUCTION

Swedish film production has increased in the last few years. Of the total 43 theatrical releases in the two years to December 2006, ten in 2005 and seven in 2006 were long documentaries. The domestic films' market share is in the 20–25% range.

The Swedish Film Institute, a foundation created in 1963 by the Swedish State and the film and media industry, administers all national financial support for film production in Sweden. There are currently no tax incentives available in Sweden.

II. PUBLIC MONEY

(a) WHAT is available?

The support available from the **Swedish Film Institute** totals approximately €27m annually. Within the legal framework of the regulations for support for film production, the Swedish Film Institute operates various schemes, such as those for feature films, shorts and documentaries, box office bonuses and development support.

The average support for feature films is around **25% of the production budget**. The average production budget is around €2m, so the average level of support is around **€0.5m**.

There are also **three regional funds** which co-finance Swedish and international productions.

(b) WHO can apply?

Production companies producing a 'Swedish film' can apply. A film is deemed to be Swedish provided that it has a **Swedish producer** and that the contribution of Swedish artists is of obvious importance. A Swedish producer is defined as a person **residing in** Sweden or a company **registered in Sweden**. The best and easiest way to benefit from the Swedish Film Institute's support system is through and together with a **Swedish producer**.

(c) HOW do you qualify?

The regulations do not exclude the possibility of a film shot mainly in a **language** other than Swedish receiving support. Decisions on support in such cases shall pay particular attention to the number of people participating in the artistic and technical work, the film's language, the location where the film is shot, and other factors of benefit to the **Swedish film culture**.

The **financial contribution** shall be in proportion to the involvement of Swedish ar .

In evaluating the project, the Institute conside. the artistic merits and the circulation / distribution potential.

(d) WHERE do you apply?

Applications should be submitted to the **Swedish Film Institute**. Applications should contain CVs of the company and the director, the Script, Production budget, Timetable, and Financing plan. It is a rolling scheme, so applications may be made at any time with no deadlines.

Swedish Film Institute
PO Box 27126
102 52 Stockholm
Sweden
T: +46 8 665 11 00
www.sfi.se
Info@sfi.se

III. OTHER USEFUL CONTACTS

Swedish Broadcasting Commission:
www.grn.se

Regional: Film I Väst:
www.filmivast.se/eng/guide.htm

Nordicom: www.nordicom.gu.se

Nordic Film & TV Fund (Scandinavia): www.nftf.net

So the 'new' UK film tax incentives have finally arrived, in the form of a **tax relief for British qualifying films**. Those of you who read the 2005/06 edition of this *Handbook* will know they've been a long time coming; the initial announcement about the impending demise of 'Sections 48 and 42' (the old system), and the introduction of a new **20% tax credit**, was first made in spring 2004. The British Government, at that time, had become increasingly disillusioned with various alleged 'abuses' of the incumbent system, and in particular felt that investors and so-called 'middlemen' were creaming off much of the benefit that had originally been intended for producers.

Hence the idea was to replace these incentives, and the 'sale & leaseback' mini-industry that they had spawned, with a new tax relief system centred around a so-called **enhanced deduction** and **tax credit**, targeted solely for the benefit of producers. The 'headline' for this new system was that:

'producers will receive an additional tax deduction of up to 80% of qualifying expenditure, amounting to a net benefit to the producer of up to 20% of qualifying production costs'

(For larger budget films — over £20m — the additional deduction is reduced, giving a maximum net benefit of 16%.)

The basic idea is that, subject to various conditions, caps, qualification tests, and so on, you get back from the government approximately 20% of what you spent in the UK on making the film. As we pointed out in the previous edition of this *Handbook*, the Government's initial proposals were littered with flaws and problems, and would never have provided the producers with the headline **20% benefit** that had been promised. But over the next couple of years, various consultation processes and revisions to the outline proposals finally resulted in legislation that seems generally to provide for a much more reasonable set of regulations.

The *Finance Act 2006*, which was passed by Parliament in the summer of 2006, sets out the regulations in detail and, despite still not quite providing the producer with the full 20% towards financing his/her budget, has broadly been welcomed by most of the industry.

To the extent that there are still a number of issues requiring clarification, the Government's **Department of Culture, Media and Sport** (**DCMS**) official **Guidance Notes** (which superseded the original published FAQs) are being continually revised, and go some way to clear up some of the outstanding detail. These and other useful publications are available on the British Government's websites. From 1 April 2007, the **UK Film Council** (**UKFC**) took over from the DCMS in dealing with British Film qualification (see below). It is anticipated that most web-based information on policy, etc, will also move across to the UKFC, but in the meantime, the Cultural Test link on the following recently updated page is a good starting point:

www.culture.gov.uk/what_we_do/Creative_industries/film

Her Majesty's Revenue and Customs (HMRC) film website is www.hmrc.gov.uk/films, and they deal with the tax aspects. The legislation itself is created by HM Treasury and information about its implementation (including the original Budget announcements, draft legislation and explanatory notes) can be found by searching for 'film' and 'Finance Act 2006' on www.hm-treasury.com, and the Finance Act itself is available on the relevant page of the Government's publications website:

http://www.opsi.gov.uk/acts/acts2006/20060025.htm.

The UK Film Council, who from 1 April 2007 will be administering the British Cultural Test and official co-production qualification, also has useful information on its website, www.ukfilmcouncil.org.uk. Search for 'tax relief' for information on the new tax credit scheme.

It can be quite tricky working your way around these websites, particularly as superseded and obsolete information is often thrown up in searches due to the requirement to keep archived information available online. In particular, note that the Cultural Test used for the definition of a British Film was changed *after* the *Finance Act 2006* was passed (as a result of to EU State Aid requirements), and so those regulations, and their various supporting and explanatory documents, therefore had to be amended. The new system came into force effectively on 1 January 2007, and this Section of this *Handbook* refers to the law as it stands on that date and to films commencing principal photography thereafter. For films which started prior to 1 January 2007 but after 31 March 2006 (when the old section 48 effectively ended), there are various transitional regulations in place, and it is suggested that specific technical and legal advice is sought to ensure qualification for either the old or new system, so as not to fall into an intermediate 'black hole'.

One other very important thing to note is the **outlawing** of so-called **GAAP fund**s by the British Government in March 2007. These were funds that used generally accepted accounting principles, rather than a dedicated film-specific tax incentive, in order to achieve reductions in tax bills for their investors. The workings of GAAP funds generally are discussed in more detail in Chapter 3 of this *Handbook*, but suffice it to say for now that, unless or until the financial whiz-kids come up with a new way to beat the system, they are **no longer** a **legitimate** source of UK funding for your movie, so beware.

Regarding the new rebate, however, and as for the other jurisdictions covered in this Chapter, we explain below what's available, who will benefit, what will (or won't) qualify under the rules, and how they will be implemented. As a large proportion of our readership has traditionally been either based in the UK and/or specifically interested in making British qualifying films, we do go into a little more detail for you in this Section. We include a few numerical examples and a simple Glossary of some of the terms introduced by the legislation. Of course the following is not intended as an exhaustive or thorough legal description of the new legislation, and any person looking to benefit from the tax incentives available is strongly advised to take legal, tax and accounting advice from his or her professional advisers.

UK Film Council Funding

Please note that, although the sums available are substantial to be considered 'financial incentives', the **UK Film Council funding** schemes are covered in some depth in Part III of this *Handbook*,, and so we have not repeated the detail in this Section.

Before we start, some brief UK facts and figures

It is claimed that the film industry contributed £3.1bn to the British economy in 2004, providing the Government with £850m in juicy tax revenues. In 2005, eight of the UK's 20 biggest box office hits were technically home-grown, and the UK reportedly has the **fastest growing** film industry of the so-called 'developed nations', currently lying fifth worldwide behind only Russia, China, India and Mexico.

UK production spending increased 48% in 2006 from £569m to £840m, with inward investment rising 80% £570m (over US$1.1bn). The number of features with budgets over £500,000 (approx $1m) increased slightly from 124 to 134, with approximately one fifth (27) being foreign inward investment films, two-fifths (57) UK co-productions and two-fifths (50) UK national films. Of these UK features, total spend was actually down 11% on the year, to £148m, but UK spend on co-productions was up 35% to £123m. However, there is still some way to go to get back to 2003 levels, where *Troy*, *Bridget Jones: Edge of Reason* and *Harry Potter and the Prisoner of Azkaban* contributed towards a massive £1.1bn UK production spend.

An average of ten films are released in the UK each week (505 in 2006, up from 467 in 2005), with an average of £600k (US$1.2m) per film spent on P&A (prints and advertising). More than 10% of these films (53) were 'Bollywood' pictures. UK box office has stayed static in 2005 and 2006 at around the £770m (US$1.5bn) mark, with about 12% of all tickets purchased being for one of *Casino Royale* or *Pirates of the Caribbean: Dead Man's Chest*, which did about £50m each at the box office. A further 17% of ticket sales were for animated features.

The UK currently has **Co-production treaties** with **Australia**, **Canada**, **France**, **New Zealand** and **Norway**. The treaties with Germany and Italy have been terminated as they have effectively been replaced by the *European Convention*, and the treaty with Norway is also due to terminate on 24 May 2007 (during the Cannes Film Market). The treaty with **South Africa** was signed in Cannes 2006 but, at the time of writing, had still not yet been ratified by the UK Parliament, and was therefore not yet in force. Likewise, the first part of a treaty with **India** has been signed, but it will not become enforceable until the second part is also agreed. Check the Film Council website for details. Following the February 2005 announcement of the intention to enter treaties with **Jamaica**, **China** and **Morocco**, negotiations are currently underway and you should keep an eye on the press for their implementation dates.

II. WHAT IS AVAILABLE?

The new incentive system has two major differences from the previous regime. First, a fundamental change to the qualification criteria for a '**British Film**', and second, a change to the tax incentives available to those films that do qualify.

In essence, the new incentive is a tax credit providing the producer with a repayment of up to 20% of the film's budget following completion, providing the film and the relevant expenditure qualify as 'British' under the regulations. In fact, the 20% is calculated as a 25% credit on (up to) 80% of the film's qualifying expenditure, as explained in more detail below.

Technically, the tax relief is split into two parts:

(i)   a **basic treatment**; and

(ii)   the **special film relief**.

The *basic treatment* covers new accounting rules dealing with films generally. It puts film investment on a 'revenue' (rather than capital) basis, and sets out how taxable income should be calculated and what can — and can't — be included as legitimate expenses. It draws the link between the costs and revenues involved in film-making, and standard accounting practice for calculating income, profit and (therefore) tax. This is covered in 'Schedule Four And The Basic Treatment', below.

The *special film relief* — which we look at first — is the 'extra bit', the specific film incentive the UK industry waited so long to hear about. It gives the producer two options, either an **80% enhancement of allowable expenses** to set against profits, or a **20% tax credit**.

III. WHO GETS THE BENEFIT?

The legal person entitled to the new special relief benefits is **the producer**, or more specifically, the **film production company** (or 'FPC'). This is the company responsible — and actively engaged in the planning and decision making — for the pre-production, principal photography and post-production (these being the **core production activities**) of the film. The FPC is the entity that directly negotiates, contracts and pays for rights, goods and services required for the production, and so will normally be the producer's regular production company, or a special company set up solely for the purpose of producing the relevant film. It doesn't have to deal with *all* the rights, or even *all* the negotiations, so it is quite feasible for (say) a studio parent to negotiate various terms on its behalf. Note that there is no requirement for the ownership of the master negative or copyright. There can't be more than one FPC per film (although there could be none) so, in the event of more than one possible company, it will be the one ultimately 'most responsible' for the core production activities.

In an official co-production, the FPC will be the UK co-producer, assuming it's not contributing just finance to the film. There are no provisions referring to the taxation of individuals or partnerships that produce films, and so they won't benefit from the new tax treatments. For certainty, therefore, it is imperative always to produce through a limited company (FPC).

IV. HOW DOES A FILM QUALIFY?

The special film relief is available for any film that satisfies four separate conditions. It must:

(i) be intended for **theatrical** release;

(ii) qualify as a '**British Film**' under the amended Schedule 1 of the *Films Act 1985*;

(iii) have the requisite **minimum** amount of UK incurred **core expenditure**; and

(iv) commence principal photography on or after **1 January 2007**.

(i) 'A film intended for theatrical release...'

This means exhibition to the paying public in a commercial cinema with a view thereby to earning a significant proportion of the film's total income. Theatrical release must be the FPC's intention from the outset, when the *film-making* activities begin (this means at the start of development! — see below), rather than at completion (as was the case under previous legislation). Accordingly, a film that is initially commissioned for TV will not qualify even if, during production, it is decided to 'promote' it to a theatrical release. This condition would have ruled out award winning films such as *Gods and Monsters*, *Mrs Brown* and *Death of a President* which, although successful at the box office, were initially commissioned for TV. Conversely, if a film does not ultimately end up in the cinemas, despite initial intentions that it should, it will still meet this qualification condition (provided the intention remains throughout production — see below). Quite how one demonstrates this 'intent' (perhaps just obtaining sales estimates on a finished script will suffice), and whether the tax authorities will believe it, is somewhat open to question. If film production continues into a second or subsequent accounting period, the theatrical intention must be present at the beginning of each period in order for relief to be granted in respect of expenditure incurred for that period. Note that a *series* of films constituting a self-contained work (or series of common-themed documentaries) with a total playing time of under 26 hours, and with less than 26 episodes, is treated as a single film, but as it must be intended for theatrical release, this would rule out TV series.

(ii) '…which qualifies as a British Film,…'

The definition of a British Film was changed significantly in November 2006, long after the original guidelines and legislation were published, so be careful what documents you read when looking at qualification criteria. The correct publication to setting out the qualification criteria for a 'British Film is the *Films (Definition of 'British Film') (No 2) Order 2006*, which came into force on 1 January 2007 and modifies the old *Schedule 1* to the *Films Act 1985*. Don't confuse this with the earlier, similarly named, *Films (Definition of a British Film) Order 2006*, which was dated 31 March 2006, and contains a 'new' British Film test that in the end was never really used (due to problems with EU State Aid requirements).

In order to obtain the tax relief, the FPC will need to present the tax authorities with a certificate of qualification as a 'British Film' from the DCMS, which grants the certificates following recommendation by the UKFC, who administers the application process. The Producer can receive an interim certificate, superseded by a final certificate on completion. This may help, for example, where production carries on into a subsequent accounting period, and tax relief is sought for both periods. The legislation provides for a two-tier test for a British Film (note the old 'maker' test no longer applies).

First, there is a new points-based '**Cultural Test**' similar to (but somewhat more complicated than) that of the *European Convention on Cinematographic Co-Productions*. And second, the original '**archive footage**' test still will apply (having not been modified by the new regulations). Taking the two parts in turn…

THE CULTURAL TEST

Under the new *Cultural Test*, the film itself will have to score at least 16 points out of a possible 31 (subject to a 'Golden Points' rule, explained at the end). To score a point, the relevant element of the film typically has to be *British*. As you will see, the administrative burden on producers wishing to demonstrate the 'Britishness' of their films is going to be fairly substantial! The Cultural Test is split into four sections, although a film does not have to score points in each section so long as it scores the aggregate of 16 points in total.

Section A — Cultural Content

This section received a huge overhaul in November 2006, a little more than six months after the original Cultural Test legislation was published (but before it came into force). It provides for a maximum possible **sixteen points**.

A1 Story Setting

Up to four points are available if the story is set in the UK, on the following basis:

1 point if more than 25% pages of the script are set in the UK

2 points if more than 50% pages of the script are set in the UK

3 points if more than 66% pages of the script are set in the UK

4 points if more than 75% pages of the script are set in the UK

A fictionalised version of the UK will count, but not a generic fictional setting. Note that it is the setting of the story which is relevant, and not where the film is shot.

A2 Lead Characters

Another four points are available for the lead characters. The Revised Guidance notes are particularly complicated on this part of the test, and need to be read very carefully (they should be updated periodically to clarify issues, so feel free to contact the DCMS or UKFC if you find them confusing!). We assume that where there is an ambiguity as to how many points should be awarded, the maximum possible points will be allowed, but this has not yet been confirmed as formal policy.

So, where there are at least four characters generally in the storyline, the points are ascribed as follows:

1 point if 1 of the *3 lead* characters is British

2 points if 1 of the *2 lead* characters is British

4 points if at least 2 of the *3 lead* characters are British

The number of 'leads' (whether British or not) clearly has an impact on the number of points available, and whether a character is a 'lead' or not depends on the centrality and prominence it has to the story (whereas under the European Convention, it is determined by the number of days worked). Take for example a film with four characters, where the obvious lead is British, as is one of the lesser three characters. If that lesser character is also considered a 'lead', then 4 points will be available (2 of the 3 leads being British). If not, it will depend on how many of two non-Brits are considered 'leads'. If one, then the film will score 2 points, and if both, the film will only score 1. If none of them are considered 'leads', leaving just one lead character, the Guidance is silent on how many points will be scored!

The situation gets even more complicated if there are less than four overall characters. If there are three characters in the film, the number of available points is as follows:

1 point if 1 of the 3 characters is British

2 points if 1 of the 2 *lead* characters is British

4 points if 2 of the 3 characters are British

Clearly there is a potential discrepancy here if 2 of the characters are British but only 1 of them is a 'lead', as it satisfies the test for both 2 and 4 points. The DCMS says it wishes in due course to conform its guidelines in relation to lead and non-lead characters, so you should check the current Guidance Notes, which are periodically updated, if this is an issue for you. Likewise check the UKFC's website. So, moving on, if there are only two characters, the points go like this:

2 points if 1 is British

4 points if both are British

As you might imagine, if there is only one character in the film and s/he is British, the film will score all **4 points**. If it is not apparent from the film whether or not a particular character is British, the applicant will be required to explain why it should be considered as such.

A3 Subject Matter or Underlying Material
4 points are awarded if either the *subject matter* (even if the events don't actually take place in the UK) or the *writer* of the underlying material (book, play, script, game, etc) is British. The Guidance Notes are silent as to how much of the subject matter needs to be British, or what happens where there is more than one writer.

A4 Language of Dialogue
The final four points in this section are awarded if the dialogue (including narrative) is in a recognised British language which, in addition to English, includes the official minor and/or regional languages of **Scottish-Gaelic**, **Welsh**, **Irish**, **Scots**, **Ulster Scots** and **Cornish**. The points are awarded in

accordance with the proportion of total words in the script as follows:

1 point if at least 25% of the total words are in a British language

2 points if at least 50% of the total words are in a British language

3 points if at least 66% of the total words are in a British language

4 points if at least 75% of the total words are in a British language

If a film scores all sixteen points in Section A, it will automatically qualify as a British Film, even though there may be no British actors, crew, locations, or production facilities or labs. This is clearly a diversion from the old thinking as to what constitutes a truly British film! However, apart from the tax relief (where the other three arms of the test still have to be passed, including a minimum 25% UK spend), the only other significant benefits available to British qualifying films are various grants and awards, and the right to be entered into certain British festivals.

Section B — Cultural Contribution

This section was added in November 2006, many months after the original 'new' Cultural Test was published. It offers up to **four points** if the film can be shown to contribute to the *'promotion, development and enhancement of British Culture'*, by reflecting or representing cultural diversity, cultural heritage and creativity.

Creativity
Points are awarded for creativity and innovation in any of cinematography, music, animation, visual effects and special effects on the following basis:

1 point for a significant degree of innovation (creativity)

2 points for an outstanding degree of innovation (creativity)

Cultural Heritage
Points are given for a contribution to, or reflection of, British cultural heritage, which involves British cultural perspectives, modern and ancient history, and an interpretation of the past and/or future. Again, points are awarded as follows:

1 point for a significant representation or reflection of British cultural heritage

2 points for an outstanding representation or reflection of British cultural heritage

Cultural Diversity

Points are given for exploring diversity issues relating to gender, ethnicity, national origin, religion, beliefs, age, sexuality, disability, and social / economic background, and how these issues (whether portrayed in the film itself or emanating from key contributors to the film) have had a significant impact on the film's final content. The number of points is awarded as follows:

1 point for a significant representation or reflection of British cultural diversity

2 points for an outstanding representation or reflection of British cultural diversity

Note that although there are a total of six individual points available from these three categories, the maximum number that can be actually be awarded under this Section B is capped at four. At the time of going to press, the DCMS was still finalising its initial Guidance on this section.

Section C — Cultural Hubs

This section covers money (or, in the case of principal photography, time) spent on the film making activities themselves. The more that take place in the UK, the more points you score. You will see that the amount of work that needs to go into calculating the relevant allocation of UK and non-UK time and money spent is arguably rather large in comparison with the total of only **3 points** that are available under this section.

Whether something 'takes place' in the UK or not depends on where services are performed and from where goods are supplied, and the relevant production costs should be allocated accordingly. If an apportionment needs to be done, it should be done with reference to time spent in or out of the UK in carrying out the particular service. Payments for UK living expenses (such as hotels) will be included, whereas non-UK ones are not, irrespective of the nationality of the person for whom the money is spent. Certain facts are expressly treated as irrelevant, such as the nationality or residency of service providers, where or by whom they are actually paid, or the currency of payment.

C1 Principal Photography / Visual Effects / Special Effects

Principal Photography (which does not include any second unit work) is measured solely on a daily rather than money-spent basis. Visual effects means any digital alteration to a film's images, by way of digital creation, recording or manipulation of the individual frames. It does not include editing. Special effects are any other techniques or processes creating an illusion in a film. In relation to these three activities, points are awarded on the following basis:

2 points if at least 50% of *any one* of the above three activities is carried out in the UK

C2 Music recording / audio post / picture post

For these purposes, music recording means commissioned rather than out-sourced music, and picture post relates to editing, copying and preparing the various forms of negatives and prints (but not 'effects' work, see C1 above). The one point available is awarded in relation to these three activities as follows:

1 point if at least 50% of *any one* of the above three activities is carried out in the UK

Section D — Cultural Practitioners

To score one of the **eight points** available under this section, the relevant person has to be a UK or EU (including EEA) citizen or resident, ie. a national of one of those countries or 'ordinarily resident' there (which does *not* include residing there simply for the purposes of making the film!). The points are allocated if (any of) the following people qualify:

1 point for the *lead* director

1 point for a scriptwriter (or any one of the three *lead* scriptwriters if more than three)

1 point for a producer (or any one of the three *lead* producers if more than three)

1 point for the composer (or the *lead* composer if more than one)

1 point for an actor (or any one of the three *lead* actors if more than three)

1 point for the majority of the cast (including stunt actors but not extras)

1 point for a 'Key Staff', ie. heads of department (see below)

1 point for the majority of the crew

The relevant departments for the Key Staff point are production design, costume design, editing, sound design, visual effects, and hair & make-up. If the head of any one of these departments qualifies, the point will be awarded. The point awarded to crew will be given if at least 50% of the production crew (meaning those who are credited, directly contracted to the production, perform services on the film itself, and are recognised PACT/BECTU members) qualify.

Golden Points Rule

Just when you thought the whole thing was complicated enough, but it appears your film qualifies, you then have to take into account the 'Golden Rule' which might still disqualify it. This rule applies to films which score all 15 points available in Sections A4 (language), C (hubs) and D (practitioners), but less than two points (ie. one or none) in both A1 (setting) and A2 (characters). The Golden Rule says that such films must also qualify for the four points available under Section A3 (story) in order to pass, even if without them it would still have the otherwise requisite 16 points.

THE ARCHIVE FOOTAGE TEST

Last, in order to qualify as a British Film, the *archive footage test* must also be satisfied. There are no new Guidance Notes on this, so it is assumed that the rules requiring no more than 10% archive footage (other than for documentaries) will apply as they always have done.

(iii) '...has the requisite amount of core expenditure incurred in the UK...'

Not less than **25%** of the *core expenditure* of the film, being money spent on pre-production, principal photography and post-production (see below for more information), must be spent *in the United Kingdom* by the FPC (or in the case of an official co-production, by the co-producers in aggregate). Note that core expenditure does *not* include development, so the question will arise as to whether items such as script commissioning, re-writing or polishing will be included. The HMRC's current official line is that the FPC will have to make the case to its tax inspector, but ultimately it is likely that standard guidance will be put in place for the sake of conformity.

The figure of 25% has been reduced from the 40% originally proposed in order to allow more films to qualify probably to bring the threshold closer to the minimum for most official co-productions. For these purposes, as in previous legislation, the definition of a *film* includes the soundtrack to it.

(iv) '...and commences principal photography on or after 1 January 2007.'

Simply, a film that started principal photography before 1 January 2007 will have to rely on the old

section 48 (or, for post 31 March 2006 films, section 42) regime, as it will not qualify for the new relief. However, the old system only covers films completed by 1 January 2007 or acquired by 1 October 2007, so if the film does not comply with either of these criteria, it could potentially fall outside the tax benefit net altogether. There are therefore transitional regulations in place to ensure that, at worst, a film will still be able to rely on s42 (even if not s48) of the old system. Any producer concerned about this should take specific legal advice.

V. HOW MUCH DO I GET?

New rules for tax treatment, including the 'additional deduction' (a.k.a. 'enhancement')

The simplest way to describe this is that a film costing £10m (such as our *Film A* example below), if it can claim the full additional deduction of £8m, will be deemed to have spent a total of £18m. Put crudely, it is this excess of £8m that can alternatively be exchanged for a tax credit. Naturally, it's not quite that simple, but hopefully the following explanation will take you through the process step by step, and describe the main issues that need to be understood by a producer looking to utilise the UK tax incentives.

So, if a film passes the four point test above (theatrical intention, British qualifying, 25% UK core expenditure and eligible start date), it will qualify for the new UK tax relief, which we know should be worth up to 20% of the film's budget (or 16% for bigger pictures). In order to qualify for this maximum relief, the producer must make sure that all the FPC's relevant expenditure qualifies. Where it doesn't all qualify, the producer needs to be able to calculate with some degree of certainty how much of a credit the FPC will get, especially if it is being discounted for production funding purposes.

The first point to note is that the FPC can only obtain the tax credit if it chooses to 'swap' its 'losses' for it. So before being able to work out how much the credit will be, it first needs to calculate how much losses it will have (this determines the level of credit, 20% being the maximum). The computation of film companies' losses is one area which has changed considerably under the new legislation.

As you will probably know, at the end of each accounting year, the FPC will have to submit its tax return to HMRC declaring its profit or loss. It will of course pay taxes on its profits, or alternatively carry forward, backwards or sideways any losses, in accordance with standard accounting practice. The new legislation updates these rules on computing profits and losses (and what can be done with the losses) in relation to film income and expenditure. This new regime for the general tax treatment of films (the '**basic treatment**') is set out in *Schedule Four* to the *Finance Act 2006*, and the new rules and their effect are covered towards the end of this Section (see below).

However, in order to calculate the tax credit, the bit you will probably want to know about first is the so-called '**additional deduction**' (also known as the **enhancement**).

This is the artificial amount that an FPC can effectively *add* to its actual expenditure, thereby reducing any profit (or creating or increasing a loss), resulting in a lower overall tax bill. If it does show a loss under the new rules, the FPC can 'surrender' part of it in return for receiving the tax credit from HMRC. The greater the loss, the larger the credit. After looking at how the additional deduction is calculated, we will explain how to 'convert' the resulting loss (or part of it) into the tax credit.

Wading through the various definitions to determine what is 'qualifying expenditure'

There is a whole host of new definitions in the new legislation covering different types of activities and expenditure which, at first, can seem quite confusing. The important ones are covered in the Glossary at the end of this Section. However, what you need to know in a nutshell, in order to work out your qualifying expenditure (which is used to calculate the additional deduction), are the following:

Film-making activities are those involved with the development, pre-production, principal photography, post-production of a film.

Production expenditure is expenditure on these film-related activities.

Core expenditure is production expenditure other than that on development.

A **limited-budget film** is one whose core expenditure does not exceed £20m (assuming transactions are on an arm's length basis).

Finally, **qualifying expenditure** is the amount of core expenditure permissible under the general basic treatment accounting rules (see below) when calculating profit and/or loss.

It follows that qualifying expenditure is, in essence, money spent on pre-production, principal photography and post-production. As we mentioned above, quite what constitutes *pre-production* (rather than *development*) expenditure is unclear. This is particularly unhelpful with regard to the timing of underlying rights options and acquisitions (but see below), and to the securing of above-the-line talent. Using 'financial closing' as a trigger date, as some have suggested, would seem inappropriate as pre-production is often well underway by that point. Note that section 41 (*Finance Act (No 2) 1992*), which had dealt specifically with 'preliminary expenditure' (development) has been repealed on the introduction of the new regime. Producers are therefore strongly advised to take professional accounting advice on any tax relief they wish to claim on development from then on.

Another potential worry is the treatment of underlying rights acquisition (eg. buying the film rights to a book) and copyright clearances (licences to use songs, pictures, etc, in the film). Whereas the phrase '*rights*, goods and services' is used elsewhere in the legislation, the definition of 'core expenditure' — which is used to calculate the additional deduction (enhancement) — simply refers to goods and services. There is no mention of money spent on rights so, despite general practice that acquisition rights are part of production rather than development, there is a danger that they will be excluded. Whether the provision of 'services' will be deemed to include rights licences — as they have been for VAT purposes — is unclear, but if not (and this seems to be HMRC's current view), it will reduce further the amount of the additional deduction available (see below).

Note also that the legislation doesn't give any further detail on what constitutes film-related activities generally and that, in particular, it doesn't mention financing or delivery. It is therefore unclear whether financing fees, executive producer fees, completion bond premiums or delivery costs will be included as core, and therefore qualifying, expenditure. However, the legislation does expressly leave the door open for the Government to make further regulations stating that certain specified elements may or may not to be included as film-related activities or (as the case may be) qualifying expenditure. Until that happens, there will be a certain level of uncertainty as to how these costs will be dealt with. Whereas producers generally accept these as standard intrinsic costs of producing their film, the HMRC may or may not conclude that they are in fact 'film-making activities'.

In particular, the existence of a completion bond is, most would argue, an intrinsic part of the production process. The guarantor often provides invaluable advice and direction, thereby increasing the quality of the finished film, and so the bond fee should be included as an expense on a film-making activity. However, there is a worry that HMRC might consider the bond to be a tool solely for the benefit of financiers, and therefore not a 'film-making activity', thereby rendering the bond fee as non-qualifying expenditure. Urgent formal guidance from HMRC on this point will hopefully be forthcoming, to enable proper financial planning.

Calculating the 'additional deduction'

The additional deduction (enhancement) is calculated by multiplying the **rate of enhancement** (being 100% for a limited-budget film, otherwise 80%) by the amount of **qualifying expenditure** that happens to be **UK expenditure**, or 80% of the total qualifying expenditure, whichever is the lower amount.

In other words, qualifying expenditure is capped at 80% (in order to comply with EU State Aid regulations) even if the UK expenditure proportion of the budget exceeds this. It follows that, if the film is 100% made in the UK, only 80% of the expenditure can be used in calculating the enhancement. For these purposes, **UK expenditure** is defined as any expenditure on goods or services used or consumed in (or fairly and reasonably apportioned to) the United Kingdom. It follows that 'British produced' films, to the extent that they are shot outside the UK, will not qualify for an enhancement, notwithstanding the fact that they may use 100% British cast and crew whilst abroad, or that they qualify as British Film under the Cultural Test. This will incentivise producers to use local crew on foreign shoots, especially as they are often less expensive and, of course, don't incur such heavy travel costs (although outbound travel costs may be included). It would knock out 'British' productions such as *Lawrence of Arabia*, *The English Patient*, *The Constant Gardener*, and *Hideous Kinky* from qualifying under the new rules, if those films

had been made today. Conversely, however, 'foreign produced' films that are shot in Britain and that meet the other conditions *will* qualify for the enhancement. Confusion may also arise as to whether or not in fact the supply of goods or, in particular, performance of services, indeed occurs in the UK (eg. equipment rented from the UK but used abroad will probably be excluded, whereas costumes made abroad but used in the UK will be included). These issues are covered more thoroughly in its Cultural Test Guidelines, and perhaps (hopefully?) the same interpretation will be used also by HMRC.

In a world where UK producers want to make international stories, these elements have arguably been the most contentious part and biggest disappointment of the new tax regime.

An Example

So, to take an example *Film A*, costing £10m (ignoring development and any other excluded costs) and made wholly in the UK, the additional deduction would be 100% (the rate of enhancement for a limited-budget film) of the qualifying expenditure, being the UK expenditure capped at 80% of the total £10m, in other words £8m. This means, effectively, that the FPC will *be deemed to have spent £18m* on the film (£12m plus the £8m enhancement). For a £30m film, *Film B*, of which half was spent in the UK, the additional deduction would be 80% (the rate of enhancement for larger films) of £15m (the UK qualifying expenditure), in other words £12m. Note that if *Film B* was made entirely in the UK, the qualifying expenditure would be capped at £24m (80% of the total), and the additional deduction would therefore be £24m multiplied by 80% (being the relevant rate of enhancement), in other words £19.2m, or 64% of the budget.

For *Film A*, we said that the entire spend was in the UK (and was therefore 'qualifying expenditure'), and so it got the maximum enhancement of £8m. If, however, only 50% was spent in the UK (thereby below the 80% cap), the enhancement would be 50% of the budget, ie £5m, and so on. You will recall that the minimum UK spend to qualify for the

Worked example

	Film A (£10m)		Film B (£30m)	
Percentage spend in the UK	100%	50%	100%	50%
Qualifying expenditure (capped at 80%)	£8m	£5m	£24m	£15m
Rate of enhancement	100%	100%	80%	80%
Additional deduction	£8m	£5m	£19.2m	£12m

special film relief is 25%, so that is the minimum enhancement available.

Surrendering losses in return for the tax credit

Remember that the additional deduction (enhancement) calculated above represents the extra expenditure that the FPC is deemed to have spent when calculating its profits / losses. These enhanced losses are a very useful tool to reduce a tax bill when they can be carried over to other periods or transferred to other group companies. However, the FPC can choose, instead of simply enhancing its permissible expenditure, to 'surrender' its loss (or part of it) to HMRC in return for a direct cash payment. This is the famed **tax credit**.

The amount of the loss that can be surrendered (the '**surrenderable loss**') is defined as the lesser of (i) the *available* qualifying expenditure (which we'll call '**AQE**', see below), and (ii) the deemed trading loss for the relevant period. The likelihood is that the lower figure will be the AQE, although this might not always be the case. For an explanation of the trading loss calculation, see 'Schedule Four and the Basic Treatment' below.

This is an important point, as a trading loss of an amount less than the AQE (or none at all) would significantly reduce the tax credit available.

In the first year of production, the 'available' qualifying expenditure (**AQE**) is equal to the whole 'qualifying expenditure' referred to above (when we looked at the enhancement calculation). After that, it is of course reduced by any qualifying expenditure that has previously already been used ('enhanced') to create an earlier additional deduction (thereby no longer being 'available' later for surrendering in return for a tax credit).

Note that any surrenderable loss that is not surrendered in any year before completion of the film can be carried forward and offset against the same film (trade), and after completion can be transferred to another British film being made by the same FPC, or by another FPC in the same group, and may, to some extent, be subject to the normal accounting treatment of trade losses, including the use of group relief.

Calculating the Tax Credit

The amount of the tax credit available is calculated by multiplying that part of the **surrenderable loss** that the FPC wishes to surrender by the **payable credit rate**, which is:

25% for limited-budget films, or

20% for other films.

So, assuming for now that the surrenderable loss equals the AQE, we can calculate the maximum possible tax credit available for our example films. This would be £2m for Film A, being 25% of the £8m surrenderable loss. This credit is equal to 20% of the budget, the headline amount. For Film B (£30m budget with half spent in the UK), the maximum credit would be £3m (20% of the £15m surrenderable loss), equal to 10% of its budget, only half the headline amount. If Film B was made 100% in the UK, the tax credit would be worth £4.8m (being 20% of the £24m AQE), or 16% of the budget. This assumes that our example films were produced in a single accounting year, ie. that no additional deduction (enhancement) was made previously.

The receipt of the tax credit is not considered income in the hands of the FPC, and HMRC reserves the right to withhold it if the FPC is in debt to HMRC for (say) income tax (PAYE) in relation to its employees, or if its claim is 'under enquiry'.

VI. HOW AND WHEN DO I RECEIVE THE TAX CREDIT?

The special film relief is normally available in respect of the accounting period in which the DCMS / UKFC have, after checking the production accounts (etc), certified that the 'completed' film has qualified under the British Film conditions. A film is considered completed when it is first *'in a form which can be*

Worked example

	Film A (£10m)		Film B (£30m)	
Percentage spend in the UK	100%	50%	100%	50%
Available qualifying expenditure / trading loss	£8m	£5m	£24m	£15m
Payable credit rate	25%	25%	20%	20%
Maximum tax credit...	£2m	£1.25m	£4.8m	£3m
...as a percentage of budget	20%	12.5%	16%	10%

regarded as ready to be copied and distributed for presentation to the general public', although the relief is also available on a film which has been 'abandoned'. Note that the definition of 'completed' doesn't state 'capable' of being distributed; it means actually 'ready...for the general public', so it should be taken to mean the date of delivery to the sales company rather than of the first test screenings.

However, for the first time, it will now be possible to obtain an interim certificate, possibly coupled with conditions and/or an expiry date. Quite how useful such interim certificates will be for financing purposes is not clear, and it will probably depend on how willing the banks (etc) are to lend against them (see below), particularly as they are revocable under certain circumstances.

That said, if the FPC wishes to claim interim tax relief (prior to completion), most likely because production spans more than one accounting period, it will need an interim certificate.

VII. SO HOW CAN I USE THE TAX CREDIT FOR PRODUCTION FINANCE?

If, taking our £10m *Film A* example, the FPC surrenders all of its available qualifying expenditure (AQE) in return for the tax credit, it could get a cheque for £2m (see above) after completion and certification of the film. This £2m tax credit might be a nice gift for the FPC once the film is completed, but the producers probably would have preferred the money up-front, and to use it as part of the finance for making the film in the first place.

Discounting the tax credit

To do this, the FPC would have to persuade someone (a lender of some sorts) that the film will definitely qualify as British, in order for that someone to lend the FPC some money against 'picking up' the tax credit cheque on completion. Of course, the tax credit is only payable to the FPC, but it can contract with the lender to pay it over once received, as part of — or outside — the recoupment waterfall. It would not be taxable income in the hands of the lender if paid as part of the loan repayment. It will probably be between six months and two years from the date the money is needed for production to the date the tax credit is paid by HMRC. Any amount lent would therefore be less than the full £2m (20% of *Film A*'s budget), as the lender would have to factor in its fees, interest, and the fact that it is potentially

a risky loan as the film may not ultimately qualify for whatever reason.

It's much more likely that the amounts lent in this way will be closer to between 15% and 17% of films' budgets (£1.5m to £1.7m for our example *Film A*). Although this doesn't quite give the producer the 20% headline benefit, it is no coincidence that it is slightly higher than the amounts traditionally available under the previous sale and leaseback regime, and this was always the Government's intention. Of course, it does require some form of financial intermediary to step in to cash-flow the tax credit, which directly conflicts with the Government's much published desire to rid the tax incentive regime of so-called 'middlemen'.

It might take a year or two before the traditional banks are willing to dip their toe in the discounting water, as they will probably first want to see the system working fully and robustly. In particular, if many claims are put 'under enquiry' (see above), causing delays, it would leave the banks somewhat uneasy. However, the HMRC now has up specially trained film tax assessors, which should speed the process up and give producers and their accountants access to officials who actually really do understand the world of film financing. In the meantime, a number of (dare we say it) 'middlemen', such as Don Star's Grosvenor Park and Jim Reeve's International Film Finance are claiming to be offering discounting services for the UK tax credit.

VIII. AT WHAT POINT DO I START PAYING TAX ON THE FILM'S 'PROFITS'?

We'll now take a brief look at the tax position of the FPC itself. The best way to illustrate this is through some simple numerical examples. Let's return to our hypothetical £10m *Film A* from before. It's a limited-budget film made 100% in the UK, and passes the new Cultural Test as a British qualifying film. It follows that it will qualify for the maximum enhancement of 80%, equal to £8m.

The initial position, therefore, is that the FPC is 'deemed' to have spent £18m (£10m to make the film plus the £8m enhancement). Ignoring for now any 'surrender' for the tax credit (we'll look at this later), the FPC can therefore receive a total of **£18m** in income, to match its deemed £18m spend, before making a profit and thereby having to start paying tax.

The important question is when will the FPC be deemed to have received £18m income? To answer this, we need to look at how the film was financed to see how much of that money (received by the FPC in order to make the film in the first place) is considered income. Let's say, for the purposes of our example, that the £10m was fairly typically financed, and made up of:

£3m pre-sales,

£3m equity,

£0.4m deferments,

£2m bank gap, and

£1.6m 'final piece' (which we'll look at later).

And, for simplicity's sake, we'll ignore interest, premiums, commissions, etc, that may be payable during recoupment of the various elements of finance.

The **pre-sales** are clearly **income**, as they are *receipts from the sale of the film or rights in it* (see Schedule Four, below). They are 'sales' in the same way that any company sells its goods or services, and therefore the FPC will be considered to have received income of £3m in this regard. It can therefore only receive a further £15m before paying tax. This income from pre-sales should be deemed received at the time the film is completed and delivered (when the distributor pays up), rather than at the earlier time of the discounting by the bank.

The **bank gap**, on the other hand, is a loan. It has to be repaid, and is therefore **not income** in the hands of the FPC. And despite its name, the '**equity**' funding is also technically a loan as it also has to be repaid, albeit on softer terms than, and ranking behind, the bank. So it too is not considered as income.

The **deferments** were never actually received in the way of cash, so are also **not** considered to be **income**. They can almost be seen as 'loans' to the FPC by the relevant producer(s), actor(s), director, etc.

So far, therefore, the FPC can receive a further £15m (total available £18m less £3m pre-sales) in income from *Film A* before paying tax.

Now let's consider the £1.6m '**final piece**' used to complete the financing of the film. Naturally, if this is additional **equity** or a **loan**, it will not be considered income, and will have to be repaid from receipts from exploitation of the film. On this basis, the FPC would 'break-even' once it has repaid £7m towards financiers' recoupment (£2m to the

bank, £3m in equity, £0.4m deferments and the £1.6m 'final piece'). This means that further post break-even revenues (ie. '**profits**') of **£8m** can be received before any tax liability kicks in (the £8m being the £18m total permitted income less the £3m pre-sales and the £7m received and paid out to financiers to reach break-even). In other words, the FPC can receive a total of £15m in net sales revenues (excluding the financing presales) before paying tax. It is, of course, no coincidence that the £8m permitted tax-free 'profit' is equal to the enhancement (80% of the £10m budget).

If, on the other hand, the 'final piece' of production finance was received in return for some actual **rights in the film** (not just a right to receive income), then just like a pre-sale, it won't have to be repaid, and will be considered income. The total 'income' received in the way of production finance would therefore be £4.6m (£3m pre-sales plus £1.6m final piece), meaning the FPC can then receive a further £13.4m (£18m permitted income less the £4.6m already received) in income before paying tax. Of this, it will have to repay £5.4m to financiers in recoupment (the bank plus the equity plus the deferments), leaving it with an additional post break-even income allowance (ie. tax-free **profits**) of, again, **£8m** (£13.4m less the £5.4m recoupment).

So, however you look at it, after paying off its financiers, the FPC for *Film A* can receive 'profits' (income after recoupment) equal to 80% of its budget before paying tax. This is effectively the additional deduction. But of course that's not the end of the story. The UK Government has acknowledged that this 'final piece' is often difficult to get hold of, and can be the make or break of producing the film. Hence the introduction of the '**tax credit**' element.

Being taxed when the tax credit is used for financing

Now, if an appropriate lender can be found, the discounted tax credit in our example could, if required, be used as the £1.6m '**final piece**'. It would not, of course, be considered 'income' for taxing purposes. If it surrenders its entire AQE for the tax credit, the tax position of the FPC would be as follows. Total production expenditure is £10m, with no 'enhancement' (you can't have both your enhancement and the tax credit!). It can therefore receive an equivalent £10m in total income before going into profit and paying taxes. Income received from financing is £3m (pre-sales only – none of the other forms of production finance were considered 'income'). Total finance to be recouped by the financiers (bank, deferments and equity) is £5.4m. Therefore the amount of tax-free income receivable once the film has broken even is £1.6m (ie. £10m expenditure less £3m financing income and less £5.4m recoupment), which, of course, is equal to the amount of the discounted tax credit 'final piece'.

There are a number of accounting issues which might favour an earlier or later surrender of the AQE for the tax credit, and professional advice should be sought as to how to maximise the available incentives and minimise the FPC's ultimate tax bill(s). One thing is for sure, however, and that is that the sooner any uncertainties in the system are ironed out, the lower the risks for discounting, and the sooner the banks (as opposed to the traditionally more expensive private financial middlemen) will enter the market.

IX. 'SCHEDULE FOUR' AND THE BASIC TREATMENT

Schedule Four of the Finance Bill sets out the general tax treatment (other than that specifically in relation to the enhancement and tax credit) for films which commence principal photography on or after 1 January 2007. It basically explains what can be included as costs, how to calculate income, and therefore how to calculate the profit or loss that the FPC makes (ignoring the enhancement and tax credit), whether or not the film qualifies as British. Without these provisions, the cost of a film would normally be dealt with as a capital investment, rather than expenses that can be written off against income. It is essential to take professional accounting advice on these matters, but below is a very brief summary of the provisions.

Film production as a trade; expenditure, income and profit

Each film produced by an FPC is considered a separate trade. The trade commences at the beginning of pre-production (unless income is received earlier), and any previous development expenditure is deemed to have been spent on the first day of pre-production. The old 'section 48' (and section 42) system treated expenditure on the production or acquisition of a master version of a film as revenue, rather than capital, in nature, and the theme of income-matching rather than capital expenditure has been continued, but only for production (not acquisition).

Under the new regime, the costs in any given accounting period that comprise permissible expenditure on a revenue basis are those incurred on *film-making activities* (see above) together with activities 'with a view to exploiting the film'. Normal exclusions apply, such as entertainment costs and interest.

Income comprises any receipts in connection with the making or exploitation of the film and specifically includes (i) receipts from the sale of the film or rights in it, (ii) royalties, (iii) payments for ancillary rights (games, merchandising, etc), and (iv) receipts of film profits. In determining profit (or loss) for each accounting period, you deduct the costs incurred in the relevant period from an apportioned 'deemed' income. Although to the 'lay' person, *receipts in connection with the making of the film* might sound like it applies to all moneys used to finance the production (including loans, equity, etc), standard accounting practices (in particular SAP 9) will be followed on a 'prudent basis', and receipts will be accounted for if they are not repayable, thereby excluding equity, loans, and so on (see above). Therefore, only revenues actually contracted for (or having an equivalent degree of certainty) will be included as receipts for the purposes of calculating income.

This deemed income is measured by calculating the percentage of total anticipated costs that has actually been spent in the relevant period, and multiplying it by the total amount of income reasonably and fairly expected from the film, considering all the relevant circumstances. For example, if at the end of the relevant period, 74% of all production costs have been spent, the company will be 'deemed' to have received in the same period 74% of its total expected income.

The issue here is how one decides what the *total* expected income is going to be, in order to work out the relevant percentage for the period, and HMRC has now provided draft guidance available on this point (speak to your accountant!). the main point to note, however, to the relief of the production community, is that HMRC has confirmed that sales estimates (projections), normally obtained by the producer prior to production in estimating total income, will not be used to determine total expected income as they are not actual contracted income (so sales will not normally be deemed to be received before they actually are).

Costs are accounted for when the relevant activities are 'represented' in the film (whether or not it's in a completed form), even if they haven't yet been paid. However, such **deferred payments** can only be included where they are (i) unconditional, and (ii) if paid from receipts of the film, a corresponding amount of income is simultaneously brought into account. No costs can be included if payment of them is still outstanding four months after the end of the relevant accounting period.

Finally, there are specific regulations outlawing artificially inflated claims, or arrangements specifically aimed at getting a tax credit that would otherwise not be available.

X. GLOSSARY OF VARIOUS TERMS DEFINED IN THE NEW LEGISLATION

additional deduction the amount of *UK Expenditure* (or, if less, 80% of the total *qualifying expenditure*) multiplied by the *rate of enhancement*.

available qualifying expenditure any *qualifying expenditure* not surrendered in previous accounting periods.

British Film a film certified as such under (modified) *Schedule 1 of the Films Act 1985*.

core expenditure expenditure on pre-production, principal photography and post-production (ie. not development).

enhancement (not to be confused with *rate of enhancement*) the same meaning as *additional deduction*.

film making activities activities on which tax relief is available: development, pre-production, principal photography and post.

film production company the company entitled to benefit from the *special film relief*.

final accounting period the accounting period in which the film is completed (or abandoned).

final certificate the certificate granted after completion of the film, certifying that it qualifies as a *British Film*.

Finance Act the Finance Act 2006, which legislates for the new tax rules brought in by the budget delivered by the Chancellor of the Exchequer in March 2006.

FPC a *film production company*.

interim accounting period any accounting period earlier than the *final period*.

interim certificate a certificate issued by the DCMS certifying that the film will certify as British if completed as planned.

limited budget film a film whose *core expenditure* does not exceed £20m.

payable credit rate 25% for a *limited budget film*, 20% for all other qualifying films.

producer (for the purposes of the Cultural Test), the person who makes the arrangements necessary for making the film, being the FPC.

qualifying co-producer the person who is the UK co-producer on a *qualifying co-production*.

qualifying co-production a co-production made under a UK Co-production Treaty or the European Convention on Cinematographic Co-production.

qualifying expenditure the *core expenditure* taken into account under *Schedule Four*.

rate of enhancement the proportion of *UK expenditure* that makes up the *additional deduction*, currently being 100% for *limited-budget films*, and 80% for other (larger budget) films.

Schedule 4 Schedule Four of the *Finance Act*, which sets out which expenditure is captured by the new regulations.

special film relief the *additional deduction* and the *tax credit* regime.

surrenderable loss the lesser of the *available qualifying expenditure* and the actual trading loss (after taking into account any *additional deduction*) for the relevant accounting period.

tax credit the amount the HMRC pays to the FPC, being the amount of the *surrenderable loss* that the FPC chooses to surrender multiplied by the *payable credit rate*.

theatrical release exhibition to the paying public in the commercial cinema.

UK expenditure expenditure on goods supplied or services performed in the UK.

Structuring the Deal

Frankfurt Kurnit Klein & Selz is pleased to have assisted in the preparation of the US Incentives chapter of this book. We are a leading entertainment law firm based in New York. Working with local counsel when necessary, we provide responsive legal services and strategic advice to filmmakers, producers, financiers, and other clients.

Client Benefits

- Structure tax-advantaged financing opportunities worldwide

- Knowledgeable about secured financing and distribution

- Protect copyrights, trademarks, and other intellectual property

- Provide script review and advice about necessary rights

- Exploit branded entertainment, video games, merchandising, and other ancillary revenue opportunities

- Negotiate and structure compensation packages

- Act as production counsel for feature films, television films, and other programming

- Assist with guild disputes

- Provide personal representation for creative talent

Top Ratings

Many of our attorneys receive high marks in *Chambers USA* and appear in *The Best Lawyers in America 2007,* the *New York Magazine* list of the best entertainment lawyers in New York, and other peer reviewed publications.

Thomas D. Selz	**Bernard C. Topper, Jr.**
(212) 826-5535	**(212) 826-5547**
tselz@fkks.com	**btopper@fkks.com**

FRANKFURT KURNIT KLEIN & SELZ PC

media & entertainment law

UNITED STATES OF AMERICA

Prepared with the assistance of Frankfurt, Kurnit, Klein & Selz (www.fkks.com)

I. INTRODUCTION

'The Sleeping Giant Awakens' or 'What Goes Around Comes Around'

While estimates vary, it seems clear that runaway productions to Canada, Europe, Australia and elsewhere have cost the US economy billions of dollars and thousands of jobs. As demonstrated in other Sections of this Chapter, one key factor attracting US films to other countries has been the many and varied tax incentives available. Well, things are changing. The US, at both the federal and state levels, has responded and responded strongly, providing attractive tax incentives for independent films, with benefits largely unconnected to the residence of the investor.

Most **state** credits are either *refundable* or *transferable* and, hence, an investor, whether US or non-US, can receive a cash payment for these credits. In addition, it may be possible to *discount* this future cash payment and use it to finance part of the cost of production.

The federal benefit consists of a *deduction* and will operate to permit an investor, again, whether US or not, to a return of his/her investment before any US income tax is payable on film revenues. As a result, non-US investors will not need other US activities or income to take advantage of either the state or federal film tax incentives. That said, an investor with US or state income may receive enhanced benefits (see below).

This Section will first explain the **federal** tax benefits now available to filmmakers and then the various US **state** tax benefits.

II. US FEDERAL TAX PROVISIONS RELATING TO FILM-MAKING — SECTION 181

The Federal Landscape – Before and After

By this, we mean before and after the new provisions applicable to film-making brought in by The American Jobs Creation Act of 2004 (explained below). Prior to its enactment, a film production company that owned the copyright to the film it was producing was generally unable to deduct any film costs prior to the delivery of the film. Rather, it was required to capitalize these costs and then recover them over a period of years, commencing with the delivery of the film. In other words, the film costs were treated as a capital investment rather than current expenditure. In addition, because of the phased recovery of these costs, the production company frequently recognized income upon its delivery of the film, even before all costs of production had been repaid from distribution proceeds.

After the introduction of the new law in 2004, the deduction for US production costs was accelerated so that an up-front deduction for these costs is permitted *in the year the costs are incurred*. (This new provision bears some resemblance to the old 'sections 42 and 48' film provisions of UK law.) The deduction is based on the total qualifying costs, frequently referred to as the production spend. This acceleration of the deduction to the year incurred will be available to an investor to offset any income from the film upon delivery or other exploitation, thus assuring that no US income tax will be paid until the production costs have been recovered (Other changes were also made and are discussed below).

This early deduction of film production costs also provides other opportunities for tax benefits. By producing a succession of films in the US, the up-front deductions from a later film may be available to offset additional income from a prior film, thereby postponing the payment of any US tax. Put simply, Section 181, at a minimum, permits an investor to recover his/her investment before any US federal income tax and, with a succession of films, may permit additional recovery from revenues generated by early films without the payment of tax until a later time.

The early deduction of costs also raises an additional possibility. If the costs are incurred in a taxable year before the production company completes production (and before the company recognizes any income), there will be a tax loss for the year. An investor in the film may be able to utilize this loss currently to offset other US qualifying income. This potentially significant benefit will be of interest to a US investor in the film or to a non-US investor with US qualifying income. An investor's ability to utilize this loss against other income is subject to limitations under the US tax law and requires specialist accounting and tax advice.

If, for reasons discussed below, the film does not qualify for the early deduction of film costs, its costs will generally be required to be capitalized and recovered over time under the income forecast method of depreciation, commencing upon the completion of the film. The new law revises these provisions to permit a more accelerated recovery of these costs, another form of timing benefit that will operate to postpone the payment of US tax.

The Technical Rules for the Early Deduction of Film Production Costs

The new rules for the early deduction of film costs are contained in Section 181 of the US tax law (known simply as '**Section 181**'). In order to qualify for this treatment, a film production must meet the following tests:

(i)   the production's aggregate cost may not exceed **$15m** (or $20m, if the costs are 'significantly incurred' in a low income community or distressed area);

(ii)   at least seventy-five percent (75%) of the production's total compensation must be for services performed **in the United States** by actors, directors, producers, and other relevant production personnel; the test generally looks to compensation paid during principal photography and to *where* the services are performed, not to the citizenship or residence of the service providers;

(iii)   the production may not be sexually explicit; and

(iv)   principal photography must commence after 22 October 2004, the date of enactment of the new tax law and before 1 January 2009 (unless the law is extended by the US Congress).

As with any new law, there are some questions concerning its application. The US Treasury Department and the Internal Revenue Service have issued temporary regulations ('regulations') addressing many of these questions. Some of the regulatory provisions produce rather harsh results; others produce rather favorable results. Suffice it to say, however, that for a US film whose budget is far less than $15m and whose structure for the production is relatively straightforward, there are probably few, if any, issues involved in applying Section 181.

Further Explanation on Certain Aspects of Section 181

(i) Films and Costs Potentially Eligible for Section 181

The regulations adopt an expansive view of the productions and types of costs potentially eligible for Section 181 subject, of course, to the $15m (or $20m) cap and other explicit limitations. It covers any film or video production, including a digital video production. As a result, productions that fall under Section 181 include not only motion pictures, mini-series, scripted dramatic TV episodes, and movies of the week, but also productions of reality programming, documentaries, sports and news programs, talk shows, commercials and infomercials. In terms of production costs, Section 181 covers development, pre-production, production and post-production costs. Development expenses may be incurred early on for such things as the development of screenplays or scripts, or for the costs of acquiring production rights to books or plays. These costs may not yet be identified with an actual production when incurred. Special rules apply that, in most instances, will allow a development cost incurred in a prior year to be deducted in the first year in which it becomes reasonably certain that a related production will occur. Once a film is released, additional costs to prepare the film for foreign distribution, rebroadcast or for release to a new market do not constitute production costs for purposes of Section 181.

The costs of acquiring a production also qualify as a production cost, with special rules that apply for an acquisition from a related party. The effect of these special rules is to require that the **greater** of the seller's production costs or the buyer's cost of acquisition be utilized to measure compliance with the $15m cap.

(ii) $15m Cap

Section 181 does not apply to '…any qualified film or TV production, the aggregate cost of which exceeds $15m' (increased to $20m in certain situations). If the $15m cap is exceeded, Section 181 does not permit *any* deduction for film costs in the year incurred.

Because only a film's projected costs will be known at the outset of production, the possibility exists that a film's actual costs will exceed the $15m cap and, if they do, the film will lose its eligibility for Section 181. A film may have a **completion bond** to cover most, if not all, costs of production in excess of the budgeted costs. While some have argued otherwise, the regulations make clear that any excess costs paid by the bond company under a completion bond (as well as the premiums paid to a bond company for the insurance) will be treated as costs that must be applied against the $15m cap.

Many in the industry strongly urged that certain costs, most notably **participations and residuals**, should *not* be included in determining compliance with the $15m cap. They represent possible future payments that are speculative and unquantifiable at the time a company invests in a film. If they are required to be included as a cost of production when they are actually paid in subsequent years, their payment could cause a film to exceed the $15m cap and retroactively lose its eligibility for Section 181. Notwithstanding these arguments, the regulations provide that participations and residuals *are* included as a cost of production and do count against the $15m cap.

If, as the facts play out, the actual costs of a production exceed the $15m (or $20m) cap because of unexpected amounts of participations and residuals and the production thereby loses its eligibility for the Section 181 deductions it previously claimed, the regulations provide a streamlined, and potentially favorable, method to 'recapture' the previous deductions. Under this approach, only the **difference** between (i) the Section 181 deductions previously claimed by the production company and (ii) the amount that it would have claimed as depreciation (under the income forecast method) if the production had used that method to recover its production costs, is included in income in the year the cap is exceeded.

As a result of this recapture approach, if the disqualifying additional costs do not arise until several years after completion of the production, as may be the case for the payment of unexpected participations and residuals, the film may have been substantially or fully depreciated at that time even if the income forecast method had been used. If so, there may be little or no recapture.

(iii) $20m Cap
The $15m cap is increased to $20m if the production's costs are **significantly incurred** in a **low income community** or **distressed area** (collectively, a '20% area'). The 'significantly incurred' test will be met if:
- at least 20% of the total, first-unit principal photography costs are incurred in connection with photography that takes place in a 20% area; **or**

- at least 50% of the total number of days of the first-unit's principal photography takes place in the 20% area.

The production costs of the first-unit principal photography include compensation to actors, directors and other personnel, location costs, camera rental, insurance and catering. It is important to note that these costs are for costs incurred while shooting takes place in a 20% area. There is no requirement that the costs be for services or equipment provided by residents of the 20% area. This approach should significantly increase the opportunity for a film to take advantage of the $20m cap.

The 50% test, based on shooting days, permits a simplified computation and avoids allocations of costs (eg. salaries) to principal photography. In the case of an animated film, the tests are determined by reference to the costs (or days) for key-frame and in-between animation, animation photography and voice over recording.

(iv) Production in the US – the 75% Test
The 75% test requires that compensation paid for actors, directors and qualified personnel, (including writers, choreographers and composers providing services during production, casting agents, camera operators, set designers, lighting technicians, ,make-up artists and others) be for services performed in the US. Generally, the test looks only to services performed during principal photography. These services will be treated as performed in the US if the principal photography to which the compensated service relates occurs in the US and the person performing the service is physically present in the US. For an animated film, special rules, similar to the rules outlined under the $20m cap, above, apply.

(v) The Production Company's Ability to Utilize the Section 181 Deduction
Section 181 merely refers to a 'taxpayer' as the person entitled to the deduction. It does not define the term. A production company that owns the copyright to the film during production and funds the production costs or, alternatively, a company that owns the copyright and funds a production services company to produce the film for it, is likely to be entitled to the Section 181 tax incentive. Loans made to the production company should not change this result. For example, funds provided by **discounting a pre-sale** with a bank should not lose the production company's ability to utilize Section 181. Actual advances by a distributor to the production company prior to the time of production against future delivery of the film will need to be analyzed

to determine the production company's continuing eligibility for Section 181.

(vi) Section 181 Sunsets After 2008

Section 181 will sunset, or terminate, for films whose principal photography commences after December 31, 2008, unless the US Congress acts to extend the time of application of Section 181.

The Technical Rules for the Income Forecast Method

If a film owned by the production company fails to satisfy the requirements of Section 181 (because, for example, the $15m cap is exceeded, or the film is produced offshore), the costs will likely be required to be capitalized and recovered over time under the '**income forecast method** of depreciation', commencing upon completion of the film. In computing its depreciation deductions, the film can take advantage of some new more favorable recovery provisions, also enacted in 2004 with a view to stemming the runaway productions.

Under these new rules, residuals and participations expected to be paid in the first 10 years may be included from the outset as part of the basis for depreciating a film. Alternatively, a taxpayer may exclude such costs from the depreciable base and deduct them in the year or years paid, even if Section 181 does not apply. In addition, in estimating income for the income forecast method, distribution costs will not reduce income. All of this is designed to speed up the recovery of production and other costs for US tax purposes.

A Further Possible New Benefit – A Production Deduction

As a part of the continuing battle between the US and Europe over subsidies, the US in 2004 revamped its tax law to provide a general production deduction for US production, and film-making can qualify for this additional deduction. Under this provision, a film production may deduct from income an amount equal to a portion of the taxpayer's qualified production income (9% when fully phased in, in 2010). Since a deduction reduces taxable income, each dollar of deduction, at a tax rate of 35%, will save 35 cents of tax and, as a result, the 9% deduction will effectively reduce the US federal income tax rate on the production income by about 3%, reducing it from 35% to 32% when it is fully phased in, in 2010.

Motion picture films or videotapes (including live or delayed TV programming, but not including certain sexually explicit productions) will constitute qualified production activities if 50% or more of the total compensation relating to their production (including projected compensation in the form of residuals and participations for the first 10 years of release) is compensation for services performed in the US by actors, production personnel, directors, and producers.

The qualified production deduction for a production company for a taxable year is limited to 50% of the wages paid by it for that year. Accordingly, depending upon whether a production company's US film activities have been arranged to permit the aggregation of more than one film for this purpose, a one film production may have little or no wages paid in that taxable year and, if so, it may not be able to claim a qualified production deduction. Additionally, the qualified production deduction may not exceed the company's taxable income for its taxable year (computed without regard to this deduction).

III. STATE TAX BENEFITS

Various States Offer a Wide Array of Attractive Credits

More than thirty states now offer tax incentives for film production activities. The more significant incentives are typically in the form of state **income tax credits**. The credits (technically referred to as a '**production credit**') range from **10% to 30%** of the qualifying production costs incurred in the relevant state. In some states, the applicable percentage varies, depending on the amount spent there (see table over for a summary).

Some states also offer a labor credit typically ranging from **10% to 20%** of incurred labor costs ('**labor credit**'). Where a labor credit is offered, in some cases, the labor costs are excluded from production costs in computing the production credit. In other states, the labor costs are included in computing the production costs for the production credit and those same costs are included again in computing the labor credit. The Schedule 'State Tax Incentives for Film Production' (below) provides a listing of the states that currently offer the more meaningful and attractive tax incentives.

In addition, many states offer an exemption (or reduction) in their sales and hotel and lodging taxes, as well as reduced 'permitting' fees and other incentives.

A few states actually offer attractive financing for a film. For example, *New Mexico* offers interest-free financing of up to $15m for approved films. The state, if it approves the script, can provide finance if at least 85% of principal photography is to be shot in New Mexico, 60% of below-the-line payroll will be paid to New Mexico residents, and both an approved guarantor (eg. a bank with at least an A rating or corporation with an investment grade rating) and distribution agreement with an acceptable distributor supporting significant sales estimates are in place.

The states are competing to enact more attractive benefits and, by the time the ink is dry on this *Handbook*, it is likely some states will have brought in a new credit for the first time or improved an existing one. The State of *Connecticut*, for example, has recently enacted a **30%** tax credit covering production costs, a highly attractive rate. The state has gone even further than most and will grant the credit on some distribution costs.

Credits Equal Cash

Most independent films in the US are produced through limited liability companies (**LLCs**). These are so-called 'flow through' entities, with the result that any tax charge flows through the company to its owners, thereby preventing the possibility of a double tax being payable at both entity level and owner level. Our discussion of state credits (and the above discussion of federal tax incentives) assumes the use of an LLC for a US production. There are, of course, corporations and other forms of entities that can be used. For a non-US investor in a US production company, other structures may also be available if the direct ownership of a US LLC is not desired as, for example, where the US film production would be the only US business of the non-US investor.

The key to an investor or production company understanding the value of credits is the recognition that they may be *converted into cash*. It doesn't matter whether the recipient of the credit is a US or a non-US investor, or whether the recipient has any US income against which to offset the credit. If an investor does not have state income against which to apply a credit, the credits are designed so that the state will either pay an amount equivalent to the credit to the investor, or alternatively issue a certificate to the investor that may be transferred (for cash) to someone else in the state who can use the credit. In either case, the credit results in a cash payment. A US or non-US investor is, therefore, assured of the return of a portion of his/her investment without regard to the success or failure of

a film. As for elsewhere around the world, the future cash payments from some states can be discounted, and the net proceeds used for production costs.

The Technical Rules for State Credits

Because of the number of states involved and their varying rules, it would not be practical to cover each state individually from beginning to end. Instead, the following is intended to give you a general basic understanding of the range of state tax credits available for film-making, and their applicable rules. We will cover various qualifications and limitations, but the central point remains: for a typical independent film, there are valuable state tax credits available.

Production Credits

i) Qualifying Productions

Generally, where a state offers a tax credit for production, it will be available for a film, video or TV production. Most states will exclude productions of athletic and news events, as well as sexually explicit productions. Some exclude one or more other types of productions. The State of *Illinois*, for example, provides a fairly expansive list of other excluded productions. In addition to news, sports and sexually explicit productions, it excludes (i) productions of current events, public programming and a program that includes weather or market quotations; (ii) talk, game and gala and award show productions; and (iii) productions for industrial, corporate or institutional purposes. Some approach their coverage from a different perspective. *Louisiana*, for example, covers feature length films, videos or TV series intended for national theatrical or TV viewing or a TV pilot.

Assuming the content of the production satisfies the tests for a qualifying production, some states require that further tests be satisfied, including:

- a '**preponderance**' test – *Massachusetts*, for example, requires that either more than 50% of the costs be incurred in Massachusetts or more than 50% of the principal photography days be in the state; *Arizona* requires that a percentage of employees (25% in 2006, increasing to 50% in 2008) be Arizona residents; in *New York*, the production must (i) use a qualified New York studio (and use it for 75% or more of the production's facility costs) and (ii) shoot at least 75% of the production's location days in New York. (NB. New York's requirement for use of a studio will be met if the total studio days are quite limited (say, a day or two) and that use is in New York.)

- a **minimum spend** test – states frequently require that a minimum amount of production costs must be spent in the state, typically ranging from $50,000 (*Connecticut*) to $250,000 (*Arizona*) or even $850,000 (*Florida*) in a year.

ii) Qualifying Costs

Most states apply their production credits to virtually the full production spend — ie., pre-production, production and post-production costs — incurred in the state. *Connecticut's* credit even applies additionally to certain distribution costs including, for example, the creation of trailers and marketing or point-of-purchase videos. *New York*, on the other hand, restricts its production credit to below-the-line costs, including costs of technical and crew production, expenditures for facilities, props, makeup, wardrobe, set construction, and background talent, but excluding costs of stories and scripts, and wages for writers, directors, producers and performers (other than extras). Also, some states' credits, such as *Louisiana* and *Massachusetts*, cap at $1 million the salary paid to a performer or other talent; and others exclude the top-earning talent (*Florida*, for example, excludes the salaries of the two highest paid individuals).

The states also take varying approaches to what qualifies as being '**incurred in the state**.' Some look to where the property or services to which the costs relate are used or performed in producing the film. *New York*, for example, covers the costs for tangible property or services used or performed within New York. Other states, like *New Mexico*, provide a credit for production costs where the recipient is subject to paying New Mexico income tax on it. In other words, the payment for services in New Mexico should be covered, provided the recipient is subject to New Mexico tax on the payment. A script will be covered by the credit if it is written by a New Mexico resident.

Labor Credits

Where a state offers a labor credit for a film production, it will frequently be available only for services provided in that state (as for *Connecticut, New York* and *Illinois*). As noted above, some states have a $1 million cap for salary payments to a person. Of these, some states permit the credit for the first $1 million of salary paid, and others exclude the entire salary. In *Massachusetts*, this may operate to the benefit of the filmmaker in that the entire payment is excluded from the 20% labor credit, but is included in the 25% production credit. *Louisiana* limits its labor credit to services provided by a resident of the state. Unsurprisingly, in most states, the payment for services that qualifies for the labor credit will *not* also be available for the production credit. This is true in *Massachusetts* and *Arizona*. However, in some states, such as *Illinois* and *Louisiana*, the payment will be included in computing *both* the production and the labor credits.

The labor credit typically covers wages and benefits. As with the production credit, there may be certain minimum requirements to trigger a state's labor credit. For example, *Massachusetts* requires total production costs in the state of $250,000.

Aggregate Maximums and Sunset Provisions for State Credits

Many states limit the amount of their state film tax incentives, such as by limiting the aggregate amount available to all productions under the state's program, utilizing either an overall or annual limit for the program, or by limiting the total amount available on each individual film production. Other states, like *Louisiana* and *New Mexico*, do not impose any overall limits on their film-making incentives.

New York's film production tax credit legislation imposes limits on the aggregate amount of credits that New York State and New York City may issue under the incentive program. Pursuant to the most recent legislation (2006), New York State is authorized to issue up to $60m of tax credits annually, and the City up to $30m annually. *Arizona* and *South Carolina* also impose annual limits on their programs. In *Massachusetts*, the credit covers the first $7m of costs per production, and *Hawaii* limits its credit to $8m per production.

The state tax credits will expire (or sunset) in some states, unless extended by further state legislation. In *New York*, for example, the provisions are scheduled to expire in 2011, in *New Mexico*, 2009 and, in *Oregon*, 2012. Generally, a film starting principal photography by the expiration date will be eligible for the credit.

Understanding the Differences Between a Transferable and Refundable Credit

If a state issues a production credit to an investor, whether a US or a non-US investor, and (as may be likely), the investor cannot utilize the credit because s/he has no (or insufficient) state income, the unused credit may be transferred by the investor (if it is a **transferable credit**) or refunded by the state to the investor (if it is a **refundable credit**). In some states, like *Florida*, the process is even more

USA: Summary of State Tax Incentives

STATE	TAX INCENTIVE	CONTACT
ARIZONA	Transferable Income Tax Credit of up to 20% for production (not in excess of $5 million per production)	www.azcommerce.com Tel: 602-771-1193 800-523-6695 Contact: Harry Tate harryt@azcommerce.com
COLORADO	Income Tax Rebate of 10% for production	www.coloradofilm.org Tel: 303-592-4065 1-800-726-8887 Contact: Kevin Shand info@coloradofilm.org
CONNECTICUT	Transferable Income Tax Credit of 30% for production and for certain distribution costs	www.ctfilm.com Tel: 860-256-2800 Contact: Heidi Hamilton heidi.hamilton@ct.gov
FLORIDA	Income Tax Rebate of 15% for production (may not exceed $2 million per production)	www.filminflorida.com Tel: 877-FLA-FILM 850-410-4765 Contact: Paul Sirmons Paul.Sirmons@MyFlorida.com
GEORGIA	Transferable Income Tax Credit of 9% for production (with additional Transferable Income Tax Credits of 3% for GA wages, 3% for rural locations and 2% for TV productions spending at least $20m annually)	www.filmgeorgia.org Tel: 404-962-4048 Contact: Lee Thomas lthomas@georgia.org
HAWAII	Refundable Income Tax Credit of up to 20% for production	www.hawaiifilmoffice.com Tel: 808-586-2570 Contact: Donne Dawson info@hawaiifilmoffice.com
ILLINOIS	Transferable Income Tax Credit of 20% for production (plus additional Transferable Income Tax Credit of 15% for wages paid to residents of impoverished areas)	www.illinoisbiz.biz/film Tel: 312-814-3600 800-419-0667
LOUISIANA	Transferable Income Tax Credit of 25% for production Transferable Income Tax Credit of 10% for LA wages	www.lafilm.org Tel: 225-342-5403 504-736-7280 225-342-FILM Contact: Alex J. Schott schott@la.gov
MARYLAND	Income Tax Rebate of 50% of first $25,000 of wages paid per employee (up to $2 million per production)	www.marylandfilm.org Tel: 800-333-6632 410-767-0067 Contact: Jack Gerbes jack@marylandfilm.org
MASSACHUSETTS	Transferable Income Tax Credit of 25% for production (excluding wages) Transferable Income Tax Credit of 20% for wages	www.massfilmbureau.com Tel: 617-523-8388 Contact: Meg M. Jarrett MassFilmBureau@aol.com

STATE	TAX INCENTIVE	CONTACT
MONTANA	Refundable Income Tax Credit of 8% for production (excluding wages) Refundable Income Tax Credit of 12% for MT wages	www.montanafilm.com Tel: 800-553-4563 406-841-2876 406-444-3960 Contact: Sten Iversen siversen@mt.gov
NEW JERSEY	Transferable Income Tax Credit of 20% for production Production Loan Assistance	www.njfilm.org Tel: 973-648-6279 njfilm@njfilm.org
NEW MEXICO	Income Tax Rebate of 25% for production Interest-Free Production Loans up to $15m per production	www.nmfilm.com Tel: 800-545-9871 505-827-9810 film@nmfilm.com Contact: Rochelle Thompson
NEW YORK	Refundable Income Tax Credit of 10% for below-the-line production Additional Refundable Income Tax Credit of 5% for New York City	www.nylovesfilm.com Tel: 212-803-2330 Contact: Pat S. Kaufman nyfilm@empire.state.ny.us
NORTH CAROLINA	Refundable Income Tax Credit of 15% for production	www.ncfilm.com Tel: 919-733-9900 800-232-9227 Contact: Joan Alford joan@ncfilm.com
OREGON	Income Tax Rebate of 10% for production Income Tax Rebate of 6.2% for wages	www.oregonfilm.org Tel: 503-229-5832 shoot@oregonfilm.org
PENNSYLVANIA	Transferable Income Tax Credit of 20% for production	www.filminpa.com Tel: 717-783-3456 Contact: Jane Saul jsaul@state.pa.us
PUERTO RICO	Transferable Income Tax Credit of 40% for production	www.puertoricofilm.com Tel: 787-758-4747 Contact: Luis A. Riefkohl lriefkohl@pridco.com
RHODE ISLAND	Transferable Income Tax Credit of 25% for production	www.rifilm.com Tel: 401-222-3456 401-222-6666 Contact: Steven Feinberg Steven@arts.ai.gov
SOUTH CAROLINA	Income Tax Rebate of 30% for production (excluding wages) Income Tax Rebate of 20% for wages	www.scfilmoffice.com Tel: 803-737-0490 803-737-3022 Contact: Jeff Monks jmonks@sccommerce.com

straightforward. Florida automatically issues a check in the amount involved to the production company.

The timing and amount of the proceeds received with respect to a transferable or refundable credit may differ depending on various factors. In *Louisiana*, for example, the credit is initially claimed by an investor on a return filed for the taxable year in which the production expenditure is incurred; in *New York*, the credit is claimed on a return filed for the taxable year in which the production is completed.

In addition, in the case of a **transferable credit**, the amount received for the credit will depend on the marketplace for the sale of these credits in the relevant state and, in some states, on local state law (in *Louisiana*, for example, a recent law requires Louisiana's film board to purchase the credit for 72% of its face amount, increasing in bi-annual 2% increments to 80%). In the case of a **refund** of the credit by a state, state law will typically determine when the refund is paid. In New York State (and City), for example, the 10% tax credit (and additional 5% City credit) is refunded, assuming it cannot otherwise be used by an investor to offset *New York* State (or City) taxable income, one-half in the year the return is filed reflecting the credit and the remaining one-half in the next year.

While not certain, the amount received by an investor from the sale of a transferable credit or the amount received as a refund for a refundable credit may constitute taxable income, subject to federal, state and local income tax.

FRANKFURT KURNIT KLEIN & SELZ PC

media & entertainment law

Thomas D. Selz
(212) 826-5535
tselz@fkks.com

Bernard C. Topper, Jr.
(212) 826-5547
btopper@fkks.com

THE BEST OF THE REST

AFRICA (SUB-SAHARA)

A number of sub-Saharan African countries are looking at introducing incentives to encourage local production. The **African Film Commission** (with headquarters in Los Angeles (where else?) is, at the time of writing, rebuilding its website (address below) but should be able to provide information if you contact them directly. Support is also available through French governmental sources (see Part III), and is available in English online.

www.africanfilmcommission.org
www.diplomatie.gouv.fr/en/france-priorities_1/cinema_2 (search for 'cinema')

BOSNIA AND HERZEGOVINA

Bosnia and Herzegovina has a small but burgeoning film industry, and official sources have been promising increases to local funding. The **National Fund for Cinematography** currently stands at approximately €750,000, of which nearly a third is earmarked for regional co-productions.

CROATIA

At the time of writing, Croatia's Ministry of Culture was in the process of setting up the **Croatian Centre for Audiovisual Services** for funding, developing, and promoting independent films. The new *Audiovisual Act* should come into effect sometime in 2007. Still under consideration, the 2007 total budget for funding film activities may end up trebling from the proposed US$6.4m to US$16.6m. No private tax incentive is in currently place, but it is being considered (see part III).

THE CZECH REPUBLIC

Recognising the need to stay competitive among its European neighbours, a study by the Czech Ministry of Culture in 2006 called for a **12.5% tax rebate** for local and international productions (but not for development of infrastructure), and the creation of a national body for overseeing overall strategy for the film industry. At the time of writing, no details had been released about the proposed rebate.

Despite earlier setbacks, the 2007 budget of the **State Fund** for the Support and Development of Czech Cinematography increased modestly to $7.6m (a rise of $4.8m but lower than the original proposal, which would have trebled the fund). Czech companies and those owned partly by foreign entities (of which less than 50% of shares are foreign) can apply for the State Fund. The fund is granted in the form of a subsidy, loan or grant-in-aid, and is limited up to **50%** of the total budget. The Czech Republic should continue to attract foreign productions as long as it stays competitive. Check details with the **Czech Film Commission** at www.filmcommission.cz/.

DENMARK

There are no fiscal incentives in the form of tax breaks currently available in Denmark. There are, however, **subsidies** available through the **Danish Film Institute** (DFI) for the development and production of exclusively Danish films and for co-productions made with international partners. It is the national agency responsible for supporting and encouraging film and cinema culture and for conserving these in the national interest, and works in a similar way to its counterparts in Sweden and Norway (see above). The Institute's operations extend from participation in the development and production of feature films, shorts and documentaries, over distribution and marketing, to managing the national film archive and cinematheque.

Danish Film Institute (DFI)
Gothersgade 55
Copenhagen1123
+45 33 74 3400
www.dfi.dk
Radio and Television Board:
www.mediesekretariat.dk

ESTONIA

The **Estonian Film Foundation** provides grants for production, development and promotion for films in which at least one of the producers is an independent Estonian production company. For co-productions, the Estonian participation must have a minimum of 10% budget and 10% film property rights. There is also a minimum local spend for international co-productions. For a quick guide, visit the website: www.filmestonia.com/index.php?page=4&

Contact the Estonian Film Foundation for the latest details.

Estonian Film Foundation

Vana-Viru 3, 10111 Tallinn
Estonia, T: +372 627 6060
F: +372 627 6061
www.efsa.ee, film@efsa.ee

FIJI

Fiji is not unique in claiming to have the **'world's best incentives'** for film production. Famous of course for the various versions of the *Blue Lagoon*, the islands have more recently hosted Sony's *Anaconda* and Fox's Tom Hanks epic *Castaway*. Fiji is only a 3 hour flight from Australia, and has daily flights to Los Angeles. Films can generally receive a **15% rebate** (to a maximum of **F$3.75m**) on **qualifying production expenditure** in Fiji (**QFPE**). For QFPE between F$250,000 and F$25m, the QFPE must represent at least **35%** of the total budget. QFPE above F$25m automatically qualifies for the rebate. To make it easier to qualify, remuneration for one above-the-line crew or cast member can be excluded from the total budget. Applicants for the rebate are excluded from qualifying for the film-making foreign employee tax exemption and F1 and F2 status.

Under the so-called F1 and F2 regime, qualifying Fiji taxpayers (including wholly foreign owned corporations) who invest in large format films, feature films, short films or telemovies can obtain up to a **150% tax concession** on their film investment. Further, up to **60%** of the **income** from that investment will be **tax exempt**. A non-resident film company intending to make a film in Fiji may also apply for a full or partial **tax exemption** for its **non-resident employees**. An application needs to be made to the Minister through the Fiji Audiovisual Commission (FAVC) on the approved form. However, neither this exemption nor the F1 and F2 are compatible with the 15% rebate mentioned above.

See www.fijiaudiovisual.com for more information.

GREECE

The **Greek Film Centre** (GFC), supervised by the Culture Ministry, oversees the Greek film industry. Tax breaks only apply to the *re*production rather than production of films, but there is money available in the form of support from the GFC for production finance, both for new and established filmmakers.

The **Horizons** scheme provides funding to feature films with a particular artistic or technical level, with high-end production values. The GFC will look in particular at the track records of the key elements and the commerciality of the project. The fund aims to participate in about 6 features per year, at least one of which should be for a first-timer. The GFC will take an equity stake in the film, and may take part-ownership of the copyright. It will finance up to **€325k** for a sub-€1m Greek picture, or for any official co-production. Whether a Greek picture or a co-production, the Greek element of the financing must be at least 30% complete in order to be approved, and shooting must start within a year of this approval. The GFC can also subsidise the distribution of films it part-financed.

Under the **Incentives** scheme, independent producers can apply for awards up to **€150k** for films budget over **€300k**. Again, the track records of the producer and director are paramount, and the GFC will also look at the financial projections and quality of script. Films must already have 60% of their finance in place before applying.

Greek Film Centre
www.gfc.gr/en/funding.asp

HONG KONG

Hong Kong has a relatively low corporate income tax rate of 17.5%. **No specific tax incentives** exist for the film industry, so general taxation rules apply. Foreign producers engaged in co-productions are likely to be subjected to the standard 'Profit Tax'. Deduction of expenses that are not of a capital nature (eg. acquisition of patent rights) are allowed. These may include deduction of interest from money borrowed and other operational costs.

The local film industry is mainly funded by **private financiers**. Each year in March, the '**Hong Kong — Asia Film Financing Forum**' (HAF) brings together film financiers, producers, bankers, distributors, buyers and funding bodies to provide them with a platform to discuss privately potential international co-productions. For 2007, it selected 25 Asian projects and expected about 700 participants.

The **Hong Kong Film Services Office** (FSO) provides two types of **funds**; the Film **Guarantee Fund** ('FGF') and **Film Development Fund** ('FDF').

The **FGF** aims to help local production companies to obtain **loans** from local participating lending institutions (PLIs) for film productions. There is a maximum annual budget commitment of HK$30m (approx. US$3.84m). A minimum of eleven films are guaranteed at any one point, with a loan guarantee of HK$2.625m (approx. USD$336k) each. To be eligible, the project must be a **feature film** for **commercial release** locally and has at least **50%** of the major cast and film crew who are **Hong Kong permanent residents**. Other conditions also apply. The fund can be in the form of equity or a loan. Application must be sent in before the start of principal photography through the PLIs or directly to the FSO.

Production companies incorporated in Hong Kong can apply for the **FDF**. It is open to applications three times a year and provides grants for recurrent and non-recurrent expenditure. For details contact the FSO Television and Entertainment Licensing Authority.

Hong Kong-Asia Film Financing Forum
7/F United Chinese Bank Building
31-37 Des Voeux Road Central, Hong Kong
T: +852 2970 3300
F: +852 2970 3011
www.haf.org.hk/haf/index.htm
info@haf.org.hk

Hong Kong Film Services Office
40/F Revenue Tower
5 Gloucester Road, Wanchai, Hong Kong
T: +852 2594 5729 / +852 2594 5726 (FGF)
F: +852 2824 0595
www.fso-tela.gov.hk/abt/index.cfm
info@fso-tela.gov.hk

INDONESIA

Indonesia is effectively a **tax-free haven** for foreign artists, although there are no specific local rebates or other fiscal incentives. However, the Bali Film Commission can offer assistance and claims to reduce budgets by up to 20%. Bali Film is an English-language organisation also geared towards helping incoming film productions.

www.balifilm.com
www.filmcommissionhq.com/listing.jsp?id=FC01636

ISRAEL

Israeli films are enjoying an increasing worldwide impact at present, with international co-production growing up to 25% year on year, and a number of films receiving top-level critical acclaim. Local films can access financial support from the **Israel Film Fund**. The tax deduction for investment in local production is no longer being championed by the authorities (there is certainly no longer promotional information in English about it on the internet), and is due to expire at the end of 2007. But the Government is currently undertaking a review of film financing policy and is looking into other larger-scale incentive packages. Watch this space.

www.filmfund.org.il

JAMAICA

As part of JAMPRO, the investment and export arm of the Government, the **Jamaica Film Commission** was established in 1984 specifically to promote Jamaica's film industry, and is mandated to increase investment, export, employment, etc. Since its inception, the Commission claims to have been involved with more than 3,000 film projects of all types, including numerous full-length feature films and documentaries.

Although Jamaica is perhaps one of the more naturally attractive locations for filming, with foreign filmmakers arriving since the early 1900s, it was only during the 1980s, when the island implemented a targeted plan to attract 'Hollywood' to Jamaica, that there was a dramatic increase in the number and type of films shooting there.

Investors wishing to put money into the country's film industry can benefit from **incentives** under the *Motion Picture Industry Encouragement Act*. Under this Act, a 'recognised film producer' is entitled to **relief from income tax** in respect of worldwide receipts for a period of up to **nine years** from the first release of the motion picture. The investor can also benefit from an **investment allowance of 70%** of the total expenditure on the production facilities' infrastructure, and this may be carried forward beyond the nine years. In addition, s/he will would be exempted from the payment of import duty on equipment, machinery and materials for the building of studios or for use in motion picture production.

Jamaica has a fairly well-developed infrastructure and investors/producers should have easy access to the necessary visas and work permits. The country also claims to have investor-friendly entry regulations.

Any company seeking incentives must be incorporated in Jamaica. It will need to complete an application for Recognition Status and provide a detailed business plan. Recognition Status may be granted for up to 15 years

Films and videos produced in Jamaica for export are **zero-rated** for **General Consumption Tax** (GCT), which would otherwise be charged at a flat rate of 15% on the total cost of most goods and services. Companies with a Jamaican budget over $30,000 can be assisted by the Commission in obtaining GCT exemption status. The producer, accountant or production manager can be authorised to negotiate purchases using a 'Waiver of GCT Letter'. Alternatively, where GCT is paid at the point of purchase, it will subsequently be refunded within 90 working days (together with interest at 2.5% per month).

> www.investjamaica.com/sectors/film
> www.filmjamaica.com
> www.caribarts.org/topics/media_arts/media.php?dis=571

JAPAN

Japan still hasn't any specific tax-breaks for film investment or production, despite increased anticipation over recent years. However, the newly-established Visual Industry Promotion Organisation (**VIPO**) aims to give all sorts of other assistance, often with a view to bringing budgets down by providing assistance in kind (mostly discounted facilities, training and advice) rather than cash.

> www.vipo.or.jp/en/index.html

MACEDONIA

At the time of writing, the **Macedonian Film Fund** was due to commence on 1 January 2007, with the aim of supporting local and international film productions. It is also looking into the concept of introducing tax breaks. A further boost is likely as the '**Film City**' of Macedonia is set to be completed at the beginning of 2008. It is aimed at establishing a 'one-stop shop' for providing infrastructure and training to aid all aspects of digital and filmed entertainment productions.

> www.culture.in.mk/default.asp

MEXICO

There is a **tax allowance** available to Mexican taxpayers. It entitles them to deduction of **100%** of any expenses outlaid and/or investments made in projects qualifying as national cinematographic film production. However, the deduction may **not exceed**

3% of the total income tax payable on the taxpayer's return for the corresponding fiscal year. There is also a limit of MXP500m annually, which is to be shared amongst all taxpayers in a fiscal year.

Any Mexican Investors (individuals or entities) are eligible to apply for the tax allowance. The expenses and outlays must occur in Mexico and must be specifically for the production of a qualifying national cinematographic film, being any production made by Mexican entities or individuals alone or under formal international co-production treaties entered into by the Mexican government.

Public Money is also available. The Cinematography Law grants incentives to the cinematography industry. A producer may receive such an incentive, by participating in international film festivals and receiving recognition or prizes. There is a Cinema Investment and Incentive Fund ('**FIDECINE**') to promote financial aid, guarantees and investments for producers, distributors, promoters and exhibitors of national film. The fund is run by a trust, to which the tax authorities are the sole trustee and the beneficiaries determined by the Trust's Technical Committee. The fund is dedicated to granting risk capital, distribution, marketing and presentation activities for national films.

Mexican Film Commission
IMCINE (C.P. Pablo Fernandez Flores Coordinador General)
Insurgentes Sur 674
Colonia Del Valle
Codigo Postal 03100
Delegacion Benito Juarez
Tel: 55 23 11 20, Ext 53 89
coordina@imcine.gob.mx
www.imcine.gob.mx

THE PHILIPPINES

The main tax break available in the Philippines is on the local **entertainment tax** (levied on local exploitation), the **rebate** being dependent on whether the film is classed as having an 'A-Rating' (which gets a 100% rebate) or 'B-Rating' (65% rebate). Film production has dived in the country from over 200 productions per year in the mid-90s to a projected 30 in 2007. And for some reason, less than ten of the 150 films made in the two years from January 2003 accessed the rebate.

POLAND

The **Polish Film Institute** was set up in 2005 and has an annual budget of about $32.6m (recently revised). The **Polish Audiovisual Fund** came into being on January 2006, providing grants that support production, distribution and promotions of films. The grants provide subsidies for both local and international co-productions (of various forms). There are also other institutes that offer limited and conditional financial support. For details, check with the Polish Film Institute.

ul. Krakowskie
PrzedmieĐcie 21/23
00-071 Warszewa
Poland
T: +48 022 42 10 518
F: +48 022 42 10 241
www.pisf.pl/index.php?kategoria=706

SERBIA

At Cannes 2006, Serbia announced the proposed implementation of a new **tax credit** worth up to a huge **21.5%** for local and international film productions. However, very little information has been released since. In the meantime, low-cost labour and a new major studio complex are the main attractions for shooting in Serbia. For details, contact **Film Centre Serbia** (part of the Ministry of Culture).

Ministry of Culture, Serbia
www.kultura.sr.gov.yu/eng/

SINGAPORE

Singapore offers a number of incentive programmes for filmmakers, mostly from the perspective of **grant** funding. Support from schemes such as the Co-investment Scheme (see below), Film Investment Program (also below), Short Film Grant, Project Development Scheme, are all run through the **Singapore Film Commission** (SFC), can be applied for by individuals or companies. Individuals must be Singapore residents or citizens, whereas companies must be at least 50% Singaporean-owned, controlled and managed. The **Scheme for Co-investment in Exportable Content** (part of the Media Development Authority's '**SCREEN**' programme), will co-invest with local production companies on a rights-sharing (and revenue-sharing) basis.

It will match local funding up to approx S$500k. International partners need to be involved in the project in order for it to qualify, and at least 30% of the budget must be financed from foreign sources. Finance is released in four equal instalments, being on financial closing, start of principal photography, delivery of first cut and delivery to sales agent.

The **Film Investment Program** supports projects with a positive contribution to the Singaporean film industry, and provide up to S$250k per feature film, so long as the producer is at least 30% Singapore-owned. The fund shares in revenues on a *pari passu* basis.

The S$10m **Film in Singapore! Scheme** (FSS), introduced in 2004 by the Singapore Tourist Board, also assists international filmmakers and broadcasters in the production (and post-production) of movies and TV programmes in Singapore. The purpose behind the programme is the promotion of Singapore as a destination for international visitors, through the medium of film and TV. Each filmmaker or broadcaster may be granted financial support of up to 50% of local qualifying spend (such as local crew, equipment, locations, transport and accommodation), determined on a **case-by-case** basis. Each project is evaluated with specific focus on how the film or programme will uniquely showcase Singapore's locations.

Singapore has co-production treaties with Canada, Japan and New Zealand.

For more detail on all the schemes mentioned above, see the Funding Directory in part 3 of this *Handbook*, or via the following websites:

www.sfc.org.sg
http://app.stb.com.sg/asp/ina/ina04.asp

SLOVAKIA

Slovakia Film Institute
Grösslingová 32, SK 811 09 Bratislava
Slovak Republic
T: +421 2 5710 1503
F: +421 2 5296 3461
sfu@sfu.sk
www.sfu.sk

Slovakia Audiovisual Information Centre
www.aic.sk

See also Part III.

SLOVENIA

The **Slovenian Film Fund** is a public fund that has supported film production and post-production for local and eligible international co-productions since 1995. It provides partial or total funding for selected projects. Funding is also available for shorts and animations. For details, visit the website

www.film-sklad.si/client.en/index.php?table=articles&ID=8

Miklosiceva 38
1000 Ljubljana, Slovenia
T: +386 1 234 32 00
F: +386 1 234 32 18/19
info@film-sklad.si

SPAIN

Spain has never been considered as one of the world's 'finance-incentives' hubs for film producers, possibly because there is very little written in the English language anywhere to attract international producers to whatever various incentives are available there. Lobbying groups have been pushing for reform in recent years, but for some strange reason, none of the local experts we approached (including specialist law-firms) were willing or able to provide us with any authoritative information on the current state-of-play that we could rely on. Apologies, and good luck!

PART III

FUNDING DIRECTORY

With over €1.5bn ($2bn/£1bn) of public money available for film and media each year in Europe alone, there's a lot out of funding out there if you know where to look. To the best of our knowledge, a directory of film funds around the world has not been collated and published before, and as such, this should be treated with caution. In some cases the most recent available information for an award is several years old, and is often not provided in English. Inevitably most of the funds listed are based in Europe, North America and Australasia, with the UK being particularly well-covered.

Needless to say schemes are being launched, closed and changed all the time. We have tried to verify every fund listed here with the organisations concerned, but some — as you may have noticed if you have tried to raise funds before — avoid the outside world unless absolutely unavoidable. So please, do not base plans on this information without first contacting the relevant organisation directly for up-to-date information. And as always, if you notice anything missing or wrong – please do let us know – funding@netribution.co.uk

With this book covering funding from all over the world, the number of awards listed has expanded from around 200 to some 1000. This would not have been possible without the support of the **European Audiovisual Observatory**, who publish the **Korda** database (korda.obs.coe.int) and whose database formed the early backbone of the expanded European part of this section, and **Catherine Allen** for her tireless work researching and updating funds.

This directory is a testament to the work over the years of **Stephen Salter**, **Caroline Hancock**, **Rachel Bibb**, **Cyndee Barlass** and **Catherine Allen**, right back to **Chris Chandler**'s *BFI Lowdown Guide* which influenced both Netribution's funding guide, and, in turn, this book. Thanks to them, **Susan Neuman Baudais** and **Markus Booms** at the Observatory and the organisations who have been helpful in providing us with information.

KEY

For
FEAT — Feature film
TV — TV
MM — Multimedia
SHORT — Short / medium length film
DOC — Documentary
ANI — Animation
YP — Young people / children's films
VIDG — Video games
WEB — Internet projects
DIGI — Digital media projects
EXP — Experimental work
FFF — First feature film from director/writer

Covering
SCRIPT — Screenwriting and script development
DEV — Project development
SLATE — Slate funding for a number of projects
PROD — Production funding
POST — Post-production funding
DIST — Distribution
PROMO — Marketing and promotion (including festivals and sales)
CULT — Support of cultural activities
DVD — For the production and distribution of DVDs and Videos
EDU — Education and training
EXH — Cinemas and exhibition
BIZ-DEV — Company and business development
PER-DEV — Personal development
AUD-DEV — Audience development

Ordering
Funds are listed alphabetically in each country with – where possible - the main national agency for the country first. Film commissions are listed at the end of the country section alphabetically. Some organisations are both funders and film commissions, so may appear in either part depending on their primary activities.

Key
For ease of reference we've tried loosely to categorise funds based on the kinds of projects and activity they support, and we list this in the directory with the abbreviations to the left. This cannot account for the different definitions between orgs (one funder's documentary is another's TV, and so forth) but should provide some kind of a guide. An index of funds offering short, animation, documentary and scriptwriting support is printed at the end of the chapter.

AUSTRALIA

Australian Film Commission

www.afc.gov.au
Level 4, 150 William Street, Woolloomooloo, NSW
2011, Sydney, Australia
T: +61 2 9321 6444 · F: +61 2 9357 3672
E: marketing@afc.gov.au

The Australian Film Commission (AFC) is an Australian Government agency established by the Australian Film Commission Act in 1975. It operates under the Commonwealth Film Programme (Department of Communications, Information Technology and the Arts) to ensure the creation, availability and preservation of Australian screen content. The goal of the AFC is to enrich Australia's national identity by fostering an internationally competitive audiovisual production industry, making Australia's audiovisual content and culture available to all developing and preserving a national collection of sound and moving image. The AFC maintains offices in Brisbane, Canberra, Melbourne and Sydney.

Funding

Applicants must be Australian citizens or permanent residents of Australia and be 18 years of age or older. The applicant can be an individual or a team of individual. The AFC provides support to projects defined as 'Australian programs'. Full details at www.afc.gov. au/funding/fd/default.aspx

New Screenwriters Program

Offers: up to A$ 10,000 · For: SCRIPT · Covering: FEAT | SHORT
For a single draft of a feature or short feature script. Writers or Directors can apply on an annual basis.

Draft Drama Funding

Offers: up to A$ 20,000 · For: SCRIPT · Covering: FEAT | ANI
For the creation of a second draft of a feature script (including feature-length animation). Applications can be made twice a year.

Draft Drama Funding: Short Features or Short TV Series

Offers: Up to A$10,000 · For: SCRIPT · Covering: FEAT | TV | ANI
For the creation of a next draft script from an existing draft for either a short feature or a short TV drama series, including animation. Applications can be made twice a year.

Seed Feature Funding

Offers: Up to A$50,000 · For: SCRIPT · Covering: FEAT
For a first draft script from an outline or treatment of a feature film only. Applications can be made four times a year.

Matched Investment Funding

Offers: up to A$ 50,000 · For: SCRIPT | DEV | DIST · Covering: DOC | FEAT
For features or feature documentaries intended for theatrical release with distributor interest.

Draft Funding

Offers: Up to A$30,000 · For: SCRIPT · Covering: FEAT
For the creation of next draft from an existing draft of a feature only. Applications can be made four times in a year.

Writer Fellowships

Offers: up to A$50,000 · For: SCRIPT · Covering: FEAT | ANI
Writer Fellowships are awarded to writers who have received significant local and international awards and/or commercial success. Funding is for the creation of a first draft feature script plus several revised drafts (subject to progress on the interim draft) for a feature (including feature-length animation).

IndiVision Project Lab & Script Development

Offers: up to A$ 22,000 · For: DEV | SCRIPT · Covering: FEAT
IndiVision supports the development, production and promotion of outstanding low-budget feature dramas.

IndiVision Single-draft Script Development

Offers: up to A$ 22,000 · For: SCRIPT · Covering: FEAT
IndiVision is a script development program for single-draft funding.

Short Features, Short TV Drama Series, & Animation Production

Offers: up to A$ 400,000 · For: PROD · Covering: SHORT | TV | ANI | FEAT
This strand offers opportunities to filmmakers who have already made strong and distinctive shorts to explore longer-form narrative drama. Applications can be made twice a year.

Shorts Production

Offers: Up to A$120,000 · For: PROD | POST · Covering: SHORT
Funding is for the production and/or post-production of digital short films under 25 minutes. Applications can be made twice a year.

IndiVision Low-budget Feature Production
Offers: Up to A$1 million · For: PROD | POST ·
Covering: FEAT | ANI
Applications can be made twice a year.

Documentary Development
Offers: up to A$25,000 · For: DEV · Covering: DOC
For the development of one-off documentaries or
documentary series. Applications can be made five
times a year.

Documentary Production
Offers: up to A$100,000 · For: PROD | POST ·
Covering: DOC
Applications can be made twice a year.

Short Animation
Offers: Up to A$80,000 · For: PROD | POST ·
Covering: ANI | SHORT
Funding is for a one-off animations up to 15 minutes.
Applications can be made once a year.

Pilot/Trailer Production
Offers: Up to A$30,000 · For: PROD · Covering:
OTHER
Funding is for a 1–3 minute pilot or trailer plus a
package of script(s) and storyboards. Only teams may
apply.

Animation Series Production
www.afc.gov.au/funding/fd/animation/default.aspx
Offers: Up to A$150,000 · For: PROD · Covering:
ANI
Funding for a 13 x 1-minute animation series.

Interactive Digital Media Matched Investment Development Funding
Offers: Up to A$50,000 · For: DEV · Covering: DIGI
For Interactive digital media projects of any length, type
or platform within entertainment, arts or education that
have been able to attract third-party financial support.

Experimental Digital Production
Offers: Up to A$20,000 · For: POST | PROD ·
Covering: DIGI
For the production and/or post-production of
experimental and innovative projects that utilise digital
technology to maximise and enhance the creative,
aesthetic and technical elements of the project.

General Development Investment
Offers: Up to A$70,000 · For: DEV | SLATE ·
Covering: FEAT | DOC | TV
This strand supports experienced producers who
are developing and financing projects, by providing
ongoing funding for infrastructure and development
slates. Applications can be made four times a year.
The programme also actively encourages and supports

producers who develop business plans, diversify
strategies, raise equity finance and develop alternative
income streams to build sustainable businesses.

Short-term Development Investment Facility
Offers: Up to A$30,000 · Covering: FEAT | DOC
For development investment at short notice for features
and one-off documentaries and series. Only for projects
likely to be financed in the immediate future.

Production Cashflow Facility
Offers: Up to A$300,000 · For: PROD · Covering:
FEAT | DOC
Loans given against committed investor drawdowns,
distribution guarantees and pre-sales. Producer must
demonstrate the urgency of loan.

Australian Film Institute
www.afi.org.au
236 Dorcas Street, South Melbourne, Victoria, 3205,
Australia
T: +613 9696 1844 · F: +613 9696 7972
E: info@afi.org.au
Founded in 1958, the AFI is Australia's leading film
and TV industry body, promoting Australian film and
TV and responsible for producing Australia's premier
film and TV awards, the annual AFI Awards. The annual
awards established by the AFI recognise and honour
outstanding achievement in the Australian film and TV
industry.

Australian Children's Television Foundation (ACTF)
www.actf.com.au/
3rd Floor, 145 Smith Street, Fitzroy, Victoria, 3065,
Australia
T: +61 3 9419 8800 · F: +61 3 9419 0660
E: info@actf.com.au
The ACTF is a national non-profit organisation
encouraging the development, production and
dissemination of TV programmes, films and other
audiovisual media for children, and the promotion of
these programmes in the community.

Independent Project Investment Program
www.actf.com.au/funding/funding.htm
Offers: up to A$125,000 · For: SCRIPT | PROD ·
Covering: YP | TV
The programme provides development finance for
producers, script writers, script editors, consultants and
funds for budget preparation. Applications are accepted
from Australian residents with four annual deadlines.

Film Australia Limited

www.filmaust.com.au
101 Eton Road, Lindfield, NSW 2070, Australia
T: +61 2 9413 8777 • F: +61 2 9416 5672
E: web@filmaust.com.au
Film Australia produces documentaries under the National Interest Program: a contract with the Australian Government to devise, produce, distribute and market productions that deal with matters of national interest or illustrate and interpret aspects of Australian life.

Hothouse Scheme for Documentary and Factual Producers

www.filmaust.com.au/production/default.asp
Offers: Up to A$100,000 a year • For: BIZ-DEV • Covering: DOC | TV
Applicant will receive cash working capital of A$100,000 (A$50,000 each from Film Australia and the FTO) over a period of 12 months in accordance with a pre-agreed business plan and set of key performance indicators. They will also access facilities and services from Film Australia for a period of 12 months with an approximate value of A$50,000.

Film Finance Corporation Australia (FFC)

www.ffc.gov.au
130 Elizabeth Street, Level 12, Sydney, NSW 2000, Australia
T: +61 2 9268 2555 • F: +61 2 9264 8551
E: ffc@ffc.gov.au
The FFC is the principal agency of the Australian government for funding the production of films and TV programmes. The government supports film and TV production to ensure that Australians have the opportunity to make and watch their own screen stories. Since its establishment the FFC has invested in over 1000 films with some A$2.5bn combined production value.
Successes include *Wolf Creek, Ten Canoes, Lantana, The Man Who Sued God, Rabbit-Proof Fence, Strictly Ballroom, The Adventures of Priscilla: Queen of the Desert* and *Muriel's Wedding*. Annual funding for 2007/08 is A$70.5m.

Funding

The FFC will only fund projects with high levels of creative and technical contribution by Australians, or projects certified under Australia's Official Co-Production Program. To support diversity, the FFC funds the most expensive programme formats (feature films, mini-series, telemovies and documentaries).

Feature Films

www.ffc.gov.au/investment/ffc_int_investment_feature.asp • Offers: up to A$5m• For: PROD • Covering: FEAT
Projects will be evaluated by the FFC to determine their merit in three key areas — Creative Potential, Market Potential, Audience Potential.

Adult Television Drama

www.ffc.gov.au/investment/ffc_int_investment_adult.asp • Offers: up to A$4m • For: PROD • Covering: TV
The FFC will finance mini-series of up to 13 hours, single telemovies and telemovie packages of up to three telemovies and animated mini-series of up to 13 episodes, each no less than a half-hour in length.

Children's Television Drama

www.ffc.gov.au/investment/ffc_int_investment_children.asp • Offers: up to A$1.5m • For: PROD • Covering: YP
The FFC will invest in telemovies, mini-series of 13 half-hours or 26 half-hours, animated mini-series of up to 26 episodes, each no less than one-quarter commercial TV hour.

Documentaries

www.ffc.gov.au/investment/ffc_int_investment | DOCumentary.asp • Offers: up to A$600,000 • For: PROD • Covering: DOC
The FFC invests in documentaries with an Australian free-to-air or pay TV pre-sale. It does not invest in other actuality programmes, such as reality TV, infotainment, current affairs, cooking, 'how to' or sports programmes. Support of up to A$200,000 for a one-off programme and up to A$600,000 for a documentary series is available.

Co-Productions

www.ffc.gov.au/investment/ffc_int_investment_co-production.asp • For: PROD • Covering: FEAT | TV | DOC
The FFC will fund only the cost of the Australian elements of a co-production and expects that the spend in Australia will be no less than 1.5 times its investment.

Film Victoria

www.film.vic.gov.au
7th Floor, 189 Flinders Lane, Melbourne, Victoria 3000, Australia
T: +61 3 9660 3200 • F: +61 3 9660 3201
E: contact@film.vic.gov.au
Film Victoria is a cultural organisation that encourages and assists the development, production, exhibition

and understanding of film, TV and new media.
Funding is available for a variety of schemes, including
development and production of feature films, short
films and digital animation.

Funding

Film Victoria offers a range of funding programs
that support Victorian film, TV and digital media
practitioners, businesses and projects. The decisions
are guided by a commitment to quality, innovation and
potential commercial viability, the support for Victorian
ideas, projects, individuals and/or businesses to
realise their potential, the opportunity to provide clear
economic and cultural benefits to both the industry and
all Victorians.

New Feature Writers

film.vic.gov.au/www/html/155-content-creation.
asp?intSiteID=1
Offers: A$13,000 · For: SCRIPT · Covering: FEAT |
TV | FFF
This program develops the scriptwriting skills of novice
screenwriters through attendance at a workshop and
provision of funds for development to next draft with
a professional Script Editor. An applicant must be an
Australian citizen or permanent resident who has lived
in Victoria for at least the last six months. There is an
annual application deadline.

Feature Film Script Development

film.vic.gov.au/www/html/155-content-creation.
asp?intSiteID=1
Offers: A$15,000 to $25,000 · For: SCRIPT | DEV ·
Covering: FEAT
This programme supports writers and creative teams
in the development of feature film scripts. The
programme encompasses funding from the early stages
of development through to higher level, 'multi-draft
funding' for projects at the final stages of development
that have attracted market interest.

Television Drama Script Development

film.vic.gov.au/www/html/155-content-creation.
asp?intSiteID=1
Offers: up to A$50,000 · For: SCRIPT | DEV ·
Covering: TV
This program supports development of TV drama
projects. 'Seed funding' is available for early stage
development. Projects beyond the early concept stage
require 'matched funding' from a network, broadcaster,
distributor or sales agent.

Documentary Development

film.vic.gov.au/www/html/155-content-creation.
asp?intSiteID=1
Offers: up to A$20,000 · For: DEV · Covering: DOC
This programme supports the research and writing
of documentary project proposals, treatments and
scripts and aims to maximise their potential to
attract production investment. Three categories of
development are available — Series development; One-
off projects; and Early Concept development.

Attachment Programme

film.vic.gov.au/www/ahtml/156-professional-
development.asp?intSiteID=1
Offers: up to A$5,000 · Covering: FEAT | TV
This programme provides professional development to
film and TV makers by placing them in a production
environment under the supervision of highly skilled and
knowledgeable personnel.

International Travel Fund

film.vic.gov.au/www/html/156-professional-
development.asp?intSiteID=1
Offers: up to A$9,000 · For: PROMO | CULT
This fund assists both new and experienced filmmakers
to attend international film festivals and markets.

Mentorships

film.vic.gov.au/www/html/156-professional-
development.asp?intSiteID=1 · For: PER-DEV
Project Mentorships provide opportunities for
practitioners to develop their own projects under
the tutelage of a more experienced mentor, and
International Market Mentorships pair new filmmakers
with experienced players and enable experienced
filmmakers to explore new markets with the assistance
of a veteran of that market.

Producer Packages

film.vic.gov.au/www/html/156-professional-
development.asp?intSiteID=1
Offers: up to A$50,000 · For: SLATE
Producer Packages assist Producers with an advance
that contributes towards the costs of developing a slate
of projects.

Digital Media

film.vic.gov.au/www/html/161-digital-media.
asp?intSiteID=1 · For: PROD · Covering: DIGI | VIDG
In May 2006, the Victorian Government announced it
would provide Film Victoria with $4.05m over 2 years
specifically for digital media programs (including video
games).

Production Investment

film.vic.gov.au/www/html/158-production-investment.asp?intSiteID=1 · For: PROD · Covering: FEAT | DOC | ANI | TV

Film Victoria provides Production Investment funds to resource and facilitate Victorian projects that show a commitment to quality, innovation and marketability.

Industry & Audience Development

film.vic.gov.au/www/html/157-industry--audience-development.asp?intSiteID=1

Offers: up to A$20,000 · For: AUD-DEV · Covering: FEAT | TV

Promotes the development of the industry and audiences by actively encouraging the appreciation, commentary and critical analysis of the Victorian film and TV sector.

Production Investment Attraction Fund (PIAF)

film.vic.gov.au/www/html/94-incentives.asp?intSiteID=1 · Covering: FEAT | TV | SHORT | DOC | ANI

The PIAF grant is designed to attract interstate or offshore productions to film or post-produce feature films, TV series, 'reality' programmes, mini-series, telemovies, animation series and documentaries in the state of Victoria.

Regional Victoria Film Location Assistance Fund (RLAF)

film.vic.gov.au/www/html/94-incentives.asp?intSiteID=1

The RLAF grant is designed to encourage local and footloose projects (ie. projects which have qualified interstate and/or international alternatives) to use locations outside metropolitan Melbourne. RLAF assists projects by offsetting some of the additional costs incurred when filming in regional areas such as accommodation, living overheads and travel.

New South Wales Film and TV Office

www.fto.nsw.gov.au

Level 13, 227 Elizabeth Street, Sydney, NSW 2000, Australia

T: +61 2 9264 6400 · F: +61 2 9264 4399

E: fto@fto.nsw.gov.au

The Film & TV Office (FTO) plays a critical role in the New South Wales (NSW) screen industry, offering programmes of assistance for content development and production, including grants for screen content creators, organisations and events. It also provides expert advice for local and international producers about NSW locations, incentives, technical and creative talent, studio space options and post production facilities. The FTO is funded by the Australian state government of NSW.

Aurora Script Workshop

www.fto.nsw.gov.au/fund.asp?id=219&subID=1 · For: SCRIPT · Covering: FEAT | TV

A two-part script development programme over six months, aimed at NSW filmmaking teams with well developed scripts. Projects are assisted towards production through creative mentoring by leading filmmakers.

Development Assistance

www.fto.nsw.gov.au/fund.asp?id=45&content=2 · For: DEV | SCRIPT · Covering: FEAT | TV

Supporting film and TV projects and creative teams from early draft through to production financing. Includes travel assistance to attend markets and festivals.

Young Filmmakers Fund

www.fto.nsw.gov.au/fund.asp?id=48&content=2

Offers: $30,000 · For: DEV | PROD | POST · Covering: FEAT | SHORT | EXP | ANI

Grants of up to A$30,000 for NSW residents aged 18-35 for production or post-production costs for short dramas, feature films, documentaries, animation and experimental screen projects.

Loan Facilities

www.fto.nsw.gov.au/fund.asp?id=51&content=2 · For: PROD · Covering: FEAT | TV

Available only for fully-financed projects that are about to begin production.

Production Investment

www.fto.nsw.gov.au/fund.asp?id=47&content=2 · For: PROD · Covering: FEAT | DOC | TV | ANI

Funding for feature films, documentaries, documentary series, TV drama and telemovies, official co-productions and animation series.

Industry and Audience Development

www.fto.nsw.gov.au/fund.asp?id=52&content=2 · For: AUD-DEV | BIZ-DEV | CULT | PROMO | DIST | EXBN · Covering: FEAT | TV | MM | SHORT | DOC | ANI

Grants supporting projects and initiatives that develop and encourage an innovative, sustainable environment in which film, TV and digital media content is conceived, produced, distributed, discussed and analysed.

Regional Finance Fund (RFF)

www.fto.nsw.gov.au/fund.asp?id=49

Offers: up to AU$50,000 or 50%

The RFF is an annual fund that is available for filmmakers that intend to film for at least one week or more in any part of regional NSW. Funds are provided by way of non-recoupable grants and not investments. The aim of the RFF is to encourage Australian productions (and eligible co-productions) to film outside metropolitan Sydney.

Film & TV Industry Attraction Fund (FTIAF)
www.fto.nsw.gov.au/content.asp?content=8&Id=29
The NSW Government has created FTIAF to further increase the State's market share in film and TV production by attracting 'footloose' productions. The attraction fund will provide a rebate to approved productions, but not investment funding.

Northern Territory Film Office

www.nt.gov.au/nreta/arts/ntfo/index.html
NT Film Office, PO Box 3521, Alice Springs, NT 0870, Australia
T: +61 08 8951 1162 · F: +61 08 8951 1165
E: film.office@nt.gov.au
The Northern Territory Film Office (NTFO) has been established to develop the region's film, TV and new media industry. The key role is to develop and support the local film industry, attract production to the territory and celebrate an active screen culture.

Screen Grants
www.nt.gov.au/nreta/arts/ntfo/doc/ntfo_screen_
grants_gdlns_2006-07.pdf
Offers: up to A$15,000 · For: DEV | SCRIPT | PROD · Covering: FEAT | TV | SHORT | DOC
The fund supports the development of original and creative screenplays that are suitable for financing and distribution, and demonstrate an economic and/or cultural benefit to the Northern Territory.

Pacific Film and Television Commission (PFTC)

www.pftc.com.au
PO Box 15094, City East, Brisbane, Qld 4002, Australia
T: +61 7 3224 4114 · F: +61 7 3224 6717
E: pftc@pftc.com.au
The Queensland Government's PFTC helps local filmmakers to get their ideas on screen, attracts production to Queensland, and celebrates an active screen culture across the state. The PFTC has 10 permanent schemes of assistance and offers development and production initiatives for new and emerging filmmakers to partner with broadcasters to create short film and TV projects.

Funding
Funding is for Queensland-based residents. The PFTC Board approves funding in excess of A$300,000.

Write Stuff Short Film Development Scheme
www.pftc.com.au/pftc/funding/content.asp?pa
geid=173&top=2&menuparent=21 · For: DEV · Covering: SHORT
The fund aims to assist emerging writers to develop short drama projects.

JUMPSTART Short Film Fund
www.pftc.com.au/pftc/funding/content.asp?pageid
=174&top=2&menuparent=21
Offers: up to A$30,000 · For: DVD · Covering: SHORT
The fund aims to assist the career development of filmmakers by providing production investment for low-budget live action short dramas.

Short Film Fund
www.pftc.com.au/pftc/funding/content.asp?pageid
=175&top=2&menuparent=21 · For: PROD | POST | PROMO · Covering: SHORT
The fund aims to assist the career development of filmmakers by providing investment and creative support to produce, post-produce and market medium to high-budget live-action short dramas.

Indigenous Filmmakers' Fund — Short Black
www.pftc.com.au/pftc/funding/content.asp?pa
geid=274&top=2&menuparent=21 · For: DEV · Covering: SHORT
The fund aims to assist indigenous writers develop short drama projects.

Project Development Scheme
www.pftc.com.au/pftc/funding/content.asp?pa
geid=172&top=2&menuparent=21 · For: DEV · Covering: TV | DOC
The scheme facilitates production opportunities for writers, producers and directors by providing funding to develop film and TV projects for which there is a market demand. The majority of production and post-production must take place in Queensland.

Digital Fund
www.pftc.com.au/pftc/funding/content.asp?pageid
=177&top=2&menuparent=21 · For: PROD | DEV · Covering: TV | ANI | FEAT
The fund facilitates the development and production of animated TV series and feature films, TV drama using digital technology, and feature films with electronic game spin-off potential.

PREMIERE Script Development Scheme

www.pftc.com.au/pftc/funding/content.asp?pageid
=176&top=2&menuparent=21 · For: DEV | SCRIPT ·
Covering: FEAT

The scheme aims to raise the quality of feature film screenplays by providing intensive development services to projects that can attract audiences in Australia and the rest of the world.

New Media Fund

www.pftc.com.au/pftc/funding/content.asp?pageid
=178&top=2&menuparent=21 · For: PROD

The fund facilitates the development and production of content for new media platforms by providing development and production investment.

Documentary Production Fund

www.pftc.com.au/pftc/funding/content.asp?pa
geid=181&top=2&menuparent=21 · For: PROD ·
Covering: DOC

The fund increases production of documentary projects created by Queensland writers, producers and directors by providing production investment.

Production Fund

www.pftc.com.au/pftc/funding/content.asp?pa
geid=179&top=2&menuparent=21 · For: PROD ·
Covering: TV | FEAT

The fund aims to increase production of film and TV projects created by Queensland writers, producers and directors by providing equity investment.

Interstate Marketing Scheme

www.pftc.com.au/pftc/funding/content.asp?pag
eid=182&top=2&menuparent=21 · For: PROMO ·
Covering: FEAT | TV

The fund facilitates the marketing and financing of feature film and TV projects by providing grants for interstate travel.

International Marketing Scheme

www.pftc.com.au/pftc/funding/content.asp?pageid
=183&top=2&menuparent=21

Offers: up to A\$5,600 · For: PROMO · Covering:
FEAT | TV

The scheme facilitates the marketing and financing of feature film and TV projects by providing grants to producers for international travel.

Revolving Film Finance Fund

www.pftc.com.au/pftc/funding/content.asp?pa
geid=184&top=2&menuparent=21 · For: PROD ·
Covering: FEAT | TV

The fund aims to increase production in Queensland by providing loans to cashflow film and TV productions and for infrastructure projects that will benefit the film and TV industry.

Business Development Scheme

www.pftc.com.au/pftc/funding/content.asp?pageid
=180&top=2&menuparent=21

Offers: up to A\$100,000 · For: PROD · Covering:
FEAT | TV

The fund enables Queensland film and TV production companies to increase production output and achieve sustainability by providing investment in a slate of film and TV projects.

Industry Sponsorship

www.pftc.com.au/pftc/funding/content.asp?pageid
=102&top=2&menuparent=21 · For: CULT | PROMO

The sponsorship aims to increase the range of activities and events which promote and encourage a vigorous and diverse screen industry and culture in Queensland.

ScreenACT

www.screenact.act.gov.au/
PO Box 243, Civic Square ACT, 2608, Australia
T: +61 02 6207 1967
E: screenact@act.gov.au

ScreenACT is the Australian Capital Territory (ACT) Office of Film, TV and Digital Media. ScreenACT aims to advance the capability and professionalism of these industry sectors in Canberra and the region, and to promote the ACT and surrounding area as a filming location.

Development Funding

www.screenact.act.gov.au/funding/index.html# ·
For: PROMO | CULT · Covering: FEAT | TV | VIDG

Some funding available to screen industry professionals in the ACT and Capital Region. Financial assistance may be given towards initiatives offering an economic development outcome such as festivals and award sponsorship.

ScreenWest

www.screenwest.com.au
PO Box 8349, Perth Business Centre, WA 6849,
Australia
T: +61 8 9224 7340 · F: +61 8 9224 7341
E: info@screenwest.com.au

ScreenWest, Western Australia's film funding and development agency, is dedicated to the growth and promotion of film and TV activity in the State. ScreenWest provides funding for film and TV productions undertaken in Western Australia in order to assist development of a local screen industry, and to encourage national and international standard production in the State.

General Development Investment Funding (Docs & TV)

www.screenwest.com.au/index.
cfm?objectId=D1154E04-65BF-EBC1-
2317192DEC6279EE

Offers: up to A$50,000 · For: DEV · Covering: TV | DOC

ScreenWest assists with the development of quality film and TV projects intended for production in Western Australia. It does so by providing financial support for well-conceived projects with market potential, which have a strong likelihood of being produced. Whilst it is not required that a Western Australian–resident Producer be committed to the project, ScreenWest will give priority to projects that have a local producer as an active part of the team.

Production Funding

www.screenwest.com.au/index.
cfm?objectId=E0F3B2B6-65BF-EBC1-
2B77C06AC63AC335

Offers: up to A$600,000 · For: PROD · Covering: DOC | TV | YP

The Production Fund is ScreenWest's principal fund for the provision of production finance.

Screen Culture

www.screenwest.com.au/index.
cfm?objectId=E0F45B4B-65BF-EBC1-
29F925C9DA3AFB8D · For: CULT · Covering: TV | DOC

Seeks to develop the local screen culture and industry through the funding of events, courses and training activities.

South Australian Film Corporation (SAFC)

www.safilm.com.au

3 Butler Drive, Hendon Common, Hendon, 5014, Australia

T: +61 8 8348 9300 · F: +61 8 8347 0385
E: safilm@safilm.com.au

Starting life as a production company in 1972, the SAFC is a statutory body established under the South Australian Film Corporation Act that has helped foster an internationally recognised industry producing hundreds of feature films, TV dramas and documentaries.

Script and Project Development Funding

www.safilm.com.au/library/SCRIPT%20AND%20PR
OJECT%20DEVELOPMENT%20FUNDING%20Guidel
ines%202005_2006.pdf

Offers: from A$4,000 -$12,000 · For: DEV · Covering: FEAT | TV | DOC

Applicants must be Australian citizens or permanent residents of Australia and be 18 years of age or older. Corporate entities cannot be applicants, but the SAFC will contract with such entities.

Producer Business Development

www.filmnz.com/production-guide/large-budget-
screen-production-grant-scheme.html · For: DEV · Covering: FEAT | TV | DOC | DIGI

Producers are eligible to apply for funding, if in the past five years they have more than two hours of broadcast TV above the line credits, or a feature film credit as a producer.

Business Travel (Traditional & Digital Media)

www.safilm.com.au/library/BUSINESS%20TRAVEL
%20Guidelines%202005_2006.pdf · For: PROMO · Covering: FEAT | TV | DOC | DIGI

The aim of Business Travel funding is to allow film, TV and interactive digital media producers to travel to international markets and set up meetings to attract finance for a project or slate.

Digital Media Project Development

www.safilm.com.au/library/DIGITAL%20MEDIA%20
PROJECT%20DEVELOPMENT%20Guidelines%2020
05_2006.pdf · For: DEV · Covering: DIGI

The aim of the Digital Media Project Development program is to support the development of interactive digital media projects which are based on strong ideas, are well-crafted, are of varying styles and content, exhibit a high level of creative ambition and can demonstrate the possibility of being financed for production and economic benefit to South Australia.

Production Investment

www.safilm.com.au/library/PRODUCTION%20INVES
TMENT%20Guidelines%202005_2006.pdf

Offers: A$200,000 · For: PROD | POST · Covering: FEAT | TV | DOC

Production Investment funding supports the production of projects that are creative and original, possess overall appeal to diverse audiences, display good market prospects, and have significant economic benefits to the South Australian production and post-production film and TV sector.

SAFC Short Film Fund

www.safilm.com.au/library/SAFC%20SHORT%20FILM%20FUND%20Guidelines%202005_2006.pdf

Offers: A$50,000 · For: PROD · Covering: SHORT

The SAFC Short Film Fund offers South Australia's filmmakers and digital media practitioners the opportunity to develop their skills as a way of progressing towards long form feature film, TV drama, documentary and digital media production.

Educational Content Fund (Traditional & Digital Media)

www.safilm.com.au/library/EDUCATIONAL%20CONTENT%20FUND%20Guidelines%202005_2006.pdf

Offers: up to A$100,000 · For: PROD · Covering: DOC | DIGI | YP | FEAT | TV

Supports the production of educational, sponsored and government related projects across all platforms, for example, documentary film, DVD, online, and CD-ROM, but excluding solely print-based media.

Digital Media Production Investment

www.safilm.com.au/library/DIGITAL%20MEDIA%20PRODUCTION%20INVESTMENT%20Guidelines%202005_2006.pdf · For: PROD · Covering: VIDG | DIGI

The SAFC provides production investment funding for digital media projects in the areas of arts and entertainment. This includes interactive/online dramas, documentaries, animations, content-rich electronic or computer games, or combinations of these.

Revolving Loan Fund

www.safilm.com.au/library/REVOLVING%20LOAN%20FUND%20Guidelines%202005_2006.pdf · For: PROD · Covering: FEAT | TV | DOC | ANI | DIGI

In addition to production investment funding, the SAFC administers a A$3 million revolving loan fund to sustain and increase film and TV production in South Australia. The fund does this by cash-flowing secured pre-sale and distribution guarantees or advances into the production budget of a project. The SAFC will also consider cash flowing productions in the final stages of contracting on a short term basis during pre-production.

Practitioner Development Funding (Traditional & Digital Media)

www.safilm.com.au/library/PRACTITIONER%20DEVELOPMENT%20FUNDING%20Guidelines%202005_2006.pdf · For: EDU

The programme provides funding for practitioners to attend workshops, conferences, courses or other industry related events that provide professional development or career enhancement, and that contribute to the applicant's skills and ability to contribute to and work within the South Australian industry.

Attachment Scheme

www.safilm.com.au/library/ATTACHMENT%20SCHEME%20Guidelines%202005_2006.pdf

The Scheme provides support to a limited number of practitioners who have appropriate skills and a demonstrated commitment to the South Australian industry to further develop their skills in a professional work environment.

Digital Media Attachment Scheme

www.safilm.com.au/library/DIGITAL%20MEDIA%20ATTACHMENT%20SCHEME%20Guidelines%202005_2006.pdf

The funding supports practitioners who have appropriate skills and a demonstrated commitment to the digital and/or traditional media industry, as a way of further developing their digital media skills in a professional work environment.

Festival and Awards Grants (Traditional & Digital Media)

www.safilm.com.au/library/FESTIVAL%20AND%20AWARD%20GRANTS%20Guidelines%202005_2006.pdf

Offers: up to A$2,000 towards airfare/travel costs and A$100 per day for *per diems*, for a maximum of 5 days · For: PROMO

To allow South Australian filmmakers and digital media practitioners to travel to key festivals and interstate award ceremonies where they are being recognised for their work.

Industry Development Events and Activities (Tarditional & Digital Media)

www.safilm.com.au/library/INDUSTRY%20DEVELOPMENT%20EVENTS%20%20ACTIVITIES%20_IDEA_%20Guidelines%202006_2007.pdf · For: EDU · Covering: FEAT | TV | DOC | ANI | DIGI

The programme provides funding for industry development events and activities, such as short courses which are strategically targeted at short-term skills development, seminars, conferences workshops, speakers' programmes and other activities of relevance to the South Australian film, TV and digital media sector. There are two deadlines per year.

Screen Culture Organisational Funding (Traditional & Digital Media)

www.safilm.com.au/library/SCREEN%20CULTURE%20ORGANISATIONAL%20FUNDING%20Guidelines%202005_2006.pdf

Funding is available to organisations whose core activities and programmes significantly contribute to the promotion and development of screen culture in

South Australia. Not for profit organisations active in the area of screen culture who are based in South Australia are eligible to apply. National organisations based outside South Australia, but with a demonstrable commitment to activities within the state, may also be eligible.

SAFC/SBSi Documentary Series & Cross Media Opportunity

www.safilm.com.au/program_detail.
aspx?p=14&id=45
Offers: A$600,000 plus office facilities. · For: PROD · Covering: WEB | DOC
The programme offers a cross platform (TV and online) opportunity as part of SBS TV's high profile half-hour Australian documentary strand INSIDE AUSTRALIA. The selected series producer will work with South Australian producers and key creatives to develop TV and online programming. The application deadline is once a year.

The Script Factory

www.safilm.com.au/program_detail.
aspx?p=14&id=49 · For: SCRIPT | EDU
The aim of the Script Factory Script Writing and Development Workshop is to provide a forum for writers and producers, directors and script editors working on feature film projects to explore and refine the way they work with scripts.

Rocket Science

www.safilm.com.au/program_detail.
aspx?p=14&id=50 · For: EDU | PROD
Rocket Science is producer-driven and designed to assist producers with developed feature film projects and to enhance their film financing and strategic skills before presenting their projects to the domestic and international market to secure financing.

Dococom.com

www.safilm.com.au/program_detail.
aspx?p=14&id=48 · For: DEV | PROD | DIST · Covering: DOC | DIGI
The SAFC offers support for the development, production and online distribution of digi-docs, telling 'real' stories from the perspective of traditionally disenfranchised or marginalised community groups.

Digital Animation Initiative

www.safilm.com.au/library/Digital%20Animation%20Guidelines.pdf
Offers: up to A$450,000 · For: DEV | PROD · Covering: DIGI | ANI
The Digital Animation Initiative funds the development and production of a 13 x 5 minute cross-platform animation series. Projects should be targeted towards a young/young adult audience.

Post Production Initiative — Drama

www.safilm.com.au/library/Drama%20Post%20Production%20Guidelines%202006.pdf
Offers: up to A$70,000 · For: POST · Covering: FEAT
The SAFC will offer investment for a drama project to be taken from an assembly stage to completion to enable the producer to attract further investment and market interest. The application deadline is once a year.

Post Production Initiative — Doco

www.safilm.com.au/library/Doco%20Post%20Production%20Guidelines%202006.pdf
Offers: up to A$30,000 · For: POST · Covering: DOC
The SAFC offers investment funds for a documentary project to be taken to fine cut stage to enable the producer to attract further investment and market interest.

Payroll tax exemption

A payroll tax exemption on eligible productions shot in South Australia (SA) reduces the film's payroll total by approximately 6%. Note that this is an up-front exemption, not a rebate. To be eligible for the exemption, projects must be produced wholly or substantially within South Australia, employ SA residents, and provide significant economic benefits to the State.

Employment rebate

A 10% rebate on all eligible SA labour expenditure on any eligible film or TV production. The employment rebate is not a tax rebate and therefore is not tied to a year-end tax return. It can be paid in instalments, with the first (potentially largest) instalment paid on the first day of principal photography.

Film Commissions

Ausfilm International

www.ausfilm.com.au
Fox Studios Australia, 38 Driver Avenue, Moore Park NSW 2021, Australia
T: 61 2 9383 4192 · F: 61 2 9383 4190
E: info@ausfilm.com.au
The Australian Federal Government has a refundable tax offset for eligible film and TV productions. The offset benefit is worth 12.5% of the production's qualifying Australian production expenditure. The refund is claimed by the production company through the company's tax return. A fact sheet, guidelines and application forms are available from the film tax offset page of the Department of Communications, Information Technology and the Arts website at www.dcita.gov.au/filmtaxoffset. In addition to the federal tax offset, the Australian States offer a variety of incentives

such as location attraction grants, post-production incentives, payroll tax rebates, cast and crew wage rebates and subsidised public service resources. The qualification criteria varies from state to state.

Melbourne Film Office

www.film.vic.gov.au/mfo
GPO Box 4361, Melbourne, Victoria 3001, Australia
T: +61 3 9660 3200 · F: +61 3 9660 3201
E: mfo@film.vic.gov.au
In addition to the Australian Government's 12.5% film tax offset, the Melbourne Film Office offers two highly competitive financial incentive programs.

AUSTRIA

Österreichisches Filminstitut

www.filminstitut.at
Spittelberggasse 3, A-1070 Vienna, Austria
T: +43 1 526 97 30 · F: +43 1 526 97 30 440
E: office@filminstitut.at
The Austrian Film Institute was established in 1981 to provide comprehensive funding for the Austrian film industry in its cultural and economic development. It is particularly aimed at strengthening the Austrian film industry and the creative and artistic qualities of Austrian film, to ensure its domestic and international success. AFI objectives include supporting the production, dissemination and marketing of Austrian films. The institute aims to improve the international position and co-production of Austrian film particularly through supporting the presentation of Austrian film domestically and abroad.

Support for Script Development
Offers: up to €15,000 · For: SCRIPT · Covering: FEAT | DOC | YP | FFF
The fund takes the form of a grant.

Support for Project Development
Offers: up to €36,000 · For: DEV · Covering: FEAT | DOC | YP | FFF
The fund takes the form of a grant.

Support for Production
Offers: €440,000 · For: PROD · Covering: FEAT | FFF | YP | DOC
The fund supports feature films with a length of 70 minute, children's films with a length of 59 minutes, and first feature films with length of 45 minutes.

Automatic Support for Production based on a 'reference' film
www.filminstitut.at/downloads/
11151230FILM%20FUNDING%20ACT%202005.pdf
· For: PROD · Covering: FEAT | FFF | YP | DOC
The fund takes the form of a grant

Support for Co-production — Co-financing
For: PROD · Covering: FEAT | FFF | YP | DOC
The fund takes the form of non-repayable advance.

Support for Distribution
Offers: up to €40,000 · For: DIST · Covering: FEAT | DOC | ANI | YP
The fund takes the form of non-repayable advance.

Support for Professional Training
A non-repayable advance.

Cine Styria Film Fund

www.cinestyria.steiermark.at/
Cine Styria, Filmcommission & Fonds,
Trauttmansdorffgasse 2, 8010 Graz, Austria
T: +43316 877 2435 · F: +43316 877 2477
E: office@cinestyria.at
A regional, national and international agency that offers film funding, information, services and support for film and TV projects that are relevant for Steiermark. Film funding applies to both commercial film and TV projects as well as more cultural projects.

Arthouse support
www.cinestyria.steiermark.at/cms/
beitrag/10224863/7684533/ · For: PROD · Covering: FEAT | DOC | SHORT | ANI | FFF
The fund supports independent, artistic and culturally relevant film and TV productions that contribute towards Austrian and European film culture.

Production support for commercial films
www.cinestyria.steiermark.at/cms/
beitrag/10224856/7684472/ · For: PROD · Covering: FEAT | TV
The fund aims to enhance the quality of commercial film and TV productions, and contribute to the strengthening of the audiovisual sector within Austria.

Cine Tirol Film Fund

www.cinetirol.com

Filmförderung Film Commission & Fund, c/o Tirol Werbung, Maria Theresien Straße 55, A-6010 Innsbruck, Austria

T: +43 512 53 52 0 · F: +43 512 53 20 140

E: cinetirol@tirolwerbung.at

Cine Tirol supports commercial film projects (including documentary) as well as telefilms and series that are relevant for international screening, that have been totally or partially made in Tirol.

Production Support

Cine Tirol offers the possibility of financial incentives, the structure of which is based on internationally accepted standards for this type of financing. The production should show a reference to Tirol. Financial support may take the form of co-funding through an interest-free, success-linked, repayable grant. There are four annual deadlines.

City of Salzburg — Culture Department

www.stadt-salzburg.at

Kulturabteilung der Stadt Salzburg, Mozartpl. 5, A 5024 Salzburg, Austria

T: +43 662 8072 3435 · F: +43 662 8072 3469

E: kulturamt@stadt-salzburg.at

The Film and Cultural Centre functions as a central institution for the promotion of culturally valuable films. For the funding of new talents are the schemes such as Action Film Salzburg.

Scriptwriting Award

www.stadt-salzburg.at/internet/themen/kultur/t2_ 90525/t2_86558/t2_84390/p2_147795.htm

Offers: €50,000 · For: SCRIPT | DEV · Covering: ANI | FFF | DOC | MM | FEAT

Applicant should have some relationship to Salzburg, either personally (native of or living and working in Salzburg); by content (film relating to Salzburg); or by production (part of film shot in the city).

Federal Chancellory film and media department

www.bmukk.gv.at/

Bundeskanzleramt, Abteilung II/3, Film und Medienkunst, Schottengasse 1, 1014 Wien, Austria

T: +43 1 531 15 0 · F: +43 1 531 15 7538

E: johannes.hoerhan@bka.gv.at

Operates as part of the Federal Ministry for Arts, Education and Culture.

Production support

Offers: up to €100,000 · For: PROD | DIST · Covering: TV | FEAT

The fund supports full-length features and TV films. The grants programme distinguishes between grants for non-profit associations and institutions, grants for events and investment grants.

Scriptwriting support

Offers: up to €5,000 · For: SCRIPT · Covering: FEAT | SHORT | TV | DOC | ANI

There are three annual deadlines.

Distribution

Offers: up to €20,000 · For: DIST

Subsidy to support the distribution of eligible films.

Development support

Offers: up to €10,000 · For: DEV · Covering: FEAT | TV | SHORT | DOC | ANI

There are three annual deadlines.

Fernsehfonds Austria (RTR-GmbH)

www.rtr.at/filmfoerderung

Mariahilfer Strasse 77-79, A-1060 Wien, Österreich, Austria

T: +43 1 58058 0 · F: +43 1 58058 9191

E: rtr@rtr.at

The Austrian TV Film Fund is intended to contribute to an improvement in the quality of TV production and the capacity of the Austrian film industry, as well as reinforcing Austria as a media location and ensuring the diversity of the cultural landscape. Grants are also intended to contribute to the strengthening of the sector in Europe.

Television Fund (Fernsehfonds Austria)

www.rtr.at/web.nsf/englisch/Foerderungen_ Fernsehfonds

Offers: up to €700,000 · For: PROD · Covering: TV

Grants — in the form of a non-repayable subsidy — can be awarded to cover a maximum of 20 percent of reasonable overall production costs. Grant limits vary by genre, with TV series being eligible for grants up to €120,000 per episode, TV films up to €700,000 and TV documentaries up to €200,000.

Digitisation Fund

www.rtr.at/web.nsf/englisch/Foerderungen_ Digitalisierungsfonds · Covering: MM | DIGI

For promoting digital transmission technologies and digital applications based on European standards. The fund supports projects which upgrade and reinforce all broadcasting transmission platforms as a special part of communications infrastructure.

Filmfonds Wien

www.filmfonds-wien.at/
Stiftgasse 6, 1070 Wien, Austria
T: +43 1 526 50 88 · F: +43 1 526 50 88 20
E: office@filmfonds-wien.at
The Vienna Film Fund is a non-profit fund aimed at strengthening and consolidating Vienna as a city of film and audiovisual media within the international arena, while also promoting the cultural diversity of Europe. Therefore it is essential for the Vienna Film Fund to help subsidise culture, the economy and employment in the film industry of Vienna, Austria and all of Europe. It is also an important aim of the fund to promote Austrian film.

Project Development Subsidy

www.filmfonds-wien.at/en/subsidy/guidelines/9--project-development-subsidy/ · For: DEV
The subsidy is provided in the form of recoupable grants which can amount to half of the total development costs up to a maximum of €50,000. A film's producer is eligible to apply.

Support for Production

www.filmfonds-wien.at/en/subsidy/guidelines/10--production-subsidy/
Offers: up to €400,000 · For: PROD · Covering: FEAT | TV
The Film Fund subsidises the production of films in the form of a Subsidy Repayable on Success. Productions for which applications have been submitted to the Film Fund for funding amounting to less than 30% of the total production costs recognised by the Film Fund will have priority for subsidy.

Joint Productions and Additional Terms Regarding Productions Subsidies

www.filmfonds-wien.at/en/subsidy/guidelines/11--joint-productions-and-additional-terms-regarding-productions-subsidies/ · For: PROD · Covering: FEAT
The grant is for an international co-production between Austrian and foreign partners.

Television Productions and Additional Terms Regarding Production Subsidies

www.filmfonds-wien.at/en/subsidy/guidelines/12--TV-productions-and-additional-terms-regarding-production-subsidies/
Offers: up to €250,000 · For: PROD · Covering: TV
Productions of TV films for all fiction and documentary types are eligible.

Distribution Subsidy

www.filmfonds-wien.at/en/subsidy/guidelines/14--distribution-subsidy/ · For: DIST | CULT · Covering: FEAT
The fund subsides the theatrical distribution of films which have received support for production for the purpose of facilitating their theatrical premiere and promotion in Austria, and in other media and their participation at international festivals, market-related events and competitions.

Success Based Funding

www.filmfonds-wien.at/en/subsidy/guidelines/13--success-based-funding/ · Covering: FEAT
Applicants who have already received funding for a financially successful film are eligible to receive additional money.

Land Carinthia Film Fund

www.kultur.ktn.gv.at/
?siid=52&pagetype=nearlyplain&root=8
Amt der Kärntner Landesregierung, Abteilung 5 – Kultur, Paradeisergasse 7, 9021 Klagenfurt, Austria
T: +435 0536 30502 · F: +435 0536 30500
E: post.abt5@ktn.gv.at
Funding applies to small film projects (short films, animation films, experimental films, diploma projects) on an artistic level as well as to documentaries that have cultural and scientific relevance.

Support for film, photography and digital media

The fund supports projects that have cultural relevance.

Land Salzburg Film Fund

www.salzburg.gv.at
Abteilung 12: Kulture und Sport, Franziskanergasse 5 a, Postfach 527, 5010 Salzburg, Austria
· F: +43 662 8042 2919
E: kultur@salzburg.gv.at
The Salzburg film fund (Culture department) is committed towards artistic film-funding, which embraces the financing of new talent, avantgarde short, animation and documentary films, video productions as well as feature films (especially script and project development for cinema films).

Support for cultural films

www.salzburg.gv.at/themen/ks/kultur/film/
filmfoerderung.htm
Offers: €10,000 · For: PROD · Covering: FEAT | DOC
| ANI | FFF | SHORT
The fund applies to independent, cultural and artistic
film productions. The applicant should be born or living
in Salzburg.

BELGIUM

Centre du Cinéma et de
l'Audiovisuel

www.cfwb.be/av
Ministère de la Communauté Française de Belgique,
Service Général de l'Audiovisuel et des Multimédias,
Centre du Cinéma et de l'Audiovisuel, 44 boulevard
Leopold IIB, 1080 BRUXELLES., Belgium
T: +32 2 413 35 01 · F: +32 2 413 20 68
E: daav@cfwb.be
The Centre du Cinéma et de l'Audiovisuel is the
film and audiovisual support office for the Wallonie
Bruxelles region. The principal organisational goal
is support for the production and promotion of
audiovisual works through financial awards. CCA
supports features, documentaries, short films, animated
films and telefilms (with the prior commitment of
a broadcaster). Recommendations are made by a
committee which meets three times a year, but the final
decision is made by the Belgian Ministry.

Production Support

www.cfwb.be/av/ · Offers: up to €450,000 · For:
PROD · Covering: FEAT | ANI | TV | SHORT
The fund offers a repayable advance to producers and
authors who produce cultural films in French or German
language. 150% of the investment must be spent in
the region, and producers must demonstrate that 30%
of the budget is already in place. Project must go into
production within a year of the support offer which is
up to 25% the budget

Finance for production companies

For: PROD | SLATE | BIZ-DEV
Supports start up or existing companies based in the
region, up to 40% of capital expenditure as equity.

Flemish Audiovisual Fund

www.vaf.be
Vlaams Audiovisueel Fonds, Handelskaai 18/3, 1000
Brussels, Belgium
T: +32 2 226 06 30 · F: +32 2 219 19 36
E: info@vaf.be
The Flanders Audiovisual Fund (VAF) supports
audiovisual production in Belgium, as well as
international co-productions with Flanders. The Fund
was set up by the Flemish government in 2002 and is
headquartered in Brussels. The aims of the Flanders
Audiovisual Fund are threefold: to develop a sustainable
Flemish audiovisual industry, to encourage and support
upcoming audiovisual talent and to promote a vibrant
audiovisual culture in Flanders. The Flemish Audiovisual
Fund received a €12.5m grant from the Flemish
government in 2006.

Support for production

Offers: €87,500 - €1.25m · www.vaf.be/frames.
asp?page=1&lang=1 · For: PROD · Covering: FEAT |
DOC | ANI | MM
A minimum of 78% of the annual budget goes
to production support, which takes the form of a
repayable advance.

Support for promotion

Offers: up to €25,000 and 50% · For: PROMO
Flanders Image attends a large number of festivals and
markets, such as Rotterdam, Berlin, Cannes and MIP
and organises and/or participates in film events abroad
that are aimed at supporting Flemish audiovisual
productions.

Support for development

Offers: €75,000 - €250,000 and up to 50% · For:
DEV · Covering: FEAT | TV | SHORT | DOC | ANI
Cofinancing for the development of films.

Support for scriptwriting

Offers: up to €12,500 · For: SCRIPT · Covering:
FEAT | SHORT | TV | DOC | ANI
A repayable advance to support scriptwriting.

Wallimage

www.wallimage.be
6 rue du Onze Novembre, BE — 7000 MONS,
Belgium
T: +32 65 40 40 33 · F: +32 65 40 40 39
E: info@wallimage.be
Set up on the initiative of the Walloon Region and its
Ministry of the Economy, the Wallimages and Sowalim
companies are structured as an investment fund which
aims to support the audiovisual sector in Wallonie.

Finance for Audiovisual Works
www.wallimage.be/comment_uk.php?lang=uk
Offers: up to €500,000
The support provided to both Belgian and international producers is broken down into 60% co-production investment and 40% loan, which can be used by the production for a maximum period of three years.

Film Commissions

Antwerp City Film Office

www.antwerpen.be/filmoffice
Desguinlei 33, 2018 Antwerpen, Belgium
T: +32 3 202 66 88 · F: +32 3 202 67 89
E: bedrijvenloket@stad.antwerpen.be
In the city of Antwerp, usage fees for the public domain are demanded for TV and film-commercials. In Belgium a federal tax shelter system is available (see Part II).

Wallonie Bruxelles Images

www.wbi.be
18 Place E. Flagey, 1050 Brussels, Belgium
T: +32 2 223 23 04 · F: +32 2 218 34 24
E: wbimages@skynet.be
The best way to get information on independent productions by the French-speaking Belgian community.

BRAZIL

Cinema Brazil

www.cinemabrazil.com
Avenida Rio Branco, 277 Sl, 102 — 20047-900, Rio De Janeiro, Brazil
T: +55 21 2210 1371 · F: +55 21 2240 2791
E: xolotl@ism.com.br
The Agência de Cinema e Audiovisuel (Cinema Brazil) supports the production, promotion and funding of films in Brazil.

Assistance to movie production in Brazil
www.cinemabrazil.com/indexen.html
The government has previously managed an investment programme, whereupon for a $1.6m subscription, investors can take 30% of gross revenues, although limited details were available at publication.

For film commission support see:
www.minasfilmcommission.com.br

BULGARIA

Bulgarian National Film Centre

www.nfc.bg
Executive Agency National Film Centre, 2A Kniaz Dondukow Boulevard, BG-1000 Sofia, Bulgaria
T: +359 2 988 3831 · F: +359 2 987 36 26
E: nfc@nfc.bg
The Bulgarian National Film Centre (BNFC) is a State institution that operates under the auspices of the Ministry of Culture. The aim is to distribute and administer state subsidies for film production. The National Expert Committee meets four times a year to select projects that will be supported by the BNFC. There is one committee for feature, documentaries and animation films.

Production support
www.nfc.bg · For: PROD · Covering: ANI | DOC | FEAT
Producers and production companies are eligible to apply for support. The fund takes the form of repayable advances. At least 50% of the production, including the laboratory processing of the picture, should be implemented in Bulgaria.

CANADA

National Film Board of Canada

www.nfb.ca/e/
Postal Box 6100, Centre-ville Station, Montreal, Quebec, H3C 3H5, Canada
T: +514 283 9000 · F: +514 283 7564
E: international@nfb.ca
The National Film Board of Canada (NFB) is a federal cultural agency within the portfolio of the Canadian Heritage Department. Initially known as the National Film Commission, it was created by an act of Parliament in 1939. Its mandate, as set forth in the National Film Act, 1950, is 'to produce and distribute and to promote the production and distribution of films designed to interpret Canada to Canadians and to other nations.' The NFB's mandate has been revised several times over the years to take into account the changing audiovisual environment and financial and social situation.

French Program
www.nfb.ca/faireunfilm/index.php?v=h&lg=en · For: PROD | DIST · Covering: DOC
The French program supports productions that are important to Francophones in Canada while promoting the growth of a national cinema and to distribute these films at home and abroad. Its mission is to

produce films that reflect the personal approaches of Canadian filmmakers, and to explore avenues of distribution appropriate to the nature of their film. The English program supports the production of Canadian documentaries.

English Program

www.nfb.ca/faireunfilm/index.php?v=h&lg=en · For: DIST | PROD · Covering: DOC | FEAT | ANI
The English Program works with documentary directors in every region of Canada. The fund produces videos and films of highly recognized filmmakers as well as emerging artists. Its aim is to reflect the cultural diversity of Canada, including the production of many Aboriginal documentaries and documentaries by women.

Co-production with the NFC

www.nfb.ca/faireunfilm/index.php?v=h&lg=en · For: PROD · Covering: FEAT | DOC | ANI
The NFC works together with over 13 different co-production studios and can give advice on co-productions and help with finding suitable co-production companies.

Distribution Funding

www.nfb.ca/faireunfilm/faire_un_film_distribuer. php?v=h&lg=en · For: DIST · Covering: DOC | ANI | FEAT
The fund supports Canadian and international documentaries (one-offs and series), animated films; socially relevant documentaries exploring health, international conflict and peace, and global environmental issues; youth-oriented educational content in science, history and civilization. Proposals can be submitted at any time of the year. The NFB has recently adopted an acquisition policy for new audiovisual products, including projects in development. The aim is to acquire Canadian documentaries and animated films as well as foreign productions that are in line with the spirit of the NFB's collection and that have obvious commercial sales potential.

Aboriginal Filmmaking Program

www.nfb.ca/faireunfilm/travaillerStudio.php?idP=0 &choix=stage&idS=15&idCat=39&v=h&lg=en · For: PROD | DEV · Covering: DOC
Projects must be directed by an Aboriginal filmmaker. The primary focus of the program is to support documentary films. other genres will be considered as long as the subject matter and its portrayal are consistent with the NFB's mandate regarding the social and cultural relevance of the content, creativity, and innovation. NFB support may be available at the development stage and during production. With co-productions, preference will be given to those that include apprenticeship or training opportunities for an Aboriginal person or persons.

Animacadie 2006

www.nfb.ca/faireunfilm/travaillerStudio.php?idP=0 &choix=stage&idS=25&idCat=55&v=h&lg=en · For: SCRIPT · Covering: SHORT | ANI
The NFB and Connections Productions, in collaboration with Film New Brunswick and the French-language TV service of CBC Atlantic, offer the opportunity to write a script for a professional-quality animated short. The program is directed to Francophones in the four Atlantic provinces.

Anime ton univers francophone 2007

www.onf.ca/faireunfilm/travaillerStudio.php?idP=0c hoix=stage&v=h&lg=fr&idS=50&idCat=79
Offers: C$5000 · For: PROD | EDU · Covering: OTHER
The program enables applicants to participate in workshops about cartoon creation that may lead to the production of an own professional cartoon film. French-speaking person living in Ontario and having already produced at least one cartoon film (irrelevant of whether the film was produced under professional conditions or not) are eligible to apply.

Cinéaste recherché(e)

www.nfb.ca/faireunfilm/travaillerStudio.php?idP=0 &choix=stage&idS=31&idCat=61&v=h&lg=en · For: PROD · Covering: FFF
Cinéaste recherché(e) gives emerging francophone animation filmmakers the opportunity to make their first professional film and to develop a unique creative approach.

Citizen Shift

www.nfb.ca/faireunfilm/travaillerStudio.php?idP=0 &choix=stage&idS=44&idCat=75&v=h&lg=en · For: PROD · Covering: OTHER | FFF
Inspired by the NFB's legendary Challenge for Change program, the community Web platforms CITIZENShift and Parole citoyenne commission projects from a wide range of socially engaged, emerging filmmakers.

Cross-Media Challenge

www.nfb.ca/faireunfilm/travaillerStudio.php?idP=0& choix=stage&idS=51&idCat=68&v=h&lg=en
Offers: a C$10,000 co-production development offer · For: PROD · Covering: OTHER
Cross-Media Challenge is a $10,000 co-production competition for innovative content creators who share an interest in producing a film with social issues.

Doc Shop

www.nfb.ca/faireunfilm/travaillerStudio.php?idP=0
&choix=stage&idS=36&idCat=67&v=h&lg=en • For:
EDU • Covering: DOC

The scheme is a documentary training program for
English-speaking CEGEP and university students
enrolled in a film, video or communications program
in the Montreal and Ottawa areas. Participating
schools put a call out to their students for proposals
for four-minute videos on a chosen theme. Directors
and their crew members are invited to attend a series
of workshops covering many aspects of film and video
production and marketing. In addition to the workshop
weekend, each team receives C$500, three DV tapes,
technical support, as well as camera and sound
equipment if needed.

Equity Training Program

www.nfb.ca/faireunfilm/travaillerStudio.php?idP=0
&choix=stage&idS=16&idCat=40&v=h&lg=en • For:
EDU

The NFB's Equity Training Program provides
professional development in film and video for members
of employment equity designated groups: persons with
disabilities, Aboriginal people and members of visible
minorities.

First Stories

www.nfb.ca/faireunfilm/travaillerStudio.php?idP=0
&choix=stage&idS=22&idCat=51&v=h&lg=en • For:
PROD • Covering: DOC

After starting in Manitoba, this program for emerging
Aboriginal directors has come to Alberta and
Saskatchewan.

Homeless Nation

www.nfb.ca/faireunfilm/travaillerStudio.php?idP
=0&choix=stage&idS=45&idCat=76&v=h&lg=en •
Covering: SHORT

Executive producer Daniel Cross and the NFB are
collaborating on Homeless Nation, a website that
empowers the street community to undertake their own
representation and foster a dialogue on homelessness.

Hothouse

www.nfb.ca/faireunfilm/travaillerStudio.php?idP=0
&choix=stage&idS=28&idCat=58&v=h&lg=en • For:
EDU • Covering: ANI | FFF

The scheme enables emerging animators from across
Canada to receive an intensive 12-week mentorship at
the NFB. The NFB created the Hothouse to encourage
new talent, to provide an A-to-Z experience in
professional animation filmmaking, and to re-imagine
ways of making animation.

Inspired

www.nfb.ca/faireunfilm/travaillerStudio.php?idP=0
&choix=stage&idS=38&idCat=69&v=h&lg=en • For:
PROD • Covering: DOC | FFF

A partnership of the NFB, CTV, IFC Canada and the
Atlantic Film Festival, Inspired provides training and
production for emerging documentary directors in
Atlantic Canada.

Momentum

www.nfb.ca/faireunfilm/travaillerStudio.php?idP=0
&choix=stage&idS=18&idCat=42&v=h&lg=en • For:
EDU • Covering: DOC

The Momentum program develops English- and
French-language emerging documentary filmmakers
in Ontario. This program provides 100 emerging
filmmakers insight into the creative and craft elements
of documentary production and provides hands-on
experience, NFB expertise and an introduction to a
network of contacts that will help new filmmakers
pursue their career.

Arts Council Mentorship Program

www.nfb.ca/faireunfilm/travaillerStudio.php?idP=0
&choix=stage&idS=32&idCat=62&v=h&lg=en • For:
EDU

The NFB and the Ontario Arts Council select four
Ontario Francophone filmmakers for a mentorship
program in pre-production, production or post-
production, as well as training in editing, story and HD
camera work.

Reel Diversity

www.nfb.ca/faireunfilm/travaillerStudio.php?idP=0
&choix=stage&idS=24&idCat=54&v=h&lg=en • For:
DIST • Covering: DOC

The NFB's Reel Diversity competition seeks submissions
by emerging filmmakers of colour. Reel Diversity gives
three promising directors the chance to direct their
documentary for broadcast on CBC Newsworld.

Alberta Foundation for the Arts (AFA)

www.cd.gov.ab.ca/all_about_us/commissions/arts/
5th Floor, Commerce Place, 10155 – 102 Street,
Edmonton, Alberta, T5J 4L6, Canada
T: +780 422 8584 • F: +780 422 8582
E: dan.chugg@gov.ab.ca

AFA is an agency of the Government of Alberta formed
in 1991 for individual artists and arts organisations in
the visual, performing and literary arts, and cultural
industries. AFA's level of contribution increases with
Albertan ownership and the employment of Albertans
in key creative positions. The foundation will contribute
between 14%-23% of all eligible expenses incurred in

Alberta (equivalent of between 25% — 42% labour tax credit).

Film and Video Project Grant
www.albertafilm.ca/web/ab_costs.php · For: PROD
Covering: FEAT | TV | SHORT | DOC | ANI
The fund aims to support the artistic development of individual Alberta artists or an ensemble of artists with a grant for a specific film and/or video project.

British Columbia Film

www.bcfilm.bc.ca
2225 West Broadway, Vancouver, British Columbia, V6K 2E4, Canada
T: +604 736 7997 · F: +604 736 7290
E: bcf@bcfilm.bc.ca
The BCF offers development and production financing to British Columbia filmmakers through a variety of funding programs and professional development to producers, writers and directors through marketing and skills assistance programs. A private, non-profit society also administers the provincial tax credit program on behalf of the provincial government.

Project Development Fund
www.bcfilm.bc.ca/projectdevelopment.php · For: DEV · Covering: FEAT
The Project Development Fund provides 'market triggered' development financing for individual projects. Applications are evaluated on a first come/first served basis, and funding is available until the budget for the program is expended. A non-recoupable advance, matching up to 50% of the broadcast or distribution commitment is available. Applicants must be British Columbia owned and controlled production companies although international treaty or interprovincial co-productions are eligible under this program.

Slate Development Fund
www.bcfilm.bc.ca/slatedevelopment.php
Offers: up to C$150,000 · For: SLATE · Covering: FEAT
The Slate Development Fund is targeted towards established producers who have demonstrated the capacity to sustain production in British Columbia.

Canada Council for the Arts

www.canadacouncil.ca
350 Albert Street, P.O. Box 1047, Ottawa, Ontario, K1P 5V8, Canada
T: +613 566-4414 or 1-800 263-5588 · F: +613 566-4390
E: info@canadacouncil.ca
The council was established in 1957 to 'foster and promote the study and enjoyment of, and the production of works in, the arts'. The council allocates grants to film, video and new media artists twice yearly, in April and November. The grants are intended to support artistic expression through innovation and experimentation with form, content or technology across a variety of genres.

Grants to Film and Video Artists
www.canadacouncil.ca/grants/mediaarts/cn127221225398593750.htm
Offers: up to C$60,000 · For: PROD | SCRIPT · Covering: FEAT | TV
The Grants to Film and Video Artists program supports Canadian professional independent artists who use cinema and video as a mode of artistic expression, and provides them with opportunities for creative renewal and for production of independent film and video works. Applications can be submitted on a biannual basis.

Grants to New Media and Audio Artists — Research and Production Grants
www.canadacouncil.ca/grants/mediaarts/pm127222998460468750.htm
Offers: up to C$60,000 · For: PROD · Covering: MM | WEB
These grants assist Canadian artists working with new media or audio technologies as means of artistic expression. Grants cover artist's subsistence costs as well as the direct costs of research, creative development and production of artworks created with new media or audio technologies.

Assistance to Media Arts Production Organizations
www.canadacouncil.ca/grants/mediaarts/pc127226373857968750.htm
Offers: up to C$100,000 · For: PROD | POST · Covering: FEAT | DOC
Assistance to Media Arts Production Organisations offers operating assistance to Canadian non-profit, artist-run media arts organisations. The level of operating assistance approved by the Canada Council for the Arts covers one or two years. Organisations that receive annual or multi-year assistance may also obtain equipment acquisition assistance.

Grants to Media Arts Production Organizations: Development Project Grants

www.canadacouncil.ca/grants/mediaarts/
yi127226375872187500.htm
Offers: up to C$20,000 • For: PROD | DEV •
Covering: DOC | SHORT
This program supports time-limited projects initiated by Canadian non-profit, artist-run organisations, groups or collectives. The projects must be intended to provide enhanced opportunities for the production of independent media artworks by Canadian artists. Projects must also address specific production needs in the communities that applicants serve or intend to serve.

Canadian Film Centre

www.cfccreates.com/
Windfields, 2489 Bayview Avenue, Toronto, Ontario, M2L 1A8, Canada
T: +416 445 1446 • F: +416 445 9481
E: rnoonan@cfccreates.com
Founded by Governor-General Award recipient and Academy Award®- winning filmmaker Norman Jewison in 1988, the CFC started as a film training centre. The CFC has added 8 new programs, 3 initiatives and labs. CFC promotes Canada's most creative ideas and voices in film, TV and new media to the world.

TELUS Innovation Fund

www.cfccreates.com/what_we_show_and_fund/
telus_innovation_fund/index.php
Offers: up to C$100,000 • Covering: TV | FEAT | MM | WEB | VIDG
The fund supports projects in the form of a recoupable contribution towards the production of innovative film, TV, new media, or cross-platform content projects.

Canadian Independent Film and Video Fund

www.cifvf.ca/
Suite 203, 666 Kirkwood Avenue, Ottawa, Ontario, K1Z 5X9, Canada
T: +613 729 1900 • F: +613 729 4610
E: info@cifvf.ca
The CIFVF is a private sector funding body which supports non-theatrical film, videos and new media projects created by Canadian independent producers to enable lifelong learning.

Film and Video Fund

www.cifvf.ca/english/filmvideopolicy-en.html
Offers: up to C$50,000 • For: PROD | PER-DEV | SCRIPT | DEV | DIST | POST • Covering: DOC | YP | TV | FEAT | ANI
The CIFVF welcomes applications for funding for educational or informational projects, whether film, videotape or a series. The producer must be a Canadian citizen or permanent resident and the company must be Canadian-owned.

Manitoba Film and Sound Development Corporation (MSFDC)

www.mbfilmsound.mb.ca
410 — 93 Lombard Avenue, Winnipeg, Manitoba, R3B 3B1, Canada
T: +204 947 2040 • F: +204 956 5261
E: bridget@mbfilmsound.mb.ca
MSFDC is a statutory corporation of the government and aims to promote Manitoba's film and sound recording artists and industries at home and to the world. MSFDC aims to facilitate the creation and stimulation of employment and investment in Manitoba by developing and promoting Manitoba companies, producing, distributing, and marketing film, TV, video and sound recording products and also promote Manitoba as a film location to offshore production companies.

Market Driven Television Production Financing
Market Driven Feature Film Production Financing

www.mbfilmsound.mb.ca/pdfs/film/
06.07EvaluationCriteria.pdf • For: PROD • Covering: TV | FEAT | OTHER
Productions must have minimum confirmed financing of 75% in order to apply.

New Brunswick Film

www.nbfilm.com • 16th Floor, Assumption Place, 770 Main Street, P.O. Box 5001 Moncton, New Brunswick, E1C 8R3, Canada
T: +1 506 869 6868 • F: +1 506 869 6840
E: nbfilm@gnb.ca
New Brunswick Film provides services and support to the film and TV industry in the New Brunswick province by giving financial assistance (development loans and equity investments) to New Brunswick residents in order to develop and produce film and TV productions, and by giving training to and professional development of New Brunswick residents employed in the film and TV industry.

New Brunswick Film Tax Credit

The Province is providing a Film Tax Credit equal to a maximum of 40% of eligible salaries paid to New Brunswick residents. Wages in excess of 50% of the total costs of production are not eligible for consideration. The value of this credit may also be included as part of the calculation of a production company's equity in a production.

Newfoundland & Labrador Film Development Corporation

www.nlfdc.ca/
189 Water Street, 2nd Floor, St John's, Newfoundland, A1C 1B4, Canada
T: +709 738 3456 · F: +709 739 1680
E: info@newfilm.nf.net
The Newfoundland & Labrador Film Development Corporation aims to fosters and promote the development and growth of the film and video industry in Newfoundland and Labrador, and to increase the national and international visibility of Newfoundland and Labrador as a location. NLFDC also provides production assistance in the form of an Equity Investment Program (EIP) and a Development Program, as well as information and advice on tax credits.

Equity investment

www.nlfdc.ca/fundingprograms.asp#1.0
Offers: 20% up to C$250,000 · For: SCRIPT | DEV | PROD · Covering: FEAT | TV | SHORT | DOC | YP
For Newfoundland & Labrador resident companies, offering up to $250,000 for drama series and features, and $150,000 for documentary and children's film, with two annual deadlines.

Development Fund

www.nlfdc.ca/fundingprograms.asp#2.0
Offers: C$15,000 to $35,000 · For: DEV | SCRIPT · Covering: FEAT | TV | DOC
An element of the Equity Investment program with four annual deadlines and funding for first draft writing and production development.

Nova Scotia Film Development Corporation

www.film.ns.ca
1724 Granville Street, 2nd Floor, Halifax, Nova Scotia, B3J 1X5, Canada
T: +1 902 424 7177 · F: +1 902 424 0617
E: novascotia.film@ns.sympatico.ca
Nova Scotia Film Development Corporation attempts to grow Nova Scotia's film, TV and new media industries with partners by stimulating investment and employment, and by promoting Nova Scotia's producers, productions, locations, skills and creativity in global markets. The Corporation administers loan and investment programs to eligible Nova Scotian companies and their co-production partners in an effort to support film and TV production in Nova Scotia.

Development Loan

www.film.ns.ca/pdfs/general_program_guidelines.pdf
Offers: up to C$15,000 · Covering: FEAT
There are three application deadlines per year.

Equity Investment

Offers: up to C$1,000,000 · For: PROD · Covering: FEAT
There are three application deadlines per year.

Ontario Media Development Corporation

www.omdc.on.ca
175 Bloor Street East, South Tower, No. 501, Toronto, Ontario, M4W 3R8, Canada
T: +1 416 314 6858 · F: +1 416 314 2495
E: mail@omdc.on.ca
The OMDC is an agency of the Ontario Government that provides a range of services and programmes to stimulate the growth of Ontario's film, TV, book and magazine publishing, sound recording and digital media industries. OMDC has a series of funding and programs available for business development, as well as information and advice on investment and tax credits.

OMDC Export Fund

www.omdc.on.ca/Page3222.aspx · For: BIZ-DEV · Covering: DIGI | FEAT | TV
The OMDC Export Fund has been developed to provide eligible Ontario companies with funding to pursue export development activities that correspond to a strategy for company growth. Primary activities supported are market event attendance and targeted sales trips that support the strategy. The Fund will cover up to 50% of a participating company's costs to engage in export development activities.

Domestic Markets and Events

www.omdc.on.ca/Page3227.aspx · For: CULT | PROMO
The fund provides indirect support to Ontario's cultural entrepreneurs by partnering with third parties to offer events and activities that stimulate the growth of the cultural media industries.

Sask Film

www.saskfilm.com/
1831 College Avenue, Regina, SK S4P 4V5, Canada
T: +306 798 9800 • F: +306 798 7768
E: kfraser@saskfilm.com
As the film commission and funding agency for the province, the Saskatchewan Film and Video Development Corporation (SaskFilm) is responsible for establishing a film and TV industry in Saskatchewan by promoting the province's resources and locations as a production centre for local and visiting producers. SaskFilm administers funding programs and the Saskatchewan Film Employment Tax Credit Program. Applicants must be Canadian citizens and Saskatchewan residents. The production company must be Saskatchewan-based.

Development Loan Program

www.saskfilm.com/databasedfiles/1456036-0-
AZ37DB11/2006SaskFilmGuidelines.pdf
Offers: up to C$15,000 • For: DEV | PROD •
Covering: DOC | TV
To augment other resources available to producers to undertake project development and bring productions to fruition.

Documentary Program

Offers: up to C$40,000 • For: DEV | PROD •
Covering: DOC
To encourage Saskatchewan-based documentary production, SaskFilm may provide financial support to projects that result in a significant benefit to the provincial film and video industry. Applications are welcome once a year.

MAX Equity Investment Program

Offers: up to C$75,000 • For: PROD • Covering: TV
| FEAT
To support Saskatchewan-based production, SaskFilm may provide equity investments in eligible projects where there is significant benefit to the province's film and TV industry and where the potential for recoupment and profits are sufficiently high as demonstrated in the application.

Filmmakers Program

Offers: up to C$15,000 • For: PROD | POST •
Covering: FEAT | TV | DOC
This initiative provides financial assistance to filmmakers for the production of films or videos in any genre. Projects will be assessed on the significance of their cultural and artistic merit, the opportunity for professional development and employment they provide to the creators, and the extent to which they advance the filmmaker's career. Applications are welcome on a biannual basis.

Societe de Development des Enterprises Culturelles (SODEC)

www.sodec.gouv.qc.ca/sodec_mandat_en.php
215, rue Saint-Jacques, bur. 800, Montréal (Québec),
H2Y 1M6, Canada
T: +514 841 2200 • F: +514 841 8606
E: info@sodec.gouv.qc.ca
SODEC is a Québec government corporation overseen by the Minister of Culture and Communications. It supports the production and distribution of Québec culture through cultural industries. Since 1995 SODEC has aggressively pursued its mission to stimulate and support the creation and development of cultural enterprises, including the media, in every region of Québec. SODEC offers a 40% production tax credit for Quebec based producers using Quebec based crews as well as funding film and TV. French productions can receive up to 80% of their funding through SODEC.

Screenwriting Support Program

www.sodec.gouv.qc.ca/documents/cinema_en/
programs/screenwriting/cine_scena_eng06.
pdf#page=1
Offers: up to C$20,000 • For: DEV | SCRIPT •
Covering: TV | FEAT | DOC
The fund aims to encourage the exploration of a diverse spectrum of film subjects by allowing screenwriters and writer-directors to develop projects independently prior to approaching a producer. Projects must qualify as 'Quebec productions'. 80% funding is reserved for projects to be shot in French.

Support for Production Companies

Offers: up to C$50,000 • For: SCRIPT • Covering:
FEAT | DOC
The fund aims to support the writing or rewriting of original, varied, high-quality scripts, contributing primarily to direct writing costs.

Selective Support for Independent Production Companies

www.sodec.gouv.qc.ca/documents/cinema_en/
programs/screenwriting/cine_scena_eng06.
pdf#page=1
Offers: up to C$20,000 • For: SCRIPT • Covering:
ANI | TV | FEAT
The fund aims to support the writing or rewriting of original, high-quality scripts, contributing primarily to direct writing costs.

Corporate Support for Feature Film Production Companies

www.sodec.gouv.qc.ca/documents/cinema_en/
programs/screenwriting/cine_scena_eng06.
pdf#page=1

Offers: up to C$125,000 · For: BIZ-DEV · Covering: FEAT

The fund aims to strengthen highly active feature film production companies that develop multiple projects each year. It encourages companies to take risks, innovate and explore new avenues.

Production Support Program

www.sodec.gouv.qc.ca/documents/cinema_
en/programs/production/cine_prod_eng06.
pdf#nameddest=mod1

Offers: up to C$2,000,000 · For: PROD · Covering: FEAT | TV | DOC

The fund encourages and gives financial support to the production of work based on production-ready scripts. Projects must qualify as Quebec productions and must be submitted by a Quebec company operating in private-sector or independent film or TV production.

Telefilm Canada

www.telefilm.gc.ca
360 rue Saint-Jacques, Suite 700, Montreal, Quebec, H2Y 4AD, Canada
T: +1 514 283 6363 · F: +1 514 283 3317
E: info@telefilm.gc.ca

Telefilm Canada is a federal cultural agency dedicated to the development and promotion of the Canadian audiovisual industry. Telefilm provides financial support to the private sector to create distinctively Canadian productions that appeal to domestic and international audiences, mainly through the Canadian Feature FIlm Fund (CFFF). The Corporation also administers the funding programs of the Canadian TV Fund (CTF).

Writer's First

www.telefilm.gc.ca/upload/fonds_prog/writers_
first_guidelines_2006-07.pdf

Offers: up to C$28,372 · For: SCRIPT · Covering: FEAT

The Program is intended to encourage and support professional screenwriters to develop original scripts that will be attractive to producers, financiers and the marketplace. Financial support is available for a first draft feature film screenplay based on an outline or a first draft feature film screenplay based on a treatment. Assistance is available in the form of a non-interest-bearing advance.

Low Budget Independent Feature Film Assistance Program

www.telefilm.gc.ca/upload/fonds_prog/low_
budget-en-guidelines-2006-2007.pdf

Offers: up to C$1,000,000 · For: PROD · Covering: FEAT

The Program supports the independent production and post-production/completion of original and culturally relevant director-driven low budget feature films from both emerging and established filmmakers.

The Versioning Assistance Program

www.telefilm.gc.ca/upload/fonds_prog/versioning_
assistance_guidelines_2006-2007.pdf

Offers: up to C$48,000 · Covering: FEAT

The Program aims to increase the availability of and therefore audiences for Canadian feature films financed through the CFFF intended for theatrical release in English, French and Aboriginal languages. The project must be a feature film that has received production financing through the CFFF or the CTF-EIP programs. The applicant must be a Canadian-controlled corporation with its head office based in Canada. There is no application deadline.

Canada Showcase

www.telefilm.gc.ca/upload/fonds_prog/canada-
showcase_guidelines_2006-2007.pdf

Offers: up to C$500,000 · For: AUD-DEV

The program provides financial assistance to festivals that contribute actively towards the promotion and presentation of Canadian works. The applicant must be a not-for profit organisation and a Canadian-controlled entity.

International Festival Participation Pilot Initiative

www.telefilm.gc.ca/upload/fonds_prog/2006-
2007_guidelines_international_festival_
participation_pilot_initiative.pdf

Offers: up to C$100,000 per year · For: PROMO · Covering: FEAT | DOC | ANI | SHORT

The initiative aims to support the promotion and international marketing strategy of Canadian productions officially selected at one of the following international festivals: Berlin, Cannes, Pusan, Sundance and Venice. There is no application deadline.

Production Financing for Producers (for French-language Films)

www.telefilm.gc.ca/upload/fonds_prog/cfff_
guidelines_2006_2007.pdf

Offers: up to C$3.5 million and 49% · French-language projects from across Canada are received, evaluated and compared at the Montreal office of Telefilm Canada.

International Sales Promotion Pilot Initiative (French-language Feature Films)

www.telefilm.gc.ca/upload/fonds_prog/2006-2007_guidelines_international_sales_promotion_pilot_initiative.pdf

Offers: up to C$100,000 per fiscal year. · For: PROMO · Covering: FEAT

The initiative aims to support the promotion of Canadian French-language feature films in foreign markets, in particular films that have received funding through the CFFF. Eligible applicants are Canadian production, distribution and sales companies.

Alternative Distribution Networks Program

www.telefilm.gc.ca/upload/fonds_prog/alternative_distribution_guidelines_2006-2007.pdf

Offers: up to C$50,000 · For: DIST · Covering: FEAT

The programs provides financing to organisations that use alternate distribution methods to the traditional theatrical distributor-exhibitor model in promoting and releasing Canadian films. Canadian owned and controlled companies are eligible. There is no application deadline.

Production Financing for Producers (for English-Language Films)

www.telefilm.gc.ca/upload/fonds_prog/cfff_guidelines_2006_2007.pdf

Offers: up to C$4 million and 49% of budget · For: PROD · Covering: FEAT

Approximately C$28 million is available for investment in films applying to the English Language Selective Component. Of this $28 million, $18 million in production financing will be earmarked for national decision-making. Projects from across the country seeking a significant investment from the CFFF must compete for these limited resources. The balance of $10 million will be distributed to Telefilm Canada's four local offices for investment in lower budget films with lower requests for financing.

Development Financing for Producers

www.telefilm.gc.ca/upload/fonds_prog/cfff_guidelines_2006_2007.pdf

Offers: up to C$300,000 · For: DEV | SCRIPT · Covering: FEAT

Development financing is available to companies of all sizes. Telefilm Canada supports the development of projects that may become official coproductions. Development support will be awarded to those projects most likely to be selected for production financing through the CFFF.

Marketing Financing for Distributors

www.telefilm.gc.ca/upload/fonds_prog/cfff_guidelines_2006_2007.pdf · For: PROMO · Covering: FEAT

Financing is available for Canadian theatrical release costs ranging from early stage Canadian marketing costs including, but not limited to, the creation of materials such as posters, teaser trailers and test screenings, to test marketing and campaign creation to prints and advertising (P&A). Telefilm Canada's financing will be in the form of a non-interest bearing advance up to 75% of the eligible Canadian marketing costs for the release of the film.

Broadcaster Performance Envelope Stream

www.canadianTVfund.ca/producers/guidelines/main0607.pdf · For: PROD · Covering: TV | DOC | YP | FEAT

The project should address Canadian themes and subject matter. Applicants must be a Canadian-controlled corporation.

Special Initiatives Stream

www.canadianTVfund.ca/producers/guidelines/main0607.pdf · For: DEV | PROD · Covering: FEAT | DOC | TV | YP

The programme supports French-language productions outside Quebec, Aboriginal-language production, development financing and versioning assistance. Applicants must be a Canadian-controlled corporation.

Canada New Media Fund

www.telefilm.gc.ca/upload/fonds_prog/cnmf-guidelines2006-2007.pdf

Offers: up to C$550,000 · For: DEV | PROMO

This Fund provides financial support for market research and prototyping, product development and marketing of Canadian cultural new media works in both official languages that are intended for the general public. Priority is given to new media products with significant market potential to reach Canadian consumers. 75% of eligible expenses must be incurred in Canada. Generally, the fund finances $100,000 in market research and prototyping, $250,000 in product development and $200,000 in marketing.

Theatrical Documentary Pilot Program

www.telefilm.gc.ca/upload/fonds_prog/theatrical | DOC_prod.pdf

Offers: C$625,000 · For: PROD · Covering: DOC

A total of $1.25 million is available for the support of theatrical documentary productions. The fund finances two projects through this program.

Yukon Film and Sound

Commission

www.reelyukon.com
Box 2703, Whitehorse, Yukon, Y1A 2C6, Canada
T: +867 667 5400 · F: +867 393 7040
E: info@reelyukon.com
Yukon Film & Sound Commission invests in its
filmmakers, both financially, through incentives
programs, and through targeted mentorship and
training initiatives. From entry level technical crew
training to business skills development to international
market participation, YFSC invests in Yukon film
and sound practitioners in cooperation with a range
of partners including international co-production
companies, industry associations, government funding
agencies and local businesses.

The Yukon Filmmakers Fund

www.reelyukon.com/programs/yfilmmakers/yff/
Offers: up to C$5,000 · For: PER-DEV · Covering:
TV | SHORT | DOC
The purpose of the program is to deliver funding to
Yukon film and video professionals to assist them in
developing viable careers and businesses making films
and videos for broadcast or commercial release. The
applicant must be a Canadian citizen and have lived
in Yukon for at least one continuous year prior to the
award deadline.

Yukon Film Training Initiative

www.reelyukon.com/programs/yfilmmakers/
training/ · For: EDU
The purpose of the Yukon Film Training Initiative is
to assist Yukon residents to undertake training in film
production or post-production.

Yukon Film Development Fund

www.reelyukon.com/programs/yfilmmakers/
developmentfund/
Offers: up to C$35,000 · For: DEV · Covering: FEAT
The purpose of this program is to encourage the growth
and development of the Yukon Film industry through
the provision of non-repayable financial contributions
to assist with the costs of development of film projects
in Yukon.

Yukon Film Production Fund

www.reelyukon.com/programs/yfilmmakers/
productionfund/
Offers: up to C$500,000 · For: PROD · Covering:
FEAT
The Fund aims to encourage the growth and
development of the Yukon Film industry through the
provision of non-repayable financial contributions to
assist with the costs of producing a film in the Yukon.

Film Commissions

Alberta Film

www.albertafilm.ca
5th Floor, Commerce Place, 10155 – 102 Street,
Edmonton, Alberta, T5J 4L6, Canada
T: +780 422 8584 · F: +780 422 8582
E: dan.chugg@gov.ab.ca
Alberta is considered as a destination for film TV
and commercial production and has garnered many
Academy Award nominations, *Brokeback Mountain*
being the most recent success.

Calgary Film Commission

www.calgaryeconomicdevelopment.com/
keyindustries/film/filmabout.cfm
Calgary, AB, Canada
T: +403.221.7868
The Calgary Region forms the heart of the film industry
in Alberta and has been in the movie-making business
for almost a century since the era of silent films.

Columbia Shuswap Film Commission

www.filmcolumbiashuswap.com
Columbia Shuswap Film Commission, 781 Marine
Park Drive NE, Box 978, Salmon Arm, British
Columbia, V1E 4P1, Canada
T: +250 832-8194 · F: +250 832-3375
E: abender@csrd.bc.ca

Hamilton Film Office

www.hamilton.ca/film
Hamilton Film Liaison Office, City of Hamilton, 1
James Street South, 8th Floor, Hamilton, ON L8P
4R5, Canada
T: +905 546 4233 or 1-800-868-1329
F: +905 546 4107

Northern British Columbia Film Commission

www.northernbcfilm.com
T: +250 649 3207 · F: +250 649 3200
E: film@initiativespg.com

Okanagan Film Commission

www.okanaganfilm.com
1450 KLO Road, Kelowna, BC V1W 3Z4, Canada
T: +250 717 0087 · F: +250 868 0512
E: info@okanaganfilm.com

Toronto Film & Television Office

www.toronto.ca/tfto
Main Floor, Rotunda North, Toronto City Hall, 100
Queen Street W, Toronto, Quebec, M5H 2N2, Canada
T: +1 416 392 7570 · F: +1 416 392 0675
E: filmtoronto@toronto.ca
The Toronto Film and TV Office are able to guide
filmmakers through any part of the permitting process.
A City of Toronto grants directory can be found at www.
toronto.ca/grants/grants_directory.htm

CROATIA

Ministry of Culture

www.min-kulture.hr
Runjaninova 2, 10000 Zagreb, Croatia
T: +385 1 486 6666 · F: +385 1 486 6155
E: web@min-kulture.hr
The Ministry of Culture aims to support national
cultural identity, democratisation of culture, freedom of
expression and creation and conservation of audiovisual
heritage.

Production support
Offers: up to €540,000 and 80% · For: PROD ·
Covering: ANI | DOC | FEAT | SHORT | FFF
Scriptwriters, film directors, (co-)producers and
production companies are welcome to apply in order to
receive support in the form of co-finance.

City of Zagreb

www.zagreb.hr
City office for Education, Culture and Sport, City of
Zagreb, Croatia
T: +385 1 6100 585 · F: +385 1 6100 590
E: maja.petric@zagreb.hr
The organisation aims to develop film culture by
improving access to, and education about, the moving
image and foster cultural and linguistic diversity.
The fund supports the qualitative and quantitative
development of both the commercial and cultural
film industry in the region, and aims to improve the
economic structure of the film and audiovisual industry.

Gradski proracun Grada Zagreba
www.zagreb.hr/dokument.nsf/
FPHW?OpenForm&2&11030
Offers: up to €68,000 · For: PROD · Covering: FEAT°
| YP | ANI | DOC | TV | SHORT | FFF | MM
The grant supports non-commercial, art film and video.

CZECH REPUBLIC

Czech Film Centre

www.filmcenter.cz
Národní t, CZ-110 00 Prague 1, Czech Republic
T: +420 22 11 05 321 · F: +420 22 11 05 303
E: info@filmcenter.cz
The Czech Film Centre (CFC) aims to increase the
visibility of Czech film worldwide. The CFC and its
activities are financed by the Audiovisual Producers'
Association (APA) and from public funds.

Audiovisual Producers' Association

www.asociaceproducentu.cz
Národní 28, 110 00 Praha 1, Czech Republic
T: +420 221 105 302 · F: +420 221 105 303
E: apa@iol.cz
For the protection and promotion of producers'
interests, dealing with professional associations, with
protective authors' organisations or with bodies of the
state administration.

State Fund for the Support and Development of Czech Cinematography

www.mkcr.cz
Milady Horákové 139, 16041 Praha 6, Czech
Republic
T: +42 257 085 247 · F: +42 224 321 053
E: fondkino@mkcr.cz
Support is available for scriptwriting, production,
distribution, promotion, the technological development
of the cinema industry, and for the work of national and
ethnic minorities living in the Czech Republic.

**Support and development of Czech
cinematography** · For: SCRIPT | DEV | PROD |
POST | DIST · Covering: FEAT
The fund takes the form or repayable advances for up
to 50% of costs. The total budget for 2007 is set to be
$7.6m.

DENMARK.

Danish Film Institute

www.dfi.dk
Gothersgade 55, DK-1123 København K, Denmark
T: +45 33 74 34 00 · F: +45 33 74 34 01
E: dfi@dfi.dk
The Danish Film Institute is the national agency responsible for supporting and encouraging film and cinema culture and for conserving those in the national interest. The Institute's operations extend from participation in the development and production of feature films, shorts and documentaries, through distribution and marketing, to managing the national film archive and the cinematheque.

Shorts and documentaries: Consultant scheme
www.dfi.dk/english/about/financialsupport/
consultant_shortsndocs/consultant_shortsndocs.htm
· For: SLATE | PROD · Covering: SHORT | DOC
The fund subsidises the development and production of Danish short and documentary films and the participation by Danish producers in international short and documentary film co-productions.

Support for Script Writing for Feature Films
www.dfi.dk/NR/rdonlyres/AEADCD44 · For: SCRIPT
· Covering: FEAT
Script subsidies may be granted to a writer, a director working on his or her own script, a producer, or a team of these. The recipient must provide proof of how the funds have been spent.

Feature film: 60/40 scheme
www.dfi.dk/english/about/financialsupport/60_
40feature/60_40feature.htm
Offers: Up to 60% of budget · For: PROD | DEV ·
Covering: FEAT
The DFI may subsidise the development and production of Danish feature films and the participation by Danish producers in international feature film co-productions. The objective of such subsidies is to ensure the continuous production of different types of film so that in terms of variety, volume, artistic quality, and audience appeal the overall range of Danish feature films maintains and develops the art and culture of Danish film at home and abroad. The fund had a DEK5.5m budget in 2005.

Development Subsidies for Feature Films
www.dfi.dk/NR/rdonlyres/AEADCD44-542D-4B8D-
A011-11B463933335/0/sf_vilkaar_2003_eng.pdf ·
For: DEV · Covering: FEAT
A development subsidy may be granted to a film project if it is assessed that development would be of considerable help in strengthening the project. The objective of development subsidies is to ensure that the project is developed in the best possible way so as to enable DFI to assess subsequent applications for production subsidies for the film project.

Production Subsidies
For: PROD · Covering: FEAT
Subsidies for the production of feature films are granted in order to promote the production of Danish films and the participation by Danish producers in co-productions. Repayment of subsidies granted by DFI to Danish producers shall commence when the private investment has been recouped by 50%.

New Danish Screen
www.dfi.dk/NR/rdonlyres/200B1127-CCF6-4D31-
91D3-C84D7DAFF9B9/0/new_danish_screen_
guidelines_uk.pdf · For: SCRIPT | PROD | DEV ·
Covering: FEAT | SHORT | FFF
New Danish Screen is a scheme for promoting and inspiring the development of film language and storytelling to sustain and strengthen the dynamics and diversity of Danish cinema. It must be ensured that new generations of filmmakers constantly strive to push the limits and create new experiences for audiences.

Coproduction subsidies
www.dfi.dk/english/about/financialsupport/
coproductionsubsidies/coproductionsubsidies.htm ·
For: PROD · Covering: FEAT | DOC
Co-productions divide into two basic categories: Danish majority productions have a Danish executive producer which can either be in Danish or in a foreign language; and Danish minority productions which have a foreign executive producer, in a language other than Danish.

Feature Film: Consultant Scheme
www.dfi.dk/english/about/financialsupport/
consultant_feature/consultant_feature.htm · For:
SCRIPT | DEV | PROD · Covering: FEAT
The DFI may subsidise the preparation of film scripts, development and production of Danish feature films and the participation by Danish producers in international feature film co-productions. The objective of such subsidies is to ensure the overall range of Danish feature films maintains and develops the art and culture of Danish film at home and abroad. The fund had a DEK11.8m budget in 2005.

West Denmark Film Pool

www.filmpuljen.dk
Kalkvaerksvej 8, 8000 Arhus, Denmark
T: +45 89 40 48 82 · F: +45 89 40 48 52
E: mail@filmpuljen.dk
Aims to support the development of the local film industry through subsidy and investment primarily in fiction film. The Pools budget in 2004 was €1.8m.

West Danish Film Pool

www.filmpuljen.dk/
Offers: Up to €269,000 · Covering: FEAT | SHORT | DOC | ANI
The fund, to support filmmaking, had a €800,000 budget in 2004.

ESTONIA

Estonian Film Foundation

www.efsa.ee
Vana-Viru 3, Tallinn 10111, Estonia
T: +372 627 60 60 · F: +372 627 60 61
E: film@efsa.ee
The Estonian Film Foundation is committed to the financing of Estonian films; establishment and development of international contacts and co-operation in the film and TV sector; assistance to promote and develop Estonian film and audiovisual culture on a national and on international level; supporting education and training of Estonian filmmakers and audiovisual professionals on an international level; creation of an up-to-date database of Estonian film production, filmmakers, producers as well of the audiovisual sector. The budget for 2007 is €3.8m.

Support for scriptwriting

Offers: up to €3200 · For: SCRIPT · Covering: YP | FFF | FEAT
Scriptwriting grants are offered to an Estonian independent production company for writing a feature screenplay.

Support for development

Offers: up to €31948 · For: SCRIPT · Covering: DOC | ANI | YP | FEAT | FFF
Development support is provided to an Estonian independent film production company in the form of a grant.

Support for production

Offers: up to €380,000 · For: PROD · Covering: FEAT | SHORT | DOC | ANI | FFF
Support offered in form of grants, co-financing and co-production.

Support based on box office results

Covering: FEAT | SHORT | DOC | ANI | FFF | YP
The support based on box office results is awarded to completed films based on audience figures, for the producer's next film project. The current threshold for being eligible for the grant is 20,000 domestic admissions during the first year after release.

Support for participation in festivals

For: PROMO
The support is provided in return for participation in major festivals and must be invested in the production company's or producer's next film project.

Support for film-related activities

For: CULT
Support is available for filmmakers and researchers – for training and research purposes, projects and initiatives that foster the development of the Estonian film culture and film promotional events.

EUROPEAN

Media 2007

europa.eu.int/comm/avpolicy/media/index_en.html
Education, Audiovisual and Culture Exchange Agency, MEDIA PROGRAMME, Office: BOUR 3/30, AVENUE DU BOURGET, B-1049 Brussels, Belgium
E: EACEA-P8@ec.europa.eu
The MEDIA Programme of the European Commission (2007 — 2012) aims to strengthen the competitiveness of the European audiovisual industry with a series of support measures dealing with training of professionals, development of production projects, distribution and promotion of films and audiovisual programmes. 50% of European films theatrically released in Europe in 2006, and 90% of those distributed in the rest of the world have received support from the MEDIA programme. The organisation supports over 300 films and 100 festivals each year. Every EC nation, and many regions, have their own MEDIA desk — a full list via snurl.com/1ckrq
Media 2007 is divided into five key strands:
· the training of professionals;
· the development of projects and companies;
· the distribution of films and audiovisual programmes;
· the promotion of films and audiovisual programmes; and including the support for film festivals
· horizontal actions/pilot projects.

Support for the development of single projects

ec.europa.eu/information_society/media/producer/
develop/single/index_en.htm
Offers: up to €80,000 or 60% · For: DEV | SLATE ·
Covering: FEAT
Grants of this type are aimed at independent
production companies that have been registered
companies for at least one year. The experience required
varies depending on the company's country of origin
and whether or not it has already received support from
MEDIA. Grants can cover up to 50% or 60% of eligible
development costs for a project, up to a maximum
amount for each type of work (€10,000 — 30,000 for
a documentary, €20,000 — 50,000 for fiction, €10,000
— 50,000 for a multimedia production and €10,000
— 80,000 for animations).

Funding in the field of vocational training

ec.europa.eu/information_society/media/training/
index_en.htm
MEDIA Training supports the creation of pan-
European training networks to help professionals in
the audiovisual industry enhance their competence in
the international market. These networks provide close
collaboration and exchange of know-how between
different partners active in the training field: cinema
and TV schools, specialised training centres, production
and distribution firms, etc.

Support for the development of a slate of projects

ec.europa.eu/information_society/media/producer/
develop/slate1st/index_en.htm
Offers: up to €150,000
Slate funding is aimed at independent European
production companies that have been legally registered
businesses for at least three years and already have
international experience as well as the financial capacity
to undertake more than one project simultaneously.
There is an annual application deadline. Companies can
apply for either 3 to 6 or 3 to 10 projects.

Selective support for the transnational distribution of European films

ec.europa.eu/information_society/media/distrib/
schemes/select/index_en.htm
Offers: up to €150,000 and 50% of budget · For:
DIST · Covering: FEAT | DOC | ANI
Selective support is for groups of at least five European
companies in countries participating in the MEDIA
programme distributing a film from another European
country in their distribution territory.

Support for the transnational distribution of European films (sales agents)

ec.europa.eu/information_society/media/distrib/
index_en.htm
Offers: up to €25,000 · For: DIST
You are eligible if you are a European company and
have contracted with the producer(s) of a film to
act as agent to market the rights to the work to
potential buyers (particularly distributors) outside the
home country or countries in at least ten countries
participating in the MEDIA Plus programme.

MEDIA Promotion

ec.europa.eu/information_society/media/promo/
markt/list/index_en.htm · For: PROMO
Supports promotion of European films, including the
building and management of databases, screening
events, festival networks and promotion to the public.

European Film Promotion (EFP)

ec.europa.eu/information_society/media/promo/
abroad/index_en.htm · For: PROMO · Covering:
FEAT | SHORT | DOC | ANI | YP
For EU producers and sales agents to promote their
films in festivals that they would not necessarily
attend for financial or logistical reasons and to adapt
their marketing strategies to these new markets. For
European companies only.

European Coordination of Film Festivals (ECFF)

ec.europa.eu/information_society/media/festiv/
index_en.htm
Offers: €250,000 · For: PROMO · Covering: FEAT |
SHORT | DOC | ANI | YP
The fund supports and promotes over 100 European
films festivals.

Support for the networking of cinemas screening European films

ec.europa.eu/information_society/media/exhibit/
index_en.htm
The fund aims to encourage the networking of
European première cinemas and the screening of
non-domestic European films by these cinemas.
Particular attention will be paid to the development of
potential in countries or regions with a low audio-visual
production capacity and/or a restricted linguistic or
geographical area. There are two deadline per year.

Promotion of Pilot Projects

ec.europa.eu/information_society/media/pilot/
index_en.htm · For: DEV | SLATE | PROD | DIST ·
Covering: DIGI
The MEDIA Plus programme takes account of rapid
technological change. In the next few years, the use
of digital technology will make European audiovisual

works more accessible, and thereby more widely available outside their country of origin, because of new ways of transporting audiovisual content. The competitiveness of the audiovisual sector will greatly depend on the use of new technologies for development, production and distribution.

Automatic distribution support

ec.europa.eu/information_society/media/distrib/schemes/auto/index_en.htm · For: DIST
You are eligible if you are a European distributor who has already distributed at least one European work from another country. Funding varies depending on the success of former films.

i2i Audiovisual

ec.europa.eu/information_society/media/producer/i2i/detail/index_en.htm
Offers: €5,000 to €50,000 · Covering: FEAT
Designed to facilitate access to financing from banks and other financial institutions by subsidising part of the cost of the guarantees required by these institutions and/or part of the financing itself. These costs include insurance, completion guarantee, financing costs. Works of fiction (min. 50') or animation (min. 24') and documentaries (min. 25') produced with significant European participation are eligible.

Support for television broadcasting

ec.europa.eu/information_society/media/producer/tv/detail/index_en.htm
Offers: up to €500,000 and 20% · For: PROD · Covering: TV | SHORT | DOC | ANI | YP
Independent European production companies legally registered in an EU country can apply for support with the production of fiction, animation and creative documentaries where there is the participation or co-operation of at least three broadcasters — and preferably more — from several member states. Sequels and series of episodes based in whole or in part on a previous project are not eligible for funding. MEDIA funding can cover up to 12.5% of the production budget for fiction and animated films, and 20% for documentaries. The maximum amount available for one piece is €500 000. There are three application deadlines per year.

Culture 2007

culturefund.eu
Cultural Contact Point UK, EUCLID, 12 Charlotte Street, Manchester, M1 4FL, UK — for rest of Europe see ccp.culture.info
T: 44 (0)7000 382543 · F: 44 (0)161 245 3322
E: info@euclid.info
The Culture 2007 programme, replacing Culture 2000, is intended as 'a coherent, global and complete tool for multicultural co-operation in Europe and should contribute actively to the development of a European identity from the grassroots'. The specific objectives of the Programme are to promote the transnational mobility of people working in the cultural sector; to encourage the transnational circulation of works and cultural and artistic products; to encourage intercultural dialogue.

There are 'Cultural Contact Points' (CCP) throughout the EU to discuss possible ideas and applications, the contact details above are for the UK CCP, EUCLID. For other CCPs see ccp.culture.info. For audiovisual production see Media 2007.

Funding

Funding provides:
· support for cultural actions;
· support for bodies active at European level in the field of culture (e.g. European cultural networks);
· support for analyses and the collection and dissemination of information and for activities maximising the impact of projects in the field of European cultural cooperation and European cultural policy developments.

Multi-annual cooperation projects

Offers: Up to €500,000 a year and 50% of budget · For: BIZ-DEV | DEV · Covering: OTHER
This support is intended to assist projects in their start-up and structuring phase or in their geographical extension phase. At least six organisations from six different eligible countries are required. The aim is to encourage them to establish sustainable foundations and achieve financial autonomy, with support offered for three to five years.

Cooperation measures

Offers: €50,000 to €200,000, up to 50% of costs · For: DEV | BIZ-DEV · Covering: OTHER
For smaller projects lasting 1-2 years, with a priority for 'creativity and innovation'. Projects which explore avenues for cooperation in order to develop them over the longer term will be 'particularly encouraged'. Partners in three EU countries are required.

EC Development Directorate Culture Section

europa.eu.int/comm/world
Unité EuropeAid/C/4 'Opérations centralisées dans les pays ACP', rue de la Loi 41, B-1049 Bruxelles, Belgique, EURO
T: +32 2 296 00 05 · F: +32 2 299 49 47
E: contact@filmfestamiens.org
To encourage cooperation between the European Union and Africa, the Caribbean and Pacific region (ACP) countries. This contributes to developing local human resources and creative skills, promoting cultural identity and favouring the participation of the local population in a development process. Within the framework of the EU cooperation and development policies with the 70 ACP countries, funding is available for the film and audiovisual sector. Available funding covers a wide range of activities from film production, distribution, promotion, to film festivals and varied project support.

Screenplay Development Fund

www.filmfestamiens.org/spip. php?rubrique9&lang=en
Offers: €7,600 · For: SCRIPT | DEV
Confirmed directors having made at least one feature film may apply. Alternatively directors proposed by a known producer from one of the participating countries may apply. Candidates may submit several projects, but only one project will be selected for the competition.

Production support

europa.eu.int/comm/europeaid/tender/index_ en.htm
Offers: Max €400,000 · Covering: FEAT | DOC | TV
Support is aimed at directors or producers in the 71 countries in Africa, the Caribbean and the Pacific which are signatories of the 1975 Lomé Convention. In the case of films, production companies based in the EU or in an ACP country may apply, provided they are associated with an ACP director. Post-production, distribution, and promotion support is also available.

Eurimages

www.coe.int/T/E/Cultural_Co-operation/ Eurimages/
Council of Europe, F-67075 Strasbourg Cedex, France
T: +33 3 88 41 26 40 · F: +33 3 88 41 27 60
E: eurimages@coe.int
Eurimages is the Council of Europe fund for the co-production, distribution and exhibition of European cinematographic works. Set up in 1989 as a Partial Agreement, it currently has 28 Member States. Eurimages aims to promote the European film industry by encouraging the production and distribution of films and fostering co-operation between professionals.

Co-production support

www.coe.int/t/e/cultural_co-operation/eurimages/ funding_programmes/coproduction/EN_2006_ GuideCoprod.pdf
Offers: up to €700,000 · Covering: FEAT | ANI | DOC
The fund supports full-length feature films and animation as well as documentaries of a minimum length of 70 minutes. All projects submitted must have at least two co-producers from different member States of the Fund. The participation of the majority co-producer must not exceed 80% of the total co-production budget, and the participation of the minority co-producer must not be lower than 10%. The fund takes the form of an Interest Free loan. Financial support will not exceed 20%. There are five deadlines each year.

Distribution support

www.coe.int/t/dg4/eurimages/Support/ SupportDistri_en.asp
Offers: up to €8000 · For: DIST · Covering: FEAT | DOC
Support for distribution is aimed at providing a system of support for distribution complementary to the MEDIA Programme of the European Union. The support is available to distributors of the member States who are not able to benefit from the support awarded by Media, ie. Bosnia and Herzegovina, Croatia, Romania, Serbia and Montenegro, 'the former Yugoslav Republic of Macedonia' and Turkey. No distributor, however, may apply for a film originating in its own country. Applications can be made 5 times each year.

Exhibition Support

www.coe.int/t/dg4/eurimages/Support/ SupportSalles_en.asp · For: EXBN · Covering: FEAT
The aim of the fund is to increase the programming of European films in cinemas in EURIMAGES member States that do not have access to the MEDIA Programme, notably the countries of central and eastern Europe. It supports initiatives by cinemas which programme and promote European films on their screens.

Europa Cinemas

www.europa-cinemas.org
54 Rue Beaubourg, 75003 Paris, France
T: +33 1 42 71 53 70 · F: +33 1 42 71 47 55
E: europacinema@magic.fr
Europa Cinemas is the first international cinema network for the distribution of European films. It operates in all 27 countries of the European Union as

well as Iceland, Norway, Switzerland and Liechtenstein. The objective of Europa Cinemas is to increase the programming of films from Europe and partner countries and thus to raise the number of people attending these films. To achieve this objective, Europa Cinemas give support to theatre exhibitors in order to encourage the programming of European films and particularly European non-national films, and to foster initiatives towards Young Audiences.

Support for initiatives by cinemas aimed at Young Audiences

Offers: between €15,000 and €50,000 · For: EXBN
The cinema's programming must include at least 30% European non-national screenings for single-screen theatres, and at least 33% for European non-national (ie. outside the country) screenings for screens in multiplexes. Grants will only be made if the exhibitor invests at least an equal sum in programming and promoting of European non-national films. Grants may not be greater than €1 per admission to European non-national films.

Support for the programming of European films in cinemas

Offers: between €15,000 and €50,000 · For: EXBN
Same requirements as Support for initiatives by cinemas aimed at Young Audiences.

Support for digital projection of European films in theatres

www.europa-cinemas.org/en/programmes/cinema_numerique/mesures_soutien.php · For: EXBN
Europa Cinemas offers funding to European exhibitors on the basis of a minimum number of European films screened by way of digital projection technology. The fund assists theatres in their transition to digital cinema and informs exhibitors about the development of digital projection technology and on the economic models available to finance its introduction.

Distribution, Programming and Promotion of European films in third countries

www.europa-cinemas.org/en/programmes/pays_tiers/documents/Distribution_promotionGB.pdf · For: PROMO | DIST
This support is available for distribution companies that market European films. Priority will be given to distribution companies that are in a position to operate in several territories.

Hubert Bals Fund

www.filmfestivalrotterdam.com/
Hubert Bals Fund , P.O.Box 21696, NL-3001 AR Rotterdam, The Netherlands
T: +31 10 890 90 90 · F: +31 10 890 90 91
E: hbf@filmfestivalrotterdam.com
Administered by the International Film Festival of Rotterdam, the Hubert Bals Fund is designed to support feature films and creative documentaries by innovative and talented filmmakers from developing countries. The fund has close to €1.2m available annually.

Funding

The fund is available to projects from countries in receipt of development aid, including the Caribbean, Africa, Asia, the Middle East, the former Soviet Union and the former Yugoslavia (excluding Croatia and Slovenia). The entry should be original, authentic and rooted in the culture of the applicant's country. The project should contribute to the development of the local film industry and local film-making skills. Applicants approaching the fund should have other interested partners in place. Selections take place twice each year.

Script and project development

Offers: up to €10,000 · For: SCRIPT | DEV · Covering: FEAT | DOC
The fund takes the form of a grant.

Post-production funding or final financing

Offers: up to €30,000 · For: POST · Covering: FEAT | DOC
The fund takes the form of a grant.

Distribution support

Offers: up to €15,000 · For: DIST · Covering: FEAT | DOC
Supports costs in the country of origin.

Training support

Offers: up to €20,000 · For: EDU
The Fund also support special projects, such as training initiatives for filmmakers in developing countries.

Hubert Bals Fund Plus

Offers: up to €50,000 · For: PROD · Covering: FEAT | DOC
Supports Dutch producers involved in international co-productions.

Digital production

Offers: up to €10,000 · For: PROD · Covering: DIGI | SHORT | FEAT
For digital production of a film with maximum budget of €100,000.

FIJI

Fiji Audio Visual Commission

www.fijiaudiovisual.com
Ground Floor, Civic House, Victoria Parade, Suva,
GPO Box 18080, Fiji
T: +679 330 6662 · F: +679 331 4662
E: bolea@fijiaudiovisual.org.fj
Tax Rebate (similar to Australian tax offset): If a
fully-funded production expends in Fiji a minimum
F$250,000 of qualifying Fiji expenditure representing at
least 35% of the budget, then it can claim back 15% of
its Fiji expenditure.

FINLAND

Finnish Film Foundation, Suomen Elokuvasäätiö

www.ses.fi/
Finnish Film Foundation, Kanavakatu 12, FIN-00160,
Helsinki, Finland
T: +358 9 622 0300 · F: +358 9 622 03050
E: ses@ses.fi
The Foundation's goal is to promote high-quality and
original Finnish film production.

Funding

There are no deadlines for production support
applications. The applicants are advised to contact the
person responsible for granting the support and to read
the support guidelines.

Script support

Offers: up to €8,500 · For: SCRIPT · Covering: YP |
ANI | DOC | SHORT | TV | FEAT
Script support can be granted to an individual or a
team for the writing of a film script. The applicant must
supply the Foundation with a working plan for the
script as part of the application.

Development support

Offers: up to €100,000 · For: DEV | PROD | SCRIPT
· Covering: YP | ANI | DOC | SHORT | TV | FEAT
A production company (a registered company) holding
the rights to the film in Finland can be granted
development support for the film project. The support
can be applied towards the writing and further
development of the script, production, shooting and set
design plans, and any other measures required before a
budget and the related financing arrangements can be
completed. The applicant must supply the Foundation
with a project development plan, a development
budget and a financing plan.

Advance support for production

Offers: around €500,000 · For: PROD · Covering:
FEAT | TV | SHORT | DOC | YP
Granted production support can cover a maximum
of 70% of the film's production costs, including any
development support already granted for the project by
the Foundation.

Marketing and distribution support

Offers: up to €70,000 · For: DIST | PROMO ·
Covering: FEAT | DOC | YP
Marketing and distribution support is open to
production companies holding the film's rights in
Finland or to the film's professional Finnish distribution
company. Support can be granted for the marketing
and distribution costs related to the film's theatrical
distribution in Finland and can cover 70% of the costs
at most. For documentaries and short films, marketing
support can also be granted for non-commercial
distribution.

Post-release support for production

Offers: up to €700,000 · Covering: FEAT | DOC | YP
| ANI
Post-release support for production can be granted,
on the basis of a domestic film's total attendance,
to a production company holding the film's rights in
Finland. Post-release support can be granted to a film
with sufficient domestic content in the Foundation's
evaluation, whose domestic theatrical release was on
1 January 1997 or after that date and which attracted
a minimum of 45,000 viewers who bought a regular-
priced ticket to see the film at domestic film theatres in
its first year of release.

Centre for the Promotion of Audiovisual Culture in Finland (AVEK)

www.kopiosto.fi/avek
Hietaniemenkatu 2, FIN-00100 HELSINKI, Finland
T: +358-9-4315 2350 · F: +358-9-4315 2377
E: avek@avek.kopiosto.fi
AVEK's goal is to strengthen the production
infrastructure of the Finnish media sector, ensuring
long-term programme production which maximizes the
resources available as effectively as possible. It also aims
to support new entrants.

Support for production of documentary films

www.kopiosto.fi/avek · For: PROD | SCRIPT | DEV |
POST | DIST · Covering: DOC
Support is selective, given either as a grant or a loan.
The productions should be intended for TV, video
distribution or some other forms of audiovisual
presentation or distribution. When considering the

applications, special attention is paid to subject matter, themes and narration, and the overall expressive impact of the project.

Support for production of short films and animation

www.kopiosto.fi/avek · For: PROD | SCRIPT | DEV | POST | DIST · Covering: SHORT | ANI
It is possible to apply for funding for scriptwriting (individual playwrights only), pre-production, production, post-production and distribution (production companies).

Support for production of multimedia and media art

www.kopiosto.fi/avek · For: PROD | SCRIPT | DEV | POST | DIST · Covering: MM | DIGI | EXP
Support is selective, given either as a grant or a loan. Installations and performance art as well as exhibition videos and small-scale video works would be supported the Visual Art Promotion Centre (VISEK).

Northern Film and Media Centre

www.poem.fi
Aleksanterinkatu 33, 90010 City of Oulu, Finland
T: +358 8 558 47527 · F: +358 8 558 47533
E: poem@poem.fi
The aims of Northern Film and Media Centre (POEM) are to develop, sustain and promote the industry and culture of moving images and to establish the city of Oulu as a major regional resource and development centre for film, TV and mobile game production in Finland.

Funding

The funds supports projects that have cultural links with North Finland and have a possible economic impact on the screen industry's infrastructure and employment in the region. Films and projects for young people will be given priority. The producer should be a permanent resident of North Finland and the production company should have a mainland office there. A majority of the creative team of the film should be North Finland permanent residents. Support is offered in various forms: grants, interest-free loans, approved development expenses, co-financing, financial input and advice, services provided and acquisition of work by the fund. Producers and writer/producer teams may apply.

Script development scheme

Offers: up to €10,000 · For: SCRIPT · Covering: DOC | FFF | YP | FEAT | ANI | SHORT
The aim is to develop scripts, increase the quality of scripts, and foster new talent.

The scheme for short films

Offers: up to €50,000 · Covering: SHORT | YP | ANI | Other
The aim is to encourage professional short film-making in Northern Finland, to foster new talent from the region, to develop new cinematic work and help first-time producers develop the skills necessary to work with a professional crew.

The scheme for documentaries

Offers: from €500 to €30,000 · For: PROD · Covering: DOC
The fund aims to develop high quality documentaries and documentary series, foster new talent, and encourage filmmakers to team up with journalists and visually talented professionals to produce films that reflect life, social processes and the reality of the people in Northern Finland.

The scheme for mobile games (narrative) and interactive TV

Offers: up to €50,000 · For: PROD · Covering: FEAT | TV | SHORT | Other_ANI | DOC | YP
The fund aims to foster new talents from the region, support the development of mobile game production, and create TV and mobile combined TV formats, dramas and series which have an impact on the TV industry and mobile telecommunications industry's infrastructure and employment in the region. Furthermore it supports research and development of new ways of expression via digital and mobile technology.

Production fund for feature films and documentaries

Offers: up to €150,000 · For: PROD · Covering: DOC | FFF | YP | FEAT
The fund supports well-developed, high quality films and audiovisual works which have cultural links in the region and/or have a significant positive impact on the region's content industry infrastructure and employment, and fulfill POEM's strategic objectives and aims of the funding schemes.

FRANCE

Centre National de la Cinématographie (CNC)

www.cnc.fr
12 rue de Lübeck, F-75784 Paris cedex 16, France
T: +33 1 44 34 34 40 · F: +33 1 44 34 34 73
E: webmaster@cnc.fr
The world's largest publicly funded screen agency with an annual budget of approximately €500m, operated under the auspices of the French Ministry of Culture.

The priorities of the CNC are: economy of the cinema and audiovisual, regulation, the promotion of cinema, the protection of film heritage and the implementation of international agreements. In regard to the economy of the cinema and the audiovisual, the CNC manages state financial support for the film industry and audiovisual programmes as well as grants by the Ministry of Culture. Support is delivered in two forms: automatic aid (reinvestment subsidies awarded under purely economic rules) and selective aid which meets qualitative and cultural needs.

Funding

Aid granted by the CNC to film production and distribution is either automatic or selective: Automatic aid is based on the performance of the producer's previous film, both at the box office, on TV and on video/DVD. The aid can be used for repaying previous loans, development costs and production. The approximate annual proportion of these three categories is 8-9% on repayment, 5-6% on development and 83-85% on production. Automatic aid is paid only to French producers, and is thus limited to French films and co-productions. Distributor and exhibitors are also eligible for automatic aid, depending on box office receipts from the previous year. Selective aid — the system of 'avance sur recettes' ('advance against revenue') is an interest-free loan repayable either from income or from any automatic aid granted to a film. The selection procedure is carried out by the Commission d'Avance sur Recettes. Money is generally advanced at script stage, with a certain number of much smaller advances made after a film has been completed. Selective aid is also available for script development. Distributors and exhibitors are eligible for selective aid where they will support smaller and less commercial films. Funding is available through strands including international, cinema, short film, multimedia and new technologies.

Automatic support for the production of feature films

www.cnc.fr/?ID=238
Offers: up to €300,000 · For: PROD · Covering: FEAT
Production of feature films by established French film producers. Producers can benefit from financial support allocated by a sliding scale of return based on earnings for their films (box office, TV, and video/DVD).

Automatic Support for Distribution

www.cnc.fr/?ID=567 · For: DIST · Covering: FEAT | DOC | ANI
Distributors may apply for support calculated according to box-office receipts of their films in cinemas on the basis of a sliding scale, provided the films in question

are of French nationality or co-productions involving France.

Automatic Support for Exhibition

www.cnc.fr/?ID=198 · For: EXBN · Covering: FEAT | DOC | ANI
Support is aimed at financing the cost of new equipment and the modernisation of cinemas, as well as the creation of new cinemas.

Scriptwriting Support

www.cnc.fr/Site/Template/T11.aspx?SELECTID=327&id=225&t=1 · For: PROD · Covering: FEAT | FFF
The funds assists and supports the scriptwriting of audiovisual TV projects. Considerable attention is placed on format, dramaturgy and realistic realisation of the project. Applications may be made by one or more authors. The applicants must be a French citizen and the project must be in French.

Automatic and Selective support for Scriptwriting and Project Development

www.cnc.fr/Site/Template/T11.aspx?SELECTID=325&id=223&t=2
Offers: up to €76,300 · For: SCRIPT | DEV · Covering: FEAT | DOC | ANI | SHORT | Other
The programme supports the writing of new film scripts and the further development of existing scripts. The fund takes the form of a grant.

Development Support for TV productions

www.cnc.fr/Site/Template/T11.aspx?SELECTID=416&ID=258&t=1 · For: DEV · Covering: TV
The fund supports innovative audiovisual TV projects and pays particular attention to the format, dramaturgy and possible realisation. The development aid is intended for production companies that work on a joint basis with one or more authors on innovative TV projects. The projects must be written in French language.

Support for Development of Feature Films

www.cnc.fr/Site/Template/T11.aspx?SELECTID=325&id=223&t=2 · For: DEV | SLATE | SCRIPT · Covering: FEAT
The fund supports production companies developing a single project or a slate of projects. Areas covered by this programme include: the different stages of writing, optioning and acquisition of rights, writing and script development and research.

Production and Distribution Support for Short Films

www.cnc.fr/Site/Template/T6B.aspx?SELECTID=1014&id=114&t=3 · For: PROD | DIST
Support can be awarded on the strength of the script or in the form of an award for quality on completion

of the film. Projects which receive production support may also receive support for the creation of an original musical score.

Support for Production of Foreign-Language Films

www.cnc.fr/Site/Template/T11.aspx?SELECTID=374&ID=182&t=3 · For: PROD · Covering: FEAT
The fund aids the production of foreign-language feature films by prominent French or foreign directors.

Support for French-Canadian Co-productions

www.cnc.fr/Site/Template/T11.aspx?SELECTID=332&id=227&t=1 · For: PROD | DEV · Covering: FEAT | DOC | ANI
The fund gives support to feature film, animation and documentary productions of common interest to both countries and which contribute to the quality of film production. The fund takes the form of repayable advances.

Selective Support for the Distribution of Films for Young Audiences

www.cnc.fr/Site/Template/T11.aspx?SELECTID=382&ID=193&t=3 · For: DIST · Covering: FEAT | ANI
This support is designed to permit renewal and diversification of the offer of films for young audiences. There are four application dates per year.

Support for Pilots

www.cnc.fr/Site/Template/T11.aspx?SELECTID=340&id=235&t=1 · For: SLATE · Covering: ANI
CNC supports applicants with slate-funding in order to help the producers to manage difficult projects and seek other financial partners.

Selective Support for the Distribution of Foreign Films from Rare Cinematographic Traditions

www.cnc.fr/Site/Template/T11.aspx?SELECTID=378&ID=190&t=3
Offers: up to €30 487 · For: DIST · Covering: FEAT | DOC | ANI
The fund aims to contribute to the discovery and commercial distribution of works originating in countries whose productions are little known in France. The programme is jointly administered by the CNC and the Ministry of Foreign Affairs.

Selective Support for Exhibitors for the Modernisation and Construction of Cinemas in Rural Areas

www.cnc.fr/Site/Template/T11.aspx?SELECTID=387&ID=199&t=3 · For: EXBN · Covering: OTHER
The fund aims to encourage the creation and modernisation of cinemas in insufficiently served areas, in particular in rural areas and the suburbs of large cities. The fund takes the form of a grant.

Support for Cinemas within the 'Art and Experimental Cinema' Network and for Independent Cinemas

www.cnc.fr/Site/Template/T11.aspx?SELECTID=388&id=200&t=3 · For: EXBN · Covering: OTHER
The fund supports film theatres programming non-mainstream films which are difficult to compete with mainstream films.

Automatic Production Support

www.cnc.fr/Site/Template/T11.aspx?SELECTID=343&ID=238&t=3 · Covering: DOC | ANI | TV | Other
The programme supports the creation of new work by producers who have already produced programmes for French TV channels. The production company must be established in France and not be controlled by non-European interests. The company's chairman, managing director or general manager should be of French or EU nationality, or resident in France for more than five years. Programme must have been presold to a French TV channel which must cover at least 25% of the budget or 25% of the French part of an international coproduction. The fund takes the form of an Investment Certificate.

Selective Support for the Development of Animations

www.cnc.fr/Site/Template/T11.aspx?SELECTID=337&ID=232&t=3 · For: DEV · Covering: ANI
There are three different types of support for animation: support for the production of animation pilots; support for French-Canadian co-production in the context of the mini-treaty on animation; support for creation of short works of animation by new creators. This last programme is run in co-operation with the Ecole de l'image at the Gobelins institute, as part of the 'Centre de la première oeuvre'

Automatic or Selective Support for Documentaries

www.cnc.fr/Site/Template/T6B.aspx?SELECTID=840&id=112&t=2
Offers: up to €7 623 · For: PROD · Covering: DOC
The scheme supports the production of documentaries within the cinema, TV or multimedia sector. A selection committee made up of CNC staff meets two or three times a year to choose around ten projects. The support can be given automatically or selectively where documentaries cannot fulfill the standard eligibility criteria.

Support for Investment by Film and Television Industry Facilities Companies

www.cnc.fr/Site/Template/T6B.aspx?SELECTID=840&id=112&t=2 · For: CULT · Covering: OTHER
This support scheme is intended to facilitate the acquisition of equipment, modernisation and restructuring of companies, the development of specific equipment and the realisation of innovatory industrial projects in the film and TV technical service sector.

Support for Research and Development

www.cnc.fr/Site/Template/T11.aspx?SELECTID=1348&id=792&t=3 · Covering: FEAT | TV | MM | SHORT | ANI | DOC | FFF | YP
The fund aims to encourage co-operation and technology transfer between research laboratories and multimedia, TV and cinema production companies, and support their in-house research and development.

Support for Multimedia Publishing

www.cnc.fr/Site/Template/T11.aspx?SELECTID=305&ID=218&t=3
Offers: up to €76 225 · For: PROD · Covering: MM
The support fund for multimedia publishing intends to encourage the production of original content on optical media (CD ROMS, DVD ROMS) and the Internet.

Support for Experimental Production

www.cnc.fr/Site/Template/T11.aspx?SELECTID=2013&ID=1283&t=3 · For: PROD · Covering: FEAT | SHORT
The programme aims to share the risk of producers who use innovative technologies (digital special effects, image modelling) or specially developed processes in the production of their works.

Automatic Support for Publication of Videocassettes for Private Use

www.cnc.fr/Site/Template/T6B.aspx?SELECTID=840&id=112&t=2 · For: DVD · Covering: OTHER
There are two forms of support for video publishing: Automatic support intended for video publishers exploiting recognised French films theatrically release during the preceding five years; selective support intended to encourage the publication of cultural programmes. This support is payable to video editors subjected to the tax on sale and rental of videocassettes.

Support for the Promotion of Audiovisual Programmes

www.cnc.fr/Site/Template/T11.aspx?SELECTID=358&id=250&t=3 · For: PROMO · Covering: DOC | ANI | SHORT
This support scheme allows producers and distributors to use effective means to promote their programmes abroad.

Scriptwriting and Development Support for Documentaries

www.cnc.fr/Site/Template/T11.aspx?SELECTID=334&id=229&t=1
Offers: €7000 or €15,000 · For: SCRIPT · Covering: DOC
The funds comprises two types of assistance: help with the writing of €7,000, which is addressed to the authors that may contribute significantly to the quality of documentaries; development aid of an average amount of €15,000, which addresses production companies that are trying to finance the scriptwriting.

Development Support for French-Canadian documentaries

www.cnc.fr/Site/Template/T11.aspx?SELECTID=465&id=231&t=1 · For: DEV · Covering: DOC
The fund supports the development of French-Canadian projects in French language. With regards to documentaries, the aim of support is to foster partnership between Canada and France.

Selective Production Support

www.cnc.fr/Site/Template/T11.aspx?SELECTID=342&id=237&t=1 · For: PROD · Covering: FEAT | TV | DOC | ANI
The programme supports the production of documentaries, fiction, animation, TV programmes and live shows for TV by companies which do not qualify for automatic aid. There are several deadlines throughout the year. Applying companies must be independent of any TV channels. At least 30% of the overall cost must be financed by French participants. About 50% of the production expenses should be spent in France. Financial assistance granted in this way cannot exceed 50% of the overall cost of work.

Support Music for Documentaries

www.cnc.fr/Site/Template/T11.aspx?SELECTID=346&id=241&t=3 · Covering: DOC
The Funds for Musical Creation (FCM), the Ministry for the Culture (Direction of music, dance, theatre and spectacle) and CNC set up the 'Funds for audiovisual music' and aims to encourage the use of music in documentaries.

Support for Videoclips

www.cnc.fr/Site/Template/T11.aspx?SELECTID=356&id=248&t=3
Offers: €1,200 · Covering: OTHER
The fund supports videoclips that include music and lyrics that are sung in French language.

Support for new Production Technologies
www.cnc.fr/Site/Template/T11.aspx?SELECTID=2013&id=1283&t=3 · Covering: OTHER
The fund assists and encourages production companies to use new and innovative technology (i.e. numerical special effects, synthesized images, development of specific processes). It takes the form of a selective subsidy and takes into account the expenditure related to the use and development of new technologies.

Support for Foreign Distribution
www.cnc.fr/Site/Template/T11.aspx?SELECTID=358&id=250&t=3 · For: DIST · Covering: FEAT | TV | DOC | ANI
Selective assistance is given to producers or distributors for the export of their films and programs. This includes support for subtitles, formatting to international standards etc. The grant cannot exceed 50% of the total cost of expenses.

Tax Incentives
www.cnc.fr/Site/Template/T11.aspx?SELECTID=849&id=508&t=3
Under particular conditions, tax credits of up to 20% may be given.

Support for Cinema Productions
www.cnc.fr/Site/Template/T6B.aspx?SELECTID=511&id=113&t=3 · For: SCRIPT | DEV | PROD | DIST | EXBN · Covering: FEAT | DOC | ANI
CNC runs 31 different schemes that support films which are intended for cinema exhibition.

Support for Video Editing
www.cnc.fr/Site/Template/T11.aspx?SELECTID=2296&id=1523&t=3
This automatic support funds video editors in relation to the sales turnover. All films must be entirely produced in France or be a French co-production.

Support for Multimedia and New Technologies
www.cnc.fr/Site/Template/T6B.aspx?SELECTID=972&id=116&t=3 · Covering: MM | Other
The fund assists companies that take risks of using new innovative technologies in long and short films. This includes the research and development of the technologies and also encourages partnerships with the government research laboratories.

Fonds Sud
www.cnc.fr/Site/Template/T11.aspx?SELECTID=361&ID=204&t=3 · For: PROD · Covering: FEAT | DOC | ANI
The Southern Funding programme was created in 1984 to support the development and realisation of productions from southern countries. The fund supports especially films that emphasise the cultural identity of

their country. In the past support has been given to countries in Africa, Latin America, the Maghreb, the Middle-East, Central Asia, the Caribbean, to Albania, and the countries of ex-Yugoslavia. The assistance is granted for the production of feature films, animations and documentaries. The projects must be filmed in the countries and the language of the film should predominantly be the national language of the country.

Support for English Subtitling
www.cnc.fr/Site/Template/T11.aspx?SELECTID=2280&ID=1513&t=3 · Covering: FEAT | DOC | ANI
This help aims to finance English subtitling in order to support the sales of French language films.

Action régionale pour la création artistique et la diffusion en Ile-de-France (ARCADI)
www.arcadi.fr
1 bis passage Duhesme, BP 30066, 75861 Paris Cedex 18, France
T: +33 1 55 79 00 00 · F: +33 1 55 79 97 79
E: info@arcadi.fr
The organisation offers information and advice for the benefit of artists who contribute to the cultural environment in France. Arcadi supports artistic creation and acts as co-producer. It support the distribution of works and contributes to the development of the projects.

Support for the Production of Medium-Length Films
www.arcadi.fr
Offers: up to €45 735 · For: PROD · Covering: FEAT | SHORT
The director must have finished a short film before, the producer must have produced several short films before.

Support for Post-Production (celluloid)
www.arcadi.fr · For: POST · Covering: DOC | ANI | FFF | SHORT | FEAT
For producers of short films that have not obtained more than €12,196 or unfinished medium-length films between 45 and 59 min; first and second unfinished full-length films not having obtained a total funding higher than €457,347.

Support for Post-production (digital)
www.arcadi.fr · For: POST · Covering: FEAT | SHORT | DOC | ANI | FFF
For producers of short films that have not obtained funding of more than €7,622; medium-length films that have not obtained more funding of more than €5,3357; first and second unfinished full-length films not having

obtained a total funding higher than €228 674 (in case of documentary films the limit is €304,898).

Africa Cinemas

www.africa-cinemas.org
54 rue Beaubourg, 75003 Paris, France
T: +33 1 42 71 53 70 · F: +33 1 42 71 47 55
E: info@africa-cinemas.org
Africa Cinémas is an interagency program of the Intergovernmental Agency for French-speaking Nations, the French Foreign Affairs Ministry and the European Union (European Development Fund) to support the distribution and exhibition of African films in France. At time of publication the nature of the programmes was under discussion, but in previous years has included the following awards.

Distribution support
www.africa-cinemas.org/en/docs/Distribution%20-%20Lignes%20Directrices.pdf · For: DIST · Covering: FEAT | DOC | ANI
Films which may receive Africa Cinémas' support must be directed by a cinematographer originating from Sub-Saharan Africa, and produced or co-produced by one or several companies in those countries.

Exhibition support
www.africa-cinemas.org/en/docs/Exploitation%20-%20Lignes%20Directrices.pdf · For: EXBN · Covering: FEAT | DOC | ANI
Applications must be received, with no exceptions, no later than one month before the announced meeting of the Committee.

Agence culturelle d'Alsace

www.culture-alsace.org
1 espace Gilbert Estève, BP 90025 — 67601 Sélestat Cedex, France
T: +33 3 88 58 87 58 · F: +33 3 88 58 87 50
E: agence@culture-alsace.org
The Film Department of the Agence Culturelle d'Alsace acts as a springboard for new film talent.

Investment 'in kind' · For: PROD · Covering: OTHER
Support is in the form of investment in kind (shooting, editing) and advice. Priority is given to professional quality film projects which by their subject or their method of production, correspond with the general objectives of the Agency. Applications may be made by writers, directors or producers. There must be a regional involvement in the project, for example, principal photography in the region, or residence of the applicant.

Aid for First Films
Offers: €7,650 · For: PROD · Covering: FFF | SHORT | DOC
The fund assists directors who have not yet directed an original film shot on professional formats (16mm, 35mm, Beta SP) and who have developed a project independently (ie not in relation with their studies).

Support for innovative projects
Offers: €4,573 · For: PROD · Covering: DOC | MM | Other
Support is intended for transversal projects which by their innovative nature have difficulty raising finance by traditional means. These projects can include production of films (research, artists videos) and in particular works using new technology in this domain. Support takes the form of financial aid, advice and assistance and investment in kind (editing, shooting, projection equipment etc). The director must be a resident in Alsace or the applying organisation must have its base in the region.

Agence intergouvernementale de la Francophonie

www.francophonie.org/
Agence intergouvernementale de la Francophonie, Direction du cinéma et des médias, 13 Quai Andre Citroën, 75015 Paris, France
T: +33 1 44 37 33 20 · F: +33 1 45 79 14 98
E: fondsaudiovisuel@francophonie.org
Operated across 55 states, the Agency exists to support and promote the use of the French language across culture.

Award for Production of Films from the Southern Hemisphere
www.francophonie.org/actions/cinema/fin-audiovisuelle.cfm · For: PROD · Covering: TV | FEAT | SHORT | DOC | ANI
Since its creation in 1988, the CNC backed fund has supported many majority world productions in the southern hemisphere, and now the Far East and Eastern Europe. 25% of the budget must already have been collected. There are three annual deadlines.

Award for the Promotion of French language Films from the Southern Hemisphere
agence.francophonie.org/actions/cinema/fin-promofilm.cfm
Offers: Up to €80,000 · For: PROMO | EXBN · Covering: FEAT | TV | SHORT | DOC | ANI
Covering the same majority world remit as the production award, the fund takes the form of a grant, with an annual deadline.

Agence pour le développement régional du cinéma

www.adrc-asso.org
4 avenue Marceau, 75008 Paris, France
T: +33 1 56 89 20 30 · F: +33 1 56 89 20 40
E: adrc@adrc-asso.org
The fund aims to support country-wide access to cinema, to encourage diversity of cinemas, films and audiences and to maintain and develop local cinemas.

Support for the Production of Additional Prints
· For: EXBN · Covering: FEAT
Managed by the ADRC, this help is financed by the CNC to support access to film by the production of additional prints. The support is intended for exhibitors in small and special medium sized towns, and for films classed as 'artistic and experimental cinema'.

Support for classic films · For: EXBN · Covering: OTHER
The fund supports the exhibition of classic films distributed by French companies.

Support for renovation
Offers: up to €1800
The organisation gives architectural and environmental advice for the renovation of cinema theatres.

Aquitaine Image Cinéma

aquitaine-image-cinema.fr
Cité mondiale, 23 parvis des Chartrons, F-33074 Bordeaux cedex, France
T: +33 5 56 01 78 70 · F: +33 5 56 01 78 30
E: aic@aic.aquitaine.fr
The organisation assists at all the stages of the cinematographic or audio-visual activities. It supports the emergence of Aquitanian talents and the development of the regional companies of production. The organisation aims to promote Aquitanian identity and culture within the media and cinema.

Support for development and production
aquitaine-image-cinema.fr/spip.php?article18
Offers: up to €100,000 · For: PROD | DEV | SCRIPT · Covering: DOC | ANI | FFF | TV | SHORT
The programme assists the scriptwriting, development and production of film and video work. Support ranges from €8,000 for screenwriting, €15,000 for short film production to €100,000 for feature production

Scriptwriting grant (short films)
aquitaine-image-cinema.fr
Offers: €2,000 · For: SCRIPT · Covering: SHORT
The fund applies to the authors living in the Aquitaine area who have already produced a short-film. The

projects must be fictional, made in the Aquitaine area and must be less than 60 min. The fund takes the form of a grant.

Atelier de Production Centre Val de Loire

www.apcvl.com
Atelier de Production Centre Val de Loire, 24 rue Renan, F — 37110 CHATEAU-RENAULT, France
T: +33 2 47 56 08 08 · F: +33 2 47 56 07 07
E: infos@apcvl.com
The APCVL is the cinema antenna of the Val de Loire region. Its mission is to give artistic and technical expertise, treatment of projects submitted to the Centre region, location office for films, support regional focus for film education and training and the diffusion and promotion of films.

Support for the production of short films
www.centreimages.fr/production_courtmetrage.php
Offers: up to €45,000 · For: PROD · Covering: SHORT | ANI
In 2006, 10 short live action films and two animations were supported. All must be under 30 minutes and finish on 35mm.

Support for TV production
www.centreimages.fr/production_pt.php
Offers: up to €20,000 · For: PROD · Covering: TV | SHORT | DOC | ANI | YP
Offers up to €15,000 for single programmes and €20,000 for series.

Support for Media Production
www.centreimages.fr/production_pa.php
Offers: up to €150,000 · For: PROD · Covering: DOC | ANI | TV
Offers up to €30,000 for single documentary productions and €60,000 for series. Support for animation up to €75,000 for a single programme and up to €150,000 for a series. Length must be over 52 minutes.

Support for Feature films
www.centreimages.fr/production_LM.php
Offers: Up to €200,000 · For: PROD | POST · Covering: DOC | FEAT | ANI
In 2006, four full-length films were supported with production (average assistance: €142,500) and four were supported with post-production (average assistance: €45 000).

Company developmnt

www.centreimages.fr/production_ia.php
Offers: Up to €15,000 · For: BIZ-DEV
Offers infrastructural support for companies operating in the region for more than a year.

Centre régional de ressources audiovisuelles de la région Nord-Pas de Calais

www.crrav.com
CCRAV (Centre Régional de Ressources Audiovisuelles), 21 rue Edgar Quinet, BP 152, F — 59333 TOURCOING CEDEX, France
T: +33 3 20 28 26 40 · F: +33 3 20 28 26 41
E: pfreville@crrav.com
The mission of the CRRAV is to develop the audiovisual sector in the region. The association administers a 'Production Fund' intended to support film, TV and multimedia works that are relevant, in artistic terms, to the historic, geographic and social diversity of the Nord-Pas de Calais region.

Funding

Applications will be accepted only from producers registered with the CNC. The applying producer must be the originator of the project, and have full artistic, financial and technical responsibility for it. Producers may submit only one application for each scheme and a total of two applications at each session of the selection committee. No minimum and maximum amounts are indicated for the awards, with figures given below based on awards made in 2006.

Support for Scriptwriting and Development

www.crrav.com/fonds_cinema_TV.htm
Offers: Up to €25,000 · For: SCRIPT | DEV · Covering: FEAT | MM | DOC | ANI | TV
Awards are made at one of four annual panels.

Support for Shorts

www.crrav.com/fonds_cinema_TV.htm
Offers: up to €35,000 · For: PROD · Covering: DOC
Support for production is through the 'Support Fund for cinematographic, TV and multimedia production'.

Support for Production

www.crrav.com/fiction.htm
Offers: Up to €450,000 · For: PROD · Covering: FEAT
Four annual deadlines.

Support for documentary

www.crrav.com/documentaire.htm
Offers: Up to €25,000
Offers small (under €10,000) investments in the development of documentaries, with larger awards (up to €25,000) for production.

Collectivité teritoriale de la Corse

www.corse.fr/
Hôtel de Région, 22 Cours Grandval, BP 215, 20187 AJACCIO cedex 1, France
T: +33 4 95 51 64 64 · F: +33 4 95 51 67 75
E: contact@corse.fr
The organisation supports and promotes film in the region by encouraging filmmakers to shoot there.

Support for short or medium length films and documentary

Offers: up to €80,000 · For: PROD · Covering: SHORT | FEAT | DOC
The fund supports a production company located in the region (open subject) or a production company located outside the region but proposing a project on a subject related to the region.

Support for scriptwriting

www.corse.fr/documents/guide_aide/ 1%20aide%20ecriture.pdf
Offers: up to €6,000 · For: SCRIPT · Covering: DOC | TV | SHORT | FEAT
The fund aims to improve artistic creations by financing the writing of a script (ie. locations, voyages, work with a scenario writer, dialogist). The author should be established in Corsica or the subject and geographical place of the project should be linked to Corsica.

Support for project development

Offers: up to €15,000 · For: DEV · Covering: FEAT | SHORT | DOC | ANI | FFF | YP
The development support aims to help finalise the possibility of a production. The fund helps to finance the expenditure of rewriting, research, filing. The production company should be established in Corsica, or there should be a link to Corsica. Furthermore, 50% of the fund should be spent in Corsica.

Support for the production of feature films, telefilms and TV series

Offers: up to €100,000 · Covering: FEAT | TV | FFF
This help is intended to support, within the framework of the funds of production aid of the CTC, the production of telefilms.

Support for mulitmedia and video art

Offers: up to €50 000 · For: PROD · Covering: MM | Other

This help is intended to support the emergent forms of audiovisual numerical and video-art.

Production support for cinema releases

Offers: up to €150,000 · For: PROD · Covering: FEAT

This help is intended to support the production of cinematographic works of fiction.

Support for first works

www.corse.fr/documents/guide_aide/ 5%20aide%201ere%20oeuvre.pdf

Offers: up to €50,000 · For: PROD · Covering: FFF | FEAT | DOC | SHORT

This help is intended to promote new talents that concentrate on audiovisual and cinematographic creation in Corsica. Eligible for the funding are films of short and medium-length and documentaries presented by a producer living in Corsica. The projects should be shorter than 60 minutes.

Communauté urbaine de Strasbourg

www.strasbourg-film.com

Aurélie Reveillaud, Service de la Culture/ Audiovisuel et Cinéma, France

T: +33 3 88 60 92 97 · F: +33 3 88 60 98 57

E: media@cus.sdv.fr

The organisation promotes the development of an audiovisual industry within the region and aims to attract inward investment. Local production companies or authors are eligible to apply. The theme of the film should be of interest or relevant to the region. The fund emphasises the use and employment of local human and material resources.

Production Support

www.strasbourg-film.com/media/fichiers/ file2006120519.pdf

Offers: up to €100,000 · For: PROD · Covering: FEAT | SHORT | DOC | ANI

The program supports film and video production.

Distribution Support

www.strasbourg-film.com/fr/aides-a-la-diffusion/

For: DIST · Covering: OTHER

The Town of Strasbourg supports institutions which distribute and promote cinematographic and audiovisual work.

Conseil général de l'Eure

www.cg27.fr

Responsable du Pôle animation cultruelle, Hôtel du Département, Boulevard Georges-Chauvin, 27021 Evreux Cedex, France

T: +33 2 32 31 51 04 · F: +33 2 32 39 91 88

E: sophie.seragin@cg27.fr

The cultural department of the Council supports film through the recognition of screenwriting.

Short film script competition: 'l'Eure: terre de cinéma'

The Short fiction film script competition is organised each year with the Moulin d'Indé-Céci foundation. Action should take place in the Eure area and should include exterior scenes. Only one script per author is permitted. The fund takes the form of an award.

Conseil général de l'Isère

www.cg38.fr

Service Culture, 7 rue Fantin-Latour, 38000 Grenoble, France

T: +33 4 76 00 33 81 · F: +33 4 76 01 09 77

E: cg38@cg38.fr

Competition for film scripts

www.cg38.fr · For: SCRIPT · Covering: ANI | YP | FEAT | DOC

Competition for scripts are organised by the Festival de Court-métrage en Plein Air de Grenoble and the Conseil général de l'Isère. The competition is open to all works of fiction, documentary, animation or experimentation and designed to be shot on film. One project per writer; a project may only be presented once. The writer should be a resident or a native of the Isère department and should be able to supply evidence. They may not be on the jury. Projects already in production are not eligible. There is one application deadline per year.

Conseil général de la Charente

www.charente-developpement.com

Frédéric Cros, Directeur du département stratégie marketing, Charante Développemnt, 7 rue du Secours, 16022 Angoulême Cedex, France

T: +33 (8) 5 45 67 36 15 · F: +33 (8) 5 45 61 46 14

E: fcros@charente-developpement.com

The council promotes cultural identity in the region through supporting different types of films and holding the annual Cognac film festival. Filmmakers are encouraged to produce in the geographical area and to work with regional film commissions.

Scriptwriting and project development

www.charente-developpement.com/uk/
Offers: Up to €4,000 · For: DEV | SCRIPT · Covering:
FEAT | TV | SHORT | DOC
The fund supports scriptwriting up to €4,000.

Production support

Offers: up to €150,000 · For: PROD · Covering:
FEAT | TV | SHORT | DOC | ANI
Assistance available for short film of fiction,
documentary and animation (max €30,000 or €3,000/
minute for short films); telefilms and series TV (max
€150,000); documentary (max €30,000); and for a
series of animation (max €15,000 per episode).

Digital media

Offers: Up to €150,000 · For: PROD · Covering: MM
| VIDG | DIGI
Multimedia projects can be funded up to €30,000 and
videogames up to €150,000.

Conseil général de la Corrèze

www.cg19.fr
9 rue René et Emile Fage, BP 199, 19005 Tulle
Cedex, France
T: +33 5 55 93 70 50 · F: +33 5 55 93 73 25
The council's aim is to support film production in the
region.

Production Support

For: PROD · Covering: SHORT | FEAT
The fund takes the form of a grant.

Conseil général de la Sarthe

www.cg72.fr
MDPH, 15 rue Gongeard, 72000 Le Mans, France
T: 02 43 54 11 92
E: contact.estc@cg72.fr
The council fosters cultural activities including short
film funding and safeguarding film exploitation by
developing the activities which revolve around the
cinema.

Support for the Production of Short Films

www.cg72.fr/GuideDesAides/iso_album/7.13_aide_
production_courts_metrages.pdf · For: PROD ·
Covering: SHORT
The fund supports short films with an artistic quality.

Conseil général de Loire-

Atlantique

www.cg44.fr/
Direction du Développement Culturel et du Tourisme,
Mission Cinéma, 3 quai Ceineray, 44041 Nantes
Cedex 01, France
T: +33 2 40 99 10 76 / 2 40 99 15 48
E: contact@cg44.fr
The Conseil general was founded in 1990 in order
to promote cultural development and support film
production.

Support for the Production of Short Films by Young People

www.cg44.fr/ · For: SCRIPT | DEV | PROD ·
Covering: SHORT | YP
This programme encourages young people to write and
produce a short film with professional assistance with
the intention to present the film in a cinema.

Conseil général de Seine-Saint-Denis

www.cg93.fr/
Direction de la Culture, de la Jeunesse et du Sport,
BP193, 93003 Bobigny cedex, France
T: +33 1 43 93 80 86 · F: +33 1 43 93 81 60
E: pgac@cg93.fr
The Council aims to develop the production of feature
films and realisation of short films in the region of
Seine-Saint-Denis.

Production support

Grants are available for shorts and features.

Conseil général des Bouches-du-Rhône

www.cg13.fr/?page=accueil
Hôtel du Département, 52 avenue de Saint-Just,
13256 Marseille cedex, France
T: +33 4 91 21 17 57 · F: +33 4 91 21 23 92
E: infos@cg13.fr
The Council works with various sectors such as the
social action, transport, teaching, the economy, the
environment, the roads and the cultural departments.
The council aims to widen diverse public access to
culture and supports artistic productions within music,
theatre, dance, visual arts and cinema.

Production Support for Short Films

www.cg13.fr/?page=accueil · For: PROD · Covering:
SHORT
The program supports documentary or fiction films
no longer than 26 minutes in length and of which the
director or producer is resident in the Bouches-du-

Rhône department. The selection committee meets twice a year: in April and October. Applications should be submitted at least two months beforehand.

Conseil général des Côtes d'Armor

www.cg22.fr · Direction de la Culture, des Sports, de l'Education et de la Jeunesse, Hötel du Département, Place du Général de Gaulle, BP 237122023 Saint-Brieuc Cedex 1, France
T: +33 2 96 62 50 49 · F: +33 2 96 62 61 13
E: info@oddc22.com
The Council supports the distribution of film and promotes local industry events and festivals.

Scriptwriting support

www.cotesdarmor.fr/fileadmin/pdf/GDA2006/PAGE164.pdf
Offers: up to €3,000 · For: SCRIPT
Scriptwriting support is given to professional authors who have already finished a scriptwriting project within the field of documentary, fiction or animation. Project Development is funded up to €5,000 (50% of the costs).

Production support

www.cotesdarmor.fr/fileadmin/pdf/GDA2006/PAGE164.pdf
Offers: UP to €12,000 · For: PROD · Covering: FEAT | DOC | ANI
Documentaries are funded to €12,000, animation productions are funded up to €10,000 and fiction films receive a grant of €8,000.

Conseil général du Finistère

www.cg29.fr · Pôle de développement culturel, Maison du Département, 32 boulevard Dupleix, 29196 Quimper, France
T: +33 2 96 62 50 49 · F: +33 2 96 62 61 13
E: contact@cg29.fr
The Council supports cultural activities and fosters creative talents from the region and the development of a network of independent cinemas.

Support for short film production

Offers: Up to 10% or €8,000
The rate of subsidy can be increased to a maximum of 20% for films in the Breton language.

Conseil général du Lot

www.lot.fr/
Service des Affaires scolaires, culturalles, sportives et des Transports, Place Chapou, BP 291, 46005 Cahors cedex 9, France
T: +33 5 65 23 15 23 · F: +33 5 65 23 15 39
E: affaires-culturelles-sportives@cg46.fr
A short film screenwriting contest has been organised by the Council since 2003.

Competition for short film and creative documentary scripts

www.lot.fr/news/suite.php?newsid=1209
Offers: up to €7,600 · For: SCRIPT · Covering: SHORT | DOC
Eligible works are Short fiction films (15 minutes' duration) which are linked to and set in Lot, and creative documentaries (26 or 52 minutes) made by a writer living (or who lived) in Lot. The fund takes the form of an award.

Conseil général du Val-de-Marne

www.cg94.fr/index2.php
Service culturel, 16 rue des Archives, Marie Aubayle, FR — 94000 Creteil, France
T: +33 1 43 99 73 69 · F: +33 1 43 99 73 60
E: marie.aubayle@cg94.fr
The council has funded film production since 1989.

Production support

www.cg94.fr/node/5552 · For: PROD · Covering: FEAT | TV | SHORT | DOC
Only one project may be submitted by a producer or company and it should have artistic originality. The fund takes the form of a grant.

Conseil régional d'Alsace

www.cr-alsace.fr/
Direction de la Culture et des Sports, 1 place du Wacken, BP 91006, Strasbourg 67070 cedex, France
T: +33 3 88 15 67 81 · F: +33 3 88 15 69 49
E: contact@region-alsace.fr
The Council promotes development of the film and video sector in Alsace and supporting the creation of jobs.

Funding

Applications may be made by individuals or production companies resident or operating in Alsace. Applications should be made by means of a detailed letter explaining the work to be done and accompanied by a description of the project and the potential costs of the work. Any development support awarded will be deducted from production support given subsequently.

Support for Scriptwriting and Development of Audiovisual Projects

www.cr-alsace.fr/

Offers: ranging from €1,500 to €7,600 · For: SCRIPT | DEV · Covering: FEAT | DOC | TV

The fund supports scriptwriting or development by an individual or a production company. It takes the form of a grant.

Support for Audiovisual Production (except long films)

www.region-alsace.eu/dn_guide-aides-edition-audiovisuel/soutien-production-audiovisuelle-courts-metrages.html?profiles=&chapitres=129&recherche=

Offers: up to €75,000 · For: PROD · Covering: FEAT | TV | DOC | ANI

This program funds the production of short and medium-length films that have regional relevance. The fund takes the form of a grant.

Support of audiovisual distribution

www.region-alsace.eu/dn_guide-aides-edition-audiovisuel/soutien-recherche-diffuseur-audiovisuel.html?profiles=&chapitres=129&recherche=

Offers: up to €7,000 · For: DIST · Covering: FEAT | TV | DOC | ANI

The fund allows producers based in Alsace to initiate distribution at interregional level, national or international, through the realisation of pilots and/or bands of demonstration.

Conseil régional d'Aquitaine

www.cr-aquitaine.fr/

Service Culture, Hôtel de Région — 14 rue François-de-Sourdis, F-33077 Bordeaux cedex, France

T: +33 5 57 57 80 00

E: cra@aquitaine.fr

The Regional Council aims to foster the development of new talent, encourage creativity and the personal growth of citizens in the Region and regards the development of the film and video sector as a priority axis of its policy. The council's aims are to support the authors of the region and help distribute their projects at cultural events, develop professional production in Aquitaine and finance the modernisation of cinemas. For the year 2007, the budget comprises €1,500,000.

Production support for regional companies

www.aquitaine.fr

Offers: up to €100,000 · For: PROD | SCRIPT | DEV

Covering: FEAT | TV | SHORT | DOC | ANI | FFF | YP

Project must be produced by a company from Aquitaine except in the case of first or second feature films. Applications from outside the region may be considered who include a contribution of at least 30% from a co-production partner in Aquitaine. Except for feature films, duration of project must not exceed one hour. There are no deadlines, although the reading committee considers projects four times a year. Support for feature films up to €100,000, for short films, documentaries, TV series and animation films up to €30,000.

Scriptwriting Support

interventions.aquitaine.fr/article106.html

Offers: up to €8,000 · For: SCRIPT · Covering: FEAT | TV | DOC | ANI

The programme offers assistance with the writing of full-length cinema films and TV fiction. Applications can be made by writers, producers or directors of film and video work. Authors established in Aquitaine or authors and producers who commit themselves to film in the Aquitaine area are eligible.

Development Support

interventions.aquitaine.fr/IMG/doc/Aide_d_veloppement_LM | DOC_ANIM_2006_site3.doc

Offers: up to €15,000 · For: DEV · Covering: FEAT | DOC | ANI

The fund supports development and writing, the first steps of distribution and co-production.

Conseil régional de Basse-Normandie

www.cr-basse-normandie.fr/

Abbaye aux Dames, Place Reine-Mathilde, BP 523, 14035 Caen, France

T: +33 2 31 06 98 44 · F: +33 2 31 06 97 61

E: courrier@crbn.fr

The film and video sector is a priority of the region. The aim of the department 'House of the Image' is to support any activity related to the development of the film and video sector in Basse-Normandie.

Support for Festivals

The Council funds six annual festivals in the region.

Support for Cinemas

This investment form functions to modernise cinemas in rural areas.

'High-school pupils to the cinema'

www.cr-basse-normandie.fr/culture-soutien-diffusion-audiovisuelle.php · For: PROD · Covering: FFF | YP | SHORT

Together with the National Centre of Cinematography (CNC) the council encourages young people with the programme 'High-school pupils to the Cinema' to discover and experiment with cinematographic culture and artistic creations.

Conseil régional de Franche-Comté

www.cr-franche-comte.fr
Direction de la Culture, 4 square Castan, F — 25031 BESANCON Cedex, France
T: +33 3 81 61 61 61 · F: +33 3 81 83 12 92
E: commission.du.film@cr-franche-comte.fr
The council supports, encourages and promotes film in the region by encouraging filmmakers to produce locally and to work with regional film commissions and other similar organisations.

Support for Short film production and documentaries

Offers: up to €20,000 · For: PROD · Covering: SHORT | DOC

Production companies from Franche-Comté are eligible to apply. Fiction and animation films should be limited to 26 minutes. The duration of documentary may exceed 26 minutes. Production companies that are not established in Franche-Comté must shoot entirely in the area.

Scriptwriting support for feature and TV films

Offers: up to €7,600 · For: SCRIPT · Covering: FEAT | TV

The producer or author must be established in the area while filming and post-production should take place in the region.

Support for the modernisation of cinemas

Offers: up to €76.200 · Covering: OTHER
The fund helps to modernise cinemas in areas where there are more than 10,000 inhabitants.

Production support for TV documentaries

www.cr-franche-comte.fr/aides/index.php
Offers: up to €40,000 · Covering: TV | DOC
Production companies established in the area that do not receive automatic assistance from the CNC (COSIP) are eligible to apply. The fund takes the form of a subsidy.

Production support of TV fiction programs and TV animation series

Offers: up to €100,000 · For: PROD · Covering: TV | ANI | FEAT

The fund aims to develop TV production in the region and promotes the decentralisation of production in France. Production companies established in Franche-Comté are eligible to apply. The production aid takes the form of a subsidy.

Conseil régional de la Bretagne

www.region-bretagne.fr/french/crb/index.htm
Direction de la Culture, 283 avenue du Général Patton, CS 21101, 35711 Rennes Cedex 7, France
T: +33 2 99 27 11 72 · F: +33 2 99 27 15 16
E: j.danielou@region-bretagne.fr
The Conseil régional de la Bretagne supports the development of film and video in the region. The funding has a cultural, artistic and an economic purpose, thus priority is given to the projects of companies established in Brittany.

Support for Cinemas

Offers: up to €135,000 · For: EXBN
The fund supports the modernisation of independent cinemas in the region.

Support for festivals

The Council hosts national and international festivals in the region and gives financial support to the organisers.

Production Support

www.region-bretagne.fr/CRB/Public/rubriques_thematique/culture_et_sport/cache_culture_et_sport/la_politique_regiona9837_11600342924244
Offers: up to €76,000 · For: PROD · Covering: FEAT | DOC | ANI | TV | SHORT
In order to receive this support, the majority of the filming should be done in Brittany and the actors and technicians should be from Brittany.

Scriptwriting and Development Support

For: SCRIPT | DEV · Covering: FEAT | DOC | ANI | TV | SHORT
The fund assists with scriptwriting and development. The support is intended in particular for Production Companies from Breton but other producers are welcome to apply. The film should be produced in Breton or be relevant to the region.

Conseil régional de la Picardie

www.cr-picardie.fr/
Service Culture, Conseil régional de Picardie 11, Mail Albert-1er, BP 2616, 80026 Amiens, France
T: +33 3 22 97 37 51 · F: +33 3 22 97 39 03
E: webmaster@cr-picardie.fr
ACAP is the film foundation for the region of Picardy. Commissioned by the Ministry of Culture and Communication, the National Centre for Cinematography and Picardy regional Council, ACAP plays a role in coordinating, coaching and conveying a specific idea and philosophy on the production of independent films. ACAP operates across production, education and distribution. The association is focused on providing opportunities for the general public to meet film directors and to view their work, establishing, through artistic and political channels, the concept of a free, vibrant and far-reaching cinema, supporting the independent cinemas in their selections and practices and providing everyone with easy access to information.

Support for Script Support for Writing and Development

www.acap-cinema.com/acap.html
Offers: up to €8,000 (€4,000 for documentaries and short films) · For: SCRIPT | DEV · Covering: DOC | FEAT | FFF | SHORT
Filming should be completed primarily in the region but any French company can apply.

Production support for short films and documentaries

www.acap-cinema.com/acap.html
Offers: up to €25,000 · For: PROD · Covering: SHORT | DOC
Majority local shoot but applications can be from companies located anywhere in France.

Production Support for feature films

www.acap-cinema.com/acap.html
Offers: up to €150,000 · For: PROD · Covering: FEAT | FFF
Most of the filming should be done in the region. Support is given as a grant or an advance to be reimbursed.

Production support for television programmes

www.acap-cinema.com/acap.html
Offers: up to €20,000 · For: PROD · Covering: TV
The Majority of the filming should be done in the region. Individual programmes should be longer than 26 minutes.

Conseil régional de Lorraine

www.cr-lorraine.fr/
Direction de la Patrimoine et de la Culture, Conseil régional de Lorraine, Place Gabriel-Hocquard, BP 81004, Metz, France
T: +33 3 87 33 62 20 · F: +33 3 87 32 89 33
E: crt@crt-lorraine.fr
The Council's aims is to make Lorraine a culturally attractive place. It promotes film production in the region and encourages filmmakers to produce in Lorraine and to work with regional film commissions.

Production support for fiction film

For: PROD · Covering: FEAT | FFF | SHORT
The company should be established in Lorraine and the subsidy should be spent in the Lorraine area. The subject of the film should have relevance to the region.

Support for scriptwriting

Offers: up to €2,000 · For: SCRIPT · Covering: FEAT | SHORT | DOC | FFF
The fund applies to authors resident in Lorraine who write about a subject significant to the area.

Support for creative documentaries

For: PROD · Covering: DOC
The support cannot exceed more than 15% of the total budget of work. The producer must fulfil at least two of the four following criteria: the company must be established in Lorraine; the subject should be relevant to Lorraine; the author should be from the region; the subsidy must be spent in the area.

Conseil régional de Poitou-Charentes

www.cr-poitou-charentes.fr
15 Rue de l'ancienne comédie, BP 575, 86021 POITIERS CEDEX, France
T: +33 5 49 55 77 00 · F: +33 5 49 55 77 88
E: postmaster@cr-poitou-_charentes.fr
The Conseil régional de Poitou-Charentes encourages young talent, promotes regional production and supports regional enterprises to innovate and develop.

Presence of the regional companies in the great festivals

www.cr-poitou-charentes.fr/fr/exergue/services/aides/aide.dml?id=42 · For: PROMO
The fund encourages regional companies to present their work at large festivals in France.

Support for the Production of Pilots

Offers: up to €8,000 · For: PROD · Covering: SHORT
Producers and distributors from the region are eligible to apply.

Production support for short films

Offers: up to €30,000 · For: PROD · Covering: SHORT | DOC | TV

The production of the film (no longer than 60 min) should take place in the region.

Support for video games

www.cr-poitou-charentes.fr

Offers: up to €150,000 · For: DEV · Covering: VIDG

The support is intended for companies established in the area which develop the games in the region. The fund is intended for preproduction.

Production support for multimedia projects

Offers: up to €30,000 · For: PROD · Covering: MM

The fund is intended for producers or editors who use a topic that is connected to the region. The fund takes the form of a subsidy.

Production support for television programmes

Offers: up to €150,000 · For: PROD · Covering: TV | ANI | DOC

Intended for production companies that produce episodes between 13 and 24 minutes. A large proportion of the subsidy should be spent in the region.

Production support for feature length fiction

Offers: up to €300,000

The films should have a minimum duration of one hour. 25% of the expenditure should be carried out in area.

Conseil régional de Provence-Alpes-Côte d'Azur

www.cr-paca.fr/

Service Culture, Hôtel de la Région, 27 Place Jules Guesde, 13481 Marseille Cedex 20, France

T: 04 91 57 50 57 · F: 04 91 57 51 51

E: info@hdr.cr-paca.fr

The council aims to give assistance to all inhabitants of the Provence-Alpes-Coast of Azure and supports associations, companies, students, high-school pupils, researchers, so that everyone has a chance to realise their project. Furthermore, the various funds were created in order to support important industries of the territory.

Support for the Production of Short Films

www.regionpaca.fr/uploads/media/Fiche_CM06.pdf

Offers: up to €25,000 · For: PROD · Covering: SHORT

Production support is intended for companies presenting work under 60 minutes which is filmed entirely in the region. Alternatively the author or producer must be resident in the area PACA. There are two application deadlines per year.

Support for Scriptwriting and Project Development — short

www.regionpaca.fr/uploads/media/Fiche_CM06.pdf

Offers: up to €5,500 · For: DEV | SCRIPT · Covering: SHORT

The fund supports writers or companies from the region who propose a project of less than 60 minutes. There are two application deadlines per year.

Support for Scriptwriting and Project Development — long

www.regionpaca.fr/uploads/media/Fiche_LM_06.pdf

Offers: up to €5,000 · For: SCRIPT | DEV · Covering: FEAT

The fund gives assistance with writing and support for the development to any writer resident in area PACA who proposes a full-length feature film. Co-producers will have to film at least 50% (minimum 3 weeks) in the region.

Research Grant

www.regionpaca.fr/uploads/media/Condition_d_acc_s06_01.pdf · Offers: up to €15,000

Research grants are intended to support the work of an author resident in PACA who wishes to make a new proposal (any format, any kind) of a piece of work that s/he is already very committed towards. The recipient must have already written five films.

Production support

www.regionpaca.fr/uploads/media/Fiche_LM_06.pdf

Offers: Up to €152,000 · For: PROD · Covering: FEAT | DOC | TV

Production support is intended for companies intending to present their full-length films in cinemas. 50% (or at least three weeks) filming must take place in the region. The assistance takes the form of a recoupable advance on receipts. There are two annual application deadlines. Up to €152,000 for feature films, for documentaries €77,000, for TV productions €54,000 is available.

Conseil régional des Pays de la Loire

www.paysdelaloire.fr

Pôle cinéma, audiovisuel et multimédia, 44966 Nantes Cedex 9, Responsable, France

T: +33 2 28 20 51 30 · F: +33 2 28 20 51 30

E: guylaine.hass@paysdelaloire.fr

The Conseil régional des Pays de la Loire supports the film and video creation through production funding and encourages cinematographic, audiovisual and multimedia productions in the Loire region.

Funding

Support is available where the production takes place in the Loire region, or the author is living in the area. Alternatively the subject of the work should be of regional interest.

Support for production

www.paysdelaloire.fr/?id=1660
Offers: up to €130,000 · For: PROD · Covering: FEAT | TV | SHORT | DOC | MM
The grant supports productions with a maximum of 25% of the estimated budget. The fund can only be given to productions that have not yet started.

Support for project development

www.paysdelaloire.fr/?id=1660
Offers: up to €7,500 · For: DEV · Covering: FEAT | TV | SHORT | DOC | MM
The fund supports research, documentation and scriptwriting up to a maximum 25% of the estimated budget.

Conseil régional du Limousin

www.cr-limousin.fr/
27 Boulevard de la Corderie, 87031 Limoges cedex, France
T: +33 5 55 45 19 00 · F: +33 5 55 45 18 25
E: documentation@cr-limousin.fr
The council supports a variety of cultural activities in Limousin such as cinema, dance, music, visual arts and over 40 festivals. Limousin encourages film productions in the region and has 24 cinemas in 23 communities as well as a mobile cinema offering cinema in the most rural areas.

Production Support

www.cr-limousin.fr/article.php3?id_article=1628
Offers: up to €80,000 · For: SCRIPT · Covering: SHORT | FEAT | DOC | FFF
Filming must not have started before the final decision and should take place in the Limousin area. There are three application deadlines per year.

Support for scriptwriting and development

www.cr-limousin.fr/article.php3?id_article=284
Offers: up to €70,000 · For: SCRIPT | DEV · Covering: SHORT
The fund is intended for projects that will later be produced in the region and funds the rewriting, research and documentation, archival work, pilot programmes, and research for partners. There are three application deadlines per year. For feature films up to €70,000 is available, for documentaries, up to €15,000 and short films up to €17,000.

Short film support

www.cr-limousin.fr/article.php3?id_article=1675
Offers: up to €10,000 · For: DIST · Covering: FEAT | TV | SHORT | DOC | FFF
The new fund supports authors, associations or companies with professional of independently produced films. The artists or the film must have a connection to the region.

Support for the modernisation of cinemas

www.cr-limousin.fr/article.php3?id_article=285
Supports the modernisation and renovation of cinemas in the region.

Conseil régional Midi-Pyrénées

www.midipyrenees.fr/
22 Boulevard du Maréchal-Juin, 31406 Toulouse Cedex 04, France
T: +33 5 61 33 50 50 · F: +33 5.61.33.52.66
The Council encourages artists and producers to create, produce and distribute their works while contributing to the development of the Midday-Pyrenees as a professional production place and strengthening regional film export. The Council lays particular emphasis on the participation of young people.

Support for Scriptwriting and/or Development

www.midipyrenees.fr · For: SCRIPT | DEV · Covering: FEAT | DOC | FFF | ANI | TV
Applications may come from outside the region but particular conditions apply for non-regionals. For TV movies the producer must have an agreement with a broadcaster. The fund takes the form of a grant.

Support for transfers to film

www.midipyrenees.fr/ · For: POST · Covering: DOC | SHORT | FEAT
The subject of the film should be of regional interest.

Production Support

www.midipyrenees.fr/ · For: PROD · Covering: FEAT | DOC | ANI | TV | SHORT | FFF
The fund takes the form of a grant.

Conseil régional Rhône-Alpes

www.cr-rhone-alpes.fr
Direction de la Culture, du Sport et de la Solidarité, Service Culture, 78 route de Paris, BP 1969260 Charbonnières-Les-Bains, France
E: contact@info-rhonealpes.fr
The Conseil Regional, which has supported film through the Rhône-Alpes Cinéma fund since 1990, created separate funds in 2001 to support documentaries, animation and scriptwriting.

Support for cinema and audiovisual creation

Offers: up to €30,000 · For: PROD · Covering: FEAT | TV | Other | DOC

Funding applies to drama, animation or documentaries of less than 60 minutes' duration. Applicants must satisfy at least two of the following criteria: they must be a producer based in or mainly active in the Rhône-Alpes region; a writer or director resident in Rhône-Alpes, and/or employing technical staff and/or actors from Rhône-Alpes; the film must be entirely shot in Rhône-Alpes and a sum equivalent to 120% of the grant spent in the region.

Support for student writing

Offers: up to €3000 · For: PROD · Covering: SHORT

The fund is for students enrolled at a further educational institution in Rhône-Alpes and working on a degree course, or for interns engaged on a professional qualification recognised by AFDAS.

Ministère des Affaires étrangères

www.france.diplomatie.fr/

Direction de l'audiovisuel extérieur et des techniques de communication, 244 Boulevard Saint Germain, 75007 Paris, France

T: +33 1 43 17 84 97 · F: +33 1 43 17 92 42

E: contact@crm-rhonealpes.fr

The Ministry for Foreign Affairs exerts a significant role in regards to cultural distribution of French programmes through arts centres and institutes, alliances, amd also in festivals, cinema clubs, universities and museums. It is increasingly called on by French professionals to support their efforts to develop the commercial exploitation of their work.

Fonds Images Afrique

Offers: maximum grant for production: €120,000; for completion: €60,000; for transfer to film: €30 000 · For: PROD · Covering: FEAT | TV | MM | DOC | ANI

An audiovisual production support fund which aims to promote the creation of local TV programmes and films in the countries of Sub-Saharan Africa. By developing national productions originating not only in public and private TV channels but also in production companies, it aims to help to enrich the programming of TV channels in the countries concerned and increase the share of African fiction films in cinemas in Africa. The director, majority of crew, and applicant production company must all come from sub-Saharan Africa. The production company must show they have finances to cover at least 40% of the budget on signature of the funding agreement.

Commercial distribution

www.diplomatie.gouv.fr/en/france-priorities_1/cinema_2/promotion-of-french-cinema_3/commercial-distribution_516/index.html · For: DIST

In other countries the Ministry ensures, in cooperation with local professionals, the promotion of French cinema by paying for the travel expenses of the filmmakers and actors, and for the subtitling of films acquired by local distributors or the organisers of promotional events. It also supports, through Europa Cinémas, the programming of French and European films in cinema theatres in Central and Eastern Europe. In Africa, the Ministry of Foreign Affairs has signed an agreement with the main operator of films theatres on the continent, CFAO, to maintain a significant presence of mainstream French films.

Non-commercial distribution

www.diplomatie.gouv.fr/en/france-priorities_1/cinema_2/promotion-of-french-cinema_3/non-commercial-distribution_5/index.html · For: DIST

The fund promotes the international distribution of films by making available to an international cultural network a collection of hundreds of films for which the Ministry currently has the non-commercial distribution rights. For each one of these titles, prints subtitled in French, Spanish and Arabic are available.

Festival Award

www.diplomatie.gouv.fr/en/france-priorities_1/cinema_2/promotion-of-french-cinema_3/circulation-in-festivals_528/festival-cinema-du-reel-in-paris-march-10-19-2006_4063.html

Offers: €15,000 · For: PROMO · Covering: DOC

The Festival Cinéma du Réel (March, Paris) receives support from the Foreign Ministry, which will award an annual €15,000 prize awarded to a French-made documentary presented in competition at the Festival. Its objective is to support the screening of French documentaries aboard.

Distribution Support Funding

www.diplomatie.gouv.fr/en/france-priorities_1/cinema_2/cinematographic-cooperation_9/distribution-support-funding_1538/index.html

Offers: up to €30,500 · For: DIST

The fund intends to promote the discovery and commercialisation of quality films from countries whose film production is little known in France. Support is given to a maximum of 15 films a year.

African film library

www.diplomatie.gouv.fr/en/france-priorities_1/
cinema_2/cinematographic-cooperation_9/african-
film-library_1847/index.html · For: DIST
The African film library aids the distribution of
films by African film directors. The works, covering
over 30 years, include fiction and documentaries
devoted to French-speaking Africa and its
developmental problems. Films are distributed in
France (in informative, educational and sociocultural
organisations, establishments and institutions), abroad,
and film festivals, on condition that permission is
granted by the interested parties.

Support fund for the production of short films in sub-saharan Africa

www.diplomatie.gouv.fr/en/france-priorities_1/
cinema_2/cinematographic-cooperation_9/
production-support-funding_10/support-fund-
for-the-production-of-short-films-in-sub-saharan-
africa_5483/index.html
Offers: €15,000 · For: PROD · Covering: SHORT
To support the emergence of new talent, production aid
is allocated to producers based in sub-Saharan Africa.
Decisions are made by an independent committee
(Commission Fonds Courts Métrages Afrique)
consisting of audiovisual professionals from Northern
and Southern countries (appointed for one year.
Appointments can be renewed once). The aid amount
is approximately €10,000 per project, and is capped at
€15,000.

Production of fictional series in sub-saharan Africa

www.diplomatie.gouv.fr/en/france-priorities_1/
cinema_2/cinematographic-cooperation_9/
production-support-funding_10/production-of-
fictional-series-in-sub-saharan-africa_5482/index.
html · For: PROD · Covering: TV
The vast majority of the TV series projects submitted
to the Fonds Images Afrique since 2004 have been
miniseries. The aim is to help African professionals
win back African audiences and thereby contribute to
the emergence of a real audiovisual economy on the
continent.

Fonds Sud Cinema

www.diplomatie.gouv.fr/en/france-priorities_1/
cinema_2/cinematographic-cooperation_9/
production-support-funding_10/fonds-sud-cinema_
11/index.html
Offers: up to €152,500 · For: PROD · Covering:
FEAT | DOC | ANI
Since its creation, the Fonds Sud Cinéma has helped
more than 300 film projects from the majority world

(Africa, Asia Latin America and Eastern Europe).
This fund concerns feature, animation and creative
documentary film projects intended for theatrical
release in France and internationally. The average aid
awarded to a film is €110,000, and can not exceed
€152,449. The greater part of the sum must be
earmarked for post-production in France.

Office régional culturel de Champagne-Ardenne

www.orcca.asso.fr/domaines/cinema.php
33 avenue de la Champagne, BP 86 51203 Epernay,
France
T: +33 3 26 55 71 71 · F: +33 3 26 55 32 59
E: infos@orcca.asso.fr
The Champagne-Ardenne has a network of almost 70
cinema screens distributed in various cities of the area
and forty rural communities. The council hosts festivals
in the region and contributes to the distribution of
French film.

Production Support (shorts and documentaries)

www.orcca.asso.fr/domaines/aide-creation.php
Offers: up to €21,500 · For: PROD · Covering: DOC
| SHORT
In order to receive funding, filming should take place
in the region Champagne-Ardenne, or the production
company should be from the region, or the subject
should be of particular interest in the region.

Pôle Image Haute Normandie

www.poleimagehn.com
43 rue des Capucins, 76000 Rouen, France
T: +33 2 35 70 20 21 / · F: +33 2 35 70 35 71
E: accueil@poleimagehn.com
The aim of the fund is the sensitisation and education
of the public to the regional film culture and its values.
The Fund gives financial helps towards the creation,
production and distribution of films from the region.

Production Support

www.poleimagehn.com/creation/fonds_aide/
creation_fds_aide.htm
Offers: up to €120,000 · Covering: FEAT | SHORT |
DOC
The fund supports producers from the region who wish
to film in the Haute-Normandie. If the producer is not
resident in the region, the complete production must
take place in Haute-Normandie. Offers up to €120,000
for full-length films, €28,000 for documentaries,
€11,000 for short-films

Support for innovative and experimental projects

Offers: up to €3,000 per project · For: PROD · Covering: OTHER

Non-regional projects may be supported on the condition that they have a regional partner for exhibition.

Support for regional production companies

Offers: up to €9,000 · For: DEV · Covering: FEAT | DOC

The fund gives support for regionally based production companies upon presentation of a 'slate' of projects to be developed. The company must be based in Haute-Normandie (longer than 12 months) and the slate must contain at least 2 projects for a total of at least 100'. Individual projects can be 26', 52', 90' or a documentary series. The projects should have distribution potential. Three are supported per year.

Support for young talents from the region

Offers: up to €11,500 · For: PROD · Covering: FFF

The program awards prizes to new filmmakers and is given directly to the filmmakers. The applicant must be a resident from the region.

Région Ile-de-France

www.iledefrance.fr

Direction de l'habitat, de la culture et des solidarités, 35 boulevard des Invalides 75007 Paris, France

T: +33 1 53 85 55 40

E: alain.losi@iledefrance.fr

The Region Ile-de-France supports local production. The financial incentives are directed at production and post-production of a number of feature films.

Support scheme for local film and audiovisual industry

www.iledefrance.fr · For: PROD · Covering: FEAT | DOC | ANI

The fund encourages French and international producers to use film and TV industries from the region. At least half of the project must be shot in the Ile-de-France region. Production must use at least two of the following services in the region: decor and costumes; make-up; technical equipment; laboratories and digital special effects; editing and sound. The reading committee will also take into consideration the expenses incurred in the region, using a points system.

Région Réunion

www.region-reunion.com

Hôtel de Région, Avenue René-Sassen, Moufia, 97497 Sainte-Clothilde Cedex, La Réunion, France

T: +33 262 48 70 00 · F: +33 262 48 70 71

E: region.reunion@cr-reunion.fr

The Région Réunion aims to contribute to the economic development of the region and therefore prioritises projects intended for the commercial sector and for export whilst implementing human and technical resources. All recipients of the funds commit themselves towards these aims and contribute to it within the framework of his project.

Support for Scriptwriting and development

www.regionreunion.com/fr/spip/spip.php?article261

Offers: up to €8,000 · For: SCRIPT | DEV · Covering: DOC | FFF | ANI | TV | FEAT | SHORT

The fund supports new talents in particular. Those resident in the region or that use a subject of relevance to the region are eligible.

Production support

www.regionreunion.com/fr/spip/spip.php?article262

Offers: up to €152,000 · Covering: DOC | ANI | FFF | TV | FEAT | SHORT | Other

The fund applies to European production companies. The subject must be of relevance to the region. For short-films up to €23,000 is available, for documentaries €30,000, and fiction and TV films €152,000.

Multimedia Productions

www.regionreunion.com/fr/spip/spip.php?article783

Offers: up to €15,000 · Covering: MM

The projects should have an educational or cultural content, or implement a major technological innovation. The commercial viability of the project constitutes one of the essential decision criteria.

Rhône-Alpes Cinéma

www.rhone-alpes-cinema.fr

24 Rue Emile Decorps, 69 100 Villeurbanne, France

T: +33 4 72 98 08 98 · F: +33 4 72 98 18 99

E: contact.rac@rhone-alpes-cinema.fr

In addition to the national funds, some of the departments and regions of France offer film funding that can benefit international co-productions, should the film be shot in their region.

Equity Investments in the Production of Feature Films · For: PROD · Covering: FEAT | TV
The fund offers co-production investment. The filming must take place in the region and the subject should be significant to Rhone-Alpes.

Support for Scriptwriting and Development of Feature Films · For: DEV | SCRIPT · Covering: FEAT | TV
The fund offers co-production investment.

Film Commissions

Alsace Cultural Agency

www.culture-alsace.org
1 Espace Gilbert Estève, BP 90025 — 67601 Sélestat Cedex, France
T: +33 3 88 58 87 58 · F: +33 3 88 58 87 50
E: agence@culture-alsace.org
The Alsace Cultural Agency provides free support to audiovisual and cinema crews wishing to shoot in Alsace. Its services include giving assistance on location, administration and logistic processes and local suppliers.

Commission National du Film

www.filmfrance.net/
33, rue des Jeûneurs, 75002 Paris, France
T: +33 1 53 83 98 98 · F: +33 1 53 83 98 99
E: film@filmfrance.net
Film France is the first stop for foreign production companies and individuals preparing to film in France. A network of 34 local film commissions throughout the country offers free information on locations, crews, labour rates and facilities.

GERMANY

German Federal Film Board (Filmförderungsanstalt)

www.ffa.de/
FFA Filmförderungsanstalt, German Federal Film Board, Große Präsidentenstraße 9, 10178 Berlin, Germany
T: +49 (0)30-27577-0 · F: +49 (0)30-27577-111
E: presse@ffa.de
The Film Board is the national body for German cinema. Funded by a levy onf distribution of between 1.8% and 3%, the board has an annual budget of approximately €70m. Its remit is to promote German cinema and to improve the structure of the German film industry, to support the national economic affairs of the film industry in Germany, to improve the foundations for the distribution and market-driven exploitation of the German cinema at home and its economic and cultural distribution abroad as well to work towards an alignment and coordination of film support operated by the Federal Government and regional states.

Funding
The different funds (either grant or loan) go to films that improve the quality and profitability of German cinema. Automatic funds are available for films which have reached a certain level of 'reference points'. This matrix is based on box office success and performance at international festivals. To reach 150,000 reference points a film would need at least 50,000 admissions.

Support for the Production of Short Films
For: PROD · Covering: SHORT | FFF
The funding is based on the 'reference-principle', meaning that a producer with German residence may qualify for a grant if a previous short film has received a quality label ('besonders wertvoll' or 'wertvoll') and/or has been selected/distinguished in a festival. The grant must be used with the 2 years following the official approval for the production of a new short film of a maximum duration of 15 minutes (or up to 59 minutes for a children's/youth film). Also eligible are films between 15 and 45 minutes if they are made at school or are the first film of that length made by an independent filmmaker.

Automatic Support for Distribution
For: DIST · Covering: FEAT | DOC
In accordance with the 'reference principle', a distribution company resident in Germany, may qualify for support, provided that it has released a German film having obtained 100,000 paying admissions during its first year of exploitation (for first feature films and chidren's films 50,000 and for documentaries 25,000 admissions are neccessary).

Selective Distribution funding
Offers: up to €600,000 · For: DIST · Covering: FEAT | DOC | YP
The FFA may grant funding support for the distribution or export of films as interest-free loans or as grants. The maximum amounts vary depending on the particular measure. The maximum amounts for loans range between €150,000 and €600,000, for grants up to €100,000. A subcommittee consisting of five members decides on the granting of this funding.

Automatic Support for Exhibition
Since 1968, there has been a calculated grant support for all of the exhibitors who pay/have paid the film levy.

Selective Support for Exhibition (Cinema)

Offers: up to €200,000
Interest-free, conditionally repayable loans may be granted for the modernisation and improvement of cinemas as well as for new constructions if it serves structural improvement.

Support for the Production of Additional Prints

For: EXBN · Covering: OTHER
Grants can be allocated for the prints of national and foreign films which are intended to be played in places with, as a rule, up to 20,000 inhabitants if the films are expected to have admissions of more than 1.5m in total.

Support for Video Distributors

Offers: loans range between €150,000 and €600,000 · For: DIST
Funding support can be granted to home entertainment companies with their headquarters in Germany for the distribution of recorded video carriers of German films, particularly the meeting of release costs, for extraordinary and/or exemplary marketing measures or the production of foreign language versions.

Support for National and International Promotion and Marketing

For: PROMO
The fund aims to enhance the position of German film on the internal and external markets.

Marketing support

For: PROMO
The FFA can rent out advertisement spaces for German cinema films. No charges apply.

Automatic production funding for Feature Films

Offers: up to €1m · For: PROD · Covering: FEAT | YP
The funding is granted for films with a running time of at least 79 minutes and for children's films of at least 59 minutes. A producer with headquarters in Germany is entitled to subsidy as a grant to produce a new film if s/he has produced a German film (or a German co-production with another country) which has reached 150,000 'reference' points in Germany within one year from first release.

Support for Scriptwriting

Offers: up to €50,000 · For: SCRIPT · Covering: FEAT
Grants of up to €25,000, in exceptional cases up to €50,000, can be allocated by the responsible sub-committee for the development of screenplays for full-length feature films. A maximum of €30,000 can be granted for further development of a screenplay. Projects submitted must already have an interested producer. A letter from the latter, confirming his interest, must accompany the application. This aid may not be combined with any other script-funding sources.

Video funding

Offers: up to €100,000
Interest-free loans are granted for the modernisation and improvement of family video stores as well as for new constructions if it serves structural improvement.

Selective production funding for feature films

Offers: up to €1m

The FFA can grant project funding as a conditionally repayable, interest-fee loan if a producer's application makes it likely — on the basis of the screenplay, budget, the financing plan, the cast and crew lists and, if applicable, the distribution contracts — that the film looks set to improve the quality and profitability of German cinema.

Filmförderung Baden-Württemberg

www.film.mfg.de.
Breitscheidstr.4, Stuttgart, 70174, Germany
T: +49 71 12 59 44 30 · F: +49 71 12 59 44 333
E: filmfoerderung@mfg.de
The Film Commission actively supports the search for locations and filming permits, artistic and technical professional, young talent, producers and other service providers in the Stuttgart region.

Production Support for Documentaries

www.mfg.de/film/ · For: PROD · Covering: DOC
The fund supports documentaries for cinema as well as TV productions.

Film & Entertainment VIP Medienfonds GmbH

www.vip-muenchen.de
Bavariafilmstrasse 2, 82031, Grunwald, Munich, Germany
T: +49 89 74 73 43 43 · F: +49 89 74 73 43 44
E: info@vip-muenchen.de
The media fund co-produces international TV and feature films, with over €100m of private finance. Former films include *The Jacket*, *Lucky Number Slevin* and *All The Kings Men*.

Bavarian Film & Television Fund

www.fff-bayern.de
Sonnenstraße 21, 80331 Munich, Germany
T: +49 89 544602 0 · F: +49 89 544602 21
E: filmfoerderung@fff-bayern.de
Founded in 1996, FFF Bayern provided €23m production finance in 2006, with further support from the Bavarian Bank Fund. In addition, the organisation offers comprehensive consulting and information services for the film and TV industry, supporting both German and foreign production companies. Financial support can be requested at each stage of the production process starting with script funding to packaging, production of theatrical and TV-movies as well as exhibition of same.

Funding
At least 150% of the production support must be spent in Bavaria, and feature films can be supported with up to €1.6m provided that the producer or co-producer is based in Germany. Foreign producers can only access funding by submitting an application through a local partner.

Story and Project Development Funding
Offers: up to €30,000 · For: SCRIPT | DEV · Covering: FEAT | YP
A conditionally repayable, interest-free loan may be granted for the development of motion picture screenplays. The producer must be a Bavarian resident.

Project development
Offers: up to €100,000 · For: DEV · Covering: FEAT
Funding may be granted for the development of motion pictures or TV films. Only producers may file applications.

Production Funding for Motion Pictures and Television Films
Offers: up to €1,6 million · For: PROD · Covering: FEAT | TV | DOC | ANI
Qualified repayable loans may be granted for the production of motion pictures and TV films. Only producers are entitled to file applications for funding. Interest payments on the loan shall cease at the end of the 18th month following the German premiere of the funded film.

Distribution and Foreign Sales Funding
www.fff-bayern.de/en/
?rub=foerderung&nav=richtlinien
Offers: up to €205,000 · For: DIST · Covering: FEAT
Distribution and worldwide sales companies may be granted qualified repayable loans for the distribution and sales of feature-length motion pictures, particularly for those produced or funded in Bavaria.

Investment Funding for Film Technology Enterprises
Offers: up to €150,000 · Covering: FEAT
Subsidies for low-interest loans may be granted for investments by film technology enterprises.

Film Projection and Presentation
Offers: up to €1.6m · For: EXBN · Covering: SHORT | YP | FEAT
Allowances may be granted to Bavarian commercial cinemas which have presented a film programme of outstanding quality during the past calendar year, with an appropriate share of German films.

Beauftragter der Bundesregierung für Kultur und Medien

www.filmfoerderung-bkm.de
MR Dr. Hermann Scharnhoop, Filmreferat K 35, Graurheindorfer Str. 198, D- 53117 Bonn, Germany
T: +49 1888 681 3643 · F: +49 1888 681 3885
E: K35@bkm.bmi.bund.de
The Fund's main aim is to improve the artistic quality of German cinema and promote the distribution of high-quality German films as an expression of cultural identity. Unlike other funding organisations, the BKM's intention is not to set economic and location limitations but to consider cultural and artistic quality foremost.

Funding
In order to receive funding, the producer must be German or the film should have relevance to Germany culture and be produced with a predominantly German crew.

German Film Award
tinyurl.com/34a6aj
Offers: up to €400,000 · Covering: FEAT | DOC | YP
The fund provides annual prizes with cash awards for outstanding new feature films intended for cinema release in the form of certificates (Urkunden) — the Silver Film Award (Filmpreis in Silber) and the Golden Film Award (Filmpreis in Gold). The cash award must be invested into the development or production of a new high-quality German film within two years.

German Short Film Award
tinyurl.com/2ttr6n
Offers: up to €30,000 · Covering: SHORT
The fund awards annual prizes accompanied with premiums intended for the production of a new quality short film. The prizes are for short films completed in the year of the award or the two years before that. Films are nominated by the BKM on the proposal of the various German film institutions and associations, and of the Selection Committee's members.

Support for Distribution and Distribution Prize

tinyurl.com/2nnjyg f

Offers: up to €50,000 · For: DIST · Covering: FEAT | SHORT | DOC | FFF

Available for films released on 25 or more prints and where the distributed invests at least 30% of the cost.

Film Innovation

tinyurl.com/2o7tou

Innovative ideas in the film sector are supported through this award. In particular projects which do not necessarily fit into the other designated categories for awards.

Distribution Prize

tinyurl.com/35ejxb

Offers: up to €75,000

Distributors can be awarded one of three distribution prizes up to €75,000. The criteria include cultural quality and proportion of German and European Films.

German Script Award

tinyurl.com/3e3t8r

Offers: up to €30,000 · Covering: OTHER

The aim of this annual award is to support the development of artistically outstanding film scripts. The award is reserved for scriptwriters who are not directors. €25 000 of the cash award must be used to finance the writing of a new screenplay.

Production support

tinyurl.com/2tsu3o

Offers: €250,000 · For: PROD · Covering: FEAT | DOC

The fund supports films that have a minimum of 79 minutes and are suitable for cinema screenings. The decision for funding is based on the script, financial plan, calculation and cast list of the project. The fund takes the form of a grant.

Production support (short films)

tinyurl.com/3cmfjd

Offers: €15,000 · For: PROD · Covering: SHORT

The fund supports new talent so that the artists can create films with financial independence and the freedom to chose the location, ie. 'innovative autonomy'. The fund promotes artistic experimentation while the maximum length should not exceed 30 minutes.

Scriptwriting Support, Project Development and Production Support for Children and Youth Films

tinyurl.com/2ll69p

Offers: up to €250,000 · For: SCRIPT | DEV | PROD · Covering: YP

The decision for funding will be taken on the basis of a dialogue scene, a treatment and the filmography of the author, if the author works together with the drama department of the organisation. Up to €50,000 for scriptwriting and €250,000 for Project Development is available.

Cinema Support

tinyurl.com/2o7tou

Offers: up to €20,000

Different awards are given each year for cinemas with the best program of the year, ie. with a particular large proportion of artistic German and European films.

Production Support for TV productions

tinyurl.com/3c2dk2

Offers: up to €30,000 (in exceptional cases €50,000) · For: DEV | SCRIPT · Covering: TV | FEAT

Project Development will be supported if the author is able to convince the panel that a producer is seriously aiming to produce the film and has a minimum of €10,000 to invest.

Support for copies

tinyurl.com/2o7tou · Covering: FEAT | DOC | YP | SHORT

The fund supports productions of additional copies of films that have an artistic relevance and a considerable audience potential.

FilmFernsehFonds Bayern

www.fff-bayern.de

Sonnen Strasse 21, D — 80331 München, Germany

T: +49 89 5446020 · F: +49 89 54460221

E: filmfoerderung@fff-bayern.de

Funding is available to increase the quality of film and TV production and enhance the efficiency of the Bavarian film industry, ensuring a diverse cultural environment. The allocated funds serve to improve the terms of competition in Bavaria, secure employment in the Bavarian film industry and support Bavaria as a media location.

Support for Project Development

Offers: up to €100,000 · For: DEV | SCRIPT · Covering: TV | FEAT | SHORT

A conditionally repayable, interest-free loan may be granted for the development of motion picture screenplays.

Production Funding for Motion Pictures and Television Films

Offers: up to €1.6m · For: PROD · Covering: TV | FEAT | SHORT

Only producers are entitled to file applications for funding. Interest payments on the loan shall cease at the end of the 18th month following the German premiere of the funded film. The producer must be a German resident or have a branch office located in Germany.

Distribution and Foreign Sales Funding

www.fff-bayern.de/en/
?rub=foerderung&nav=richtlinien

Offers: up to €205,000 · For: DIST · Covering: FEAT

Distribution and international sales companies may be granted qualified repayable loans for the distribution and sales of feature-length motion pictures, particularly of those produced or funded in Bavaria. The fund takes the form of an interest loan.

Investment Funding for Film Technology Enterprises

Offers: up to €50,000 per annum · For: BIZ-DEV

The fund takes the form of an interest-bearing loan.

Support for the Production of First Films

The fund takes the form of a grant. A total of €1.2m was available in 2004.

Support for Distribution and Sales

The fund takes the form of an interest-free loan.

Film Projection and Presentation

Offers: up to €1.6m

Funds may be granted to Bavarian commercial cinemas which have presented a film programme of outstanding quality during the past calendar year, with an appropriate share of German film (including short subjects) and children's films.

Filmförderung Hamburg GmbH

www.ffhh.de

FilmFörderung Hamburg GmbH_& Hamburg Film Commission, Friedensallee 14-16, D-22765 Hamburg, Germany

T: +49 40 398 37-0 · F: +49 40 398 37-10

E: filmfoerderung@ffhh.de

The fund's purpose is to develop and strengthen Hamburg's film industry, both culturally and economically. Its support goes particularly to films which are important in cinema terms (first films, documentaries, shorts, experimental films and big international co-productions), but it also backs TV films and serials aimed at a large international audience, as well as TV and video productions. The fund wishes to create and develop employment in cinema and audiovisual sectors in Hamburg.

Funding

The fund gives interest-free loans — with repayment being determined by the project's successes — usually to producers, for production, preparation, scriptwriting, distribution and sale of films. Producers are not required to live in the region, or even in Germany, but 150% of the allocated sum must be spent in the Hamburg area.

Incentive Funding

Offers: up to €160,000 · Covering: FEAT | TV

Depending on success funding may be given towards the development of cinema or TV films. The application must include a project draft, finance plan, business development plan etc. Small and medium-sized production and distribution companies with projects that have a cultural relevance to Hamburg are eligible to apply. The fund takes the form of repayable advances.

Support for Scriptwriting

Offers: up to €50,000 · For: SCRIPT · Covering: DOC | FEAT

The fund takes the form of an interest-free loan. Authors and producers are eligible to apply for funding. A dialogue scene must be submitted with the application as well as proof of the production rights.

Production Support

ffhh.lbhh.de/art/mediaCenter/Downloads/ Sonstiges/Guidelines.pdf · For: PROD · Covering: FEAT | TV | DOC | SHORT | YP

Producers are eligible to apply. Applicants must invest an appropriate amount of their own funds in the financing of the film project (no less than 5% of the production cost). The fund takes the form of an Interest-free loan.

Support for Television Production · For: PROD · Covering: TV

The production of TV movies and series of excellent quality may be financially supported if there seems to be a good chance of refinancing via the national and international markets. Grants for these films shall not exceed 30% of the total production budget or the German share of the entire production costs.

Support for Project Development

Offers: up to €110,000 · For: DEV · Covering: FEAT | SHORT | DOC | TV

The fund supports the development of TV or cinema production. Producers are eligible to apply if their project takes places primarily in Hamburg. The fund takes the form of an interest-free loan.

Support for Distribution and Sales

Offers: up to €200,000 · For: DIST | PROMO · Covering: FEAT | SHORT | DOC | FFF | YP

Distribution and sales companies are eligible to apply. In some cases producers may also submit applications. The fund takes the form of an interest-free loan.

Support for Screenings and Film Presentation

Offers: up to €50,000 · Covering: FEAT | DOC | YP | SHORT

Operators of Hamburg cinemas and screening locations are eligible to apply. Cinemas which screen high quality film programmes, which include an appropriate percentage of European and German films, children's and youth films, short films and documentaries are eligible for a special award.

Filmstiftung Nordrhein Westfalen GmbH

www.filmstiftung.de
Kaistraße 14, D-40221 Düsseldorf, Germany
T: +49 211 930 500 · F: +49 211 930 505
E: info@filmstiftung.de

The aims of the Filmstiftung Nordrhein-Westfalen GmbH are to increase the quality and quantity of film production in North Rhine-Westafalia, to strengthen the economic viability of NRW film companies, to facilitate a high standard of film production and to promote the distribution and exhibition in North Rhine-Westphalia.

Support for Project Development and Pre-production

Offers: up to €40,000 · For: SCRIPT | DEV · Covering: TV | FEAT

An interest-free loan; applications may be made by producers with a registered business location in Germany, as well as by screenwriters whose primary place of residence is in North Rhine-Westphalia.

Support for Film Exhibition in North Rhine-Westphalia

Offers: up to €100,000 · For: EXBN · Covering: FEAT

Funding of up to 30% of the approved costs for the modernisation and construction of film theatres can be granted; the amount of the loan will be reduced correspondingly if the applicant also receives a loan or support from the FFA (German Federal Film Board).

Support for the Production of Feature Films and TV Projects

Offers: up to €750,000 · For: PROD · Covering: FEAT | TV

Feature films can only be supported if there is reason to believe that the film will be a commercial success in the cinema and will prove a boost to cinematic culture. The production of TV projects can be supported when the project is of a particularly high programme quality; when the film is being co-produced with international, in particular European partners or is expressly intended for distribution on the international, in particular the European market; and when the project is of special interest to the State of North Rhine-Westphalia. The fund takes the form of an interest-free loan.

Support for Post-production

Offers: up to €7,500 · For: POST · Covering: TV | FEAT

In individual cases support can be granted for the post-production of feature or TV films, insofar as the cinema film or TV project in question has not already received support. The fund takes the form of an interest-free loan.

Support for Distribution and Sales

www.filmstiftung.de/English/guidelines_for_support.php · For: DIST · Covering: FEAT

The interest-free loan may amount to a maximum of 50% of the costs of the measure. Loans are given in cases where film productions were supported in North Rhine-Westphalia.

Hessische Filmförderung

www.hessische-filmfoerderung.de
Am Steinernen Stock 1, D-60320 Frankfurt/M., Germany
T: +49 69 155 45 16 · F: +49 69 155 45 14
E: postmaster@hessische-filmfoerderung.de

The federal state government of Hessen supports the region's film and cinema culture with the goal of increasing its variety and quality, and in establishing Hessen as an important location. It aims for as close a co-ordination as possible with the Hessen Rundfunk film fund (HFF HR).

Funding

Three independent juries (HFF-Land, HFF-HR, HFF-Land-Screening) decide on the level of financial support. Their primary consideration is artistic quality and topical relevance. Projects must have a connection with the state of Hessen. A connection with Hessen exists if the applicant (director or producer) has the central focus of his or her work in Hessen, if the project was filmed predominantly in Hessen, or if the subject involves the state of Hessen. All the funds awarded are grants that do not need to be repaid after the completion of the project.

Hessen Film Award
www.hessische-filmfoerderung.de/richtlinien_hff_03_03.doc
Offers: €75,000 · Covering: FEAT | SHORT | Other | DOC | ANI
The award goes to directors that have produced aesthetic and artistic films.

Hessen Cinema Prize and Film Prize
Offers: €7,500 to €75,000 · Covering: FEAT | DOC | ANI | FFF | YP
The award goes to cinemas with an outstanding commitment to support cultural films.

Hessen Art-film Prize
Offers: up to €20,000 · Covering: DOC | ANI | FFF | YP | TV | FEAT | MM
The award goes to non-commercial communal cinemas and art-houses for non-commercial art-film screenings.

Hessen University Film Prize
www.hessischer-filmpreis.de/de/hochschulfilmpreis.aspx
Offers: €7,500 · Covering: FEAT | TV | SHORT | DOC | ANI | FFF | YP
The annual prize is awarded to the best graduation film by a graduate from an educational institute in Hessen. Any graduation film by a student of a university, completed no more than 2 years before the date of application (1 August each year).

Hessen script prize
www.hessischer-filmpreis.de/de/drehbuchpreis.aspx
Offers: €7,500 · For: SCRIPT · Covering: FEAT | TV | SHORT | DOC | ANI | FFF | YP
The annual prize is awarded to authors who have produced original scripts with a reference to Hessen.

Production and Post-production support
www.hessische-filmfoerderung.de/foerdermemo06.doc
Offers: up to €75,000 · For: PROD | POST · Covering: FEAT | TV | SHORT | DOC | ANI | FFF | YP
The funding supports all genres, lengths and formats. There are two application deadline per year. Production support up to €75,000, Post-production support up to €10,000.

Scriptwriting support
www.hessische-filmfoerderung.de/foerdermemo06.doc
Offers: up to €15,000 · For: SCRIPT · Covering: FEAT | TV | SHORT | ANI | FFF | YP
The fund supports scripts with fictional content. There are two application deadline per year. The applicant must be a resident of Hessen.

Exhibition support
www.hessische-filmfoerderung.de/foerdermemo06.doc
Offers: up to €15,000 · For: EXBN · Covering: FEAT | SHORT | DOC | ANI | FFF | YP
There are two application deadline per year. The application requires a detailed distribution plan.

Project Development Support
www.hessische-filmfoerderung.de/downloads/Förderung/Produktonsvorbereitung_Fördermemo.doc · For: DEV · Covering: FEAT | TV | DOC | SHORT | ANI | FFF | YP
The fund supports projects with fictional content as well as documentaries.

Kulturelle Filmförderung Bremen

www.filmbuero-bremen.de
Filmbüro Bremen e.V., Waller Heerstrasse 46, 28217 Bremen, Germany
T: +49 421 387 67 40 · F: +49 421 387 67 42
E: post@filmbuero-bremen.de
The Filmförderung Bremen, created in 1951, is an institution covering 16 counties which supports the ministry of Hessen for science and art. The aim is to promote film and video in all forms through handing out the award 'wertvoll' and 'besonders wertvoll' (valuable and extremely valuable).

Support for scriptwriting
www.filmbuero-bremen.de/15.0.html · For: SCRIPT · Covering: DOC | Other_SHORT | FEAT
The fund supports documentaries, experimental and artistic film and video work in Bremen.

Support for Project Development and Pre-production
www.filmbuero-bremen.de/uploads/media/KFF_Bremen_Richtlinien.pdf
Offers: both grants are up to €6,000 · For: DEV · Covering: FEAT | OTHER
The fund takes the form of an interest-free loan and has to be paid back if the film goes into production.

Support for production

Offers: up to €30,000 · For: PROD · Covering: FEAT | DOC | ANI | YP
The fund supports films of all genres.

Documentary film Award

www.filmbuero-bremen.de/dokpreis.0.html
The prize supports the development of two documentary projects up to production stage. There is an annual application deadline.

Art-Video Award

www.filmbuero-bremen.de/13.0.html · Covering: OTHER
Each year two art-video concepts submitted by media artists from Germany or Partner-towns of Bremen/Bremerhaven are funded. After one year the projects will be exhibited in museums or galleries in Bremen.

Diploma Film Funding

www.filmbuero-bremen.de/122.0.html
Offers: between €500 and €6,000
Funds are given to final year students in order to support new talent and develop their networking with Bremen professionals. The subsidy must be spent in the Bremen area.

Kulturelle Filmförderung Sachsen

www.kulturstiftung.sachsen.de
Karl-Liebknecht-Str. 56, 01109 Dresden, Germany
T: +49 351 8 84 80 15/14 · F: +49 351 8 84 80 16
E: kulturstiftung@kss.smwk.sachsen.de
The fund promotes the development of arts and culture, education, the promotion of young talents and the transnational, transcultural collaboration. The fund will give support to the production of artistic short films and documentaries, script development, the creation of subtitles for international presentation, national and international workshops and the presentation of national and international cinema. As of 2005 the fund is managed by the Kulturstiftung des Freistaates Sachsen.

Scriptwriting, Pre-production and Production funding

www.kulturstiftung.sachsen.de/foerili.pdf · For: PROD | SCRIPT | DEV · Covering: DOC | SHORT
The fund supports productions with supraregional and international interest. The project should have a noncommercial intentions and can be funded up to 50% of the overall cost.

Support for subtitle development for international exhibition

www.kulturstiftung.sachsen.de/kultfoer/index.htm
Provides funds for the subtitle of films intended for export or international sales.

Kulturelle Filmförderung Sachsen-Anhalt

www.sachsen-anhalt.de
Kultusministerium des Landes Sachsen-Anhalt, Referat 73 Postfach 3780, D-39012 Magdeburg, Germany
T: +49 391 / 567 3624 · F: +49 391 / 567 3855
E: info@kunststiftung-sachsen-anhalt.de
Since 1991 Sachsen-Anhalt is able to support the development of a film-culture, especially film projects of public - utility associations, festivals as well as short films and documentaries. The funding includes new media and audiovisual digital media. In general, the funding concentrates on artistically innovative and culturally relevant projects.

Support for Pre-production (Script)

For: SCRIPT · Covering: FEAT | TV | DOC | SHORT
Support for film script development for artistic films, videos and documentary films as well as radio plays and similar projects.

Support for Production

For: PROD · Covering: FEAT | TV | MM | SHORT
Funds for production of short and long works.

Support for Exhibition and Cinemas

Promotion for special programmes, festivals and other cultural and artistic events involving other regions.

Kulturelle Filmförderung Schleswig-Holstein E.V.

www.filmbuero-sh.de
Filmbüro, Haßstrasse 22, D-24103 Kiel, Germany
T: +49 431 551439 · F: +49 431 51642
E: info@filmbuero-sh.de
The aim of the cultural film fund is the qualitative and quantitative development of a film-culture in Schleswig Holstein and the promotion of this region on a national and international level.

Support for Project Development

Offers: €5,000 · For: DEV · Covering: FEAT | SHORT | DOC | ANI | FFF | YP
The fund supports film and media projects. TV programmes cannot be funded. Film creators from Schleswig-Holstein are eligible to apply or the project can have a relevance to the region. The fund takes the form of a grant.

Support for Production

Offers: up to €50,000 · For: PROD | POST ·
Covering: FEAT | DOC | ANI | FFF | YP | SHORT
The fund supports applicants from Schleswig Holstein
or projects that have cultural relevance to the region.

Support for Distribution, Licensing and Exhibition

Offers: up to €7,500 · For: EXBN
The programme supports attempts to exhibit and
publish film and media products. Funding may be given
to distributions that aim to improve the film production
of Schleswig Holstein with films that concentrate on the
culture and history of the region.

Kulturelle Filmförderung Thüringen

www.thueringen.de/de/tsk/
Thüringer Staatskanzlei, Referat 37
'Medienwirtschaft, -förderung, -kultur',
Regierungsstraße 73, 99084 Erfurt, Germany
T: +49 361 37 92 371 · F: +49 361 37 92 302
E: HennebergerE@tsk.thueringen.de
The funding aims to develop and strengthen the
cultural film industry in Thüringen. Support can be
given for development, production, and various other
phases of the filmmaking process.

Support for Scriptwriting and Production

www.thueringen.de/tkm/hauptseiten/grup_presse/
zuwend_f.htm · For: SCRIPT | DEV | PROD ·
Covering: FEAT | TV | MM | SHORT | DOC | ANI | FFF
| YP | Other
The fund supports projects from young talents with
a noncommercial interest. It particularly encourages
Childrens' and Youth films. The funding supports films
that depict Thüringen as a cultural location and are
distributed in the region. There is an annual application
deadline.

Mecklenburg-Vorpommern-Film E.V

www.landesfilmzentrum.de/
Landesfilmzentrum MV, Bürgermeister-Haupt-Straße
51-53, D-23966 Wismar, Germany
T: +49 3841 618 200 · F: +49 3841 618 209
E: filmfoerderung@film-mv.de
The MV Film E.V. is a non-profit association
that promotes the development, promotion and
conservation of the film and media culture in
Mecklenburg-Vorpommern. The association represents
the cultural film fund and supports cultural media-
projects and activities in the region.

Funding

In order to receive funding, the project should have a
reference to the region, ie. the applicant is a resident of
Mecklenburg-Vorpommern, or the region is part of the
filming location. There are two application deadlines
per year.

Support for Production

www.landesfilmzentrum.de/uploads/media/
Richtlinien.pdf
Offers: up to €250,000 · For: PROD · Covering: TV
| FEAT | FFF
Applications need to include a script, treatment or
another detailed project description, including a
financial and budget plan.

Support for Scriptwriting and Project Development

Offers: up to €16,000 · For: DEV · Covering: TV |
FEAT | FFF
Authors and producers are eligible to apply for the
fund. Funding applies in cases where the project has a
realistic chance of being made.

Support for Distribution, Licensing and Exhibition Support

www.film-mv.de/index.php?id=filmfoerderung
Offers: up to €16,000 · For: DIST | EXBN · Covering:
FEAT | FFF
The fund supports various measures associated with
film distribution and exhibition, including print costs,
advertising and subtitling. The fund takes the form of
a grant.

Medien- und Filmgesellschaft Baden-Württemberg GmbH

www.film.mfg.de
MFG Filmförderung, Breitscheidstr. 4, D-70174
Stuttgart, Germany
T: +49 711 90715 — 400 · F: +49 711 90715
— 450
E: filmfoerderung@mfg.de
The main objectives of the MFG are to develop, sustain
and promote film culture, to develop and promote
film production services and opportunities in Baden-
Wurttemberg both nationally and internationally.

Funding

Producers or authors resident in Germany and/or
producers who intend to produce the planned project
in Baden-Wurttemberg are eligible to apply. The
following films will have funding priority: culturally
significant films of diverse genres; film productions that
significantly contribute to advancing the film industry in
Baden-Wurttemberg; and culturally significant TV and

video productions. At least 120% of the total financial support awarded annually should be spent in Baden-Wurttemberg.

Support for Pre-production and Project Development

Offers: up to €75,000 · For: PROD | POST · Covering: TV | FEAT

As a rule, the amount is awarded in the form of a conditionally repayable loan. The loan can cover up to 80% of the applicant's share of the project development budget. If the project is also awarded production support, the project development support can, instead of being repaid, be converted into a portion of the production support. Producers, in particular young producers from Baden-Wurttemberg, are eligible to apply.

Support for script development

www.mfg.de/sixcms/media.php?729/MFG%20Dreh buchf%F6rderung%20Richtlinien.pdf

Offers: up to €25,000 · For: SCRIPT | DEV · Covering: DOC | FEAT | TV | FFF | YP

Normally the loan is repayable on the first day of principal photography or if the rights to the project are exploited in any other way. If the script is not exploited within 36 months of payment of the last installment, the MFG can request that all rights to the script that were acquired using the support be transferred to the MFG.

Support for the Production of Feature Films with Budgets under €500,000

Offers: up to 70% · For: PROD · Covering: SHORT | FFF | FEAT | DOC | TV | YP

Producers and filmmakers, especially young film professionals, are eligible to apply. Preference is given to productions by young authors and/or graduates in film and media studies from an educational institution located in Baden-Wurttemberg. The fund takes the form of an interest-free loan.

Support for the Production of Feature Films with Budgets over €500 000

Offers: up to €1m or 50% · For: PROD · Covering: FEAT | DOC | ANI | TV | YP

As a rule, the producer is obliged to repay the amount awarded with 50% of his/her receipts from the supported film for eight years after release. A feature film awarded support must have a theatrical window of at least six months in length following its theatrical premiere. A national TV broadcast may not take place within 24 months following the theatrical premiere. Special arrangements will be made for pay TV and other similar broadcasting formats. If other German funding institutions are involved in the financing of

the film, proportional repayment can be agreed to. The repaid sum shall be made available to the producer as automatic funding towards the development or production of a new project.

Baden-Würtembergische Documentary Film Prize

The prize is awarded every two years by an independent jury.

Support for distribution and licensing

Offers: up to €125,000 · For: DIST · Covering: FEAT | TV | DOC | ANI | FFF | YP

Distribution and sales are eligible for support if they are of special cultural and/or economic interest to Baden-Wurttemberg, and if they were awarded production support by the MFG. Support will be awarded in the form of a conditionally repayable loan as a rule of up to 50% of the distribution or sales costs.

Support for cinemas

The fund gives out grants for cinemas and for new prints of important films. Representatives of cinema associations, who are resident in Baden-Wurttemberg, are eligible to propose films.

Support for film-related productions with interactive content

Covering: MM

Companies active in the audiovisual and/or multimedia branch are eligible to apply. A script or another equivalent project description together with a budget for the project submitted must be included with the application. A separate allocation committee decides on the applications.

Digital Content · For: DEV | PROD | PROMO · Covering: MM

The Digital Content funding programme is intended to support fiction, documentary and experimental projects, which combine an interactive version of cinematic narrative and content with the technical possibilities of the Internet and digital media. Development, production and marketing projects may be submitted.

Incentive Funding

For: SLATE | DEV · Covering: FEAT | TV

Development funding of a slate of projects for film or TV is open to producers.

Fifty-Fifty

www.mfg.de/sixcms/media.php?729/merkblatt_ fifty_fifty.pdf

Offers: up to €400,000 · Covering: FEAT | TV

The programme was created in collaboration with two major public TV channels in order to fund the works of new talent and contribute to the strengthening of

Baden-Württemberg as a location. The projects should have a contemporary subject and a realistic chance of going into production.

Medienboard Berlin-Brandenburg

www.medienboard.de
August-Bebel Strasse 26-53, 14482 Potsdam-Babelsberg, Germany
T: +49 331 743 87 0 • F: .+49 331 743 87 99
E: info@medienboard.de
Medienboard Berlin-Brandenburg GmbH is the central access point for all players in the region's media industry. The board is a joint venture of the two states in the area of film promotion and location development. The aim of Medienboard is to support qualitative and quantitative development of the commercial film industry in Berlin-Brandenburg; to strengthen the economic power of film companies together with the infrastructure in the Berlin-Brandenburg region; to foster the varied and creative talents of high-standards for the production of film and TV in Berlin-Brandenburg. Since 1994 more than 1400 film projects have obtained €171m in grants and claims that for every Euro spent on aid to moviemakers, an average of just under three Euros is injected into the local economy.

Funding

Producers that both live and have a company registered in Germany may apply. There are different deadlines throughout the year. Medienboard Berlin-Brandenburg supports films and film-related projects in the categories of script development, project development, package promotion, production, distribution and sales, and other activities. A single authority, the board's director, makes the final decision in consultation with a team of advisers.

Support for Script Development and Project Development

http://tinyurl.com/232kfa
For: SCRIPT | DEV • Covering: FEAT | DOC | ANI
Filmboard Berlin-Brandenburg puts strong emphasis on script and project development. The Filmboard may allocate funding covering up to 70% of the total development costs. Repayment of the funding must occur by the first day of principal photography or upon other utilisation of the rights of the supported project. The fund takes the form of an interest-free loan.

Slate-Funding

Offers: up to €150,000 • For: SLATE • Covering: FEAT
Generally takes the form of a development package composed of 3 to 5 projects already in various stages

of script- or project development. The scheme does not aim to help the initiation of new projects, but to finance a longer development period. Only production companies registered in the region for a minimum 3 years and for whom the principal activity is the production of feature films and TV productions, are eligible for this scheme.

Support for Production

Offers: up to €800,000 • Covering: FEAT
An amount corresponding at least to the amount of funding awarded, must be spent in Berlin or Brandenburg relating to direct costs for the production. The maximum percentage-rate of production costs which may be covered by funding from the Filmboard is between 50% and 70%, depending on the level of the total budget: 70% for budgets under €250,000; 60% for budgets up to €1.5m; 50% for budgets above €1.5m; 30% for TV productions. A signed distribution contract for a release of the film in cinemas in Germany is a pre-requisite for the awarding of production support. The fund takes the form of an interest-free loan. Funds repaid by a producer will be made available again to the producer as so-called 'reference funds', ie. funds held in reserve and specifically earmarked for use by the producer for the preparation or production of a new film project.

Support for Distribution, Licensing and Foreign Sales

Offers: up to €150,000 • For: DIST | PROMO • Covering: FEAT
The fund takes the form of an interest-free loan. Funding from this scheme can cover up to 50% of the calculated costs. A sum equivalent to the sum awarded must be spent in Berlin-Brandenburg. Whenever technically feasible, prints must be printed using local facilities.

Miscellaneous Activities in Line With Promotion Objectives

www.medienboard.de/WebObjects/
Medienboard.woa/1/wa/CMSshow/
1004529?wosid=cc1yfNK23Hncb1LVdltEFw
For: PROMO
For measures to improve film quality and moviemaking profitability, special marketing operations, programme placement and work on further audiovisual products.

Package Promotion

www.medienboard.de/WebObjects/
Medienboard.woa/1/wa/CMSshow/
1004526?wosid=cc1yfNK23Hncb1LVdltEFw
For: DEV • Covering: FEAT | TV | DEV
Support of project packages is the fund's way of aiding production companies who aim to develop feature

films and TV broadcasts or to produce documentaries to be screened initially in the cinema and comes after script and development funding. Package promotion is focused on small and medium-sized motion picture and TV companies in the region. This part of Medienboard GmbH operations consists of nurturing three to five unripe movie projects in one go that are either at the material development or project development stage.

Newcomer Funding

Offers: up to €200,000 · For: PROD · Covering: FFF
Particular attention is paid to the funding of the region's film newcomers. In this context, apart from independently funded projects — ie. those without the support of the film academies — two films can be subsidised yearly from each of the Berlin-Brandenburg region's two film academies, the DFFB and the HFF 'Konrad Wolf'.

Mitteldeutsche Medienförderung GmbH

www.mdm-online.de/
Hainstr. 19, D-04109 Leipzig, Germany
T: +49 341 269 87 0 · F: +49 341 269 87 65
E: info@mdm-online.de
The fund's aim is to support film and media productions which depict regional qualities authentically; are concerned with cultural and historical heritage; address issues of cultural identity; and tell an original story to which European and international audiences can relate to. In addition MDM supports festivals, workshops, seminars and projects relevant to the media location.

Support for Script development

Offers: up to €25,000 · For: SCRIPT · Covering: FEAT | SHORT | DOC
Funding can be granted for the development of a script. This includes production of screenplays, script consultation and research. Eligible applicants are producers, authors and directors intending to shoot in Central Germany.

Production funding

For: PROD · Covering: FEAT | TV | SHORT | DOC
There is a particular focus on new talent, children and young people and multimedia. The fund takes the form of an interest-free loan and totalled €6.8m in 2004.

Project development

Offers: up to €100,000 · For: DEV · Covering: FEAT | DOC | SHORT
Funding can be granted for acquisition of the rights on scripts, script consultation, research, location and casting, etc. For multimedia projects this especially includes: acquisition of the rights on image and sound

footage, research, production of a demo version. If possible, the funding should be spent in Central Germany.

Support of distribution and sales

For: DIST · Covering: FEAT | TV | MM | DOC | SHORT | YP
Support can be granted for measures of distribution and sales of film and media productions which are of special cultural or economic interest to the three German states and/or whose production has been funded by the MDM already. The loan covers 50% of the cost.

Support of screening, presentation and OTHER projects

For: PROMO · Covering: FEAT | MM | DOC | ANI | SHORT | FFF
Loans or subsidies can be granted to promote screenings and presentations of German and European films, especially those funded by MDM.

Support for education and training

To operate media-specific education and training. Training providers with a high degree of professionalism and media specific experience are eligible.

Package Funding

www.mdm-online.de/en/funding/f_antrag.html
Offers: up to €150,000
Funding can be granted for the development of several projects. Eligible for application are producers and multimedia developers, who contribute to the development of the economy of media culture in Saxony, Saxony-Anhalt and Thuringia and who are in the position to adequately produce of the project.

MSH Institute for development of audiovisual works in Schleswig-Holstein

www.mshfoerderung.de
Schildstrasse 12, D-23552 Lübeck, Germany
T: +49 451 719 77 · F: +49 451 719 78
E: info@mshfoerderung.de
The aim of this fund is to support the film, TV and radio industry of the region in order to strengthen the economic capabilities of production companies, improve the formation of the regional film, TV and radio culture and promote market development.

Support for Pre-production

Offers: up to €50,000 · Covering: FEAT | TV | DOC
The fund should be spent in the region and can be given up to 80% of the calculated costs.

Support for Script Development

Offers: up to €30,000 · For: SCRIPT · Covering: FEAT | TV | DOC

Funding may be available if the script is of exceptional quality. The application must include a treatment with a dialogue scene. The funding takes place in three instalments. The applicant must agree to continue with the production in the region of Schleswig-Holstein.

Support for Film and TV Production

www.mshfoerderung.de/formulare/ FoerderungsrichtlinieFilm.pdf · For: PROD · Covering: FEAT | TV | DOC

The fund finances up to 50% of the production cost. The fund should be spent in the region.

Training and education

The programme is project-orientated. Institutions that have more than five years of professional experience in the area of broadcasting training and education are eligible for funding.

Support for Radio broadcasting

The fund supports the qualitative, quantitative and market-orientated development of radio broadcasting in Schleswig Holstein. The subsidy should not exceed 80% of the total cost.

Nordmedia

www.nordmedia.de/

Expo Plaza 1 , 30539 Hannover, Germany

T: +49 511 123456-0 · F: +49 511 123456-29

E: info@nordmedia.de

Nordmedia Fonds is the central funding institution of the regions Lower Saxony and Bremen for creative people and media companies in the film, TV and multimedia branch. The aim of the Fund is to support the quantitative and qualitative strengthening and economic development of the cultural film industry in Lower Saxony and Bremen. For all funds there are three application deadlines.

Support for script and project development

www.nordmedia.de/scripts/contentbrowser. php3?ACTION=SHOWARTIKEL&ID=597

Offers: up to €100,000 · For: SCRIPT | DEV · Covering: FEAT | DOC | TV | SHORT | ANI | FFF | YP | VIDG

The Producers and authors are eligible to apply for funding that will supports the research, production of a script, archive costs, driving miles, casting and general preparation. The funding can cover up to 100% of the calculated costs. Developers of entertainment software are welcome to apply for project development. Offers up to €100,000 for development (pre-production), up to €25,000 for script development.

Support for production

www.nordmedia.de/scripts/contentbrowser.php3?ACTION=SHOWCONTENT&menuepunkt=382

For: PROD · Covering: FEAT | TV | MM | DOC | SHORT | ANI | FFF | YP

The fund covers in general 50% of the production cost and supports films of all lengths and genres. Besides financial support Nordmedia offers possible co-production partners.

Support for sales, distribution and promotion

www.nordmedia.de/scripts/contentbrowser. php3?ACTION=SHOWARTIKEL&ID=595 · For: DIST | PROMO · Covering: FEAT | SHORT | DOC | FFF | TV | ANI | YP

The fund covers up to 80% of the cost. The funding supports the development of a European film culture in Niedersachsen/Bremen and therefore emphasise the importance of the subject to the region.

Support for screening and exhibition

www.nordmedia.de/scripts/contentbrowser. php3?ACTION=SHOWCONTENT&menuepunkt=383 · For: EXBN | CULT · Covering: FEAT | MM | SHORT | Other | DOC | ANI | FFF | YP

The fund is for cultural films, film series, exhibition, festivals and other forms of presentation. It covers up to 80% of the cost.

Support for investments

www.nordmedia.de/scripts/contentbrowser.php3?ACTION=SHOWCONTENT&menuepunkt=384

Offers: up to €100,000 · For: BIZ-DEV

The fund supports investments up to 50% of the calculated costs that are directed towards the set-up, modernisation, expansion and rearrangement of an organisation such as cinema or cultural centre in Niedersachsen/Bremen.

Funding of copies

www.nordmedia.de/scripts/contentbrowser.php3?ACTION=SHOWCONTENT&menuepunkt=199

Nordmedia finances further film copies of well-visited films for cinemas in less populated regions (up to 20,000 inhabitans) .

Scholarship

www.nordmedia.de/scripts/contentbrowser.php3?ACTION=SHOWCONTENT&menuepunkt=387

Nordmedia awards two scholarships per year for producers who want to make a short film in Hannover.

Saarland Medien GmbH

www.Saarlandmedien.de
Nell-Breuning Allee 6, 66115 Saarbrücken, Germany
T: 49 681 3 89 88 53 · F: 49 681 3 89 88 20
E: info@saarlandmedien.de
Created in 1999 Saarland Medien promotes Saarland as
a film location, supports the local regional film industry,
and aims to support the economic area of the industry.
The fund supports various cinemas in the region and
hosts small film festivals.

Film production fund
Offers: up to €20,000 · For: PROD · Covering: Other
| DOC | SHORT | ANI
The fund supports films of all genres that have a
thematic or organisational relevance to Saarland. The
producer should be a resident from the region.

Film Music Fund
www.saarlandmedien.de/front_content.
php?idcat=142
Offers: up to €10,000 · Covering: SHORT | Other |
DOC | ANI
Since 2003 the fund supports with a total of €10,000
the use and composition of film music and the use of
acoustic sounds in general. With an annual film music
prize, the fund awards €3,000 at the Max-Ophüls-
Festival to good film music.

Support of copies
www.saarlandmedien.de/front_content.
php?idcat=143 · For: DIST
Funds duplication of successful films for the more
regional parts of the county.

Stiftung Kuratorium Junger
Deutscher Film

www.kuratorium-junger-film.de/
Schloß Biebrich, Rheingaustraße 140, D-65203
Wiesbaden, Germany
T: +49 611 60 23 12 · F: +49 611 69 24 09
E: kuratorium@t-online.de
This fund supports the production of films for children
and new talent by German residents.

Support for Script Writing
Offers: for Childrens' films up to €30,000; for
First Feature films up to €15,000 · For: SCRIPT ·
Covering: FFF | YP
The fund supports children and 'talent' films of
upcoming artists with exceptional artistic quality. The
projects should aim to be screened in cinema. The fund
takes the form of a conditionally repayable, interest-
free loan.

Support for Project Development
Offers: up to €50,000 and 80% · For: DEV ·
Covering: YP | FFF
Supports script and project development costs for a first
time feature filmmaker.

Support for Production
Offers: for Childrens' films up to €250,000; for First
Feature films up to €50,000 · For: PROD · Covering:
YP | FFF
The production fund functions as first aid that makes
other funds more accessible for the production
companies. The fund generally funds the first and
second full-length film within the 'Talent' films
category. Usually low budget films (under €1.5m) are
eligible for funding.

Support for Distribution
Offers: up to €13,000 and 50% · For: DIST
For the distribution of children and youth films, or first
films.

Support for Subtitling
Offers: up to €5,000
For works intended for export.

Support for Project Development of Children's
Films
Offers: up to €41,000

World Cinema Fund

www.berlinale.de
c/o Berlin International Film Festival, Potsdamer
Straße 5, 10785 Berlin, Germany
T: +49 30 259 20 516 · F: +49 30 259 20 529
E: worldcinemafund@berlinale.de
In co-operation with the German Federal Cultural
Foundation (Kulturstiftung des Bundes) the Berlin
International Film Festival runs the World Cinema
Fund to support filmmakers from 'transition' countries,
Latin America, Africa, South East Asia, the Caucasus,
the Middle East and Central Asia. The aim of the
World Cinema Fund is to help the realisation of films
which otherwise could not be produced, ie. feature
films and creative feature-length documentaries with
a strong cultural identity. Another important goal is
to strengthen the profile of these films in German
cinemas. The fund provides support in the fields of
production and distribution.

Production funding
www.berlinale.de/en/das_festival/world_cinema_
fund/wcf_profil/index.html
Offers: up to €100,000 · For: PROD
Eligible for funding are production companies with
directors from the above mentioned regions as well as

German production companies working with a director from these regions. In order to receive such funds, a German partner is required. However, the film does not necessarily have to be a co-production. The budgets of the projects should range between €200,000 and €1,000,000. The funds should be spent in the countries in which the film is to be produced. There are six application deadlines per year.

Distribution support
www.berlinale.de/en/das_festival/world_cinema_fund/wcf_profil/index.html
Offers: up to €15,000 per project
German distributors can apply for distribution support. The funds have to be spent on distributing the film in Germany. There are six application deadlines per year.

Best First Feature Film
www.berlinale.de/en/das_festival/preise_und_juries/uebersicht_auszeichnungen/index.html
Offers: €50,000 · Covering: FFF
Since the Berlinale 2006 a three-person international jury awards the Best First Feature Award to a debut film in the Competition, the Panorama, the Forum or the Generation section. The prize is donated by the Gesellschaft zur Wahrnehmung von Film-und Fernsehrechten (GWFF).

Film Commissions

Berlin Brandenburg Film Commission

www.bbfc.de
August-Bebel-Straße 26-53, 14482 Potsdam-Babelsberg, Germany
T: (0331) 743 87-30 · F: (0331) 743 87-99
E: location@medienboard.de

Focus Germany

www.focusgermany.de
T: +49 211 930 500 · F: +49 211 93050 85
E: info@focusgermany.de
FOCUS Germany is a coordinating service for film professionals seeking information and professional guidance regarding Germany's broad range of funding and production possibilities. Established in 1990 as an umbrella organisation for the major German film funding institutions, it was launched at a time when regional funding in Germany was becoming increasingly important on the national an international production scene. FOCUS Germany supplies the necessary contacts for an efficient co-production with Germany including every aspect of production from location research to post production.

Schleswig-Holstein Film Commission

www.shfc.de E: info@m-s-h.org
MSH GmbH, Regional filmfund, Schildstr. 12, 23552 Luebeck, Germany
T: 0451 — 790 76 65 · F: 0451 — 719 78

GREECE

Greek Film Centre

www.gfc.gr
10 Panepistimiou Str., GR — 106 71 Athens, Grece
T: +30 210 3678500   · F: +30 210 3614336
E: info@gfc.gr
The aim of the Greek Film Centre is the protection, support and development of the art of film in Greece and the dissemination and promotion of Greek film productions both domestically and internationally.

Horizons Programme
For: DEV · Covering: FEAT | FFF
For the development of the art of film in Greece through the creation of film works with outstanding artistic, technical and financial specifications, it provides for the funding of at least six feature films annually, of which at least one must be the work of a new director.

Incentives Programme
For: PROD · Covering: FEAT
A development programme for the support of independent productions whose objective is the creation of popular films with a satisfactory production standard and aesthetic competence. It provides for the funding of up to eight projects annually.

Short Cuts
For: PROD · Covering: DOC | SHORT | FEAT
The programme's basic goal is to operate as a springboard and showcase for young scriptwriters, directors, actors, technicians and producers. It provides for the funding of up to 12 shorts annually.

Animation Programme
www.gfc.gr/en/funding/index.asp
Supports for the production of up to three shorts and one feature-length animated film each year.

New Perception
For: PROD · Covering: FFF
A selection programme administered jointly with the Hellenic Broadcasting Corporation ERT S.A. Its objective is to constitute a springboard for the renewal of the art of film by supporting creators with first or second feature film projects.

Documentary Programme

A selection program that considers the documentary a distinct audiovisual work, which reaches broader audiences chiefly and initially through TV. It provides for the funding of up to six documentaries with a running time of 45-50 minutes and two documentaries with a running time of 80-90 minutes each year

Scriptwriting Programme

For: **SCRIPT** · Covering: **FEAT**
A selection program that provides for the funding of up to 10 projects annually for the development of scripts for feature films.

SEE Cinema Network

www.gfc.gr/see/contacts.html
T: +30 210 36 78 501 · F: +30 210 36 48 269
E: see@gfc.gr
The aim of the fund is to encourage the development of collaborations between film professionals in the 11 member-states of the SEE CINEMA NETWORK (Albania, Bosnia Herzegovina, Bulgaria, Croatia, Cyprus, Fyr of Macedonia, Greece, Romania, Slovenia, Turkey, Serbia & Montenegro). The main goals are to promote and develop the national filmmaking industry of each participating country, to strengthen bilateral and multilateral co-operation among the Network members. It is financed by the Greek Film and by the National Film Centres of the participating countries.

Co-production Development Funding

www.gfc.gr/see/fundingCorp.html
Offers: up to €15,000 · For: **DEV** · Covering: FEAT
The network provides funding for co-production project development such as expenses related to the search for co-producers, financial backing, artistic resources and distributors. The funding will have the form of a non-repayable loan and will be paid in three instalments.

The Balkan Fund

www.filmfestival.gr/balkan_fund
Balkan Fund (Script Development Fund), c/o Thessaloniki International Film Festival, 9 Alexandras Avenue, 11473 Athens, Grece
T: +30 210 870 6000 · F: +30 210 64 56 251
E: balkanfund@filmfestival.gr
Script development fund for south eastern Europe: Albania, Bosnia & Herzegovina, Bulgaria, Croatia, Cyprus, 'Former Yugoslav Republic of Macedonia', Greece, Romania, Serbia & Montenegro, Slovenia and Turkey. The Balkan Fund awards its support once a year at the Thessaloniki Film Festival in November. The applications have to be submitted in English.

Script Development Fund

www.filmfestival.gr/balkan_fund
Offers: €10,000 · For: SCRIPT
The fund takes the form of a grant and awards 4-5 prizes a year. The applicant should be the film's producer or the film's director. The prime consideration of the panel which considers the projects will be of the artistic qualities of an application. The entry should be further original, authentic and rooted in the culture of the applicant's country.

HAWAII

Big Island Film Office

www.filmbigisland.com
County of Hawaii Department of Research and Development, 25 Aupuni St. Rm. 219, Hilo, HI 96720, Hawai
T: (808) 327-3663 · F: (808) 935-1205
E: film@bigisland.com
Incentives for Film, TV, Commercials, and New Media. 20% refundable tax credit on money spent in Hawaii.

Honolulu Film Office

www.filmhonolulu.com
Honolulu Film Office, City and County of Honolulu, 530 South King Street, Suite 306, Honolulu, Hawai'i 96813, Hawai T: 808 527-6108 · F: 808 527-6102
E: info@filmhonolulu.com

Hawaii Film Office

www.hawaiifilmoffice.com
No. 1 Capital District Building, 250 South Hotel Street, 5th Floor, Honolul, HI 96813, Hawai
T: (808)586-2570 · F: (808)586-2572
E: info@hawaiifilmoffice.com
There are two different tax credits that may be applied to TV and film production in Hawaii. One is the High Technology Business Investment Tax Credit (commonly known as 'Act 221,' Session Laws of Hawaii 2001, or 'Act 215,' Session Laws of Hawaii 2004), which is applicable to a TV or film production company that establishes a long-term presence in Hawaii. The other, the Motion Picture and Film Production Income Tax Credit, is a refundable tax credit (see Part II)

Maui County Film Office

www.filmmaui.com
County of Maui, Office of Economic Development,
Maui Film Office, One Main Plaza, 2200 Main Street
Suite 305, Wailuku, Hawaii, 96793, Hawai
T: 808.270.7415 · F: 808.270.7995
E: info@filmmaui.com

HONG KONG

Hong Kong Film Services Office, TELA

www.fso-tela.gov.hk
40/F, Revenue Tower, 5 Gloucester Road, Wan Chai,
Hong Kong, Hong Kong
T: (852) 2594 5745 · F: (852) 2824 0595
E: info@fso-tela.gov.hk
No monetary incentive simply because there is no sales
and services tax in Hong Kong. The fund's service to
filmmakers' requests is free.

HUNGARY

Motion Picture Public Foundation of Hungary

www.mmka.hu
H-1068 Budapest, Városligeti fasor 38., Hungary
T: +36 1 351 7696/351 7697 · F: +36 1 352 8789
E: mmk2@axelero.hu
The Hungarian Motion Picture Public Foundation
was established in 1998 by the Government of the
Republic of Hungary and 27 organisations of the
cinema profession. The aims of this fund is promote the
production of films and development of the motion
picture industry, to preserve and protect the products of
the motion picture industry, to improve the conditions
of the motion picture activities and to enhance the
income of those working in the film industry.

Funding
The basic objectives of the foundation include support
of the production of Hungarian films of all genres,
the enhancement of the distribution of productions
of the Hungarian as well as the representation of the
Hungarian cinema.

Feature film production support
Offers: up to €200,000 · For: PROD · Covering: FEAT

Support for animation film
Offers: up to €20,200 · For: PROD · Covering: ANI

Support for documentary production
Offers: from €2000 to €20,500 · For: PROD ·
Covering: DOC

Production support for popular science films
Offers: up to €20,000 · For: PROD

Support for film research, education, publishing and experimental film
Offers: up to €40,500 · For: EDU

Support for film distribution
For: DIST | EXBN_AUD-DEV
The fund provides support for film distribution,
exhibition, film clubs, festivals, etc.

Support for scriptwriting and development
For: SCRIPT | DEV · Covering: TV | SHORT

Support for coproduction
For: PROD · Covering: FEAT

Support for TV films and short films
For: PROD · Covering: TV | SHORT

Foundation of the Hungarian Historical Motion Picture

www.mtfa.hu E: mtfa@mtfa.datanet.hu
H-1014, Budapest, Kapisztrán tér 2-4., Hungary
T: +36 467-0627 · F: +36 1 251-8170
The aim of the Foundation is to support the production
of historical features and documentary films which
represent ways of life, historical events and issues
affecting the present. The foundation promotes the
representation of social trends brought into being
by the revolution and the events of 1956, the vital
questions of Hungarians living outside the borders and
the drastic changes in lifestyles over the past 50 years.

Support for feature film production
A subsidy from a fund which in 2003 totalled €197,000.

Support for scriptwriting
Total funds in 2003 were €15,000.

Support for documentary film production
A subsidy from a fund which in 2003 totalled €375,000.

National Cultural Fund of Hungary

www.nka.hu/
Gyulai Pál utca 13., H-1085 Budapest, Hungary
T: +36 1 327 4300 · F: +36 1 327 4470
E: elnok@nka.hu
The National Assembly set up the National Cultural
Fund to support the creation and preservation of

Hungarian cultural values and their propagation domestically and abroad. The National Cultural Fund is operating under the supervision of the Ministry of Cultural Heritage.

Moving Pictures

www.nka.hu · For: PROD · Covering: FEAT | TV | MM | DOC | ANI | FFF | YP

The Fund was created to support the preservation of Hungarian cultural values and their propagation domestically and abroad. Natural and legal entities as well as business organisations without incorporation may apply for support from the Fund. Applicants who do not have Hungarian citizenship need to have an assistant executive who does. Support may be provided in the form of repayable, partly-repayable loans or subsidies.

National Radio and Television Commission

www.ortt.hu
vizió Testület, Reviczky utca 5, H-1088 Budapest, Hungary
T: +36 1 429 8600 · F: +36 1 267 2612
E: ortt@ortt.hu

Subsidy for feature films, TV films and TV plays

www.ortt.hu
Offers: up to €400,000 · For: PROD · Covering: FEAT | TV

The fund supports public service film and TV film production. It is open to companies registered in Hungary with no public debts. The minimum duration of film or TV programme is 45 minutes. Support is paid in two parts: the first 80% in the form of an advance against receipts; the remainder is paid on completion of the production.

Hungarian Film Commission

www.hungarianfilm.com
Budapest 1015, Szabó Ilonka 63/c, Hungary
T: +36 1 225 30 69 · F: +36 1 214 48 51
E: info@szamak.film.hu

The Hungarian Film Commission provides a detailed listing of feature and TV films shot on location in Hungary and information about locations, companies and services.

Magyar Filmunio

www.filmunio.hu
H-1068 Budapest, Városligeti fasor 38, Hungary
T: +361 351 7696 · F: +361 352 8789
E: mmk2@axelero.hu

Magyar Filmunió was established in 1992 by the Motion Picture Public Foundation of Hungary to promote awareness of Hungarian film-making at an international level within the circle of professionals as well as of a wide public. Hungarian feature film, short, documentary and animation production is offered for selection and is nominated by Magyar Filmunió at international film festivals.

ICELAND

Icelandic Film Centre

www.icelandicfilmcentre.is
Kvikmyndamidstöd Íslands, Túngötu 14, 101 Reykjavík, Iceland
T: +354 562 3580 · F: +354 562 7171
E: info@icelandicfilmcentre.is

The Icelandic Film Centre is a public organisation that allocates funds for the development and production of features, shorts, TV live action, and documentaries. The centre promotes Icelandic films abroad and supports the general development of film culture in Iceland. Activities include the promotion of 'Film in Iceland', a government organisation which offers 12% tax reimbursements for film and TV production costs incurred in Iceland. Furthermore it supports Icelandic participation in international bodies, such as Eurimages, the Nordic Film and TV Fund, Media, Filmkontakt Nord, North by North West, European Film Promotion and Scandinavian Films.

Icelandic Film Fund

Offers: up to €800,000 · Covering: FEAT | TV | SHORT | DOC | ANI | FFF | YP

The fund supports both films that are produced and sponsored by Icelandic companies and films that are co-productions with foreign parties. A project supported by the Icelandic Film Fund must have connections with Icelandic culture unless special cultural grounds exist for deciding otherwise. Production companies registered in Iceland can officially apply for this support.

Film In Iceland

www.filminiceland.org
Skolavordustigur 11, 101, Reykjavik, Iceland
T: +354 561 5200 · F: +354 561 5205
E: info@filminiceland.org
Film in Iceland is a project set up to promote film production in Iceland. The project is run by the Invest In Iceland Agency, an agency of the Ministry of Industry and Commerce. Producers can apply for reimbursements from the State Treasury of 14% of the costs incurred in the production of films and TV programmes in Iceland.

INDONESIA

Bali Film Commission

www.balifilm.com
T: (62-361) 744 4246 · F: (62-361) 286 425
E: Contact@BaliFilm.com
Indonesia is a tax free haven for foreign artists. And although Indonesia has no tax rebates or incentives in place, they are able to cut most production budgets by 10-20%.

IRELAND

Irish Film Board

www.irishfilmboard.ie
Queensgate, 23 Dock Road, Galway, Ireland, Ireland
T: +353 91 561398 · F: +353 91 561405
E: info@irishfilmboard.ie
The Irish Film Board provides loans and equity investment to independent Irish film-makers to assist in the development and production of Irish films. The Board also acts in co-operation with other Irish regional agencies to improve the marketing, sales and distribution of Irish films and to promote training and development in all areas of film-making. Employment of Irish film workers and the use of ancillary Irish services is a vital factor in the Board's consideration of applications.

Company Development Initiative

www.irishfilmboard.ie/stop_press.php?press=45 ·
For: BIZ-DEV
Support awarded to five companies to develop slate of projects. For the first 3-year period, funding from IFB is completed by debt funding of €380,000 from Anglo Irish Bank.

Development Loans for Feature Length Fiction Films

www.irishfilmboard.ie/guidelines.php?type=g&id=1
Offers: up to €75,000 · For: DEV · Covering: FEAT
The fund is targeted at teams that seek to reach a broad international audience. The loan is aimed at producer/director/screenwriter teams. You must have an Irish producer attached to the project.

Production Loans for Feature Length Fiction Films

www.irishfilmboard.ie/guidelines.php?type=g&id=14
Offers: up to €750K · For: PROD · Covering: FEAT
This loan is aimed at Irish production companies and directors with distinctive voices and commercial films that want to connect with a broad range of audiences.

Short Shorts

www.irishfilmboard.ie/guidelines.php?type=s&id=5 ·
For: PROD · Covering: SHORT
Short Shorts aims to produce ultra short pieces (one to three minutes long), which can be screened theatrically in front of feature films.

Animation Development Loans

www.irishfilmboard.ie/guidelines.php?type=g&id=2
Offers: up to €80,000 · For: PROD | DEV · Covering: ANI
This loan is aimed at producer, animator, screenwriter teams and individual animators, with up to €10,000 for individual animators.

Short Cuts

www.irishfilmboard.ie/guidelines.php?type=s&id=1
Offers: up to €80,000 · For: PROD · Covering: SHORT
Scheme run in conjunction with RTE (national broadcaster). A minimum of five films will be supported from a total fund of €370,000 but not all films will receive equal funding.

Development and Production Finance Loans for Documentaries

www.irishfilmboard.ie/guidelines.php?type=g&id=3 · For: DEV | PROD · Covering: DOC
The fund supports examples of high-quality documentary making with potential for theatrical / festival screening. This loan has been restructured to accommodate the development process as well as production. Applicants must have an Irish production company attached to their project.

Frameworks VI

www.filmboard.ie/guidelines.php?type=s&id=3
Offers: up to €250,000 · For: PROD · Covering:
SHORT
Scheme run in conjunction with the Irish Arts Council.
Applicants are not required to submit a full budget
but short-listed applicants will be required to provide a
detailed budget. The intention is to commission six new
Irish animations for theatrical release and TV broadcast.

Animation production loans

www.irishfilmboard.ie/guidelines.php?type=g&id=2
Offers: €750,000 · For: PROD · Covering: ANI
The funding is designed as recoupable loan-equity
participation

The Louth, Newry & Mourne Film Commission

www.filmcommission.ie/
Dundalk Office, Louth, Newry & Mourne Film
Commission, County Hall, Millennium Centre,
Dundalk, County Louth, Ireland
T: 042 9324126 / 9324354 · F: 042 9334549
E: info@filmcommission.ie

ITALY

Direzione Generale per il Cinema

www.cinema.beniculturali.it
Ministero per i Beni e le Attività Culturali, 51 Via della
Ferratella in Laterano, I — 00184 ROMA, Italy
T: +39 06 704 75 450 · F: +39 06 773 2493
E: segreteria@cinema.beniculturali.it
The Direzione Generale per il Cinema is the national
institute promoting the development and distribution of
Italian cinema and the national film industry. Activities
include supporting and promoting Italian film culture
financially while acting as a financial intermediary for
production and distribution, as well as in exhibition. As
part of its remit, the Direzione Generale oversees the
allocation of funds dedicated to cinema of the Fondo
Unico dello Spettacolo and manages the work of the
related committees.

Funding

Film policy and funding is managed through the
Dipartimento dello Spettacolo of the Ministeri per i Beni
e le Attività Culturali. The Dipartimento is responsible
for the Fundo Unico dello Spettacolo (F.U.S), which
provides support to all areas of the performing arts.
Limited information was available on the Direzione on
their funding schemes.

Loan for Feature Film Production

Offers: Up to €3.7m · For: PROD · Covering: FEAT
| FFF
The BNL loan can cover at maximum 90% of the cost
of production, and is only available for films deemed in
the national cultural interest.

Support for the Production of 'National' Feature Films

Offers: Up €500,000 and 70% · For: PROD ·
Covering: FEAT
The decision is based on evaluation of the subject,
script, budget and production schedule of the project.
The support provided to films in this category is
awarded in the form of grants. Films which do not
promote 'National cultural interest' may also apply for a
low-interest loan.

Support for the Production of Short Films

€1m was available in 2002.

Support for films by new directors

Up to €11m was available in 2002, to fund up to 90%
of the budget.

Automatic funding for feature film production

In 2002 the fund had a budget of €18m for feature film
grants.

Friuli Venezia Giulia Film Commission

www.fvgfilmcommission.com
Via Milano, 34132 Trieste, Italy
T: +39 40 3720142 · F: +39 403720142
E: info@fvgfilmcommission.com
With the Regional Audiovisual Fund the Autonomous
Region Friuli Venezia Giulia can directly help finance
audiovisual projects made in the region. The agency
had a budget of €350,000 in 2004.

Regional Audiovisual Fund

www.fvgfilmcommission.com/regolamentoen.htm
Offers: up to €120,000 · For: PROD · Covering:
FEAT | TV | SHORT | DOC | ANI
Productions filming in Friuli Venezia Giulia will be
entitled to apply for a grant in cash, depending on the
production's period of stay in the regional territory.
At least 150% of the regional grant must be spent
in the region itself, with the exception of crews and
investment expenses. Filming in the region must equal
at least 70% of the entire external filming of the film,
and at least 50% of the total filming of the finished
film.

Salento Film Fund

www.provincia.le.it/fondi/film%20fund.htm
Servizio Politiche Culturali, presso il Museo
Provinciale Sigismondo, Castromediano, Viale
Gallipoli, Lecce, Rag. Salvatore Viva, Italy
T: +34 0832 683532
E: ufficiocrediti@provincia.le.it
The Salento Film Fund provided direct financial support
to the production, distribution, and promotion of films
and TV programmes. Priority goes to co-productions
involving companies based in other regions. The
beneficiaries of the new fund can either be production
companies based in the Province of Lecce, production
companies which intend to spend a significant amount
of time filming within the Province of Lecce and would
hire local professionals, or production companies which
bring projects co-produced by at least one company
from the Province of Lecce. There are no specific
conditions to apply but the Fund prioritises projects
which identify the importance of the Province of
Lecce in the Mediterranean area and support Euro-
Mediterranean relationships.

Production support

www.provincia.le.it/fondi/film%20fund.htm
Offers: up to €100,000 or 30% of budget · For:
PROD · Covering: FEAT | TV | DOC | ANI | SHORT |
DIGI
The fund supports the development of the local
audiovisual industry, through direct funding and by
encouraging co-productions between local enterprises
and those of other regions, as well as national and
international levels. It also supports local professionals
working in the region of Salento. For documentaries
under 75 minutes, the maximum investment is €30,000
and for other TV content it is €20,000.

Film commissions

Campania Film Commission

www.campaniafilmcommission.org/
Via Lago Patria, 200 — IT-80014 Napoli, Italy
T: 0039 081 5091533 · F: 0039 081 5091533
E: info@campaniafilmcommission.org
The local film fund offers assistance of €70,000 per
Feature Film, €20,000 per Documentary Film, €3,000
per Short Film, tax Rebate, free shooting permits and
authorisations and other discounted services.

Italian Film Commission

www.filminginitaly.com
E: losangeles@losangeles.ice.it
The Italian Film Commission (IFC) is a division of
the Italian Trade Commission (ITC) and operates as
the promotional office for the Italian Entertainment
Industry. The Italian Film Commission provides
information and assistance to the audiovisual industry
by showcasing, promoting and assisting with Italian
locations, facilities and Italian crews above and below
the line. Their role as a liaison between the Italian film
community, its services and products and the global
industry, has helped increase productions in Italy.

JAMAICA

JAMPRO/Jamaica Film, Music

www.filmjamaica.com/
Jamaica Film Commission, 18 Trafalgar Rd, Kingston
10, Jamaica
T: (876) 978-7755, 978-3337 · F: (876) 978-0140
E: film@investjamaica.com

LATVIA

National Film Centre of Latvia

www.nfc.lv
Elizabetes iela 49, Riga, LV-1010, Latvia
T: +371 750 50 74/750 50 85 · F: +371 750 50 77
E: nfc@nfc.gov.lv
The National Film Centre's main objectives are to
administer the government's financial support to
Latvian films, prepare legal acts and governmental
documents to secure film-making in Latvia, preserve
the national audiovisual heritage, promote Latvian
films abroad and to co-operate with the relevant
international and national organisations.

Support for film

Covering: ANI | FEAT | DOC | SHORT
Awards are made once a year.

Support for festivals and film events

For: PROMO

State Culture Capital Foundation

www.kkf.lv
Vilandes iela 3, Riga, LV-1010, Latvia
T: +371 750 3177 · F: +371 750 3176
E: kkf@kkf.lv
The aim of the State Culture Capital Foundation (SCCF)
is to promote a balanced development of creativity in all

areas of art and preservation of the cultural heritage in the country in line with state cultural policy. The SCCF does not deal with any commercial activities.

LITHUANIA

Ministry of Culture of the Republic of Lithuania

www.lrkm.lt/index.php/en/39548/
Basanaviciaus g. 5, LT 2001 Vilnius, Lithuania,
T: +370 52 619 486 · F: +370 52 620 768
E: culture@muza.lt
The Ministry of Culture is the governmental body of the Republic of Lithuania in charge of formulating and implementing the state culture policies as well as the safeguard of copyright and neighbouring rights and the protection of cultural values.

LUXEMBOURG

Film Fund Luxembourg

www.filmfund.lu
5 rue Large, L-1917 Luxembourg, Luxembourg
T: +352 478 20 65 · F: +352 22 09 63
E: info@filmfund.etat.lu
The Film Fund of the Grand-Duchy of Luxembourg exists to promote and to encourage the development of the country's audiovisual production sector, and to administrate film-making incentive and assistance schemes.

Audiovisual Investment Certificates

www.filmfund.lu/filmfund.lu/cu/iandg/index.php ·
For: PROD · Covering: FEAT | TV | MM | ANI | DOC
The production costs covered by the Investment Certificate Programme include personnel costs incurred and spent in Luxembourg or involving training of local industry staff, as well as goods and services acquired from firms or individuals based in the Grand Duchy. The financial assistance is provided on completion of the production and following presentation of audited accounts.

Support for Scriptwriting and Development

Offers: up to €75,000 · For: SCRIPT | DEV ·
Covering: FEAT | DOC | ANI | TV
A project can only benefit from this aid if it has a Luxembourg producer attached. A public competition for the selection of projects is held. In addition to the costs related to scriptwriting and development, funding can support translation of the final script and costs linked to the search for and conclusion of financing.

Support for Production

Offers: up to €500,000 · For: PROD · Covering: FEAT | TV | SHORT | DOC | ANI
This aid is primarily intended for Luxembourg-based production companies. For co-productions, the Luxembourg participation must be between 10% and 90%. Rights linked to the production must reflect the respective proportions of financing and and ownership must be shared jointly by all the co-producers. The Luxembourg co-producer must participate both artistically and technically in the production of the project.

Support for Distribution

Offers: up to €50,000 · For: DIST · Covering: TV | FEAT | DOC | ANI | SHORT
The scheme promotes the distribution of Luxembourg productions and co-productions in Luxembourg. The fund is open to Luxembourg-based producers and distributors, having produced or co-produced films recognised as being of Luxembourg nationality. The applicants must provide proof that they are able to cover a reasonable proportion of the costs of distribution for the films or audiovisual projects for which application is made.

Support for promotion

For: PROMO · Covering: FEAT | TV
The fund gives support for the promotion of Luxembourg films at festivals and other events.

MACEDONIA

Broadcasting Council of the Republic of Macedonia

www.srd.org.mk
Ilindenska 9, 1000 Skopje, Macedonia
T: +389 2 3109338 · F: +389 2 3126704
E: proekti@srd.org.mk
The programs financed by this fund are designed to protect, promote and preserve the Macedonian cultural and historical tradition, as well as the traditions of the ethnic groups living in 'The former Yugoslav Republic of Macedonia'. They should also promote quality and creativity, and support the production of programs which are of interest to all citizens of the state, their work and life.

Fund for Financing Radio and Television Programmes of Public Interest

www.srd.org.mk/default-en.asp
Offers: up to €90,000 · Covering: TV | OTHER
The scheme aims to contribute to enriching national radio and TV production. Original fiction and

documentary, as well as new content are favoured with the basic principles for selection that the project must have an impact on the people living in the country and preferably be produced in one of the languages used. Projects are selected for the quality of the content and should not have a commercial agenda.

MALTA

Malta Film Commission

www.mfc.com.mt
The Trade Centre, San Gwann, SGN 09, Malta, Malta
T: +356 21 497 970 • F: +356 21 499 568
E: info@mfc.com.mt
The Malta Film Commission, a non-profit making organisation, offers its services to foreign film and TV productions. In order to encourage further investment in the film industry, the Government of Malta offers rebates and tax reductions to production companies shooting on the islands and companies operating from Malta on a case-by-case basis. The MFC promotes Malta as a film location around the world (see further info in Part II).

Malta Film Commission
www.mfc.com.mt/page.asp?p=14253&l=1 •
Covering: FEAT | TV | SHORT | DOC | ANI
Productions filming in Malta before 31 December 2008 are eligible for financial incentives in the form of a cash grant given to eligible productions on the qualifying expenditure incurred in Malta. Up to 20% of the eligible expenditure can be obtained as a cash rebate by a qualifying production company once filming is complete.

Co-productions
www.mfc.com.mt/page.asp?p=14255&l=1
The Film Commission promotes the development of European multilateral cinematographic co-production. In order to obtain co-production status, the work must involve at least three co-producers, established in three different signatories to the Convention. The participation of one or more co-producers who are not established in such Parties is possible, provided that their total contribution does not exceed 30% of the total cost of the production.

National Film Commission

www.conafilm.org.mx
Av. División del Norte # 2462 5to. piso, Col. Portales
C.P., 03300 D.F, Mexico
T: +1 525 688 7813 • F: +1 525 688 7027
E: conafilm@conafilm.org.mx
With the cooperation of the Federal Government, the States Governments and public and private organisations and institutions, the National Film Commission of Mexico and its network of State Film Commissions head the efforts to promote the production of films, TV programs and commercials in Mexico and to give assistance to all companies and producers interested in developing their projects in the country.

THE NETHERLANDS

Dutch Film Fund

www.filmfund.nl/
1071 CM Amsterdam, Netherlands
T: +31 20 5707676 • F: +31 20 5707689
E: nff@filmfund.nl
Film production in the Netherlands is funded through the Dutch Film Fund (Nederlands Fonds voor de Film), which was established in November 1993 by bringing together the 'Production Fund for Dutch Films' and the 'Fund for the Dutch Film. The Fund's objectives are to encourage film production in the Netherlands, with the focus being on both quality and diversity; and to 'engender a good climate for Dutch film culture'. The Film Fund gets its money from the Ministry of Education, Culture and Science (Ministerie van Onderwijs, Cultuur en Wetenschappen). In 2005, 49% of the 931 projects submitted for support were funded.

Holland Film, affiliated with the Dutch Film Fund, is the official marketing & promotion agency for Dutch film abroad. The organisation, financed from public funds, and some private sponsors offers a wide variety of services for Dutch filmmakers and producers to enhance the perception of Dutch filmmaking worldwide. It acts as a consultant when Dutch films are presented at international film festivals and film markets and it provides the international film circuit with information on current activities within the Dutch film industry.

Funding
Financing is in the form of a loan which is repayable from revenues (including revenues generated from ancillary rights). If there are no revenues, there is no repayment and no interest is charged, no profit points are taken and the Fund's recoupment position is negotiable.

International co-productions are dealt with on a case-by-case basis and will be judged on its cultural links with the Netherlands, and its interest to a Dutch audience from recognisable cultural elements. The Fund requests that any funding is spent either in the Netherlands or on a Dutch crew and cast. The applicant must be a Dutch producer and the film must have theatrical distribution in the Netherlands. The DFF's guidelines do not specifically mention economic criteria such as setting up a sustainable industry.

Support for feature film scriptwriting & development

Offers: up to €35,000 · For: SCRIPT | DEV · Covering: FEAT
Script development support covers all possible stages of development, including the development of a synopsis, a treatment, and rewriting.

Support for production (feature films)

Offers: up to €450,000 · For: PROD · Covering: FEAT | FFF
Claims must be submitted by a producer established for at least two years in the Netherlands. Producer and director cannot be the same person. The fund supports no projects of applicants who are still following professional training. First-time directors are advised to submit a claim in combination with an experienced producer

Support for Distribution

www.filmfund.nl/categorieen/lange_speelfilm/index.htm
Offers: up to €27,000 · For: DIST · Covering: FEAT | TV | DOC | ANI
Aids the distribution of feature films.

New Media

www.filmfund.nl/categorieen/nieuwemedia/index.htm
Offers: Up to €6,806 · Covering: MM | DIGI
The fund gives financial support for new media projects in the field of art and design with the intention to support innovative new media projects which do not qualify for other support programmes operated by the Dutch Film Fund. Claims may be submitted by organisations such as a theatre group or a film production company. Individual artists or designers can submit claims for small-scale, preparatory research projects up to maximum of €6,806.

Public film

www.filmfund.nl/categorieen/publieksfilm/index.htm
Offers: up to €900,000 and 30% · For: PROD · Covering: FEAT
The fund gives support to films aimed at the Benelux market and which are likely to appeal to a 'broad audience'. The production budget should be between €1.4m and €4.5m. The project must have sufficient Dutch characteristics. The forecast promotion and marketing costs must amount to at least five per cent of the production costs and at least €70,000.

Documentary production

www.filmfund.nl
Offers: up to €160,000 and 45% of budget · For: PROD · Covering: DOC
Maximum award for documentaries longer than 75 minutes is €160 000; for documentaries between 60 and 75 minutes, maximum is €110,000, for less than 60 minutes, maximum is €70,000. An applicant can apply for up to two projects at a time.

Animation production

www.filmfund.nl/categorieen/animatie/
Offers: up to €120,000 · For: PROD · Covering: ANI
Support for production and completion of Dutch animated films, with a €536,000 budget in 2005 and seven films supported. There are three annual deadlines.

Documentary development

www.filmfund.nl
Offers: up to €14,000 · For: SCRIPT · Covering: DOC
At least 20% of the estimated costs must be invested in the development by the producer (or third parties).

Animation script development

www.filmfund.nl
Offers: up to €15,000 · For: SCRIPT · Covering: ANI
Application must be submitted by a producer established in the Netherlands for at least two years. The fund will not support applicants who are still on a training course.

Short film production

Offers: Average €30,000 · For: PROD · Covering: SHORT
The size of the fund in 2005 was €315,000 and 10 films out of the 91 submitted were funded.

Support for experimental films

Covering: OTHER
Support takes the form of a subsidy from a fund which in 2005 was €835,000.

Project development/scriptwriting support for feature films

Offers: up to €45,000 · For: DEV | SCRIPT · Covering: FEAT

Up to €35,000 is available for kunstzinnige' (arthouse films). The total script and development budget was €920,000 in 2005 with 96 projects supported.

Jan Vrijman Fund

www.idfa.nl/jvf_content.asp
Jan Vrijman Fund / IDFA, Kleine Gartmanplantsoen 10, 1017 RR Amsterdam, Netherlands
T: +31 20 627 3329 · F: +31 20 638 5388
E: janvrijmanfund@idfa.nl

The Jan Vrijman Fund provides financial support for documentary projects from developing countries which are aimed at research and script development, production and post-production, distribution and sales. In addition, other activities for the promotion of the production and distribution of documentaries, like for example the organisation of workshops, documentary film festivals and other education programs, are eligible for support. The Fund seeks to support projects that would otherwise not have been realised, or to a lesser standard. In selecting the projects, the Jan Vrijman Fund will not apply rigid criteria but judge each project on its merits. A binding condition, however, is that the filmmaker lives and works in a developing country or country in transition.

Script and project development

Offers: up to €4,000 · For: SCRIPT | DEV · Covering: DOC

There are two annual deadlines.

Production and post-production

Offers: up to €15,000 · For: PROD | POST
Applicants must submit a full synopsis, script, budget and finance plan.

OTHER activities

Can be for the support of local activities that aim to promote the documentary film genre; the organisation of workshops; or activities aimed at the distribution of documentaries in developing countries. The fund is receptive to alternative and innovative ideas, as long as these are well-founded by a clear plan of implementation.

Rotterdam Film Fund

www.rff.rotterdam.nl/
Rotterdam Film Fund, Rochussenstraat 3c, 1315 EA Rotterdam, Netherlands
T: +31 10 436 07 47 · F: +31 10 436 05 53
E: info@rff.rotterdam.nl

The Rotterdam Film Fund (RFF) focuses on encouraging audiovisual activities in the Rotterdam region. The Fund provides facilities and financial support for feature films, documentaries and TV productions that are produced by companies based in the Rotterdam area. The RFF is especially interested in productions that contribute to a long-term strengthening of the audiovisual sector. The Fund also develops relevant training courses (postgraduate courses and workshops).

Support for Production

www.rff.rotterdam.nl/site/eng/rff/financieel.htm
Offers: up to €130,000 · For: PROD · Covering: FEAT | TV | MM | SHORT | DOC | ANI | FFF | YP

The RFF is especially interested in productions that contribute to a long-term strengthening of the audiovisual sector. The most important condition for financial support is that 150% of the sum that is borrowed must be spent in the Rotterdam area. Foreign producers must find a co-producer based in Rotterdam. The Fund can decide to provide a higher financial contribution if virtually the entire production (from pre- to post-production) takes place in Rotterdam or the region.

Support for Project Development

Offers: up to €9,000 · For: DEV · Covering: FEAT | TV | MM | SHORT | DOC | ANI | FFF | YP

The fund promotes the development of high-profile audiovisual projects by Rotterdam-based production companies. It takes the form of an interest-free loan.

Rotterdam Shorts

www.rff.rotterdam.nl/site/eng/rff/kortrotterdams.htm
Offers: up to €30,000

The program invites five Rotterdam production teams each year to prepare a short film (5-7 minutes in length). The films must include recognisable Rotterdam elements in terms of location and choice of subject. The productions are presented each year during the International Film Festival Rotterdam (IFFR), after which they circulate as shorts in cinemas throughout Holland.

Stimuleringsfonds Nederlandse Culturele Omroepproducties

www.stimuleringsfonds.nl
Korte Leidsedwarsstraat 12, 1017 RC AMSTERDAM, Netherlands
T: +31 20 6 233 901
E: info@stimuleringsfonds.nl
The aim of the Dutch Cultural Broadcasting Promotion Fund is to provide grants to encourage the development and production of cultural radio and TV programmes. The programmes concerned are mainly cultural programmes, largely of Dutch origin with a high level of artistic merit. These are to be broadcast by one of the national broadcasting companies, an educational broadcaster, or a religious denomination with national broadcast time. Moreover, these programmes need to be in Dutch language for at least 60%.

Support for the Production of Audiovisual Programmes with Cultural Content

For: PROD · Covering: FEAT | DOC | TV | YP
This funding is only given to recognised public broadcasting organisations. Projects must be Dutch, ie at least 65% filmed in Dutch and using Dutch technical facilities. Funding is available for fiction films, serials and for documentaries, providing they are cultural programmes.

Support for Script Writing for Audiovisual and Radio Works

www.stimuleringsfonds.nl/page.ocl?mode=&version
=&pageid=10&MenuID=0 · For: SCRIPT · Covering: TV | FEAT
The programme provides funding for the writing of a synopsis/treatment from which a first draft of a script can be written.

The Dutch Co-production Fund for Broadcasting Companies

www.cobofonds.nl
CoBO-fonds, Postvak M.54, Postbus 26444, 1202 JJ Hilversum, Netherlands
T: +31 35 677 53 48 · F: +31 35 677 19 55
E: cobo@cobofonds.nl
The CoBO Fund (National Broadcasters Coproduction Fund) was established in 1986. Its main source of income is the broadcasting fees from performance rights paid by Belgian and German cable operators for the simultaneous broadcast of Dutch channels in their own regions. The CoBo Fund encourages co-productions between national broadcasters and independent producers in the Netherlands, the BRTV Belgian TV channel and cinemas.

Co-production funding

sites.omroep.nl/cobofonds/ · For: PROD · Covering: FEAT | TV | SHORT | DOC
The CoBO Fund gives financial support to co-productions to broadcasters. A co-producer can be: an independent film producer; an institution or person in the field of the performing arts; the Flemish Radio and TV public broadcaster (VRT); one of the German public broadcasters (ZDF, WDR, ARD etc.).

Private funds

Film Investors Netherlands (FINE BV)

www.fine.nl
Sarphatikade 12, Amsterdam, 1017 WV, Netherlands,
T: +31 20 530 4700 · F: +31 20 530 4701
E: info@fine.nl
FINE BV acts as an intermediary between producers and potential investors, seeking venture capital for film projects through a network of financial institutions such as banks, and forming limited film partnerships for tax purposes.

NEW ZEALAND

Film New Zealand

www.filmnz.com
PO Box 24142, Wellington, New Zealand
T: +64 4 385 0766 · F: +64 4 384 5840
E: info@filmnz.org.nz
New Zealand Film provides financial assistance for New Zealand feature film projects and New Zealand filmmakers, by way of loan or equity financing. The New Zealand Government has introduced a Large Budget Screen Production Grant (LBSPG) scheme whereby an eligible applicant will be granted a sum totalling 12.5% of the Qualifying New Zealand Production Expenditure on films of budgets greater than NZ$15m. Film New Zealand commits up to 8% of their annual budget to feature film development financing, and up to 60% to feature film production financing. Development decisions are made by either the senior staff group (up to NZ$15,000 per project) or the Development Committee (up to NZ$75,000 cumulative per projects).

Large Budget Screen Production Grant Scheme

www.filmnz.com/production-guide/large-budget-screen-production-grant-scheme.html · For: PROD · Covering: FEAT | TV | DOC | ANI | Other
Applicants will be granted a sum totalling 12.5% of the Qualifying New Zealand Production Expenditure

(QNZPE). To access the scheme the applicants QNZPE must be at least NZ$15 million. Applicants must be either a New Zealand resident company, or a foreign corporation operating with a fixed establishment in New Zealand. The fund also encourages international co-productions.

Film South New Zealand

www.filmsouth.com
PO Box 330, Christchurch, New Zealand
T: +64 3 365 5865
E: info@filmsouth.com
The fund offers a large budget screen production grant (LBSPG) scheme whereby an eligible project will be granted a sum totalling 12.5% of the Qualifying New Zealand Production Expenditure (QNZPE). Where the value of the QNZPE is between NZ$15 million and NZ$50 million, QNZPE must be at least 70 % of the film's total production expenditure. Where the value of the QNZPE is NZ$50 million or more it will qualify for the grant regardless of the percentage ratio of QNZPE to the screen production's total production expenditure. For TV series, individual episodes, which have completed principal photography within any 12 month period and with a minimum average spend of NZ$500,000 per commercial hour, may be bundled to achieve the total of NZ$15 million.

Film Wellington

www.filmwellington.com
Jean Johnston, Film Wellington, Level 9, AMI Plaza, 342 — 352 Lambton Quay, Wellington, New Zealand
T: +64 4 494 2546 · F: +64 4 494 2569
E: film@filmwellington.com

NORDIC

Nordic Film & TV Fund

www.nftf.net
PO Box 275, 1319 Bekkestua, Norway
T: +47 64 00 60 80 · F: +47 64 00 60 87
E: nftf@nftf.net
The Purpose of the NFTF is to promote the production of audiovisual projects in the Nordic area by participating in top-up financing of feature films, TV fiction, TV series, short films and creative documentaries. The Fund also promotes audiovisual productions by supporting project development, distribution and promotion, and Nordic language dubs. It also administers funds from the Nordic Council of Ministers, which are earmarked for distribution and film

cultural initiatives. There are no pan-Nordic thematic requirements, national quotas, or requirements with regards to the artistic or technical staff. Productions aimed at youth and children will receive special attention.

Funding
Nordic Production Companies are eligible for support. The fund cannot take part in the financing of projects which are presold to, or co-produced with a Nordic broadcaster that is not a partner in the fund. There are no application deadlines and applications including enclosures should be submitted in a Scandinavian language or English.

Production Support
For: PROD · Covering: SHORT | FEAT | ANI | YP | TV
The fund supports production of audiovisual projects in the Nordic area by participating in gap financing of feature films. Films must be suitable for theatrical release, TV broadcasting or other forms of distribution and have satisfactory marketing/audience potential within the Nordic Area. Productions aimed at youth and children will receive special attention.

Project Development
For: DEV · Covering: DOC | ANI | FEAT | YP | TV
Top-up financing support is primarily given to feature films and TV-fiction/series and to a lesser extent documentary projects and occasionally other forms of audiovisual projects. Priority is given to projects with a Nordic perspective where the Fund has an interest in participating in the production itself.

Support for Distribution, Promotion and Nordic Language Versions ·
For: DIST | PROMO · Covering: YP | ANI | DOC | SHORT | FEAT
The scheme aims to enhance circulation of Nordic films within the other Nordic countries. Applying for support for distribution in the country of origin is not allowed; the film should have been well received from the national audience before applying for distribution support from another country. The Fund primarily gives support for special promotional purposes. Nordic distribution companies in the country where the film shall be distributed are eligible for support.

Film Cultural Initiatives
www.nftf.net/guidelines/nftfenglish.pdf · For: CULT
Funding for special workshops, forums, festival programs or seminars, which can strengthen the competence of the Nordic film & TV environment.

Nordic Language Versions
Covering: YP | FEAT | TV | SHORT | DOC | ANI
This support is granted to create a version of a Nordic film in another Nordic language, primarily through dubbing. Films that receive support for dubbing should have been well received in the country of origin. Support is normally given only to films aimed at children and young people from Nordic production and distribution companies.

NORWAY

Norsk Filmfond

www.filmfondet.no/
Norwegian Film Fund, P.O.Box 752, Sentrum, Dronningens gate 16, NO-0106 Oslo, Norway
T: +47 22 47 80 40 · F: +47 22 47 80 41
E: mail@filmfondet.no
The Norwegian Film Fund administers the state support for film productionand is charged with administering all national support for film production in Norway. According to its Statutes, the Film Fund also advises the Ministry for Cultural and Church Affairs on film policy. Norsk Filmfond replaces AV-Fondet, Norsk Film A/S and the Norwegian Film Institute.

Funding
The Fund has private film producers as its target group. Available support totals approximately €35m annually. Support is available to professional, independent audiovisual production companies registered in Norway, for the production of films in the Norwegian or Sami languages. A ceiling of NOK 30 million (CPI-adjusted annually) applies to support of any one, single project (production support and automatic support combined). Support is provided as conditionally repayable loans. There are no deadlines for applying for production support. Applications are screened on the basis of artistic merit and financial solidity by one of the Film Fund's four Commissioning Editors (a.k.a. 'consultants'), whose recommendations for support are formalised through decision of the Film Fund's seven-member Board of Trustees, meeting on an average eight to ten times a year. In addition, the Film Fund may provide development grants and marketing (P&A) support upon application.

Support for production of minority co-productions
For: PROD · Covering: FEAT | TV | DOC | ANI | YP | SHORT
Support may be granted to the Norwegian participation in international co-productions, produced in languages other than Norwegian and Sami. The following

particular conditions must be met: a Norwegian production company must be responsible for the Norwegian participation in the project; the Norwegian production company shall be responsible for any artistic, technical and financial contribution to the production; there shall be a reasonable proportionality between the participation and capital investment of the Norwegian and foreign production companies in the production, and between the Norwegian and foreign artistic and technical contribution.

Support for short films and TV documentaries ·
For: PROD · Covering: SHORT | FFF | TV | DOC
Support may be awarded to independent Norwegian audiovisual production companies for the production of Norwegian short films, intended for screening in cinemas, on TV or through other media, including single documentaries for TV screening. The projects shall be evaluated on the basis of artistic, production-related, economic, technical and market-related criteria. The amount of support will be determined from a combined assessment of these criteria.

Support for full-length feature film (development, production)
For: DEV | PROD · Covering: FEAT | TV | SHORT | DOC | ANI | FFF | YP
Support may be awarded to independent Norwegian audiovisual production companies for the production of full-length Norwegian feature films. The projects shall be evaluated on the basis of artistic, production-related, economic, technical and market-related criteria. The producer's equity funding shall be minimum 25% of the approved budget of the film. The Norwegian Film Fund may, in particular cases, determine a lower equity funding for documentaries and films for children.

Support for television series
For: PROD · Covering: TV | YP
Support may be awarded to independent Norwegian audiovisual production companies for the production of TV series, drama and documentaries. The support is intended for the production of TV series, recorded in Norwegian or Sami language.The production company's equity financing shall be a minimum 50% of the approved budget of the production. The Norwegian Film Fund may, in particular cases, determine a lower equity financing for documentaries and for productions aimed at children.

Support for interactive productions
www.filmfondet.no/icm.aspx?PageId=713 · For: DEV
Support may be awarded for the project development of interactive productions that employ Norwegian or Sami language. The projects shall be evaluated on the basis of artistic, production-related, economic, technical

and market-related criteria. The amount of support will be determined on the basis of a combined assessment of these criteria. A reasonable proportionality shall exist between the production company's equity financing, support from the Norwegian Film Fund and other sources of financing. The production company's equity financing shall be a minimum 25% of development costs.

Production support

Offers: Up to NOK 30m · For: PROD | DEV · Covering: FEAT | TV | DOC | ANI | YP | MM | SHORT
Support is available in different strands covering production of feature-length films (national films and majority co-productions), production of short films and TV documentaries, production of minority co-productions, development of interactive productions and production of TV series.

Support for production of films on commercial criteria

For: PROD · Covering: FEAT | Other | DOC | ANI | YP
Applications for support for production of films on commercial criteria are accepted, provided that the producer has raised at least 50% of the budget, and is awarded on the basis of an evaluation of the commercial potential of the film. There are no application deadlines.

Box-Office Bonuses (automatic support in proportion to ticket sales)

www.filmfondet.no/icm.aspx?PageId=712 · For: EXBN
Box-Office Bonuses are awarded automatically to any film which is distributed theatrically in Norway, currently standing at 55% of ticket revenue until the ceiling amount is reached (100% for children's films). The ceiling on Box-Office Bonuses is calculated in relation to the producer's investment and risk.

North Norwegian Film Centre

www.nnfs.no
Postboks 94, NO-9751 Honningsvåg, Norway
T: +47 78 47 64 00 · F: +47 78 47 64 10
E: info@nnfs.no
The purpose of the Filmcentre is to administer funds on behalf of the Ministry of Cultural Affairs to support the production of shorts and documentary films with connection to northern Norway. The Filmcenter supports the producers and filmmakers in Northern Norway with advice and assistance. The Filmcentre supports distribution, marketing, information and training of the professional filmmakers. In addition, children and youths an important target group.

Support for production

For: PROD · Covering: SHORT | DOC
Producers from Norway who want to produce the film in North Norway are eligible to apply.

Norwegian Film Commission

www.norwegianfilm.com
Georgernes Verft 12, Bergen, N-5011, Norway
T: +47 55 56 43 43 · F: +47 55 56 43 48
E: post@norwegianfilm.com
The NFC is an autonomous, national foundation whose purpose is to encourage and support production of international films in Norway.

Norwegian Film Development

www.norskfilmutvikling.no/
Filmens Hus, Dronningens gate 16, Postboks 904, Sentrum, NO-0104 Oslo, Norway
T: +47 22 82 24 00 · F: +47 22 82 24 22
E: mail@nfu.no
The Norwegian Film Development is one of three public film institutions for professional training and development, financing and distribution. It directs itself to the creators of ideas, principally writers and directors, and is responsible for professional training of filmmakers. Accordingly, it supports the development of scripts and projects of all genres and lengths. Furthermore, the Norwegian Film Development administrates a screenplay development fund for full length fiction, animation and documentary.

Support for scriptwriting

www.norskfilmutvikling.no/dok.php?id=24 · For: SCRIPT · Covering: FEAT | DOC | ANI
Writer-based screenplay development fund for full-length fiction, animation, TV-drama and documentaries supports 30-50 projects at any one time with script editors as well as bursaries for the writers (from a €600,000 fund). In addition additional project development, such as 'cold readings', rehearsal of various scenes in the script development process, research, etc. is also available.

West Norwegian Film Centre

www.vestnorskfilm.no
Vestnorsk Filmsenter, Georgernes Verft 12, NO-5011 Bergen, Norway
T: +47 55 56 09 05 · F: +47 55 56 03 55
E: line@vestnorskfilm.no / gry@vestnorskfilm.no
The West Norwegian Film Centre funds the development and production of independent short and documentary films. The Centre's main objective

is to support and stimulate short and documentary film production along the western shores of Norway. However, projects that both thematically and in terms of production have an international level and perspective are of interest.

Funding for short and documentary films · For: PROD · Covering: SHORT | DOC
Producers can receive funding at and for various stages of production, starting with screenplay development through to post-production and launch. Most funding is given at the early stages of project production. Producers are strongly encouraged to procure funding either from the private sector or through other cultural institutions or funds in Norway.

POLAND

Polish Film Institute

www.pisf.pl/
ul. Krakowskie Przedmie cie 21/23, 00-071 Warszawa, Poland
T: +48 22 42 10 518 · F: +48 22 42 10 241
E: pisf@pisf.pl
The Polish Film Institute (PISF) is the newest film institute in Europe, established in 2005 in accordance with the new cinematography law, passed by Polish Parliament. It is set up similarly to the mechanisms of film industry support existing in many countries of Europe. The Polish Film Institute wants to draw Polish viewers back to the theatres to watch Polish films and, at the same time, to make them worth of seeing and accessible to international audiences, particularly in Europe. The institute aims to support the preparation of film projects; film production; film distribution and dissemination; promotion of the Polish film creativity; and popularising film culture.

Funding
Financial aid can be given in form of subsidies, loans and pledges. The institute emphasises artistic, cognitive and ethical qualities, including: precision of the dramatic construction, the psychological depth of the characters and quality of dialogues application of innovative forms of expression; identification of new theme areas and up-to-date social problems; promotion of ethical and educational values, also among children and young people; significance for the national culture and strengthening of the Polish tradition and mother tongue; and enriching the European cultural variety. In addition to production support, outlined below, funding is available for promotion of Polish films abroad, distribution, film culture education and training, but further details were not available at publication.

Production Support
www.pisf.pl/pliki/c0/d1/c0d1ce96201c347/
rozporzadzenie_decree.doc
Offers: up to PLN 4 million · For: PROD · Covering: FEAT | SHORT | DOC | ANI | YP
Offers no more than 50% of budget up to PLN 4 million for feature film, PLN 500,000 for a standard documentary, PLN 2 million for feature documentaries, PLN 500,000 for a standard animation and PLN 3 million for feature animations. For a low-budget or 'difficult' film up to 90% is available.

Film Polski

www.filmpolski.pl
ul. Mazowiecka 6/8, PL — Warszawa 00-148, Poland
T: +48 22 826 84 55 · F: +48 22 826 08 49
E: info@filmpolski.com
The Agency deals with the promotion of Polish films at home and abroad.

Financial support for promotion of films in cinema distribution
Offers: up to €10,000 · For: PROD · Covering: FEAT | DOC | SHORT | ANI | YP | FFF
The fund supports non-commercial Polish film production intended for cinema release.

PORTUGAL

Instituto do Cinema, Audiovisual e Multimédia

www.icam.pt/
Rua de S. Pedro de Alcantara 45 — 1e, PT — 1269-138 LISBOA, Portugal
T: +351 213 23 0800 · F: +351.21.3428717
E: mail@icam.pt
The Institute for Cinema, Audiovisuals and Multimedia (ICAM) is a public body with autonomy in the management of its affairs and assets, reporting to the Minister of Culture. ICAM's aim is to affirm and to strengthen cultural identity and diversity in the area of cinema, audiovisual and multimedia, by supporting innovation and creativity as well as by reinforcing the content creation industries and promoting Portuguese culture and the Portuguese language.

Funding
Financial support for film production is granted as follows: Selective Financial Support System, taking in account production content and the aesthetic, technical and artistic aspects; Direct Financial Support System, completing financing obtained by the producer for his

film project.

Direct Financial Support System for Film Production

Financial support to be granted is a complement for other funds already obtained and is intended for fictional feature films and documentaries. Creative documentaries are considered to be those that present an original approach to any aspect of reality, provided they have not a predominantly informative, didactic or advertising nature, nor are meant to act as a mere complement of a work in which image is not the essential element.

Selective financial support system for the production of fictional feature films and First Films

The fund supports feature films that are either the first or the second film from film director. Film directors and film producers are eligible for this fund.

Selective Financial Support System for Co-Productions

For: PROD

The fund supports co-productions made within the scope of bilateral Agreements or International Conventions signed by the Portuguese Government and having more than 50% of the project's total capital investment guaranteed by a foreign producer. In addition, the support system considers co-productions produced by one or more Portuguese producers and, at least, a producer from a Portuguese speaking-country, made within the scope of bilateral agreements establishing reciprocity terms.

Selective Financial Support System for Short Films for Children and Youngsters

For: PROD · Covering: SHORT | YP

The fund supports fictional short films for children and youngsters, made in any format. Fictional short films for children are considered to be those lasting up to 15 minutes, aimed at children between 4 and 11 years. Fictional short films for youngsters are considered to be those lasting up to 60 minutes, aimed at young people between 11 and 17 years.

Support for the Development, Research and Production of Creative Documentaries

For: DEV | PROD · Covering: DOC

Creative documentaries are considered to be those that present an original approach to any aspect of reality, provided they have not a predominantly informative, didactic or advertising nature, nor are meant to act as a mere complement of a work in which image is not the essential element.

Selective Financial Support System for Animated Films (Full-length, Medium-length, Short Films and Series)

For: PROD | DEV · Covering: ANI

Project development for medium-length animated films lasting more than 25 minutes, for full-length animated films and for animated series.

Support for Distribution

For: DIST · Covering: FEAT | DOC | ANI | FFF | YP

ICAM provides financial support for film distribution, by participating in the cost of prints and promotion materials, as well as by supporting the making of inter-negatives and inter-positives of films.

Financial Support for Audiovisual Production ·

For: PROD

The fund supports projects of audiovisual programmes and series in Portuguese language, by independent producers, in any genre. Financial support for each project varies from 20% to 50% of the total cost for each project.

Cinema Exhibition

www.englishversion.icam.pt/

For: EXBN · Covering: OTHER

Financial support for Cinema exhibition is specially intended to fund the creation of new cinemas or to improve the existing ones, as well as to fund the acquisition of all necessary equipment.

Computerisation of Box Offices Programme

For: EXBN · Covering: SHORT

The programme's aim is to fund ticket-offices computerisation on as wide a scale as possible.

Alternative Film Exhibition Network Programme

www.englishversion.icam.pt/

For: EXBN · Covering: OTHER

The creation of an alternative film exhibition network is an initiative developed by ICAM, which aims to promote and support the implementation of a network of cinemas, either commercial or non-commercial, to exhibit films that usually do not circulate in commercial distribution networks, in particular short films, animated films and documentaries by Portuguese and European producers.

Promotion

ICAM offers several activities for film promotion, such as financial support for film festivals, financial support for film exhibitions and fairs, support for subtitling and transcription of prints.

ROMANIA

National Cinema Centre

www.cncinema.abt.ro/
Centrul National al Cinematografiei, Str. Dem. Dobrescu nr. 4-6, Sector 1, Bucuresti 010026, Romania
T: +40 21 310 43 01 · F: +40 21 310 43 00
E: cnc@cncinema.ro
The NCC aims to encourage and protect national film production, and stimulate the filmmaking and distribution of films of artistic value. The NCC is funded through a levy on cinema and video releases, and TV advertising. The budget in 2004 was €4.3m.

Cinema fund

www.cncinema.abt.ro/
Offers: up to €405,000 or 65% · For: DEV | PROD | POST | EXBN · Covering: DOC | ANI | FFF | YP | FEAT | SHORT
The fund assures the financial means necessary for the development of cinematographic activity. The budget limit of 65% applies to feature films; for short films and first feature films the limit is 80%. Funding is available for several phases of intervention and is offered in several forms: repayable advances on receipts, a loan with interest, interest-free loan, co-financing, co-production, distribution agreement and acquisition of work by the fund.

SINGAPORE

Stingapore Film Commission

www.sfc.org.sg
c/o Media Development Authority, 140 Hill Street, 04-01 Mica Building, Singapore, 179369, Singapore
T: 657062.9773 · F: 6563361170
E: sfc@sfc.org.sg
Singapore offers several incentive and financing plans including a SFC Co-Investment Scheme, a Film Incubator Programme, the Short Film Grant, the Project Development Scheme, the Script Development Grant and Overseas Travel Grants.

SLOVAKIA

Ministry of Culture of the Slovak Republic

www.culture.gov.sk
Program Pro Slovakia, Nám. SNP 33, 813 31 Bratislava, Slovenská republika, Slovakia
T: +421 2 59 39 11 05 · F: +421 2 54 41 96 70
E: mksr@culture.gov.sk

Film and Video

For: PROD · Covering: FEAT | DOC | ANI | OTHER
The fund takes the form of a subsidy.

Pro Slovakia Programme

For: PROD · Covering: FEAT | DOC | ANI | FFF | YP | SHORT | TV
The fund promotes the creation and expansion of cultural values, the development of cultural heritage, representation of Slovak culture abroad. Grants are provided for companies based in Slovakia.

SLOVENIA

Slovenian Film Fund

www.film-sklad.si/
Miklosiceva 38, 1000 Ljubljana, Slovenia
T: +386 1 23 43 200 · F: +386 1 23 43 218
E: info@film-sklad.si
The Slovenian Film Fund enables planning and facilitates film production co-funded by the state. It monitors the work and public expenditure of producers involved in the national film programme. The fund facilitates the presentation and marketing of Slovenian film at home and abroad and encourages the production and distribution of art films, and carries out other tasks connected with film in Slovenia.

Public tender for co-financing of films and audiovisual productions

For: PROD · Covering: FEAT | TV | SHORT | DOC | ANI | FFF
Applications may be submitted by persons resident in the Republic of Slovenia. An individual producer may submit a maximum of three feature film or documentary projects and any number of short, short documentary or animation projects. Proposals must be in the Slovenian language.

Public tender for co-financing of cultural events, professional meetings and training
www.film-sklad.si/client.en/index.
php?table=articles&ID=8 · For: CULT
Applications may be submitted by people registered in the fields of performing cultural and art activities in the field of cinematography in the Republic of Slovenia. An individual applicant may submit a maximum of three programmes.

SOUTH AFRICA

South African Film Finance Corporation

www.theimaginarium.y.co.za
Glenmain Bldg, 1st Floor, 359 A Main Road, Sea Point, Cape Town, 8005, South Africa
T: +27 21 434 2851 · F: +27 21 434 1229
E: info@theimaginarium.y.co.za
The Imaginarium provides financing of feature films in Southern Africa and executive production services. Funding is secured through the South African Film Finance Corporation (SAFFCO). SAFFCO secures financing in a variety of forms, including equity, gap, tax incentives and facilities deals.

African Film Commission

www.africanfilmcommission.org
468 North Camden Dr. Suite 200, Beverly Hills, CA 90210, USA
T: 310.860.7527 · F: 310.860.7500
E: nelle@africanfilmcommission.org

SPAIN

Instituto de la Cinematografia y las Artes Audiovisuales

www.mcu.es/cine/index.jsp
Plaza del Rey 1, Ministerio de Cultura, 28071 Madrid, Spain · F: +34 91 701 70 05
E: info.cine@mcu.es
The national Spanish film institute, ICAA aims to develop the film and video production sector through the provision of aids for production and distribution as well as for the creation and modernisation of cinemas. Furthermore, the institute contributes to the national and international distribution of Spanish films, by supporting participation in festivals and other events and representing in Spain in key international events and forums. It also supports the preservation and restoration of works of cinematographic heritage,

through the Filmoteca Española.

Support for the production of feature films by new directors
Offers: up to €500,000 · For: PROD · Covering: FEAT | FFF | ANI | DOC
The fund encourages new directors and the production of experimental films. Applicants must be a producer registered with ICAA. The Production company must prove that it has financial capability to deliver a project. The budget should be less than €2,000,000. A 'new director' is defined as one who has directed less than three films released in cinemas. 'Experimental works' are films of outstanding quality and artistic value that have difficulty in finding financing. The project must be capable of qualifying as a 'Spanish film'. The amount awarded cannot be more than 60% of the budget.

Support for short films
Offers: up to €60,000 or 75% · For: PROD | POST · Covering: SHORT
The fund encourages new directors to apply. The applicant must be a registered producer. The short/medium-length film should have a running time of less than 60 minutes. There are two types of support available: one for production of short/medium-length films, the other for short/medium-length films that have been completed. A film can obtain both types of support. The film must also have received an official exhibition rating and certificate. Projects are assessed on the basis of: quality, artistic value and purpose of the project; budget; financial plan; the producer's solvency, and financial background; the director's and screenwriter's track record.

Support for the amortization of feature film costs
Offers: up to €1,000,000 · For: PROD · Covering: FEAT | FFF
The fund encourages the production of commercially successful feature films. This is an automatic scheme and the aid is based on objective criteria in terms of the critical acclaim and box office takings.

Support for Distribution of European Union Films
Offers: up to €60,000 · For: DIST · Covering: FEAT | SHORT
The fund encourages theatrical distribution in Spain of EU films of quality. Distributors registered with the ICAA may apply for support covering up to 50% of the cost of distribution of EU films, and collections of short films, up to a maximum of €60,101. The distribution campaign in question must include at least 15 Spanish provinces and five autonomous communities. In the case of a collection of short films it must include four

Spanish provinces and two autonomous communities.

Loans for the Production of Feature Films
Offers: up to €1,000,000
ICAA has signed an agreement with the Instituto de Credito Oficial (ICO) for the provision of a line of credit available for the production of feature films. Loans can be up to 50% of the budgeted cost of the film. Exceptionally, and only on application, requests for loans totalling €5,000,000 may be considered. Applicants are also required to provide an undertaking stating that the project should be able to acquire Spanish nationality, and confirmation from the tax and social security authorities that there are no outstanding liabilities.

Support for Script Development
Offers: up to €15,000 · For: SCRIPT · Covering: TV | FEAT
Applications may be made by individual authors for development of scripts for feature-length films in any of the official languages, for theatrical or TV exhibition. Scripts to be developed can only be original works. Applications are evaluated on the following basis: author's track record, originality of the script idea, quality and viability of the project. Successful applicants have a period of 9 months after the award to develop the script.

Loans for creation and modernisation of cinemas and upgrading and modernisation of production and other technical facilites
www.mcu.es/principal/servicios.html
The fund gives out loans for creation and modernisation of cinemas and upgrading and modernisation of production and other technical facilities.

Support for participation in international festivals of Spanish films
For: PROMO · Covering: FEAT | SHORT
The fund contributes to the diffusion of cultural and artistic values of the Spanish culture by supporting participation in international festivals and other events of the Spanish films. Producers registered at the ICAA may apply for support to participate in major festivals (Cannes, Berlin, San Sebastián, Venecia, Mar del Plata, Locarno, Karlovy Vary, Moscow, Valladolid, Montreal, Hollywood Oscars).

Support for the organization of film festivals and other audiovisual events in Spain
The support could be for festivals, trade shows, fairs, competitions, markets, as well as other activities and events which aim to promote and disseminate the cinematography and audiovisual arts in Spain.

Support for the conservation of negative and original medium of films, in Spain
Producers or right holders of films who commit themselves not to export the negative of their films could be granted up to the 50% of the cost of the production of the internegative and interpositive of the film which must be deposited in a laboratory, in Spain.

Loans for the Distribution of European and Ibero-American Films
The fund supports the distribution of European and Iberoamerican films. Two different types of loans are available: conventional distribution (loans can be up to 50% of the total investment in acquisition of rights, copies and advertising, with a maximum amount of 300,000 per film); and online distribution (loans can be up to 70% of the total investment in digitisation and those costs necessary to put the works on internet).

Asesoría de Cine de la Comunidad de Madrid

www.madrid.org
Consejeria de Cultura y Deportes, Direccion General de Promocion Cultural, Alcala 31, 28014 MADRID, Spain
T: +34 91 720 81 98 · F: +34 91 720 82 65
E: atencionalciudadano@madrid.org
The main objective of the Madrid film office is to promote culture in the region with specific support for film production and distribution in the region of Madrid.

Support for Scriptwriting and Production of Short Films & Audiovisual Works
For: PROD | SCRIPT · Covering: SHORT
Applications may be made by small and medium-sized companies (less than 250 persons), registered as production companies with the ICAA. Projects must be delivered on 35mm for theatrical exhibition and should be no more than 25 minutes long. Applications may be accepted for co-productions. The main criteria for receiving funding are artistic and cultural quality and viability of the project.

Catalan Finance Institute

www.icfinances.com
Generalitat de Catalunya, Gran Via de aes Cortes Catalanas 635, 08010 BARCELONA, Spain
T: +34 93 342 84 10 · F: +34 93 487 37 87
E: info@icfinances.com
The Institut Catala de Finances (ICF) aims to provide financial support for the establishment of new companies and the modernisation of existing ones, in order to increase the overall competitive edge of

different sectors of industry. The ICF is authorised to set up specific credit schemes and one such scheme is intended for Film and TV production. The distribution sector may also access loans but through the general scheme.

Credit Line for Investments in Audiovisual Production

www.icfinances.com · For: PROD · Covering: FEAT | TV | DOC | SHORT | ANI | YP

Applications may be made for production of features, documentaries, shorts, TV series and TV films, as well as for dubbing of TV series. Applicants must be audiovisual or film production companies and members of the Asociacion Catalana de Productores Cinematograficos y Audiovisuales (ACPCA) or of Barcelona Audiovisual Asociacion de Productores Catalanes. Applications should be made directly to the ICF.

Communidad de Aragón

portal.aragob.es/

Gobierno de Aragón, Dirección General de Cultura, Paseo María Agustín 36, 50004 Zaragoza, Sr. José de Uña, Spain

T: +34 976 45 60 50 · F: +34 976 45 60 51

E: portal@aragob.es

For the support of creative professionals in the audiovisual sector from Aragon.

Support for film and audiovisual production

portal.aragob.es/

Offers: up to €12,000 · For: PROD · Covering: SHORT | DOC

The fund supports non-commercial film and audiovisual production. Film professionals born in or resident of Aragón are eligible to apply. A short film or documentary should not be longer than 30 min.

Comunidad Autonóma de Extremadura

www.cedrama.com

Dirección General de Promoción Cultural, Comunidad Autonóma de Extremadura, C/ Almralejo 14, 2 planta06800 MÉRIDABadajozEspaña, Spain

T: +34 924 007174 · F: +34 924 007028

E: cedrama@clt.juntaex.es

Support for film and TV production

www.cedrama.com/audiovisuales/

Offers: up to €30,000 · For: PROD · Covering: TV | SHORT | DOC

The fund supports the development of cinema and the TV industry in the Autonomous Region of Extremadura.

The financial aid is for production of films running under 60 minutes. Applicants must be companies based in and registered in Extremadura. Projects must be of cultural interest to the region.

Conselleria de Cultura, Comunicacion Social e Turismo, Xunta de Galicia

www.xunta.es/conselle/cultura/

Direccion Xeral de Comunicacion Social e Audiovisual, Conselleria de Cultura, Comunicacion Social e Turismo, Xunta de Galicia, Edificion Administrativo San Caetano, Bloque 3ES — 15771 SANTIAGO, Spain

T: +34 981 54 54 00

E: cultura@xunta.es

The Department of Culture, Social Communication and Tourism provides support for film and video production in the Galician language with the aim of stimulating the growth of the sector in Galicia.

Funding

Applications are evaluated on the following grounds: potential and artistic quality (originality and creativity of the idea); feasibility of execution within the context of the local industry; and coherence of the budget and of the financing plan. Development must be intended to be finished for 1 December of the year of application.

Support for Development of Audiovisual Projects

For: DEV · Covering: FEAT | TV | MM | DOC

Applications may be made for support for development to include such activities as: scriptwriting, preparation of the budget, production schedule and the marketing/distribution plan. Support could also be used for preparation of an animation pilot film, archive research and software development. The projects/scripts must be in Galician. Total support cannot exceed 50% of the cost of the project.

Support for Audiovisual Production

For: PROD · Covering: FEAT | TV | MM | SHORT | Other | DOC | ANI | DIGI

Applicants must be producers or multimedia production companies, legally registered and having their headquarters in Galicia. Sometimes applications may be accepted from producers based outside of Galicia.Short films, documentaries, multimedia and experimental video projects may request support up to 60% of the total cost of the project. Feature films and telefilms may request up to 40% and TV series pilot programmes may request up to 50% of the total cost of the project.

Support for script development and audiovisual productions by new directors

For: SCRIPT | PROD · Covering: MM | SHORT | Other

The fund supports the production of creative work by new directors. A new director is defined as having, at the date of opening of applications, directed no more than three works. The amount of support awarded may not be more than 60% of the total cost of the project.

Subsidies to support marketing of productions in Galician

For: PROMO · Covering: FEAT | TV | MM | DOC

The fund is open to production companies registered in any European Union country with a permanent office in Galicia.

Subsidies for cinemas

For: CULT | EXBN · Covering: OTHER

The fund supports cinemas in rural areas or which, due to competition, have low profitability.

Consorcio Audiovisual de Galicia

www.consorcioaudiovisualdegalicia.org
rúa do horreo no. 61, 1° andar, 15702 Santiago de Compostela, Spain
T: +0034 981 545 098 · F: +34 981 545 847
E: info@consorcioaudiovisualdegalicia.org

Following the passing of a 1999 law to encourage film activity in the north-western region of Galicia, the Galician Ministry of Culture, Social Communication and Tourism, in conjunction with various other bodies and with local broadcaster RadioTV de Galicia, set up the Consorcio Audiovisual de Galicia in 2002. Its aim is to encourage both the production of individual films and the establishment of a local audiovisual industry. Production aid is available at various levels of the local government. The Consorcio is also the supervising body for the Galicia Film Commission. Details of funds at www.consorcioaudiovisualdegalicia.org/web/asp/index.asp?id_idioma=1&id_menu=18&int1=34

Departamento de Cultura y Turismo, Gobierno de Navarra

www.cfnavarra.es/cultura
Institución Príncipe de Viana, Gobierno de Navarra, Sección de Actividades Culturales, C/ Navarrería 39, 31001 PAMPLONA, Spain
T: +34 94 842 46 78 · F: +34 94 842 46 24
E: culturayturismo@cfnavarra.es

The organisation supports film and video production in the region of Navarra.

Support for short films

www.cfnavarra.es/cultura/cas/accion/ay-audio.htm
Offers: up to €60,000 · For: PROD · Covering: SHORT

The fund supports the production of short films on 35mm film and DV.

Support for feature length films

www.cfnavarra.es/cultura · For: DEV | PROD · Covering: FEAT | TV | DOC | ANI

The director should be from Navarra, or the subject matter related to the region, or the filming must be done in the region.

Diputación Provincial de Almería

www.dipalme.org
Palacio Provincial, C/ Navarro Rodrigo 17, 04001 Almería, Spain
T: +34 950 211 100 · F: +34 950 269 785
E: cultura@dipalme.org

The regional cultural support body for the province of Almeria in south-eastern Spain, whose remit covers all forms of cultural activities. The main objectives are the distribution, promotion, and training of film culture.

Support for audiovisual production in Almería

www.dipalme.org
Offers: up to €12,000 · For: PROD · Covering: FEAT | TV | SHORT | DOC | ANI | FFF | YP

Production companies or associations based in the province of Almeria may apply, as may persons living or born in the region.

Direccion de Creacion y Difusion Cultural, Gobierno Vasco

www.ej-gv.net
Departamento de Cutura, Viceconsejeria de Cultura Juventud y Deportes, Direccion de Creacion y Difusion Cultural, Donostia — San Sebastian, 1CP 01010 VITORIA — GASTEIZ, Spain
T: +34 945 01 94 66 · F: +34 945 01 95 35
E: difusion@ej-gv.es

The institution promotes cultural relations between the different historical areas of the Basque Autonomous Community and the wider area of Basque cultural influence. The fund encourages the development of film with the ultimate aim of supporting and strengthening audiovisual infrastructure, a vital element of the cultural future of the Region.

Support for Script Writing

Offers: up to €12,000 · For: SCRIPT · Covering: FEAT | SHORT | DOC | ANI | TV | Other_YP | FFF | WEB

Applications will be assessed by the Commission using the following scale: the quality of the script to be developed (50%); general interest of the project, in terms of commercial, thematic and geographic feasibility, and in particular with regard to whether the script is to be written in the Basque language (30%); track record of the author (20%). Three awards are made each year. Awards are repayable within two years after delivery of the script (which must take place within 9 months of the award).

Support for Film and TV Project Development

Offers: up to €21,000 · For: DEV · Covering: FEAT | TV | DOC | Other_FFF | ANI

Sometimes applications may be accepted for other TV formats which are considered of cultural interest, innovative, of particular commercial potential and those that are difficult to develop without support of this kind. Applicants must be companies registered in a Member State of the European Union. In cases of co-productions, the applying producer must have a participation of at least 30% of the budget, and in this case the support offered may not exceed 50% of the applying producers participation.

Support for Feature and Television Film Production

Offers: up to €180,000, for documentaries up to €60,000 · For: PROD · Covering: FEAT | TV | ANI | DOC

Application can be made for the production of feature films, TV movies, in the fiction, animation or documentary genres, in any languages. Applicants must be companies registered in a Member State of the European Union. For co-productions, the applying co-producer must contribute at least 30% of the budget. Total public support for the project may not exceed 50% of the budget. Repayment of the advance starts once the film has recovered 80% of the cost of production through commercial release or sales of rights.

Subsidies for dubbing and subtitling films in Euskera · For: DVD

The fund promotes the exhibition of commercial movies dubbed or subtitled in Euskera.

KIMUAK — Production, distribution and promotion support for short films

Offers: · For: PROMO | DIST | PROD · Covering: SHORT

The fund produces, promotes and distributes short films made within the Basque audiovisual community. Films should not be longer than 30 minutes and may be on either 16mm or 35mm.

NINIAK — Support for promotion

The fund supports production and distribution companies operating in the Basque region access audiovisual markets internationally.

Direccion General de Fomento y Promocion Cultural, Junta de Andalucia

www.juntadeandalucia.es/cultura/
Consejeria de Cultura, Junta de Andalucia, Direccion General de Fomento y Promocion Cultural, C/ Levies 17, ES — 41004 SEVILLA, Spain
T: +34 955 036 600 · F: +34 955 036 609
E: infofomento@ccul.junta-andalucia.es

The aim of the fund is to boost the perception of film and video as cultural and artistic works, by applying to them criteria such as quality and artistic value as well as that of their contribution to the cultural heritage of Andalucia. Furthermore the fund supports young and new Andalucian talents and operates, in a first phase, through development, and in a second, consolidation, to create a competent corporate and professional infrastructure in the region.

Funding

Applicants must be producers or production companies with at least two years stable activity. In the case of newly created companies, the track records of those involved in the company will be taken into account. Companies must be registered as producers with the ICAA and should be based in or operating principally in the Andalucia region. Projects are evaluated on the following basis: the quality, artistic value and originality of the project; coherence of the proposed budget for the project and the financing plan; contribution of the project to the enhancement of Andalucian audiovisual heritage; potential for national and international exploitation; track records of the cast and crew; track record and financial situation of the applying producer; impact of the project on employment in the sector in the region.

Support for Project Development

Offers: up to €30,000 for feature films, up to €6,000 for documentaries · For: DEV · Covering: FEAT | DOC

The fund gives development support to feature films, creative documentaries and documentary series made for TV. The total of support from public and private entities must in no case exceed 100% of the cost of development. Successful applicants have 16 months for development of the project.

Support for the Production of Audiovisual Works

Offers: up to €180,000 · For: PROD · Covering: FEAT | SHORT | DOC | FFF

Applications may also be made for the production of feature films to be directed by new directors (having directed no more than three films that have been commercially released). For feature films up to €180,000, first feature films up to €132,000, for documentaries up to €24,000, for short films up to €12,000.

Support for the Distribution of European Feature Films

Offers: up to €60,100 · For: DIST · Covering: FEAT

The fund aims to consolidate a stable and unified exhibition network and facilitate the exchange of audiovisual productions that reflect cultural diversity by supporting and promoting the diffusion of Andalucian works and creators.

Support for participation in festivals and film markets

www.juntadeandalucia.es/cultura/

The fund supports the participation of documentaries and features at various cultural events.

General Directorate of Language Policy of the Region of Catalunya

www6.gencat.net/llengcat/

Departament de la Prèsidencia, Secretaria de Política Lingüística, Passatge de la Banca, 08002 Barcelona, Spain

T: +34 93 567 10 00 · F: +34 93 567 10 01

E: splcinema.presidencia@gencat.net

Operating out of the central office for Catalunya, the organisation aims to support films and audiovisual work in Catalan language.

Support for Distribution of dubbed DVD's and VHS Cassettes

Offers: up to €75,000 · For: DIST · Covering: FEAT

The fund supports initiatives aimed at increasing the number of DVDs and VHS cassettes dubbed or subtitled in Catalan in videoclubs, libraries and other commercial circuits.

Subsidies for commercial films dubbed or subtitled in Catalan

Offers: up to €100,000 · For: EXBN

Company should sell at least 1,500 tickets per year. There is one annual application deadline.

Institut Catala des Industries Culturals

cultura.gencat.net/icic

Rambla de Santa Mònica, 8 (Palau Marc), ES-08002 Barcelona, Spain

T: +34 93 316 27 00 · F: +34 93 316 28 65

E: icic.cultura@gencat.net

An autonomous body within the Catalan Department of Culture, the Institut Catala des Industries Culturals is a general regulatory body overseeing the various cultural industries (including cinema) which operate in the Catalan languages in Catalunya.

Funding

Unless otherwise stated, all funds are open to production companies registered in Catalunya and to EU companies with a permanent office in Catalunya.

Subsidy to independent production companies for the production of TV films

Offers: up to €160,000 · For: PROD · Covering: TV

Producers must have raised financial guarantees for the whole project, including at least one broadcast agreement. The producer must invest a similar amount into the project as the sum awarded and must act as the executive producer of the film. The award may cover 20% of total cost for productions in Catalan. The award may cover 10% of total cost, with a maximum amount of €80,000 for productions in any other language.

Grants for promotion of Catalan films at international festivals

For: CULT | PROMO · Covering: FEAT | SHORT | DOC | YP

The fund gives grants for participation in and promotion of Catalan films at international festivals.

Subsidies for the production of documentaries by independent producers

Offers: up to €25,000 · For: PROD · Covering: DOC

The fund supports the production of TV documentaries by producers in Catalunya. Producers must have raised financial guarantees for the whole project, including at least one broadcast agreement. Producer must invest in a similar amount in the project as the sum awarded.

Exhibition for Catalan-language versions of feature films

Offers: €6,000 · For: EXBN · Covering: FEAT

The institute supports the exhibition of films in Catalan made by independent producers in Catalunya.

Subsidies for the production of short films

Offers: €6,000 · For: PROD · Covering: SHORT

Subsidies for development of film projects

Offers: up to €30,000 · For: DEV · Covering: FEAT

Subsidies for the creation of scripts in Catalan

For: SCRIPT

Any EU national resident in Catalunya is eligible to apply. Ten awards will be made per year.

Production of feature films in Catalan by new directors

Offers: up to €120,000 · For: PROD · Covering: FEAT | DOC | ANI | FFF

The fund gives out subsidies for the production of feature films in Catalan by new directors and with clear artistic and cultural content. For purposes of this programme, 'new director' means one who has directed no more than two feature films which have been released to the public. Films of cultural or artistic merit will also be taken into consideration.

Distribution of Catalan-language versions of feature films

Offers: up to €12,000 · For: DIST · Covering: FEAT

The fund gives out subsidies to film distribution companies for the distribution of Catalan language versions of films produced by independent producers based in Catalunya.

Support for audiovisual education and training

Offers: €6,000 · For: EDU · Covering: OTHER

The institute supports education and further training in the audiovisual field by students and professionals.

Subsidies for animation development

Offers: up to €50,000 · For: DEV · Covering: ANI

The fund subsidises the development of animated series for TV by independent producers. Animated series should be between 13 and 26 episodes, 26 minutes in duration. Feature film projects are also eligible.

Subsidies for production, distribution and exhibition of IMAX films

Offers: up to €160,000 · For: PROD | DIST | EXBN · Covering: FEAT | DOC | ANI

In the case of Catalan-language films, support for distribution will represent 5-17% of the producer's investment.

Premier and production of feature films in Catalan as original language · For: PROD · Covering: FEAT

The institute gives funding for the production of feature films made in the Catalan language which are also being premiered in Catalunya.

Instituto Valenciano de Cinematografia Ricardo Munoz Suay

www.ivac-lafilmoteca.es

Plaza del Ayuntamiento 17, ES — 46002 VALENCIA, Spain

T: +34 96 35 39 300 · F: +34 96 35 39 330

E: ivac-lafilmoteca_inf@gva.es

The aim of the Valencian Institute of Cinematography is to manage and develop the cultural policy of the Autonomous Community of Valencia, in the domains of acquisition, preservation, restoration.

Support for Audiovisual Production

For: PROD · Covering: FEAT | DOC | SHORT | TV

For features films the limit is 50% of the investment of the Valencian producer. There is no limit for the other types of productions (short, doc, etc.). Applications will be accepted from audiovisual production companies registered with the Autonomous Community of Valencia Register of Audiovisual Companies.

Support for Scriptwriting for Feature-Length Films

For: SCRIPT · Covering: FEAT

The fund encourages scriptwriting for feature-length films by means of financial awards intended to stimulate such activity. Applications will be accepted from Valencian authors wishing to develop/write scripts for feature length films. Projects must be for original scripts and not adaptations.

Bursaries for training

For: EDU · Covering: OTHER

The fund facilitates participation by audiovisual sector professionals in both national and international training programmes designed to improve and increase their knowledge of the field. Applicants must be resident in the Autonomous Community of Valencia. Applicants must propose to undertake a course of study of particular interest in the audiovisual domain.

Grants for audiovisual activities

For: CULT · Covering: OTHER

The institute supports audiovisual activities such as exhibitions and festivals organised by city councils or not-for-profit organisations in Valencia.

Junta de Castilla-La Mancha

www.jccm.es

Consejería de Cultura, DG de Promoción Cultural, Servicio de Audiovisual y Publicaciones, Trinidad 8, 45071 Toledo, Spain

T: +34 925 26 74 00

E: jselgas@jccm.es

The aim of the institute is to support local audiovisual production and creativity, encourage film making in the region of Catilla-La Mancha and contribute to the development of film making and its cultural importance.

Support for audiovisual production

sacm.jccm.es/Siaci/descripcion. asp?CodigoServicio=IBV

Offers: up to €90,000 · For: PROD | PROMO | CULT · Covering: FEAT | SHORT | Other_FFF

The fund supports the production of short and feature films of special interest to the people and region of Castilla-La Mancha. This programme also includes support for festivals and 'film weeks.' Up to €12,000 for short films and up to €90,000 for feature films is available.

Projection of films on VHS/DVD

sacm.jccm.es/Siaci/descripcion. asp?CodigoServicio=IMP · For: DVD_EXBN · Covering: FEAT

The fund supports exhibition of films from VHS and DVD in towns and villages without a commercial cinema. The region should be without a commercial cinema and have fewer than 20,000 inhabitants.

SWEDEN

Svenska Filminstitut

www.sfi.se

Box 271 26, SE-102 52, Stockholm, Sweden

T: +46 8 665 11 00 · F: +46 8 666 37 60

E: info@sfi.se

The aims of the Swedish Film Institute include the promotion, support and development of film in its cultural and broader contexts, the allocation of grants for the production, distribution and public screening of Swedish films at home, and the promotion for Swedish cinema at international level. The Institute is also extensively involved in the preservation and promotion of Sweden's cinematic heritage. The Institute is financed largely by grants from the Swedish government and from Sweden's cinema owners who contribute a levy of 10% of their gross ticket sales.

Funding

The funds are used for international cooperation, production support for Swedish film, support for the distribution and screening of film throughout the country and support for international launches of Swedish film.

Fees for international cooperation

www.sfi.se/sfi/IMAGES/_SFI_PDF/RAPPORTER%2 0OCH%20DOKUMENT/THE%202006%20FILM%20 AGREEMENT%20.PDF

Part of the funds accruing to the Institute each financial year shall be used for fees for cooperation in Eurimages and the Nordic Film and TV Fund and also for Swedish coordination measures in connection with the MEDIA Programme. The size of these fees and measures are determined within the framework of international cooperation.

Support for distribution and exhibition

www.sfi.se/sfi/IMAGES/_SFI_PDF/RAPPORTER%2 0OCH%20DOKUMENT/THE%202006%20FILM%20 AGREEMENT%20.PDF

Offers: up to SEK 500,000 · For: DIST · Covering: FEAT | DOC | ANI

The fund is for film launch support, support for parallel distribution and cinema support. Following a needs assessment, film launch support shall be provided to distributors of Swedish feature films in an amount equal to the distributor's own financial investment, but no more than SEK 500 000. The amount of the support shall be determined by the Board prior to the film's release.

Production support for Swedish film

www.sfi.se/sfi/IMAGES/_SFI_PDF/RAPPORTER% 20OCH%20DOKUMENT/THE%202006%20FILM% 20AGREEMENT%20.PDF · For: PROD · Covering: FEAT | SHORT | DOC | YP

Production support for Swedish films shall consist in form of audience-related support, advance support, development support and support for regional production centres.

Support for international launches of Swedish film

www.sfi.se/omsfi/ostod/ostsvev/mostsvev.htm · For: DIST

After settlement for fees for international cooperation and for audience-related support, at least 2 per cent of the funds accruing to the Institute in a financial year shall be used for support to producers and distributors for international launches of new Swedish film.

Support for measures to combat the unauthorised use of films in all screening formats

www.sfi.se/omsfi/ostod/ostbarn/mostbarn.htm

After settlement for fees for international cooperation and for audience-related support, at least 2% of the funds accruing to the Institute in a financial year shall be used for support for measures to combat the unauthorised use of films in all screening formats. This form of support shall be distributed by the film industry and the TV companies after consultation with the Institute.

Development Support

For: DEV | EDU | BIZ-DEV

Development support shall consist of project-based support for scriptwriters, producers and directors, 'greenhouse grants' to young filmmakers, support for further professional training for established filmmakers and business support for independent producers. In distributing this support particular attention shall be given to the need for increased gender equality in the area of film. Business support paid to an independent producer may not exceed SEK 1 million per year.

Cinema Support

For: EXBN

Support for the exhibition of Swedish films to the general public, for the upgrading of cinemas and for organisers of cinematic performances that are not liable to value-added tax. Where applicable, the support shall be technology-neutral in terms of whether analogue or digital technology is used. In the distribution of funds special consideration shall be given to cinemas in small and medium sized communities.

Swedish Film Commission

www.swedenfilmcommission.com

PO Box 27183,, S-102 52 Stockholm, Sweden
T: +46 8 665 11 00 · F: +46 8 666 37 48
E: info@swedenfilmcommission.com

Sweden Film Commission is the national commission marketing Sweden as a location for shooting commercials, feature films and TV. The unit co-ordinates the regional film commissions and facilitates contacts with the local technical infrastructure. Sweden Film Commission is a first stop for information, support, and local assistance.

Film i Dalarna

www.filmidalarna.se/
Villavägen 3, S-79137 Falun, Sweden
T: +46 023 26 2 75 · F: .+46 023 26 279
E: info@filmidalarna.se

The aim is to stimulate the production of films and video in the Falun region with an annual budget of €400,000.

Film i Skåne

www.filmiskane.se
Stortorget 27 1 tr, SE- 211 34 Malmö, Sweden
T: +46 40-30 91 60 · F: +46 40-30 91 65
E: info@filmiskane.nu

Film i Skåne is a regional centre for film and video with the task of promoting all aspects of film. It aims to create an interested and demanding audience for film in the region through film education programmes. The centre creates meeting places, workshops, festivals and marketplaces to create new distribution opportunities for filmmakers. It supports co-production of short, documentary and feature films with the aim of attracting capital expenditure in the region that help develop the audiovisual infrastructor in Skåne.

Support for Production

www.filmiskane.se/ · For: PROD · Covering: FEAT | SHORT | DOC

The fund supports the co-production of short, documentary and feature films in the region. Production companies are eligible to apply. Non-Swedish companies must apply in partnership with a Swedish partner. Applicants must spend twice the amount of Film i Skane's loan in the region. Film i Skane's support is in the form of a co-production investment.

Film i Väst

www.filmivast.se/
Box 134, 46123 TROLLHÄTTAN, Växel 0520-49 09 00, Sweden
T: +46 520 49 09 00 · F: +46 520 49 09 01
E: info@filmivast.se

The best known area of Film i Väst's activity is the support of feature films. Film i Väst also works to support local film activity in the development of short and documentary film, film distribution in Sweden, and in the advancement of young filmmakers in the region. Strategic initiatives in education for filmmakers and support for developing regional film festivals and film events are other important commitments.

Support for production and development
Offers: Up to €326,000 or 30% · For: PROD | DEV ·
Covering: FEAT | SHORT | DOC | YP | ANI
In order to qualify for co-production finance from FiV
a production must be chiefly localised in the 'four
towns' region comprising the local authorities of
Lysekil, Trollhättan, Vänersborg and Uddevalla. The
main producer, or a significant co-production partner,
must have an established, permanently manned office
in one of these regions have a well-developed business
plan for future operations in the region. Co-production
finance is given to film productions considered to have
artistic quality and public appeal. The project must be
considered to have a significant positive impact on
the film industry's infrastructure and employment in
the region. Films with significant cultural links to the
Västra Götaland Region, or films for which most of the
production expenditure occurs in the region, will be
given priority. Films for children and young people will
be given priority.

Filmpool Nord

www.fpn.se
Kronan A 2, S-974 42 Luleå, Sweden
T: +46 920 43 4000 · F: +46 920 43 4079
E: info@fpn.se
The main objective of Filmpool Nord is to create a
strong infrastructure that makes it possible for the
film and multimedia industry in the Norrbotten region
to develop. Among other services, Filmpool Nord can
provide co-production financing for features, shorts,
documentary and TV productions. It offers studio
facilities, location guides, film service companies and
professional film workers. Filmpool Nord is responsible
for the distribution of films to festivals, institutions and
events and also offers special programmes for young
filmmakers. The annual budget is €3.3m.

Co-production financing
www.fpn.se/site/page.asp?id=1019 · For: PROD ·
Covering: FEAT | SHORT | DOC | TV

**Distribution of films to festivals, institutions
and events & Young filmmakers' programmes**
www.fpn.se/site/page.asp?id=1001

Göteborg Film Festival Filmfund

www.filmfestival.org/
Olof Palmes plats, S-413 04 Göteborg, Sweden
T: +46 31 339 30 00
E: filmfund@filmfestival.org
Göteborg Film Festival Film Fund supports film
production in the developing countries and aims
to strengthen the opportunities available to the

filmmakers of the world.

Gothenburg Film Festival Filmfund
www.filmfestival.org
Offers: €10,000 — €40,000 · For: EDU | POST | DEV
· Covering: FEAT | DOC | SHORT
Projects must be original and firmly rooted in the
culture of the country of the filmmaker. Projects must
contribute to the development of the local film industry
and local film-making skills. Applicants for the GFFF
must have other supporting partners and must be able
to clearly indicate that they are able to secure all the
necessary remaining financial assistance. GFFF support
will be awarded only when the rest of the financial
support has been secured. Applications must be
submitted in English.

SWITZERLAND

Canton of Aargau Film support

www.ag.ch/bks/de/pub/kultur.htm
Departement Bildung, Kultur und Sport, Abteilung
Kultur, Bachstrasse 15, 5001 Aarau, Switzerland
T: +41 62 835 23 00 · F: +41 62 835 23 49
E: ak@ag.ch
The Canton of Aargau Film supports and promotes film
projects of all genres (including co-productions) with a
thematic or biographical tie to the Canton Argovia.

Production and screenplay support
Offers: up to CHF 50,000/ €33,400 · For: PROD ·
Covering: FEAT | TV | MM | SHORT | DOC | ANI | FFF
| YP | Other
The fund supports screenplay and production
contributions of film projects of all genres and co-
productions with a thematic or biographical tie to the
Canton Argovia.

Canton of Bern Film support

www.erz.be.ch/site/index/kultur/kulturfoerderung.
htm
Amt für Kultur (AK), Sulgeneckstr. 70, 3005 Bern,
Switzerland
T: +41 31 633 85 85 · F: +41 31 633 83 55
E: ak@erz.be.ch
The institute for culture supports the work of
filmmakers of Canton Bern who engage with an artistic
and professional project that has some relevance to
Canton Bern.

Project development and Production support

www.erz.be.ch/site/index/kultur/kulturfoerderung/
kulturfoerderung-kultursparten/kulturfoerderung-
sparten-film.htm
Offers: up to €65,000 · For: PROD · Covering: FEAT
| DOC | FFF
Only films destined for theatrical distribution or for
festivals, and in some instances graduation films, will be
considered.

Canton of Lucerne Film support

www.kultur.lu.ch/
Bildungs- und Kulturdepartement, Kultur- und
Jugförderung, Bahnhofstrasse 18, CH — 6002
Luzern, Switzerland
T: +41 41 228 52 06 · F: +41 41 210 05 73
E: kultur@lu.ch
The Canton of Lucerne Film promotes film projects
of all genres and co-productions with a thematic or
biographical tie to Lucerne.

Support for production and screenplays

www.kultur.lu.ch/index/kulturfoerderung/film.htm
Only films destined for theatrical distribution or for
festivals, and in some instances graduation films, will be
considered. There are four deadlines per year.

Canton of Solothurn Film Support

www.so.ch/de/pub/departemente/dbk/aks.htm
Kantonales Kuratorium für Kulturförderung, (neue
Anschrift ab 8.4.05), Kultur Schloss Waldegg,
Schloss Waldegg 1, 4532 Feldbrunnen-St.Niklaus,
Switzerland
T: +41 32 624 49 49 · F: +41 32 624 49 50
E: aks@dbk.so.ch
The office for culture and sport was established in
1991 and reorganised in 2001. The promotion and
support of contemporary art, cultural activities and
the preservation of traditional culture in the region is
central for the office.

Support for filmmaking

www.so.ch/de/pub/departemente/dbk/aks/
kunstundkultur.htm
Offers: up to €67,000 · For: SCRIPT | PROD | POST
· Covering: FEAT | TV | MM | SHORT | Other | DOC |
ANI | FFF | YP
The fund supports screenplay, production, post-
production, and release contributions for film projects
of all genres, including co-productions with a thematic
or biographical tie to Solothurn. The Fund's maximum
contribution is CHF 100,000 / €67,000 up to 10% of
the budget.

Canton Ticino film support

www.ti.ch/decs/dc/
Divisione della cultura e degli studi universitari, viale
S. Franscini 30a, 6501 BELLINZONA, Segreteria
generale, Switzerland
T: +41 91 814 13 00 · F: +41 91 814 13 09
E: decs-dc@ti.ch

Production support

www.ti.ch/decs/dc/
Offers: up to €80,000 · For: PROD · Covering: FEAT
| TV | MM | SHORT | DOC | ANI | FFF | YP
The fund supports production contributions for
theatrical projects of all genres, including co-
productions with a thematic or biographical tie to
Tessin.

Canton-City of Basel Film Support

www.baselkultur.ch
Erziehungsdepartement, Kanton Basel-Stadt, Ressort
Kultur, Fachauschuss Audivison & Multimedia,
Leimenstr. 1, 4001 Basel, Switzerland
T: +41 61 267 84 13 · F: +41 61 267 68 42
E: kultur@bs.ch
The Film Fund supports contemporary, culturally,
thematically and aesthetically relevant films, videos,
photographs and media art. Applicants should have
lived in Canton Basel for at least a year while cultural
institutions should be based in the Canton Basel or
Basel region. Alternatively, foreign applicants with
projects that have a strong relevancy to the Cantons
will be considered. The projects should be made in the
region.

Support for production and screenplays

For: PROD · Covering: FEAT | DOC | ANI | Other_
MM | SHORT | YP
The fund supports screenplays and productions for all
types of films (except TV films) which have a thematic
or biographical relation with Basel.

City of Bern Film Commission

www.bern.ch/stadtverwaltung/prd/kultur/
foerderung
Abteilung Kulturelles, Peter Schranz,
Gerechtigkeitsgasse 79, 3011 Bern, Switzerland
T: +41 31 321 72 24 · F: +41 31 321 72 26
E: peter.schranz@bern.ch
The Commission supports screenplay, production and
promotion contributions for film projects of all genres
and co-productions with a thematic or biographical tie
to Bern.

Production support

www.bern.ch/stadtverwaltung/prd/kultur/
foerderung
Offers: up to CHF 200,000 · **For:** PROD · **Covering:**
FEAT | DOC | ANI | YP
Applications can be made four times a year. The film
must be of interest to the region. The main criteria are
professionalism, quality, innovation, relevance to the
region, coherence and feedback.

Scriptwriting and Project Development support

Offers: up to CHF 200,000 · **For:** SCRIPT | DEV ·
Covering: FEAT | DOC | ANI | YP
Applications can be made four times a year. The film
must be of interest to the region. The main criteria are
professionalism, quality, innovation, relevance to the
region, coherence and feedback.

City of Geneva Film Support

www.ville-ge.ch/culture
Ville de Genève, Division Art et Culture, Route de
Malagnou 19, case postale 9, 1211 Genève 17,
Switzerland
T: +41 22 418 65 00 · F: +41 22 418 65 01
E: patrice.mugny@dac.ville-ge.ch
The City of Geneva Film support promotes screenplay,
production and distribution of film projects, including
co-productions with a thematic or biographical tie to
Geneva.

Production and screenplay support

Offers: up to CHF 1.500,000 · **For:** PROD ·
Covering: FEAT | SHORT | DOC
The fund supports productions and feature screenplays
that have a subject relevant to the region of Geneva.

Federal Office of Culture — Film Section

www.bak.admin.ch/bak/
Bundesamt für Kultur, Office fédéral de la culture,
Ufficio Federale della Cultura, Hallwylstrasse 15, CH-
3003 Bern, Switzerland
T: +41 31 322 92 71 · F: +41 31 322 92 73
E: cinema.film@bak.admin.ch
The promotion of film through support of independent
film productions and distribution activities is a
key priority for the Federal Office of Culture. The
organisation's budget in 2005 was €21m.

Project development

For: DEV · **Covering:** FEAT | TV | SHORT | DOC | ANI
| FFF | YP
Projects will be considered under conditions of:
independent and artistic quality; creative and economic
independence; feasibility of the project; whether a
particular audience is addressed; whether the project
contributes to cultural-political aspects of diversity,
exchange and collaboration. Projects by Swiss
filmmakers that strengthen the film industry of the
country are particularly favoured.

Production

For: PROD · **Covering:** FEAT | TV | SHORT | DOC |
ANI | FFF | YP
Production support for films of all genres can be
obtained either through a selective funding process
or automatic funding conditional on former success.
In both cases Independent production companies are
eligible to apply.

Distribution, Sales and Exhibition

For: DIST | EXBN · **Covering:** FEAT | SHORT | DOC |
ANI | FFF | YP
To promote the distribution of high quality independent
Swiss films.

Funding linked to box office success

www.succes-cinema.ch · **For:** EXBN · **Covering:**
FEAT | DOC | ANI
The fund aims to strengthen the presence of Swiss films
in national cinemas and enables more continuity for the
national film industry of the basis of films which have
succeeded at the box office (up to 100,000 cinema
tickets). Films should be at least 60 minutes.

Fondation Vaudoise pour le Cinéma

www.vaudfilm.ch
Rue Charles-Monnard 6, 1003 Lausanne, Switzerland
T: +41 21 351 05 11 · F: +41 21 351 05 13
E: info@vaudfilm.ch
The FVC encourages the culture of film in the Canton
of Vaud. With private and public funds it supports the
production and distribution of cinematography and
audiovisuals.

Selective aid for small projects

Offers: up to €14,000 or 50% · **For:** PROD ·
Covering: FEAT | SHORT | DOC | ANI
The fund covers 50% of the production costs and aims
to support in particular young talents. The production
should be of short or medium length.

Fonds Regio Films

www.regiofilms.ch/
rue des Vieux-Grenadiers 11, CH — 1205 Genève,
Switzerland
T: +41 22 800 2024 · F: +41 22 800 2020
E: contact@regiofilms.ch
To support independent production in the cantons of
Geneva, Vaud and Fribourg and the cities of Geneva
and Lausanne.

Fonds Regio Films
Offers: up to €100,000 · For: PROD · Covering:
FEAT | DOC | ANI | SHORT
The funds supports independent audiovisual production
in the partner regions. Independent producers or
producer/directors living in one of the partner regions
(Geneva, Vaud, Lausanne or Fribourg), or producers of
a project on which the director is living in one of these
regions, are eligible.

Kulturfonds Suissimage

www.suissimage.ch
Kulturfonds SUISSIMAGE, Neuengasse 23, Postfach,
CH — 3001 Bern, Switzerland
T: +41 31 313 36 36 · F: +41 31 313 36 37
E: mail@suissimage.ch
The SUISSIMAGE cultural fund provides support for
long films (feature and documentary) destined for
theatrical distribution, on the basis of an advance on
receipts.

Funding
The fund is open to Swiss nationals, or producers who
have been active in Switzerland for at least three years.
The production company must be based in Switerland.
In the case of official co-productions with foreign
companies, the executive producer must be Swiss and
the share of Swiss partners at least 30%. Only films with
a duration of 60 minutes or more will be considered.
There are five application deadlines per year.

Support programme for transfer of Swiss films to DVD
Offers: up to €10,000 · For: DVD · Covering: FEAT
To support the producers or rights owners of Swiss films
in releasing their films on DVD.

Funding for Swiss films (fiction and documentaries) in the form of advance on receipts
Offers: up to €200,000 · For: PROD | SCRIPT ·
Covering: FEAT | DOC
Support the production of Swiss films.

Visions sud est

www.visionssudest.ch
Visions sud est, case postale 407, CH-5430
Wettingen 1, Switzerland
T: +41 56 426 15 33
E: info@visionssudest.ch
The Fund supports film productions from Africa,
Asia, Latin America and Eastern Europe and assures
screening in Switzerland and worldwide promotion. All
the projects, for which a financial support is requested,
must be proposed exclusively by a company based in a
country from the South (Africa, Latin America and Asia)
or from Eastern Europe and regularly producing in these
countries. Therefore, the main part of the project must
be shot in these countries and in the local or regional
language, except in exceptional circumstances.

Production support
Offers: up to €31,000 for feature films, up to
€18,600 for documentaries · For: PROD · Covering:
FEAT | DOC
In granting financial support to the production of a
feature project, Visions Sud-Est hopes to support the
approach of a small production or, in the case of a
bigger budget, improve the conditions of production.
All the projects, for which a financial support is
requested, must be proposed exclusively by a company
based in a country from the South (Africa, Latin
America and Asia) or from Eastern Europe and regularly
producing in these countries. Therefore, the main part
of the project must be shot in these countries and in
the local or regional language, except in exceptional
circumstances. There are two application deadlines per
year.

Post production support
www.visionssudest.ch/?index&language=en
Offers: up to €12,000 · For: POST · Covering: FEAT
| DOC
The fund supports the completion of a film on the basis
of a first cut and a completion concept. There are two
application deadlines per year.

Zürrich Film Foundation

www3.stzh.ch/internet/zuerichkultur/home/
foerderung/home/redirect_fi/film/home/
filmstiftung.html
Neugasse 10, 8005 Zürich, Switzerland
T: +41 43 960 35 35 · F: +41 43 960 35 39
E: info@filmstiftung.ch
The Fund supports the promotion of professional film
making in Canton Zürich, through financial support of
scriptwriting, project development and evaluation of
audiovisual projects. The fund takes the form of a grant,

loan or a conditionally repayable loan.

Project development
Offers: up to €40,000 · For: DEV · Covering: FEAT | DOC
Project development support may be given to applications resident in the Canton of Zürich. The fund is not available for TV productions and short films.

Production support 1
www.stadt-zuerich.ch/internet/zuerichkultur/home/foerderung/home/redirect_fi/film/home.html
Offers: up to €500,000 · For: PROD · Covering: FEAT | DOC | ANI | Other_TV
The fund supports productions that are aiming for theatrical release and independently produced TV films. 150% of the funding has to be spent in the canton of Zürich.

Production Support 2
For: PROD · Covering: FFF
The programme supports funding for new directors and graduation films made by students registered in recognised film programmes.

Film commission

Tenerife Film Commission
www.tenerifefilm.com
Sociedad de Promoci Exterior de Tenerife (SPET), C/ Aurea Diaz Flores, s/n, 38005 Santa Cruz de Tenerife, Tenerife
T: +34 922 237871 · F: +34 922 237872
E: film@webtenerife.com

TRINIDAD & TOBAGO

Trinidad & Tobago Film Commission
filmtnt.com/
Level 1, Maritime Plaza, Barataria, Trinidad, Trinidad & Tobago, Trinidad and Tobago
T: 868 675 7034 ext 222 · F: 868 675-7338
E: cfoderingham@tidco.co.tt
Film Incentives have been introduced offering between 12.5% to 30% rebates for projects shot on location.

UNITED KINGDOM

UK Film Council
www.ukfilmcouncil.org.uk
10 Little Portland Street, London, W1W 7JG, UK
T: 020 7861 7861 · F: 020 7861 7862
E: info@ukfilmcouncil.org.uk
The UK Film Council is the Government-backed strategic agency for film in the UK. Its main aim is to stimulate a competitive, successful and vibrant UK film industry and culture, and to promote the widest possible enjoyment and understanding of cinema throughout the nations and regions of the UK.
The UK Film Council distributes Government grant-in-aid and National Lottery money in film development and production; training; international development and export promotion; distribution and exhibition; and education. The agency's mission is to deliver lasting benefits to the industry and the public alike through:

CREATIVITY — encouraging the development of new talent, skills, and creative and technological innovation in UK film and assisting new and established filmmakers to produce successful and distinctive British films;
ENTERPRISE – supporting the creation and growth of sustainable businesses in the film sector, providing access to finance and helping the UK film industry compete successfully in the domestic and global marketplace;
IMAGINATION — promoting education and an appreciation and enjoyment of cinema by giving UK audiences access to the widest range of UK and international cinema, and by supporting film culture and heritage.

STRATEGIC PRINCIPLES
Advocacy and leadership. To lead on issues where a single powerful voice reflecting properly considered views is most effective.
Partnership. To work in partnership with government, industry and the private, public and voluntary sectors in the UK and overseas.
Economy. To work with the grain of the market to stimulate competitiveness and enterprise, and to deliver sustainable development and best value.
Diversity and inclusion. To promote social inclusion and celebrate diversity so that every citizen in the nations and regions of the UK has access to film culture and so barriers to working in the industry are reduced.
Excellence and innovation. To encourage excellence and innovation particularly through the use of new digital technologies.
Openness, transparency and accessibility. To be open, transparent and accessible to stakeholders, industry and public alike.

THE BOARD

Funding

· **The Development Fund** with £12 million over three years to support the development of a stream of high quality, innovative and commercially attractive screenplays. This fund is the largest of its type in Europe.

· **The Premiere Fund** with £24 million over three years to facilitate the production of popular, more mainstream films.

· **The New Cinema Fund** with £15 million over three years to back radical and innovative filmmakers, especially new talent, and to explore new electronic production technologies. Its short film schemes have produced over 450 films.

· **The Prints and Advertising Fund** of £6 million over three years to support the distribution of a broader range of films to audiences across the UK.

· **The Digital Screen Network** is a world first providing over £11 million to equip around 240 screens in over 210 cinemas (approximately 1 in 4 cinemas) with state of the art digital projection equipment.

· **International** – the UK Film Council's International department promotes UK film exports; develops international relations and supports UK production, while the British Film Commission encourages international productions from outside the UK to use Britain's production and facilities.

· **Diversity** — The UK Film Council's diversity strategy aims to help the sector to: achieve a more diverse workforce behind and in front of the camera, across the film sector value chain; enable all groups within our society to participate in and enjoy film culture as audiences and learners; and ensure that equality and diversity commitments are fully integrated into every aspect of all core UK Film Council activities.

In addition the UK Film Council distributes National Lottery and grand in aid funds to:

· **First Light** — a £1.1 million a year Lottery funded digital short filmmaking scheme aimed at helping young people to gain first hand experience of filmmaking.

· **Skillset** — the first ever comprehensive training strategy for the British film industry was launched in September 2003. A package of measures is being rolled out backed by an investment of around £50 million (including £6.5 million of National Lottery funding per year)over the next five years which as a whole aim to build a bigger and better future for the film industry in the UK.

· **bfi** — The British Film Institute (bfi) receives £16.5 million (grant-in-aid) per year from the UK Film Council and plays a key role in achieving the UK Film Council's goals and fostering public appreciation of film through improved access to cinema, film heritage and educational provision.

· **Regional Screen Agencies** — £7.9 million a year is allocated to regional film bodies across England, all working to create a clear film strategy for each English region and provide cash support for production, screen commissions, cinema exhibition, training, archives and education.

Premiere Fund

www.ukfilmcouncil.org.uk/filmmaking/funding/features/premierefund/

Offers: Up to 35% of budget · For: PROD · Covering: FEAT | ANI

With £8m available each year, the Premiere Fund is the UK's biggest public fund, focusing on projects with solid commercial potential. Sally Caplan took over from Robert Jones as fund helmer in early 2006. Investments include Chris Smith's *Creep* and *Severance*, Gary Chapman's *Valiant*, Robert Altman's *Gosford Park*, Christine Jeffs's *Sylvia*, Mike Leigh's *Vera Drake*, the Oscar winning *The Constant Gardener*, Chris Noonan's *Miss Potter*, Roger Michell's *Venus*, Julian Jarrold's *Becoming Jane*, Anand Tucker's *And When Did You Last See Your Father?*, *Magicians* from Peep Show creators Sam Bain and Jesse Armstrong and Gillian Armstrong's *Death Defying Acts*.

Given that the Premiere Fund is a major funded in film projects, the fund tends to be favoured by established companies which have a track record and industry relationships in place, key ingredients for securing deals which offer a return for investors.

New Cinema Fund — Feature Films

www.ukfilmcouncil.org.uk/filmmaking/funding/features/ncf/

Offers: Between 15% and 50% of the feature film's budget. · For: PROD · Covering: FEAT | DOC | ANI

Since 2000, with a £5m annual budget, the New Cinema Fund has supported over 50 films including Andrea Arnold's *Red Road* (Jury Prize Cannes 2006; The Carl Foreman Award for special achievement by a British director in their first feature BAFTA 2007), Ken Loach's *The Wind that Shakes the Barley* (Palme D'Or Cannes 2006), Kevin Macdonald's *Touching the Void* (BAFTA Best British Film 2004), Peter Mullan's *The Magdalene Sisters* (Golden Lion Award, Venice International Film Festival 2002), Saul Dibb's *Bullet Boy*, Paul Andrew Williams' *London to Brighton* (Grand Prix Winner,

Dinard 2006), Louise Osmand and Jerry Rothwell's *Deep Water*, Sarah Gavron's *Brick Lane* and Shane Meadows' *This is England* (Best British Independent Film BIFA 2006). The New Cinema Fund also funds a number of short filmmaking schemes including Cinema Extreme with Film4 and the Digital Shorts programmes with the national and regional screen agenices. Other NCF initiatives include the Warp X Low Budget Feature Film scheme partnerhed with Film4, EM Media and Screen Yorkshire and Moving Image Initiative (MII), run in conjunction with Arts Council England.

In September 2006 Lenny Crooks took over from Paul Trijbits as fund head. The New Cinema Fund seeks:
 · fresh original and dynamic work in any style or genre;
 · diverse innovative and cutting-edge filmmaking talent;
 · films from across the UK and/or from black, Asian and other ethnic minority filmmakers;
 · films that utilise the benefits offered by digital technology in the making and showing of films;
 · films that have secured or are in the advanced stages of securing the services of a director and principal cast;
 · films that have contractually secured or in our opinion have the potential to secure a UK theatrical release or a high profile digital release with a distributor, or with a web broadcaster acceptable to the New Cinema Fund Funding typically takes the form of an equity investment. Films must have a fully developed script in place, be intended for — and likely to gain — theatrical release and be British qualifying. Documentaries are funded — with seven to date — but must be suited for cinemas as opposed to TV.

New Cinema Fund — Pilots

www.ukfilmcouncil.org.uk/filmmaking/funding/features/ncf/ncfpilot/
Offers: Up to £10,000. · For: DEV
The New Cinema Fund will invest in pilot projects to establish the potential of a project that is already in development with the Fund or the Development Fund.

Development Fund — Single Projects — Seed Funding

www.ukfilmcouncil.org.uk/filmmaking/funding/features/development/devsnglwhat/
Offers: Not stated · For: SCRIPT · Covering: FEAT | DOC | ANI
The Development Fund has an annual budget of £4m. As of October 2006, the fund had invested £8.84 million in 224 'single' film projects, £7.4 million in 176 projects developed via 2001/04 slate partner deals and £2.5 million in 6 slate partnerships for 2005/08.
The aim of the Development Fund is to develop high quality scripts. Seed funding will cover: writer's fees, research fees, overhead costs of producer, option rights,

producer fees, producer's legal costs, script editor's fees, executive producer/mentor, financial/presentation 'package', and training courses. In April 2007, Tanya Seghatchian replaced Jenny Borgars who has headed the fund since September 2000.

Development Fund — Single Projects — Partnered Development

www.ukfilmcouncil.org.uk/filmmaking/funding/features/development/devsnglwhat/
Offers: Up to 75% of 'hard' costs · For: SCRIPT · Covering: FEAT | DOC | ANI
As with seed funding but for producers who have a financial partner on board.

Development Fund — Single Projects — Pre Production

www.ukfilmcouncil.org.uk/filmmaking/funding/features/development/devsnglwhat/
Offers: Up to 50% · For: DEV · Covering: FEAT | ANI
Funding for projects at a more advance stage of development will be considered as long as interest from investors is established. Pre-pre production funding will cover: writer's fees for polish only, location survey/recce, casting, preparation of production budget, preparation of production schedule.

Development Fund — Slate Projects

www.ukfilmcouncil.org.uk/filmmaking/funding/features/development/devsnglwhat/
Offers: Between £250,000 and £500,000 per year up to three years. · For: SLATE | DEV | SCRIPT · Covering: FEAT | ANI
Slate funding offers substantial resources to up to eight companies to develop a slate of projects each year. The fund has three facets to it. The first, called Working Capital Facility, is an optional element of slate funding. It allows for up to 20% of the annual slate fund (the total amount including the UKFC's investment and the partnership investment) to be channelled towards the company's overhead costs. The second element Third Party Umbrella Deals, which insists on 30% of the annual slate fund going towards producing relationships with other UK production companies. The third obligatory element is the Slate Development Projects, for which the company must spend the remaining slate funding on developing individual projects. Applicants must be able to match at least 100% of the slate funding applied for. This means that more established companies will form the main applicant base for this scheme. As the scheme is intended to boost growth and production for the company and within the UK, a performance review will be carried out at the end of each year of the three year term. The renewal of the UKFC's investment will depend on the outcome of this review.

Development Fund — 25 Words or Less

www.ukfilmcouncil.org.uk/filmmaking/funding/
features/development/25woldcgdlns/

Offers: £10,000 · For: SCRIPT · Covering: ANI |
FEAT

The initiative offers up to three writers/writing teams
per round the opportunity to develop a feature idea
based around selected genres which for 2006 were
'comedy of manners', 'stalker' and 'fighting the
system'. The initiative will assist the successful writers
to develop their idea to first script stage. The UKFC
will provide the services of a script editor assigned to
support the writer through the development process.
This initiative is open to all but is aimed particularly at
writers early in their career. One of the conditions of
applying is that the writer either has an agent or is a full
member of the Writers Guild.

Prints & Advertising Fund

www.ukfilmcouncil.org.uk/filmmaking/funding/
features/development/sltfndapp/

Offers: Between £50,000 to £100,000 · For: DIST |
PROMO

The aim of the £2m P & A Fund is to support and
encourage distributors in the theatrical release of
'specialised films' within the UK, by increasing a film's P
& A budget to expand the size of a release. Support can
cover, for example, production and design of marketing
campaigns, prints and distribution, media costs,
publicity, promotions and research.

International Festival Sales Support

www.ukfilmcouncil.org.uk/cinemagoing/ifss/

Offers: £1500 · For: PROMO

Any British film selected into a major international
film festival receiving a World or Continent premiere
is automatically eligible for at least £1500 in support.
Eligible festivals are Sundance, Berlin, Rotterdam, San
Sebastian, Venice, Cannes, Toronto, Karlovy Vary or
Locarno. The money can support a subtitled print, travel
and accommodation costs of talent, and advertising
and marketing expenses.

Digital Screen Network

www.ukfilmcouncil.org.uk/cinemagoing/
distributionandexhibition/dsn/

The Digital Screen Network is one of the most
advanced Digital cinema networks in the world. It
consists of a 'virtual network' of 240 screens, located
in approximately 200 cinemas equipped with digital
projectors, managed by Arts Alliance Digital Media. In
return for the UKFC's support in covering the costs of
installation, cinemas have agreed to allocate a certain
amount of screen time to showing 'specialised' films.

Capital Funding — Cinema Access Programme — Film Print Privision

www.ukfilmcouncil.org.uk/cinemagoing/
distributionandexhibition/cap/capprintprov/

The £60,000 fund supports the provision of soft-titled
and audio described prints suitable for hard of hearing
and blind or partially sighted audiences for up to 20
films a year.

New Cinema Fund — Digital Shorts

www.ukfilmcouncil.org.uk/filmmaking/shorts/
digitalshorts/

Offers: Up to £10,000 · For: PROD | SCRIPT ·
Covering: SHORT

100% finances 100 digital shorts nationally each year
no longer than 10 minutes with an accompanying
training programme. Delivered in partnership with B3
Media for black and ethnic filmmakers, and each UK
regional screen agency where further details can be
found.

New Cinema Fund — Cinema Extreme

www.ukfilmcouncil.org.uk/filmmaking/shorts/
cinemaextremefaqs/

Offers: Up to £50,000 · For: PROD | SCRIPT ·
Covering: SHORT

Backed by Film Four with UKFC for experienced
filmmakers with an orginal and evocative short film
idea. The applicant should be able to use this project
as a springboard to getting the first feature off the
ground. Applpications normally open in July and close
in September each year with 6 films produced in 2006.

New Cinema Fund — Completion Fund

www.ukfilmcouncil.org.uk/filmmaking/shorts/
completionfund/ · For: POST · Covering: SHORT

The fund, managed by MayaVision, supports the
completion of short films that show orginality and
cinematic flair. Funding supports the post production
process for films which have reached the rough cut
stage but not simply the transfer of finished films from
one format to another. Deadlines in Novemeber each
year.

SCREEN AGENCIES

EM Media

www.em-media.org.uk
35-37 St Mary's Gate, Nottingham, Nottinghamshire,
NG1 1PU, UK
T: 0115 934 9090 · F: 0115 950 0988
E: info@em-media.org.uk

After securing £6m in European Regional Development
Fund (ERDF) investment, EM Media, the screen agency
for the East Midlands, has committed to investing in

six feature films and four video games in the region by 2009. In addition EM Media 'will continue to work towards developing audiences and markets through investment in Digital Cinema and film and media centres, while bringing cinema to rural locations and working to increase media literacy in schools and also promoting film heritage'. Sources of funding include RIFE (UK Film Council Regional Investment Fund for England), Treasury and Lottery funds, ERDF, ESF (European Social Fund), emda (East Midlands Development Agency), ITV Central, Nottingham City Council, Leicestershire Economic Partnership, Skillset, East Midlands Tourism. Major investments to date include low budget studio Warp X, which has received £750,000 over three years.

Funding

Funding is largely open (ie not linked to specific programmes) across four strands. Applications are made through one of two forms — funding for organisations and funding for individuals. EM Media asks potential applicants to talk through their project with the organisation ahead of making an application. Eligible applicants must be either an individual living and working in the region, a company based in the region, a company moving into the region to base production activity in the region, or a company in partnership with a company based in the region EM Media looks for returns on investment. This can mean short term reimbursements, but it can also mean long term economic impact: for example there may be no possibility for a project to generate profit, but it might increase the production company's credibility and allow it to increase its overall activity and staffing within the next two year. Terms of returns on investment are negotiated project by project and will be appropriate to the level of EM Media investment.

Audience and Market Development

www.em-media.org.uk/pages/culture/exhibition
Offers: Up to £20,000 and 75% of project costs · For: DIST | EXBN
Supports 'projects that develop audiences for film and media product, particularly for specialised film, develop knowledge and understanding of film and media product and assisting in getting film and media product to market' such as Broadway Media Centre in Nottingham, Metro Cinema in Derby, Phoenix Arts in Leicester and the Media Archive for Central England (MACE).

Business Development

www.em-media.org.uk/pages/services/busdev
Offers: £1,000 — £5,000 · For: BIZ-DEV
After meeting to discus business needs, EM Media will develop a tailored programme which can include

expert, practical advice on business planning, financial management, market development, development needs assessment, coupled with mentoring opportunities or short courses. This can lead onto small and larger scale product and project investment. EM will pay for up to 50% of the cost of consultancy up to £1,000 and up to £5,000 as a start-up loan .

Product and Project Development

www.em-media.org.uk/pages/navigator_07
Offers: Up to £250,000, 50% of costs · For: PROD | DEV | SCRIPT | BIZ-DEV | PER-DEV · Covering: FEAT | TV | MM | SHORT | DOC | ANI | FFF | YP | VIDG | WEB
EM Media invests in the development and production of films, broadcast media and interactive media, including computer games. They are looking for projects that have the potential to attract buyers, that have a clearly identified audience and strategy for reaching that audience and that offer the potential of establishing companies for the long term, or that make a genuine difference to individual's careers. Priority will be given to projects with vision, which push forward creative technological or commercial boundaries and contribute to a sustainable and diverse production sector in the East Midlands.

Typical awards for short films range from £500 to £5,000 and rarely exceed £10,000; the investment in development of larger scale projects (feature films, projects for TV, games development etc) ranges from a very small initial investment up to a maximum of £95,000 for the development of slates. Production co-finance for features and large scale projects will be up to a maximum of £250,000.

Skills Development

www.em-media.org.uk/pages/services/skills
Offers: £1,000 per person, 50% of costs · For: BIZ-DEV | PER-DEV | EDU | PROMO
EM will support — for companies and individuals — technical and skills development training with a training provider; bespoke tailor made training and development; one to one training and mentoring support; attendance at festivals and other networking events. For company training, £1,000 per employee can be provided up to 10 employees and 50% of project costs.

DV Shorts

www.em-media.org.uk/pages/investment/dvshorts
Offers: up to £10,000
The DV Shorts scheme runs annually with a deadline in September, offering a combination of training, development and production support for a short film shot on digital of no greater length than 10 minutes.

Film Agency for Wales

www.filmagencywales.com/
Suite 7, 33-35 West Bute Street, Cardiff, Wales, CF10
5LH, UK
T: 02920 467 480 · F: 029 20 333320
E: anneli.jones@artswales.org.uk
Established in July 2006 to replace Sgrin, which closed
in March 06, the Film Agency for Wales is the new
slimmed-down Agency for film in Wales, with a remit
to ensure that the economic, cultural and educational
aspects of film are effectively represented in Wales, the
UK and the world. The Agency offers:
· Project specific advice and assistance in identifying,
preparing for, approaching and dealing with targeted
potential third party financiers, distributors and/or sales
agents and industry markets;
· Assistance in profiling talent with third party
financiers, distributors, commissioners and at market
events;
· Co-financing for a minimum of 2 — 3 low budget
films per annum;
· Support for new talent with experienced production
personnel and mentors where appropriate, facilitating
access to hands-on production training opportunities
where possible;
· Advice and information regarding industry
opportunities, working with training organisations to
facilitate access wherever possible.

Funding

Films selected for funding are assessed on the quality
of the work, the benefit to Welsh talent, the viability
of the project and its market appeal. Applications
for funding up to £25,000 will be made by the Chief
Executive, Head of Talent & Talent Development
Executive. Decisions on funding applications between
£25,000 and £50,000 will be made by the above and
the Agency Board's Chairman. Funding decisions above
£50,000 will be subject to Board approval.

Production Funding

www.filmagencywales.com/production.php
Offers: Up to £200,000 and 50% of budget · For:
PROD · Covering: FEAT | ANI
Offers co-financing for a minimum of 2-3 low budget
films each year. Budgets for these feature-length
films, intended for theatrical release, will ordinarily be
between £400,000 and £750,000. But ultra low budget
projects (ie £50,000 £100,000) will be considered
provided that they meet best industry practices and fair
pay agreements. Completion funding is also available
up to 50% of total costs capped at £50,000.

Development Funding

www.filmagencywales.com/development.php
Offers: 100% of development costs · For: DEV |
SLATE | SCRIPT · Covering: FEAT
Around 20 projects are in development at any one time.
Support is available for a range of development activity,
including script re-writes, scheduling, budgeting,
casting, location recces and costs associated with
raising finance /sales and distribution interest.

Exhibition Core Funding

www.filmagencywales.com/exhbition.php
Offers: From £1,500 · For: EXBN_AUD-DEV
Support for exhibitors who show more than 10
'specialist films' to more than 1000 people each year
with a sliding scale of support dependent on the
audience size.

Exhibition Project Funding

www.filmagencywales.com/exhibition.php
Offers: Up to £5,000 or 75% of project costs · For:
PROMO | AUD-DEV
To support events and festivals or film societies without
core funding.

Education Funding

www.filmagencywales.com/education.php
Offers: Up to £5,000 or 75% of costs · For: EDU
Supports education and training providers with support
for one to three projects (with total support capped
at £10,000 per organisation a year). The main focus is
on projects which increase film literacy and stimulate
interest in specialist films.

Film London

www.filmlondon.org.uk
Suite 6.10 The Tea Building, 56 Shoreditch High
Street, London, E1 6JJ, UK
T: 020 7613 7676 · F: 020 7613 7677
E: info@filmlondon.org.uk
Film London is the capital's film and media agency.
Film London sustains, promotes and develops London
as a major international film-making and film cultural
capital. This includes all the screen industries based
in London – film, TV, video, commercials and new
interactive media. Film London is supported by the UK
Film Council and the London Development Agency
through Creative London. Film London also receives
significant support from Arts Council England London,
the European Regional Development Fund, the Mayor
of London and Skillset. As well as supporting exhibition,
education, training, research, sales, locations and three
funds, the agency runs the London Artists Moving
Image Network (flamin.filmlondon.org.uk).

Microwave

www.filmlondon.org.uk/microwave

Offers: Up to £100,000 · For: PROD · Covering: FEAT | DOC | EXP | FFF

Microwave challenges filmmakers to shoot a full length feature film, intended for theatrical release, for no more than £100,000 with cash and in-kind support. The scheme provides an intensive approach to filmmaking, with training throughout the production and a professional mentoring scheme from leading industry figures. Microwave is open to filmmakers working in documentary, fiction and to artists working with the moving image. Backed by the BBC and Skillset, the scheme has previously offered up to £50,000 (and in 'exceptional circumstances' £75,000) of direct funding per project. This is accompanied with in-kind support from facilities and services companies, reduced location fees and a revenue share model for a total accounted-for budget of no more than £100,000.

Copyright in films is owned by Film London until expenses are recouped when 40% of revenues after sales commissions are returned to the filmmakers. Completed films, which must be shot and edited in London, are guaranteed a BBC broadcast (no further fee is paid for this broadcast). In addition a mentoring and training scheme is provided from leading industry figures.

Pulse Digital Shorts

www.filmlondon.org.uk/pulse

Offers: Up to £10,000 · For: PROD · Covering: SHORT | ANI

PULSE was launched in 2002 in partnership with the UK Film Council's New Cinema Fund. The ambition is to produce a new generation of filmmakers who use digital technology creatively to tell stories in groundbreaking ways. At least 8 films will be commissioned every year with awards up to £10,000 depending on the nature of the project. The running time should be between 1 and 10 minutes.

Film London Artists Film & Video Awards (LAFVA)

www.filmlondon.org.uk/lafva

Offers: Up to £20,000 · For: PROD · Covering: EXP | SHORT | ANI | DOC

LAFVA is managed by Film London in partnership with Arts Council England. Awards of up to £20,000 are available to artists working in the context of contemporary moving image practice and producing work intended for exhibition in galleries, cinemas, festivals, specialist venues and as site specific installations. Awards are intended for fully developed projects with a realisable exhibition and distribution plan. Full details of the next round of LAFVA will be available in mid 2007.

North West Vision

www.northwestvision.co.uk

Manchester Film Office, tBBC New Broadcasting House, Oxford Road, Manchester, M60 1SJ, UK
T: 08706094481 or 0161 244 3742 · F: 0161 244 3755
E: info@northwestvision.co.uk

North West Vision is the TV, film and moving image development agency for England's North West, working to support, fund and produce film, TV and digital production in the region. NWV's missions is to 'champion our film and TV industry, celebrate our talent and diversity, and build on our production success to be the best in Europe'.

Funding

Funding comes from National Lottery funding, the Regional Attraction Fund and the Merseyside Film and TV fund. North West Vision also run the short film production schemes, Virgin Shorts and Digital Shorts. At time of publication the organisation had announced a scheme to produce content for mobile phones called Short Sharp Shots, but further details were not available. There are eight annual deadlines.

Heritage, Access to Film and Audience Development Fund

www.northwestvision.co.uk/page/cinemas-archives-and-film-festivals

Offers: up to 70% of project costs · For: AUD-DEV | EXBN_PROMO

Supports cinemas, archives and festivals. Awards for projects running April 07 — March 08 was closed at time of publication with no further details about the 2008/09 round. Applicants must be a legally constituted organisation with a written constitution or set of rules and be based in the region.

Merseyside Film & TV Production Fund

www.northwestvision.co.uk/page/feature-film-production-finance

Offers: £10,000 to £250,000 up to 37% · For: BIZ-DEV | DEV | PROD · Covering: FEAT | TV | DOC | ANI | VIDG | WEB | MM

The Merseyside Film and Television Fund is available to new and established local businesses, companies locating into Merseyside and joint ventures between local companies and companies from outside the area. Between £15,000 and £100,000 (38% of costs) is available for production development, and up to £250,000 (and 25% of costs) for production finance. Awards within this range are also available for company development for facilities and production companies in the region.

Feature Film Script Development

www.northwestvision.co.uk/page/feature-script-development

Offers: Up to £5,000 · For: SCRIPT · Covering: FEAT
For the development of a feature script from an established writer.

New Feature Film Writers Development Scheme

www.northwestvision.co.uk/page/new-feature-film-writers-development-scheme

Offers: Between £500 and £5000
A two stage scheme which offers 3-5 days training to up to 30 first time feature script writers in the region, after which 8 will be chosen to have a feature idea developed to first draft over an eight month period.

Training

www.northwestvision.co.uk/section/training

Offers: Between £500 and £5000
Professional development and skills for people working in the screen industries.

Virgin Shorts

www.northwestvision.co.uk/page/virgin-shorts

Offers: Up to £1000 · For: PROD · Covering: SHORT
Production bursaries for 12 short narrative films made by new filmmakers.

Digital Shorts

www.northwestvision.co.uk/page/digital-shorts

Offers: £3,000 — £9,000
Part of the UK DV Shorts scheme split into two strands:Mini — funds six films with £3,000 budget for emerging writer/producer/director teams; and Maxi — funds four films with a £9,000 budget for more experienced production teams, aimed at an international festival audience.

Digital Departures

www.digitaldepartures.co.uk/

Offers: £250,000 · For: PROD · Covering: FEAT
100% financing for three microbudget feature films to be shot in the Liverpool and premiering by Autumn 2008 with distribution on the UK Digital Screen Network.

Northern Film & Media

www.northernmedia.org
Central Square, Forth Street, Newcastle, NE1 3PJ, UK
T: 019 1269 9200 · F: 019 1269 9213
E: info@northernmedia.org
Northern Film & Media, the RSA for the north-east of England, provides funding and support to encourage more people to make, watch and work in film, TV and interactive media in the region. They are supported by the UK Film Council, One North East, Skillset, EU Regional Development Fund and the Northern Cultural Skills Partnership.

Their stated mission is 'To lead the building of a commercial and expert regional media sector with an international reputation which thrives on creativity, competition and success, attracting investment and talent to the North East of England. To establish a world class moving image culture throughout the region that enriches community life and in which more people participate by watching, learning, creating and celebrating.'

Funding

The bulk of funding is cleanly split between Economic Impact (including development and production awards) and Social Impact funding strands. In addition, funding is available under an Accelerator fund for new ideas on emerging platforms, a Network TV fund and skills placement support.

TV Development

www.northernmedia.org/?&pageid=24

Offers: Up to £1500 · For: Project Development (includes pre-PROD)_DEV · Covering: TV | ANI | DOC
Aimed at individuals and companies looking to develop ideas and pitches to network broadcasters. Applicants must show a detailed knowledge of schedules and broadcaster requirements, although they do not need to have previously delivered for network.

New Media

www.northernmedia.org/?&pageid=24

Offers: Up to £5,000 · For: DEV · Covering: MM
Aimed at developing strong new media ideas to a stage where they can be pitched to investors/funders. Applicants are expected to come with a well thought out idea – this fund is not for developing a fledgling idea (for this please see Accelerator Fund).

Writers Awards

www.northernmedia.org/?&pageid=24

Offers: £5,000 · For: SCRIPT · Covering: FEAT
Individual writers are eligible to apply for one of two awards to fund the writing of a script (not treatments). Project must already have a strong 8+ page treatment, with a clear idea of who audience is and any co-creators.

Feature Production

www.northernmedia.org/?&pageid=24

Offers: Up to £30,000 and 75% of costs · For: PROD · Covering: FEAT
The provision of funding towards micro-budget features with commercial potential, a distribution plan and a budget not greater than £300k.

Development Packages

www.northernmedia.org/?&pageid=24

Offers: Up to £7,000 · For: DEV · Covering: FEAT | ANI

To support packaging of feature ideas, including script development, pre-production, trailers, casting, legal, etc. Companies applying will be expected to show how they plan to deliver the project and which experts they are attaching to the project to ensure its success. Companies need to show an existing production track record, and can be located outside the region if they are working with local talent.

Digital Shorts

www.northernmedia.org/?&pageid=56

Training, development and production for short films.

Marketing & market access

www.northernmedia.org/?&pageid=24

Offers: £300 — £1,500 · For: PROMO · Covering: SHORT | ANI

Up to £300 for marketing activity (showreels, duplications and specific marketing materials etc); £300 for market access (attending festivals and markets); and £1500 for strategic market access, which covers a number of events in a 12 month period.

Training for individuals

www.northernmedia.org/?&pageid=24

Offers: £5,000 · For: PER-DEV | EDU

Support for indivudals to attend training events, courses and workshops and mentoring opportunities.

Training for companies

www.northernmedia.org/?&pageid=24

Offers: £5,000 · For: BIZ-DEV | EDU

Support for companies to develop internal skills through placements, mentorships or attendance on training programmes.

Social Impact Fund

www.northernmedia.org/?pageid=28

Offers: £300 — £40,000 · For: BIZ-DEV | PER-DEV | AUD-DEV | EXBN | EDU | CULT | PROMO

The social impact fund supports projects where the benefit is measured socially rather than economically. This includes:

· Exhibition and Education — supporting access and learning
· Community Film — supporting participatory production
· Festivals — supporting the region's international moving image festivals
· Training and Networking — supporting professional development to deliver work and projects of social impact (ie not Skillset / career development)

Awards average between £5,000 and £10,000 and are open to both individuals and organisations. For 2005-06, including grant-in-aid to established organisations, 40 awards were made totalling £362,000.

Accelerator Fund

www.northernmedia.org/?pageid=30

Offers: Up to £3,000 · For: DEV | BIZ-DEV · Covering: MM | EXP | WEB

To develop new, innovative and entrepreneurial projects the fund — operated across the social and economic impact funds — invites people to submit a 150 word pitch by email. If successful the following stage involves a 5 minute pitch to a panel and 15 minute Q&A after which up to £3,000 may be availble.

Northern Ireland Film Television Commission (NIFTC)

www.niftc.co.uk

Alfred House, 21 Alfred Street, Belfast, Northern Ireland, BT2 8ED, UK

T: 028 9023 2444 · F: 028 9023 9918

E: info@niftc.co.uk

The NIFTC was established in 1997 as a Film and TV Commission for Northern Ireland, with the objective of attracting film production to the region. In 2002, the Arts Council of Northern Ireland designated it with the responsibility of distributing the annual lottery film funds.

Funding

NIFTC offers funding across all sizes of projects, as well as skills, market, company development and distribution support. The key funds are the Northern Ireland Film Production Fund for larger investments, and the Made in Northern Ireland (MINI) scheme which offers up to 90% of production costs. Ideally any project applying to the NIFTC Lottery funds will be of cultural relevance to Northern Ireland, have a member of the creative team who is a Northern Ireland resident, intend to maximise the use of Northern Ireland resident cast, crew and facilities while exposing Northern Ireland locations to the fullest potential. However this is an ideal scenario, and the NIFTC invites any potential producer to discuss their project with them.

Deviate (ie. Digital Shorts)

Offers: Up to £8000 · For: PROD | DEV | POST · Covering: SHORT

Production scheme for digital short films with an annual deadline normally in March.

Project Development (lottery)

Offers: Up to £40,000 and 50% of costs · For: PROD | DEV | SCRIPT · Covering: ANI | DOC | FEAT | MM | TV | SHORT | FFF | EXP

The NIFTC award will be made available over a series of stages and not in one lump sum. The completion of each stage to the NIFTC's satisfaction is essential to enable an applicant to access the full award. The NIFTC may award up to 75% on an initial development budget up to £10,000 but beyond the first £10,000 the NIFTC will not exceed 50% of the remaining development budget. The NIFTC expects development applications to be realistic and appropriate for the scale of the production to be developed.

Made in Northern Ireland (MINI) Individuals

www.niftc.co.uk/page.asp?id=137

Offers: Up to £2,500 and 90% of costs · For: PROD · Covering: SHORT | DOC | ANI | EXP

The NIFTC will accept applications from individuals for support to produce ultra low budget experimental work and those new to film-making. This could include:
· Short narrative films (normally of up to 5 minutes)
· Short experimental films (normally of up to 5 minutes)
· Animation production (normally of up to 2 minutes)
· Single documentaries (normally no longer than 30 minutes)

For productions with a total budget of less than £2,500 up to 90% of the budget may be awarded. The NIFTC's maximum cash contribution will therefore be £2,250. NIFTC does not aim to make a recoupment and there are no deadlines.

Made in Northern Ireland (MINI) Small Awards

www.niftc.co.uk/page.asp?id=137

Offers: £2,501 — £5,000 · For: AUD-DEV · Covering: SHORT | DOC | ANI | EXP

As with MINI individuals, except for groups, organisations and companies, with a higher budget.

Made in Northern Ireland (MINI) Low Budget Awards

www.niftc.co.uk/page.asp?id=137

Offers: £5,000 to £30,000 and up to 75% of costs · For: PROD · Covering: SHORT | EXP | ANI | DOC | TV | MM | FEAT

Funding is available towards the costs of production of: short narrative films (normally of up to 10 minutes); short experimental films (normally of up to 10 minutes); short animation films, including series; Culturally relevant documentaries, including series; experimental films; digital media products with a high proportion of moving image content. There is no deadline .

Made in Northern Ireland (MINI) High Budget Awards

www.niftc.co.uk/page.asp?id=137

Offers: £30,000 to £100,000, up to 50% · For: PROD · Covering: TV | FEAT | SHORT | DOC | ANI | EXP | MM

With the same eligable products as for the MINI Low Budget awards, but with participation limited to 50%. For investments over £50,000 there are four annual deadlines for applications.

Company Development Fund

www.niftc.co.uk/page.asp?id=88

Offers: £3,000 — £80,000 · For: BIZ-DEV

A two stage fund to provide funding for the development of a business plan (up to £3,000, or 50% of costs) and an operating grant of up to £80,000, or 40% of the total budget to support a business strategy.

Product Development Fund

www.niftc.co.uk/page.asp?id=88

Offers: £10,000 — £20,000 · For: SLATE · Covering: FEAT | TV | DOC | ANI | YP

The NIFTC will provide recoupable loans of between £10,000 and £20,000 to support a Northern Ireland based production company's slate of projects intended for network and international audience.

Completion Fund

www.niftc.co.uk/page.asp?id=159 · For: POST · Covering: SHORT

Awards are available to enable projects to complete post-production (picture and sound post and delivery materials). Projects must have a final running time of normally less than 30 minutes; been edited to a rough-cut or beyond; have main elements (e.g. producer, writer, director, location, story) which are substantially Northern Ireland based; and when completed will be capable of being fully cleared for cinema.

Skills Development Bursary Fund

www.niftc.co.uk/page.asp?id=13

Offers: £1,000, up to 75% · For: EDU | PER-DEV

Eligible costs include course fees, travel and accommodation. Applications are accepted on a rolling basis, 6 weeks ahead of the intended course.

Low Budget Feature Film Production

www.niftc.co.uk/page.asp?id=86

Offers: Up to £150,000, no more than 50% · For: PROD | POST | DEV · Covering: FEAT | ANI

Priority is given to projects with a very strong cultural resonance for Northern Ireland, that support local talent, that use a digital format appropriate to this budget level and projects with broadcasters, sales agents or distributors already attached.

Northern Ireland Film Production Fund

www.niftc.co.uk/page.asp?id=8
Offers: £150,000 — £600,000 · For: DEV | PROD | POST · Covering: FEAT | ANI | TV
NIFTC will invest in a live action or animated feature film or a live action or animated TV drama single, series or serial where the production has a strong cultural relevance to Northern Ireland. Applicants must normally be able to demonstrate that their project is 65% funded at the point of application. The investment takes the form of a recoupable loan with profit participation. There are four deadlines throughout the year.

Markets, festivals & Conferences

Offers: Up to £2,000 or 50% · For: PROMO | PER-DEV | BIZ-DEV
Offers Northern Irish talent financial support to attend established markets, festivals and industry conferences. Applications should be made four weeks before the event.

Distribution and promotion

www.niftc.co.uk/page.asp?id=96
Offers: Up to £5,000 and 10% of total budget · For: PROMO | DIST · Covering: SHORT | FEAT
Offers support with costs including transfers, telecine, DVD copies, shipping, entry fees, promotional materials, design and print. NIFTC is particularly interested in packages of short films which hence will show economies of scale.

Scottish Screen

www.scottishscreen.com
249 West George Street, 2nd Floor, Glasgow, Scotland, G2 4QE, UK
T: 0845 300 7300
E: info@scottishscreen.com
Scottish Screen develops, encourages and promotes every aspect of film, TV and new media in Scotland. Scottish Screen's work focuses on five priority areas: Education, Talent & Creativity, Market Development, Enterprise & Skills, and Inward Investment and Communications. From April 2007, the Scottish Screen Archive will come under the stewardship of the National Libraries of Scotland. From 2008 Scottish Screen is expected to form part of Creative Scotland with the Scottish Arts Council. The agency is funded by £3m from the Scottish Executive and has a further £3m National Lottery funds to distribute.

Funding

To receive funding for Content Development, Short Film Production and Content Production all projects must meet specific 'Eligibility Criteria' to establish that the project will have a benefit for Scotland. This covers the nationality of key talent, the cultural relevance of the story, and the distribution of production spend. To be eligible for funding a project needs to have accumulated a certain score based these elements and also be capable of qualifying as a British Film. The scoring system is similar to that used for the classification of a British film. At time of publication further funding strands were still to be announced.

Content Development

Offers: Up to £50,000 and 50-75% of costs · For: SCRIPT | DEV · Covering: FEAT | DOC | ANI | TV
Scottish Screen's investment in Content Development aims to assist Scottish talent in developing projects to take to the marketplace. Scottish Screen will therefore place a strong emphasis on supporting projects that have a significant chance of being realised and distributed through an appropriate medium whether that be via TV or cinema. Applicants must be able to demonstrate that Scottish Screen's investment will significantly enhance the quality of the their project. Awards are normally made for six months followed by a review and an extension of either three or six months granted. With £150,000 available each year, awards can make up to 75% of total budget for a £25,000 investment and 50% of costs for awards up to £50,000.

Short Film Production

Offers: Up to £50,000 and 75% of costs · For: PROD · Covering: SHORT | ANI | DOC
Scottish Screen's investment aims to encourage strong cinematic voices to be exploited and produced that are capable of winning international recognition and significantly raising the profile of the team attached. Projects should be creatively and commercially ambitious and have high production values. The quality of the writer, producer and directors previous work will be assessed rigorously. Total fund size is £150,000 with 25% partnership funding required (10% of which can be in kind).

Content Production

Offers: Up to £500,000 and 25% of budget · For: PROD · Covering: FEAT | DOC | ANI
Scottish Screen's investment in the production of Content aims to provide the necessary support to production companies to finance the physical production of the intended project. Projects should be distinctive, high quality and commercially viable. They should provide opportunities for Scotland's talent to demonstrate their ability in an international arena. With £1.5m available for 2006/07, projects should be distinctive and commercially viable, providing an opportunity for Scottish talent to demonstrate their ability in an international arena.

Exhibition

To support policies, initiatives and organisations which provide access to the broadest range. £380,000 was available in 2006/07.

Distribution

Offers: Up to £15,000 and 50% of costs · For: DIST | PROMO

To support the release of certified British and specialised films and to increase access to these films amongst Scottish audiences. Eligible films must conform to the UK Film Council definition of a 'British' or 'specialised' film £50,000 is available for 2006/2007 and 50% partnership funding is required.

Festivals

Offers: Up to £50,000 and 50% of costs · For: PROMO

To support Scottish festivals and events and widen access and awareness amongst Scottish audiences. Eligibility applies to Scottish based companies and activities. Fund available for 2006/2007 is £175,000 and 50% minimum partnership funding is required.

Audience Development

Offers: Up to £15,000 and 50% of costs · For: AUD-DEV | CULT

Can support educational events, programmes, workshops and research in Scotland which serves to increase cinema literacy. Eligible projects should bring new audiences to moving image media, increase range of content available to Scottish audiences and encourage attendance by under represented groups. The total budget is £75,000 and 50% partnership funding is required.

Festival and market attendence

Offers: £250 to £1,500 and 75% of budget · For: PER-DEV | PROMO

Scottish Screen's investment aims to support Scottish talent to attend markets and festivals to promote themselves and their projects. Attendance at markets and festivals should significantly enhance the prospect of an individual, a company or a project in securing future investment from the marketplace.

New Talent Initiatives

Offers: £25,000 to £75,000 and 50% of project costs · For: PER-DEV | EDU · Covering: FFF

Scottish Screen's investment aims to broaden the opportunities and support available to emerging talent through investment in targeted initiatives which Scottish based companies can apply to run. The aim of these initiatives is to provide Writers, Producers and Directors with a combination of tailored and open access training and to create innovative work which will be promoted to an appropriate audience. Will increase

tailored and open access training for emerging writers, producers and directors to benefit from a combination of. £250,000 available for 06/07 with 50% minimum partnership funding required and up to half of the partner contribution can be in-kind.

Digital Access Fund

Offers: £5,000 to £20,000 · For: EDU | BIZ-DEV

The Digital Access Fund is supported by Scottish Screen and the Scottish Arts Council. The aim of the fund is to support organisations who can offer opportunities for individuals and groups who are currently under represented in the field of moving image culture, by creating a programme of activities that produces and explores digital content across a range of platforms. 50% match funding is required of which 25% can be in-kind.

Education Development

Offers: £10,000 to £25,000 · For: CULT | AUD-DEV | EDU

Investment is given to local authorities or organisations with a remit for education in Scotland who aim to develop and integrate moving image education in their schools or institutes. Investment is also available for these organisations to provide training for professionals to teach moving image education. £80,000 is available for 2006/2007. Maximum funding level applies to consortium and partnership applications and 50% partnership funding is required.

Business Development Loan

Offers: £10,000 to £40,000 p.a. · For: BIZ-DEV

Scottish Screen's investment in Business Development Loans aims to provide companies with an opportunity to access finance where access to commercial finance may be restricted. Scottish Screen's Business Development Loan will provide companies to sustain, develop or grow an aspect of their business for a period of up to two years without having to repay the loan or pay interest during that time. Business Development Loans aim to stimulate the development of the screen sector in Scotland creating sustainable and dynamic businesses for the future.

Screen East

www.screeneast.co.uk
2 Millennium Plain, Norwich, Norfolk, NR2 1TF, UK
T: 01603 776920 · F: 01603 767191
E: info@screeneast.co.uk

Screen East is the regional screen agency dedicated to developing, supporting and promoting film and media industry and culture in the East of England. Four departments deliver provision: Locations, Productions, Audiences and Education; and Enterprise and Skills.

Funding

Screen East provides project investments (not grants) that fit within one of three priority areas:
· Priority One: Talent and Content Development. Developing and promoting talent in the East of England
· Priority Two: Enterprise and Skills Development. Developing adaptable, competitive and sustainable film, TV and moving image businesses in the East of England.
· Priority Three: Audience Development. Enabling audience access and participation through moving image education, cinema exhibition and archive activity. Screen East also runs the production scheme Digital Shorts. Regional eligibility criteria apply for all funds.

Archive Services
Offers: Up to £5000 for individuals and up to £10,000 for organisations.
Support for film archive and conservation services.

Company Development Investment
Offers: Up to £20,000
Development of a slate of projects for promising regional production companies.

Development Finance
Script and project development prior to pre-production.

Digital Shorts
Offers: Up to £8000
Training, development and production for short films.

Educational Projects & Initiatives
Offers: Up to £5000 for individuals and up to £10,000 for organisations.
Development of film education in schools, colleges and the community.

Featurelab Tender
Offers: Full cost of course paid for.
Training and development for screenwriters to produce first draft scripts at the University of East Anglia.

Investment to Support Access for Audiences
Offers: Up to £10,000
Support for specialist and mainstream exhibitors to bring diverse cinema to a wider audience.

Production Finance
Offers: Up to £20,000
Short film production, post production and distribution

Small Scale Capital Awards
Offers: Up to £5000
Investment in hardware and software to develop applicant's business.

Content Investment Fund
www.dcvirtual.net/screeneast/pdfs/Screen%20East%20Content%20Investment%20Fund.pdf
Offers: Total fund £2m · For: PROD · Covering: FEAT | TV | MM | DOC | ANI | FFF | YP | VIDG | DIGI
Companies based in the Screen East region, or partnering with a regional organisation are eligible to apply for 10 to 40% of proposed equity finance from a total pool of £2m, which must all be spent by September 2008. Screen East seeks repayment of investment, a share of profits and a share of copyright ownership.

Screen South

www.screensouth.org
The Wedge, 75-81 Tontine Street, Folkestone, CT20 1JR, UK
T: 01303 259777 · F: 01303 259786
E: info@screensouth.org
Screen South has set its regional priorities as the need for a sustainable media industry, to increase opportunities for audiences, and to develop talent. Its lottery programme is structured in three priority streams. Screen South activity areas include archive, exhibition, education, production & development, vocational training, film commission and inward investment. ScreenSouth ALSO supports a number of production hubs which provide free equipment, facilities and support to a number of shorts each year, including Oxford Film & Video (ofvm.org), City Eye (city-eye.co.uk) and Lighthouse (lighthouse.org.uk).

Funding
Screen South's established priority areas for funding are:
· Priority One: Talent. To support and promote the development of companies and individual talent within the region
· Priority Two: Infrastructure. To support a sustainable, professional film community and infrastructure
· Priority Three: Audience Development. Increasing audience participation, access and choice in the South of England.

Screen South offers a straightforward funding structure with the bulk of UK Film Council RIFE funds administered through an open award scheme with a rolling deadline. For all funds the maximum available to an individual or organisation is £10,000. In 2006 £205,000 was available and in 2005 132 awards were made for an average of £1,500 each. Potential applicants are asked, but not required, to first attend and information day. Screen South also runs the Dreamcatcher and Digital Shorts production schemes. Applicants must be based in the region.

Open Funding — small awards

www.screensouth.org/pages/funding/funding_intro.html

Offers: Up to £500 · For: DEV | PROD | POST | DIST | PROMO | CULT | DVD | EDU | EXBN | BIZ-DEV | PER-DEV | AUD-DEV · Covering: FEAT | TV | MM | DOC | ANI | WEB | EXP | VIDG

Open funding supports education, exhibition, market access, training. company and project development. It does not support shorts or script writing. Applications are taken on a rolling basis, and can take up to six weeks for a decision from first receipt of application. Projects must meet one of Screen South's priority areas for funding.

Open Funding — large awards

www.screensouth.org/pages/funding/funding_intro.html

Offers: £500 — £10,000 · For: AUD-DEV | PER-DEV | BIZ-DEV | EXBN | EDU | DVD | CULT | DIST | PROMO | POST | DEV | PROD · Covering: FEAT | TV | MM | DOC | ANI | VIDG | WEB | EXP

As with small awards but with a different application process and a cap of £5,000 for individuals and £10,000 for businesses. Funding decisions are made quarterly.

Festival and Exhibition Fund

Offers: up to £10,000 · For: EXBN | PROMO | AUD-DEV

With a budget for 2006/07 of £45,000, awards are made to events and festivals with an annual deadline in early March. Capped at £5,000 for individuals and £10,000 for companies.

Dreamcatcher

Offers: £5000 · For: SCRIPT

Script development for screenwriters.

Digital Shorts — Long Shots

Offers: £6,400 · For: PROD · Covering: SHORT | DOC | ANI | EXP

Entries called for in summer each year, and in 2006 funded six 5-9 minute shorts.

Digital Shorts — Close ups

Offers: £1,000 · For: PROD · Covering: SHORT | ANI | EXP | DOC

Funding for five one minute shorts of any genre. 2006 deadline was July.

Digital Shorts — One minute wonders

Offers: £500 · For: PROD · Covering: SHORT | ANI

Funding for ten one minute animations. 2006 deadline was in July.

Screen West Midlands

www.screenwm.co.uk
9 Regent Place, Birmingham, B1 3NJ, UK
T: 0121 265 7120 · F: 0121 265 7180
E: info@screenwm.co.uk

Screen West Midlands works to support, promote and develop the screen media industries throughout the West Midlands through areas such as production, education, exhibition, archive and skills development. Core funding is through the UK Film Council RIFE, Advantage West Midlands and The Learning and Skills Council.

Funding

Screen West Midlands covers several operational areas, including feature film investment, short film initiatives, freelancer and company training schemes, and RIFE Lottery investment to support, promote and develop the screen media industries in the West Midlands.

Film & Media Production Fund

www.screenwm.co.uk/production-and-development/production-investment/index.asp

Offers: Lesser of £300,000 or 25% of budget · For: PROD · Covering: FEAT | DOC | ANI | TV | MM | VIDG

Primarily focussed on features but will invest in other formats including video games and TV dramas. In 04/05 supported four features including Confetti and Road to Guantanamo. Applications must be made after an initial contact with the department and subsequent completion of an expression of interest form. Unsolicited applications are not accepted.

Lottery Script Grants

Offers: £5,000 · For: SCRIPT · Covering: FEAT

Supports writers and producers for first and second draft feature film scripts. A further £2,000 is available to cover script editor costs. Applications are accepted twice a year.

Advantage Development Fund

Offers: £5,000 — £30,000 · For: DEV | SCRIPT | SLATE | BIZ-DEV · Covering: FEAT | TV | MM | SHORT | DOC | ANI | VIDG | WEB | EXP

Supports higher risk projects from companies in the region which require research and development investment ahead of being brough to market. This can include script development, pre-production packaging, ideas generation and slate project funding.

Acccess Grants

www.screenwm.co.uk/funding/access-fund.asp
Offers: £5,000 to £15,000 · For: BIZ-DEV | PER-DEV
| EDU | PROMO | CULT | EXBN_AUD-DEV
Provides grants for education, new talent, exhibition
and audience development projects. An R&D Access
Grant is also available to explore ideas before making a
fuller application.

Digital Shorts

www.screenwm.co.uk/production-and-
development/digital-shorts/index.asp
Offers: Up to £9,000 · For: PROD · Covering:
SHORT
Eight filmmakers are supported annually to produce a
DV short of no more than 10 minutes length.

Digital Extreme

Offers: Up to £20,000 · For: PROD · Covering:
SHORT
Award for one director / writer who has previously
completed a digital short to make a higher budget short
of any length.

Screen Yorkshire

www.screenyorkshire.co.uk
Studio 22, 46 The Calls, Leeds, Yorkshire, LS2 7EY,
UK
T: 011 3294 4410 · F: 011 3294 4989
E: info@screenyorkshire.co.uk
Screen Yorkshire is the gateway to film, broadcast and
digital media in the Yorkshire and Humber region. They
are responsible for inspiring, promoting and supporting
a successful long-term film and media sector for the
region. In May 2006 the organisation secured £10.2m
funding from Yorkshire Forward to deliver a four year
development programme, the largest ever made in
the UK by a regional development agency to a screen
agency. Part of the investment will be in multi-platform
programming to help place the region at the forefront
emerging content devliery methods. Recent films shot
in the region include *Mischief Night, History Boys* and
Garfield II.

Funding

Lottery funding comes under Low Budget Shorts;
Up Short; SPARK Writers Scheme; Development
of Skills and People; Audiences, Programming and
Education; and Community and Youth Projects, and are
assessed quarterly for any application over £1000. The
application process and guidelines are largely the same
for each and up to 30% of costs must have been raised
from other sources (of which a third can be in kind).
The Yorkshire Production fund provides investments,
and Business Development Awards are set to be revised

considerably with the investment from Yorkshire
Forward.

Yorkshire Production Fund

www.screenyorkshire.co.uk/default.asp?id=581
Offers: Up to £200,000 and 5% of costs · For:
SCRIPT | DEV | SLATE | PROD · Covering: FEAT | TV
| MM | DOC | ANI | VIDG
Provides substantial recoupable investments. For
features this will be rarely more than two-three a year,
and for budgets under £1m filmmakers are urged to
approach Warp X.
For development, up to £20,000 (and in some cases
£40,000) is available for up to 50% of costs of
individual projects, and up to £100,000 for 'high risk,
high growth' slates.
For production, up to £600,000 is available to finance
the producer tax credit for a 10% fee. Up to £200,000
is available for production investment although this
would not normally be more than 5% of the total
budget. For films from production companies not based
in the region the local expenditure would be expected
to be twice that of any investment.

Business Development Awards

screenyorkshire.co.uk/default.asp?id=362
Offers: Up to £25,000 · For: BIZ-DEV | PER-DEV
At time of publication these were being restructured
after the Yorkshire Forward investment, but in previous
years have supported activities from R&D projects to
assisting with marketing & networking and consultancy
& advisor costs ranging from £500 to £25,000.

Up Short

screenyorkshire.co.uk/default.asp?level=3&id=224
Offers: Up to £20,000 · For: PROD · Covering:
SHORT
Advanced level short film funding scheme for a
filmmaker with a relationship with Screen Yorkshire.
One award made annually.

Caught Short

screenyorkshire.co.uk/default.asp?id=358
Offers: Up to £9,000 · For: PROD · Covering:
SHORT
Digital Shorts scheme, run annually with a deadline
typically in June, to fund 8 projects.

Low budget shorts

Offers: Up to £2,000 · For: PROD · Covering:
SHORT
Applicants must raise 20% of the budget in cash
themselves. 12 films are funded a year.

SPARK — Feature Film Development Programme

screenyorkshire.co.uk/default.asp?id=283

Offers: Up to £5000 for individuals and up to 80% of project costs. • For: SCRIPT • Covering: FEAT

Writers apply to take part in a one day development workshop following which a treatment will be prepared and further workshops offered to successful applicants with the potential of an option on the script idea from Screen Yorkshire.

Development of Skills and People

Offers: Up to £2,000 • For: EDU

Individuals and organisations can apply for support with 70% of the costs of attending or providing training.

Audiences, progamming and education

screenyorkshire.co.uk/default.asp?id=363

Offers: £500 to £20,000 • For: AUD-DEV | CULT | PROMO | EDU

Aimed primarily at cinemas, festivals, education consortia, archives and non theatrical exhibition section, eg mobile cinema and film societies.

Community and Youth Projects

screenyorkshire.co.uk/default.asp?id=363

Offers: £500 to £5,000 • For: AUD-DEV | CULT • Covering: YP

Support for projects involving young people or under-represented sections of the community.

South West Screen

www.swscreen.co.uk

St Bartholomews Court, Lewins Mead, Bristol, BS1 5BT, UK

T: 0117 952 9977 • F: 0117 952 9988

E: info@swscreen.co.uk

South West Screen works to develop and sustain all areas of film, TV and digital media activity in the South West. Funds are channelled into a wide range of creative initiatives, management and support services and outreach. In addition, South West Screen seeks to 'influence and inform policy-makers, decision-takers and public opinion about the contribution, value and needs of film, TV and digital media in the region'.

A lot of support is delivered locally through networks such as Cornwall Media Focus (cornwallmediafocus. co.uk), Bristol Media (bristolmedia.co.uk), Plymouth Media Partnership (pm-p.com), Wessex Media Group (wessexmediagroup.co.uk), and workshops such as The Engine Room (theengineroom.net).

Funding

The agency is supported by the UK Film Council, the Southwest Regional Development Agency, Arts Council England, Skillset, European Social Fund and the European Regional Development Fund. Funding is not available for film production other than through the Digital Shorts scheme. Instead the agency focuses on 'building capacity and infrastructure, especially by providing the information, advice, training and broad investment that will help individuals, organisations and business to develop.'

Funding priorities are to:

• Build the capacity for growth of the film, TV and digital content industries in the region

• Drive innovation and the sector's understanding and adoption of changing technologies

• Support the development of individual and professional creativity and talent

• Increase access to moving image by enabling more people to make, show, see and discuss it.

Awards under £2,000 are accepted on a rolling basis and require at least 30% match funding. Awards between £2,000 and £10,000 require 40% match funding, while those over £10,000 need 50%.

Any award over £2,000 is considered at quarterly assessment meetings. Details of Business Development Awards for 2007/08 were not available at time of publication but are likely to include R&D support, trade event bursaries, placements and skills training.

Digital Shorts

www.swscreen.co.uk/WhatWeFund/112.aspx

Offers: Up to £8,000 • For: PROD • Covering: SHORT

DV Shorts scheme with 11 films financed in 2006/07. Run in partnership with Cornwall Film, ITV West, Calling the Shots and The Engine Room.

Production Alliances

www.swscreen.co.uk/WhatWeFund/74.aspx

Offers: Up to £8,000 • For: BIZ-DEV | CULT | DEV

Support the collaboration between 2-3 small businesses / freelancers in the region to develop a project (with £2,000 match funding) that explores:

• New and creative ideas or new uses of technology

• Ideas that increase access to new markets (territory, commissioner or genre)

• Ideas that focus on social inclusion

Film Festival Fund

www.swscreen.co.uk/WhatWeFund/ LOTTERY%20FUNDING.aspx

Offers: £2,000 to £20,000 • For: PROMO | EXBN_ AUD-DEV

Fund had a budget of £50,000 in 2006/07 with an average award of between £2,000 and £5,000 for emergent festivals and between £8,000 and £15,000 for more established nationally recognised 'strategic festivals'.

Audience Development Fund

www.swscreen.co.uk/WhatWeFund/
LOTTERY%20FUNDING.aspx
Offers: £1,000 to £8,000 · For: AUD-DEV | EXBN |
PROMO | CULT
Fund was £54,000 in 2006/07. Awards available to
organisations for audience development, training and
screening programmes, with £20,000 of the fund
earmarked for audiovisual archives projects.

Talent Development Fund

www.swscreen.co.uk/WhatWeFund/
LOTTERY%20FUNDING.aspx
Offers: £500 to £8,000 · For: EDU | AUD-DEV |
PROMO
With a budget of £45,000 in 2006/07, the fund
supports script and skills development initatives,
discretionary awards and festival attendence from
organisations and individuals.

Private Funds

Aurelius

www.aureliuscapital.com
Aurelius House, 3 Lower James Street, Soho,
London, W1F 9EH, UK
T: 020 7287 1900 · F: 020 7287 2314
E: info@aureliuscapital.com
One of the UK's leading facilitators of equity and tax-
based financing for motion film productions. Offers gap
finance and brokering, press and advertising finance,
and a host of other services.

Baker Street

www.bakerstreetfinance.tv
96 Baker Street, London, W1U 6TJ, UK
T: 020 7487 3677 · F: 020 7487 5667
E: enquiries@bakerstreetfinance.tv
Baker Street Media Finance specializes in the co-
production, financing and structuring of British
feature films, and British qualifying international
co-productions. Baker Street has established strong
relationships with major production companies and
studios as well as industry bodies. Typically Baker Street
has provided around one third of a films budget, which
includes any Sale & Leaseback deal.

Grosvenor Park Media Limited

www.grosvenorpark.com
4/5 Arlington Street, London, SW1A 1RA, UK
T: +44 (0) 20 7493 8030 · F: +44 (0) 20 7493 4143
E: funding@grosvenorpark.com
With offices in New York, Toronto, LA and London,
Grosvenor Park is a leading provider of tax based film
finance to producers around the world. Over 25 years
Grosvenor Park has raised more than $5 billion for over
400 film and TV productions and manages investments
on behalf of five thousand investors.

Ingenious Film & Television Limited

www.ingeniousmedia.co.uk
15 Golden Square, London, W1F 9JG, UK
T: 020 7319 4000 · F: 020 7319 4001
E: enquiries@ingeniousmedia.co.uk
One of leading providers of private finance to British
film through equity investment and P&A support.

Invicta Capital

www.invictacapital.co.uk
33 St James's Square, London, SW1Y 4JS, UK
T: 020 7661 9376 · F: 020 7661 9892
E: info@invictacapital.co.uk
A film investor and tax/co-production advisor. Through
the provision of debt, equity and structured finance,
Invicta has developed an influential position in the
UK and US film industries. Invicta advises private
clients and corporations on equity and tax efficient
investments in film production and distribution.

Matrix Film Finance LLP

www.matrix-film-finance.co.uk
Matrix Group, One Jermyn Street, London, SW1Y
4UH, UK
T: 020 7925 3300 · F: 020 7925 3301
E: enquiries@matrix-film-finance.co.uk
Matrix is a financial services company specialising in the
creation and promotion of innovative financial products
and services.

Movision Entertainment Ltd

www.movision.co.uk
Kingfisher House, Hurstwood Grange, Hurstwood
Lane, Haywards Heath, RH17 7QX, UK
T: 0870 3891415
E: mpollins@movision.co.uk
One of the UK's leading private film financiers, having
backed titles including The Da Vinci Code.

Prescience Film Finance

www.presciencefilmfinance.co.uk
Tim Smith, 45 Wycombe End, Beaconsfield,
Buckinghamshire, HP9 1LZ, UK
T: +44 (0) 1494 670 737 · F: +44 (0) 1494 670 740
E: info@presciencefilmfinance.co.uk
A financier of British, European and international
feature films and TV programming, working with
leading producers through the Foresight limited liability
partnerships and studio productions' EIS offering.

Scion Films

www.scionfilms.com
18 Soho Square, London, W1D 3QL, UK
T: 020 7025 8003 · F: 020 7025 8133
E: info@scionfilms.com
Co-produces and co-finances a small number of high
quality feature films each year such as The Constant
Gardener, Phantom of the Opera and Pride and
Prejudice.

ScottsAtlantic

www.scottsatlantic.com
3 De Walden Court, 85 New Cavendish Street,
London, W1W 6XD, UK
T: 020 7307 9300 · F: 020 7307 9292
E: info@scottsatlantic.com
Scotts Atlantic provides funding for British films,
traditionally though sale and leaseback. In addition it
may provide mezzanine or equity finance dependent on
a strict investment requirement.

Other UK Funds

Arts Council of England

www.artscouncil.org.uk
14 Great Peter Street, London, SW1P 3NQ, UK
T: 020 7333 0100 · F: 020 7973 6590
E: enquiries@artscouncil.org.uk
The Arts Council is the national development agency for
the Arts in England and is responsible for distributing
lottery money to the Arts. Funding is spread across
Grants for the arts, Regular funding for organisations,
Cultural leadership programme, Own Art (loans for
people to purchase art), Managed funds. Funding is
normally operated through regional offices — a full
list is available from www.artscouncil.org.uk/aboutus/
contact.php.

Funding
Funding from the Arts Council is aimed towards all
the Arts, including the moving image. However, film
financing is not available from the Arts Council — the
focus instead on 'supporting artists work with the
moving image'. Applications involving the moving
image must be works of art, rather than the kind of
screen and broadcast productions that would be funded
by a Screen Agency. Eligible activities could include:
· the production of artists' moving image work,
· education, participatory and training initiatives where
the focus is on artists' work in the moving image
· organisational development, or capital items such as
equipment
· cinemas or production facilities for projects
specifically concerned with the development,
production or exhibition of artists' work in the moving
image
· education and participatory work, eg animation
workshops for children which have an emphasis on
creativity · programmes of artists' work in the moving
image at film or media arts festivals
· animation projects which are experimental in form or
content, or technologically innovative

Grants for the Arts — Individuals, organisations and national touring
www.artscouncil.org.uk/funding/gfta2006.php
Offers: Up to £3m, avg between £5,000 & £20,000
For: DEV | PROD | POST | DIST | BIZ-DEV | EDU |
EXBN | CULT · Covering: EXP | DIGI | SHORT | ANI
This fund supports arts-based activities, organisations
and practitioners in England. Applications are made
on a rolling basis with decisions made within six
working weeks for applications for £5,000 or less and
12 working weeks for applications for over £5,000.
In 2005/06 4,707 grants were made totalling £81.7
million. Typically at least 10% of costs are expected to
come from other sources.

Arts Council of Northern Ireland

www.artscouncil-ni.org
MacNiece House, 77 Malone Road, Belfast, BT9
6AQ, UK
T: 028 9038 5200 · F: 028 9066 1715
E: reception@artscouncil-ni.org
The Arts Council of Northern Ireland will support film and video artists in their development towards producing artwork for gallery installation. Production companies and filmmakers seeking to produce and distribute film projects are not eligible for funding. Film and video artists can apply for funding through the Arts Council's 'Support for the Individual Artist' programme, or through its National Lottery programmes.

Support for the Individual Artist Programme

www.artscouncil-ni.org/award/award.htm
Offers: Up to £5000. · For: PROD | EDU | CULT ·
Covering: Other | EXP
This award is for artists resident in Northern Ireland seeking support for specific projects, travel and residencies. Production companies and filmmakers seeking to produce and distribute film projects are not eligible for funding.

General Arts Awards

www.artscouncil-ni.org/subpages/funding.htm
Offers: Up to £5,000 · For: PROD | CULT | EDU ·
Covering: EXP | Other
Awards can be for specific projects, specialised research, personal artistic development and certain materials/equipment for artists of all disciplines and in all types of working practice.

Major individual awards

Offers: Up to £15,000 · For: PROD | CULT | EDU ·
Covering: Other | EXP
Two annual awards for artists of all disciplines and in all types of working practice who have not previously received a major award.

Arts Council of Wales

www.artswales.org.uk
9 Museum Place, Cardiff, Wales, CF10 3NX, UK
T: 029 2037 6500 · F: 029 2022 1447
E: info@artswales.org.uk
The Arts Council of Wales is responsible for the development and funding of the arts in Wales. It distributes the National Assembly for Wales funding to the arts, and is also the distributor of National Lottery funding to the arts in Wales. There are three offices covering North, South and Mid & West Wales.

Funding

Up to 90% of project costs are available for artists work in the moving image, resident in Wales and who plan to undertake their project in Wales. For grants above £5,000 applicants must have been in practice for at least two years.

Funding for individuals — Project Grants

www.artswales.org.uk/publications/General_Guide_
to_ACW_FundingInds_06_07(1).pdf
Offers: Individuals can apply for between £250 and £5000. · For: PROD | DEV · Covering: SHORT | ANI | DIGI | EXP
This grant is to allow individuals to explore project ideas or to build their creative, artistic and professional capability over time. If your project includes an element of production you must have a partner organisation who will present your work in Wales.

Funding for individuals — Production Grants

www.artswales.org.uk/publications/General_Guide_
to_ACW_FundingInds_06_07(1).pdf
Offers: £5001 to £20,000 · For: PROD | DEV ·
Covering: SHORT | DIGI | EXP | ANI
To support artists in the creation of a new artistic product in collaboration with a new partner organisation who will present their work in Wales. For new touring product, existing partnerships will be considered. Work must be innovative and artistically challenging.

Creative Wales Awards

www.artswales.org.uk/publications/General_Guide_
to_ACW_FundingInds_06_07(1).pdf
Offers: Between £500 and £25,000 · For: PER-DEV | PROD | DEV · Covering: DIGI | EXP | ANI | SHORT
Standard grants are between £5,000 and £12,000 to enable artists with a track record to develop their creative practice, eg the creation of new, experimental and innovative work, taking time away from their usual commitments, or refreshing skills, creativity and creative partnerships. In addition, for artists who demonstrate a consistent level of achievement and contribution within their area of practice in Wales £20,000 is available and for projects with a strong element of production £25,000 is.

Funding for organisations — low level

www.artswales.org.uk/publications/General_Guide_
to_ACW_FundingOrgs_06_07.pdf
Offers: £250 to £5,000 · For: EXBN | EDU | BIZ-DEV | DEV | PROD | CULT · Covering: ANI | SHORT | DIGI | EXP
This level of grant is to support organisations planning and running small scale projects, pilot projects or projects that have significant levels of funding from

other sources.

Funding for organisations — higher level

www.artswales.org.uk/publications/General_Guide_
to_ACW_FundingOrgs_06_07.pdf
Offers: £5,000 to £50,000 · For: DEV | PROD | BIZ-
DEV | EXBN | EDU | CULT · Covering: DIGI | EXP |
SHORT | ANI
This level of grant is for organisations that have an
established track record in arts development and project
management and projects that are in line with ACW's
funding priorities.

Awards for All

www.awardsforall.org.uk
Ground Floor, St Nicholas Court, 25-27 Castle Gate,
Nottingham, NG1 7AR, UK
T: 0845 600 20 40
E: general.enquiries@awardsforall.org.uk
Awards for All England is supported by the Arts Council
England, the Big Lottery Fund, the Heritage Lottery
Fund and Sport England and gives grants of between
£300 and £10,000 for people to take part in art, sport,
heritage and community activities, and projects that
promote education, the environment and health in the
local community.

Awards for All

www.awardsforall.org.uk/england/
www.awardsforall.org.uk/scotland/
www.awardsforall.org.uk/cymraeg/
www.awardsforall.org.uk/ni/
Offers: Between £300 and £10,000 · For: CULT ·
Covering: SHORT | DOC | YP | DIGI
The scheme (which only supports not-for-profit
organisations) can fund projects that enable people
to take part in art, as well as projects promoting
education, the environment and health in the local
community. Funds are distributed by local offices, with
the minimum award for Scotland, Northern Ireland and
Wales being £300 against £500 for England.

BBC Films

www.bbc.co.uk/bbcfilms/
Grafton House, 379 Euston Road, London NW1 3AU
T: 020 7765 0251 | F: 020 7765 0278
BBC Films is the feature film-making arm of the
BBC. It is firmly established at the forefront of
British independent film-making and co-produces
approximately eight films a year from an annual
budget of approx. £10m. Working in partnership with
major international and UK distributors, including
Miramax, PolyGram, Fox, Buena Vista, Pathé,

Momentum and UIP, BBC Films aims to make strong
British films with range and ambition. Recent projects
include *Revolutionary Road*, reuniting Kate Winslett
and Leonardo DiCaprio, and Woody Allen's *Scoop*.
Production companies and Agents may submit scripts
to: Beth Richards, Development Editor.

B3 Media

www.b3media.net
B3 Media, PO Box 41000, London, SW2 1HN, UK
T: 44 (0) 207 274 2121
E: studio@b3media.net
Nurtures, develops and showcases creative talent
— filmmakers, visual artists, musicians — from
communities that are underrepresented by the
mainstream. B3 works across a range of media including
short film, spoken word, moving image and feature film.
Our work and events are hosted locally, regionally and
internationally to support talent across these mediums.

Blank Slate — Digital Shorts

www.b3media.net/digitalshorts/
Offers: Up to £9,000 · For: PROD · Covering:
SHORT
Funds eight black and minority ethnic DV shorts.

Big Lottery Fund

www.biglotteryfund.org.uk
1 Plough Place, London, EC4A 1DE, UK
T: 0845 4 10 20 30 · F: 020 7211 1750
E: general.enquiries@biglotteryfund.org.uk
The Big Lottery Fund was set up by the Department of
Culture, Media & Sport in June 2004 to absorb the New
Opportunities Fund, and the Community Fund into one
entity. The fund will give out more than £2.3 billion
between 2006-2009. It also backs Awards For All, which
is covered separately.

Funding

Funding from this body is concerned with aiding local
communities, particularly those which face hardship and
disadvantage. Film and video work could take place as
part of an activity — such as to engage local people
creatively, to document a process or produce resources
which support another project.

England: Young People's Fund — Grants to Individuals

www.biglotteryfund.org.uk/prog_ypf_individuals_
eng.htm
Offers: Between £250 and £5000 · Covering: SHORT
| YP
Young people in England with an idea for a project
that can make a difference in their community are

encouraged to apply for this award. This award is designed for 11-25 year olds applying individually or in small groups.

Scotland: Investing in ideas
www.biglotteryfund.org.uk/prog_investing_ideas. htm
Offers: Between £500 and £10,000 · For: BIZ-DEV | DEV
The fund has £4.6 million to test and develop ideas that could eventually become fully-fledged projects — all driven by community groups to strengthen the area.

Scotland: Young People's Fund
www.biglotteryfund.org.uk/prog_ypf_individuals_ eng.htm
Offers: Between £5,000 and £1 million
Funds are made over one to four years to organisations to support new ideas or projects that involve groups of young people who share common concerns, experiences or issues in the local area.

Northern Ireland: Live and Learn
www.biglotteryfund.org.uk/prog_live_learn.htm
Offers: Stage 1 — £20,000 to £50,000; Stage 2 -£600,000 to £1 million
Will fund projects where 'people have the opportunity to achieve their full potential' and attain 'physical and mental health for all people.' The project must also address disadvantage or the reduction of poverty.

CBA — DFID Broadcast Media Scheme
www.cba.org.uk
Commonwealth Broadcasting Association, 17 Fleet Street, London, EC4Y 1AA, UK
T: +44 (0)20 7583 5550 · F: +44 (0)20 7583 5549
E: dfidfund@cba.org.uk
Founded in 1945, the Commonwealth Broadcasting Association (CBA) promotes broadcasting throughout the British commonwealth. The CBA has partnered with the UK Department for International Development to increase awareness of the majority (ie developing) world in the UK on mainstream media. With funding secured until 2009, a further 70 programmes to the 100 already supported are expected to receive funding.

DFID Programme Development Fund
www.cba.org.uk/funds/dfidinformation.html
Offers: Up to £10,000 or 80% of budget
To support established documentary production companies wishing to produce programmes that increase understanding of the majority world. Can support development, research, pilot filming and rights / access.

Channel 4 British Documentary Film Foundation
www.britdoc.org
E: info@britdoc.org
Channel 4 British Documentary Film Foundation exists to promote British documentary by looking beyond TV to develop, fund and distribute the work of a new generation of UK documentary filmmakers. The organisation backs 'short films, particularly by new filmmakers, feature-length projects with the potential to break through, experimental films, passion projects by established filmmakers, documentaries by artists from other mediums such as photography or art and ambitious development projects'. Headed by Jess Search, the Foundation also runs the BritDocs festival. In its first year of operation to May 2006 they funded 23 projects out of 600 proposals with just in excess of £500k.

Rolling Fund
https://www.britdoc.org/foundation/filmmaker.php
Offers: £3,000 to £100,000 · For: PROD · Covering: DOC | TV | FEAT | SHORT
Awards bursaries on a rolling basis to any UK based filmmaker or a British filmmaker working anywhere in the world. Proposals are accepted through the website online, and must be made by the filmmaker, not the producer. Channel 4 have a 'first look' option on all films and development that are funded for TV rights. Funding can support short films and development or completion of a feature documentary.

Campaigners Fund
https://www.britdoc.org/foundation/campaigners. php
Offers: Up to £35,000 · For: PROD · Covering: DOC | TV
In partnership with the Joseph Rowntree Reform Trust for one or more documentary projects that focus on issues of social justice, human rights and democracy in Britain today. Match funding from the foundation takes the total potential amount available to £70,000, and is open for hour or feature length documentaries on relevant subjects.

BRITDOCART
https://www.britdoc.org/foundation/britdocart.php
Offers: Up to £30,0000 · For: PROD · Covering: TV | SHORT | DOC
Launched with the Institute of Contemporary Arts and Arts Council England, the fund is aimed at established artists interested in making documentaries between 3 and 30 minutes long, to be shot on any format.

City of Westminster Arts Council

www.cwac.org.uk
Council House, Marylebone Road, London, NW1 5PS, UK
T: 020 7641 1017 · F: 020 7641 1018
E: paula@cwac.org.uk
The City of Westminster Arts Council is funded by the Westminster City Council and run by the council and Film London.

Westminster Film, Video & Moving Image Bursaries
www.cwac.org.uk
Offers: Up to £1000 · For: PROD · Covering: SHORT | EXP
Production funding for new work in film, video or digital multimedia. Applicants must work, live or study in Westminster. There is one deadline each year, usually in the spring.

Ealing & Hounslow: Ealing & Hounslow Short Film Production Fund

West London Film Office, 5th Floor, Perceval House, 14-16 Uxbridge Road, London, W5 2HL, UK
T: 020 8825 5975
E: willmotte@ealing.gov.uk
Operated by the London Borough of Ealing and the London Borough of Hounslow to encourage new and emerging talent in film-making.

Short Film Production Fund
www.hounslow.gov.uk/applicationform.doc
Offers: Up to £4,000 · For: DEV | PROD | POST | SCRIPT · Covering: SHORT
The award may be used for any production costs, from pre- to post-production and the applicant must be a resident, working or studying within either Borough. The content of the short film must address an aspect of the relationship between people of Asian origin and other ethnic communities in West London.

Eastern Edge Film Fund

www.redbridge.gov.uk/leisure/artsfilm.cfm
UK
T: 01708 456 308
E: chris.cole@havering.gov.uk.
The fund aims to support emerging filmmakers in the London Boroughs of Barking & Dagenham, Havering & Redbridge into making their first steps into independent film-making.

Short film production
For: PROD · Covering: SHORT
Assistance will be offered ranging from office space and administrative support to cash input, training and hands on advice from a professional executive producer.

FilmFour

www.channel4.com/films
124 Horseferry Road, London, SW1P 2TX, UK
T: 020 7306 5190 · F: 020 7306 8638
E: hvarty@channel4.co.uk
The feature film division of Channel 4 TV. FilmFour continues to develop and co-finance theatrical films, which a focus on working with British talent, co-financing eight features a year. Due to the sheer volume of material received FilmFour cannot consider unsolicited material that does not come from a producer or agent. The company seeks projects intended for cinema that can also play on Channel 4 following their cinema life. Ideas will tend to be contemporary stories which are British talent lead.

National Film & Television School
www.nftsfilm-tv.ac.uk · For: DEV | SCRIPT · Covering: FFF
Each year FilmFour awards a development bursary to two graduating teams from the NFTS, to develop a feature film project. This offers newly graduated students a chance to make strong links with the industry and give them experience of the professional script development process.

Coming Up
www.iwcmedia.co.uk/news · For: SCRIPT · Covering: TV
Channel4's drama department run, in partnership with IWC Media, the Coming Up scheme. This scheme offers the opportunity for new writers and directors to have their work professionally produced and aired on TV.

Future Perfect
www.painesplough.com · For: SCRIPT · Covering: Other
FilmFour and Channel 4 drama sponsor a new theatre writing scheme run by Paines Plough Theatre. Future Perfect is a year-long project, for six new writers aged 18-26, specially chosen for their potential and ambition to become a new generation of playwrights.

Mesh
www.channel4.com/culture/microsites/M/mesh/
Offers: Up to £20,000 · For: PROD · Covering: SHORT | ANI
Mesh is the first national scheme to nurture new talent in computer generated and interactive animation. Each

of the directors will receive a fee of £2000 for his/her work during the 4 months development period and a further fee of £5000 for their work during the 4 months of production. MESH will also provide the animators with additional software or hardware that may be required to complete the development work.

A-I-R
www.a-i-r.info/
Offers: Up to £4,600 · For: PER-DEV · Covering: ANI
The Channel 4 / NMPFT Animator in Residence scheme offers new animators the chance to develop their short films in the new animation gallery at the National Museum of Photography, Film & TV. The animator receives advice from a professional Producer, £1600 materials budget and £3000 grant.

animate!
www.animateonline.org/
Offers: £5,000 to £20,000 · For: PROD · Covering: ANI | SHORT
animate! TV commissions films up to 6 minutes which will receive their premieres on Channel 4 in autumn 2008. To be eligible you must be an artist or animator with experience of experimental practice in film or digital media, and be based in the UK. Celluloid, tape and digital technologies are all acceptable, in pure or hybrid form.

First Light

www.firstlightmovies.com
Unit 6, Third Floor, The Bond, 180-182 Fazeley Street, Birmingham, B5 5SE, UK
T: 0121 7534866 · F: 0121 766 8744
E: info@firstlightmovies.com
First Light receives funding from the UK Film Council to support short filmmaking by young people. Funding and resources are offered to organisations across the country who work with people between the age of 5 and 18, and who would like to make short films with them.

Funding
Funding falls into three schemes. The Pilot Award is designed for groups which are used to working with young people but who are first time filmmakers. The Studio Award is for groups who are familiar with working with young people and with filmmaking. The Youth Media Fund was announced ahead of the books publication, offering £6m for young people's media. First Light will fund:
· Films where young people (aged 5 –18 years) take a lead role in all aspects of the production process
· Live action, animated fiction or creative documentary productions in any genre
· Films mainly shot on digital cameras
· Films that explore and develop creative filmmaking techniques with young people
· Films that are under 5 or 10 minutes (depending on the scheme applied to)
· Films that are based solely in the UK, and that are of a direct benefit to young people living in the UK

Pilot Award
www.firstlightmovies.com/assets/Pilotform18.doc
Offers: Up to 80% of project costs with a ceiling of £4000 · For: PROD · Covering: SHORT | ANI | YP
The Pilot Award supports organisations that allow the production of one a short film of no more than 5 minutes long by young people. This award is aimed towards groups who are new to filmmaking but experienced at working with young people between the ages of 5 and 18. All funded projects must involve young people in key roles of the project ensuring it is authored filmed and produced by young people.

Studio Award
www.firstlightmovies.com/assets/Studioform18.doc
Offers: Up to 60% of project costs with a ceiling of £20,000 · For: PROD · Covering: SHORT | ANI | YP
The Studio Award supports organisations that allow the production of 2-4 short films of no more than 10 minutes long by young people.

Youth Media Fund
www.media-box.co.uk/
Offers: £1,000 to £80,000 · For: PROD · Covering: YP | SHORT | DIGI | WEB | EXP | TV
A £6 million fund supported by DfES, has been created to give young people in England a positive public voice. The fund will offer grants to young people to create and distribute high quality media projects that inspire positive change for 13-19 year olds and their communities, through film, radio, TV, print, photography and interactive media. Young people will be at the core of the Youth Media Fund from its inception, influencing the vision, development and delivery.

What's the big idea?
Offers: £1,000 · For: SCRIPT | DEV · Covering: SHORT | YP
To develop stories and ideas for film.

Gaelic Media Service

www.gms.org.uk/
Seaforth House, Seaforth Road, Stornoway, Isle of
Lewis, HS1 2SD, UK
T: +44 1851 705 550 · F: +44 1851 706 432
E: fios@gms.org.uk

The GMS, in partnership with broadcasters and
producers, strives to ensure that high quality Gaelic
TV programmes are available to viewers throughout
Scotland at appropriate viewing times, and that the
range and quality of Gaelic sound programmes is
improved. The Service also has a consultative role in
relation to Gaelic programmes on digital TV.

Television & radio production grants
www.gms.org.uk/funding/ · For: PROD · Covering:
TV | DOC | YP | ANI
For projects that have a UK commissioning broadcaster
on board and that match GMS' funding criteria. Grant-
aid funding is available to independent producers or
the in-house production arm of broadcasters. The level
of grant-aid ranges from co-production partnership
funding to full grant-aid.

Development grants
www.gms.org.uk/funding/programme.php
Offers: Up to £3,000 · For: SCRIPT | DEV · Covering:
TV | DOC | ANI | YP
GMS offers grant-aid funding to assist independent
producers to develop programme ideas to a level that
will help induce a broadcaster to accept the project for
broadcast.

Training grants
www.gms.org.uk/funding/training.php · For: EDU ·
Covering: SHORT | ANI | YP | TV
Supports individuals to enhance their skills by funding
short courses and short-term placements in the
freelance, independent and broadcast sectors.

Glasgow Film Office

www.glasgowfilm.org.uk
City Chambers, Glasgow, G2 1DU, UK
T: 014 1287 0424 · F: 014 1287 0311
E: info@glasgowfilm.org.uk

Since 1997 Glasgow Film Office has supported in excess
of 40 high value productions spending over £36m
Glasgow. The aim in Phase 2 is to build on that success
by supporting both local companies and mobile high
value TV and film producers. Grants will now focus on
expanding the City's production capacity, boosting the
creative content capacity of identified local growth
companies and enhancing their location liaison service.
GFO offers various awards and support, all designed to
bring new talent together with established companies.

Recce Support Fund
www.glasgowfilm.org.uk/filming_in_glasgow/
Financial_Incentives.asp · For: DEV
GFO can provide support to productions by offering
an organised recce for key personnel including up
to two nights accommodation and the services of a
professional location scout. Transport for this will also
be provided.

Infrastructure Support Fund
www.glasgowfilm.org.uk/developing_your_
business/Business_Services.asp · For: BIZ-DEV
GFO can provide subsidy for the engagement of
consultants to assist in the creation of strategic business
plans. Small grants can also be accessed for generic
business planning needs, e.g. purchase of specialist
software, staff development requirements or upgrading
of business premises. Much of the assistance will be
direct and at zero cost.

Production Support Fund
www.glasgowfilm.org.uk/filming_in_glasgow/
Financial_Incentives.asp
Offers: Up to £50,000 · For: PROD · Covering: FEAT
· Visiting productions can apply for support via
the production support scheme. If successful, the
contribution forms part of the finance plan of the film
and will be recoverable – recoupment position to be
negotiated on an individual project basis.
· Indigenous productions can also apply for the
production support scheme. Following on from the
success of our original winter work scheme, Glasgow
Film Office will continue in its commitment to support
new directors.

The level of GFO contribution will be determined on the
basis of an estimated local spend report provided by the
production. The production must spend at least double
the GFO contribution on deals with Glasgow facility and
service companies which will be pre-agreed by GFO.
GFO expects that where possible, local crew are used
on the production.

Glasgow Media Access Centre (GMAC)

www.g-mac.co.uk
3rd Floor, 34 Albion St, Glasgow, G1 1LH, UK
T: +44141 5532620 · F: +44141 5532660
E: info@g-mac.co.uk
Scotland's longest running open access facility for
young filmmakers, provides training, information and
facilities hire as well as running a number of short film
production schemes.

Little Pictures

Offers: £1,000 · For: PROD · Covering: SHORT

Little Pictures is for first time filmmakers and is looking for strong ideas inspired by given themes. Little Pictures has a rolling commissioning process with a themed commissioning round every 4 months. Successful applications receive a cash budget of up to £1,000 and free access to GMAC production and post-production resources.

Cineworks

Offers: Between £6,000 and £10,000 and between £13,000 and £15,000 for animation · For: PROD · Covering: SHORT | ANI | DOC

Cineworks commissions five short films a year in the genres of drama, documentary and animation, by new filmmakers. The scheme was initiated by Glasgow Media Access Centre and Edinburgh Media Base and supported by Scottish Screen, The Film Council's New Cinema Fund and BBC Scotland. Each film is eligible to receive between £10,000 and £15,000 for production, as well as receiving support from industry professionals who will act as mentors throughout development. Producers and Directors are teamed up with projects in need of them and selections are made to allow production of five of the ideas.

Digicult

www.digicult.co.uk

Offers: £6,000 to £10,000 · For: PROD · Covering: SHORT

Digicult is principally for emerging Scottish based directors — members of the Digicult talent pool receive access to training and support to develop their project with 4-5 films commissioned a year.

Heritage Lottery Fund

www.hlf.org.uk

7 Holbein Place, London, SW1W 8NR, UK

T: 020 7591 6000 · F: 020 7591 6001

E: enquire@hlf.org.uk

The Heritage Lottery Fund is a non-departmental public body, assigned by the Department of Culture, Media & Sport to distribute lottery money to local, regional and national heritage projects and schemes. They will only fund a film as a small part of a wider project where for example a film or video maker collects and records personal histories as part of a project which involved the wider community in learning about and having access to their heritage.

Funding

The fund administers various grants aimed at supporting local heritage. Those schemes that might be of interest to readers of this book are Your Heritage, Heritage Grants and Young Roots. The Heritage Lottery Fund offers a range of grant-giving programmes.

Your Heritage

www.hlf.org.uk

Offers: Between £5000 and £50,000. · For: CULT | PROD · Covering: TV | SHORT | DIGI | WEB

This fund supports a wide range of projects that meet two broad aims, which are to, 'conserve and enhance diverse heritage' and to encourage communities to identify, look after and celebrate their heritage. Projects could be focused on traditions, sites and places, buildings, records and objects.

Heritage Grants

www.hlf.org.uk

Offers: £50,000 or more. · For: PROD | CULT · Covering: TV | SHORT | WEB | DIGI

This fund has similar priorities and aims as the Your Heritage grant, but the scope is larger.

Young Roots

www.hlf.org.uk

Offers: Between £5000 and £25,000. · For: CULT · Covering: TV | SHORT | YP | WEB | DIGI

This scheme is designed to assist youth organisations to actively involve young people in the UK's heritage. The applicant organisation must work with young people between the age of 13 and 20.

Isle of Man Film Commission

www.isleofmanfilm.com

Hamilton House, Peel Road, Douglas, Isle of Man, IM1 5EP, UK

T: 016 2468 7173 · F: 016 2468 7171

E: iomfilm@dti.gov.im

The Isle of Man Film and TV Fund offers equity investment for films and TV productions that are shot at least in part on the island. The Isle of Man is self-governing with its own laws. The government has made available equity funding for films shot on the island, to encourage film production and to boost the local economy.

Isle of Man Film & TV Fund

www.gov.im/dti/iomfilm/mediadevfund.xml

Offers: Up to 25% with a ceiling of £350,000. · For: PROD · Covering: FEAT | TV | ANI

Investment to attract film production to the island. All productions must be for theatrical release or broadcast with at least 50% of principal photography taking place on the island and at least 20% of below-the-line costs spent on local services. Applicants must also have a sales agent or distributor on board.

Lewisham and Southwark: South London Film Fund

www.lewisham.gov.uk/LeisureAndCulture/
ArtsService/LewishamFilmInitiative/default.htm
Lewisham Film Initiative, 1st Floor, Town Hall
Chambers, Rushey Green, London, SE6 4RU, UK
T: 020 8314 7733
E: Elizabeth.Mitchell@lewisham.gov.uk
Offered through a partnership between Lewisham Film
Initiative and the Southwark Film Office.

South London Film Fund

www.lewisham.gov.uk/LeisureAndCulture/
ArtsService/LewishamFilmInitiative/default.htm
Offers: £2,000 to £5,000 · For: PROD · Covering:
SHORT | DOC | ANI
With an annual deadline in the fourth quarter of each
year, funds are available to three groups of filmmakers
resident in either boroughs to produce and promote
their work.

NESTA

www.nesta.org.uk
1 Plough Place, London, EC4A 1DE, UK
T: +44 (0)20 7438 2500
E: information@nesta.org.uk
NESTA is the National Endowment Science, Technology
and the Arts. It was set up by an Act of Parliament in
1998 to invest in individuals and projects that display
innovation, creativity, dynamism and longevity. Since
its launch NESTA has invested over £105 million in over
1000 UK projects and companies. Every £1 invested by
NESTA in early-stage companies is matched with £5 in
private capital.

Funding

In 2006 its endowment was expanded by £75m and
the organisation was restructured offering, in addition
to policy and research, funding through Innovation
Programmes — to foster skill and attitudes required for
innovation to flourish (eg Pocket Shorts (see below), to
encourage creation of content for mobile phones); and
Investments — providing seed capital and commercial
support for innovative start-ups.

NFTS Inc

www.nftsfilm-tv.ac.uk
Offers: Up to £15,000 · For: BIZ-DEV · Covering:
FEAT | TV | MM | SHORT | DOC | ANI
An incubator environment dedicated to supporting
graduates develop start-up businesses in moving image,
with the offer of mentors, office space and start up
funding.

Nesta Ventures

www.nesta.org.uk/insidenesta/hwf_fellow.html
Offers: Up to £500,000 · For: BIZ-DEV | DEV
Invests directly in UK-based, early-stage companies,
with innovative technologies usually taking a minority
equity stake, for example the Short Fuse filmmaking
software Moviestorm.

Ideasmart — Scotland

www.ideasmart.org
Offers: Up to £15,000 · For: BIZ-DEV
Innovation programme to support new projects and
ideas from creative businesses in Scotland.

One World Broadcasting Trust

www.owbt.org
River House, 143-145 Farringdon Road, London,
EC1R 3AB, UK
T: 020 7239 1422 · F: 020 7833 8347
E: oneworld@owbt.org
Founded in 1987 the trust aims, through encouraging
the effective use of media, to promote a clear and
balanced awareness of human rights and global
development issues among the UK public.

Student Bursaries

www.owbt.org/pages/Bursaries/
bursariesbackground.html
Offers: £600 to £6,000 · For: PROD · Covering:
SHORT | DOC
Support for finishing a documentary about or in the
majority world to a higher standard, covering, for
instance, travel costs or post production. Grants are
available to film/video students and postgraduates in
the UK with documentary-making experience, including
overseas students based in the UK. In 2005, a film
student in Pune, India was funded to travel to the
UK to complete their documentary. Calls are made in
February with screenings each November.

Scottish Arts Council

www.scottisharts.org.uk
12 Manor Place, Edinburgh, EH3 7DD, UK
T: 013 1226 6051 · F: 013 1225 9833
E: help.desk@scottisharts.org.uk
The Scottish Arts Council distributes lottery funding
across the Arts through streams covering Crafts, Dance,
Drama, Literature, Music, Visual Arts, and Capital funds.
Within each stream the two priorities are for individual
artists and non profit-making arts organisations.
At publication plans to merge the Arts Council with
Scottish Screen into a new entity, Creative Scotland,
were set to be debated in parliament.

Funding

Artists working in film and/or video can apply to the Visual Arts Department scheme: Creative and Professional Development as well as studio residencies in New York and Amsterdam. In previous years a Scottish Artists Film and Video Award of £5,000 — £15,000 has been run in conjunction with Scottish Screen.

Visual Artists Awards

www.scottisharts.org.uk/1/funding/apply/individuals/visualarts.aspx
Offers: Up to £15,000 · For: DEV | PER-DEV | EDU · Covering: Other | EXP
Available for exploration of new ideas and/ or realisation of significant projects.

Creative and Professional Development

www.scottisharts.org.uk/1/funding/apply/individuals/visualarts.aspx
Offers: £1,000-5,000 · For: PER-DEV | DEV | EDU · Covering: EXP | Other
To assist individual artists with the immediate costs involved in producing and presenting work. Visual artists including film and video artists at any stage of development in their work, with a body of work outside formal education who are based in Scotland are eligible.

Creative Scotland

www.creativescotland.org.uk/home.aspx
Offers: up to £30,000
The £30,000 awards reward, honour and celebrate established and leading artists in Scotland and raise the profile of the arts and their contribution to Scotland. 10 are awarded each year.

Scottish Documentary Institute

www.scottishdocinstitute.com
Edinburgh College of Art, 74 Lauriston Place, Edinburgh, EH3 9DF, UK
T: 0131 221 6125 · F: 0131 221 6100
E: scottishdocumentaryinstitute@eca.ac.uk
The institute aims to create a synergy between the practice and study of documentary film, linking industry and academia through public talks, screenings and production and training initiatives (Bridging the Gap, AfricaDoc, Constructing Reality) for new filmmakers.

Bridging the gap

www.scottishdocinstitute.com/projects
Offers: £16,000 (50% in kind) · For: PROD | EDU · Covering: SHORT | DOC
The fund includes training for 12 filmmakers and seven annual awards offering 100% of project funding for 7 short themed documentaries.

The Prince's Trust

www.princes-trust.co.uk
18 Park Square East, London, NW1 4LH, UK
T: 020 7543 1234 · F: 020 7543 1200
E: webinfops@princes-trust.org.uk
The Prince's Trust offers a range of activities, schemes and grants that encourage young people under 30 who have undergone hardship in one way or another and are particularly in need of support. Funding varies depending on region, so check with your local office. For instance, people in Loondon with degrees are not eligiible for Start Up Business Support, and in Scotland applicants must be under 25, as opposed to 30 for the rest of the country.

Start-up Business support

Offers: loan of £3,000 to £5,000 & grant of £1,500 · For: BIZ-DEV
For individuals and companies eligible for support, a low interest loan of up to £4,000 for a sole trader, or up to £5,000 for a partnership (the average loan is between £2,000 and £3,000 but varies regionally) is available, alongside support from a mentor, a test marketing grant of £250, and in some circumstances a further £1,500 grant.

Grants for education, training and work

www.princes-trust.org.uk/Main%20Site%20v2/14-30%20and%20need%20help/grants%20for%20jobs%20and%20training.asp
Offers: £50 to £500 · For: EDU | PER-DEV
Grants to help applicants get into education, training or employment.

The Big Boost

www.princes-trust.org.uk/Main%20Site%20v2/14-30%20and%20need%20help/grants%20for%20group%20projects/funding%20and%20support.asp
Offers: £1,000 to £5,000 · For: CULT
A grant for projects initiated by those between 14 and 25 in England to create a project that brings benefit to the community. Eligible applicants include the unemployed, ex offenders, care leavers and educational underachievers. £1,000 is available for 14-16 year olds and £5,000 for those aged 16-25.

The Wellcome Trust

www.wellcome.ac.uk
Gibbs Building, 215 Euston Road, London, NW1 2BE, UK
T: +44 (0)20 7611 8888 · F: +44 (0)20 7611 8545
E: contact@wellcome.ac.uk
The Wellcome Trust is an independent charity set up by Sir Henry Wellcome in 1936. It has an endowment

of about £10m to fund biomedical research aimed at improving human and animal health.

Funding

Funding for filmmakers is available through 'Public Engagement' awards, which supports arts and communication projects which help the general public have a better understanding of biomedical issues. Most awards are aimed at arts and science practitioners or organisations.

People Awards

www.wellcome.ac.uk/node2510.html
Offers: Up to £30,000 · For: PROD | EDU · Covering: SHORT | DOC
Grants in the field of biomedical science that focus on communicating to and educating the public about the field which improve understanding. Workshop, art and teaching projects will be considered.

Society Awards

www.wellcome.ac.uk/node2540.html
Offers: Above £50,000
Grants will be awarded to academic research or acitivies in the field of biomedical science that focus on communicating to and educating the public about the field and which improve understanding. Projects should intend to make a significant nationwide impact.

Sciart Research & Development Awards

www.wellcome.ac.uk/node2530.html
Offers: £15,000 · For: DEV · Covering: TV | DOC | ANI | EXP
The Sciart project is aimed at supporting innovative projects at the intersection of arts and science. This fund supports ideas and initiatives at their early stages. Funding can cover research, small-scale productions, performances, broadcast proposals or digital media.

Sciart Production Awards

www.wellcome.ac.uk/node2530.html
Offers: Up to £120,000 · For: PROD · Covering: TV | DOC | FEAT
Supports the production of projects which engage the public in science. Funding can cover major activities run by arts, science and broadcast organisations. Individuals can apply so long as they are attached to a recognised organisation.

Pulse

www.wellcome.ac.uk/node2550.html
Offers: £10,000 to £50,000 · For: PROD · Covering: TV | DOC | EXP
Up to £10,000 is available for workshops, project development while up to £50,000 is available to support the full production costs for a regional project or part of the costs of a national tour.

Tri-Pod Film Fund

www.greenwich.gov.uk/Greenwich/
News/NewsArchive/2006/August/
TripodFilmFundApplicationPack.htm
Studio 2B1, The Old Seager Distillery, Brookmill R, Greenwich, London, SE8 4JT, UK
T: 020 8694 2211 · F: 020 8694 2971
E: filmofficer@greenwich.gov.uk
The TriPod Film Fund is operated across three London boroughs of Bexley, Bromley and Greenwich in partnership with Film London.

Tri-pod Film Fund

For: PROD · Covering: SHORT
The Tri-Pod Film Fund will provide full training in the area of script development for all short-listed applicants, who must be resident in one of the three London boroughs backing the fund. Additionally one of these projects will be taken from script to screen and will receive mentoring throughout the process. Applications should be made via each local borough: For Bromley — Kiaran Hall on 020 8323 1714 / email: kiaran.hall@bromleymytime.org.uk | For Bexley — Saskia Delman on 020 8294 6991 or email: saskia. delman@bexley.gov.uk | For Greenwich — Suzanne Hutchinson/Nicola Hogan on 020 8921 6146/6048 or email: filmofficer@greenwich.gov.uk

Triangle Film Fund

www.haringey.gov.uk/index/business/filming_in_
haringey/filmfund.htm
T: 020 8489 6903
E: filmoffice@haringey.gov.uk
Triangle films is a collaboration between the Enfield Film Fund, the Haringey Film Fund and the Waltham Forest Film Fund. For an application form and further details, contact the local borough:
Enfield: Alexandra Lowe on 020 8379 1467 / alexandra. lowe@enfield.gov.uk | Haringey: David Waterson on 020 8489 6903 / filmoffice@haringey.gov.uk Waltham Forest: Martin O'Connor on 07851 936 268 / martin. oconnor@walthamforest.gov.uk

Triangle Film Fund

Offers: £1,900 to £2,500 · For: PROD · Covering: SHORT
Offers seven awards for film-makers living in the three boroughs, as well as development seminars.

UnLtd

www.unltd.org.uk
123 Whitecross Street, London, EC1Y 8JJ, UK
T: 020 7566 1100 · F: 020 7566 1101
E: info@unltd.org.uk
Unltd was formed in 2000 as the foundation for Social Entrepreneurs. It took over the management of the Millennium Awards from the Millennium Commission in 2002 with an endowment of £100m of lottery money. UnLtd's awards provide practical and financial support to social entrepreneurs in the UK – people who have both the ideas and the commitment to develop projects which will benefit their community. In the past moving image related funding has been provided for workshops and training, media literacy, documentaries and community based video.

Level 1

www.unltd.org.uk/template.php?ID=10&PageName=level1_examples
Offers: £500 — £5,000 · For: DEV | BIZ-DEV | PER-DEV | CULT
UnLtd gives out 1,000 Level 1 Awards each year across the UK. Level 1 Awards are aimed at individuals or informal groups of people who have an idea and want help getting it off the ground. The money is to help with the running costs of the project.

Level 2

www.unltd.org.uk/template.php?ID=33&PageName=level2_examples
Offers: £10,000 to £20,000 · For: DEV | PER-DEV | BIZ-DEV | CULT
Awards support people whose ideas are already developed or to pay for the living expenses of Award Winners to help them devote more time to their projects. These Awards are given out once in the spring and once in the winter.

Wandsworth Film Fund

www.wandsworth.gov.uk/Home/LeisureandTourism/Arts/artsgrants.htm
London Borough of Wandsworth, Arts Office, Room 224A, The Town Hall, Wandsworth High Street, London, SW18 2PU, UK
T: 020 8871 8711
E: arts@wandsworth.gov.uk
The annual award with a September deadline is run by the Wandsworth Arts Office, the Wandsworth Film Office and Film London. Individual filmmakers or filmmaking organisations that work, study or live full time in Wandsworth are eligible to apply for up to £5,000 to produce or complete a short film. The film must have a budget of no more than £25,000.

Wandsworth Film & Video Awards

www.wandsworth.gov.uk/Home/LeisureandTourism/Arts/artsgrants.htm
Offers: Up to £5000 · For: PROD · Covering: SHORT | DOC | ANI
Short film production fund with total annual budget of £8,000 for fiilmmakers based in the borough

Warp X

www.warpx.co.uk
The Workstation, Paternoster Row, Sheffield, S1 2BX, UK
E: info@warpx.co.uk
Warp X was set up to exclusively manage and co-produce films for the Low Budget Feature Scheme tendered by UK Film Council and Film4 in 2005, with further support from Optimum Releasing, EM Media and Screen Yorkshire. Warp X makes digital films with budgets between £400,000 and £800,000 for theatrical distribution in the UK and internationally.

Digital Feature

www.warpx.co.uk/submissions.asp
Offers: up to £800,000 · Covering: FEAT | DIGI
Between 2006 and 2008 Warp X is producing seven digital films. Warp X will harness cutting edge digital technology and low budget production methods to make high value movies that can reach cinema audiences across the world. Warp does not accept unsolicited submissions.

Competitions

DepicT!

www.depict.org
Brief Encounters Short Film Festival, Watershed Media Centre, 1 Canon's Road, Bristol, BS1 5TX, UK
T: 0117 927 6444 · F: 011 7930 9967
E: madeleine@watershed.co.uk
Invites filmmakers to shoot a 90 second short, with prizes of £2,000 to live action and animation categories. Previous judges have included Peter Jackson and Terry Gilliam.

Oscar Moore Screenwriting Prize

www.screendaily.com/omf.asp
Screen International, 33-39 Bowling Green Lane, London, EC1R 0DA, UK
T: 020 7505 8080
E: admin@screeninternational.com
An annual prize of £10,000 to the best first draft screenplay in a genre which changes each year. No

award was made in 2006 after trustees of the awards decided none of the 154 entries were of sufficient quality.

Pocket Shorts

www.pocketshorts.com
The Old Caretakers House, Turnbridge Mills Quay Street, Huddersfield, West Yorkshire, HD1 6QT, UK
T: 014 8430 1805
E: info@pocketshorts.co.uk
Pocket Shorts gives new filmmakers opportunities to experiment with mobile technologies and is backed by NESTA and regional screen agencies.

Pocket Shorts — North England

www.pocketshorts.co.uk/
Offers: Up to £2,000 · For: PROD · Covering: SHORT
Pocket Shorts is a production funding scheme which gives early career filmmakers the opportunity to make original content for mobile phones. Applicants needs to have graduated within the previous five years and live in the North East, North West or Yorkshire. Contact — Lisa Roberts on info@pocketshorts.co.uk

Pocket Shorts — Scotland

www.pocketshorts.com/scotland/
Offers: Up to £2,000 · For: PROD · Covering: SHORT
For the production of content for mobile phones, for 'early career' filmmakers based in Scotland. Contact — scotland@pocketshorts.com

Turner Classic Movies Short Film Competition

www.tcmonline.co.uk/classicshorts
Turner House, 16 Great Marlborough Street, London, W1F 7HS, UK
E: classic.shorts@turner.com
Offers an annual prize fund of £10,000 for the best British short, with an illustrious panel of judges, that has previously included Ewan McGregor, Bernado Bertolucci, Kate Winslet and Gurinder Chadha.

UK Jewish Film Festival

www.ukjewishfilmfestival.org.uk
11a Jew Street, Brighton, BN1 2PN, UK
T: +44 (0) 1273 735522
E: shortfilmfund@ukjewishfilmfestival.org.uk
The UK Jewish Film Festival launched a short film fund in 2004, with an annual call for entries in January and a complete date at the end of August each year.

Short Film Fund

www.ukjewishfilmfestival.org.uk/Short-Film-Fund/
Offers: Up to £15,000 · For: PROD · Covering: SHORT | DOC | ANI
Any UK resident is invited to apply to produce a film with a Jewish theme of significance to both Jewish and general public audiences and a maximum length of 10 minutes.

Film Commissions

Most of the screen agenices lsited at the start of the UK section also act as film commissions for their region.

Bath Film Office

www.visitbath.co.uk
Abbey Chambers, Abbey Church Yard, Bath, BA1 1LY, UK
T: 01225 477 711 · F: 01225 477 279
E: maggie_ainley@bathnes.gov.uk

Guernsey Film Commission

www.filmguernsey.com
P.O Box 459, St Martin, Guernsey, Channel Islands, GYI 6AF, UK
T: 44 (0) 1481 234567 · F: +44 (0) 1481 238755
E: jason.moriarty@commerce.gov.gg
For short shoots the Film Commissioner can act as a Location Manager and pre-shoot will act as a location scout. There may be a charge for the services of the commission but there is no permitting scheme operating in the Islands. Many locations are available free of charge and the Island is extremely film friendly.

USA

Private funds

Salem Partners LLC

www.salempartners.com
11111 Santa Monica Boulevard, Suite 1070, Los Angeles, California, 90025, USA
T: +1 310 806 4208 · F: +1 310 806 4201
E: dmerritt@salempartners.com
A full service investment bank, providing services to the media and entertainment industries.

Public grants

Alabama Humanities Foundation

www.ahf.net
1100 Ireland Way, Suite 101, Birmingham, Alabama, 35205, USA
T: (205) 558 3980 · F: (205) 558 3981
Founded in 1974 the AHF offers the people of Alabama opportunities to explore the humanities through public programs such as seminars, workshops, lectures, exhibitions, documentary videos, and films.

Media Grant

www.ahf.net/grants.html
Offers: up to $5,000 · For: DEV | SCRIPT · Covering: DOC | FEAT | YP
Media Grants provide support for films, videotapes, slide/tape presentations, as well as TV and radio programs which have an Alabama-specific focus. All must be accompanied by interpretive study guides.

Media Grant

www.ahf.net/grants.html
Offers: up to $20,000 · For: PROD · Covering: FEAT | DOC | YP
The grant supports preliminary TV documentaries and study guides to stimulate discussion on issues, and dramas based on oral histories .

Alaska Humanities Forum

www.akhf.org
421 W 1st Ave, Ste 300, Anchorage, AK 99501, USA
T: (907) 272-5341 · F: (907) 272-3979
E: grants@akhf.org
The Alaska Humanities Forum is a non-profit organisation affiliated with the National Endowment for the Humanities, established in 1965. Its purpose is to promote the exploration of ideas, human values, and public issues that concern Alaskans today. The Forum believes that projects rooted in history, philosophy, literature, traditional wisdom, and other studies in the humanities contribute to our quality of life in meaningful ways and so supports humanities-based projects by Alaskans with grants, volunteer work, and educational workshops.

Grants Program

www.akhf.org/grants/application_materials/mini_grant_guidelines_5_05update.pdf
Offers: around $3,500 · For: SCRIPT | DEV | DIST | AUD-DEV · Covering: FEAT | TV | DOC | ANI | YP
Makes possible innovative humanities-based projects across the state, including oral history, films and other media, lectures, exhibits, conferences, public meetings, and research. Non-profit organization or institutions, individual scholars, and ad-hoc groups may apply for grants.

Astraea

www.astraea.org
116 East 16th Street, 7th Floor, New York, NY 10003, USA
T: 1212 529 8021 · F: 1212 982 3321
E: info@astraeafoundation.org
Offers general grants, scholarships and funds for sexual minorities.

US Panel Grants

www.astraea.org/PHP/Grants/USPanelGrants.php4
Offers: up to $10,000 · For: PROD · Covering: FEAT | DOC | SHORT
The grant is offered to US-based lesbian, trans and LGBTI social change organisations and projects, including cultural and film/video projects.

Visual Arts Fund

www.astraea.org/PHP/Grants/AstraeasUSGrantsProgram.php4
Offers: $2,500 · Covering: MM
The Astraea Visual Arts Fund promotes the work of contemporary lesbian visual artists.

International Fund Panel Grant

Offers: up to US $50,000
Astraea's International Fund for Sexual Minorities gives priority to groups with limited access to traditional funding.

CPB — Funding Educational Programs

www.cpb.org/
Corporation for Public Broadcasting, 401 Ninth Street, NW, Washington, DC 20004-2129, USA
T: 202-879-9600
E: press@cpb.org
The Corporation for Public Broadcasting offers grants to producers of educational programming.

Greenhouse Fund

www.cpb.org/grants/greenhousefund/ · For: EDU
The Greenhouse Fund awards grants for industry training and professional development projects for public TV professionals and independent producers.

National Programming Outreach Fund
www.cpb.org/grants/tvoutreach/
Offers: up to US $250,000 · Covering: TV
The fund awards grants in support of innovative outreach projects that maximise the impact and reach of public TV programming. There are four application deadlines per year. The proposal must be formally submitted by a US-based film producer, production company, or public TV station.

Program Challenge Fund
www.cpb.org/grants/07challengefund/ · Covering: DOC | TV
The Program Challenge Fund supports high profile, primetime limited series and specials for the national public TV schedule. There are four application deadlines per year. Any person or institution may apply.

Experimental Television Center

www.experimentaltvcenter.org/
ELECTRONIC and FILM ARTS GRANTS PROGRAM, Sherry Miller Hocking, Program Director, Experimental TV Center, 109 Lower Fairfield Rd., Newark Valley, NY 13811, USA
T: (607) 687-4341 · F: (607) 687-4341
E: etc@experimentaltvcenter.org
The Experimental TV Center provides support to electronic media and film artists and organisations in New York State to encourage creative work; to facilitate the exhibition of moving-image and sound art to audiences in all regions of the State; and to strengthen organisations with active media programs.

Finishing Funds
www.experimentaltvcenter.org/GrantsIndex.html
Offers: up to US $1,500 · For: POST · Covering: FEAT | DIGI | MM | DOC
Finishing Funds helps with the completion of electronic media and film art works which are currently in progress. Eligible forms include film, audio and video as single or multiple channel presentations, computer-based moving-imagery and sound works, installations and performances, and works for new technologies, multimedia and the Internet. There is a single deadline each year of March 15th. Applicants must be residents of New York State.

Presentation Funds
Offers: up to US $1,000
Presentation Funds provides grants to not-for-profit organizations throughout New York State. Support is available for personal presentations by independent electronic media and film artists. The program seeks to encourage events which increase understanding of and appreciation for independent media work in all areas of the State.

Media Arts Technical Assistance Fund
Offers: up to US $2,000
The fund is designed to help non-profit media arts programs in New York State stabilise, strengthen or restructure their media arts organisational capacity, services and activities.

Film Arts Foundation

www.filmarts.org
145 Ninth Street, #101, San Francisco, CA 94103, USA
T: (415) 552-8760 · F: (415) 552-0882
E: info@filmarts.org
The San Francisco filmmaking organisation is a non-profit pioneer in the media arts field, providing comprehensive training, equipment, information, consultations, and exhibition opportunities to independent filmmakers.

Grants program
www.filmarts.org/services.php?function=grants · For: PROD | DEV | EXBN · Covering: FFF | FEAT
The Grants Program encourages new and diverse works by film and video artists who have little likelihood of being supported through traditional funding sources. These awards are targeted for film and videomakers in categories that are normally the most difficult areas in which to raise money.

Fiscal Sponsorship
www.filmarts.org/services.php · For: BIZ-DEV
Film Arts' fiscal sponsorship program allows individual projects to become eligible for funding — particularly from foundations and government entities — which would normally only be distributed to nonprofit organisations (ie it acts as an alias for the applicant)

Ford Foundation Media, Arts and Culture Grants Database

The Ford Foundation, 320 East 43rd Street, New York, NY 10017, USA
T: (212) 573-5000 · F: (212) 351-3677
E: office-secretary@fordfound.org
The Ford Foundation is an international grant making organisation with offices in New York and 11 international locations. The foundation tries to advance human welfare by making grants to develop new ideas or strengthen key organisations that address poverty and injustice, and also promote democratic values, international cooperation and human achievement. Within these aims the organisation focuses the grants on fields within Asset Building & Community

Development, Peace & Social Justice and Knowledge, Creativity & Freedom.

Main award

www.fordfound.org/program/media.cfm
Offers: up to $200,000 or above · For: PROD · Covering: FEAT | DOC
The fund strengthens free and responsible media that address important civic and social issues. It supports productions that enrich public dialogue on such core issues as building democratic values and pluralism.

Frameline Completion Fund

www.frameline.org
145 Ninth Street, #300 San Francisco, CA 94103, USA
T: 415-703-8650 · F: 415-861-1404
E: info@frameline.org
Frameline's mission is to strengthen the diverse lesbian, gay, bisexual and transgender community and further its visibility by supporting and promoting a broad array of cultural representations and artistic expression in film, video and other media arts.

Completion Fund

www.frameline.org/fund
Offers: up to $5,000 · For: PROD · Covering: FEAT | DOC | ANI | YP
Lesbian, gay, bisexual and transgender film and videomakers are encouraged to apply to Frameline for the Frameline Film & Video Completion Fund. Grants are available once annually for projects in the final stages of production.

Funding Exchange/Paul Robeson Fund for Independent Media

www.fex.org
666 Broadway, Suite 500, New York, NY 10012, USA
T: 212-529-5300 · F: 212-982-9272
E: info@fex.org
The Funding Exchange was founded in 1979 as a network of community-based foundations committed to supporting movements for progressive social change. The organisation is a partnership of activists and donors dedicated to building a permanent institutional and financial base to support progressive social change through fundraising for local, national, and international grantmaking programs. It supports progressive independent media with community organisation component.

Independent Media Fund

www.fex.org/content/index.php?pid=29
Offers: up to $20,000 · For: PROD | DIST · Covering: FEAT | DOC | Other
The Fund supports media activism and grassroots mobilisation by funding the pre-production and distribution of social issue film and video projects and the production and distribution of radio projects, made by local, state, national or international organisations and individual media producers.

Independent Television Service

www.itvs.org
Independent TV Service (ITVS), 651 Brannan Street, Suite 410, San Francisco, CA 94107, USA
T: (415) 356 8383 · F: (415) 356 8391
E: itvs@itvs.org
ITVS was established by Congress to fund and present innovative public TV programs. ITVS is committed to programming that addresses the needs of underserved audiences, particularly minorities and children. ITVS funds, distributes and promotes new programs produced by independent producers primarily for public TV and beyond. ITVS is looking for proposals that increase diversity on public TV and present a range of subjects, viewpoints and forms that complement and challenge existing public TV offerings.

Funding

Applicants must be independent producers, which means that they must a) own the copyright of their production; b) have artistic, budgetary and editorial control of their project, and; c) are not regularly employed by a public or commercial broadcast entity or film studio. Producers representing foreign-based production entities are not eligible. Accepted applicants will receive funding in the form of a 'Production License Agreement' for production (Open Call or LInCS) or a 'Development/Option Agreement' for development (DDF). Both of these contracts assign ITVS certain important rights over the production.

International Call

www.itvs.org/producers/international_guidelines.html
Offers: from $10,000 to $150,000 · For: PROD · Covering: TV | DOC | ANI | YP
The ITVS International Call enables independent producers from outside of the US to create documentaries for US TV. Applications can be made once in a year.

Diversity Development Fund

www.itvs.org/producers/ddf_guidelines.html
Offers: up to $15,000 · For: DEV · Covering: DOC | TV

The Fund seeks minority producers to develop projects for public TV. It encourages minority artists to tell their stories and reach audiences often overlooked by conventional programming. Projects must be in the research or development phase, and cannot have begun production. Applications can be made once a year.

LINCS (linking independents and co-producing stations)

www.itvs.org/producers/lincs_guidelines.html
Offers: up to $100,000 · Covering: TV

LINCS provides matching funds to partnerships between public TV stations and independent producers. To apply for LINCS funds, independents must first approach a public TV station and establish a partnership. Single shows in any genre will be considered. Projects may be in any stage of development. Applications can be made once a year.

Research and Development/Commissioning Funding

For: DEV | SCRIPT | PROD

ITVS accepts proposals on an ongoing basis for research funding, development funding and production funding for projects that do not fit within the parameters of its standing initiatives (Open Call, LINCS and DDF), including limited series.

Jerome Foundation

www.jeromefdn.org
400 Sibley Street Suite 125, St. Paul, MN 55101-1928, USA
T: 651 224 9431_or 1 800 995 3766
E: info@jeromefdn.org

The Jerome Foundation, created by artist and philanthropist Jerome Hill (1905-1972), makes grants to support the creation and production of new artistic works by emerging artists, and contributes to the professional advancement of those artists. Jerome Foundation grants are made primarily to nonprofit arts organizations. The Foundation supports emerging media artists producing new works in all genres, with an emphasis on experimental work.

Funding

Production grants are made to individual artists residing in Minnesota and New York City. Subject matter of the proposed project is secondary to evidence of talent as demonstrated by work samples, except for projects in which the subject clearly requires special expertise.

Minnesota Production Grant Program

www.jeromefdn.org/IV~Grant_Programs/
B~Minnesota_Film_and_Video/b~Guidelines_and_
Procedures.aspx
Offers: from US $8,000 to $30,000 · For: PROD · Covering: FEAT | ANI | DOC

Preference is given to personal work in which the artist exercises complete creative control over all aspects of production. There is one application deadline per year.

Media Arts

www.jeromefdn.org/IV~Grant_Programs/A~General_
Program_Grants/1~Policies/a~Program_Focus.aspx
· For: PROD | DEV · Covering: FEAT | MM | WEB | DIGI | EXP

The Foundation supports emerging media artists producing new works in all genres, with an emphasis on experimental work.

New York City Film and Video

www.jeromefdn.org/IV~Grant_Programs/D~New_
York_City_Film_and_Video/Default.aspx · For: PROD · Covering: ANI | DOC | FEAT | Other

This program serves film and video artists who work in the genres of experimental, narrative, animation and documentary production.

Marin Arts Council

www.marinarts.org/grants.htm
555 Northgate Drive, Suite 270 (2nd floor), San Rafael, CA 94903, USA
T: (415) 499-8350 · F: (415) 499-8537
E: marinarts@marinarts.org

Funded by the Marin Community Foundation, this grant program awards money to residents of Marin County, California for works in a variety of media.

Community Arts Partnership

www.marinarts.org/grants_apply.htm
Offers: up to US $5,000

Community Arts Partnership Grants are available to Marin-based arts organizations or to partnership projects in all media. This program encourages people to experience and practice the creative process through local, community-based art activities, and encourages professional artists to become involved in the cultural life of their home communities.

Media Artists Resource Center

www.mtn.org/marc/grant.html
125 SE Main Street, Minneapolis, MN 55414, MN
55414, USA
T: (612) 331 8575 · F: (612) 331 8578
E: video@mtn.org
The non-for-profit organisation's mission is to promote
the production of media works by independent artists
from all communities.

Marc Access Grants

www.mtn.org/marc/guidelines_page1.pdf
Offers: US $2,250 · For: DEV
This program provides selected media artists free
access to its media equipment and facilities to create
a proposed project. The program is designed to foster
diversity and present alternative views of Midwestern
life, women, people of colour, the physically disabled,
are especially encouraged to apply.

Minnesota Independent Film Fund

www.ifpmn.org
IFP Minnesota, 2446 University Avenue West, Suite
100, St. Paul, MN 55114, USA
T: 651-644-1912 · F: 651-644-5708
E: word@ifpmn.org
IFP Minnesota is a nonprofit charitable organization
supported in part by contributions from individuals,
corporations and foundations. Minnesota residents are
eligible to apply.

SCREENWRITING FELLOWSHIP

www.ifpnorth.org/
Offers: $25,000 · For: SCRIPT
At the national screenwriting competition two winning
Fellows receive an award for excellence in the art of
screenwriting.

Professional Development

www.ifpnorth.org/
Offers: $25,000 · For: PER-DEV | EDU · Covering:
FEAT | SHORT | DOC | ANI
The program is intended to support mid-career
artists by providing financial assistance, professional
encouragement and industry recognition. IFP
Minnesota gives awards to two Minnesota filmmakers
annually.

National Asian American Telecommunications Assoc.

www.asianamericanmedia.org
145 Ninth Street, Suite 350, San Francisco, CA
94103, USA
T: (415) 863-0814 x103
E: info@asianamericanmedia.org
The Center for Asian American Media's mission is to
present stories that convey the richness and diversity
of the Asian American experience to the broadest
audience possible. It funds, produces, distributes and
exhibits Asian American films, videos and new media.

Media Fund

asianamericanmedia.org/rf_cms/index.
php?cmd=showPage&page_id=1.3.1&section=1.3 ·
For: PROD | DEV · Covering: TV
The funds aims to increase visibility of Asian American
programs on public TV and have impact on the way in
which Asian Americans are perceived and understood.
To date, over $3 million has been granted to over 150
projects.

National Black Programming Consortium

www.nbpc.tv/
68 East 131st Street, 7th floor, New York, NY 10037
T: 212 234 8200 · F: 212 234 7032
E: info@nbpc.tv
The Media arts and funding organisation dedicated to
the promotion, funding, preservation, and distribution
of diverse films from African American communities.
Funding is open to independent producers.

Annual Open Solicitation Fund

Offers: up to US $80,000 · For: DEV | PROD | POST |
DIST · Covering: FEAT | DOC | ANI | Other
Through the Open Call, producers can seek the
funds they need to begin or complete their projects,
launch an outreach campaign, or develop new media
components for their public TV programs. There is one
application deadline per year.

Discretionary Fund

Offers: up to US $30,000
Discretionary requests are accepted year round.

Acquisition Program

www.nbpc.tv/media/files/40/NBPC-FUNDING-
GUIDE07.pdf · For: DIST · Covering: TV
The program reviews completed programs from
producers and directors whose work has the potential
for airing on national or regional public TV and the
potential for distribution to the educational or home
video market.

National Foundation for Jewish Culture

www.jewishculture.org
330 Seventh Avenue, 21st Fl., New York, NY 10001
T: (212) 629-0500 · F: (212) 629-0508
E: nfjc@jewishculture.org.
The National Foundation for Jewish Culture invests in creative individuals and ideas in order to nurture a vibrant and enduring American Jewish identity, culture and community. Since 1996 the Fund for Jewish Documentary Filmmaking has supported 63 filmmakers with more than $1.35 million dollars to produce thought-provoking and award winning documentaries that have reached audiences in the millions.

The Fund for Jewish Documentary Filmmaking

www2.jewishculture.org/film/film_fund.html
Offers: up to $50,000 or 50% · For: PROD | POST · Covering: TV
Priority in funding will be given to those works-in-progress which combine intellectual clarity with creative use of the medium, can be completed within one year of the award, are standard one-hour or half-hour broadcast length, and are likely to be broadcast. Applicants must be US. citizens or permanent residents. Projects must be in production at the time of application.

New York Foundation for the Arts

www.nyfa.org
New York Foundation for the Arts, 155 Avenue of the Americas, 6th Floor, New York, NY 10013-1507, USA
T: 212-366-6900 · F: 212-366-1778
E: nyfainfo@nyfa.org
The foundation offers financial and informational support to the artists in New York State and throughout the United States.

Artists' Fellowships

www.nyfa.org/level2.asp?id=1&fid=1&sid=44
Offers: $7,000
This program accepts work that has been initially shot with a film camera. Filmed material that has been transferred to videocassette or computer for editing and processing is acceptable.

New York State Council on the Arts

www.nysca.org
175 Varick Street, New York, NY 10014, USA
T: (800) 510-0021
NYSCA accepts grant proposals each March 1 from nonprofit organisations incorporated in New York State. Individuals are not able to apply.

Electronic Media & Film

www.nysca.org/public/guidelines/electronic_media/index.htm · For: DEV | CULT | EXBN · Covering: FEAT | Other
The Program supports a variety of activities that assist diverse people in the development and realisation of film, video, sound, art and new media programs and opportunities. The fund supports grassroots and volunteer operated programs, youth media, community communications centers, independent cinemas, museums and broadcasters.

Individual Artists Program

www.nysca.org/public/guidelines/individual_artists/index.htm · For: PROD · Covering: DIGI | Other | EXP
The program offers support for the creation of artist-initiated projects in electronic media (video, sound art, installations, and new technologies) and film production, and the commissioning of new work by composers and theatre artists. Artists at various career stages are welcome to apply to this program.

Nicholl Fellowships

www.oscars.org
Academy of Motion Picture Arts and Sciences, 1313 North Vine Street, Los Angeles, California, 90028, USA
T: +1 310 247 3059
E: nicholl@oscars.org

Institutional Grants

www.oscars.org/grants/institutional/index.html
Offers: from US $5,000 to $15,000
The purpose of the Grants Program is to foster educational activities between the public and the film industry. The application deadline is in January. Grants are available for organisations.

Pacific Pioneer Fund

www.pacificpioneerfund.com
P.O. Box 126, College Park, MD 20741 , USA
T: 650-996-3122
E: armin@stanford.edu.
The aim of the fund is to support emerging documentary filmmakers. The term 'emerging' is intended to denote a person committed to the craft of making documentaries, who has demonstrated that commitment by several years of practical film or video experience.

Filmmaker grants

Offers: US $1,000-$10,000 · For: PROD · Covering: DOC

Grants to support filmmakers are limited to filmmakers or videographers who live and work in California, Oregon and Washington. Applications are accepted on an ongoing basis.

Rhode Island Committee for the Humanities

www.rihumanities.org/
385 Westminster Street Suite 2, Providence, RI 02903, USA
T: 401-273-2250 · F: 401-454-4872
E: maitrayeeb@rihumanities.org

The mission of the Rhode Island Council for the Humanities (RICH) is to inspire and support intellectual curiosity and imagination in all Rhode Islanders through lifelong learning in the humanities.

Media Production Grant

www.uri.edu/rich/grants_guides/categories.
html#media
Offers: above $5,000 · For: DEV | PROD | DIST · Covering: FEAT | Other_TV

The fund provides opportunities for humanities programs to reach a broad audience. All applications seeking support for films, videotapes, audio tapes, slide/tape presentations or live programming produced for TV, radio or cable broadcast, shall be considered.

Script Development Grants

Offers: up to $5,000 · For: SCRIPT · Covering: FEAT | SHORT

Southern Humanities Media Fund

www.southernmediafund.org/
Southern Humanities Media Fund, Virginia Foundation for the Humanities, 145 Ednam Drive, Charlottesville, VA 22903-4629, USA
T: 434-924-6895 · F: 434-296-4714
E: shmf@virginia.edu

The Southern Humanities Media Fund (SHMF) supports inventive film, TV, and radio programs and is particularly interested in media productions that focus on the 'new face' of the South, offering insights into the region's changing social, economic, and political conditions.

Southern Humanities Media Fund

www.southernmediafund.org/about.html
Offers: up to $110,000 · For: PROD · Covering: FEAT | TV | DOC

The Southern Humanities Media Fund has an annual grant cycle with a two-step application process to fund one to three projects.

Squeaky Wheel

www.squeaky.org
712 Main St, Buffalo, NY 14202, USA
T: 884-7172
E: office@squeaky.org

Squeaky Wheel / Buffalo Media Resources is a grassroots, artist-run, non-profit media arts centre founded in 1985 to promote and support film, video, computer, digital, and audio art by media artists and community members. The organisation provides low-cost access to video and film equipment rental, editing suites, workshops, and screenings of independent and avant-garde film and video.

Local Artist Access Residency

www.squeaky.org/opportunities.html · Covering: FEAT

The program is offering four equipment access residencies to local artists. The residency includes forty hours free access to the digital lab, 6-plate film editing suite, digital video editing systems as well as two days free rental of a production kit; including camera, light kit, tripod and microphone.

Texas Filmmakers Production Fund

www.austinfilm.org/tfpf/
Austin Film Society, 1901 E. 51st St., Austin, TX 78723, USA
T: 512-322-0145 · F: 512-322-5192
E: afs@austinfilm.org

The Austin Film Society (AFS) supports independent film with screenings in public venues all over Austin. In addition, it has instituted programs that award grants to filmmakers and internships for students in the film industry. The Texas Filmmakers' Production Fund is an annual grant awarded to emerging film and video artists in the state of Texas.

Texas Filmmakers Production Fund

www.austinfilm.org/for_filmmakers/texas-filmmakers-production-fund/ · For: PROD · Covering: FEAT | DOC | ANI

Since 1996 the Austin Film Society has awarded $550,000 to over 190 film and video projects.

The National Endowment for the Humanities

www.neh.gov
National Endowment for the Humanities, 1100 Pennsylvania Avenue NW, Washington, DC 20506, USA
T: 202-606-8400
E: info@neh.gov
The Independent federal agency funds media, including films, that enrich the arts, education, and humanities in America. Its budget for 2008 is $141m.

Funding

Any U.S. nonprofit organization with IRS 501(c)3 tax exempt status is eligible, as are state and local governmental agencies. Grants are not awarded to individuals. Independent producers who wish to apply for NEH funding are advised to seek sponsorship by an eligible organisation before submitting an application to NEH.

Television Projects: Planning, Scripting, and Production Grants

Offers: from $400,000 to $800,000 (for Production Grants) • For: DEV | SCRIPT | DVD_PROD • Covering: TV | DOC
NEH supports TV documentary programs or historical dramatisations that address significant figures, events, or developments in the humanities and draw their content from humanities scholarship. Projects must be intended for national distribution during prime time hours, whether on public TV, commercial TV, or cable networks. Support is also available for DVDs and Web sites that expand the content of the TV program.

We the People Grant Initiative

www.neh.gov/news/humanities/2000-05/slavery.html
Offers: from $400,000 to $800,000 • For: PROD • Covering: TV | DOC
The program aims to help Americans make sense of their history. Through this initiative NEH encourages applications that explore events and themes in the nation's history and culture.

The Open Society Institute

www.soros.org/initiatives/media
Open Society Institute, 400 West 59th Street, New York, NY 10019, USA
T: 1-212-548-0600
E: OSF-London@osf-eu.org
The Open Society Institute (OSI), a private operating and grantmaking foundation, aims to shape public policy to promote democratic governance, human rights, and economic, legal, and social reform. On a local level, OSI implements a range of initiatives to support the rule of law, education, public health, and independent media.

Media Program

www.soros.org/initiatives/media/about
The Media Program seeks to promote independent, professional, and viable media and quality journalism, primarily in countries undergoing a process of democratisation and building functioning media markets. Crisis assistance is available for outlets that operate in extremely oppressive environments such as conflict and post-conflict zones. The aim of this assistance is to enable media outlets to survive hardship. These grants can provide basic running costs.

Roy W. Dean Film and Video Grants

www.fromtheheartproductions.com/
From The Heart Productions, 1455 Mandalay Beach Road, Oxnard, California, USA
T: 93035-2845
E: Caroleedean@att.net
From the Heart Productions is a non-profit organisation dedicated to funding films that are 'unique and make a contribution to society'.

LA Film Grant

www.fromtheheartproductions.com/grant-lafilm.shtml • For: PROD • Covering: DOC | SHORT
There is one application deadline per year.

The Roy W. Dean Editing Grant

www.fromtheheartproductions.com/grant-editing.shtml • Covering: DOC | SHORT | FFF | FEAT
Go Edit gives two months free access to a filmmaker for editing their film. This grant is available to low, low budget ($500,000.00 and under) indie films, documentaries and shorts that are unique and make a contribution to society.

Writing Grant

www.fromtheheartproductions.com/grant-writing.shtml • For: SCRIPT • Covering: DOC | FEAT | TV | SHORT | FFF | YP

The grant is for writers who need uninterrupted time to work on projects in a beautiful, remote setting with a good computer, VCR, TV car and a few sheep to tend.

Thousand Words

www.thousand-words.com
110 S. Fairfax, Suite 370, Los Angeles, CA 90036, USA
T: (323) 936-4700 · F: (323) 936-4701
E: info@thousand-words.com

Finishing Fund
Filmmakers with incomplete projects can apply to this production and finance company for completion funds.

WriteMovies.com

www.writemovies.com
11444 Washington Blvd, Suite C-227, Los Angeles, CA. 90066 , USA
T: 310-281-6213 · F: 310-578-2452
E: info@writemovies.com
Screenwriter consultants sponsor this contest for short films and videos, awarding $500 and industry exposure to the winner.

Film commissions

Alabama Film Office

www.alabamafilm.org
401 Adams Avenue, Suite 630, Montgomery, AL 36104, USA
T: 334 242-4195 · F: 334 242-2077
E: hobbieb@ado.state.al.us

Alaska Film Group

www.alaskafilmgroup.org
P.O. Box 92008, Anchorage, AK 99509-2008, USA
T: 907 561-6445 · F: 907 248-0239
E: afg@alaskafilmgroup.org
Alaska has no state sales tax

Arizona Film Commission

www.azcommerce.com
1700 W. Washington, Suite 600, Phoenix, Arizona, 85007, USA
T: (602) 771.1193
E: harryt@azcommerce.com

Baltimore Film Commission

www.marylandfilm.org/faq.htm
417 E Fayette St, Room 601, Baltimore, MD 21202, USA
T: 410 396-4550 · F: 410 625-4667
E: rose.greene@baltimorecity.gov

Buffalo Niagara Film Commission

www.FilmBuffaloNiagara.org
617 Main Street, Suite 200, Buffalo, NY 14203, USA
T: 716.852.0511 ext 227 · F: 716.852.0131
E: clark@buffalocvb.org

California Film Commission

www.film.ca.gov/state/film/film_homepage.jsp
7080 Hollywood Boulevard, Suite 900, Hollywood, CA 90028, USA
T: 323 860-2960 · F: 323 860-2972
E: filmca@commerce.ca.gov
Free permits and no location fees for California state properties. 5% sales tax exemption on post-production equipment. No state hotel tax on occupancy.

Chicago Film Office

www.cityofchicago.org/filmoffice
1 North LaSalle, Suite 2165, Chicago, IL 60602, USA
T: 312 744-6415 · F: 312 744-1378
E: filmoffice@cityofchicago.org
20% Illinois Film Tax Credit on all local project related expenditures: labour, rentals, leases, purchases, services, housing, etc. The program is applicable to all phases (pre-production, production and post-production) of feature film, movies for TV, TV series and commercials.

Colorado Film Commission

www.coloradofilm.com/
Advance Colorado Center, 1625 Broadway, Suite 950, Denver, Colorado 80202 , USA
T: 303.592.4075 · F: 303.592.4061
E: info@coloradofilm.org
A production company can qualify for a 10% cash rebate on spending if at least 75% of below the line spending is with Colorado businesses and 75% of crew are Colorado residents. To qualify an in-state production company must spend at least $100,000 and an out-of-state production company must spent at least $1 million (rebate applies to first dollar spent once the minimum is met). Production companies must fill out a 'Statement of Intent' and receive written approval before principle photography begins.

Dallas Film Commission

www.filmdfw.com/
325 North St. Paul Street, Suite 700, Dallas, Texas, 75201, USA
T: 214-571-1050 · F: 214-665-2907
E: info@filmdfw.com

Delaware Film Commission

dedo.delaware.gov/filmoffice/default.shtml
99 Kings Highway, Dover, DE 19901, USA
T: (800) 441-8846 · F: (302) 739-5749
E: nikki.boone@state.de.us
Delaware has no state or local general sales tax. A low accommodations tax of 8% is ideal for large crews.

East Tennessee Television & Film Commission

www.ettfc.com
17 Market Square, #201, Knoxville, TN 37902, USA
T: 865-637-4550 · F: 865-523-2071
E: mbarnes@kacp.com

Eastern North Carolina Film Commission

www.filmeast.net orwww.ncfilm.com/region_eastern.asp
c/o Foundation for Renewal for Eastern North Carolina, 1645 E. Arlington Boulevard, Suite C, Greenville, North Carolina, 27858, USA
T: 252.756.0176 · F: 252.756.0717
E: fdooley@filmeast.biz

Film Division, Connecticut Commission on Culture and Tourism

www.ctfilm.com
One Financial Plaza, 755 Main Street, Hartford, CT 06103, USA
T: 860-256-2800 · F: 860-256-2811
E: Heidi.hamilton@ct.gov
Connecticut offers 30% digital media and motion picture tax credit and spends $50,000 for expenses.

Film Office of the Atlantic City Convention & Vistitors Authority

www.atlanticcitynj.com
2314 Pacific Avenue, Atlantic City, NJ 08401, USA
T: 609-348-7100 · F: 609-345-7287
E: brhoads@accva.com

Florida Governor's Office of Film & Entertainment

www.filminflorida.com
Governor's Office of Film and Entertainment, Executive Office of the Governor, The Capitol, Tallahassee, FL 32399-0001, USA
T: (850) 410-4765 · F: (850) 410-4770
E: Paul.Sirmons@MyFlorida.com
Florida offers an Entertainment Industry Financial Incentive, which reimburses up to 15% on the total Florida budget of a filmed entertainment program that spends at least $850,000 in qualified expenditures, up to $2 million. Furthermore, the state offers a State Sales Tax Exemption of 6% valid on production purchases and rentals of certain items used exclusively as an integral part of the production activities in Florida.

Fort Lauderdale/Broward County Film Commission

www.browardalliance.org/film
110 E. Broward Blvd, Suite 1990, Fort Lauderdale, FL 33301, USA
T: 800.741-1420 · F: 954.524.3167
E: info@browardalliance.org
Qualified productions during fiscal year 2006-2007 may receive a cash rebate of up to 15% of their Florida qualified expenditures, up to a maximum of $2,000,000, provided they spend a minimum of $850,000 in Florida on Florida cast, crew, businesses and vendors.

Georgia Film, Video & Music Office

www.georgia.org
75 Fifth Street, N.W., Suite 1200, Atlanta, GA 30308, USA
T: 404.962.4052 · F: vburr@georgia.org
Incentive Program: Comprehensive NEW tax credit effective now. Additionally, Georgia offers a point of purchase sales tax exemption for qualifying productions.

Idaho Film Bureau

www.filmidaho.com
700 W. State Street, Box 83720, Boise, Idaho, 83720-0093, USA
T: 208 334-2470 · F: 208 334-2631
E: peg.owens@tourism.idaho.go or kat.haase@tourism.idaho.gov
Sales tax exemption for productions spending $200,000 on a wide variety of qualifying expenses; tax incentives

for facility development when certain wage/job development criteria are met; no sales or lodging taxes with stays of 30+days.

Imperial County Film Commission

www.filmimperialcounty.com/body.htm
230 South Fifth Street, El Centro, CA 92243, USA
T: 760 337-4155 · F: 760 337-8235
E: filmhere@earthlink.net
At present the county does not offer incentives, local establishments offer discounts for lodging and rental facilities and cheaper labor costs.

Iowa Film Office

www.filmiowa.com
200 East Grand, Des Moines, IA 50309, USA
T: 515 242-4726 · F: 515.242.4718
E: filmiowa@iowalifechanging.com

Jacksonville Film & Television Commission

www.filmjax.com
220 E. Bay Street, Jacksonville, FL 32202, USA
T: (904) 630-2522
E: Silog@coj.net

Kankakee County Convention & Visitors Bureau

www.visitkankakeecounty.com
One Dearborn Square, Suite 521, Kankakee, IL 60901, USA
T: (815) 935-7390
E: kccvb@visitkankeecounty.com
The State of Illinois film office offers statewide tax incentives.

Louisiana Governor's Office of Film and Television Development

www.lafilm.org
T: 504.736.7280
Louisiana offers 25% Motion Picture Investor Tax Credit, 10% Louisiana Employment Tax Credit 15% Sound Recording Tax Credit, 15% Digital Media Tax Credit, 15% Infrastructure Tax Credit.

Maine Film Office

www.filminmaine.com
State House, Station 59, Augusta, ME 04333-0059
T: 207 624-7631 · F: 207 287-8070
E: filmme@earthlink.net

Maryland Film Commission

www.marylandfilm.org
217 E. Redwood St, 10th floor, Baltimore, MD 21202, USA
T: (800) 333-6632 · F: (410) 333-0044
E: kpelura@choosemaryland.org

Employer Wage Rebate Grant Program
This program allows a qualified production company to claim a rebate of 50% of the first $25,000 of wages paid per employee while filming on-location in Maryland for qualifying film and TV productions. Employees earning $1 million or more are excluded. Rebates may not exceed $2 million per project and are funded by an annual appropriation. The rebate is distributed in the form of a grant. To qualify, the production must incur at least $500,000 in total direct costs in the State and at least 50% of the production's filming must occur in Maryland . In addition, the production must have nationwide distribution.

5% State Sales & Use Tax Exemption
An exemption from the 5% state sales tax is available to qualified feature, TV, cable, commercial, documentary, music video, etc, projects.

Memphis & Shelby County Film & Television Commission

www.memphisfilmcomm.org/
50 Peabody Place, Suite 250, Memphis, TN 38103,
T: 9015278300 · F: 9015278326
E: info@memphisfilmcomm.org

Metro Orlando Film & Television Commission

www.filmorlando.com
301 East Pine Street, Suite 900, Orlando, FL 32801
T: 407.422.7159 · F: 407.841.9069
E: info@filmorlando.com

Michigan Film Office

www.michigan.gov/filmoffice
Michigan Film Office, P.O. Box 30739, Lansing, MI
48909, USA
T: 800-477-3456 • F: 517-373-0638
E: jlockwood@michigan.gov
Michigan offers a cash incentive on a sliding scale for
film, TV and commercials. The MI spending threshold
is $200,000. From $200,000-$1 million, a 12% refund;
$1 mil-$5 mil, a 16% refund; $5 mil-$10 mil, a 20%
refund.

Minnesota Film & TV Board

www.mnfilmandtv.org
2446 University Ave. West, Saint Paul, MN 55114
T: 651.645.3600 • F: 651.645.7373
E: info@mnfilmandTV.org

Mississippi Film Office

www.visitmississippi.org/film
501 North West Street, Woolfolk Building, Suite
501B, Jackson, MS 39201, USA
T: 601 359-3297 • F: 601 359-5048
E: wemling@mississippi.org

Montana Film Office

www.montanafilm.com
301 South Park, Helena Montana, 59620, USA
T: 800.553.4563 • F: (406)841-2877
E: mgoodrich@mt.gov

Monterey County Film Commission

www.filmmonterey.org/
Monterey County Film Commission, P O Box 111,
Monterey, CA 93942-0111, USA
T: (831) 646-0910 • F: (831) 655-9250
E: info@filmmonterey.org

New Hampshire Film and Television Office

www.nh.gov/film
20 Park Street, Concord, NH 03301, USA
T: (603) 271-2220 • F: (603) 271-3163
E: film@nh.gov

New Jersey Motion Picture/TV Commission

www.njfilm.org

153 Halsey Street — 5th Floor, P.O. Box 47023,
Newark, New Jersey, 7101, USA
T: 973-648-6279 • F: 973-648-7350
E: NJFILM@njfilm.org

New Mexico Film Office

www.nmfilm.com
418 Montezuma Avenue , Santa Fe, NM 87501, USA
T: 505-827-9810 • F: 800-545-9871
E: film@nmfilm.com

New York State Governor's Office for Motion Picture & TV Development

www.nylovesfilm.com
633 Third Avenue, 33rd Floor, New York, 10017, USA
T: 212.803.2330 • F: 212.803.2339
E: nyfilm@empire.state.ny.us_

North Carolina Film Office

www.ncfilm.com
4324 Mail Service Center, Raleigh, North Carolina,
27699-4324, USA
T: 919.733.9900 • F: 919.715.0151
E: joan@ncfilm.com

Oklahoma Film & Music Office

www.oklahomafilm.org
Oklahoma Film & Music Office, 120 N. Robinson,
Suite 600, Oklahoma City, OK 73102, USA
T: (800)766-3456 • F: (405)230-8640
E: jessika@oklahomafilm.org

Oregon Film & Video Office

www.film.org
Greater Philadelphia Film Office, 100 S. Broad Street,
Suite 600, Philadelphia, PA 19110, USA
T: 215.686.2668
E: mail@film.org

Otero County Film Office

www.filmotero.com
1301 N White Sands Blvd, Alamogordo, NM 88310-
6659, USA
T: 505-434-5882 • F: 505-437-7139
E: jan@filmotero.com

Palm Beach County Film and Television Commission

www.pbfilm.com
1555 Palm Beach Lakes Blvd, Suite 900, West Palm Beach, Florida, 33401, USA
T: 818.508.7772
E: filmflorida@earthlink.net

Park City Film Commission

www.parkcityfilm.com
PO Box 1630, Park City, UT 84060, USA
T: 435 649-6100 · F: 435 649-4132
E: lynnw@parkcityinfo.com

Pennsylvania Film Office

www.filminpa.com
Commonwealth Keystone Building, 400 North Street, 4th Floor, Harrisburg, PA 17120-0225, USA
T: 717-783-3456 · F: 717-787-0687
E: jsaul@state.pa.us

Pittsburgh Film Office

www.pghfilm.org
D.L. Clark Building, 503 Martindale Street, 5th Floor, Pittsburgh, PA 15212, USA
T: 888.744.3456 · F: 412.471.7317
E: info@pghfilm.org

Ridgecrest Regional Film Commission

139 Balsam Street, Ridgecrest, CA 93555, USA
T: 800-847-4830 / 760-375-8202 · F: 760-375-9850
E: racvb@filmdeserts.com

Rio Rancho Convention & Visitors Bureau

www.rioranchonm.org
4011 Barbara Loop, Suite 208, Rio Rancho, NM 87174, USA
T: (505) 891-7258 · F: (505) 892-8328
E: info@rioranchonm.org

Rochester/Finger Lakes Film & Video Office, Inc.

www.filmrochester.org
45 East Avenue, Suite 400, Rochester, NY 14604-2294, USA T: 585.279.8308 · F: 585.232.4822
E: dwightc@visitrochester.com

San Diego Film Commission

www.sdfilm.com
1010 Second Avenue, Suite 1500, San Diego, CA 92101-4912, USA
T: 619 234-3456 · F: 619 234-4631
E: info@sdfilm.com

San Francisco Film Commission

www.sfgov.org/site/filmcomm_index.asp
Office of the Mayor, City Hall, Room 473, 1 Dr. Carlton B. Goodlett Place, San Francisco, CA 94102-4649, USA
T: (415) 554-6241 · F: (415) 554-6503

Santa Clarita Film Office

www.santa-clarita.com
23920 Valencia Blvd, Suite 235, Santa Clarita, CA 91355, USA
T: 661-284-1425 · F: 661-286-4001
E: film@santa-clarita.com

Savannah Film Commission

www.savannahfilm.org
PO Box 1027, Savannah, GA 31402, USA
T: 912 651-3696 · F: 912 651-3696
E: Jay_Self@savannahga.gov

South Carolina Film Commission

www.FilmSC.com
1201 Main Street, Suite 1600, Columbia, SC 29201
T: 803.737.0490 · F: 803.737.3104
E: Email: filmsc@sccommerce.com

St. Joseph CVB — Film Division

www.stjomo.com
St. Joseph, Missouri Convention & Visitors Bureau, 109 South 4th Street — St. Joseph, Missouri, 64501,
T: (816) 233-6688 · F: 816-233-9120
E: cvb@stjomo.com

St. Petersburg-Clearwater Area Film Commission

www.floridasbeachfilm.com
13805 58th Street, Suite 2-200, Clearwater, FL 33760, USA T: 727-464-7240
E: Jennifer@floridasbeachfilm.com
Soft incentive packages available locally to qualified projects. State entertainment incentive fund, available July 1 (go to filminflorida.com for details).

State of Alaska Film Program

www.alaskafilm.org
550 W 7th Avenue, Suite 1770, Anchorage, AK
99501, USA
T: 907-269-8190 · F: 907 269-8125
E: alaskafilm@commerce.state.ak.us

Tampa Bay Film Commission

www.FilmTampaBay.com
401 E. Jackson Street, Suite 2100, Tampa, FL 33602,
USA
T: 813-223-1111 · F: 813-229-6616
E: ksoroka@VisitTampaBay.com

Vermont Film Commission

www.vermontfilm.com/
10 Baldwin St., Drawer 33, Montpelier, Vermont,
05633-2001, USA
T: 802-828-3618 · F: 802-828-0607
E: vermontfilm@vermontfilm.com

Virginia Film Office

www.film.virginia.org
901 East Byrd Street, Richmond, VA 23219-4048,
USA
T: 804.545.5530 · F: 804.545.5531
E: vafilm@virginia.org

Washington State Film Office

www.filmwashington.com
Department of Community, Trade and Economic
Development, Washington State Film Office, 2001
Sixth Avenue, Suite 2600, Seattle, Washington,
98121, USA
T: 206.256.6151 · F: 206.256.6154
E: wafilm@cted.wa.gov

West Virginia Film Office

www.wvfilm.com
90 MacCorkle Avenue SW, South Charleston, WV
25303, USA
T: 304.558.2200, x-320 · F: 304.558.1662

Western Reserve Film Commission

www.filminohio.com
25 East Boardman Street, Suite 442, Youngstown,
OH 44503, USA
T: 330 743-3900 · F: 330 743-3950
E: info@filminohio.com

Wichita Convention & Visitors Bureau, Greater

www.visitwichita.com
100 S. Main, Suite 100, Wichita, KS 67202, USA
T: (316) 265-2800 · F: (316) 265-0162
E: JCommer@visitwichita.com

Wyoming Film Office

www.filmwyoming.com
1-25 College, Cheyenne, WY 82002, USA
T: 307 777-3400 · F: 307 777-2877
E: info@wyomingfilm.org

Resources

Association of Film Commissioners International (AFCI)

www.afci.org
314 North Main Street, Helena, Montana, 50601,
USA
T: +1 406 495 8040 · F: +1 406 495 8039
E: info@afci.org
AFCI is the official professional organisation for film
commissioners who assist film, TV and video production
throughout the world. It is a non-profit educational
association whose members serve as city, county, state,
regional, provincial or national film commissioners for
their respective governmental jurisdictions.

Foundation Center

foundationcenter.org/
79 Fifth Avenue/16th Street, New York, NY 10003-
3076, USA
T: (212) 620-4230 or (800) 424-9836 · F: (212)
807-3677
E: communications@foundationcenter.org
The Foundation Center was established in 1956 and
supports over 600 organisations. It is an online resource
for researching funders, with tips on proposal writing.
The Center maintains the most comprehensive database
on U.S. grantmakers and their grants. The Foundation
Center's mission is to strengthen the nonprofit sector by
advancing knowledge about U.S. philanthropy.

Index of funds

The following lists of organisations offering funds for animation, documentary, shorts and script development is in no way meant to be exhaustive. It is based on indications given by the bodies and our research which may have changed or been misinterpreted. But while not intended as a definitive list of all sources of funding in a particular area, providing this index will hopefully make searching a little easier.

Animation

Australia : Australian Film Commission, Film Victoria, New South Wales Film and TV Office, Pacific Film and TV Commission, South Australian Film Corporation | **Austria** : Cine Styria Film Fund, City of Salzburg — Culture Department, Federal Chancellory film and media department, Land Salzburg Film Fund, Österreichisches Filminstitut | **Belgium** : Centre du Cinéma et de l'Audiovisuel, Flemish Audiovisual Fund, Bulgarian National Film Centre | **Canada** : Alberta Foundation for the Arts (AFA), Canadian Independent Film and Video Fund, National Film Board of Canada, Societe de Development des Enterprises Culturelles, Telefilm Canada | **Croatia** : City of Zagreb, Ministry of Culture | **Denmark** : West Denmark Film Pool | **Estonia** : Estonian Film Foundation | **Pan-European** : Eurimages, Media 2007 | **Finland** : Centre for the Promotion of Audiovisual Culture in Finland, Finnish Film Foundation, Suomen Elokuvasäätiö, Northern Film and Media Centre | **France** : Action régionale pour la création artistique et la diffusion en Ile-de-France (ARCADI), Africa Cinemas, Agence intergouvernementale de la Francophonie, Aquitaine Image Cinéma, Atelier de Production Centre Val de Loire, Centre national de la cinématographie (CNC), Centre régional de ressources audiovisuelles de la région Nord-Pas de Calais, Collectivité teritoriale de la Corse, Communauté urbaine de Strasbourg, Conseil général de la Charente, Conseil général de l'Isère, Conseil général des Côtes d'Armor, Conseil régional d'Alsace, Conseil régional d'Aquitaine, Conseil régional de Franche-Comté, Conseil régional de la Bretagne, Conseil régional de Poitou-Charentes, Conseil régional Midi-Pyrénées, Ministère des Affaires étrangères, Région Ile-de-France, Région Réunion | **Germany** : Bavarian Film & TV Fund, Hessische Filmförderung, Kulturelle Filmförderung Bremen, Kulturelle Filmförderung Sachsen-Anhalt, Kulturelle Filmförderung Schleswig-Holstein e.V, Kulturelle Filmförderung Thüringen, Medien- und Filmgesellschaft Baden-Würtemberg GmbH, Medienboard Berlin-Brandenburg, Mitteldeutsche Medienförderung GmbH, Nordmedia, Saarland Medien GmbH | **Grece** : Greek Film Centre | **Hungary** : Motion Picture Public Foundation of Hungary, National Cultural Fund of Hungary | **Iceland** : Icelandic Film Centre | **Ireland** : Irish Film Board | **Italy** : Friuli Venezia Giulia Film Commission, Salento Film Fund | **Latvia** : National Film Center of Latvia | **Luxembourg** : Film Fund Luxembourg | **Malta** : Malta Film Commission | **Netherlands** : Dutch Film Fund, Rotterdam Film Fund | **New Zealand** : Film New Zealand | **Norway** : Nordic Film & TV Fund, Norsk Filmfond, Norwegian Film Development | **Poland** : Film Polski, Polish Film Institute | **Portugal** : Instituto do Cinema, Audiovisual e Multimédia | **Romania** : National Cinema Centre | **Slovakia** : Ministry of Culture of the Slovak Republic | **Slovenia** : Slovenian Film Fund | **Spain** : Catalan Finance Institute, Conselleria de Cultura, Comunicacion Social e Turismo, Xunta de Galicia, Departamento de Cultura y Turismo, Gobierno de Navarra, Diputación Provincial de Almeria, Direccion de Creacion y Difusion Cultural, Gobierno Vasco, Ibermedia, Institut Catala des Industries Culturals, Instituto de la Cinematografia y las Artes Audiovisuales | **Sweden** : Film i Väst, Svenska Filminstitut | **Switzerland** : Canton of Aargau Film support, Canton of Solothurn Film Support, Canton Ticino film support, Canton-City of Basel Film Support, City of Bern Film Commission, Federal Office of Culture — Film Section, Fondation Vaudoise pour le Cinéma, Fonds Regio Films, Zurich Film Foundation | **UK** : Arts Council of England, Arts Council of Wales, EM Media, Film Agency for Wales, Film London, FilmFour, First Light, Gaelic Media Service, Glasgow Media Access Centre (GMAC), Isle of Man Film Commission, Lewisham and Southwark: South London Film Fund, NESTA, North West Vision, Northern Film & Media, Northern Ireland Film TV Commission (NIFTC), Scottish Screen, Screen East, Screen South, Screen West Midlands, Screen Yorkshire, The Wellcome Trust, UK Film Council, UK Jewish Film Festival, Wandsworth Film Fund | **USA** : Alaska Humanities Forum, Frameline Completion Fund, Independent TV Service, Jerome Foundation,

Minnesota Independent Film Fund, National Black Programming Consortium, Texas Filmmakers Production Fund,

Documentary

Australia : Australian Film Commission, Film Australia Limited, Film Finance Corporation Australia Ltd (FFC), Film Victoria, New South Wales Film and TV Office, Northern Territory Film Office, Pacific Film and TV Commission, ScreenWest, South Australian Film Corporation | **Austria** : Cine Styria Film Fund, Cine Tirol Film Fund, City of Salzburg — Culture Department, Federal Chancellory film and media department, Land Salzburg Film Fund, Österreichisches Filminstitut | **Belgium** : Flemish Audiovisual Fund | **Bulgaria** : Bulgarian National Film Centre | **Canada** : Alberta Foundation for the Arts (AFA), Canada Council for the Arts, Canadian Independent Film and Video Fund, National Film Board of Canada, Newfoundland & Labrador Film Development Corporation, Sask Film, Societe de Development des Enterprises Culturelles, Telefilm Canada, Yukon Film and Sound Commission | **Croatia** : City of Zagreb, Ministry of Culture | **Denmark** : Danish Film Institute, West Denmark Film Pool | **Estonia** : Estonian Film Foundation | **Pan-European** : EC Development Directorate Culture Section, Eurimages, Hubert Bals Fund, Media 2007 | **Finland** : Centre for the Promotion of Audiovisual Culture in Finland, Finnish Film Foundation, Suomen Elokuvasäätiö, Northern Film and Media Centre | **France** : Action régionale pour la création artistique et la diffusion en Ile-de-France (ARCADI), Africa Cinemas, Agence culturelle d'Alsace, Agence intergouvernementale de la Francophonie, Aquitaine Image Cinéma, Atelier de Production Centre Val de Loire, Centre national de la cinématographie (CNC), Centre régional de ressources audiovisuelles de la région Nord-Pas de Calais, Collectivité teritoriale de la Corse, Communauté urbaine de Strasbourg, Conseil général de la Charente, Conseil général de l'Isère, Conseil général des Côtes d'Armor, Conseil général du Lot, Conseil général du Val-de-Marne, Conseil régional d'Alsace, Conseil régional d'Aquitaine, Conseil régional de Franche-Comté, Conseil régional de la Bretagne, Conseil régional de la Picardie, Conseil régional de Lorraine, Conseil régional de Poitou-Charentes, Conseil régional de Provence-Alpes-Côte d'Azur, Conseil régional des Pays de la Loire, Conseil régional du Limousin, Conseil régional Midi-Pyrénées, Conseil régional Rhône-Alpes, Ministère des Affaires étrangères, Office régional culturel de Champagne-

Ardenne, Pôle Image Haute Normandie, Région Ile-de-France, Région Réunion | **Germany** : Bavarian Film & TV Fund, Beauftragter der Bundesregierung für Kultur und Medien, Filmförderung Baden-Württemberg, Filmförderung Hamburg GmbH, German Federal Film Board (Filmförderungsanstalt), Hessische Filmförderung, Kulturelle Filmförderung Bremen, Kulturelle Filmförderung Sachsen, Kulturelle Filmförderung Sachsen-Anhalt, Kulturelle Filmförderung Schleswig-Holstein e.V, Kulturelle Filmförderung Thüringen, Medien- und Filmgesellschaft Baden-Würtemberg GmbH, Medienboard Berlin-Brandenburg, Mitteldeutsche Medienförderung GmbH, MSH Institute for development of audiovisual works in Schleswig-Holstein, Nordmedia, Saarland Medien GmbH | **Grece** : Greek Film Centre | **Hungary** : Foundation of the Hungarian Historical Motion Picture, Motion Picture Public Foundation of Hungary, National Cultural Fund of Hungary | **Iceland** : Icelandic Film Centre | **Ireland** : Irish Film Board | **Italy** : Friuli Venezia Giulia Film Commission, Salento Film Fund | **Latvia** : National Film Center of Latvia | **Luxembourg** : Film Fund Luxembourg | **Malta** : Malta Film Commission | **Netherlands** : Dutch Film Fund, Jan Vrijman Fund, Rotterdam Film Fund, Stimuleringsfonds Nederlandse Culturele Omroepproducties, The Dutch Co-production Fund for Broadcasting Companies | **New Zealand** : Film New Zealand | **Norway** : Nordic Film & TV Fund, Norsk Filmfond, North Norwegian Film Centre, Norwegian Film Development, West Norwegian Film Centre | **Poland** : Film Polski, Polish Film Institute | **Portugal** : Instituto do Cinema, Audiovisual e Multimédia | **Romania** : National Cinema Centre | **Slovakia** : Ministry of Culture of the Slovak Republic | **Slovenia** : Slovenian Film Fund | **Spain** : Catalan Finance Institute, Communidad de Aragón, Comunidad Autonóma de Extremadura, Conselleria de Cultura, Comunicacion Social e Turismo, Xunta de Galicia, Departamento de Cultura y Turismo, Gobierno de Navarra, Diputación Provincial de Almería, Direccion de Creacion y Difusion Cultural, Gobierno Vasco, Direccion General de Fomento y Promocion Cultural, Junta de Andalucia, Ibermedia, Institut Catala des Industries Culturals, Instituto de la Cinematografia y las Artes Audiovisuales, Instituto Valenciano de Cinematografia Ricardo Munoz Suay | **Sweden** : Film i Skåne, Film i Väst, Filmpool Nord, Göteborg Film Festival Filmfund, Svenska Filminstitut | **Switzerland** : Canton of Aargau Film support, Canton of Bern Film support, Canton of Solothurn Film Support, Canton Ticino film support, Canton-City of Basel Film Support, City of Bern Film

Commission, City of Geneva Film Support, Federal Office of Culture — Film Section, Fondation Vaudoise pour le Cinéma, Fonds Regio Films, Kulturfonds Suissimage, Visions sud est, Zurich Film Foundation | **UK** : Awards for All, CBA — DFID Broadcast Media Scheme, Channel 4 British Documentary Film Foundation, EM Media, Film London, Gaelic Media Service, Glasgow Media Access Centre (GMAC), Lewisham and Southwark: South London Film Fund, NESTA, North West Vision, Northern Film & Media, Northern Ireland Film TV Commission (NIFTC), One World Broadcasting Trust, Scottish Documentary Institute, Scottish Screen, Screen East, Screen South, Screen West Midlands, Screen Yorkshire, The Wellcome Trust, UK Film Council, UK Jewish Film Festival, Wandsworth Film Fund | **USA** : Alabama Humanities Foundation, Alaska Humanities Forum, Astraea, CPB — Funding Educational Programs, Experimental TV Center, Ford Foundation Media, Arts and Culture Grants Database, Frameline Completion Fund, Funding Exchange/Paul Robeson Fund for Independent Media, Independent TV Service, Jerome Foundation, Minnesota Independent Film Fund, National Black Programming Consortium, Pacific Pioneer Fund, Roy W. Dean Film and Video Grants, Southern Humanities Media Fund, Texas Filmmakers Production Fund, The National Endowment for the Humanities

Shorts

Australia : Australian Film Commission, Film Victoria, New South Wales Film and TV Office, Northern Territory Film Office, Pacific Film and TV Commission, South Australian Film Corporation | **Austria** : Cine Styria Film Fund, Federal Chancellory film and media department, Land Salzburg Film Fund | **Belgium** : Centre du Cinéma et de l'Audiovisuel, Flemish Audiovisual Fund | **Canada** : Alberta Foundation for the Arts (AFA), Canada Council for the Arts, National Film Board of Canada, Newfoundland & Labrador Film Development Corporation, Telefilm Canada, Yukon Film and Sound Commission | **Croatia** : City of Zagreb, Ministry of Culture | **Denmark** : Danish Film Institute, West Denmark Film Pool | **Estonia** : Estonian Film Foundation | **Pan-European** : Hubert Bals Fund, Media 2007 | **Finland** : Centre for the Promotion of Audiovisual Culture in Finland, Finnish Film Foundation, Suomen Elokuvasäätiö, Northern Film and Media Centre | **France** : Action régionale pour la création artistique et la diffusion en Ile-de-France (ARCADI), Agence culturelle d'Alsace, Agence intergouvernementale de la

Francophonie, Aquitaine Image Cinéma, Atelier de Production Centre Val de Loire, Centre national de la cinématographie (CNC), Collectivité teritoriale de la Corse, Communauté urbaine de Strasbourg, Conseil général de la Charente, Conseil général de la Corrèze, Conseil général de la Sarthe, Conseil général de l'Eure, Conseil général de Loire-Atlantique, Conseil général des Bouches-du-Rhône, Conseil général du Finistère, Conseil général du Lot, Conseil général du Val-de-Marne, Conseil régional d'Aquitaine, Conseil régional de Basse-Normandie, Conseil régional de Franche-Comté, Conseil régional de la Bretagne, Conseil régional de la Picardie, Conseil régional de Lorraine, Conseil régional de Poitou-Charentes, Conseil régional de Provence-Alpes-Côte d'Azur, Conseil régional des Pays de la Loire, Conseil régional du Limousin, Conseil régional Midi-Pyrénées, Conseil régional Rhône-Alpes, Ministère des Affaires étrangères, Office régional culturel de Champagne-Ardenne, Pôle Image Haute Normandie, Région Réunion | **Germany** : Bavarian Film & TV Fund, Beauftragter der Bundesregierung für Kultur und Medien, FilmFernsehFonds Bayern, Filmförderung Hamburg GmbH, German Federal Film Board (Filmförderungsanstalt), Hessische Filmförderung, Kulturelle Filmförderung Bremen, Kulturelle Filmförderung Sachsen, Kulturelle Filmförderung Sachsen-Anhalt, Kulturelle Filmförderung Schleswig-Holstein e.V, Kulturelle Filmförderung Thüringen, Medien- und Filmgesellschaft Baden-Würtemberg GmbH, Mitteldeutsche Medienförderung GmbH, Nordmedia, Saarland Medien GmbH | **Grece** : Greek Film Centre | **Hungary** : Motion Picture Public Foundation of Hungary | **Iceland** : Icelandic Film Centre | **Ireland** : Irish Film Board | **Italy** : Direzione Generale per il Cinema, Friuli Venezia Giulia Film Commission, Salento Film Fund | **Latvia** : National Film Center of Latvia | **Luxembourg** : Film Fund Luxembourg | **Malta** : Malta Film Commission | **Netherlands** : Dutch Film Fund, Rotterdam Film Fund, The Dutch Co-production Fund for Broadcasting Companies | **Norway** : Nordic Film & TV Fund, Norsk Filmfond, North Norwegian Film Centre, West Norwegian Film Centre | **Poland** : Film Polski, Polish Film Institute | **Portugal** : Instituto do Cinema, Audiovisual e Multimédia | **Romania** : National Cinema Centre | **Slovakia** : Ministry of Culture of the Slovak Republic | **Slovenia** : Slovenian Film Fund | **Spain** : Asesoría de Cine de la Comunidad de Madrid, Catalan Finance Institute, Comunidad de Aragón, Comunidad Autónma de Extremadura, Conselleria de Cultura, Comunicacion Social e Turismo, Xunta de Galicia, Departamento de Cultura y

Turismo, Gobierno de Navarra, Diputación Provincial de Almería, Direccion de Creacion y Difusion Cultural, Gobierno Vasco, Direccion General de Fomento y Promocion Cultural, Junta de Andalucia, Institut Catala des Industries Culturals, Instituto de la Cinematografia y las Artes Audiovisuales, Instituto Valenciano de Cinematografia Ricardo Munoz Suay, Junta de Castilla-La Mancha | **Sweden** : Film i Skåne, Film i Väst, Filmpool Nord, Göteborg Film Festival Filmfund, Svenska Filminstitut | **Switzerland** : Canton of Aargau Film support, Canton of Solothurn Film Support, Canton Ticino film support, Canton-City of Basel Film Support, City of Geneva Film Support, Federal Office of Culture — Film Section, Fondation Vaudoise pour le Cinéma, Fonds Regio Films | **UK** : Arts Council of England, Arts Council of Wales, Awards for All, B3 Media, Big Lottery Fund, Channel 4 British Documentary Film Foundation, City of Westminster Arts Council, DepicT!, Ealing & Hounslow: Ealing & Hounslow Short Film Production Fund, Eastern Edge Film Fund, EM Media, Film London, FilmFour, First Light, Gaelic Media Service, Glasgow Media Access Centre (GMAC), Heritage Lottery Fund, Lewisham and Southwark: South London Film Fund, NESTA, North West Vision, Northern Film & Media, Northern Ireland Film TV Commission (NIFTC), One World Broadcasting Trust, Pocket Shorts, Scottish Documentary Institute, Scottish Screen, Screen South, Screen West Midlands, Screen Yorkshire, South West Screen, The Wellcome Trust, Triangle Film Fund, Tri-Pod Film Fund, Turner Classic Movies Short Film Competition, UK Film Council, UK Jewish Film Festival, Wandsworth Film Fund | **USA** : Astraea, Minnesota Independent Film Fund, Rhode Island Committee for the Humanities, Roy W. Dean Film and Video Grants,

Script Development

Australia : Australian Film Commission, Film Victoria, New South Wales Film and TV Office, Northern Territory Film Office, Pacific Film and TV Commission | **Austria** : City of Salzburg — Culture Department | **Canada** : Canadian Independent Film and Video Fund, Newfoundland & Labrador Film Development Corporation, Societe de Development des Enterprises Culturelles, Telefilm Canada | **Czech Republic** : State Fund for the Support and Development of Czech Cinematography | **Denmark** : Danish Film Institute | **Pan-European** : EC Development Directorate Culture Section, Hubert Bals Fund | **Finland** : Centre for the Promotion of Audiovisual Culture in Finland, Finnish Film Foundation, Suomen Elokuvasäätiö |

France : Aquitaine Image Cinéma, Centre national de la cinématographie (CNC), Centre régional de ressources audiovisuelles de la région Nord-Pas de Calais, Conseil général de la Charente, Conseil général de Loire-Atlantique, Conseil régional d'Alsace, Conseil régional d'Aquitaine, Conseil régional de la Bretagne, Conseil régional de la Picardie, Conseil régional de Provence-Alpes-Côte d'Azur, Conseil régional du Limousin, Conseil régional Midi-Pyrénées, Région Réunion, Rhône-Alpes Cinéma | **Germany** : Bavarian Film & TV Fund, Beauftragter der Bundesregierung für Kultur und Medien, FilmFernsehFonds Bayern, Filmstiftung Nordrhein Westfalen GmbH, Kulturelle Filmförderung Sachsen, Kulturelle Filmförderung Thüringen, Medien- und Filmgesellschaft Baden-Würtemberg GmbH, Medienboard Berlin-Brandenburg, Nordmedia | **Hungary** : Motion Picture Public Foundation of Hungary | **Luxembourg** : Film Fund Luxembourg | **Netherlands** : Dutch Film Fund, Jan Vrijman Fund | **Switzerland** : City of Bern Film Commission | **UK** : Ealing & Hounslow: Ealing & Hounslow Short Film Production Fund, EM Media, Film Agency for Wales, FilmFour, First Light, Gaelic Media Service, Northern Ireland Film TV Commission (NIFTC), Scottish Screen, Screen West Midlands, Screen Yorkshire, UK Film Council | **USA** : Alabama Humanities Foundation, Alaska Humanities Forum, Independent TV Service, The National Endowment for the Humanities

Looking for your next European partner?

Whether you're looking for your next European

- Co-production partner
- Distributor
- Funder

Visit the online directory available in
French, English, German, Italian and Spanish language

www.filmfileeurope.com

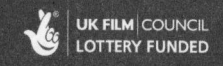

REFERENCE SECTION
GLOSSARY

The following descriptions are based on the use of these terms specifically in the film industry, rather than their general meanings. Many have more detailed explanations in the main text of this Handbook. Capitalised terms in the following descriptions have their own listings in this Glossary

A

Above-the-line the fundamental elements of a Budget whose costs and contracts are typically individually negotiated, usually comprising Underlying Rights / Screenplay, Producer (and Executive Producer), Writer, lead cast, Director and occasionally some heads of department, and which are highlighted by being listed at the beginning of the Budget, above the ruled 'line' that differentiates them from the more mundane 'Below-the-line' elements (see also Below-the-line, Budget)

Academy Awards® see Oscars®

Accelerated Deduction (in relation to tax) the right to deduct capital investments as costs from income at a faster rate than otherwise permitted (see relevant section in Part II)

Access Letter see Lab Access Letter

Acquisition Agreement the lead agreement under which a) the producer acquires the underlying rights needed to produce the film, or b) a sales company acquires from the producer the rights to sell it, or c) a distributor acquires from the sales company the rights to distribute it

Adaptation a derivative work (such as a film based on a novel or play)

Adjusted Gross Receipts (AGR) Gross Receipts less certain costs (typically those of the Collection Agent, 9taxes and Residuals, and sometimes Prints and Advertising, but *before* deduction of the Sales Commission), as specified in the relevant contractual definition of AGR (see also Net Profit)

Advance an up-front payment in relation to (and in anticipation of) amounts that would otherwise be payable in the future (see MG and relevant section in Chapter 3)

AFM the annual American Film Market in Los Angeles, where rights to independent films are bought and sold, and which now takes place every November (having recently shifted from February)

Agent someone who represents and is legally authorised to negotiate on behalf

of another (such as a talent agent for an actor, or a Sales Agent for a Producer)

AGR see Adjusted Gross Receipts

Allowance (in respect of tax) see Tax Allowance

AMPAS see Oscars®

Ancillary Rights (in relation to Distribution) also referred to as Secondary Rights, being those Rights other than Primary Rights (those of exploiting the film itself), and including Merchandising, Remake / Sequels, internet, music publishing, sound recordings and soundtrack, adaptations (into books, plays etc), etc

Ask Prices (aka Highs) the amounts referred to by a Sales Agent in its Sales Estimates as being the 'High' prices it will initially ask for when negotiating sale contracts for the various territories

Assign a legal term meaning to transfer (ownership)

Associate Producer typically the initial owner who brings a project (often already Packaged) to the main Producer, but is not necessarily integrally involved in the actual Production of the film

Attached (usually referring to Talent) contractually secured to work on the project, albeit often subject to certain conditions such as agreeing dates and fees, the film being fully financed, etc

Audit a formal, independent inspection and checking of accounts and records, often specifically in relation to the receipt of income (eg. to ensure that Overages are being paid when due, etc)

Auteur the French term for the 'filmmaker', suggesting that the creator of the film is the director rather than the producer

Automatic Support a Grand or Award that a producer has an absolute entitlement to so long as he (or the fim) meets certain prescribed conditions (see also Selective Support)

Award (regarding Soft Money), a type of Grant

B

Back-end colloquial term for Net Profits

Bankable in terms of Talent, a name with strong enough appeal who, if Attached to the project, could entice a financier to invest or lend production finance

Bankable Contract a contract to receive future income that a bank feels is strong enough to lend money against

Bank Gap Gap Finance (provided by a bank)

Below-the-line all the production costs (other than those Above-the-line) of actually making the film, as set out in the Budget

Beneficiary the person in whose favour something is done, such as granting a Charge, the setting up of a trust bank account, or the issuing of an insurance policy or Letter of Credit

Berne Convention a treaty between most of the progressive nations aimed at providing a more unified and reciprocal approach to, and treatment of, copyright laws and protection around the world

Bilateral (eg. in relation to Treaties) between two countries

Boiler Plate the various 'standard', non-commercial provisions found at the end of a long-form contract (see relevant section in Chapter 1)

Bond abbreviation for Completion Bond

Bond Company alternative term for a Completion Guarantor

Box Office (Gross) the total amount, before any deductions, paid to cinema (theatre) owners by movie-goers around the world to watch a particular film Theatrically

Break-even the point where all recouping financiers have been fully repaid as per their contracts, and the film thereby goes into profit

Break-out refers to a movie that becomes more popular after an initial limited release

Bridge Finance a short-term loan made in anticipation of the Closing of Production Finance, often to allow time-sensitive production to start on time (see relevant section in Chapter 3)

Budget a detailed, standard-form schedule of all the costs required to produce the film

Budget Top-Sheet the first page of the Budget, which summarises the costs under the main headings

Business Angel a business or individual, often affiliated to or acting through a relevant association, specifically looking for new business opportunities in which to invest

Business Plan a document prepared to demonstrate the likely commercial success of a film, and the attributes of the team producing it, and how they intend to market it (often used for the purposes of attracting finance)

Buyer for our purposes, someone acquiring film rights, such as a Distributor purchasing territorial distribution rights from a Sales Agent

C

Cap a prescribed limit or maximum amount

Cash Budget the amount of actual cash (money) needed to be paid out in order to produce the film, ie. roughly equal to the full Budget less any Deferments or Post Deals

Cash Flow Schedule a time-related statement of when Budget items are projected to be paid/payable, often used in determining the amount of total production funds the producer can Draw Down, and have control of (in the bank) at any one time

CGI computer generated imagery

Chain of Title the successive contracts, certificates and other documents demonstrating how the copyright required to make and distribute the film has been transferred from the original author(s), via whomever, to the present owner (probably the Producer)

Charge a type of security over an asset (similar to a mortgage), such that if the asset's owner defaults on its agreement with the Chargee, the Chargee can take possession of the asset

Chargee the Beneficiary of a Charge

Chargor the person granting a Charge

Claw Back payment from future revenues of an owed amount that has already accrued but has been deferred

Closing the finalisation and execution (signing) of legal contracts, all the parties having agreed every last point

Collection Account the account into which income from sales is received and from where payments to financiers and profit participants is made (see relevant

section in Chapter 3), as distinct from the Production Account

Collection Agent the company whose responsibility is to administer the Collection Account (see relevant section in Chapter 3)

Comfort Letter see Letter of Intent

Commission see Sales Commission

Commissioning Producer the head Producer when (eg. for tax reasons) another entity (a Production Services Company) is commissioned to actually make the film on its behalf

Company generic term for incorporated legal entity such as LLCs and corporations (in the US) and private or public limited companies (in the UK)

Completion Agreement the contract between the Completion Guarantor and the Producer (see Table of Contracts)

Completion Bond another term for Completion Guarantee

Completion Guarantee an insurance-like policy that protects financiers' money by ensuring that the film is completed and Delivered on time and on budget, or else the Completion Guarantor will repay the money to the financier (see relevant section in Chapter 3)

Completion Guarantor the company issuing the Completion Guarantee, also know as a Bond Company

Completion Guaranty see Completion Guarantee

Compound Interest Interest charged on previous Interest that has already accrued

Contingency the item in the Budget that is set aside for unforeseen overspend, usually required (by the Bond Company and financiers) to be at least 10% of the total Budget

Co-producer one of the Producers of a Co-production

Co-production a collaboration where two or more producers get together to jointly produce a film (see also Official Co-production, and the section on Co-productions in Chapter 3)

Co-production Treaty an agreement between governments setting out the qualification criteria for an Official Co-production between those countries (see section on Co-productions in Chapter 3)

Copyright the bundle of transferable legal rights in a work, initially attributable to its original author, preventing the unauthorised copying, adapting, publishing, distribution (etc) of the work (see section on Copyright in Chapter 1)

Corridor an allocation of a proportion of income as it is received, eg. 'all receipts to be paid to the bank except for a 10% corridor which goes to the producer' (see also *Pari Passu*)

Cost of Production the actual amount it cost to make the film (see also Overspend, Underspend, Production Costs, Negative Cost)

Coverage in terms of financing, the amount of anticipated income available for repayment that exceeds the amount being invested or lent (see relevant section in Chapter 3)

Creative artistic rather than financial or commercial

Credit a different number of meanings relating to accounting, but can also mean an On-Screen Credit

Cross Collateralisation the use (offset) of receipts from one source (eg. a film, territory, format, etc) to recoup from another loss-making source where receipts were inadequate

D

Dailies (aka Rushes) raw footage delivered daily from the set / laboratory to those who have the right to review them (director, financiers, etc) before editing

Day and Date a requirement that a film's release is simultaneously synchronised across a region or territory

Deal Memo a (usually legally binding) short-form term sheet setting out the salient terms of a contract, similar to a Memorandum of Understanding (see relevant section in Chapter 1)

Debenture a document evidencing debt, usually also granting the right to take a fixed and/or floating Charge over a company (or a group of its assets) as a form of security

Debt money actually owed (as opposed to Equity), such as loan repayments, payments for goods received, etc

Defamation a false written or oral statement that diminishes somebody's perceived reputation (includes slander and/or libel)

Deferments/Deferrals the pre-agreed delaying of payment of all or part of a fee, often referring to the Producer and/or Talent being paid a proportion of their contractual fee out of Receipts from Distribution / Exploitation of the film (either before or after Break-even), rather than from the Production Finance comprising the Budget, and thereby reducing the Cash Budget (see relevant section in Chapter 3)

Delivery on completion of the film, the physical delivery (or granting of laboratory access), which often triggers payment of some or all of the purchase price (eg. an MG), to those that have acquired the relevant Distribution Rights (typically being the Sales Agent from the Producer, and Distributors from the Sales Agent), of all the elements necessary for distributing and marketing of the film, including (in accordance with the relevant Delivery Schedule) negatives, prints, soundtracks, copy contracts and documents, etc (see relevant section in Chapter 3)

Delivery Costs the costs incurred in Delivering (as opposed to making) the film

Delivery Date the date contractually agreed for Delivery of the Film (from the Producer to the Sales Agent or, as the case may be, from the Sales Agent to the relevant Distributor(s))

Delivery Items those listed on the Delivery Schedule

Delivery Materials see Delivery Items

Delivery Schedule the itemised list of required Delivery elements, as attached to the relevant contract(s) (see sample Delivery Schedule in the reference section)

Development the initial stage of preparing for the film up until Production Finance is required in order to make it, including acquiring Underlying Rights, commissioning script-writers and polishers, preparing an initial Business Plan and draft Budget (and other documents), sometimes identifying and securing Talent and Heads of Department, and so on (see Chapter 1)

Development Costs the costs of Development

Development Finance / Funding finance available specifically for the Development process rather than for Production

Director the person controlling the front-of-camera action and dialogue, and who is generally primarily responsible for the creative outcome of the film interpreting the Screenplay and overseeing the artistic side of the Production from beginning to end (not to be confused with the 'director' of a company, being a specific corporate office-holder)

Director of Photography sometimes referred to as DP (in the US), DoP (in the UK) or Cinematographer (Europe), the person who ensures the Director's vision is actually captured on film (being responsible for framing, lighting, exposure, camera crew, etc)

Discounting lending (typically a smaller amount) against a future (larger) known income, such as a bank providing certain Production Funds up-front in return for the right to receive the income contractually payable by a Distributor on Delivery under a Pre-sale agreement, together usually with a discounting fee (see relevant section in Chapter 3)

Distribution the process involved in bringing the film to the public, through cinema (Theatrical) exhibition, cable, satellite and television broadcast, video / DVD sales and rentals, internet downloads, etc, and requiring a licence of the necessary rights

Distribution Agreement / Contract / Deal (aka a Sale Contract) an agreement under which a Distributor agrees, in return for the necessary licence and a Distribution Fee, to distribute the film, or sublicense its distribution, on all (or some) formats in its local territory for a specified period

Distribution Rights the rights of Distribution for a particular Territory or Territories

Distribution Expenses the local costs incurred in Distribution, including local advertising, transportation/shipping, creation of prints, Video / DVD production, dubbing, taxes, etc

Distribution Fee actually more of a 'commission' than a fee, the percentage(s) of income that a Distributor can keep for itself (see relevant section in Chapter 3)

Distributor (at markets sometimes referred to as a Buyer) the person responsible for Distribution, either by directly dealing with cinemas, manufacturing DVDs / Videos and/or broadcasting the film, or alternatively by Sublicensing these roles to Sub-distributors in its relevant territory

Documentary a (non-fictional) film portraying real people rather than actors, usually relating to real events

Domestic Distribution Distribution in the USA or North America

Domestic Distributor a Distributor specialising in the north American (or just US) territory

Domestic Rights Distribution rights for the USA or North America

Domestic Sales Agent a Sales Agent whose rights are typically limited to North America, and who sublicenses ('sells') the rights to Sub-distributors locally for various formats and/or regions

Domicile the country which someone considers their 'home' (or for a company, where it is established), and to where they will ultimately always return (used for some National Film qualification criteria)

Downside the outcome if things go wrong, ie. if commercial performance does not meet expectations (see Upside)

Drawdown (Draw Down) the transfer into the production account from financiers' accounts of the Production Funds (often in accordance with a pre-agreed **Drawdown Schedule**, linked to

the Production Schedule and Cashflow Schedule)

Drawdown Notice / Request / Certificate a formal request to financiers for Drawdown of Production Funds into the Production Account, submitted in an agreed form

....
E
....

E & O Insurance see Errors and Omissions Insurance

EIS the UK's Enterprise Investment Scheme (see relevant section in Chapter 3)

Electronic Press Kit (EPK) recordings of interviews, trailers, stills, etc, that are sent out for promotional purposes, typically to broadcasters

End User the member of the public who ultimately watches the film at the cinema, on TV, on DVD, via the internet, etc

Equity (1) ownership in or of (rather than loans to) a project, with a right to receive a share of any profits (but with the risk of losing any investment in the event of a loss) (see relevant section in Chapter 3)

Equity (2) the UK actors' union

Equity Investor a financier who invests Equity and thereby takes (part-)ownership of the project, but consequently being at risk of not recouping (see relevant section in Chapter 3)

Errors and Omissions Insurance (aka E&O insurance) an insurance policy taken out by a Producer to cover against being sued in relation to matters arising from Distribution of the film, eg. for defamation, infringement of copyright (see Chain of Title) or other rights, etc

Escrow the holding of money by a third party as a security protection, to be paid out only if a certain pre-agreed event occurs or conditions met (eg. fees paid to actor, to be released if and when Production Financing is raised)

European Convention abbreviation for the *European Convention on Cinematographic Co-Production*, see relevant section in Chapter 3

Execution (of documents) the signing, dating, stamping, sealing (etc) of agreements, such that they become valid and enforceable

Executive Producer someone who brings something major or fundamental to the party (usually the finance) that allows the film to 'get off the ground', or is instrumental in its Packaging

Exhibition the showing of a film to the public for a charge, usually referring to Theatrical presentation

Exhibitor a cinema (theatre) owner or chain

Exploit(ation) to generate income from a film through various methods of Distribution

F

Facility Letter a letter (often in the form of a contract) from a bank setting out the terms of an offered loan (or other banking facility)

Favoured Nations (Terms) the best terms available, such that no-one else will be given better (more favourable) terms

Feature Film a non-documentary, full-length (at least 70 minutes) dramatic film intended as the principal attraction at a cinema (ie. not made-for-TV)

Film Commission a government body set up for the purposes of promoting a certain region or country as a place for film production, and assisting those that choose to produce there

Film Festival a cultural event usually aimed at offering the public an opportunity to see a number of films, typically new releases and/or films based around a specific theme, genre or location (see also Film Market)

Film Market an event specifically set up for industry players to buy, sell and license film Distribution Rights, often coupled with a local Film Festival (such as at Cannes, Berlinale / European Film Market, etc)

Film Rights all the Rights in a film, including all Distribution Rights (and usually Remake / Sequel Rights, Merchandising Rights, etc)

Final Cut the ultimate Right when it comes to editing the film to create the final version for the Master Negative (usually retained by financiers, but sometimes given to producer or director)

Finance Plan the schedule setting out the respective contributions to the Budget by the film's various Financiers

Financial Closing the Closing of the Production Financing agreements

Financier for our purposes, *any* contributor of *any* type of money to the Production Budget (some limit the term 'financier' to banks and lending institutions only, but we don't)

Financing Agreements the contracts relating to or regulating the Production Finance (see Table of Contracts)

Finishing Funds finance required to complete a film where all the production finance has already been used up, typically because the film has gone over budget or additional Post-Production is required (see also Rescue Finance)

First Dollar usually defined as the first money actually received by the Sales Agent (or, as the case may be, a Distributor) from Exploitation of the film

Flat Sale (aka Outright sale) a sale with no 'Splits' or 'Overages', ie. the distributor pays a fixed amount for the rights for a specified period, and does not need to account to the Producer for any income it receives during that period (see relevant section in Chapter 3)

Floating Charge a security charge over a company's entire assets, but which allows the company to deal in those assets in the ordinary course of business, unless or until the company defaults on its agreement with the Chargee, at which point the charge 'crystallises', giving the charge possession over whatever assets the company owns at that time

Foreign Rights distribution rights for all countries worldwide *other than* North America (Domestic); the terms **Foreign Sales Agent, Foreign Distributor, Foreign Distribution** and **Foreign Sales** can be construed accordingly (see also International Rights and Domestic Rights)

Format the media (film, DVD, video cassette, digital, broadcast, etc) and/or size ratios (widescreen, 4:3, 16:9, etc) on or through which the film is distributed

Free Television publicly broadcast television programming that is free to watch without paid subscription to any specific channels or cable / satellite services

Fund a single pool of money, often originating from more than one source

G

GAAP funds film production funds which claim to be able to provide investors and/or producers with benefits based on, and calculated with reference to, with generally accepted accounting principles ('GAAPs') as opposed to specific film-related legislative incentives (see relevant section in Chapter 3), not to be confused with Gap Finance

Gap Finance as the final piece of Production Finance (filling the shortfall or 'gap' between the aggregate finance already committed and the full Budget), a loan to the Producer - usually, but not always, from a bank - repayable out of future sales income (see relevant section in Chapter 3); the terms **Gapping Bank** and **Gap Loan** can be construed accordingly

General Partner usually the management and decision-making side

of a Limited Partnership (see also Limited Partners) or LLP

General Release a film being shown in a large proportion of commercial cinemas, typically 500 in the US or 100 in the UK

Genre the 'type', category or theme of a feature film, usually being one or a hybrid of *action, adventure, art-house, biopic, children, comedy, crime, drama, erotic, family, fantasy, farce, horror, musical, mystery* (and *murder mystery), period (historical), political, rites of passage / coming of age, road movie, romance* (and *'rom-com', a romantic comedy), science fiction, teen / high school, thriller* (and *psychological thriller), western,* and so-called *'World Cinema'*

Grant (1) money given by a government, public or private body for a specific purpose (such as investing locally in film production); see also Subsidy(ies), Soft Money, and the relevant section in Part II

Grant (2) to legally give, convey, transfer and/or license rights, such as Distribution Rights, pursuant to a contract

Gross Participant someone with an entitlement to a share of Gross Receipts (rather than Net Profit), usually either from First Dollar or after Break-Even; the term **Gross Participation** can be construed accordingly

Gross Receipts usually a contractually defined term referring to all monies from Exploitation received at a specified point in the distribution chain (such as sales proceeds and Overages received in the Collection Account) *before* any deductions (such as Sales Commissions and Sales Expenses)

Guild a labour organisation or union, such as SAG (US) and Equity (UK) for actors, DGA (US) and DGGB (UK) for directors, etc.

H

High Net Worth Individuals very wealthy people with an extensive personal asset base who may be inclined to invest (usually equity) in film production

High Estimate see Ask Price

Hold-back a contractual period of time during which a film may not be released on particular formats or in particular territories

Home Video the sector of the film industry dealing with video cassettes, DVDs, and other physical storage units capable of being purchased or rented for use in the home

I

Indemnify to reimburse following a financial loss

Indemnity an obligation to Indemnify

Independent Film a film that is not a Studio Picture, and/or whose finance is provided by more than one source (see relevant section in Chapter 1)

Independent Sector that part of the film industry that deals with independent Films

In Profit for a film, once it is past Break-even

Interest a charge levied on money loaned, usually expressed as a percentage of the amount lent (Principal), and calculated with reference to the amount of time that the loan or any part of it remains unpaid or outstanding (eg. 10% per year)

Internal Rate of Return (IRR) a method of calculating an equivalent or effective profitability of an investment, taking into account the timing of the outlays and of the (projected) income, which investors use as a tool in comparing investment returns with interest rates available at a bank

International Rights usually equivalent to Worldwide Rights (but occasionally means the more limited Foreign Rights - so check!); the terms **International Distributor, International Distribution** and **International Sales Agent** can be construed accordingly

Interparty Agreement (IPA) the agreement regulating the contractual relationship between all the Financiers, the Producer, the Sales Agent, the Collection Agent, etc (see Table of Contracts)

Investment the commercial use of capital (as opposed to loans) in a venture with a view to creating income by way of profits (see also Equity)

Investor someone who invests in a project because of its deemed commerciality and anticipated profits (rather than lends in return for Interest payments, thereby taking commercial risks

IRR see Internal Rate of Return

Irrevocable unable to be withdrawn or altered

J

Joint Venture a business venture undertaken jointly by more than one entity, with a view to sharing risks, profits, losses, control, responsibilities, etc on agreed terms

Jurisdiction an area (usually a geographical territory such as a country or state, but also potentially an area of commerce such as, say, employment) governed by a body with the authority to deal with certain matters and/or make binding decisions

K

Key Elements those people and documents (including the Script, Budget, most Above-the-line personnel, etc) considered so fundamental to the film production process that changes to them cannot be made without approval of a number of interested parties (such as the Financiers, Bond Company, etc)

L

Lab(oratory) the place where the shot film (and recorded sound elements) is physically and chemically developed to create the Master Negative and other subordinate prints

Lab Letter either (depending on the context) a Lab Access Letter or Lab Pledgeholder Agreement

Lab(oratory) Access Letter (LAA) see Table of Contracts

Lab(oratory) Pledgeholder Agreement (LPA) see Table of Contracts

Lending Bank a bank (that lends!)

Letter of Credit in essence, a letter from a bank guaranteeing that its customer will have a certain amount of funds (or credit) available for a specified period and purpose, such that if in the event it does not, the bank itself will make its own funds available

Letter of Intent a non-binding (if properly worded!) letter stating the writer's sincere intention (but without any obligation) to enter into a later contract or arrangement, usually specifying certain conditions that must be met before any further consideration or commitment will be made (see also Letter of Interest)

Letter of Interest similar to a Letter of Intent, but usually with weaker wording specifying just a mere interest in entering into the future contract or arrangement

Leverage a financial term relating to the ratio of debt to equity in a particular investment

LIBOR the London Inter-Bank Offered Rate, ie. the lowest interest rate available in the UK banking market (see also Prime)

Library a large number of films whose copyright and/or Distribution Rights are ultimately owned by a single entity

Licence (spelt '**License**' in US) the Grant of a right (eg. copyright), usually in writing, by the owner of the rights (Licensor) for a period of time and subject to specific ongoing conditions (a Distribution Agreement is effectively a Licence of Distribution Rights)

Licensee the recipient of a Licence

Licensing (or **to License**) the act of granting a Licence, ie. of giving someone (the Licensee) the legal right to do something s/he would otherwise not be permitted to do

Licensor the grantor of a Licence

Lien put crudely, the legal right in some cases to retain possession of (ie. hold onto) an item of property until its owner pays a due debt

LLP a Limited Liability Partnership, being a type of legal entity similar to a Limited Partnership

Limited Partners usually the investor side of a Limited Partnership (as opposed to the managing partner)

Limited Partnership the type of legal entity sometimes used for a Fund or Producer, being a kind of hybrid between a partnership and a limited company

Limited Recourse where there is some risk to the borrower or other protection for the lender, such as a guarantee from the borrower's parent company (see also Non-Recourse, Recourse Loan)

Limited Release the exhibition of a film in a limited number of venues, sometimes for test purposes, such as for risk mitigation on a film whose likely success is unknown

Line Item an item of production expenditure specified (on its own 'line') in the Budget

Line Producer the person responsible for organising the Production in respect of the Below-the-line Budget items (sometimes combined with the role of the Production Manager)

Litigation legals proceedings (fighting a 'case')

Loan the provision of money on the basis that there is a contractual obligation to repay it (usually with interest)

Loan-out Agreement an agreement for the provision of an individual's services (usually those of Talent) to be made through a Loan-out Company

Loan-out Company a vehicle sometimes used by Talent for tax or liability purposes which contracts with the Producer to provide the services of its owner / controller (the Talent individual), the individual him/herself thereby avoiding a direct personal contract with the Producer

Long-form Agreement a multi-page contract (hopefully) covering each and every provision relevant to the deal

Low Budget Films a bit of a moveable feast, but typically films with budgets in the region of US$1m to (say) US$12m, although a $30m picture may still be considered low-budget these days

Low Estimate see Take Price

....

M
....

Mainstream intended for viewing by all of the general public rather than only certain sectors

Majors colloquial term for the Studios (and their subsidiaries)

Major Territories the traditionally more expensive Territories to Sell, including the USA (Domestic), Germany, UK, France, Scandinavia, Australia and Japan

Master Negative the original, first generation fully edited film reel (ie. made from the one exposed in the camera during shooting), usually preserved and held in a lab so as never to be damaged, from which all other prints derive

Memorandum of Understanding (aka an 'MoU') similar to, but sometimes fuller, longer or more detailed than, a Deal Memo (see relevant section in Chapter 1)

Medium Budget Films films with budgets ranging approximately from US$10m to US$40m

Merchandising Rights the right to exploit trademarks and copyright from the film (eg. names, pictures, characters, etc) on other tangible goods (eg. on clothing, crockery and toys, via fast-food outlets, in books, etc)

MG Minimum Guarantee

Microbudget Films although no definitive range, generally films with budgets between US$0.1m and US$1.5m

Mid Price in relation to Sales estimates, the price somewhere (often arbitrarily) between the Ask and Take Price, which reflects what the Sales Agents would (should?) expect to achieve in a normal market

Mini-Majors increasingly obsolete term referring to the larger Production Companies which, until recently, had considerable 'clout' but have since mostly been swallowed up by the Studios

Minimum Guarantee a commitment to pay over a minimum amount from revenues received, often by way of an Advance (see relevant section in Chapter 3)

Movie of the Week a film made for US prime-time television audiences

MOW Movie of the Week

MPAA Motion Picture Association of America, which awards Ratings in the US

....

N
....

National Film for our purposes, a film made in such a way that it meets certain locally-determined criteria, usually in order for it to qualify for local financial incentives (see Part II)

Negative Cost the full, actual costs of producing the finished film, including all fees and charges, and any Overspend (see also Cost of Production, Budget)

Negative Pick-Up the acquisition of a finished film (and all the rights in it) for a fixed price (see relevant section in Chapter 3)

Net Profit (not to be confused with Producer's Net Profit) a contractually defined term relating to whatever income (from Exploitation) is left after all relevant distribution Fees and Expenses have been deducted, and all relevant Financiers are fully Recouped, such that Net Profit Participants are allowed to share in it (see relevant section in Chapter 3)

Net Profit Participants those who have a contractual entitlement to (Participation in) a share of Net Profits (see relevant section in Chapter 3)

Net Profit Participation simply, a Participation in Net Profits

Net Receipts sometimes simply a synonym for Net Profits, or alternatively a contractually defined term where not all costs have yet been deducted (ie. therefore not yet Net Profit)

No Budget Films (1) film with budgets under about US$0.1m (see Microbudget)

Non-Theatrical Rights the right to give a film a 'public' viewing other than in the cinema (theaters), such as in/on airlines, hotels, ships, oil-rigs, schools, military barracks and prisons (it does *not* mean the rights on all formats other than Theatrical)

Non-Recourse in relation to a loan or debt, where the borrower has no personal liability and therefore is considered to have little or no personal risk other than, where there is a debenture or other Charge, in relation to the asset in respect of which the loan was made (see also Limited Recourse, Recourse Loan)

North America the USA and Canada, and occasionally (if so defined) including Mexico and some of the Caribbean islands

Notice of Assignment (NoA) (used mostly in relation to distribution deals) the letter to a Distributor, from a bank which has lent production funds, informing it that the bank has security over all the Film Rights (until fully repaid), giving it effective 'ownership' of the Producer's benefits under the sales contract, so that the Distributor should therefore pay amounts due to the bank directly, rather than into the Collection Account

nVOD (Near Video on Demand) films or programmes scheduled to repeated / restart at regular intervals (often every 15 minutes) in order to provide a similar service to VOD, but at a much reduced cost

....

O
....

Official Co-production a bi- or multi-national Co-production that meets the criteria set out in the relevant governmental co-production Treaty (or European Convention), thereby allowing access to benefits available to National Films of each relevant country (see relevant section in Chapter 3)

Off-the-Top deductions made *before* the remainder is split between interested parties

On-Screen Credits the long list of names of contributors (cast, crew, back-office, etc) to the production, appearing usually in a scrolling format at the end (and/or for a few people at the beginning) of the film (see also Single Card Credit)

Opinion Letter a letter issued by a law firm, usually (but not always) in relation to Chain of Title, stating its opinion as to the quality, shortfalls and adequacy of various previously executed contracts which it has been asked to read and consider

Option (as a legal concept) the contractual right to enter into a subsequent contract (such as to acquire Rights) within a prescribed time period

Oscar® nickname given to the coveted Academy Awards® (statuettes) issued annually by the Academy of Motion Picture Arts and Sciences (AMPAS)

Output Deal an arrangement where a party has the first opportunity (and sometimes the obligation) to buy from another party everything available for sale that meets the criteria of the deal, eg. film Distribution Rights (see also Put Deal)

Outside the Pot colloquial phrase relating to income from certain rights (eg. Soundtrack and/or Merchandising) or Territories that does not have to be paid into the Pot (Collection Account) because it is not included in the definition of Gross Receipts

Outright Sale see Flat Sale

Overages amounts payable under a Distribution Deal in excess of the MG (see relevant section in Chapter 3)

Overhead the costs of running a business generally, rather than those directly attributable to production of the Film

Overspend the excess (if any) of the Cost of Production over the Budget

....

P

....

Packaging (in relation to film financing rather than video / DVD distribution) the securing of the fundamental elements of the project, such as the Script, Production team, Talent and sometimes Sales Agent (with Sales Estimates), with a view to attracting Production Finance

P & A see Prints and Advertising

pari passu Latin phrase meaning side-by-side, so for (say) a 50/50 *pari passu* entitlement, *each* dollar is split as and when received, so that both parties are entitled to 50c straight away, rather than one party having to wait for the other to be paid first

Participation the right to be paid (participate in) a share of something (eg. Net Profits, Gross Receipts, etc), by virtue of having a legal interest in it

Partnership where more than one person jointly carry out a business together, other than through a limited company, thereby being taxed (and liable!) individually for the business, despite the venture being a legal entity in its own right

Party(ies) (contract law) the person(s) or entity(ies) entering into a contract

Passive Investor someone who invests in something without taking an active personal involvement in the day-to-day running of it

Pay or Play a bit of a misnomer meaning that the relevant Talent will be paid *whether or not* they ultimately are required to perform, or their performance is actually used

Pay Per View (PPV) payment made only for programmes actually watched

Pay Television television channels (rather than individual programmes) requiring paid subscription

Perpetuity for ever

PFA / PFD see Table of Contracts

Pitch a brief presentation by a Producer to potential Financiers

Pledgeholder Agreement see Lab Pledgeholder Agreement

Points (usually relating to Back-End Participation) colloquial term for percentage of profit awarded to a participant

Pornography books, magazines, pictures, films, etc, containing gratuitous graphic sexual images, often with little or no 'artistic' content (whatever that means!)

Post Deal a type of Deferment whereby a Post-Production studio / lab agrees to do work on the film for a discounted (or no) fee up front, being paid the remainder out of income from Exploitation, in return for a Net Profit Participation (see relevant section in Chapter 3)

Post-Production the work carried out on a film following Principal Photography in order to create the Master Negative, including editing, CGI, sound effects and music, special effects, On-Screen Credits, etc

Pot colloquial term for the Collection Account

Premiere the first official public viewing in a particular Territory

Premium (in relation to Financing and Recoupment) a fixed amount, rather than time-dependent Interest, to be recouped over and above (and usually expressed as a percentage of) the original Principal

Pre-Production that part of Production that takes place (usually after Financial Closing) in order to prepare fully for actual shooting (Principal Photography), as distinct from (but sometimes overlapping with) Development

Pre-sale a sale / purchase of Distribution Rights that takes place at any time prior to the Production being completed (or even started):see relevant section in Chapter 3

Primary Rights the rights required for exploiting the film on the main distribution media, ie. Theatrical (cinema), television and DVD / Video Rights (perhaps soon also to include Internet)

Prime Rate the lowest published interest rate available for borrowing in the US

Principal (1) the person who appoints an agent and on whose behalf the agent acts, such as a Sales Agent (agent) acting on behalf the Producer (Principal)

Principal (2) the amount originally lent or invested

Principal Photography the period of actual filming (or 'rolling of cameras')

Print a reel of celluloid film containing the entire picture

Prints and Advertising (P&A) the amount a Distributor has to spend (although it may have access to outside finance for this purpose), as part of the Distribution Expenses, on making 'positive' copies of the negative for projection (Prints, costing perhaps $5,000 each), and on advertising the film locally in its Territory, often amounting to several $m

Producer the person ultimately responsible for making the film (and therefore usually the owner of the finished product), including acquiring the necessary rights, raising the Production Finance and engaging the cast and crew

Producer's Net Profit (PNP) the Producer's agreed share of (ie. Participation in) Net Profits, from which he usually has to pay Talent Net Profit Participants, the remainder of Net Profits typically going to Financiers (see relevant section in Chapter 3)

Producer's Share the proportion of Distributor's Receipts that, in accordance with the Splits in the Distribution Deal, it must pay over into (or, where an MG was paid, account to) the Collection Account for Recoupment and/or as Net Profits (so in fact a bit of a misnomer as the Producer itself may not receive any of it, see relevant section in Chapter 3)

Production the actual making of the film, comprising Pre-Production, Principal Photography and Post-Production (and may or may not include Delivery), but typically excluding Development and Packaging

Production Account the segregated bank account into which all the Production Funds are placed (Drawn Down from the Financiers), and from which all expenses of Production are paid by the Producer; as distinct from the Collection Account

Production Accountant the person responsible for the accounts, bookkeeping and payroll (who may also have prepared the Budget) during Production

Production Company the company that produces the films

Production Costs general term for the costs of producing the film (see also Cost of Production, Negative Cost, Budget)

Production Finance / Funding the money needed for Production, ie. to make the film (see also Development Finance)

Production Finance (and Distribution) Agreement see Table of Contracts

Production Funds the money used for Production Financing

Production Overhead the Overhead of the Production Company, sometimes prevented from being included in the costs of producing the film (ie. not forming part of the Budget)

Production Manager the person responsible for implementing the Below-the-line Budget items and the day-to-day management of the Production (see also Line Producer)

Production Risk the risk that the film will not be completed on time, on Budget, or at all

Production Schedule the document setting out the detailed timetable for Principal Photography (and often including Pre- and Post-Production)

Production Services Company a company engaged by the Producer (ie. the owner of the necessary rights) to make the film on its behalf

Production Value the generally perceived quality of the Production

Product Placement the contracted inclusion in the film, for a substantial fee, of third party commercial products (see relevant section in Chapter 3)

Profit the excess of income (receipts, revenues, etc) over expenses (costs)

Profit Participation see Net Profit Participation

Project colloquial term for a film at any time from concept to Principal Photography

Projections see Sales Estimates / Projections

Promotional Tie-in a marketing deal that combines the advertising of a film with that of a third party product (see also Product Placement, Merchandising Rights)

Property US term relating to a Packaged or part-Packaged Project (and the rights in it)

pro rata Latin term meaning 'in proportion', eg. where profits are shared in proportion to financial contributions

Provisions (in relation to a contract) the clauses setting out the terms and conditions

Public Funds money available from a public body (see relevant section in Parts II and III)

Put Deal an arrangement where a party has the obligation to buy from another party, on pre-agreed terms, everything available for sale that meets the criteria of the deal, eg. film Distribution Rights (see also Output Deal)

R

Rating film classification by a formal body (MPAA in the US, BFCC in the UK), with reference to suitability for viewing by different age groups within society

Rebate a regulated repayment or reimbursement of part of an amount spent (see also Refund)

Receipts general term for money received from Exploitation of the film

Recouped repaid (with interest and/or premium, as per the relevant financing contract, see relevant section in Chapter 3)

Recoupment repayment to Financiers of Production Finance from income generated by the film (see relevant section in Chapter 3)

Recoupment Schedule the document, appended to most of the Financing Agreements, setting out the agreed Recoupment Waterfall in detail (see Reference Section for a sample)

Recoupment Waterfall the strict order in which Gross Receipts are distributed for Recoupment by Financiers, and then for Participation by Net Profit Participants (see also Recoupment Schedule, and the relevant section in Chapter 3)

Recourse Loan a loan which requires an enforceable guarantee by or on behalf of the borrower (see also Non-Recourse, Limited Recourse)

Refund repayment of part or all money spent (see also Rebate)

Refundable Tax Credit a tax credit that is payable by the tax authority whether or not the payee owes taxes to set it off against (see Chapter 3 and Part II)

Release Date the date a film opens Theatrically in a particular Territory

Release Schedule a Distributor's timetable for the respective Release Dates of its films (on all formats)

Remake / Sequel Rights the rights needed to produce a remake (based on the original story) or sequel (following on from it) of the original film

Rentals (a term used mostly in the US) the Receipts received by a Distributor that derive from Theatrical Exploitation (ie. the amount the exhibitor pays over to the Distributor)

Rescue Finance additional money, in excess of the initial budget, needed in order to prevent the collapse of a film that is in production but has run out of funds due to overspending (see also Finishing Funds)

Residuals payments, required by the Guilds, made to Talent (often, but not always, paid by the local rights-holding Distributor) based on the level of Exploitation in the particular Territory

Return the profit received from an investment, often expressed as a percentage of the amount invested

Right crudely, a legally enforceable power or authority (to do something)

Rights as defined in the relevant contract, but in relation to film, typically the Right to do any of develop, adapt, produce, show theatrically, make copies, broadcast (and so on, see Chapter 1)

Rights-Based Financier someone who finances a film in return for being granted some form of Distribution Rights, eg. a Sales Agent, Distributor or broadcaster

Royalties payments specifically for the Right to use something, such as Copyright

Rushes another term for Dailies

S

SAG the Screen Actors Guild (in the US)

Sale usually in fact a Licence (to Distribute); the term **Sell** can be construed accordingly

Sale Contract several meanings, but usually a Distribution Agreement of some form

Sale and Leaseback particularly popular in the UK until recent legal changes there, a complex transaction based around film incentive tax laws, whereby a film is sold by, and leased back to, its original owner (usually the Producer), providing both parties with a substantial financial benefit (see the Reference Section for more details)

Sales Advance an advance (similar to an MG) given by a Sales Agent in return for the Right to Sell (or Subdistribute) the finished Film (see relevant section in Chapter 3)

Sales Agent the entity appointed or authorised to Sell (ie. License) a film, usually on behalf of the Producer, but sometimes in its own right (see relevant section in Chapter 3)

Sales Commission the percentage of Sales income that the Sales Agent can take as its fee for securing the Sale

Sales Estimates / Projections Territory-by-Territory estimates of Sale prices of a film considered likely and/or possible by a Sales Agent (see also Ask Price and Take Price, and the relevant section in Chapter 3)

Sales Expenses the (pre-agreed) expenses of the Sales Agent in marketing and advertising the film to potential buyers (Distributors), at Film Markets and elsewhere

Sales Projections see Sales Estimates

Scale the minimum wage / fee set by the Guilds and Unions for their members

Screenplay (shooting script) technically the final Script that is ultimately shot in a film

Script a document (which often goes through several drafts) setting out the full dialogue together with certain scene descriptions and 'stage' directions for a film

Secondary Rights similar meaning to Ancillary Rights

Section 42 / Section 48 now obsolete UK statutory provisions setting out salient parts of the old UK tax incentives

Secured Creditor a creditor who takes out a mortgage, Charge or other form of Security in order to protect its investment or loan

Security collateral offered by a debtor to a creditor, which the creditor may take possession of in the event of default by the debtor

Seed Capital early Development Finance, often used primarily for Overhead

Sell-through (in terms of Video / DVD) the end-user market for purchases rather than rentals

Sequel Rights see Remake / Sequel Rights

Selective Support a Grant or Award available at the discretion of the relevant issuing body (see also Automatic Support)

Shareholders the owners of a company

Shooting Schedule similar to a Production Schedule, but usually just relating to Principal Photography

Short a short film, technically under 50 minutes, but usually between 5 and 20 minutes

Single Card Credit an On-Screen Credit appearing alone, without any other name on the screen at the same time, typically negotiated specifically by Above-the-line Talent, and placed 'front-end' (at the beginning of the film, before or after the main title) or 'back-end' (at the end of the film)

Single Picture Financing the separate financing of individual films (see also Slate Financing)

Single Purpose Vehicle see SPV

Six-Tenths Rule the (not always followed) rule-of-thumb stating that an Equity Investor's Net Profit Participation should be approximately equal to six tenths of his/her/its Budget contribution

(ie. 0.6% of Net Profit for each 1% of the Production Finance provided)

Slate multiple Properties / Projects owned and/or controlled by the same Producer

Slate Financing a transaction providing Production Finance for an entire Slate

Soft Money Production Finance that generally does not have to be repaid or, if it does, then on a Non-recourse basis, and on highly favourable commercial terms (see relevant section in Chapter 3)

Soundtrack (1) the part of the negative containing the sound elements

Soundtrack (2) a re-recording of the musical score, or a compilation of featured songs, available for purchase by the general public

Splits colloquial term for the ratios determining the division of proceeds in terms of what Receipts the Distributor may keep for itself, and the Producer's Share (see relevant section in Chapter 3)

Split Rights Deal where one Financier puts up or arranges a proportion of Production Finance in return for the ability to deal exclusively with (say) Domestic Rights, and another Financier does the same in relation to Foreign Rights, one of the Financiers often being the Producer (see relevant section in Chapter 3)

Sponsorship the provision of goods (or even cash) in return solely for an On-Screen Credit (see relevant section in Chapter 3)

SPV a 'single purpose vehicle', a Company (or similar entity) set up specifically for a distinct function (such as producing a single film or owning copyright in it), rather than for carrying out business on a more general basis, usually established in order for its owner(s) to avoid any potential liability in respect of the 'purpose'

Stills photographs taken during Principal Photography used for publicity

Straight Sale usually, a Sale without an MG, such that Producer's Share is paid in accordance with the Splits from First Dollar received by the Distributor, although (confusingly) can also mean a Sale that is not a Pre-sale (see relevant section in Chapter 3)

Streaming the delivery via internet of video or audio content which begins to play in real time without having to wait for all the data to download

Strike Price the Cash Budget from the Bond Company's perspective, ie. the amount the Bond Company requires the Financiers to provide in order for the Bond to be effective and the film to be made (see relevant section in Chapter 3)

Studios the (now) six major Hollywood multilayered film production, financing and distribution conglomerates, being Disney, Fox, Paramount, Sony, Universal and Warner Brothers (see relevant section in Chapter 1)

SubDistributor a Distributor (usually handling a specific Format or sub-Territory) who is licensed the necessary Rights by a Distributor who is itself already a Licensee

Sublicence a (subordinate) Licence granted by someone who is already a Licensee

Subsidy(ies) direct Grant payments made by governmental (or quasi-governmental) organisations to subsidise the costs of film makers producing locally qualifying films (see Parts II and III)

....

T
....

Take Prices (aka Lows) the amounts referred to by a Sales Agent in its Sales Estimates as the lowest prices it will accept when negotiating Sale contracts for the various Territories, and which (usually) it may not reduce without prior approval of the Producer and/or Financiers

Talent the main artistic contributors, being primarily the Director and lead actors

Talent Agreement the agreement engaging an actor (or other Talent) to provide services for the production of the film

Taxable Income the amount of income that is used in the calculation for computing Tax Liability (see Chapter 3)

Tax Allowance a specially sanctioned amount of income that is tax-free, ie. not subject to taxation (see also Tax Credit, Tax Rebate, Part II and relevant section in Chapter 3)

Tax Avoidance the legal and legitimate structuring of transactions, usually pursuant to specialist advice, so as to minimise Tax Liability (compare with Tax Evasion)

Tax-based Finance Production Finance that has come about as a result of film-related Tax Incentives (see Part II and relevant section in Chapter 3)

Tax Benefit see Tax Incentive

Tax Break colloquial term for Tax Incentive

Tax Credit a Credit on (or reduction in) Tax Liability (see Part II and relevant section in Chapter 3)

Tax Deduction a form of Tax Relief, usually in the form of a reduction in Taxable Income (eg. by way of a Tax Allowance)

Tax Evasion the illegal non-payment of tax that is actually properly due (compare with Tax Avoidance)

Tax Incentive a statutory benefit or concession, implemented through the relevant tax authority, targeting a particular group of tax-payers within the business and/or investment community (see Part II and relevant section in Chapter 3)

Tax Liability the amount of taxes actually owed (or to be owed)

Tax Offset see Tax Set-off

Tax Set-off generally, the ability to set off an amount against taxable income or tax liability (such as in the form of a Tax Credit), thereby reducing Tax Liability

Tax Rebate a Rebate of taxes paid (see Part II and relevant section in Chapter 3)

Tax Relief a reduction in ultimate Tax Liability

Tax Shelter a scheme utilising a Tax Incentive

Telemovie a film made specifically for TV

Term (1) the length of time that a contract is in force (eg. the licence period)

Term (2) contractual Provision (see relevant section in Chapter 1)

Term Sheet another term for Deal Memo

Territory a country (or region) or geographically close group of countries (or regions)

Theatrical in the cinemas (theaters)

Trades the periodical publications dedicated to film industry readers (such as *Variety, Hollywood Reporter, Screen International, Screen Digest*)

Turnaround where a Studio no longer wants to produce a film project (Property) it originally acquired and developed, and therefore makes it available for acquisition and production by an Independent Producer, often the one who took the Project to the Studio in the first place (hence the Property can 'turn around' and leave the Studio)

U

Underspend the (unlikely) amount by which the Budget exceeds the actual Production Costs

Unions official trade bodies, including the Guilds, collectively representing and looking after the interests of their Talent and crew members

Underlying Rights the Rights in the work (eg. a novel, play, Script / Screenplay, biography, etc) upon which the film is based, and from which it is adapted

UPM Unit Production Manager (usually requiring Guild recognition / certification)

Upside potential profits and/or Return on investment if things go well

V

Venture Capital money earmarked under a high-risk investment strategy for growth business (see relevant section in Chapter 3)

Video on Demand (VoD) the ability to watch a film or programme at any desired time rather than waiting for a scheduled broadcast

W

Warranty a contractual promise or assurance about a fact which, if it turns out not to be true, gives rise to a contractual claim

Window the period during which a particular Right (eg to Distribute on a particular Format) may be exercised exclusively

Worldwide Rights Distribution Rights for the entire world (ie. Foreign and Domestic); the term **Worldwide Distribution** can be construed accordingly

Sample delivery schedule

Below is a sample Delivery Schedule, reproduced with kind courtesy of International Delivery Film and Television Limited ('ID Films'). Naturally, in practice, each Delivery Schedule will be different, depending on a number of factors. The size of the budget obviously has an impact on what might be made available, as the items generally have to be paid for by the Producer from the production funds (although, in some cases, the proceeds of the MG will have to be used under certain distribution deals). The entity to which the materials are being delivered will also have its own requirements, and will not pay for the film until these are met.

The Delivery Schedule on the back of the Sales Agency Agreement should contain the aggregate of everything that any of the Sales Agent's buyers (Distributors) are likely to need, so that it has all the necessary materials to deliver on to them. As for the Distributors themselves, some have greater requirements than others. German buyers, for example, have higher technical requirements than most, and American (especially Studio) Distributors usually insist on an inordinate amount of paperwork. The Completion Guarantor will usually agree to bond most of the essential elements on the Sales Agent's Delivery Schedule, but not all; paperwork and publicity materials usually being the first casualties. For any one film, therefore, there may be a number of conflicting Delivery Schedules, and care must be taken in ensuring that the underlying agreements provide for who must pay for what in the event of a discrepancy.

One last point relates to '**Access**' as opposed to '**Delivery**'. Sometimes the recipient is entitled to receive actual hard copies of the materials, and sometimes it is given the right to attend the laboratory at which the masters are stored in order to make its own copies (again, on whom the relevant costs fall can be a major issue). If all copies are made at the Producer's own lab, s/he will have a little more control over the number of copies in existence. It is also cheaper for the Producer if s/he doesn't have to pay and deliver the copies around the world him/herself.

Delivery Schedule

A   FEATURE ELEMENTS

1   **Laboratory Access to 35mm fully cut and assembled Original (or Output) Negative of Feature**, complete with Main and End Titles.
2   **35mm Combined Stereo Answer Print** of Feature from Original (or Output) Negative, fully corrected and approved by Producer, complete with Main and End Titles.
3   **35mm Feature Interpositive**, fully timed, complete with Main and End Titles.
4   **2 x 35mm Feature Internegatives**, fully timed, complete with Main and End Titles.
*** NOTE FOR ITEMS 3 & 4 – If feature has subtitles inherent in reels then textless reels will have to be supplied for domestic and international use ***
5   **2 x 35mm Feature Optical Sound Track Negatives**, fully cut with Main and End Titles, edited, scored and assembled, synchronised with picture negative elements.
6   **2 x 35 Combined Check Print From I/Negatives**, full timed, complete with Main and End Titles.
7   **35mm Magnetic 2-Track Stereo Print Master (SVA)** of Feature and MO Disk if Digital.
8   **35mm Magnetic 6-Track 5.1 Print Master Digital Version of Feature** (L/LS/R/RS/C/Sub).
9   **35mm Magnetic Stereo International Music & Effects Track of Feature**, fully fitted with full 4+2 configuration (L/C/R/S/Clean Dialogue/Additional Material).
10 **35mm Magnetic Stereo International 6-Track Digital SRD Music & Effects Track** (L/LS/R/RS/C/Sub) of Feature, fully filled, with full 6-Track Digital configuration.
11 **35mm Magnetic Stereo 6-Track D/M/E of Feature** (Stereo Dialogue, Stereo Music, Stereo Effects).
    *** ITEMS 7-11 ABOVE CAN BE DELIVERED ON DA88 At 24 FPS, 25 EBU, 48 KHz. However, if items 7-11 are delivered on DA88, then item 7a and 10a shown below must also be delivered. ***

| 7a | DAT 2-Track Final Mix at 25 FPS, 25 EBU, 48 KH |
| 10a | DAT 2-Track Music & Effects Track at 25 FPS, 25 EBU, 48 Khz |

12 **Full QC (Quality Check)** of above Sound Elements (items 7-11).

13 **35mm Interpositive and Internegative of Textless Backgrounds of Main and End Titles**, and any captions or subtitles contained in the picture – to include all optical fades and dissolves, to length of title sequence.

13a **35mm Check Print** from above internegative.

14 **Access to Television Version of the Film**, if created by the Producer as well as access to the Negative and Positive Print of all available alternative takes, cover shots, looped dialogue lines and other material not used in the final version of the Film.

15 **Electronic Press Kit** or other documentary material if created, access to and loan of master elements as well as delivery of the EPK on a Digital Video Tape format.

16 **Digital Audio Tape of all Master Music** specifically recorded for the Film.

17 **1 x High Def Master** 4 x 3 Pan and Scan Full Frame Video Master of Feature.

17a **1 x Digi Beta PAL** 4 x 3 Pan and Scan Full Frame Video Master of Feature.

17b **1 x Digi Beta NTSC** 4 x 3 Pan and Scan Full Frame Video Master of Feature.

18 **1 x High Def Master** 16 x 9 Full Height Anamorphic Video Master of Feature.

18a **1 x Digi Beta PAL** 16 x 9 Full Height Anamorphic Video Master of Feature.

18b **1 x Digi Beta NTSC** 16 x 9 Full Height Anamorphic Video Master of Feature.

19 **1 x High Def Master** 16 x 9 Original Ratio (ie Letterbox 1.85:1 or 1:2.35) Video Master of Feature.

19a **1 x Digi Beta PAL** 16 x 9 Original Ratio (ie Letterbox 1.85:1 or 1:2.35) Video Master of Feature.

19b **1 x Digi Beta NTSC** 16 x 9 Original Ratio (ie Letterbox 1.85:1 or 1:2.35) Video Master of Feature.

*** ITEMS 17-19b TO HAVE TEXTLESS BACKGROUNDS ADDED AT THE END OF THE FEATURE AND AUDIO FINAL MIX ON 1&2 AND M/E ON 3&4 ***

*** IF THE FILM IS MASTERED ONTO HIGH DEF, THEN WE WILL REQUIRE COPIES AS PER ITEMS 17-19b, IF NOT AN AGREED DELIVERABLE THEN DIGI BETAS AS PER 17a-19b WITH ACCESS TO ORIGINAL HIGH DEFS IF CREATED ***

20 **DA88 5.1 Print Master** conformed to Video Master.

21 **DA88 5.1 M&E** conformed to Video Master.

22 **Full QC (Quality Check)** by video house to approve above Masters.

23 **Full Dialogue Continuity and Spotting List of Feature** including all spotting information. Both hard copy and on disc.

B   PUBLICITY / DOCUMENTATION

Detailed Synopsis (minimum 500 words). Also to be delivered on disc.

Credit List of full Cast and Technical Personnel. Also to be delivered on disc.

Production Notes, Biographies and Filmographies of Principal Cast, Producer, Director and Writer, and descriptions or locations used. Copies of all available Press Clippings, Press Kits, Books, Synopses, Flyers and other Publicity Material. (Also to be delivered on disc)

Black and White Stills and Original Negatives of Stills maximum of 250 10'x8'. (These are also to be delivered on CD – and are to include full contact sheets detailing each image)

35mm Original Colour Transparencies maximum of 250. (These are also to be delivered on CD – and are to include full contact sheets detailing each image)

Note: All Stills and Transparencies to have been taken during production and to be titled and captioned with all persons appearing, to be identified and to be supplied together with written clearances from any party featured who has any Stills Approval Rights.

Key Art if created by the Producer, a first generation Dupe Transparency of the Key Art created for the One-Sheet. (this must also be delivered on CD).

Final Billing Blocks for Posters, Video Packaging, Paid Advertising and Trailers, approved by all parties, as well as camera-ready Black and White Stats of all the Logos required by the Producer to be included in the Billing Block (this must also be delivered on CD, with separate files for the fonts and logos included as well as the text itself).

Notarised copy of the E&O Certificate.

Credit Statement of both the contractual Screen Credits and the Paid Advertising Credits applicable to the Film. The Statement should include each credit in one column and a summary of the credit obligation in the adjacent column, including form, placement, type size and exclusions. If there is no obligation to accord a certain credit which has been accorded on screen or is included in your Billing Block, the 'obligation' should be stated as 'Producer's Discretion'. Also to be delivered on disc.

Statement of Restrictions, a statement listing all dubbing, cutting and other restrictions applicable to the Film. Also to be delivered on disc.

Music Cue Sheets stating for each composition in the Film the Title, the Composers, Publishers, Copyright Owners, Performers, Usage, Performing Rights Society, as well as in the film footage and running time. Also to be delivered on disc.

Original notarised Chain of Title Report

Full copy of all Chain of Title agreements

Final Certified Cost Statement

MPAA Rating Certificate (if applicable).

Certificate of Nationality – 5 original, signed copies to be supplied.

Certificate of Origin – 5 original, signed copies to be supplied.

Cast/Talent/Personnel Agreements, access to copies of fully executed agreements for the Writer, Director, Producer, Composer and Principal Cast members, as well as Other Cast members, Talent and Personnel whose names are accorded Paid Advertising Credit.

Final Certified Cost Statement, prepared by either a certified public accounting firm or the production company auditor, setting forth the final actual negative cost of the Film.

Dolby License, if applicable, a copy of the executed Licence Agreement in full force and effect between the Producer and Dolby Laboratories Inc. in connection with the Film.

Editor's Script Notes, a copy of the final shooting script marked with Slate and Take numbers used in photographing each script scene, indicating the portion of each script scene covered by each Slate and Take number with notations as to camera movements used, if requested.

Editor's Code Book, a copy of the Code Book bearing identification of Slate and Take numbers of each scene by cutting print code numbers, if requested.

Music Licenses, copies of fully executed synchronisation and master use Licenses for each item of licenses music in the Film, fully executed agreements for each Composer of Underscoring, and evidence of payments under such agreements.

C   TRAILER PICTURE AND SOUND ELEMENTS

1. **35mm Fully Timed Action Internegative** of Trailer.
2. **35mm Optical Sound Track Negative** of Trailer, fully edited, scored and assembled, synchronised with Trailer Picture element.
3. **35mm Check Print of Trailer**, fully graded and in sync.
4. **35mm Master Timed Interpositive** of Trailer.
5. **35mm Textless Internegative and Interpositive of Trailer,** if applicable.
6. **35mm 4-Track Magnetic Master of Sound Track** of Trailer which will contain separate Music, Effects and Dialogue (N/D/M/E), plus 4-Track Stereo (L/C/R/S) and 6-Track Digital M&E if mixed digitally.
7. **35mm Stereo 2-Track SVA Magnetic Master** of Sound Track to Trailer & MO Disc if Digital.
8. **Full Dialogue Continuity List** of Trailer including all spotting information.

*** ITEMS 6 & 7 CAN BE DELIVERED ON DA88 AT 24 FPS, 25 EBU, 48 KHz

Sale & Leaseback

Sale & Leaseback (S&L) has existed in a number of countries across various industries for at least thirty years, typically working in conjunction with legislation on tax incentives. Within the film industry, its most prolific use was in the UK between the late '90s and early 2007. However, recent changes in UK tax law, replacing the incumbent 'section 48' legislation with a new tax credit, have ended the sale & leaseback's reign there for the time being. S&L transactions are still available elsewhere, and are potentially feasible anywhere that has a tax break based around a **deduction or allowance** for the **acquisition** of films or film rights (see section on Soft Money in Chapter 3 for how an allowance works). They may well pop up in new jurisdictions at any time in the foreseeable future. The schemes offer comparatively risk-free benefits to both the Producer and the investor, as the benefits do not necessarily depend on the film's success in the market place. The following is a step-by-step explanation of how these so-called 'complex transactions' actually work, and why.

'Vanilla' Sale & Leasebacks

Recently in the UK, there was a spate of companies offering 'Sale & Leaseback money' up-front in the form of production funding. However, traditionally, the transaction only took place when the relevant film was **'completed'**, as it was only then when the relevant tax break kicked in. We will first consider how this type of generic or **'vanilla'** Sale & Leaseback works, and then look at the more advanced 'products' that have been available to the Producer in more recent times.

Say a Producer has made a film for $10m (or whatever the relevant local currency is) in a country offering an income tax allowance (or deduction) on the acquisition of film rights (let's call the relevant law **'Rule AA'**, for 'acquisition allowance'), and the Producer now wishes to enter into a Sale & Leaseback transaction. Once s/he has completed the film, and obtained any necessary certificate from the appropriate government department confirming the film qualifies for Rule AA, s/he will identify a Sale & Leaseback business (usually in the form of a partnership) to purchase the film. The partnership will be made up of various investors, who all wish to avail themselves of Rule AA. The partnership will also include a 'managing partner' as part of the administrative set-up.

As the film has already been 'completed' and certified as qualifying for Rule AA, the partnership (effectively being the investors) can legitimately write off their investment (ie. the purchase price) as an **'acquisition'** under Rule AA for tax purposes. This reduces their personal income tax bill by 40% of the amount invested (assuming their income tax rate is 40%, as it would have been in the UK). Note that much of their investment may actually have been borrowed from a bank. Anyway, the partnership would typically pay the Producer $10m to buy the film, as that is the amount it had cost to make, and the authorities would accept that is an appropriate price. So, under Rule AA, the investors are treated as if they earned $10m less in that year than they really did (because they spent $10m on the acquisition of a qualifying film, so it notionally comes off their income). With a reduction of $10m in their taxable income, the investors save a total of $4m in tax liability.

However, on its own, this simple 'sale' transaction would leave the partnership of investors owning a film they have no idea how to exploit, and the Producer with a cheque for $10m (most of which would have to go back to pay the original financiers), but no film. In practical terms, this is no good for either party. So the partnership, acknowledging that the Producer is probably better placed to exploit the film than it is, immediately 'leases' the film back to the Producer in return for periodical lease payments. This is technically a licence of all the exploitation rights whereby the Producer gets all the rights s/he needs to exploit the film for a period of up to 15 years ('**the Term**').

Reverting to our Building Analogy at the beginning of Chapter 3, this would be equivalent to an investor partnership buying the building from the Developer because it (the partnership) can get a tax allowance on the acquisition of a completed building. However, as the investor partnership isn't really in the business of renting out apartments, it will **lease back** the whole building to the Developer in return for a fixed income over 15 years, and the job of renting out (or sub-letting) the apartments also reverts to the Developer.

With the film valued at $10m (the purchase price), the lease payments required by the purchasing partnership will be fairly substantial, and it will want to be sure that it actually gets paid throughout the entire 15 year term. It will therefore typically insist that most of the $10m it paid to the Producer on acquisition of the film goes straight into a separate secured bank account, from which the lease payments will be made. Depending on local interest rates, and using simple numbers, one could say that about $8m (plus the interest earned on it) would probably be enough to pay the lease payments for the whole term. Another $0.5m will be required for the various transaction fees (especially legal costs), and the remaining $1.5m (equal to about 15% of the budget) can go straight into the Producer's pocket (or, more likely, to start paying back the film's original financiers).

Although the partnership paid $10m for the film, only $6m of this was actually '**at risk**' because the other $4m effectively comes from the taxman, having been a saving in the investors' tax bill. It works out that $8m is an adequate sum such that, when placed in the designated bank account to generate the lease payments, the investors get an acceptable return on their at-risk investment. It also generates some of the large fees charged by the Sale & Leaseback facilitators, something about which the UK Government in particular expressed its disquiet. In any event, it is calculated so that, by the end of the 15 year Term, there will be nothing left in the bank account, the lease comes to an end, and the exploitation rights to the film revert to the partnership (who will then own the film outright as part of its '**library**'). This means that the Producer has 15 years to make as much money out of the film as possible, before it reverts to the Sale & Leaseback partnership. That said, it is rare for pictures to continue bringing in substantial revenue after that point and, in any event, the film is sometimes sold by the partnership to a company connected with the Producer for a nominal fee at the end of the lease Term.

The receipts from the lease payments are themselves usually taxable in the hands of the partnership, so it could be said that, in reality, the investors actually only obtain an interest free **loan** from the relevant Government. In most jurisdictions, income received during the Term from the lease payments can be set off against other losses and/or allowances that the investors may have in whatever year the payments are received.

Where the partnership also takes a profit participation (which is not uncommon), the investors will additionally end up with a 'share' in any Net Profits made.

Discounted Sale & Leaseback

Many Producers feel that, as much as receiving a present of 15% of the budget might be considered well-earned once they have finished the picture, in fact they would rather have some money up front in order to help finance the film in the first place, production funding being extremely difficult to obtain. So, more recently, Sale & Leaseback facilitators started offering to '**discount**' the amount available and, through a bank (often the one already involved in the Sale & Leaseback transaction), provide the windfall gift - known as the '**net benefit**' - to the Producer in time for production, albeit on certain conditions.

Naturally, in these cases the partnerships will be concerned that they are be providing money up-front without the benefit of a Rule AA certificate of qualification, and therefore without the guarantee of being able to access the tax allowance. The individual investors want to be sure that they will be able to write off their investment as soon as the film is completed (which is the point at which the tax allowance becomes effective). Accordingly, the Completion Bond company (see Chapter 3) will, amongst other things, make sure that the Producers make the film strictly in accordance with the criteria required for the film to qualify under Rule AA (this usually means satisfying a '**national film**' test), and also make sure that the film is delivered on time so that the investors can utilise the tax-break within the anticipated financial year. However bond companies are often reluctant to take on these added obligations, depending on how easy it is to ensure the relevant film qualifies

The amount of the budget available in this way will depend on the magnitude of the tax break, the type of partnership used, the bank and its 'discount' rate, the amount that would otherwise have been available had the money been provided after completion, the profit participation taken (if any), the time of year of the transaction (it all gets very competitive as the financial year begins to close), and so on. In the UK, numbers were hitting close to 15% before the tax allowance was scrapped.

Other Incentives

As the market for films to invest in became tighter in the UK, Sale & Leaseback facilitators began offering Producers more and more incentives to use their product(s). Many offered much more than the traditional 12% or 15% contribution to the budget by coupling the Sale & Leaseback with other deals. For example, some offered up to 20% (although more typically usually 16% to 18%) by also taking the UK (including Republic of Ireland) distribution rights by way of pre-sale.

More popular in recent years were transactions known as 'Super Sale & Leasebacks'. Here, the partnership would offer a large proportion of the budget in return for doing the Sale & Leaseback transaction and taking an **equity stake** in the film. If (say) 35% was offered, this would be seen as approximately 15% representing the Sale & Leaseback transaction itself, and 20% representing a pure equity investment. In this regard, the Producer would have to give a percentage of the 'back end' (Net Profit) to the investors, in the above example between 12% and 20% (depending how strictly the 'Six Tenths Rule' was followed – see Chapter 3).

International Co-production Treaties

This table details the Co-production Treaties in force for most major territories. It has been carefully compiled and, to our knowledge, does not exist elsewhere. However, is is almost impossible to keep 100% on top of the movements of more than 50 governments, and the announcement, implementation and termination of each and every bilateral Co-production Treaty. So if you notice an error or change in this table, please inform us at funding@netribution.co.uk.

In addition:

Canada also has Treaties with Algeria, Bosnia & Herzegovina, Bulgaria, Chile, Columbia, Estonia, Hong Kong, Latvia, Malta (MoU), Mexico, the Phillipines, Senegal, Serbia & Montenegro, Slovenia, Uruguay, Venezuela and Vietnam.

Brazil also has Treaties or other arrangements with Argentina, Chile, Columbia, Equador and Venezuela.

Germany also has Treaties with Bosnia & Herzegovina, Bulgaria, China, Cuba and Iran

Key

x - Treaty in force

m Memorandum of Understanding (MoU) in place

p Treaty or MoU planned, pending or proposed

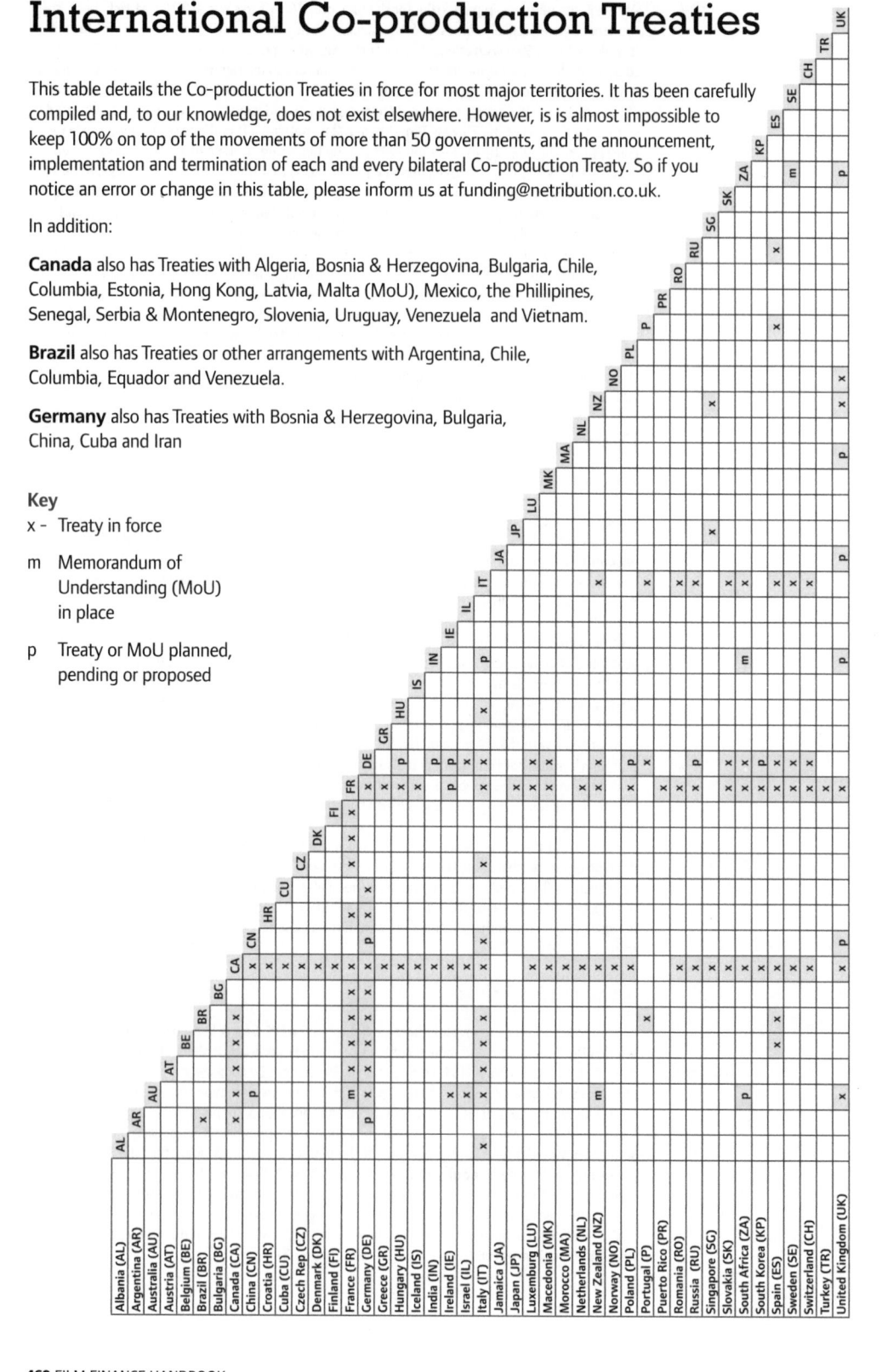

Country codes (rows and columns):
Albania (AL), Argentina (AR), Australia (AU), Austria (AT), Belgium (BE), Brazil (BR), Bulgaria (BG), Canada (CA), China (CN), Croatia (HR), Cuba (CU), Czech Rep (CZ), Denmark (DK), Finland (FI), France (FR), Germany (DE), Greece (GR), Hungary (HU), Iceland (IS), India (IN), Ireland (IE), Israel (IL), Italy (IT), Jamaica (JA), Japan (JP), Luxemburg (LU), Macedonia (MK), Morocco (MA), Netherlands (NL), New Zealand (NZ), Norway (NO), Poland (PL), Portugal (P), Puerto Rico (PR), Romania (RO), Russia (RU), Singapore (SG), Slovakia (SK), South Africa (ZA), South Korea (KP), Spain (ES), Sweden (SE), Switzerland (CH), Turkey (TR), United Kingdom (UK)

Recoupment schedule

Below is a simple form of Recoupment Schedule which might be used where the financing has been fairly straightforward. As you will see, the equity investors are entitled to an aggregate of 30% net profit so you could assume, applying the six-tenths rule, that they put up about 50% of the budget between them, the rest coming from a mixture of bank gap, deferrals, soft money and pre-sales.

The capitalised terms in the Schedule will be defined in the Collection Account Management Agreement ('CAMA') to which the Recoupment Schedule is appended. These definitions should reflect those used in the Interparty Agreement, Sales Agency Agreement, Commissioning Agreement, etc (which will also have the Recoupment Schedule attached). A couple of points to note:

Where a bank has discounted a pre-sale, the Distributor will occasionally be instructed or permitted to pay the MG balance into the Collection Account upon delivery (rather than directly to the bank). In these circumstances, provision in the Recoupment Schedule needs to be made for those amounts to be paid from the Collection Account straight to the Bank with little or no deduction. Also, in cases where it is agreed that receipts from certain countries (often called 'collateral territories') are allocated exclusively to repay a specific financier, rather than mixed with other receipts and distributed generally from the 'pot', a separate 'waterfall' is drawn up specifically for the receipts from those collateral territories. Sometimes, therefore, a Recoupment Schedule has a number of waterfalls, but to keep things simple, we have included just one for all world receipts.

Sample recoupment Schedule

All Gross Receipts derived from the exploitation of the Film shall be paid directly by all Distributors into the Collection Account [details]. The Collection Agent shall allocate and pay such Gross Receipts in accordance with the terms of the Collection Account Management Agreement in the following order:

(1)   The Collection Agency Fee to the Collection Agent; thereafter
(2)   The Non-Deferred Sales Commissions to the Sales Agent; thereafter
(3)   The Sales Expenses to the Sales Agent; thereafter
(4)   The Deferred Director's Fee to the Director; thereafter
(5)   The Gap Loan Amount to the Bank; thereafter
(6)   The Deferred Sales Commission to Sales Agent; thereafter
(7)   Repayment on a parri passu basis of Investment A to Financier A, Investment B to Financier B and Investment C to Financier C; thereafter
(8)   Repayment of any Completion Bond Production Contributions made by the Completion Guarantor under the Completion Guaranty, as notified by the Completion Guarantor to the Collection Agent in writing, to the Completion Guarantor; thereafter
(9)   The Deferred Producer's Fee to the Producer; thereafter
(10)   All further Gross Receipts (less the Sales Commission) shall be deemed 'Net Profits' and shall be paid on a pari passu basis in accordance with the following Net Profit Schedule:

BENEFICIARY	PERCENTAGE OF 100%
Investor A	15
Investor B	10
Investor C	5
Producer	50
Director	5
Actor A	5
Actor B	2.5
Actor C	2.5
Writer A	2
Writer B	2
Costume Designer	0.5
Set Designer	0.5
Total	**100**

Glossary of financing agreements

AGREEMENT NAME	PARTIES	MAIN PURPOSE
Acquisition Agreement	Depends on type	To acquire necessary rights in a film, eg. a) Producer acquiring the underlying rights needed to produce the film, b) Sales Agent acquiring from the producer the rights to sell it, or c) a Distributor acquiring from the Sales Agent the rights to distribute it (sometimes referred to as a Sale Agreement or Distribution Agreement)
Ancillary Agreements	Various	The huge number of contracts which are subordinate to the primary financing and sales agreements, and cover anything from individual profit participations to merchandising arrangements
Artist's Agreement	(1) Producer (2) Lead Artist	Artist's services and contribution (sometimes via a loan-out agreement). Similar agreements exist for the Director, Composer, Heads of Departments, etc
Charge/ Security	(1) Bank / Chargee (2) Copyright owner	Similar to a mortgage. Gives the bank or chargee a right to take possession of the asset (usually including part of the copyright) if certain conditions in other agreements are not met.
Collection [Agent's Management] Agreement (CAMA)	(1) Collection Agent (2) Sales Agent (3) Producer (4) All Financiers (5) All Profit Participants	Provides for the distribution by the Collection Agent of income as it comes into the 'pot', based upon the terms of the Recoupment Schedule. Covers recoupment of production finance and distribution of Net Profits
Commissioning [Producer] Agreement (CPA)	(1) Commissioning Producer (2) Production Company	Commissioning Producer (CP), in order for CP to obtain necessary tax breaks, engages and pays Production Company to make the Film on CP's behalf. Production Company may be a single purpose vehicle or a production services company.
Completion Agreement	(1) Completion Guarantor (2) Producer	Gives Completion Guarantor rights over the production of the film, including take-over rights, in order to make sure it is completed on time and on budget.
Completion Guaranty/ Bond	(1) Completion Guarantor (2) All Financiers	Guarantees to the financiers that the film will be completed on time and on budget, or they get their money back.
Delivery Schedule	Schedule to various Agreements	List of items that must be delivered from Producer to Sales Agent, or from Sales Agent to Distributor, on completion of the film, usually triggering payment
Distribution (or Sale) Agreement	(1) Producer (2) Distributor	Arranged by the Sales Agent, who will sometimes sign on behalf of the Producer. Grants territorial rights to local Distributors (aka Sale Agreement).
Facility Agreement	(1) Financier (2) Producer	Confirms the terms of a financing facility, usually provided by a bank.

Interparty Agreement (IPA)	(1) All Financiers (2) Producer (3) Completion Guarantor (4) Collection Agent (5) Sales Agent (6) Production Services Company (if any)	Overrides all other agreements. Ensures that all Financiers make their money available at the same time. Expresses the respective rights and obligations of all parties that are not expressed elsewhere. Sets out the definitive Recoupment Schedule (copied on the CAMA)
Laboratory Access Agreement (LAA or 'Lab Letter)	(1) Laboratory (2) Sales Agent (3) Producer (4) Distributor (sometimes)	Sometimes combined with LPA. Ensures that the laboratory provides access as necessary to Sales Agent / Distributors in order for them to make necessary distribution copies of the film at the lab.
Laboratory Pledgeholder Agreement (LPA)	(1) Laboratory (2) Production Services Company (3) Producer (4) Sales Agent (5) All Financiers (6) Completion Guarantor	Ensures that the Laboratory (at which the film is made / stored / copied) holds the materials formally on behalf of the Producer and Financiers (etc), and doesn't interfere, lay claim or prevent access to any of the materials.
Letter of Credit (L/C)	From a Bank	Guarantee from a bank that if its client does not pay up when due, the bank will pay instead. The recipient of the L/C is often another bank (eg when discounting a distributor's MG on a pre-sale).
Non-disturbance Letter	From Producer to Distributor	Confirms that if, for some reason, the SAA (through which the Distributor was granted rights by the Sales Agent) is terminated prematurely, the Producer (copyright owner) will not prevent the Distributor from continuing to exploit the film under the Distribution Agreement entered into with the Sales Agent
Notice of Availability (NoA)	From Sales Agent to Distributor	Informs a Distributor that the film elements are ready to be delivered. Clock starts ticking for Distributor to check quality and pay balance of MG.
Production, Finance (and Distribution) Agreement (PFD)	(1) Financier(s) (2) Producer	Provides for the Producer to produce the film and — usually — grant the financier(s) distribution rights in return for the financiers providing the production funds. Similar to a CPA. Not necessarily used where there is a thorough IPA and a CPA.
Sales Agency Agreement (SAA)	(1) Producer (2) Sales Agent	Appoints Sales Agent to sell film on behalf of Producer (the copyright owner). Has an agreed form Distribution Agreement attached to the back.
Sales Estimates / Projections	From a Sales Agent	Territory-by-territory list of estimated high (ask), mid, and low (take) prices for the sale of film distribution rights

Further reading

Filmmaking

'The Guerilla Filmmakers Handbook and the Film Producers Toolkit' by Chris Jones & Genevieve Jolliffe (Continuum)

'The Guerilla Filmmakers Movie Blueprint' by Chris Jones (Continuum)

'Independent Feature Film Production' by Gregory Goodell (St Martin's Griffin)

'The Beginning Filmmaker's Guide to a Successful First Film' by Renee Harman, James Lawrence and Jim Lawrence (contributor) (Walker & Co)

'Media Law' by Rhonda Baker (Routledge Press / Blueprint Press)

'Hollywood Dealmaking - negotiating talent agreements' by Dina Appleton & Daniel Yankelevits (Allworth)

'Raindance Writers Lab: Write & Sell the hot screenplay' by Elliot Grove (Focal Press)

'Film and Video Budgets' by Deke Simon and Michael Wiese (MWP)

Short Films

'Making Short Films' by Clifford Thurlow (Berg)

'In Short: A guide to Short Filmmaking in the Digital Age' by Eileen Elsey and Andrew Kelly (BFI Publishing)

'Making the Winning Short: How to Write, Direct, Edit and Produce a Short Film' by Edmond Levy (Henry Holt)

'Shooting People Short Film Directory' (Shooting People Press)

Funding

'The Film Finance Handbook' edited by Mike Downey (The Media Business School)

'The Art of the Deal' by Dorothy Viljoen (PACT)

'Filmmakers & Financing, Business Plans for Independents' by Louise Levison (Focal Press)

'Film Financing & TV Programming: A Taxation Guide' (KPMG)

'Film Finance and Distribution: a Dictionary of Terms' by John W Cones (Silman-James Press)

'Financing and distributing independent films' by Mark Litwak (Silman-James Press)

Low Budget books

'Filming on a Microbudget' by Paul Hardy (www.pocketessentials.com)

'What They Don't Teach You at Film School' by Camille Landau and Tiare White's (Hyperiion books)

'$30 Film School' by Michael W Dea (Thomson Course Technology - www.courseptr.com)

'Before You Shoot' by Helen Garvy (Shire Press)

'Planning the Low Budget Film' by Robert Latham Brown (www.chalkhillbooks.com)

'Shooting Digital' by Marcus Van Bavel (www.DVFilm.com')

'HDV Filmmaking' by Chad Fahs (Thomson Course Technology - www.courseptr.com)

Reference

'Blu book Production Directory' by Hollywood Reporter (www.HCDonline.com)

'Kays Production Manual' (Kay Media)

'Kemps' (KFTV.com)

'The Knowledge' (Miller Freeman Information Services)

'The PACT directory of independent producers' (PACT)

'The Production Guide' (Emap)

'The Writer's and Artist's Yearbook' by A C Black (A & C Black)

'Ernst & Young Guide to International Film Production' (Ernst & Young LLP)

Other Publications

'A Filmmakers Guide to Distribution & Exhibition' (BFI) free to download from www.bfi.org.uk

'The Media Business File' by the Media Business School, updated three times a year

'The Producers' Tim Adler (Methuen)

'The Wealth of Networks' by Yochai Benkler (Yale University Press)

'The Long Tail: How Endless Choice Is Creating Unlimited Demand' by Chris Anderson (Random House)

A few useful websites

Industry news
   Africa Film and TV - www.africafilmtv.com
   Box Office, www.boxoff.com, North American trade journal
   Box Office Mojo - www.boxofficemojo.com
   Cinematech - cinematech.blogspot.com
   Film Journal - www.filmjournal.com, American trade journal with international outlook
   Hollywood Reporter - www.hollywoodreporter.com,
   Le Film Francais - www.lefilmfrancais.com,
   Longtail - www.thelongtail.com
   Netribution - www.netribution.co.uk
   Screen Digest - www.screendigest.com,
   Screen Finance - www.informamedia.com,
   Screen International - www.screendaily.com
   Variety - www.variety.com,
   Indiewire - www.indiewire.com

Industry info
   Association of Film Commissioners International - www.afci.org
   BritFIlms - British FIlm Catalogue - www.britfilms.com
   Electronic Frontier Foundation - www.eff.org
   European legislation - www.europa.eu.int/eur-lex/en
   European trade mark and design office - www.oami.eu.int
   FIlm FIle Europe - directory of European funds, producers and distributors - www.filmfileeurope.com
   International Federation of Film Producer Associations - www.fiapf.org
   IMDb Links - www.imdb.com/links
   Movie Making Manual (Wikibook) - en.wikibooks.org/wiki/Movie_making_manual
   Resource 411 - www.resource411.com
   Skillset Film resources - www.skillset.org/film
   KORDA - directory of European Film Funds - korda.obs.coe.int
   Without a box, festival database and submissions - www.withoutabox.com

International Producer Associations

Argentina - Asociacion General De Productores Cinematograficos
www.acceder.buenosaires.gov.ar
aries@fibertel.com.ar
T: +54 1147770404·

Argentina - Instituto Nacional De Cine Y Artes Visuales
www.incaa.gov.ar
info@incaa.gov.ar
T: +54 11-6779-0900

Australia - Screen Producers Association of Australia - SPAA
www.spaa.org.au
spaa@spaa.org.au
T: 61 2 9360 8988

Austria - Fachverband der Audiovisions und Filmindustrie
www.fafo.at · mueller@fafo.at
T: +43 (0)5 90 900 3010

Canada - Canadian Film and Television Production Association
www.cftpa.ca · ottawa@cftpa.ca
T: 800-656-7440/613-233-1444 ·

China - China Filmmakers Association
www.sfs-cn.com

Czech Republic - Audiovisual Producers' Association (APA)
www.apa.iol.cz
apa@asociaceproducentu.cz
T: (420) 221 105 302

Denmark - Danish Film and TV Producers
www.pro-f.dk/sw269.asp
info@pro-f.dk
T: +45 33 86 28 80

Egypt - Egyptian Chamber of Cinema Industry
egycinemachamber@hotmail.com
T: 2025741638

Finland - Suomen Elokuvatuottajien Keskusliitto (SEK)
www.filmikamari.fi

France - institut national de l'audiovisual
www.ina.fr/formation/afic/index.en.html · international@ina.fr
T: (33) (1) 49832930 94366

Germany - Arbeitsgemeinschaft Neuer Deutscher Spielfilmproduzenten e.V.
www.ag-spielfilm.de
mail@ag-spielfilm.de
T: +49-89-2 71 74 30

Iceland - Association of Icelandic Films Producers
www.producers.is
sik@producers.is
T: +354 5117060

India - Film Federation of India
T: 912224952062

India - National Film Development Corporation Ltd.
www.nfdcindia.com
nfdc@nfdcindia.com
T: +91 22 2496 5643

Iran - The Iranian Alliance of Motion Picture Guilds - Khaneh Cinema
www.khanehcinema.ir
intl@khanehcinema.ir
T: 982177525977

Italy - Unione Nazionale Produttori Film (ANICA)
www.anica.it · anica@anica.it

Japan - Motion Picture Producers Association of Japan
www.eiren.org

Netherlands – Netherlands Feature Film Association (NVS)
www.speelfilmproducenten.nl ·
info@speelfilmproducenten.nl
T: +31 (0)206270061

New Zealand - Screen Production and Development Association (SPADA)
www.spada.co.nz
info@spada.co.nz
T: +64 4 939 6934

Norway Film & TV Produsenters Forening
www.produsentforeningen.no
pf@produsentforeningen.no
T: (47) 23 11 93 11

Russia - Film Producers Guild of Russia
www.kinoproducer.ru
guild@kinoproducer.ru
T: +7 095 143-90-28

Spain - Federacion de Asiociaciones de Produtores Audiovisuales de Espana
www.fapae.es · web@fapae.es
T: (34) 91 512 16 60

Sweden - Swedish Filmproducers' Associations
www.swedishfilmproducers.com ·
lisa@filmproducenterna.se
T: 08-6663742· F: 08-6663748

Switzerland - Swiss Film Producers' Association
www.swissfilmproducers.ch
info@swissfilmproducers.ch
T: +41 31 370 10 60

UK - Producers Alliance for Cinema and Television (PACT)
www.pact.co.uk · iptf@pact.co.uk.
T: +44 207 0674367

UK - New Producers Alliance
www.npa.org.uk
queries@npa.org.uk
T: +44 207 6430440

USA - Independent Film & Television Alliance
www.ifta-online.org
info@ifta-online.org
T: 310.446.1000· F: 310.446.1600

USA – Independent Feature Project (IFP)
www.ifp.org · info@ifp.org
T: (212) 465-8200

USA – Motion Picture Association of America (MPAA)
www.mpaa.org

Part I Index

35MM 61, 75

A
admissions 5
advance 100, 118
advertising revenue 173
agent 116
ancillary 117
attachments 24
automatic funding 104
awards 103

B
back-end 101
bank gap 99
bilateral co-production 112
bilateral treaties 111
blog 163
bond company 129
box office 5–7
Brave New Theaters 159, 174
break even 101, 120
budget 23, 32
business angels 137
business plan 19, 28–59
buyer 116

C
carbon neutral filmmaking 64
cash budget 130, 131
cash rebate 104
chain of title 121
charge 127
claw back 134
Cluetrain Manifesto 160
co-production 107–109
co-production treaty 107
collection account 99, 118
collection agent 99, 134
commission 133
competent authority 109, 110
completion agreement 129
completion bond 122, 127, 128
completion guarantee 128, 132
contingency 130–131
Convention co-productions 109
copyright 41–43
corridor 100, 126
coverage 125
Creative Commons 157, 171
crowd sourced financing 17, 154

D
day-and-date 15
deal memo 39
deferments 16, 98, 130, 131, 134
delivery schedule 120
development 12, 22
digital 60–63
digital cinema 174
Digital Rights Management 167, 169–170
digital TV 6
direct support 103
discounted sale & leaseback 459
discounting 98, 104, 122, 136
distribution agreements 117
distributor 116, 117
domain name 162
domestic 123, 126
domestic distributor 116
domestic sale 125
DVD 6
Video/DVD rental 14
Video/DVD sale 14

E
End User License Agreement (EULA) 169
Enterprise Investment Scheme 137
equity 98, 113
equity investor 96, 113, 123
European Convention 109, 111
executive producer 11, 97

F
festivals 21
financial incentives 102, 103
finishing funds 129
flat sale 123
foreign 116, 123
free-TV 14
Fundable.org 155

G
GAAP funds 125, 133
gap finance 16, 125–128
grants 103
gross receipts 102, 134

H
High Definition 62–63
holdback window 15, 124
home video 117

I
incentives 16

indemnities 40
independents 4, 8
international distributor 116, 135
internet rights 143

K
key elements 121

L
lending bank 96
letter of credit 122
letter of intent 24–25, 125
library 113
limited company 44
Linux 157
long-form agreements 39
longtail 168

M
majors 8
major territories 118
markets 21
merchandising rights 117
MG (minimum guarantee) 100, 118
microbudget 4
mini-majors 9
mortgage 127
multilateral co-production 112

N
national film 108
negative pick-up 16, 136
negotiating 34
net profit 101, 102
net receipts 102
networking 21
non-theatrical 117

O
official co-productions 108–110
open source 157
option 23
option agreement 23
outright sale 123
overages 12, 118, 124

P
packaging 25
pari passu 100
partnerships 45
pay-per-view (PPV) 14
pay-TV 14
piracy 169
pitch 19, 30
post-production deals 132

Further reviews and feedback

"The handbook is packed with valuable information on the structure of independent film finance and, most importantly, provides details of who can "give" you the money to make a film "
Tim Willis, Director of Film, Producers Alliance for Cinema & TV (PACT)

"There are few people in the world of film finance as well equipped as Adam P Davies is to co-write such a guide. Comprehensive, spanning many countries, meticulously researched and very well written, this is a completely indispensable guide for all people in the field of film finance, from layman to the most experienced of producers."
Peter James, Film Financier / Fund Director / Producer

"After reading The UK Film Finance Handbook I've gathered all the ammunition I'll need to successfully fund and distribute my film. It covered all my questions and gave me better advice than some high priced London lawyers have!"
Tamara Gregory, 1st time producer

"Indispensable for film-makers, producers, financiers and their advisers."
Independent on Sunday

"After reading the book you will understand every type of financing available to filmmakers... Highly recommend to any filmmaker attempting to finance either a short or a feature, it is difficult to find as detailed or easily understandable finance book anywhere else."
Six Degrees Film

"I must say it is excellent. Congratulations. The last version was good but this is in a league of its own - it is very well written and structured too"
Katharine Robinson, producer Cheeky Monkey Films (including 2004 Nokia Shorts winner)